The Slamming Door
Bone Cancer, Asperger's, and Loss

By Clarisse N. Rénard, J.D.

The Slamming Door
Bone Cancer, Asperger's, and Loss

By Clarisse N. Rénard, J.D.

QueenBeeBooks

Copyright © June 29, 2011

All rights reserved.

All rights reserved. Published in the United States by QueenBeeBooks, Connecticut.

Library of Congress Cataloging-in-Publication Data
Name: Rénard, Clarisse N., author.
Title: The Slamming Door: Bone Cancer, Asperger's, and Loss / Clarisse N. Rénard.
Description: Connecticut: QueenBeeBooks, [2011].
Identifiers: ISBN 978-1-7343743-7-7
 (paperback)
Subjects: 1. FAMILY & RELATIONSHIPS / Death, Grief, Bereavement. 2. SOCIAL SCIENCE / Death & Dying. 3. BIOGRAPHY & AUTOBIOGRAPHY / Personal Memoirs.

www.queenbeeedit.com

Cover design by Clarisse N. Rénard
Cover art by Clarisse N. Rénard
Printed in the United States of America

The Slamming Door
Bone Cancer, Asperger's, and Loss
By Clarisse N. Rénard, J.D.

The Slamming Door is a true story.

In September of 2008, Clarisse N. Rénard was asked to move in with a man who had just been diagnosed with bone cancer...by his daughter, Berta, who knew that she was a writer and available. Berta had to work in an office, so she couldn't be her father's caregiver.

He was her husband's older cousin, Bryn, a Harvard-educated, retired New York City social worker, and Clarisse and her husband Damon had stayed with him many times. He was also one of her best friends after eight years of visits, a confidante, and like another dad to her.

Damon, a scientist, was often away, struggling to make a success of his career as a Ph.D. immunologist, which took him to rural Connecticut, Iraqi Kurdistan, Kuwait, and Hungary.

Clarisse was unhappy in Connecticut, where she was staying with her parents, who didn't want her husband in their house anymore. Both Clarisse and Damon had Asperger's, but their understanding and tolerance was limited to their daughter.

The request, which was also an invitation of sorts, felt like an escape.

It also felt like a chance to pay her cousin-in-law back for all of the emotional and other support he had given to Clarisse and Damon.

She didn't know Berta very well, but had been excited to find that her marriage came with a female cousin her own age (plus another – Berta's first cousin). Clarisse looked forward to getting to know her better.

When he realized that he couldn't stay home alone while terminally ill, Bryn wanted Clarisse with him and told her so the evening that she arrived. However, he warned her that Berta and her older half-sister were very jealous of the fact that she was there with him.

Despite this, Clarisse's time in Manhattan was great...for a while.

But gradually it changed.

Berta resented Clarisse in many ways, and gradually revealed her true self: a bully.

With her father's time drawing to a close, Berta demanded Clarisse's departure, on the pretext that she was angry when Clarisse had done her a favor by cleaning a closet. Clarisse had been anxious and scared, with no one to talk to, alone and silently watching Bryn decline late at night. She had been very careful to preserve everything in that closet.

A week and a half later, Clarisse's parents drove her home to Connecticut, and made her feel welcome and wanted. Bryn died four days after that.

But that wasn't the end of it.

Clarisse wrote something to honor Bryn with at the memorial service, but was blocked by Berta.

Read on to find out how an articulate and meticulous Aspie dealt with all of these problems and situations, and how she viewed it all.

People with Asperger's are not broken; their brain patterns merely differ from those of the majority of the population. Aspies have produced great novels, scientific discoveries, and the foundations of the best legal system on the planet, namely *The Declaration of Independence*.

Asserting oneself, knowing that no good deed will be judged with appreciation by a bully, is an act of courage and defiance, but also a necessary one.

Find out how an Aspie who has learned social skills by rote, one who has earned respectable academic credentials but does not function well in many work environments, navigates a labyrinth of death, dying and loss, and how she copes with anxiety induced by travel and changes in her environment, and how she slowly, painstakingly comes to recognize the signs of hostility around her while making no apology for who she is.

There is nothing wrong with those who are different.

The problem is those who won't accept or respect them.

This book is dedicated to social workers.

They are secular saints.

And to caregivers.

They are everywhere.

This is a true story.

Table of Contents

If you ever take care of someone 1
Chapter 1: A Travesty of Luck 3
Chapter 2: Getting There 22
Chapter 3: Settling In 29
Chapter 4: Berta 44
Chapter 5: The Goddaughter, and Other Neighbors 62
Chapter 6: Chelsea, Shopping, and a Celebrity 76
Chapter 7: At MoMA with Albert and June 99
Chapter 8: The Rock Star of the Henry George School 104
Chapter 9: Alissa, Art Galleries, and June 114
Chapter 10: Signing Up for the Process of Misery 120
Chapter 11: The Page-Torn Salon for the Arts 138
Chapter 12: Diane/Dionne – The Split Personality 142
Chapter 13: Misery Round One: Chemotherapy 153
Chapter 14: Dr. Leonardi Invites Me Out 177
Chapter 15: Computing – Even When It Didn't Compute 190
Chapter 16: Dead Boiler – To TriBeCa 202
Chapter 17: Hallowe'en in Chelsea 216
Chapter 18: Obama! Obama! Obama! 227
Chapter 19: Cassie Visits – I Like Her 236
Chapter 20: TV and Take-Out 239
Chapter 21: Asperger's, Bones, and Me...Not That I Knew 249
Chapter 22: Damon Visits 259
Chapter 23: Misery Round Two: More Poison 266
Chapter 24: Bryn's Last Birthday Party 275

Chapter 25: Thanksgiving in a Brooklyn Brownstone 282
Chapter 26: The Big Apple Circus 301
Chapter 27: Bryn Throws a Party at the Hahvahd Club 312
Chapter 28: Misery Round Three: The Final Set 342
Chapter 29: *Twilight*...and Milkshake Time 385
Chapter 30: Valentine's Day Visit 412
Chapter 31: A Double Birthday Party 416
Chapter 32: At Desmond's Tavern Again After All 423
Chapter 33: Blood Transfusion...with Toby Talking Boner Pills ... 425
Chapter 34: Mommy Visits 428
Chapter 35: La Chatte Nikita 432
Chapter 36: Enjoying Life Until He Can't 442
Chapter 37: Helping Alissa 463
Chapter 38: "Rip Torn Gave Me the Clap!" – and Other Stories 469
Chapter 39: Distractions: Letterman and the Morgan Library .. 474
Chapter 40: Leila, and an Air Conditioner 486
Chapter 41: About His Papers... 497
Chapter 42: Uncle Damon Dies...on Damon's Birthday 502
Chapter 43: Craigslist and Calligraphy 507
Chapter 44: Vianne Visits 522
Chapter 45: Hospice, and His Papers Again 533
Chapter 46: 20th Precinct Business Cards 553
Chapter 47: Wedding Anniversary...and Bryn's Leg Swells 562
Chapter 48: Moonwalking with a Cane 574
Chapter 49: July Birthdays...But the Party's Over 576
Chapter 50: Alena Visits 602

Chapter 51: Walden 606

Chapter 52: Moving Furniture – Berta Freaks Out 610

Chapter 53: Bombshells and Teddy Bears 630

Chapter 54: That Son-in-Law 639

Chapter 55: Anxiety and Cleaning 648

Chapter 56: Berta's Meltdown 655

Chapter 57: Being Sent Home...and Seeing the Movie Adam 667

Chapter 58: Packing, Shopping, and More Packing 687

Chapter 59: A Foley Catheter 694

Chapter 60: A Good-Bye Party 707

Chapter 61: Home Again 712

Chapter 62: Bryn Died 718

Chapter 63: Aspie and Proud of It 724

Chapter 64: Memorial Service Plans 730

Chapter 65: Blocked 732

Chapter 66: Glowing Letters 745

Chapter 67: Not My Family – The Door Has Been Slammed 760

Chapter 68: My Home Feels Like Home Now 762

Epilogue: No Regrets 766

If you ever take care of someone who is dying, someone who has other people besides you in the picture, at least some of those people will find fault with your efforts, and insist that they could have done a better job.

But those people were not there; you were.

Don't let those who second-guess you later make you regret your efforts after the fact.

Just do your best for your charge as long as it is yours to keep.

Chapter 1

A Travesty of Luck

Only nice people get cancer – and the most painful form of it at that. Watch the first person who bothers to research this prove me wrong, but for once I have no interest in the idea of historical or histological research.

I'm just angry.

In August of 2008, Damon's cousin Bryn, the nicest member of my family of in-laws, was diagnosed with bone cancer – the most painful kind that there is, called osteosarcoma. I found out about this in mid-September.

We often called Bryn the family saint, because he was always such a sympathetic listener and friend. He let us stay with him for months in 2005 when we came home from a six-month stay in Kuwait and found that a deal that Damon had worked on for years, one that would have marketed a nutraceutical treatment and generated a permanent, continuous income for us, had fallen through thanks to some dishonesty by the corporation involved.

As the daughter of a prostate cancer nurse, I had known what cancer is for years: it is a mutated parasite, with each cell part-mutated and part whatever organ it has latched onto. Once formed, like a computer virus, it reproduces exponentially in the host's body, consuming it.

Damon – my husband – had scared me long ago by saying that if he ever got cancer, he would just kill himself rather than endure it. He wouldn't take that statement back, either. I was left with the ominous foreboding sense that someday he would abruptly abandon me forever.

I had been seriously unhappy – depressed – for quite some time. The previous August, my husband and I had had to separate against our wills due to financial and logistical circumstances. I was a writer-editor, so I could work wherever there is a computer, but Damon was a Ph.D. immunologist with no paying position at any particular university. Aside from that kind of income, scientists subsist on grant money. Damon had had grant money, but that had run out, as had our lease at a beautiful university apartment in Connecticut.

Despite Damon's constant efforts during our 8-month lease, plus some last-ditch ones, no chance of continuing at the apartment had materialized. We had been forced to move our household possessions into a storage unit – again – at the end of August 2007. I was despondent, and convinced that it would be at least 3 full years before we could live together again. By then, I would be 40 years old. Life was passing me and Damon by, while we could see other couples enjoying a calm sense of progress and togetherness.

Damon was 14 and a half years older than me, which scared me. I never want to live as a widow, and I felt a looming certainty that that was precisely what would eventually happen to me. (Damon wasn't so sure: he kept pointing out one of his grandparents, who had lived into his 90s and only died because he fell off of a chair. Plus, he intended to tinker with his genetic makeup and slow down the aging process. I was skeptical about that, but let him enjoy the idea.)

When our lease ended, Damon went back on the road – to Maryland, where his business partner lived; to Iraqi Kurdistan, to work on bringing health care training to Kurdish nurses and EMTs; to Hungary, as a guest lecturer and part-time faculty member at a university near Romania; to Kuwait, to work with the doctor he met after the Kuwait War; and to the university in Connecticut, where he would sleep on the laboratory floor and do experiments aimed at eventually getting a product on the market, based on one of his many inventions.

He had yet to succeed at generating a continuous income from any of these projects.

I had yet to make a steady income of any kind either. Moving constantly since our 2002 wedding hadn't helped, but the travel certainly gave me plenty of notes for a book about Kuwait, plus a children's book about our cat, Scheherazade, who had died in 2005 while we were staying with Bryn. Another project was co-authoring a memoir of an Iranian woman politician who had moved to the U.S. It was always moving in tiny fits and starts, thanks to the general instability of both ours situations. She was applying for a green card when I found out about Bryn's illness.

So Damon and I had no retirement money, no stable place to live, and had stayed for at least half of our marriage with relatives. We were soul mates with no viable economic pattern to our lives. We were independent, we didn't like authority, and we didn't want children. We wanted a cat and a home together. And we liked to travel.

We couldn't do that, except in a state of anxiety, traveling to earn an income that would only stop a short time later. I found it difficult to calm down enough to write anything substantial, which was what I needed to do in order to make a living at it.

What I wanted to do was almost impossible: become a published author of books sold in places like Barnes & Noble and Borders Books & Music. I was terrified of dying forgettable, unpublished and insignificant. I didn't want kids – I wanted publications. That was how I wanted to leave a piece of myself behind. A literary agent – who died shortly after laughing as he told Damon the inside scoop – had confided that this was nearly impossible because the publishing world had become a closed club. Without an insider, forget it.

I had already gotten a taste of this from one publishing company. They kept my book about the cat for 3 and a half months, then told me that they wouldn't publish it and sent the manuscript back. Seeking to learn from the experience, we called to ask why. The reply was that the book was a great story, well-organized, presented and written, perfectly good, and that the junior editors wanted it and pushed the sorely tempted senior editors to publish it. At long last, the senior editors said no, for one reason and one reason only: I was not already known, and therefore a poor economic risk.

Wonderful. Perhaps the political memoir would help me…if it ever happened.

Meanwhile, my parents decided, in the spring of 2008, that they wouldn't let my husband in the house any more, and that's where I stayed while Damon wasn't around. They were angry with him for writing to them to say that he didn't like them. He had done so after my father had put his finger in the frame of my door as I was getting out of the car and closing that car door. I was in the front seat; he was in the back, and my mother had driven. It was an accident, and it was his own stupid fault, but it hurt, so he had tried to punch me. My mother intervened by threatening to make my father move out, and said he could take our cat, Cookie, with him. Damon's attempt at distraction had totally backfired; he just didn't know how to help.

So I had nowhere to be with him after that. Granted, it wasn't logistically feasible most of the time for him to be there – it was far away from the university, and I had no car after 2004. We were effectively stranded after the old car died, with no money for another one.

This left one place to meet and be together: Bryn's apartment in Chelsea, Manhattan.

Bryn Warne Otterman was a cousin of Damon's. He and his younger brother Albert had babysat Damon when he was 9 years old and living in Manhattan with his mother and 2 younger sisters, Vianne and Alena. Damon's father was dead by then. Later, when Bryn was married and living in Oneonta, New York, Damon, his sisters, their mother, and their maternal grandparents had lived on the same street in the same town.

But for most of his life, Bryn lived in Manhattan. The exceptions were attending Harvard University, a summer interning as a social worker at the Institute of Living in Hartford, Connecticut, and those years in Oneonta. After his divorce, Bryn moved back. He lived in a few different apartments before settling into the one I knew him at, on West 21st Street between 8th and 9th Avenues. Damon said that Bryn would never leave, because he was addicted to the place.

A Travesty of Luck

Manhattan certainly is an addictive, endlessly fascinating place. I loved it, partly because I felt a sense of home and safety while staying at Bryn's place, and partly because of the fun of walking around lower Manhattan to see historic sites, stores, people, monuments, and restaurants. Manhattan is a reasonably safe place for a lone woman to walk now – not as it was during the 1980s, when I used to go with my grandmother to visit a great-aunt in Stuyvesant Village. Aunt Sharon wouldn't let us go out at night, so we would take a taxi home from the Metropolitan Ballet, which she considered to be a great but justified extravagance.

I have always had a deep dread of being alone – living alone, in particular. I won't live with another girl in some apartment. She would just get married and either stick me with the entire cost of the rent, which I wouldn't be able to afford, or expect me to move out. No – I held out for what I wanted: marriage. But that hadn't worked. I didn't have stability in my living situation – only in my emotional one. I had married my best friend, and I had him all to myself. He loved me and only me, and we both liked and disliked the same things: we loved cats and didn't want kids. There were other similarities, but that's the general idea.

Bryn was a quiet, friendly, bespectacled man in his early 60s when I met him. This was at Damon's May 2001 graduation from the Ph.D. program in Connecticut, back when Damon and I were still in the friendship phase of our relationship. He and Albert came up from New York City for the day to attend the festivities. I liked them both, but barely remembered them at first, other than the fact that Bryn had tied Damon's tie (a gift from me that depicted aliens in sunglasses). Damon had forgotten how to do that.

I didn't see or hear of Bryn again until that December, by which time I had moved in with Damon; he had an apartment near the UConn Health Center. We went to Manhattan to see the relatives for the holidays. It was a Hanukkah visit; many of Damon's relatives are Jewish. (The Otterman relatives, however, were Unitarians.) Damon had three Christian grandparents, and one Jewish grandfather, who was a founder of the New School for Social Research after Harvard ousted him for being an atheist. It was an interesting family history, which only served to further draw me and Damon together; I too, have an interesting family history.

We arrived by car – in my old grey Mercedes sedan. Damon didn't drive, so we had a joke, thanks to my uncle, that he had just married me so that I could drive him around in that grey car of mine. We parked in front of Bryn's building in a light snowstorm. It was across from an elementary school, overlooking the playground. The school, P.S. 11, has appeared in movies (including *Miss Congeniality 2* and *No*

Reservations). It was early evening when we arrived, and I asked Damon, as I pulled up, which one of his relatives we would stay with. Bryn, he said. Bryn? I felt some anxiety over the fact that we would be staying with a man.

Damon pointed him out – all bundled up with a wool hat pulled down over his thick white hair, his glasses like round magnifying lenses, with eyes that seemed to squint; he was smiling cheerfully at us. I remembered him. "Oh! He's the one who tied your tie on you at graduation!" I said. When I saw him again, I had stopped worrying. It was going to okay, staying with him.

We went upstairs with our stuff to find an old, two-bedroom apartment, one flight up in a building with no elevator. The place had hardwood floors and a lot of beautiful wooden bookcases full of books, Art Deco furniture in the living room, diner signs in the kitchen, and a big bathtub in the bathroom. Our room was on the left, and the door had been painted to cover up glass panes, which covered most of the surface of the door, and which sat a full inch off of the floor. Our two windows looked out at the school playground, with a fire escape on the left.

I remained a bit standoffish from Bryn at first, but quickly took to him.

We went to the party, which was held at the apartment of one of Damon's two "aunts" – his mother's best friends – and saw Albert again, and met June, his wife, who was very quiet, both Aunt Summer and Aunt

A Travesty of Luck

Johanna (the party was at her apartment) and some cousins, a couple named Nicola and Aaron who lived near Boston, with their new baby girl, and we saw Alena again, this time with her husband Josh, a cardiologist, and their daughter, 2-year-old Roselyn Elin, whom I had met the previous spring at Damon's graduation.

There was also a 9-year-old girl named Hilda, Bryn's goddaughter. She lived across the hall from him, and she was wearing a beautiful black dress with a gauze skirt. The gauze was folded in half and filled with a rainbow of glitter, then sewn onto the bodice of the dress. The girl had chin-length, wavy brown hair and brown eyes, and a large freckle in the center of her chin. She wanted to be involved in everything, including handing Roselyn her gifts from me, one by one. I was annoyed by this, and resisted the effort without being too obvious about it, but the kid was offended anyway. I didn't care – I never do in such situations. I just try to get through them without a major incident, which I did this time. Damon later agreed; this kid was annoying.

The party went well enough, and we headed back. Soon I found myself chattering to Bryn about all sorts of things, relaxing around him. This continued the next time we visited him, and the next. We loved staying at Bryn's place, going places with him and on our own, and I began to look forward to my next conversations with him.

Bryn had worked on a Ph.D. in sociology for many years and come away with a master's degree and membership in the dirty little secret of Ph.D. programs: the ABD club. He had earned an All But Dissertation Ph.D., which happens to a lot of Ph.D. candidates. Damon had explained this to me, sounding sympathetic toward his cousin. As time went on, I learned more details: Bryn had been trying to do his dissertation while his marriage was failing, while he was teaching at Oneonta, while going through a divorce and driving a cab in Manhattan, and was ultimately unable to make it work. He had been too busy surviving, and was too upset.

I had cheered Damon on through his Ph.D., kept him from working too much by dragging him off to movies, coffee shops, and walks around the local mall, and I noticed that other than those trips out in the car with me, he really did little else. He was a single guy doing his Ph.D., and a workaholic. The work sometimes included something frowned on in U.S. academia: attempts to start business ventures with his inventions, and the publication of a journal article about one of them while still in graduate school, plus a trip to Iran to see the victims of mustard lung disease (from the chemicals the Iraqis used in the Iran-Iraq War, 1980-1988). This was of great interest to Damon because he had been a chemical weapons officer in the Kuwait War.

The Slamming Door

I had it relatively easy: I went through law school during those 6 years, completing that degree in 3 years, 2 years before Damon graduated. My J.D. dissertation was a 33-page paper on outer space law for a seminar, relatively painless, and fascinating to me. I knew early on in the program that I wouldn't be practicing law. It just wasn't something that I would be able to do without a mentor, and I hadn't passed the bar exam. I didn't test well. I think it was sheer determination that helped me score high enough on the LSAT to go to a top-tier law school.

But I wasn't surprised when halfway along, a professor of international law informed me, in a serious but not belittling tone, that he didn't think I had the aptitude for work as a lawyer. I told him: "I'm not quitting." I meant the degree, and he knew it. "I'm not suggesting that you do," he replied. I think many of my professors liked me, and I enjoyed the program. But I graduated with nothing more than a sense of self-esteem...not a clear sense of career direction, and not a sense of how I would earn a living. It was frustrating, scary and lonely.

But back to Bryn; the next time I saw him, I barely spent any time with him. The reason was that he was one of many visitors from out of town who came to Connecticut to attend our wedding, which took place on the evening of the summer solstice in June of 2002. The wedding was absolutely perfect in every way that I could have wanted. There was lots of pink, there were bouquets and vases of pink roses and blue irises, great music and food, and everyone we wanted to see at the event was there (Except for my cousin Bradford, the artist; it was not his fault. His boss reneged at the last minute on a promise to let him off that evening.). It was a fairy tale.

Recently, however, I noticed something that really pleased me in our photos: Bryn was standing right behind me in a group family photo, taken in the garden just after the ceremony. There he is, with his thick, straight white hair, glasses, and big happy smile. He loved to have a good time, and would travel a considerable distance and stay in an unfamiliar place to enjoy a good time, with no sense of anxiety about being someplace new or far away. I couldn't do that.

Several months passed before our next visit, which was in the spring of 2003. We had been staying in McLean, Virginia for a while, at the home of a urologist that Damon knew from graduate school, while Damon wrote a grant at George Washington University. We drove up to see Bryn again, and he showed us his haunts: McNulty's Tea & Coffee Company, founded in 1895, in Greenwich Village, where he would buy his coffee (plus he showed me exactly what he always bought there: Mandeeling Sumatra blend, ½ regular and ½ decaf, fine ground), and the Henry George School of Social Science, where he taught classes in social economic theory.

A Travesty of Luck

Both the coffee shop and the school became synonymous in my mind with Bryn and his life in New York City, even though by day he had a different job: he was a city social worker. To me, this meant that he was a secular saint. He had made a career of helping people for low pay: homeless people, drug addicts, AIDS patients, and non compos mentis types (insane or otherwise mentally unstable people). By the time I met him, he was doing a dull shadow of a social worker's job, one that he called a retirement job: he would go to court on behalf of the city to make sure that no one was milking the system unfairly. The job was mostly paperwork.

It was the job he had had for a long stretch just before this one that he had truly loved: he was given a hotel room as an office, where he would see people who lived in the other rooms and help them with their problems. It was an AIDS hotel. The people there typically had a combination of the problems listed above – sick, homeless, crazy, etc. Bryn had a wonderful time just chatting with people and needing to do very little in the way of paperwork.

Before that, he was out in the field in other venues, visiting elderly residents in decaying neighborhoods. He would approach a group of drug dealers on a street corner before going to see a client: "Hi, my name is Bryn Otterman. I'm a social worker, and I'm here to see Mrs.

The Slamming Door

McGillicuddy on the 4th floor over there." They would take this information in, and then he would proceed through the dangerous area unmolested.

By then he had dealt with a problem with alcohol – his own – plus a divorce from his second wife, who was the mother of his adopted stepdaughter and their daughter, and met his girlfriend, whom he called the love of his life. Her name was Cassie, and she was engaged when they met at a bar in 1978. Her fiancé didn't care if she had a boyfriend as well as a husband, and so the relationship continued for 30 years, with the guys as friends. Both Bryn and Cassie quit drinking, and Cassie, an artist and horse-lover, got a job in upstate New York as a social worker. She still lived there with her husband, a retired professor of English.

Bryn had photos of Cassie in his bedroom, which doubled as a place to chat. He would sit in the corner facing his little television and puffing on his pipe while the visitor sat down on the bed (as if it were a sofa) and chatted. This was his standard way of socializing at home, and I quickly got used to it. I would knock – he kept the door shut to contain the smoke, as Damon and I didn't smoke – and he would invite me in to chat. The smoke smelled pleasant to me for some reason; probably because I could visit in it for a while and then walk away from it.

Bryn would invite us out with him, usually to the Greek diner nearby, a place with horridly bland, over-cooked food called the Chelsea Square Restaurant. It was a classic case of the familiar being comfortable, and he usually ate dinner there alone when he was working, in a tiny both away from the windows, he told us. When we were visiting, however, we sat by the windows at a table for four, watching people walk by on the sidewalk, on the other side of the glass. The staff included Greek guys (the owners) and Mexican guys (the waiters). The food was unhealthy – scant raw fruit or vegetables, and little variety or taste as the choice was between over-boiled/broiled and fried stuff. This was where Bryn usually ate, and he never ate in.

When he ate out, he would always get a beer or two, or a glass of wine or two, and offer to get us one as well. I usually declined; one drink knocks me out unless I have a meal with it. But Bryn seemed to have found a way to have his alcohol and not let it control him. I wondered how he did that, but never asked. Drinking tends to be a different experience for everyone, so I didn't think that this mystery could be unraveled with one person's analysis or data. One year for Christmas, I gave Bryn a book about the 6 drinks that humans have consumed throughout history, which include soda, beer, wine, "spirits" such as rum, tea, and coffee; he loved it.

At home, Bryn only ever ate breakfast; all other meals he ate out. What he really loved was his Mandeeling Sumatra coffee from

A Travesty of Luck

McNulty's. I bought some of the toasted praline blend, and pumpkin spice for Damon. But how was I supposed to make coffee without a machine? Bryn showed me how he did it: he had two plastic coffee sieves, one brown and one orange, and he would just boil water in an old pot, put a brown paper filter in one (usually the brown one), add a scoop of the fine-ground coffee, and then pour water from the pot slowly into the filter. It was so easy that it was fascinating; I made coffee that way every day whenever I was in his apartment.

Damon and I went back to see Bryn in 2004 before heading to Kuwait – with our cat – for nearly six months. Damon was being paid to do an asthma study there by a California company that, unfortunately, was involved with him solely to get his data and then make a product without compensating him for it. We got nothing of a financially lasting nature from them, and Damon had to watch as they put a couple of products on the market that he received no royalties from. Coming back in 2005 was both depressing and terrifying. I had a treasure trove of notes and photos, hopefully the makings of a travelogue, but was too upset to do much. (I have since written and copyrighted the travelogue, complete with my photos.)

We came back to my parents' place in May of 2005, and from there took a bus – with our cat hidden in Damon's army duffel bag – to Manhattan, where we stayed with Bryn for the next four and a half months. Damon was working with some of the ophthalmologists at the New York Eye and Ear Infirmary – and he still does. It was discouraging…they were millionaire businessmen with homes to share with their wives, and we were still broke and homeless. They knew how to make lots of money, and would allegedly include Damon in a deal when conditions were right. Of course, the conditions, in the form of a wealthy investor, were not yet right, and we weren't getting any younger.

The summer of 2005 was the one that Al Gore pointed out in his famous PowerPoint presentation movie, *An Inconvenient Truth*, as being the hottest one on record since the Industrial Revolution, or some such frightening declaration. On Father's Day, when Bryn was away at Cassie's place, his daughter and her boyfriend had showed up to replace the old air conditioner in his room. That was the one cool room in the place during hot weather.

We sweated out that summer, seeking air conditioning like shelter from a firestorm, and watched our poor cat die of squamous cell carcinoma – cancer that ate a hole in the right side of her face and in her mouth. We had her put to sleep on the same day that Damon's Uncle Rex, who lived in Florida, died, on August 11th. It was a bad summer. Bryn let us stay with him during that awful, hopeless time, and we were glad that he did. He never said anything severe or judgmental to us; only some concerned, worrying tones came through.

Our Kuwaiti cat, asleep on a windowsill in our room in Bryn's apartment. She had a runny right eye that turned out to have cancer growing just underneath it, behind her cheekbone. We loved her.

Bryn had each of us lecture at the Henry George School, a free evening school for adults on East 30th Street that focused on land taxes, rent control, and social and political economic theories. Bryn was one of the professors there. Damon talked about mustard lung disease and its effects on the Kuwaiti population, and I described Kuwaiti life, art, culture and history with my collection of digital photographs.

The students interrupted a lot with questions about the economics of the place, which left me clueless – all I could give them was a picture of what I had learned there, and I hadn't gone with the idea of focusing on that particular topic. It didn't seem to matter to Bryn; he was pleased with my effort, and he had known what sort of materials I had, and what his students might do. We had fun, and we ate at the restaurant near the school afterward. It was a nice, dark, modern, Italian place with good food called Zana's, and the professors all got a discount there.

At one point, Bryn invited us to the Harvard Club with him during that summer. Damon and I dressed up, with me in a black linen sleeveless dress. When we got there, Bryn gave the entire family a grand tour of the library, the balcony overlooking the back reception room with Teddy Roosevelt's African elephant head on the wall, and the painted portraits. I noticed that he was wearing a new shirt that I had bought for him a day earlier; it was just like the old one, with a white collar and white cuffs. I had bought it at Filene's Basement when I saw that the collar on the old one was frayed. It had come back from the laundry like that, pressed and folded flat. His daughters weren't around enough to take care of his wardrobe, so he just kept it clean. Men can be funny about such details, not noticing when an item has too many miles on it.

We went back to Connecticut after that, returned briefly in November, and then Damon began looking into a place for us to stay at the University of Connecticut, where he hoped to get funding for a grant to study mustard lung disease. We spent the next year limping along, with Damon working without pay and me unable to go anywhere without a ride, and unable to find work, even as a freelance editor/tutor. We got an apartment at the university, and Bryn lent us a month's rent once. So Bryn took care of us in a rather significant and obvious way twice. We were elated when, after Damon's pay from the grant began, we could pay Bryn back.

We visited some more over the next couple of years, staying for a week or so at a time. Bryn invited Damon to give another lecture, and he brought us to some special ones there, including one about the game of *Monopoly*, originally called *The Landlord-Tenant Game*.

During these years, Damon and I would discuss where we were willing to live and compare that with where we wanted to live. The biggest problem was the lack of funds to do anything one way or the other. The fact remained that we were living in the Great Recession, and this was affecting not only the United States, but also other countries around the planet.

When I went to Kuwait, I had had a massive anxiety attack. Any change of environment freaks me out. I knew I had to go and see the country and experience the culture, and I did go, bringing our cat, which was complicated. But I had a nervous breakdown over it the night before leaving. I had stayed behind for six weeks because of the cat's vaccination papers, while Damon went on ahead first to Tehran, where he attended a scientific conference, and then to Kuwait.

My mother enjoyed having me around, but the night before I went, I had laid out my clothes and books and gifts to bring, and began to panic about actually packing them and going. How would they all fit neatly, what about the weight, etc.? I had never been very calm about packing. The hyperventilating starts, and it's all downhill from there. I hated any change of environment, and I was about to make a huge one. I had gone through this every time I went back to college for another term. When I study for one term in London, England, the anxiety had manifested itself as a gray haze. Law school was easier: I lived with my parents and drove the 12 minutes each day. But I was determined to go to Kuwait.

The Slamming Door

My mother had ended up helping me pack, and my parents drove me to Newark Airport, where I took an Air France plane so that the cat could ride in the cabin with me. After I checked in, as we walked around the airport, my mother saw that the hyperventilation was not abating. She bought me an *Archaeology* magazine, offered to take me home, said I didn't have to go, etc. That offer only made me more determined to face the anxiety and go on the trip.

To deal with anxiety, during law school and until shortly after I got married, my mother, a nurse, had sent me to first one psychiatrist and then another. Each one managed to fatten me up with pills, and the second one added the most weight. The maddening part of it is that she diagnosed me with Asperger's Syndrome, told me nothing about the condition, and even said that our main agenda should be to treat my anxiety and depression. So she focused exclusively on that, without telling what Asperger's was. The pills she prescribed just made me so relaxed that I was able to eat and eat and eat until I felt sick – overweight, with a tight, water-pressure feeling in my face, and wheezing up 6 steps.

As if that wasn't bad enough, I found that my thought processes were too slow and complacent for any writing efforts. I had become fat and useless. As Damon put it, I had lost my intensity while I was on those pills, and that was what he found so wonderful about my personality. So I stopped taking the pills, and promptly shrank back down to a reasonable size and shape over the ensuing summer of 2003. And I found that I could write again.

I have been asked by some very stupid people: "Wouldn't you rather be fat and happy than thin and anxiety-ridden?" The answer is a definite and emphatic NO. I want to be beautiful – and when I am a normal weight, I look pretty good. Damon has called me his knockout. As for my thought processes, I won't give up the ability to write. What am I supposed to do, dope myself up so that I fit in very nicely in an office job where I am fat, ugly, intellectually nullified, and utterly forgettable? No way. I wish there had been a book to read about Asperger's then.

I was doing my best to stay calm and continue to write.

And I didn't want to live in a foreign country, away from my culture, away from my own language, again. Kuwait was a brief adventure that generated enough data for a book. Living in an Islamic society was interesting, but I would not do it again. The Ayatollah Khomeini summed it up quite succinctly: "Islam is not fun." I want fun. I have too little happiness in my life to surrender the last of it to a place where the men hissed at me and I couldn't go where I wanted when I wanted. There was nothing for me to do while I was away but observe and document, and feel alone. Occasionally I dragged Damon to a museum, but I hated it there.

A Travesty of Luck

Hungary, the other place where Damon went, was full of, blustering people who didn't listen – and didn't care to. I was willing to listen, but I needed listeners, too. I would not simply accompany Damon and just be there, hating it. I wouldn't be able to pursue my own career if I did that. I needed to calm down and write.

But how would I calm down? Bryn could help me with that to some extent. My mother called the idea emotional intelligence, but didn't really know how to teach it. She seemed to prefer using medication first, and then take the drugged effects from there to build on the calm and add social interaction skills. But that would leave me fat, placid, and intellectually nullified. It wasn't a solution.

Talking to Bryn seemed to be the answer. Doing that was endlessly intriguing, because talking to him included taking questions about New York City to him and hearing the place and the culture explained. It was American culture, and I needed a seasoned New Yorker and social worker to help make any sense of some of the things that went on there. Reading homeless people was one thing he would talk to me about. Dealing with upsets about life in general was another. And since we were both inclined to study whatever fascinated us, we both read a lot and would discuss our fields with each other.

Whenever I came back to the apartment after meeting and talking with a homeless person somewhere on the streets of Manhattan, I would knock on Bryn's door. He would be in there with his light on, reading, watching the economic news on television, and relaxing. "Yo!" he would call, and invite me in to chat, whereupon he would get his corncob pipe going, looking almost sleepy as he did so, with his small eyes almost squinted shut behind his huge eyeglass lenses, focused as they were on igniting the wad of tobacco he had just inserted in his pipe. I would settle onto his bed like it was a sofa, and start to tell the latest tale of why New York City and/or human nature had puzzled me. We repeated this ritual many times over the years.

Bryn was genuinely interested in whatever knowledge I had to either seek or share, even though I was over 30 years younger and female. This ceased to surprise me later, as I realized that he just really liked talking to women, especially intelligent, intellectually curious women. And I just loved talking to him and hanging out with him. He was like another dad to me.

My father was a very interesting, learned person – but not emotionally intelligent. He had anger management issues, and my mother once threw him out because he had hit me. He ended up living in a rented room for 10 months. He had had no good reason for hitting me. I was looking for a camera that he had put in some odd spot, and he had just fallen asleep. I tried to be quiet, but he woke up to ask what I was doing, so I told him. He jumped up, looked enraged, said venomously "You woke me up!" and pounded the sides of my head with his fists.

When he almost hit me again in the fall of 2007, it took him over a year to admit that he shouldn't have put his finger there, and that he was responsible for his own fingers. By then Damon had written my mother that letter about her latest threat to make my father move out. My mother wouldn't let him in the house, wouldn't ever speak to him again, and wouldn't even consider his point of view. So that ruined any holidays with my parents.

The following April, they told me he couldn't be in the house unless they were home, when I was in New York City with Damon and Bryn, just after Damon returned from Iraqi Kurdistan. They were also angry that Damon had not made a home for me yet – a permanent one. More hyperventilating and panic ensued. How would I cope with this new problem, I wondered?

It was during this visit that we noticed something ominous: Bryn was walking with a cane. He said that he had an orthopedic problem that had started when he put his right foot onto a chair to tie his shoe, and that the orthopedic surgeon had started him with the cane. He had been assured that it would get better after a while. We hoped so; Bryn had just retired and wanted to spend the next 10 years or so teaching at the Henry George School and volunteering with his land tax group at the United Nations. And – to be honest – he represented our calm, safe haven. It felt good not only because it was a place to go, but because it was his.

Life certainly gave me plenty of misery to cope with…and then I got accused of not being emotionally intelligent. To add insult to injury, some people who just didn't understand me very well would suggest more medications. I was sick and tired of explaining my whole life to make them forget the idea, and completely unwilling to hear the suggestions in the first place.

It was starting to look to me as if the only calm place I had to go to was Bryn's.

We visited him in the summer of 2008 again. It was our anniversary, and we had no better idea of where we might be together without breaking the bank…the nearly empty bank…and we wanted to see him. We hoped that he would be in better shape when we got there. We hoped that a little physical therapy would have helped him. It hadn't.

Bryn was still using the cane in late June, when we arrived. Still, the physical therapy was being touted as the solution, so we had a nice summer visit and didn't worry. He chatted with me like usual, asking how things were (they were the same), and I promised myself not to call him too often when I got home again. I didn't want him to think of me

A Travesty of Luck

as the sort of person who was always crying or complaining on the phone.

I had his home and cell phone numbers, but he didn't seem to like being on the phone. He would usually find some reason, shortly into any conversation, to end it. A favorite excuse would be the lousy reception, which was a source of frustration with most cell phone calls. If I called the land line, he would opt out for some other reason. So I wouldn't bug him, I decided. It wasn't not like he could fix things, anyway.

I went home after about a month with Damon, with the two of us reluctant to part as usual. I called Bryn a couple of times to tell him how I was, and then kept my promise to myself.

August came.

I knew that his daughter, Berta, had been considering a trip to Ireland with her boyfriend, Matt, who was from Ireland, to meet his relatives. We had corresponded by e-mail a few times, in addition to meeting occasionally at Bryn's place and in some restaurants. I had also met Bryn's older daughter, Dionne, and his niece Alissa. I had even met Dionne's husband when they had just begun to date, but Damon and I were away for their wedding, so we had missed it.

I wondered about Berta's trip to Ireland. She had worried, and so had the rest of us, about whether or not Matt's Catholic, Irish family would like her, a Unitarian American who differed from them in religion and culture. But what could they expect, I thought? That Matt would somehow find himself another Irish Catholic after leaving Catholic Ireland? Not a guarantee...

September came.

I e-mailed Berta when I thought enough time had elapsed for her to go to and return from Ireland. Why not, I thought? Being interested in my in-laws' lives seemed like a good thing, even though I hardly knew her. She e-mailed back 5 days later:

Hi Clarisse!

Ireland was amazing and I have a ton of photos to show. I haven't uploaded them yet, but I will get organized soon. I'll tell you all about it another time, but I wanted to suggest something to you.

I will call you in person either tomorrow or Thursday, but I wanted to see if you could think about coming down to stay with my father for a few weeks to take care of him. I hope by now that you have talked to him so you know that he definitely has cancer. We don't know what kind yet, as

The Slamming Door

the biopsy was first inconclusive, so they did a second one yesterday and we are awaiting the results. He has had about 5 or 6 radiation treatments, but will start chemo soon. He is in a lot of pain and can't really walk. He was in the hospital for the past five days and came out today. I asked him over the weekend how he would feel if I asked if you could come down and he said that would be nice. I was with him tonight and brought up the idea again, and he said he thought it would be a very good idea if you could come down and stay for a couple of weeks and he said that would really like that. My sister is coming back to New York on October 1st, and I can come over every night, but I don't think he should be alone right now. I am worried that he might fall and he can't really cook or shop. My uncle bought him a Lazy Boy chair which seems to be the most comfortable place for him, and his new bed is being delivered on Saturday. I am also not doing well emotionally, and [incomplete sentence.]

So I am not sure what your schedule would be like, or how you would feel about coming down but would you give some thought to it? No pressure at all, and I would completely understand if you don't think you are up to it, but I'll pay for your train, pick you up at Grand Central, and he'll pay for all the groceries, etc. for anything you would need. I would come down every night after work of course, but I don't think he should be alone. So give some thought to the idea, and I'll call you either tomorrow or Thursday to chat with you in person.

Much Love,
Berta

I stared at that line about cancer in shock for a moment, and thought I HAVE TO GO TAKE CARE OF HIM!!!!!!! I thought this before I even read on and saw Berta's request.

I could do that, I told myself. I had taken care of my grandmother through a cataract surgery, a broken wrist (a lengthy stay involving helping her bathe), another cataract surgery, and some random doctor visits. My other grandmother had died of lung cancer after I returned from my first term at college. With the exception of getting her some hot tea and a heating pad while still in high school, I hadn't been able to do much for her. I took care of my father when he had a herniated disk in

A Travesty of Luck

his lower spine (a shot of cortisone fixed it after an MRI). I had spent a winter break taking care of him, preparing food, running hot baths, and driving him to a meeting. I had even watched my Great-Aunt Susan when she had Alzheimer's disease for 2 weeks, just before she went to an elder care facility. Yes, I could do that.

But seemed perfect in an upsetting way: I was available to help, and all I needed to keep working was a computer, which Bryn had in the living room, complete with a printer that I had helped him choose, buy and install that summer. Damon had come with us to a Staples store in Union Square to carry it home. So this was lucky for both me and Bryn: he needed help, and I was available and totally willing.

Luck…what a travesty, considering that it put us together for a terrible reason. I realized that I loved Bryn. I forwarded Berta's letter to my husband, along with the following:

DAMON!

I HAVE TO GO THERE!

Love,
Clarisse.

Then I called Damon, upset and unwilling to wait for him to check his e-mail, and told him what was going on. He was at the university laboratory, working. Go there and take care of him? What about paying for food? Let me talk to them and see about it, I said.

I e-mailed Berta back, then began to think about Bryn some more. He couldn't walk, so it must be about his hip. What kind of cancer could it be? Probably bone cancer, I thought glumly, assuming the worst, and deciding that it made sense considering his orthopedic problems. But how did he get stuck with *that*? I wondered.

Next, I called Berta and said I had just seen her letter. She confirmed my suspicions: it was definitely bone cancer; an MRI scan in August had revealed that, and Bryn had spent some time – a couple of weeks, it seemed – at the Mount Sinai Hospital having radiation treatments. I could hardly wait to get there and help, was just worried about affording food, but otherwise it would be so easy to go there and help. I would just take a memory stick full of my data to Bryn's computer and insert it there, then resume whatever I had been working on there.

This was perfect to her. She said, "Don't worry; we'll pay for your food."

The Slamming Door

I called Damon back. I repeated the conversation, and suddenly he thought that this would just be the best thing for me – out of my parents' place, where I never went out because I had no car, and off to New York City, where I could safely go anywhere and everywhere on foot. I hadn't really thought about the city-as-a-playground aspect of the situation. Something wonderful was ending, and some serious misery was about to get underway as soon as a doctor could be appointed to direct it all.

Damon would send his secret recipe for ImmuneACCORD – his invention of a spice mixture – to help Bryn. Perhaps we could prolong Bryn's life a bit while reducing inflammation, and therefore pain. Inflammation causes pain, the reasoning went, and Damon wrote to both me and Berta promising to give me the secret recipe.

Berta had said not to call Bryn until the next night – to let her tell him – which was fine with me. I started planning. I told her I would come down there on Saturday, when my parents weren't working and could bring me to the bus station in Hartford. It was Wednesday evening, and I could take the two days to pack and organize whatever occurred to me.

We had just seen my mother's former boss, Dr. Leonardi, at his house the previous Saturday for his annual apple-picking party. He had an orchard outside. We had lots of apples, and I planned to make 2 pies, one for my parents and one for my grandmother and uncle who lived 5 minutes away. Then I would make a loaf of whole wheat honey bread; I could worry about breakfast foods later on. This would keep me from obsessing about the upcoming change.

Packing didn't feel too frantic this time. I felt like I was running away. I would just pack a few things and see how it went. I could arrange to get more of my clothes later…somehow. Meanwhile, I felt as though I were heading home.

I wanted to spend time with Bryn before the time was all gone, so I had to hurry up.

What an awful way to have to look at quality time with someone, on a timer, with an unknown setting for the alarm, with the remaining time looking like a great treasure.

A door had just been pulled back – and it had been pulled wide, to give a good swift swing to the entity that was about to slam it.

Chapter 2

Getting There

The evening after making these decisions, I called Bryn. He was glad to hear from me, and said that he wanted me to come and stay with him. Berta had spoken to him as planned, and he had agreed that he would need someone there with him. Until then, he hadn't really thought that far ahead or realized that it would be necessary to have a companion. It was like he understood it in theory, and had agreed, but he had also agreed because he felt that if he could have me there with him, he wouldn't mind. He liked living alone, and was rather set in his ways.

I too am set in my ways, so we would make good roommates. I liked to be on my own, I liked to read and learn and keep up with current events, and to have someone who cared about them to have conversations with. The difference was that I was a bit of a misanthrope – I didn't like a lot of noise or people. I liked my in-laws, however, so I imagined that being among the New York relatives would be a pleasant experience.

Bryn asked me when I thought I would arrive, and I said Saturday afternoon or early evening, depending upon the bus schedule, but that I would take an afternoon bus. "Don't make it too late," he said, and I promised to get an early afternoon bus.

I had already begun to get ready to go; that afternoon I had made the pies and informed my father that I would need a ride to the bus station on Saturday afternoon, because Bryn had bone cancer and I was going to go take care of him. My father responded with his usual deadpan gravity: he listened, but did not look directly at me, and said almost nothing. I understood that he had taken in the information and would give me the ride, and most likely approved of my plan. That was it. My father was rather quiet when he wasn't lecturing endlessly about whatever fascinated him or was going on in his life.

As I told my father about my plans, I was making the apple raisin pies, with my usual cut-out decorations on top. It felt different this time, like a last hurrah of baking. I most likely would not be doing any more serious baking for a very long time, as the family referred to Bryn's kitchen as a bachelor's kitchen. It had extremely limited space, few cook's tools, a gas stove, and an oven that I didn't know how to use. To top it all off, there was no way to know the temperature of said oven, as the dial was an ancient, crud-coated, blackish thing that lacked numbers. Apparently, no baking had happened in that kitchen for years...only cooking.

The Slamming Door

The next afternoon I made a loaf of whole wheat honey bread – one long loaf, which I wrapped up to take with me – and laid out some books to pack, including some on Iranian history and culture.

I was involved in a project to write a memoir of a famous feminist's career, but it felt almost like a rumor, as we hardly ever seemed to make progress on it. My co-author and the subject of the book was an Iranian woman politician, an outspoken activist who had served one term in the Majlis – Parliament – before being forbidden to run again by Iran's mullahs. Human rights, women's rights, students' rights and freedom of speech are not popular causes in Iran. Her name was Massoumeh Parsi, Ph.D., and our project was on hold while she applied for her green card, along with her husband and little girl. I had taught myself, by reading, everything and anything I could about Iranian history and Iranian women's studies, plus watching Marjane Satrapi's *Persepolis*. I was learning all about the culture so as to not waste Massoumeh's time or mine. Perhaps we would do more work while I was in Manhattan.

I did not know how long I would be gone, so I laid out some recreational books also: French history, historical novels, etc. I really don't remember precisely what I threw in; I was forcing myself not to get bogged down in an anxiety-ridden rut this time. The clothes were a problem, but I figured I would just bring what I needed for the current season and ask my mother to send others later if the visit stretched on…which I expected it to. This wasn't really a visit, after all. I was going to Bryn's place as a caregiver, though I had yet to hear this term.

My mother and her mother were nurses, so I realized that I must have it in me to take care of sick relatives properly. My mother was an office nurse who did triage (that means deciding what each patient needs in the immediate future and directing them on to that phase of treatment), which she handled mostly over the telephone.

My grandmother trained in Boston at the Brigham and Women's Hospital in the 1930s. It was a 1-year course, and she had lived in a dormitory with a head nurse as the dorm mother and instructor. She worked there briefly before following a patient home to Hartford, Connecticut, where she was a home care nurse until the woman died. When the undertaker came to collect the corpse, it was my grandfather. I have always found this circumstance hilarious, as did the patient's widower. He derived great pleasure and amusement from the whole thing, following the news of their relationship over the ensuing year of courtship until their wedding, when he gave them money for furniture. Nana's subsequent nursing career, resumed when their children were a bit older, was ever after as a home care nurse.

I would be Bryn's de facto home care nurse, I thought, though the term "caregiver" was really a more accurate title for the role I took on,

Getting There

and the definition of the role was revealed to me in detail as time went on. Whatever the title, it made me think of my grandmother on her first live-in home care nurse job often over the course of the time I spent with Bryn.

By this time, Bryn had known what was wrong with him for a month and a half.

He had been through some radiation and a hospital stay.

This meant that he was probably exhausted, demoralized, and sad.

Yet he had told me on the phone that he was still going out every day to buy himself a copy of *The New York Times*, something that he wanted to read every day. This meant that he had no energy for any other trips out of his apartment each day after getting the newspaper. He had a computer with an Internet connection, but he wasn't very adept at using it, and was frankly a bit intimidated by the technology. I had given him a couple of lessons in August, but he had been so timid with the technology that he barely remembered what I had showed him.

Well, I could take care of that problem: I called the customer service people of *The New York Times* – that number was easy enough for me to find online – and ordered him a subscription. It would have his name on the delivery address and my name on the billing address. [I didn't know it yet, but this would set a precedent for the way that we would operate my daily caregiving and acquisition of supplies for the duration of my stay with him. I would keep records, and he would reimburse me at the end of each month.] I called Bryn after placing the order, and told him that it would start before I arrived. He was delighted.

Berta told me that she was worried that he might fall in the shower, so I also ordered a shower seat (to be assembled after delivery) from Bed Bath & Beyond. It arrived the same day that I did, but Bryn didn't need it until months later. Still, it was good to plan ahead and be prepared. I didn't bother mentioning that right away.

I continued my preparations for departure, figuring that I would find out whatever else was needed after I got there.

The only thing I would miss at Bryn's place, aside from being able to do any serious baking, would be seeing what became of Cookie, my black-and-white cat. He had some maddening, mysterious problem that was causing him to lick himself bloody and bald here and there all over…on his head, between his shoulder blades, etc. It was driving both me and him crazy; me because I could hear the relentless licking, knowing that he was just making it all worse, and him because he was endlessly uncomfortable with no end in sight.

My father was going to take him to a pet allergist that our neighbor had told us about. I hoped that would solve the mystery and begin a recovery, but it would have to be up to my parents to deal with that. I

The Slamming Door

didn't know everything about what it would be like to die of cancer, but I knew that it would be too difficult for Bryn to do all by himself. So I was leaving.

My mother ended up helping me a little bit with the packing after all – because she offered and I accepted. It felt better that way, and she said she would send on more stuff later somehow if necessary. That was a relief. It was also a relief to leave; I was out in rural Connecticut away from a bus line and beyond any reasonable walking distance for purposes of employment or recreation.

I had been totally dependent upon my parents for transportation, and was unwilling to spend time trapped in a car with either of them in order to get rides on any routine basis. That meant no rides to work even if I had actually had a job. We had entered the Great Recession, though it was not yet being called by that term, and finding employment was a grim proposition at best. Being trapped in a moving vehicle with my mother making endless unsolicited suggestions on the days that she drove me to Curves – my only chance to go out most weeks, on Wednesdays, her day off – was stressful.

I had not been able to do much of anything at home – I had a beautiful new Windows Vista computer, but that was my only distraction aside from books, crime shows on CBS, and *Bones* on another channel. I wanted out, even if I hadn't known where life would take me next.

I went through the usual routine of reminding my father yet again why I wanted to leave from Hartford rather than from Farmington (only one stop in New Haven, thus a shorter ride and only one time to watch and make sure that my bag didn't get unloaded or stolen there).

On Saturday, September 20, 2008, I bought the ticket at Union Station in Hartford, and was off, cell phone ready and with a memory stick sewn into my pocket. Not much could go wrong on this run, I told myself. I now knew the ride to New York City well, having made the trip by bus often in the past 3 years: down Interstate-91 to 95, off to New Haven, back on, and on to Manhattan, entering through a northern point of the island.

I don't remember calling Bryn during this ride – I was just thinking and daydreaming, which I do a lot of, and watching out the windows. I had a window seat, and no one sat next to me. I kept my carry-on bags there. Bryn called me as the bus entered northern Manhattan, though. He wanted to know when I thought I would arrive, so I told him where the bus was, and said he would have to know based on that, because I couldn't explain it in minutes. What was out the windows? Triple-X night clubs with huge billboards, and seedy-looking brick buildings, I said. He knew that area too – so that meant I would arrive soon. This was

Getting There

good, he added, because everyone was there. He seemed satisfied with this, and sounded very cheerful.

We rang off and I watched as the bus moved southwards through Manhattan, passing through Haarlem and Morningside Heights, bypassing Central Park on the north by the northwest corner (wasn't this the set of twin buildings where Alissa had an apartment, I wondered?), and then on down Columbus Avenue until it became 9th Avenue, into the underground parking area of the Port Authority Bus Station.

It was now quite familiar to me, thanks to countless trips here with Damon. It was easier and cheaper to come here this way; the costs and hassle of parking a car in Manhattan just aren't worth it. One either parks in a garage and pays outrageous fees while being unable to go back and put in or take out anything (the garage people drive it up or down a level, put it on a rack, or otherwise make it inaccessible, thus ensuring receipt of the parking fees), or else one keeps moving the car on alternate street sweeping days. Better to just arrive without a car.

The bus pulled into the station and we all hurried out at a sloth's pace, impatient but stuck in a narrow space. I retrieved my new, bright blue duffle bag on wheels and found that the zipper had popped open in transit. Wonderful; I had thought that this stupid bag would make travel easier. I dragged it inside and found an out-of-the-way spot to wrestle the zipper into submission. As I did so, I glanced up to see a seventysomething lady, African-American, with bangs and straight, chin-length hair, glasses, a prim-looking dress, and a straw hat with a big bow on the front of it. She was pursing her lips and regarding my bright blue nuisance with disapproval.

"This is the first time that I used this bag, and it will probably be the last," I said to her. She shook her head and disgust and sympathy, and replied, "They don't make things like they used to." "Probably made in China," I agreed, as I rolled it toward the escalator.

The routine was so firmly recorded in my mind that it was now as though my memory was playing a DVD to indicate the route out of the labyrinth: up the escalator, out past fast-food joints, shops, newsstands and kiosks to reverse direction and exit at 9th rather than 8th Avenue. The 8th Avenue side was mobbed with people and taxi cabs, and although getting a cab was easier on that side, one would then have to pay a higher fare in the end, because it would include crossing to 9th Avenue. I would get a cab on 9th Avenue, ride it straight south, and get out on the left/east side of the street at the north side of 21st Street. From there, I would just walk up to Bryn's building. I really had this routine down pat…though I sensed that I would not need this information ever again. I expected to remain with Bryn until he no longer required me.

The Slamming Door

Getting the cab didn't take long. I quickly hopped in with my stuff, explained what I wanted to the driver, and we took off. As we headed down 9th Avenue, I almost called Bryn again, but then decided it wasn't worth it; I would be there shortly, and would not have time to think quietly again.

The cab pulled up next to the new bicycle lane and I paid up and got out.

There was the familiar corner: northeast, with the high-end florist shop right on the end, facing the Avenue, followed by a high-end hair salon with ornate, curlicued metal-work and Billy's Bakery, known for pastel-iced, too-sweet cupcakes. I glanced at the other corners, now like a second home: southeast, with Rafaella on 9th, a café with Moroccan and Italian food; southwest, with a construction project underway – thanks to a sale by the Episcopal Seminary of one of their buildings, the neighborhood was soon to acquire yet another apartment building that could rent its ground floor out as small business spaces; northwest, with Le Grainne Café – it served French food (my favorite), had a 1951 LaRousse French-English dictionary over the booth area seating, and occupied a building that is protected as a National Historic Landmark because Clement Clark Moore wrote *T'was the Night Before Christmas* in the upper floor.

Le Grainne Café seen from outside and Rafaella on 9th seen from inside.

I turned to face the stretch of 21st Street between 8th and 9th Avenues. It was mid-September, so it was still officially summer. The leaves were still green on the trees, the air was a comfortable, pleasant temperature without being hot or humid, and the sun was still shining. People were out walking together holding hands – both gay and straight couples, as

Getting There

this was Chelsea – or walking their dogs, or both. I didn't see any familiar faces yet.

Bryn had given me and Damon keys a few years ago, and had deliberately and pointedly not taken them back. The reason was convenience and welcome combined: he would not have to meet us to let us in if we had our own keys. We could just arrive and depart. We were easy guests, I thought: we cleaned everything we used, and we cleaned his apartment for him whenever we visited, thus saving him money on cleaning lady fees. We had made a habit of buying replacements for any household items that were worn out, which made his life more comfortable. And I had bought him various household gifts to make him more comfortable, things that he would not otherwise think to buy on his own.

It felt ominous yet inviting as I looked east on 21st Street; time to go in and see everyone, and greet Bryn. I headed up the street, into the gray brick building, and let myself into the apartment.

Chapter 3

Settling In

There was no point in trying to guess the details of the future. I sensed what the final outcome would be, and that was why I was here – to spend as much time as I could with him before that time was all gone. Hurry up before it's all gone, I would say to myself whenever I thought about why I was doing this. I would say that to myself a lot, and would have to tell myself to say it out loud to Bryn. He deserved to hear it.

This was an old building, and the apartments that weren't completely renovated and rented out at the market rate were adequately though not beautifully maintained. Everything worked, a superintendent would help with whatever problems cropped up, and plumbers and electricians were available. But the overall appearance of the place was a bit antiquated to the point of shabby. Neither Bryn nor the family cared; what mattered was that the place was in a nice area of lower Manhattan at a low price. Bryn had been very happy here for decades.

The building's superintendent was new to the job, a nice Puerto Rican man named Luis. His newly retired predecessor was an old Cuban man named Teo. Teo was a bit of a legend in the building, cranky, quiet, and still a resident, up on the fifth floor – the top one. He had wisely gotten himself one of its rent-controlled apartments. Teo had a long, wavy white beard that hung like a curtain in front of his chest, and he always wore jeans and a Panama hat. He liked to sit outside on a folding chair in warm weather, but I hadn't seen him as I arrived that evening.

Bryn had told me about Teo a few years earlier: he had allegedly fought the Communist regime of Castro in the Bay of Pigs fiasco in April of 1961, after which time the C.I.A. had found him this job as superintendent of a building on West 21st Street. That was the rumor; Bryn had warned us not to say a word to him about it, so we never did. Teo rarely smiled, and he tended to scowl at Bryn and Damon. But he always smiled when I greeted him, nodded, and said "Hi" back to me. Bryn explained that he liked women, and me in particular. Damon cheerfully added, "Everyone likes Clarisse!" Damon was biased, of course.

It was a lovely evening, and Teo's pair of giant potted plants still stood on either side of the entrance like sentries. The decaying list of tenants was behind a glass panel to the left of the front door which, just like the inner one, was made of glass and opened with the same key. Old white-and-black tiles covered the floor, and ivory paint, the latest of many coats since the building's construction, covered the walls. The apartment doors were an attractive shade of dark green, and small signs

Settling In

indicated the floor and letter of each one. Around the corner to the right were the mailboxes and the stairwell.

Up the stairs, half facing the stairwell window and half facing each floor, I had dragged my suitcase and hauled my other bags. I knew that I was about to see a lot of people all at once in there. I took out my keychain, complete with the extra little ring on it that contained the set of 3 keys for Bryn's place, and let myself in. A chorus of greetings rang out and people called me into the back of the apartment.

Everyone was there: Albert (Bryn's younger brother – they were 2 years apart in age), June (Albert's wife), Alissa (their daughter), Berta (Bryn's daughter), Matt (Berta's boyfriend), and Bryn. They were all in Bryn's room.

I dumped my stuff in the guest room and went in there, curious about the changes that had taken place in there. Berta was sitting on the latest change, a new, full-sized bed with pretty sea-green sheets and the new sage green quilt from L.L. Bean that Damon and I had sent to Bryn at Christmas. At last it was in use; Bryn hadn't even taken it out of the packaging since we had given it to him, but today Berta had done so and thrown the ugly old brown one in the closet.

Bryn was seated in his usual corner to the left of the windows, holding court in his bedroom-that-doubled-as-visiting room. Something was different there, too. It was a very good something: he had a beautiful new Lazy-Boy chair, upholstered in a light blue fabric. The new chair

The Slamming Door

was a gift from Cassie, as was its predecessor, which had been literally falling apart at the seams. (Berta had been mistaken in her letter; she had thought that Albert gave it to him.) The matching ottoman that came with the old chair was still there, serving as a place for Bryn's current reading material. The usual piles of other reading material and yet-to-be-dealt-with mail lay here and there on the floor – so nothing else was new. Just the reason for my presence here…

I greeted Bryn and everyone else, got a hug, and was pleased to hear Bryn call out to me, dragging out my name with his customary enthusiasm and big toothy grin. He looked sort of okay, but then I realized that the most significant damage yet done by the medical profession was diagnosing him too late to save him. The real damage was yet to come – poison and strange pharmaceuticals followed by surrender to the inevitable. I was morbidly relieved to realize that we wouldn't have to face that just yet. A second, surreptitious scrutiny revealed that his eyelids had taken on that odd, waxy appearance of someone who has had radiation treatments.

I was looking forward to spending lots of time with Bryn. He was like another dad to me, one who didn't get angry, but who was intellectually curious like my own father – even more so. I had that in common both with him and my own father. And I have always loved being around older people, whereas I hate to be around babies and little kids. Older people have wonderful stories to tell, great stores of knowledge of whatever interests them, and they have enough life experience and wisdom to be able to gauge the effect of their remarks on others before saying anything upsetting. That was Bryn. Here was the most fun and interesting and beloved member of the family, he was in need of careful attention, and I was happy to be able to give it to him. He certainly deserved it.

As usual, right after greeting everyone, I had to use the bathroom and clean myself up – I have an evil bladder that makes me desperate for the bathroom if I feel the slightest bit of you-know-what in it. (The only reason I mention this is that living with Bryn and only one bathroom would make it an issue – more on that later.) I quickly got clean and comfortable, and then changed into something suitable for a trip to the local diner and touched up my makeup. June, who had Alzheimer's disease, joked with me, saying that she always had to do that too.

We were going to the diner called Moonstruck (named after the movie), where we thought we could get a table all together. (Bryn's usual haunt, the Greek's, was right across the street, but it didn't have a table for 8 or 9 people, so we weren't going there.) In typical fashion, whenever any large group of people intends to head out together, we didn't go as soon as I imagined we would. I had gotten ready as fast as I

Settling In

could, only to have what I wanted: a couple of minutes to spare during which I managed to put away every dish in the kitchen dish rack, which I had noticed was full as I walked by with my luggage. The family promptly remarked about this, complimenting me.

All this is really is my obsessive compulsive tendencies at work, which I channel in a useful way: cleaning, straightening, neatening, and organizing. Maintaining a neat and clean environment, has the added dividend of leaving me with less work to do, less stress, and no complaints from the other people around me. It seemed to work well, so I kept it up. This means routine cleaning and daily chores, which just seems normal. Apparently, my in-laws did not see it that way; they were amazed and impressed by something that I thought of as a requirement. I was pleased, though I didn't show them much of a reaction; I didn't want to seem smug over it.

But this was, I was sure, part of what they hoped for in asking me there: I would keep Bryn's environment clean and organized, and make sure that he ate well and lived in comfort, no longer having to do any chores at all.

It was Hilda's job to remove the garbage and recycling; Bryn paid her a weekly allowance for that. He informed me of this fact, and so I cheerfully refrained from trotting the stuff down to the creepy basement, and warned Damon that he was no longer to do that when he visited.

The Slamming Door

Damon used to consider that to be his duty, until we knew that it was Hilda's. It's wrong to take a kid's chance to earn money away; kids don't have many chances to do that.

So I just bagged it up as Bryn directed; the building had a lot of specific rules for this. Garbage was kept separate, of course, and all recyclables except for paper went together, while paper went into huge, clear and hard-to-find plastic bags. I ended up searching many of the area stores for those bags, and ultimately getting several packages via the Internet, of all things, stocking up so as to not have to bother with it again for several months. That lasted until I left.

It wasn't long before we were all ready to head out to the diner.

When Bryn got up, I watched him move. He used the cane, leaning heavily on it, and that the bone cancer was primarily in his right hip joint. It was hurting him so much now that he was really only truly comfortable either in his new chair or lying in bed. He couldn't possibly carry a bag of laundry to and from the laundromat down the street any more, I thought, or much else. I would take care of it all.

We headed out, and the Matt said that his sister and her husband were visiting from Ireland, and were walking around in Greenwich Village. They would meet us at the Moonstruck Diner when they got there, and they intended to walk. Albert and Bryn warned me that the brother-in-law was a doctrinaire Catholic with rigid political and religious views. I took this to mean that he was an anti-choice type on the subject of abortion. I am pro-choice – with the attitude that men had a hell of a nerve to ever tell women what to do with our bodies. I wouldn't start any trouble over this, but if asked point-blank, well…I felt a devilish amusement just contemplating it. It wasn't anything I was particularly concerned about, though. Why would that come up? We were just going to eat together.

I walked alongside Bryn, chatting with him and watching him surreptitiously. He wasn't going as fast as before. But he wasn't exactly moving at a snail's pace, either. I made no attempt to predict how long his illness would be, how it would go, how much of it would be enjoyable time for him and how much would be miserable, or anything else. Everyone's demise was different, I reasoned, and that was a good thing. I didn't want to know. If I knew the answer to that, I really would feel depressed and terrified. I would rather just see how it all played out. I sounded like Morgan Freeman in *The Bucket List*, which I had just seen that summer.

It looked as though Bryn would have some more enjoyment before the end of his story, so I decided not to think about it further just now. I found out that I would have a different, more comfortable bed than ever before, because he had thought to put his old mattress in my room, on

Settling In

top of the horrible, flat, futon. The delivery guys who had brought in the new bed had taken the old box spring away and moved the mattress for me, and Berta had brought some new sheets for my bed as well as her father's. I was psyched about it; my back had gone out once on that futon.

Bryn's old mattress was something of a joke combined with a legend in the family. It was probably older than me, and I was 38 years old at the time that all this was happening. The mattresses had belonged to his and Albert's mother, who had died in 1981, and she had had it for many years before that. When she died, Bryn – who was divorced and living in his bachelor pad with not much furniture – had inherited all of her things, including the bedding. Rather than get new mattresses, he just used those. As if that wasn't enough frugality (or perhaps lack of interest in his surroundings) he always used the same side of the mattress, never turning them.

He never noticed that he had what I liked to call an avalanche bed.

Damon and I discovered this during a hot week alone together in Bryn's place during the summer of 2005. By "hot" I don't mean a steamy, sexy time. I mean it was a record hot weather summer in terms of humidity and discomfort. Bryn had gone away for a week to Philadelphia for a Henry George School historical pilgrimage to the social economist's house museum and grave with his colleagues. That left us in the apartment alone, and Damon immediately availed himself of Bryn's air conditioner, shutting himself in the room with the cool air.

I had followed, intending to sleep next to Damon, but when I lay down next to him, I rolled right into him. With great effort, putting tense pressure on my left side, I managed to stay on my half of the bed, but it was immediately obvious that sleep would not be possible like that. And despite the fact that I was hotter than I normally preferred, I decided that the air conditioning was just too cold. So it was back to the guest room with the fan, my own television, plenty of books, and the ability to lie flat effortlessly. Much as I loved to be next to Damon, an avalanche bed made the idea an exercise in futility.

When I found out about the avalanche mattress being mine, I expressed thanks with enthusiasm. This was a very nice thing that Bryn had thought of for me, and I knew I could eliminate the avalanche factor with the horrid old pillows and unwanted quilts of varying sizes that were tossed into the closets. This was going to be a very comfortable pad in short order.

I was curious to get to know Albert's wife June and daughter Alissa, whom I had only met a few times and who were both rather quiet. June was slowly declining into the abyss of Alzheimer's disease, but she hadn't yet descended very far. I had had a great-aunt with the same problem, so I knew about the use of distraction to get the patient off of the idea of wandering off on her own, and I knew that the memories she had weren't gone yet – they were just getting harder and harder to access at will. It is only later that even this isn't possible, when the unfortunate person's brain breaks down and the cells containing those memories disintegrate. June wasn't there yet, so I thought I would be getting to know her over the next several months, and I looked forward to it. (It turned out that I was right about that, too.)

June had aced her way through graduate school not once but twice, studying first art and then psychology. She had worked as a counselor in New York City's public schools, offering art therapy. She liked horses. She liked cats and dogs, and had had several pets; right now they had a Sheltie dog named Phoebe. June was petite, small-boned, and blonde; Albert adored her and was determined to do whatever he could to keep her happy at all times. He had bought a house on Martha's Vineyard with her so that she could go away and ride horses, which they still had. They were selling it now.

Alissa was not only quiet, she barely spoke. The family had told me that she used to speak even less than she did now, and I was curious about her. She seemed very nice. She loved dogs, and thought cats were okay but preferred dogs. Alissa lived in her own apartment at the northwest corner of Central Park, and visited her parents often. I had the distinct feeling that being on her own was not really that big of deal to her, or that important. She seemed to prefer staying with her parents. She was fluent in French and Italian, and had studied for her master's degree in medieval European history at Columbia University. That was why she had not been to my wedding – final exams had conflicted with it.

Berta seemed really happy to see me, and she and her boyfriend Matt walked along with us in a good mood. I was curious about her. I hadn't

Settling In

spent much time with her yet. I knew that she worked as a secretary/receptionist (both) at Deutsche Bank on Wall Street. She had returned to New York City in 2006 after being away for several years, first in Los Angeles for 4 years, then a couple of years in Oneonta, upstate in New York, where her mother had a house. Since meeting her, I had only seen her perhaps 2 or 3 times, usually in connection with an event at the Henry George School.

I walked with Bryn most of the way, first heading west to 9th Avenue, then crossing to the other side and walking up two blocks to the Moonstruck Diner. When we arrived, the diner wasn't crowded; it was early, so only a few booths were occupied. The waiter took us straight back to an area I hadn't seen before, with a large table, close to the rest rooms. The place was lighter, more open, and cleaner than the Greeks across the street – but I kept my opinion to myself. Bryn loved the Greeks. (Eventually I would get him to explain why.)

Bryn told the waiter that 2 more people were on their way, and a small table for 2 was shoved up against a table for 8. Bryn took the seat at the end farthest from me, and Alberta sat down next to me. I was with my back to the wall (my favorite way to sit in a public place – it feels safe to me), next to the table for 2. The family settled around us and I began to observe them all. Bryn kept getting up and standing with his cane; he said that it hurt to either sit or stand for very long. I wondered about getting him a cushion to carry around, but it was too late to do that for this evening.

Dinner went well enough. Matt's sister and her husband showed up as we were ordering and settled in next me. June and Albert had settled with Alissa across from us, and Bryn had installed himself at both ends of the table, alternating whenever sitting became unpleasant. It was like a huge bone-spur was bothering him. He spent half the meal standing with his cane, chatting.

I don't remember what he ate that evening, but he did eat. I ordered trout and green beans, and was pleased that it came with an orange rather than a lemon (I don't like lemon). Berta got turkey with gravy and mashed potatoes. The Irish relatives almost talked politics with me, but I stared the husband down with a stony smile when he tried to discuss abortion, saying something like, "So…you are anti-choice, religiously Catholic, and so on." He got the message and gave up on the idea of berating me, which is what I suspected he wanted to do. I don't like religion or religiousness, and I won't let anyone harangue me about it. Being older or male or a guest won't induce me to allow someone to do that. Nothing will.

Eventually, we all headed back to Bryn's place. The Irish couple rode back to Long Island with Matt. His relatives always stayed at his house when they toured New York City, so he drove them in his SUV. Berta rode with them; he would drop her off at the Stuyvesant apartments, where she lived with her mother. She and I planned to meet and go out together the next afternoon, after sleeping late.

Albert, June and Alissa went home after a while, and Bryn and I found ourselves walking back to his place together. It was dark at that point, but the air was perfect. I wore a light jacket, and he was in his usual khaki Dockers and a loose, dark blue sweatshirt with a thin gray stripe across the middle of it. We walked slowly because he was using the cane.

Bryn's corn-cob pipes, on the ash-tray with the television, and more on the windowsill, his supply for future use.

Upstairs, we realized that it was so early in his illness that the evening could be fun and relaxing. It was only nine o'clock, so we didn't even start getting ready for bed. I busied myself with straightening up his room, and then flopped on the new bed, enjoying the ugly brown pillows, a pair of long ones that made the bed into a sofa in its daytime mode. I sat there facing Bryn, who leaned back in his new blue Lazy-Boy chair and lit his corn-cob pipe.

From that spot, I had a view of the drop-leaf table that was straight across from the bed, between Bryn's habitual corner and the door to his room. To its right was Bryn, next to his partially open window, with his tins of tobacco on the sill and his little television on the small wooden table to his left. A bureau stood in the other corner of the room, to my right, and the air conditioner was in the right-side window. The room had two windows in a row looking out at the street. There was a small screen for the left-side window, and Bryn was careful never to open any of them too wide and leave them; he didn't want any birds to fly in.

There was just one lamp in there, and it was on the drop-leaf table close to Bryn. The leaves of the table were always kept down. On the table was so much stuff that it was hard to make sense of it all, but I would become intimately familiar with it quickly. It had to be kept neat and organized, clean and dusted, and the things on it within easy reach so that Bryn wouldn't have to keep getting up. Funny how I was able to plot this logistics out at a mere glance, but that was one of my talents.

On the floor were his piles of papers. They were a mess. These were the piles that I had always lifted up and shaken dirt out of whenever Damon and I had visited. We would clean the room while Bryn was out, with me dusting and mopping, and Damon changing the sheets. We never spoke about our intention; we would just suddenly find ourselves working on his room.

I didn't comment about the mess in front of me now; I was waiting to see what Bryn would ask me to do. I didn't have to wait long.

Shortly, he asked me if I would go through all those piles for him. "I don't want Dionne and Berta to have to do this," he told me. They contained his unopened or not-dealt-with mail, such as bills and personal correspondence. The papers amounted, in part, to the documents of his estate, I realized. He wanted me to help with this because I was a lawyer and therefore by definition trustworthy and good at sorting through such things with efficiency. He had that right, I thought, but I just nodded.

Of course he didn't want them to do this; it would be upsetting to Berta because of what it would mean – imminent death for her father, or else it wouldn't be dealt with at all. Neither of them would be able to sort it all out anyway.

With that, I promised to take care of it during the next week, and thus clear it all off the floor. For now, I placed all of the piles neatly together in the corner so that walking around in there would be easier.

Next, Bryn told me that his daughters were jealous of me for being able to be with him and to take care of him. I did not ask why; I figured it was fairly self-explanatory. Still, I was curious to learn more about them, particularly their personalities.

Bryn said he was going to get a haircut the next day; his hair was now so long that it looked like one of the appalling shaggy dos of the 1970s (I hated the aesthetics of that decade). In the past, his daughters had each told me that he usually went to a cheap place nearby and came back with a not-so-attractive haircut. (I think Damon might have gone there, too, referred by Bryn, but he looked okay afterward.) They had also informed me that he would occasionally go to a pricier place staffed by gay stylists, and come back looking great. Wherever he went, I had a glum sense that this would be his last haircut ever. I hated cancer treatments. They were barbaric, and I just knew that they would take away all of Bryn's beautiful thick, white hair.

At that point, Bryn told me something: he didn't want either of his daughters – not Berta, and not his older, married stepdaughter Dionne – to take care of him. That surprised me a little, except for the fact that I had been brought in to do that. Silly me; I had thought that logistics had informed this decision. Berta had to work all day every weekday at Deutsche Bank, so she wasn't available, and Dionne was married and often in Colorado or Wyoming with her husband. Both were artists, and he was independently wealthy.

But no; that was not why. The reason that Bryn gave was that he felt uncomfortable with having them know the details – and messiness – of his illness. He was embarrassed by the mere idea of it, and wanted to conceal it. That made sense, considering the fact that he had gone to such extreme lengths to conceal his first bout with cancer.

"This is going to get messy," he confided. "Do you think you can handle that?"

"Well, yeah, I can handle that, and I will aid and abet you in concealing all of the evidence, too," I promised him.

He perked up at that, looking greatly relieved.

"I will clean up any mess you make before visitors come in and see it, and if it involves anything to do with needing the toilet, I won't tell people," I clarified.

He looked even happier. Then he asked me something even more serious. Would I promise to stay with him until he didn't need me anymore?

Yes.

Well...that took care of all the important stuff.

We spent some more time talking, and at one point – the only time that I cried to Bryn about the fact that he was sick and therefore doomed to leave me – I did so. He was leaving all of us, and I'm not sorry to have shown him at least once that I was upset. But I don't think it would have been good to do it repeatedly. That's not to say that I never cried about anything again while I was with him. Sometimes the stress of my own problems would set me off, but as always, he was my friend and would offer advice that settled me down.

On this night, however, he said, "Don't you think that I am upset about being sick?"

I said that of course I did, but that it was unrealistic of him to expect the family not to get upset and cry about his illness.

Settling In

He told me that that was why he had concealed his first bout with cancer, in 2005. He hadn't wanted to deal with people getting upset about him. He had hoped to hide this illness too, but unfortunately, he just didn't see how to pull that off.

So…he had been sick before, and during that horridly hot summer in 2005.

I was about to find out all of the relevant, basic facts of the matter, and I did over the next week or so. When I understood how this illness had come about, I was infuriated; Bryn didn't have to be terminally ill with bone cancer. He could have been limping along with prostate cancer, with several more years of life to live. But that is an explanation for later.

For now, we settled in for the evening. Bryn pulled a chair up to the refrigerator, sitting in the front hall, while I opened the door and he told me what food was too old and what was okay. Lots of take-out containers went into the trash.

The living room of Bryn's place with our old laptop on the desk/table. By 2008, there was a desktop computer with a small flat-screen monitor there.

I settled my food and cookware into place, and was glad that I had bought him little gifts here and there on my many past visits. This bachelor pad kitchen still had some awful cookware in it, including a wooden-handled wok with its black paint chipping off and a huge, flat-bottomed, Revere-ware fry pan that food always stuck to, but at least I could work in there.

I checked the computer when the kitchen was in order, plugging in my memory stick and transferring all of my files to the hard drive. Later that month, I bought a second stick with even more storage space on it, and kept them both in the computer tower's USB ports at all times after that. I had also brought my Wi-Fi gadget from home so that I could pirate an Internet signal off of the airwaves in the building. That worked sporadically, but it worked.

My favorite part of the desk where that the computer sat on was the left side, where Bryn had piled stacks of books in such a way that they would not fall. The family liked to say that he had built a fort of books there. They were stacked like bricks, one way and another, but so that one could still read the titles.

This is exactly how the fort of books looked during Bryn's illness, and that chair and cushion were the ones that I sat on for hours on end almost every day.

About a week or so later, Bryn decided that he should learn – for real this time – how to use the Internet so that he could edit a new Henry George book with his colleagues. As he did so, he began to understand that the Internet system we had was not adequate.

It was with silent elation that I responded to his request that I set up a cable Internet system in the apartment, which he and I arranged by

Settling In

phone with Time-Warner Cable. The cable boxes needed updating and replacing, and the Internet could be wired into the same box.

I ended up walking down 23rd Street past Madison Square Park to the Time-Warner company to get the necessary items. While there, I met a tall, muscular, stubble-haired guy who was going gray. He was the one who waited on me and explained what he would give me to take home and how to set it up once he realized that I could do it all myself. I had told him all about Bryn, that he was my husband's wonderful cousin, sick with terminal bone cancer, and that I was taking care of him now. It was a habit, telling people about my life, but I didn't care. I never told people things that would threaten my security or anyone else's, but talking eased stress.

When he heard this, he told me that he had recovered from cancer a few years ago, and that a friend had moved in to take care of him. Wow. He was well now and back on his own. I didn't ask what kind of cancer it had been. It was just nice to know that it was gone, and to see that this guy was back to living his life. He might have been in his mid-forties.

He brought out a huge, ugly, orange bag with handles with a Time-Warner logo on it, plus two cable boxes, new remote controls, another box that was small and black and with lots of connectors protruding from it, and a lot of cords, including a really long one that would go from the living room computer to the television setup in Bryn's room. Bryn had insisted on giving me cab money, and when I felt the heaviness of that bag, I appreciated it.

The setup was simple, and soon I had the wires hooked up properly and the little connector box on the floor under the window behind Bryn's Lazy-Boy chair. The long cord went behind it and out to the living room. I taped it down in several places with clear packing tape so that no one, least of all Bryn, would trip over it. That worked; he never tripped over it.

And we were hooked up to a super-fast Internet connection! It was a thrill to have a reliable line to the World Wide Web. But that was later on. Meanwhile, I struggled with Bryn's old computer, even going so far as to buy memory upgrades for it. It was a hand-me-down from a friend of Alissa's, and I had already invested in a surge-protector for it over the summer.

That had been amusing; Bryn had come in while Damon and I were watching a movie to say that I shouldn't have spent money on anything for it. I had just bought him a mouse-pad with an image of Van Gogh's *Starry Night* on it at Staples, and the surge protector. It was late June, and a lightning storm had motivated me to do that.

"And what would you say to Alissa if a lightning storm fried that nice new computer that she just gave you?" I had asked him.

The Slamming Door

Bryn had paused for a moment; this very real possibility had not occurred to him. "Good point," he had said, and let the matter drop, accepting the new gadget. He really didn't know much about computers, even though they had become indispensable in everyone's lives.

Now that he had me there, and he knew that my career revolved around the machine, he let me take possession of it most of the time, and arrange its settings to suit myself. I don't think he knew what that involved, but he understood that enabling me was enabling himself right back. It was a necessary and fair exchange.

That first night, I thought I did a decent job of settling in. I had the computer in order, and soon the bed was more or less leveled off from underneath by the old pillows and quilts that no one wanted any more. The food was put away, and my stuff was unpacked.

I felt as though I had escaped from something, albeit into a tough situation.

The next day, I was to meet Berta, get something to eat with her, and chat.

Chapter 4

Berta

There was something familiar about Berta even though I barely knew her; it was as though I had met her personality type before, but I just couldn't place it. Not a problem, I told myself; I would have plenty of time to figure it out. The fact of the matter was that I would have to collect a lot more data on her, and that in time, she would no doubt unwittingly supply it.

The next day, we were to meet at 1 p.m. at the corner of 14th Street and 7th Avenue on the northwest corner. She had called to say that she would be at a bakery close to that intersection.

Bryn was not pleased to hear that. "She'll probably be eating something she shouldn't when you find her," he told me. He often commented about his displeasure over her girth.

I promised to do what I could to steer her away from baked goods and toward a healthy meal, and added that I had a plan: up the street from that corner, on 7th Avenue, was a Le Pain Quotidien, a Belgian franchise with wonderful wheat breads, jams, hazelnut spreads (I planned to get a jar for my homemade bread), and open-faced sandwiches with fresh vegetables, fresh fruits, chicken, turkey, and smoked salmon. The place also sold pureed vegetable soups such as carrot ginger, and kept a daily chalkboard menu. There was coffee, café au lait, hot chocolate, and of course, tarts, cakes and cookies. But I was going to suggest lunch – real food.

Inside Le Pain Quotidien.

The Slamming Door

Meanwhile, I had gotten myself up by 11 a.m., eaten breakfast in the apartment, and made sure that we had basic items such as toilet paper, paper towels, orange juice, yoghurt, and so on. That meant a fast run around the corner to the grocery store on 8th Avenue. It was the closest one to Bryn's apartment, and he had always shopped there.

I got his newspaper, which was downstairs in between the two glass doors, and he was delighted. He told me that he had not realized what a drain it had been to go out and buy a copy of *The New York Times* until he didn't have to do so. It was also cheaper this way, I pointed out. He told me to keep a running list of expenses, and he would reimburse me each month.

Thus began a long Word file on the computer entitled *Expenses for Taking Care of Bryn*, which ran month by month. On it, I would list, by date followed by the name of the store, the total amount of money spent at each place on each occasion. At the end of the month, using the computer's calculator, I would tally it up, print the month's pages out, and submit it to Bryn. He would go over it carefully in his chair, approve it, and write me a check. I paid the debt on my credit card with that money.

At first, I had been mortified as I had handed the expense sheet over, wondering what he was thinking of it, but he never objected. It probably had something to do with the fact that I would bring the purchases into his room and show him everything – partly hoping to tempt him into eating more – and then put it all away, or else just recite the list of purchases. At one point after several months of this, Albert had looked at the tally sheet and pronounced the total expense for two people living in a Manhattan apartment to be quite low and reasonable. I was amazed; all that worry over nothing.

It was a good system, and I still have my copy of that file. I kept vigilant track of it, entering all new data straight off of the receipts almost immediately upon arrival back at the apartment every time I came home.

I quickly found myself referring to Bryn's apartment as home.

It was home to me. It felt like home, complete with my own niche in it, and Bryn treated me like it was my home. I was happy there. I just wasn't happy that it was ending and I would never be able to talk to him again when it finally did.

With the first round of errands done, I took off, satisfied that the fridge was stocked, the toilet paper and Soft Scrub and sponges were newly supplied (I had even found lavender Soft Scrub!) and Bryn was okay.

It was time to spend some one-on-one time with Berta and learn more about her.

Berta

She had been a subject of curiosity to me for quite some time.

Bryn had framed photographs of both of his daughters, plus a couple of his niece, on the walls in his room. (He also had one or two of his brother, his girlfriend, his long-dead Golden Retriever, and his also long-dead, short-haired cats, Carmen and Guido. Carmen was a black-and-white tuxedo female; Guido was a tiger-striped male. When the cats had died, Bryn had been so upset that Cassie spent a weekend with him. He didn't get any more cats after that.)

Bryn had told me and Damon all about his daughter back in the summer of 2005, when we staying in the guest room, which used to be her room. Some of her stuff was still in it.

We were flopped on that dreadful futon with the television on and tuned into a movie. Like in Bryn's room, the bed occupied a back corner, so I was using pillows and the wall as a sort of sofa in there. Damon occupied the open side of the bed, next to the closet. The television was straight across from us, between the windows, with the fire escape on the left. A pair of antique bureaus on either side completed the room, as did Diane's nuclear blast oil paintings.

Bryn had stood there and described his daughter. At that point in time, Berta and I had never met. (We didn't meet until the following summer, as it turned out.) She was living in Los Angeles, where she had had a job with the Mattel Corporation, supervising four other secretaries, from 2000 to 2004. Unfortunately, even though she absolutely loved it out there, she had been fired, but had remained out there for another year. She came back to the state of New York in 2005, but not to her old room. Her father didn't want her in it.

That caught my attention. My parents would always let me have my old room back. Why didn't her dad want her to be here?

It turned out that she was not a good roommate, to put it succinctly.

But that doesn't tell much. So, to make a short story long, I will explain it all in detail.

She had lived in that room on high school breaks and during college, after sharing an apartment with friends. She had partied with the friends and flunked out of one school, so after enrolling in yet another, she had ended up back with her father. Her mother had lived where she was now, in the Stuyvesant apartments, but Berta had preferred to be with her father.

Oddly, her mother taught at the school across the street, and often Berta would see her out the window at recess, supervising the kids in the playground then.

When she lived with Bryn, she had had a cat, which he had inherited when she left for California (where she had then adopted another). The cat was a long-haired, gray-and-white female named Gracie, the

The Slamming Door

counterpart to Hilda's short-haired, tiger-striped male across the hall named George. I had known them both; but both had died...of cancer. They were both nice cats, and Bryn had loved and taken good care of Gracie. He had even taken care of Nikita, the fluffy, black-and-white tuxedo female cat from California, when Berta had gone away with Matt.

The image that Bryn painted for us was vivid enough: Berta would be lying on her futon bed, watching trash TV, eating junk food, and not moving much. Gracie the cat would have to take a flying leap to get from point A to point B in her room due to the mountains of trash from used bags of junk food. Berta didn't clean up much while she lived with her father. This was while she was taking twelve years rather than four to complete college.

He just found it too depressing to live with her, so when she had come back from L.A., he had avoided the whole mess by inviting Cassie's "project", a girl named Maggie from upstate New York, to stay in that room, thus deliberately making it unavailable to Berta. Rather than face any confrontation over the room, that was how he had prevented her from repossessing it.

Interesting.

But there was much, much more to the story.

It is probably better to go back to circumstances which predate her very existence.

Her mother was Bryn's second wife, and he was her second husband.

Before that, Bryn had attended Harvard University, married a woman who later became a physician in Manhattan, and then gotten divorced. The woman had fallen in love with someone else. "Damn her! What did she do that for?!" I exclaimed, when he had told me that. "That is exactly what my mother said," he replied. Wife number one went on to work as a physician in some Manhattan hospital, and that was that.

That was when Bryn had come back to Manhattan after graduating from Harvard in 1959. His own father had died when he was 20 years old and still in college. A couple of years later, Albert graduated from Hamilton College with a degree in French and joined him in Greenwich Village.

They enjoyed sharing a cheap apartment together, and both smoked cigarettes at the time. They also shared another thing in common: obsessive compulsive tendencies. To that end, they kept an ashtray on the back of the toilet to see how high the pile in it could get. It ceased to accumulate when their mother visited, used the bathroom, and flushed it in disgust, unaware of their bizarre competition.

But soon Albert met June in a bookstore, and it was love at first sight. June was a beautiful, petite, blonde, divorced child bride who had married a drummer at age seventeen, then moved from St. Louis, Missouri to lower Manhattan. It wasn't long before they moved in together.

Sometime after that, Bryn met Elvira, who was divorced with a little girl named Diane. (The ex-husband, a heroin addict, had moved to California.) Elvira was from Alabama, and had some African-American ancestry. This meant that although she was smart enough for any ivy-league school, she could just forget it thanks to apartheid in the school systems of the South. She had been forced to attend an all-black school thanks to some vicious record-keeping. That school lacked the necessary math rigor to qualify her for Smith College, so she was rejected, and that upset her badly – perfectly understandable.

Elvira looked like what the majority of her DNA had made her: a white woman. She had brown eyes and brown hair, was about the same height as Bryn, and pretty. Bryn started dating her in part because he thought that her little girl was "cute as a button." Bryn always liked little girls, and when Elvira gave him another one (Berta), he was thrilled. By that time, he had married Elvira and formally adopted Diane, who thought of him as her real father.

The family moved to Oneonta, in upstate New York, and Bryn began graduate school while teaching college courses there. Elvira, meanwhile, had become a grammar school teacher. Bryn once told me that she had actually gone to nursing school first, but been expelled. Expelled?! How? "She did something terrible," he said. "What?" "She destroyed a laboratory when she got angry over something." Wow…that would do it, I thought.

Anyway…Bryn was married to Elvira for approximately six years. They had Berta, he bonded with both girls, and then things fell apart. Elvira wasn't so nice to him after a while, and he noticed that she wasn't all that nice to Diane. To escape, Bryn lapsed into alcoholism and quietly smoking his pipe (off of cigarettes, I suppose – Albert too had seen the insanity of paying for the most pernicious form of tobacco poisoning and quit by then).

Berta told me that a big part of the problem was that her father needed some quiet time to himself to relax, and her mother kept bothering him whenever he tried to do that, asking him, "Why aren't you working on your thesis?!" He ended up with just a master's degree after all that effort, and that was that.

When they got divorced, Elvira kept the house, which was up the hill from the one that Damon and his mother and sisters and maternal grandparents had lived in when he was in his teens. Elvira still went to stay there often, and Berta kept some of her stuff there.

The Slamming Door

Bryn came right back to Manhattan and got a job driving a cab. He stayed in a boarding house at first, and adopted two cute kittens: Carmen and Guido. He got along well with everyone he met, and the next one he met was Cassie…at a bar on June Street in Greenwich Village. She was an artist who loved cats and horses, and like Bryn, an alcoholic. Cassie was also engaged to an English professor.

Life is complicated in different ways for different people. Chip, Cassie's fiancé, was an unusual sort of guy; he said he didn't care if she had a boyfriend, and said that as long he got to marry her, she could have both of them. So Bryn and Chip became friends, and when Cassie and Chip moved upstate so that Chip could teach college there, Bryn would go to visit, and the guys would watch sports on television together. Cassie used to come to Manhattan to stay with Bryn for a few days at a time, but when Chip's health deteriorated, she stopped. They talked on the phone every day.

By this time, Albert and June had their apartment in TriBeCa, on Greenwich Street. A little while later, Bryn found another place directly above the Chelsea Square Restaurant, a.k.a. the Greeks diner. Greek guys owned it, hence the nickname. Bryn ate there every night, and that was his entire reason for going back there so much after he found the next place, which is where I moved in to take care of him.

He got it by paying some friends who lived there but were moving out $10,000 to get in under a statue that would allow him to keep the place as a rent-controlled apartment. That statute was ending soon. There are no more fabulous deals like that anymore; my generation couldn't possibly afford lower Manhattan, much to my disappointment. I don't want to live in some other area and commute; I would want to already be there, in walking distance of everything.

When Bryn got that Chelsea apartment, he swore he'd never move again, and he meant it. He got his wish. Berta was in high school by then, and she preferred to live with her father when she wasn't boarding at the Emma Willard School in Troy, New York. It was an all-girls school, and not too far from where Cassie lived, and Bryn was paying for it. Because he and Albert had attended the Hackley School in Tarrytown, New York, her father wanted to give her the same advantages that he had grown up with.

Bryn had a story about driving past the campus on Halloween night one year with Cassie and Berta in the car when they all noticed a group of girls running naked through the trees and tossing rolls of toilet paper up into the branches. When the adults commented about it, Berta told them that those were her friends; lovely.

Berta was into Stevie Nicks' music then; Cassie introduced her to it. She became a fan, and decided that she liked the rock star's style, too.

Berta

That meant fringed leather handbags and cowgirl hats. I don't know what that music is like; I prefer orchestra scores of movie soundtracks, some rock music if it relates to a movie, plus Mozart symphonies and operas.

Berta told me that she found the sound of a soprano voice annoying. I told her that I liked it and left it at that; no need to say that I wished I had perfect pitch and a soprano voice myself. What fun that would be...but I can't sing as well as I would like to.

As a teenager, Berta was a pretty girl of normal size. She dyed her long, wavy hair blond with peroxide, and had a good time. Her father paid for the private school education at that famous, prestigious, all-girls institution. She had a wonderful time as a hell-raiser with her friends, then graduated and began college. She wanted to major in television production.

As I listened to him describe this, and later heard her supplement some details, I noticed a pattern: private school followed by a great college. Bryn had also sent her to camp in New Hampshire, at Lake Winnipesaukee. She loved that, too. My parents had done all of the same things for me: camp (I hated it! Being sent away to a cabin and a lake to swim in was misery to me, plus the other kids were bullies to a loner who didn't fit in or care to); private school for girls (MacDuffie in Springfield, Massachusetts); and on to college.

And there the similarity ended. I was a serious, quiet and anxious student who hated to party. When I got to college, I was terrified of not doing well and threw myself into getting used to the new environment, acclimating myself to it and academia, and organizing my major and minor – history and women's studies. In four years, I was finished and glad to be able to go home. I had applied to law school, but the timing was bad; the Persian Gulf War had induced a glut of applicants to apply, worried that a draft might be instituted (it wasn't).

So I worked at museums in Hartford, Connecticut as a historic interpreter – the Harriet Beecher Stowe and Mark Twain Houses. I also worked at the graduate medical library where Damon was studying for his Ph.D., though we were just best friends at that point. After 5 years, a boyfriend at the dental school encouraged me to reapply for law school, and I was accepted.

Meanwhile, Berta was still working on her bachelor's degree.

She had partied and screwed up and wasted her father's money on tuition, and flunked out of one or two schools. Ultimately, she ended up at the New School for Social Research, which Damon's grandfather had helped found. I wondered whether Bryn had engineered her acceptance by mentioning that ancestor, but didn't ask.

During that time, Berta got a job as an executive assistant for investment bankers (1993), which was a couple of years after she should

The Slamming Door

have completed her college degree (she and I both completed high school in 1987, so 1991 would have been "on time"). Twelve years after beginning her degree in television production, Berta graduated with a degree in general studies.

She had also managed to pack on an enormous amount of weight, which was evident from the photos in her father's apartment. It was hard to understand; she had such a pretty face and great hair. My mother had told me that a lot of fat women have pretty faces.

Bryn struggled with his weight too, but I saw a double-standard there; men get away with being fat much more easily than women do, at least socially. But obesity puts a person at an increased risk of cancer, heart trouble, and diabetes. Bryn had tachycardia – rapid heartbeat during a state of rest. And of course, he came down with cancer. His mother had died at age 71 of bladder cancer. His father had been a quiet alcoholic – one who didn't hurt anyone or get loud or menacing. He died when he was 54, and it might have been heart failure.

When I went to take care of Bryn, he was 70 years old.

But there was more about Berta. She had moved to L.A. to work for the Mattel Corporation as a production administrator. It was close enough (geographically) to television production to be exciting to her. At work, Berta was the supervisor of various employees as she dealt with toy marketing. She loved her life out there. It was much slower-paced than New York, which she really didn't like all that much. She learned a lot about Barbie dolls and how they are marketed and sold around the world, and later told me a few interesting things about that.

But there were some problems. She had a conflict at work. The upshot of it was that she had bullied someone in her department, someone over whom she had had supervisory authority. Terrific; Berta had been an authority figure who had abused her position. She was fired.

Bryn offered to pay for an attorney so that she could sue and get her job back, but she turned him down. When I first heard that, I figured that I didn't know much about her, so I had no way of knowing what to make of that. But now I understand that it was an admission of guilt.

It was at that point that Bryn had become well acquainted with me and told me what was happening. He gave me a book on Barbie dolls that he had bought for Berta because he thought that it would just depress her after that. I thanked him and took it back to Connecticut with me.

Berta managed to stay on in California through the summer, during which time Bryn paid for her to go to a fat farm. I don't know what it was called, just that he was concerned about her ballooning weight problem, worried that she wouldn't be able to get another boyfriend like that, and wanted to help. She hated it; the experience was humiliating. The people who ran it would bus the group of residents to a park to walk around and exercise. It was a public park, and L.A. is full of gorgeous, thin people in the movie business. The obese group attracted a lot of stares, and Berta was mortified. I don't blame her; it sounded awful.

She came home to New York after that, having run out of money to keep her apartment, and found that Maggie was in her old room, and that a lot of her things were in a pair of tall cardboard boxes in the living room.

Berta did not know that this was by design, but she was upset. She hated Cassie for having packed – and therefore touched – her old things. When I got there, some of her things were still in that room, untouched since the outrage of touching and moving. They were in the upper shelves of the closet collecting dust, plus in the walnut-and-white-marble bureau on the left with the drawers jammed shut because they were so packed with…Wonder Woman dolls, among other things. She showed them to me a few months later. There were also in the three drawers of the futon frame, the middle one of which lacked a handle. I wasn't the sort of person to rifle through someone else's things, so I didn't look at them.

For a year, Berta stayed with her mother in Oneonta and worked as a secretary at Hartwick College, which happened to be a party school, and in the same town. I don't know that she did much partying there, but by now it should be clear that she was the antithesis of me.

Then she got a job at Deutsche Bank and moved to Manhattan, where she stayed with her mother, paying half of the rent in the Stuyvesant apartment, and met Mike, her nice, quiet, red-headed boyfriend at a bar. He was Irish, from Galway, wore glasses, and was a tad overweight, though not much. He repaired refrigerators for grocery stores, and had a house on Long Island. He had recently, after eighteen years in the U.S., become a citizen, and was soon going to vote in his first presidential election. I liked him; we all did.

I had met Berta for the first time at a place called East of Eighth in 2006; her father was throwing a lunch party for her 37th birthday. She was back, she was still somewhat thinner after her weight loss program, and she looked pretty in her black shirt with a thin, green-patterned peasant blouse over that. Her long, thick hair was back in a barrette.

Three years earlier, when Damon and I had been planning our wedding, I had known that she could not attend. Plane tickets are expensive. But that was not the point; you invite people anyway, just to be polite and friendly. So I had written Bryn's address on the envelope, with his and Cassie's names on the first line and his daughters' on the next. He was the only one of them to show up. (I had no idea about his love triangle with Cassie and Chip yet, but so what.)

The Slamming Door

At that point, I really didn't know Berta at all, but I was also meeting her cousin Alissa on that day, and Diane was back from living in Milan, Italy for sixteen years. I was delighted with all of this because it meant having two female cousins who were my age, plus another one who was a talented artist. Who cared that they were in-laws?! They were what I had always wished for, and I said so, explaining that I had a male cousin who was two years younger than I was, plus a female cousin eighteen years younger, both of whom did not live near me.

When I told Berta that I was thrilled to finally meet her, she grinned widely. I took her picture then and there, and I still have it. Now I see something that I did not understand or recognize at that time: she is clenching her teeth in it, and very tense.

Why was that? I have thought about that meeting since then. My best guess is that I was sitting across from her, thin, married, educated with a bachelor of arts degree (not one in general studies), which I had completed in precisely four years, plus a doctor of laws. When I had introduced myself, I had told her about myself, saying that I was a writer and editor, and when I had finished with that, I had asked her about herself. Her soliloquy was shorter.

I just completely missed that, so pleased was I to meet a female cousin my age. She was just 6 months older than I was; we had grown up enjoying many of the same television shows (we both liked *Wonder Woman*, for example), and several of the same rock groups as teenagers.

By the time that Bryn was sick and I was moving in with him, however, Berta had gained all of her old weight back and more, and was approximately 300 pounds. (My mother, a nurse, took one look at a current photograph and gave that assessment.) Mike was frustrated with her, and her mother, a horrid woman who liked to bully both of her daughters – Bryn had warned me about her, and so did Berta – would walk around the apartment in Stuyvesant Village calling her a disgusting fat pig in front of her boyfriend. Did Elvira think that such behavior would help her daughter to shrink? What an absurd idea; mean and nasty behavior never works.

At one point, Berta told me, "I hate my mother and I wish she would die."

I was appalled, but didn't reply. My mother had upset me badly many times, but I would never wish her dead. Once she's gone, that's it; it's quite final. And I wanted her alive. Upset as I was about her, I didn't want to never be able to interact with her again. That idea was scary.

So the day after arriving at Bryn's and settling in, I went to meet Berta, worried about being late. I needn't have worried, despite the fact that I am no expert at being on time. I took my cell phone, and promised Bryn to steer Berta toward some healthy food.

Berta

I dashed on foot down 8th Avenue and across the north side of 14th Street (Manhattan's grid, which runs from just north of Greenwich Village and on up the island, has several large, two-way streets: 14th, 23rd, 34th, 42nd, 57th, and so on). There were a couple of bakeries, and I peered anxiously into each one. No Berta. I stood on the corner for a while, pondering my next move, and finally called her.

She answered right away and said that she was coming, almost there, and we chatted as she walked. Soon she said she saw me and we rang off. As I put my phone back into my pocket, I spotted her. She had her hair in a ponytail, was wearing jeans and a tee shirt, and was just finishing a regular-sized cup of what was most likely frozen yoghurt. She tossed it into a trash bin before crossing to meet me.

When she suggested getting something to eat, I immediately suggested showing her Le Pain Quotidien, saying it was just up the street and that I planned to buy something there anyway. She was all for it; I thought, "Mission accomplished!" I had steered her away from the bakeries. She told me that the yoghurt was the first thing she had eaten all day. As we had both planned to sleep late, I believed her, but Bryn didn't. Oh well…

Berta loved Le Pain Quotidien, but told me that she hated France. I didn't say anything more than that I loved France, and that I really learned to speak and understand French when I had gone there. (I would find out much more about Berta and France later, and it wasn't pretty.) Meanwhile, she enjoyed the food, which included a huge bowl of carrot soup, a sandwich, and several tastes on the huge slice of bread (it came with the soup) from each jar of jam and the hazelnut spread – there was one of those on each white marble table. Then she bought some 4-berry jam for Bryn, and I got the hazelnut spread.

Throughout my stay in Manhattan, she would pay for our food when we ate out, and that was very, very often. That was our deal, though all this eating out amazed me. It was expensive! But it was normal for her and for most of my in-laws. I guessed that they didn't cook much. I just kept saying thank-you, cooking for people when we stayed home, and taking care of Bryn. What else could I do? I couldn't pay those bills, and they couldn't take care of Bryn. Being a writer who stayed near a computer most of the time was what made me available, and that worked for them, and for me.

But back to this first lunch visit: We discussed logistics a bit, then lapsed into talking about what fun we would have together as she showed me Manhattan over the next several months. So I was meant to hang around with her as well as be with Bryn….good. He had lots of people he liked to visit with.

The Slamming Door

After a few hours, I went home to Bryn and she took off, not to be seen again until after work the next day. She appeared around 6 o'clock, when Bryn and I were sitting in his room, relaxed and doing little of anything. I was in the chair by the door. She was standing facing him in his Lazy-Boy chair. Naturally, the subject of how he was doing came up right away.

"Have you had trouble having a bowel movement?" she asked, all seriousness and concern, as if it were the most normal and reasonable of questions to have asked. As she stood there, I suddenly noticed that she loomed large over the two of us in a brown pants suit, looking like the subject of her impertinent inquiry personified. How gross.

Her question was just vulgar and intrusive. The way she asked it – her tone, her expression, her general demeanor – was calculated to convey a disingenuous impression of care-giving concern, thus justifying having asked it. That didn't make it any less wrong.

Bryn looked horrified; I kept my expression neutral, waiting for Bryn to respond first.

He did so in much the way that I had expected: "That's between me and my doctor."

At this point, I felt free to speak, keeping my tone as calm and non-threatening as possible. "Berta, that's gross! No one likes to even think about such things, much less get asked about them."

Fortunately, the conversation obligingly moved on to other things.

She had just come back from her job at Deutsche Bank on Wall Street, where she worked as an administrative secretary. Her job was to make limo and travel arrangements, restaurants and hotel reservations, field phone calls, type memos, and so on.

Her boss had retired a year or so earlier, promising in all insincerity that she could be the secretary for his replacement, but the new guy had brought his own secretary with him. Berta thus became a floating secretary. It didn't sound very stable to me, but apparently she was holding steady in her position.

Bryn guessed that she made between fifty and eighty thousand dollars per year, which made little sense to me. She was a secretary. Why did the bank pay her so much? Was it because the job was in an expensive city, and they wanted her able to live close by? How could it pay her so much? Didn't they prefer to funnel that money into the salaries of Wharton School graduates and holiday bonuses?

I never did understand this, and gave up trying. I had better things to think about.

At least Berta was talking about other things. It was early in her father's illness anyway, and there wasn't much point in demanding to know the gory details up front. Perhaps she was testing the waters, just to confirm that he would not be sharing much information about it.

I never expected to know much beyond whatever he volunteered, and had no wish to dig deeper. What was the point? I wouldn't like that if I were sick, and the salient points of it all were now known to all: Bryn had bone cancer and was doomed to die of it…at some point.

When that would be was anyone's guess, including that of the specialist, the osteo-oncologist. No one said this, but I had been around nurses, doctors, and scientists long enough to understand this intuitively. Everyone's DNA, environmental exposures, health care decisions, food and exercise choices, and death is different. Everyone's combination of these factors adds up to a different result.

To be honest, I was glad not to know how this illness would play out.

What good would it do? It would be sad and unpleasant, and that was enough data.

That movie called *The Bucket List* had just come out over the previous summer, and it had dealt with this particular question. The guys who were doomed to die of cancer in that story hadn't thought it was so great to know the answer either. Morgan Freeman's character had the most interesting combination of feelings about this: at first he had always leaned toward wanting to know the best guesstimate of the moment of his own death, but when the oncologist provided it, he changed his mind.

I knew that at some point, Bryn would ask a health care professional this same question, and that because this was not a scripted movie but reality, he would just be told that it was different for everyone, so they couldn't possibly tell him.

To this day, I don't think that knowing would have been good for us. In fact, I think it would have made the experience of his death more upsetting for all of us. We were all going to experience his death – his friends, his family, his caregiver (that was me), and himself. The closer one of us was to him, and the more time one of us was to spend with him, the more up close and personal…and intense the emotional experience of losing him would be.

I realized this early on, but I kept reminding myself that it wouldn't be too upsetting for a while. Not until Bryn was really at the end of the illness, near death. I can avoid feeling really and truly miserable until it is actually time to deal with the consequences. Meanwhile, I understand them without allowing myself to have a full-blown meltdown and panic attack.

I could still have bouts of terrible anxiety, but there were plenty of ways to deal with them: call Damon and chat; read interesting books, explore the historic areas of Manhattan with my street atlas; buy books

The Slamming Door

in little specialty shops; try hot chocolate and coffee and tea and pastries at various cafés; watch movies; accept any invitation to go out with Bryn or any other relative; watch my favorite television shows plus Letterman and Ferguson's shows each night.

That anti-bucket list could keep me busy and distracted.

I was frustrated at not being able to do more writing, but taking notes for this book during the actual experience of the death process was problematic. Ultimately, I only got 53 pages of data saved, but that was enough when one considers all the photographic evidence of the experience I managed to accumulate. I even had this same title all picked from the start. Bryn knew about it and didn't object.

I had another writing project to do with an Iranian feminist politician – her memoirs – but she wasn't ready to work yet. She had her green card application to concentrate on.

And I had a travelogue about a trip to Kuwait that I had extensive notes for from over three years earlier, complete with photos, a 345-page journal, several books and newspapers with an accompanying bibliography, and some other mementos of the experience.

All this, and I realized that taking care of Bryn was going to stress me out too much to relax and concentrate, in part because of the endless parade of visitors and relatives through the apartment. So I decided that I would wait until after it was all over.

I need quiet to work anyway, and so I wait until everyone is asleep and I am shut in my room. Just as Virginia Woolf said, a woman must have a room of her own if she is to write, and I fit this description to a tee. I figured it didn't matter; I would get the writing done eventually.

And I did; after my time with Bryn, the Kuwait book was written and copyrighted, and so was a dystopian science fiction novel. I didn't even realize I had that one in me, but I did. Funny how it works when you can concentrate and don't feel as though someone is looking for you, wanting your attention…

Writing is relaxing for me; when I do it, I forget my problems and the anxiety that tends to grip me goes away. That gray haze – the visual manifestation of my anxiety – doesn't haunt me. I am free to get things done, and the fact that I may actually be solving my own problems by fulfilling my dream of being a published author who can earn money from her efforts adds to that feeling.

Strange; writing manages my anxiety now, and that is better than those stupid, fattening, anti-anxiety and anti-depressant pills ever were. Plus it's productive, unlike pills that cost money and run up food bills, and dull my thoughts so that I am happy for no valid reason and fat. I told Berta shortly after settling in that I used to be on those pills, and why I had stopped them.

Berta

Berta had explained to me that she was on antidepressant and anti-anxiety pills, and that she knew that they made her want to eat a lot. She added that she couldn't stand to skip a meal or just eat less; she got too hungry. She just couldn't face going off of those pills and having to handle her emotions on her own.

To top it all off, she told me that she also had ADD – Attention Deficit Disorder – and OCD – Obsessive Compulsive Disorder – which manifested themselves by, respectively, an inability to pay attention to any detailed story, and a need to tap an interesting moon-faced gate each time we passed it (it was near Bryn's place). Self-discipline was not something that she seemed to be able to find within; she chose to rely on pharmaceutical solutions to that deficit.

I knew that there would eventually be terrible trouble with Berta as I thought all this over. She was my exact polar opposite in just about every way possible, and we were not attracted to each other. She needed me, and I needed to be near her father, my cousin, my alternate father figure, for as long as I could. It was a purely emotional need on my part, and I'm not sure that she understood that. She knew I was unhappy in Connecticut, but I'm not so sure that understood how attached I was to Bryn; he was like another dad to me.

Hurry up and spend time with Bryn before he's dead and the time is all gone, I had told myself. That was really why I had rushed to move in and take care of him. That and the fact that I knew he would accept and want me for that purpose.

It was like a sleep-over party for two intellectuals who liked to stay up late but pursue our own interests, complete with our own rooms and televisions and collections of books for that exact purpose. Bryn totally accepted me as I was, and of course I accepted him. Older people always have the upper hand this way; I look to them to accept me, having already accepted them.

Bryn didn't need me in the mornings except in rare emergencies, in which cases we left the apartment for the hospital. Most days, we got up late, when recess began at P.S. 11's playground across the street.

Those sustained noise levels of children's shrieks that emanated from the playground were the same ones that had bothered and depressed me as a child; I had spent recess periods pacing the perimeters of the playground, silently waiting for the recess to end. No wonder I stood out; I got the highest grades in my class, but hated recess. I liked the free time to think, just not the racket made by my classmates. Now I just slept through them, grateful to have aged past being among little kids.

Bryn heard about all this and just accepted it.

Berta heard about it – I don't recall precisely when – and said nothing, but I sensed that she didn't approve. I should have just fit in, I

The Slamming Door

should have liked little kids as an adult, I should have not minded the noise. She didn't say so, but I could tell that she didn't like me as I was.

I know that I am not endearing to most people, but to my surprise, I have come to realize that to some, I am a source of intimidation. Despite having had the reasons for this explained to me at various times in my life, it continues to amaze and occasionally mystify me.

How could I be intimidating? Aren't we all supposed to control our impulses to overeat? Aren't we all supposed to complete our educations on time regardless of how tempting it is to get sidetracked by either fun or anxiety? Aren't we all supposed to build up a set of skills that should be in order by our thirties – or earlier?

Well – yes to all of that, but that doesn't mean that we all do so.

Therein lies the rub.

Berta had the opportunity to do these things, complete with a father ready and willing to pay her tuition at the college level, but she had not done so. Instead, she could get only the most dull and ordinary of jobs. She was a source of disappointment to him for that reason, and for her weight. She was the size of two people – 300 pounds on a medium-boned, 5-foot, 8-inch frame.

A few months later, she e-mailed me a copy of her résumé. It was precisely one page, and she had paid someone to prepare it, $100 with unlimited corrections. It looked nice, but very different from my CV. Its format was what was different: whereas I had each item listed in short form, with the institution, location, position and time period in 2 lines followed by a line or so to explain what I did at each place, she had a long paragraph for each position, plus a bulleted list of duties. I listed my degrees first, and she listed hers last. I was fascinated by the differences, because most of my edits were of academic CVs – not résumés.

I supposed that that was normal for an administrative assistant, just as mine was normal for a person with a varied career in academia. Berta's jobs had all been to answer phones, type letters, and make travel arrangements and dinner reservations.

My jobs had been to lecture extensively on topics that I had made a thorough study of, to correct and prepare elaborate journal article manuscripts, to write novels and non-fiction narratives, to tutor students in writing and speaking, and to handle the logistics of complex projects…including legal papers. I hated phones – both their interruptions, and their noise.

Which brings me back to Bryn's request to organize his papers: he wanted me to do that for him for various reasons. One was that I was eminently qualified to do that thanks to being a lawyer. Another was that I was good at it. Yet another was that he knew that his brother and daughters could never focus on the job long enough to get on with it.

Berta

He explained that to me, and I understood what he meant quickly.

All that was on the evening of my arrival; after that, I made an excellent beginning of it, then put the result aside until later, when I would inevitably be asked to complete it. It wasn't my business to peruse Bryn's papers in detail, only to organize them all. Later on, I would go through it all in more detail; meanwhile, I just got those piles off of the floor.

Berta seemed pleased with all that I was doing in the early days of the illness.

She wanted someone staying with her father, and we all knew that he couldn't stay home alone with bone cancer. He could fall and not be able to get up. He could injure himself in any number of ways. He could have some other crisis and need someone to be there. Walking around on a cane meant that he was already having difficulty moving around. Who knew what would go wrong when? It was just unwise to try to be sick and all alone, and it was needless.

For a long time, the job was mostly to just be there.

Of course, I did more than just hang around: I cleaned the apartment every few weeks, dusting with furniture polish and mopping, and changing Bryn's sheets. I would pull the furniture out and get all dust and cobwebs off of it. I would go around the perimeter of each room with the stick mop, outlining it and then filling in the rest. It was relaxing to see the dirt disappear. I would dust the ceilings with a dry rope mop, and wash the windows. The first time I did that was the day after I arrived, when I came back from visiting with Berta. Bryn commented that I was the most efficient person he had ever known, which made it fun.

On a regular basis, so that these areas never had a chance to become dirty, I scrubbed the bathroom fixtures. That meant washing the tub with Soft Scrub and a scratchy sponge before and after every bath that Bryn ever took while I was there, plus putting down his pebble-pattern bath mat with the suction cups that I had bought for him over the summer. No sense letting him get any more health problems than he already had – nothing that would shorten whatever amount of time he had left. I wanted to prevent slip-and-fall accidents, and infections. It worked, too.

That wasn't all; I washed every dish and put it away immediately, and this was my most noticeable habit. The family wasn't used to such efficiency, and Albert kept commenting on how great that was. This amused me; I have always done this. I just don't like to see work sitting around, waiting to be done. It's so much more relaxing to know that it's all done.

As I considered all that I knew and had recently learned about Berta, I still wondered how she could have turned out the way she did. I decided to add to this small store of data as new bits of information became

The Slamming Door

available to me, without being obvious about acquiring them. I didn't want my amazement to show.

The one question that nagged at me was how someone whose father was Bryn – a cheerful, friendly, Harvard-educated, talented, intellectually curious person who was genuinely interested and concerned about others – be the way that she was? As time went on, I decided that only one answer could work: somehow, Elvira's DNA and influence had crowded out a significant share of Bryn's. Berta had spent enough of her formative time with her mother to have absorbed the woman's character and personality traits. The result was not good.

I meanwhile, not knowing any better that to attempt to make great friends with Berta, told her all about the negative aspects of my own life. She was probably building up her own converse impression of me all that time, and likewise seeing that we were polar opposites.

Chapter 5

The Goddaughter, and Other Neighbors

Bryn's goddaughter – Hilda – lived across the hall with her parents and cat, Puma.

Hilda's parents were Rudy and Elah. The cat was a little tortie calico.

Rudy and Elah had a one-bedroom, rent-controlled apartment directly across the hall from Bryn, and they had moved in sometime in 1989. It was their second apartment together, from what Elah told me. Elah loved cats, and Rudy was indifferent to them. He used to have a pet snake – or maybe a pair – but when the female tried to bite him, he gave her away. She was a boa constrictor; when they get that big, they could eat their human caregivers. I hate snakes!

The family were Jews, but not observant. Still, Elah tried to keep connected to Jewish culture, working on Thursdays at a place that kept the Yiddish language alive. I don't know whether she spoke or read it herself, but she was interested in it. For years, she had no job, but the year that Bryn's bone cancer started bothering him – before we knew what was wrong – she had been doing this for a while.

She also worked on her laptop three times a day – or maybe it was four – for a real estate service, posting listings over and over again on Craigslist so that they would always be first on the list. Rudy commented that it seemed insane to him, saying that unless it was a porn site, why keep moving stuff to the front of the list? I don't know what that meant, but I could see that she was chained to this task, with barely time to go to the Yiddish place. She only had six hours free in between posts, and that didn't leave enough time to go to the Yiddish place and return before the next posting time. She got this posting job sometime in the year before Bryn got sick.

Elah adopted Puma, a beautiful but reticent, tiny, small-boned tortie cat that year by volunteering at the ASPCA shelter on East 95th Street until she was allowed to adopt one of the cats. Hilda was thrilled, but Rudy kept saying it was temporary. Meanwhile, the cat loved him and climbed into his lap often. It was amusing. Once, out on Bryn's street on a sunny day in July, he said that, and I laughed and said, "Yeah, right. She's your cat now." He just looked glum, and Damon and I cracked up.

Bryn was thrilled to be a godfather to Hilda. He loved little girls. Not in a creepy or disturbing way – in just the right way. He loved being a dad to little girls, or an uncle, or a godfather, or whatever role worked for all parties involved. He never intruded upon anyone's lives in order to enjoy a little girl's company – he was often invited, and accepted happily.

The family had an abundant supply of girls: first Bryn married a woman with a little girl – Diane – whom he had formally adopted and once surprised with a trip for just the two of them to see the museums of Washington, D.C. Diane had a wonderful time. Next, Bryn and Elvira had another daughter together – Berta.

Meanwhile, his brother Albert and sister-in-law June had gotten married shortly after Bryn did. They had been living in sin (not a big deal) until June got pregnant (suddenly it was a big deal), whereupon Margery, who was Bryn and Albert's mother, marched the two of them down to City Hall in Manhattan with Bryn in tow as a witness. Alissa was born less than a year after that, and so Bryn had a niece who was just a year younger than Berta.

That kept him occupied for years, but eventually they both grew up and had their own lives and interests to pursue. It was during this dry period that the neighbors straight across the hall from him had a daughter, Hilda Mae Ranger Stone. Bryn was delighted to hear of it, but she was theirs, and he wasn't about to involve himself uninvited…until they did so by making him her godfather. Berta was living with him then, working as a secretary and going to school for her bachelor's degree in nothing in particular. That was in 1993.

But then they both got a bit more involved with Hilda when her parents, Rudy Stone and Elah Roni Ranger, opened a restaurant off of 10th Avenue near Chelsea Pier. It only lasted for a short time, but it was awesome, at least from what Bryn described.

When I assess a restaurant, the first thing that I judge is the food. I love gourmet food made from scratch using fresh ingredients. Throw in a ghost and you've got a winning combination – great meals and atmosphere. The place allegedly had more than one ghost, including someone who died in the bar area while attempting to elude a thug, and a woman who was murdered on site at another time.

Bryn walked us past there once – me and Damon – and told us the whole tale of woe. Rudy's food was fantastic, which was no surprise, and Elah had helped him full time. It was during this stint of perhaps a year or more as Rudy pursued his life's dream that Bryn and Berta baby-sat for Hilda and Bryn was made her godfather. At least, that's how I remember the story. Perhaps he got the title when she was born, but in any case he was so pleased to have been awarded the job that he took it very seriously for the rest of his life.

Unfortunately, the restaurant failed, but not because of Rudy. It really doesn't seem to have been his fault – just rotten luck. It failed for lack of a liquor license, which is death to any Manhattan restaurant.

The Goddaughter, and Other Neighbors

Without influence and an in for speeding the application process along, restaurateurs can find a horrendous time lag between the opening of their business and receipt of a liquor license. Then they lose money when customers get frustrated by not being able to have wine or beer with dinner. That's what spoiled it for Rudy and Elah.

Elah got very depressed after that. I know what it's like to watch a husband try very hard to make a success of his career with all of the necessary skills but get nowhere fast; that is part of how Damon and I ended up staying with Bryn so much, and why I got to know and love him so well. Anyway…Elah got involved with marijuana at some point in her life, perhaps this point, perhaps some other point. It was the perfect escape. Add to that a cigarette addiction and her health proceeded to decline, though not farther than to speed up her aging process.

And no matter how much I remember Bryn thinking that she should have controlled her emotions and gotten it together and displayed more sociability towards the people around her (he would say "I don't understand what's wrong with that woman" to me sometimes), I just can't blame her for any of it. Not the pot, not the depression and sleeping, not whatever else.

It's not like I know everything that was going on, so why have a detailed judgment and opinion of her response to stress and disappointment? Besides, I don't respond well to that either, so I'll be damned if I'll expect anyone else to do so. She was always nice to me; hard to reach by phone, but nice. She never said anything judgmental or unpleasant to me in the entire time that I knew her. When I think about her, I find that I like her.

Rudy, however, was very different from his wife. He kept himself in good shape physically by riding his bike to work across the city, where he had a series of jobs as a chef in various restaurants or diners. I don't know whether he was the boss – the head chef – or just a highly competent one among a team of chefs, but he was always working as a chef somewhere. He didn't smoke or use drugs.

In addition to that, Rudy was a talented musician who hired himself out for various gigs around the city, participating in orchestras and chamber groups, sometimes for free but often for pay, and in bands as well. He played classical music as well as jazz, and he taught students on occasion in their apartment. Most of the time, he played a bass violin, which he wheeled around the city in its huge, padded, black canvas case. He also played a bass guitar – electric – and there was a small piano in the apartment.

Rudy wrote for fun – screenplays, short stories, and I didn't know what else – and once, Hilda told me about giving one of her father's screenplays to an actor who lived on the same street, in a townhouse

The Slamming Door

closer to 9th Avenue. (Rudy knew about this and was okay with it, of course.) I don't know that anything more ever came of it, but it was a good idea.

From what I was able to observe from my conversations with Rudy – which came at odd moments when he was returning from work and dragging his bicycle into the building, in a rare moment of sociability – he was the sort of person who would have loved college if he had gone. Instead, he had gone to chef school. I don't know why he didn't go to college, but I suspect that finances might have played a role in the decision. He was intellectually curious; he loved to go to a museum to see ancient scrolls and art or look up stars and planets on the Internet after seeing them in the sky as he was about to come into the building.

Hilda was gradually growing into a Goth teenager. She morphed into one over the course of the year that I spent with Bryn. She had started off as a little girl with naturally pale, pasty skin, a huge freckle/mole in the center of her chin, and brown eyes and hair that grew in waves down to her shoulders.

She liked wild colors – reds, in particular – and didn't like pinks or blues, which happen to be my favorite colors. For a couple of years, whenever Damon and I visited, I would give Hilda a pedicure, in alternating colors on each nail: red and black. It was fun, even though the kid typically showed up with utterly filthy feet, and I would make her scrub them in the bathtub before I proceeded with the job. I think now that these pedicures were very much about pleasing Bryn; he liked Hilda, so I was doing her nails.

Bryn once complained to me that he didn't like her style at all, and characterized it as Puerto Rican. I don't think he was disparaging that style in general, just saying that it simply did not look attractive or tasteful on Hilda. But he let well enough alone.

Hilda lived in a room that wasn't really a room, and had managed well enough until she became a teenager. The room was basically half of what was meant to serve as the apartment's living room. Entering from the long hallway which led from the front door, one faced the room with a desk against the wall to the right, with the seat facing back at the door. Directly across from the front door was the piano, which was backed up against a long set of thin, red blinds affixed to the ceiling. The blinds separated the living room from Hilda's area.

That was what passed for her room: an area. To go into it, one walked between the piano and the desk, turning right, and then left into the area, which included the window at the back wall. One bunk bed was behind the blinds, reached by a ladder, and with a low, comfortable seat underneath. There was a television and DVD player against the wall, and Hilda's artwork. Puma liked to sleep up on the habitually unmade bed.

The Goddaughter, and Other Neighbors

That was it – no soundproofing, no real privacy. A couple of years earlier, when Hilda was thirteen, Bryn had come back into his own apartment and told me and Damon and Hilda had bitterly remarked that she was very unhappy to be entering her teen years without her own room, complete with a door and a lock on it. He said he thought that it was uncool of her to say so, but I refused to agree with him. The fact was, I agreed with her, and would have felt guiltless about complaining if I had been in the same situation, with parents who could not afford to give me my own space to retreat into. Terrible of me, but my own space and quiet is one of the most important things to me and always has been.

The entire apartment was packed to the hilt with stuff, but there was no other option; Rudy had paintings by relatives, and Elah, who was originally from Ohio, had family photos all over the place. It had been painted various colors by them over the course of a couple of decades: pale lavender in the long hallway that led into it; purple and blue in the kitchen, red in the living room, and lavender in Rudy and Elah's bedroom. The coats of paint looked thick and crusty, as they did in Bryn's Spartan place, which was all ivory.

The other rooms in the place were all on the left: first the kitchen, with its built-in dish cabinet with glass on the upper doors, ancient gas stove and oven that didn't work at all, and the toaster oven, microwave and coffee machine straight ahead in the tall set of shelves. Next, through the music and desk area, to the left, were the bathroom and Elah and Rudy's room. Going that way, the bathroom was on the right and stretched to the back of the building, followed by the bedroom, which occupied the corner of the floor, with a window on two sides of it. It had a big bed, a television, and pretty, floral-upholstered, Victorian furniture. Elah sat by the back window, smoking and working.

Rudy would get frustrated at the close quarters, sometimes wishing that Hilda weren't in there with her friends, who would show up in groups to meet her and either stay for a bit or go directly out with her. But he was the one who had begged and begged for a child, and Elah had agreed. She was glad she had Hilda, but Rudy seemed like someone who had lost interest in a pet once it grew too big, like his snake.

Berta had enjoyed Hilda thoroughly while she was still living there, taking her shopping for pretty dresses and out to movies. She had told me so, and there were photos of them together in Bryn's apartment, dressed up and smiling. Berta loomed shapelessly over Hilda in a black dress, her pretty, long wavy hair cascading around her face, complete with flawlessly applied cosmetics. Berta added that she missed Hilda as a little girl. They were still close, but Hilda wasn't a cute little doll to play dress-up with; Berta preferred much more conventional styles.

The Slamming Door

Bryn played his role as godfather to Hilda with enthusiasm, visiting her and having her over at his place, hearing reports of schoolwork, plays, musicals and other things that she was participating in at school, meeting her friends, and watching her live her life. He paid for her to go to camp at the same place that he had sent Berta, which was a girls' camp across Lake Winnipesaukee in New Hampshire from the one that he and Albert had attended. He also took her to Broadway shows and musicals, and to museums.

Once, he sent Hilda to the Museum of Natural History with me and Damon to see a special exhibit on Charles Darwin. It was fabulous, and I had read every single placard and display, and learned a lot. Hilda was not so interested, and it was awkward when we got home and Bryn called me into his room to report on how much of it Hilda had absorbed. She had certainly looked at quite a bit of the information, but she had not taken a great fascination from it and really studied it.

I told him the truth – I don't know how to lie or gloss things over – and he seemed reasonably satisfied even though he wasn't thrilled to pieces over the report. What he really would have enjoyed was a sense of scholarship, but not everyone is a scholar. I hope I made up for it, describing the exhibit in painstaking detail, which I couldn't resist doing as a way of showing my appreciation for the museum visit. He was very happy with that, and enjoyed hearing what the exhibit contained. Bryn was another scholar after all – intellectually curious.

When Damon and I went to stay with Bryn during the hot summer of 2005, we had just returned from Kuwait, so we had our old laptop, printer, and a new, shared cell phone. I had set the cell phone up with my name in blue letters and a beach scene for its wallpaper – choices that came with the phone. One day, after Hilda had been in the apartment, I flipped it open and it said "Hey Dude!" in red letters. Damon and I were horrified; was this our phone, or had we gotten some else's by mistake? It turned out that Hilda had fooled around with the greeting message. I changed it back. We were outraged; Bryn just said, "It's a kid." We didn't think that that made it okay, but didn't say anything more about it.

As Hilda got older, she began to change her style even more dramatically, dying her hair blond, adding pink highlights, and wearing heavy eye makeup. She loved camp and made friends who would visit from out of state, and Bryn would let Hilda and her visitor take over his guest room. Hilda and her parents had their own keys to Bryn's apartment so that Rudy could use the oven anyway, so arranging things like visits was easy.

When I visited, I would always bring something for Hilda: once it was a Norman Rockwell tee shirt of his painting called *The Gossips*; each

The Goddaughter, and Other Neighbors

Hanukah, it was a CD of some musical, because Hilda had a soprano singing voice and would memorize all of the songs quickly, enjoying herself in the process; another time, it the lyrics of a *Harry Potter* song called *Double Trouble* that we both liked. I had looked them up on the Internet for her as a surprise.

I would take her out to movies each time I was in town, and it would either be something educational or else something that we were both really enthusiastic about. We saw at least one *Harry Potter* movie together, and *Marie Antoinette*, a herstorical feast of eye candy. Speaking of candy and junk food, Hilda was addicted to it as a preteen. It was so bad that one weekend, she hardly ate anything but popcorn – paid for by Bryn, who doled out cash from the ever-present wad he kept in his pants pocket (he didn't use a wallet) – coated with melted butter and every last type of powdered, synthetic crap that the movie houses provided at their concession areas.

Fortunately, her eating habits had improved by the time we saw *Marie Antoinette*; she was a bit older, and perhaps my phone call to her mother on the way home from the third movie in the space of weekend...as Hilda's stomach lurched repeatedly and she moaned in discomfort...had an effect. I took her to Balducci's on 14th Street, a gourmet grocery store, where she chose a salad to take into the theater for her dinner.

There was just one feature of Hilda's transition to her teens that grated on me: she developed a strong sense of what was cool and what was not. Such senses are highly subjective and vary with each successive generation. When she criticized my comfortable black pants with deep pockets, I was really annoyed. She preferred tight, uncomfortable pants and had the straight, skinny physique that made such things look good on her. I am somewhat curvy, short-waisted, and have always – including during my teens – chosen comfort and function first and foremost, yet managed to look up-to-date and attractive...even stylish.

The very idea that a particular age group should be the arbiter of coolness infuriates me. It always has. I am cool on my own, as an individual, attractive, thin enough, and determined to wear only what I like. How dare the fashion industry even attempt to tell me what to like and spend money on and wear?! If people like Hilda had their way, only teens and twentysomethings would ever be cool, and the rest of us would be has-been geeks. That's ridiculous.

During the summer before we knew that Bryn was sick, Hilda decided that she was too old to return to camp the next year, and no one disagreed. She would be sixteen the next year. But when she came home, she spent some time with the wrong person, a girl who got them both picked up for shoplifting. Elah had to go down to the local precinct to

The Slamming Door

pick her up, which was embarrassing. The cops had gone easy on Hilda, and let her go with a warning, apparently choosing to believe that Hilda did not know what her friend was up to, but her parents forbade her to associate with that kid again. It was awful; I could hear Bryn and Berta talking about it in the next room when Berta came over. "She's a damned liar!" Bryn roared, convinced that Hilda had stuck around in that store, fully aware of her friend's actions. But it all blew over.

By the time I arrived to stay with Bryn, Hilda had become a teenager who preferred the company of her friends to anyone else's. There would be no trips to the movies with her. She was busy attending *The Rocky Horror Picture Show* with them each and every Friday evening, and they would all dress a particular way that changed each week. She had a succession of boyfriends, and was seeing a tall, thin, dark-haired boy named Riley whose parents had divorced. His mother had moved upstate with her new husband, taking his younger siblings with her, leaving him to stay with his dad. He was a nice enough kid, and he and Hilda were inseparable.

Diagonally upstairs from Bryn, overlooking the street on the second floor (we thought of the levels in the building as ground floor, 1st floor, 2nd, 3rd, 4th and 5th), lived two teachers who certainly fit that description: Piper Firman and Melissa Farber. They were married for tax reasons, Bryn said, but otherwise so unconscious of convention that it was of little concern to them. Both wore glasses and had long, scraggly, wavy hair. Piper's was gray, and he had a beard. Melissa's was black and somewhat tightly curled, with many white strands. It was roughly parted in the middle, and she wore no makeup. She listened to people with a serious expression.

Their apartment was, Bryn had informed me long ago, a dark morass of books, papers, and old, antique furniture, most of which had been scavenged from the discarded items left at various curbs nearby. Piper and Melissa shared Bryn's subscription to *The Economist* with him. They went out to dinner or lunch or brunch with him sometimes, met him at the Henry George School for lectures, and traveled together during school breaks, leaving a set of keys with Bryn so that he could take in their mail and water their plants when they traveled. My father would have called them dirty intellectuals; I found them intriguing. They were nice enough.

I took over that chore – for pay – when Bryn got sick, and saw that the apartment was a fascinating place full of books and antiques and many old things collected from sidewalks, just as Bryn had described. The entire wall on the right-hand side of their bedroom was a white set of cubbyholes. In the cubbyholes was every paper from every year that Melissa had ever taught in her career. They weren't cooks, preferring to subsist on whatever leftovers they could gather from almost anywhere plus uneaten food from their own restaurant outings.

Melissa saw to it that their laundry was taken out and brought back, doing it herself. Once, a few years earlier, I had heard an odd thumping sound in the stairwell and went out to see what was going on. Melissa was hauling up a cage-on-wheels laden with a massive laundry bag; she must have let it pile up and then tried to drag it all upstairs at once. She turned and saw me, and said that she had hurt her back a while ago, but was better and had thought she could get this upstairs. I dragged the bag out of that cage and walked quickly upstairs to her door with it, surprising her with my strength. I'm no Amazon, but I am a bit stronger than I look.

Piper had a Ph.D. in sociology and taught at Montclair State College in New Jersey. He took a train to get there. Melissa was a special education teacher of English in Manhattan. They were in their late fifties or early sixties, and they usually took off for Europe or San Francisco together when school was not in session, with Piper going earlier than Melissa and staying later than she did due to the difference in their teaching schedules.

Shortly after Bryn welcomed me as his caregiver, Piper got some Chinese food and brought it in to eat with Bryn. Bryn told me that he was coming. He added that he was going to assert himself, a rare thing with Piper, but necessary; otherwise, if Piper could get away with it, he would just open all of the containers of Chinese food on Bryn's bed and likely spill it all over the new quilt, sheets, mattress…everything. "Don't interfere," Bryn warned me, "I'll handle it."

I might have left the apartment rather than risk an awkward moment; I don't remember. But Bryn did protect his new bed, and Piper did indeed attempt to unpack the food on it, whereupon Bryn had said, "It's my apartment, and I want this opened on the kitchen counter." Whereupon Piper had cooperated, marched into the kitchen, opened something, and promptly spilled smelly eel sauce all over everything.

The only preparation I had made was to get an old, forest green colored towel out and leave it for Bryn to spread over the quilt, just in case. He had put it down before letting Piper sit there and eat. Piper hadn't understood the need for it until he dripped a few drops of eel sauce.

Why mention this at all? To describe a key part of Piper's personality: a playful and careless lack of interest in appearance, table manners, and neatness. It would crop up from time to time, and Bryn fondly remembered – his friendship with Piper and Melissa dated back decades – eating out with them while he was still married to Elvira. It was a hot summer night, and Piper had put the little foil-wrapped packets of butter into his shirt pocket to take home. They melted there, oozing all over the front of his shirt as he walked home. The end result was that that story just put me at ease with Piper.

Bryn forbade me to mention any of this, so I kept quiet. There was no need to bring that up, but somehow he worried that I might say something. Asperger's wasn't on our minds as yet, but just watch someone who has the condition enough in social situations, and the urge to warn the person not to do anything impulsive or say anything too honest will make itself known.

These were the key residents in the building, but there were others worth describing.

Smack in between Bryn and Hilda's place, directly across from the stairwell, was another apartment, and it was probably even tinier than Hilda's. It occupied a stretch of wall that had windows only on one side, only one bedroom, and was rent-controlled. It was also occupied by at least five people. An Ecuadoran family lived there.

They were extremely noisy, and the whole building was frustrated with them. Rudy hated them. There was Luisa, the mother, who was the original tenant, her son by her first husband, a Chinese man whom she had divorced after a visit home to Ecuador where she had met and fallen in love with a man from there. She had moved him in with her and her son, and they had gone on to have three little girls. They also had an older, female relative living on the ground floor for while – in the first door on the right at the foot of the stairwell – from whose apartment the most delicious smells had emanated, but she had moved on. We didn't know any more about that.

They had had a blue van for a while, with an alarm. The kids liked to sit outside, just below my bedroom window all day long during the summer. They did it every year, and the sound of that alarm repeatedly going off all day drove me and no doubt many other people crazy. I got so at ease with the situation that shouting "Shut up!" was something that I soon ceased to be shy about doing. There were other car alarms that went off nearby, but none with such regularity.

The boy also had a mini-motorcycle that he rode noisily up and down the sidewalk. I hated that sound, but what could anyone do? To top it all off, he and his sisters would race through the front door and up to their apartment shouting – often. It annoyed everyone.

But the worst had ceased before I knew them. Bryn told me that Luisa used to burn off stress by shrieking "AAAAAHHHHH!" at the top of her lungs often and without warning. It would startle and infuriate people all over the building, and could be heard throughout the structure. It was also illegal. As a lawyer, I can provide the label for her offense. She was interfering with the other tenants' right to quiet enjoyment of the premises. It ceased because Luisa was called to court, where the judge told her that it was illegal and she was thereby ordered to cease and desist. Problem solved, albeit with much fanfare and hassle.

Bryn knew her and her story from a time when she had locked herself out of her apartment. He had let her in to call her husband, and to wait for him to arrive and let her back in. She had told him the story of her life. When I was there, he insisted that I go out and buy some nice Halloween candies for her kids, and again for other holidays. I got the idea, and kept it up for Christmas, Valentine's Day, and Easter.

The people who lived to the right of us were an older Greek-American couple named Andreas and Amy Stavros. Andreas had actually been born in that apartment, and had lived there for his entire life. He and Amy had raised their children there. It was rent-controlled, too. They were very nice, concerned about Bryn but not overly inquisitive, and I gave updates when they asked, without revealing anything that Bryn wanted kept back. I had told him up front to be specific about what was secret and what was not, and it worked out well enough for us.

Downstairs, on the left as one entered the building, was another neighbor, a very strange woman by the name of Karen Carter. She was a hoarder and an old maid with short gray hair, glasses, jeans, sneakers and sweatshirts, and a slight mustache. She had a one-bedroom, rent-controlled place, and a sister who checked on her occasionally. Bryn had told me that once, years ago, he had to call the fire department to break into her place through the window on the street because she had said that she was going to kill herself.

She was the sort of person whom everyone knew about and avoided, trying to creep unnoticed past her door on the way into the building. She usually stayed inside, but she drove them all crazy imagining that she smelled gas, calling the gas company to check the whole building. No one was ordered out of their homes for this, but it happened a lot and induced some stress. The superintendent knew to keep his distance from her, or she would have driven him crazy with demands to check every inch of the building incessantly.

But the most exasperating thing that she did was to constantly call Bryn and ask whether he was running water in his bathroom. He wasn't, and he had no idea why anything was dripping in her apartment. Nevertheless, she kept on calling, and once or twice she called when I was home alone to ask the same question. This went on for a couple of years, ending a few months before Bryn started using a cane. Karen Carter had sounded rather irked at me when I answered that no water was running. "You sound annoyed," she said. I lost patience at that. Why shouldn't I be annoyed?! She kept calling back over and over again after

The Slamming Door

I had said that it wasn't running! "I am annoyed. The water is not running, and I'm trying to get some writing done."

That worked; she stopped calling. I really didn't care about the water – especially after checking and tightening the faucets. Once I have honestly checked and tested something, I get very upset if people don't believe me and leave me alone to concentrate. I hate phones.

In the spring of the year that I took care of Bryn, the impossible happened: Karen Carter moved out. Bryn found out what had happened: the landlord and his daughter, who managed the building (they owned several apartment buildings), had paid her off. Renovators went in and, with much noise and ado, destroyed the place and then put it back together over the course of a month or so. Bryn and I peered in whenever we walked by, and saw the transformation.

It was a miraculous rising of a newly refurbished unit out of the ashes and plaster fragments of the old one. The building dated back to 1926, and it showed. The old radiator was pulled out. The old bathroom fixtures including, alas the beautiful big tub, were yanked out. The wiring and plaster was all replaced, as were the outlets and the entire kitchen, plus the wooden flooring and bathroom tiles. The windows were not changed, but the place was completely brought up to code and no longer rent-controlled. So this was what happened when an older tenant left: the landlord could arrange to charge full market price.

The landlord had no choice in the matter of the renovations; it was the law. But the prices were prohibitive. What had once been rented out for perhaps $650 per month was now going for something like $1,800 a month. The two-bedroom unit above Bryn cost over $2,400 – which led to a succession of new tenants as people found the cost to be just too much for them. When I was Bryn's caregiver, a family with little kids lived there, and they stayed. The husband tended to whoop and leap about annoyingly during football season – more damned noise. I hate team sports and the noise that their fans make…

There was one more tenant worth describing. She lived on the third floor. Bryn did not like her at all. Her name was Rita Matthews. She had lived there for a long time, and she looked and dressed as though she had stepped out of a cheesy, 1950s sci-fi horror flick. Granted, that is a nasty description, but this woman was rather horrible and nasty herself, so that made her fair game for this sort of jab. She lived 2 floors straight up from the noisy Ecuadoran family, directly across the hall from the stairwell. The only time I went up there was when she needed help with her heavy grocery bags and I happened to hear her in the hall; I plunked them in front of her door and went right back into Bryn's place.

This woman devoted her spare time to organizing tenants' meetings over whatever the landlord had done or failed to do – there was always something – and took it upon herself to post signs on the front glass doors of the building claiming all sorts of unlikely things about others. She was just a nuisance and a bit malicious for no good reason. At one point, she posted a nasty sign about bed bugs in the Ecuadorans' apartment, and we were all insulted on their behalf.

She had no evidence and no justification; she just wanted to harass them. Not even Hilda's parents thought it was right, and Elah ripped the signs down. Rita Matthews put them up once more, only to have them disappear again, and then gave up. I saved one and scanned it for Bryn, but ultimately we let the matter drop when she did.

I will leave you with an image of her: medium height, medium-boned, short white hair styled in spikes that stuck out every which way from her head, and sunglasses…black with green plastic rims. The glasses gave her the freakish appearance of an overgrown, alien insect who had just disembarked from a U.F.O. with the worst of special effects that Hollywood ever provided. Add a slightly beaked nose and pursed, somewhat full lips to it, plus a hood on cold days, and the impression of an insectoid refugee from a sci-fi flick is complete.

Downstairs, across from Karen Carter's place, was a couple with two dogs. The guy was a tall, thin, cigarette-smoking guy in sweats with curly brown hair and brown eyes. His fiancée was a beautiful nurse who worked in a nearby hospital on the urology ward. She was Latina or Philippina, I never asked which, and she had tanned skin with long, straight black hair cut with bangs and streaked with blond.

They were rather quiet, especially the thin guy, but he often sat with his ground floor windows and shades open watching television, which was awkward. I made a point of not staring in at him. The most interesting thing about them was their two dogs, however. One was a little Shih Tzu, gray and white, and the other was a huge English Bull Mastiff, gray and black speckled. His name was Harlem, and he was a friendly puppy whose appearance reminded me of the Hound of the Baskervilles every time I saw him. I never learned the little dog's name.

Aside from Teo, whom I have already described, that sums up the motley crew.

Other people lived there, of course, and many of them were in non-rent-controlled units. They tended to be yuppies, fairly nondescript and ultra-conventional. They were nice, quiet, and dull. They made no trouble, no noise, and did nothing interesting to write about.

In fact, the only people I ever found anything about were in the apartment just across the hall next to Hilda's place. The woman was a pediatrician doing a residency somewhere in the city, and her boyfriend was a financier who had lived in Paris for a few years but just moved back to the U.S. Both were Americans, and blond. They showed me the

The Slamming Door

inside of their refurbished unit once, because I was curious. It had smooth, white walls, new hardwood flooring, a pass-through in the kitchen leading to the living room, and two very small bedrooms. I suppose that this further justified the increased rent.

When I saw these expensive units, I despaired of ever affording a life in Manhattan, but didn't let that worry me. Who knew what would happen in the future with my writing efforts and Damon's immunotherapeutic products? Who knew where we would ultimately choose to live?

As long as we could have variety and travel, and never be bored, but also get a stable place of our own to come back to forever after, we would be satisfied. It didn't have to cost a million dollars. We just needed some money – not riches, but solvency. But I had other things on my mind during that time with Bryn. I tried to just focus on that, and for the most part, I did.

Chapter 6

Chelsea, Shopping, and a Celebrity

Chelsea is a great place to live.

The trouble with being a great place to live is that it is usually unaffordable except for a select few. Those few include wealthy celebrities, upper middle class professionals, the few hangers-on of the rent-control system, and the well-entrenched elderly who have long held a foothold in lower Manhattan and thus gotten the best the deals so as to be able to remain in their old and familiar environment.

To others, it is just a place to visit, closed off to many who would love to remain.

There are plenty of attractions: historic buildings, gourmet restaurants, grocery stores that include Chelsea Market, specialty bakeries, florists, beauty salons, boutiques, the General Theological Seminary, the Geraldine Page Salon for the Arts, and with Greenwich Village in easy walking distance.

Chelsea, being just north of Greenwich Village, is on the grid plan for the island that was mapped out in the nineteenth century, by John Randel Jr. He began his work in 1808 and it was published in the Commissioner's Plan in 1811. The maze that is Greenwich Village and the area south of the line along its northern border already existed, so the grid began in Chelsea and extended up and across Manhattan Island in that plan for the future development of the city.

Walking around is easy enough; just watch out for the newly installed biker's lanes, remember that even-number avenue traffic goes north and odd-numbered avenue run south, and that odd numbered streets run west while even-numbered ones run east, with the exception of a few two-way, larger ones that begin with 14th Street; no jay-walking.

Exploring is endlessly fascinating. Bryn got me hooked early on, when Damon and I visited back in 2003, traipsing around the Chelsea boutiques with me so I could see the high-end, hilariously over-priced items for sale (I later learned that New Yorkers say "on sale" even though the price is not marked down and that they wait "on line" rather than "in line"). He laughed ruefully and ushered me out when I started reading the prices out loud, but enjoyed the scene nonetheless. He told me that he and his friend Toby, a former foreign correspondent for NBC News, used to amuse themselves looking in those stores.

None of us would ever buy any of the things that he showed me. He was showing me the high-fashion, top-dollar boutiques in the art district of Chelsea that catered to wealthy gay men. A large percentage of Chelsea residents are gay men. Bryn once told me that many of them

The Slamming Door

were actually upset to see families moving in – the kind with a married mother and father. They felt as if their special area had been intruded upon.

But everyone has to live somewhere, and they don't seem upset anymore.

Still, part of the entertainment to be had from the area is the collection of businesses that cater to the gay community. New York City even has a fun Gay Pride Parade in late June of each year, complete with floats, rock music blaring from the 1980s, and drag queens. To complete the celebration, the Empire State Building uses mauve-colored lights for its spire at night. That building changes the colors of its lights according to the occasion, and maintains a website were the schedule can be seen: http://www.esbnyc.com/tourism/tourism_lightingschedule.cfm

There was a gay bar called The Rawhide across from Bryn's street, on 8th Avenue between 20th and 21st Streets, a card and souvenir shop one block down called Rainbows and Triangles that sold gay jokes and memorabilia, and a DVD store called Rainbow Station across the street from it. A pet store on 9th Avenue, directly on the other side of the block from the DVD place, offered books entitled *Is Your Dog/Cat Gay?* Bryn bought one for Albert and June. I doubted that Pearlie was a lesbian dog, and so did he, but that wasn't the point. We all laughed.

That store was right around the corner from Bryn's apartment; we went to the right, crossed the street facing south, walked to 9th Avenue, turned the corner, and it was a few doors down on the left. On the way, we passed the restaurant called Rafaella's, which offered a mix of American, Italian and Moroccan dishes. It was one of Bryn's favorite places, and he had taken me there alone for brunch shortly after I had married Damon, just to talk and get to know me. I remember getting the granola breakfast with fresh berries, fresh-squeezed orange juice, and coffee. We ate there often over the next year that I took care of him.

Bryn and I were both very set in our ways about food, always wanting to eat the same things over and over, unless we were in a fancy restaurant, in which case we might try something new. I had wondered how we would get along about food, but there was nothing to worry about. He expected me to eat whatever I could eat, and not whatever others deemed appropriate. I loved that about him; he just accepted this before he had any problems of his own with food. He ended up having such trouble with his own taste buds as soon as his treatments started that we often had to eat separately. Every smell bothered him, and only certain things went down without bothering him.

But for now, before he was even signed up with an oncologist, we both decided to have some fun. We might as well do that while he merely knew he had a terrible problem but wasn't yet feeling utterly miserable from it. A couple of days after I got settled in and had cleaned the place, taken out the laundry, gotten used to taking in his daily edition of *The New York Times*, and stocked us up on basic supplies like milk, orange juice, yoghurt, coffee, toilet paper and paper towels (with a 2-ply and a pattern – Bryn was very specific, as he used this in place of Kleenex!), he took me out.

The place we went to was one that I hadn't seen before. Perhaps it was new, or perhaps I hadn't noticed it previously. It was called La

The Slamming Door

Bergamote, and it was French; therefore it promised to be thrilling and offer delectable treats in a chic environment. It was on 9th Avenue, on the southwest corner of 20th Street. Inside were glass cases of souris au chocolat (chocolate mice) with toasted almond ears, linzer tarts, pates de fruits, chocolate and fruit tarts, and so on. The walls were painted to look like 18th century French salons.

Chelsea, Shopping, and a Celebrity

Bryn was in a great mood, and I had brought my camera, so he grinned cheerfully as I took a photograph of him at our table, and smiled and said it was fine when I told him I wanted to take photos of the rest of the place, because it was so beautiful. He knew I loved France and French things; I had studied the language in high school, traveled to Paris, Toulouse and Provence as a student, and appreciated the food and art. Bryn liked it too; he had been taking French lessons when he retired from being a social worker.

The Slamming Door

We both ordered the same things: café au lait and a linzer tart. Bryn looked so happy at the booth, watching people sit and enjoy each other's company in there, that it was hard to believe he was about to fight bone cancer. Except for the cane he now carried, he looked the same as ever – grinning from ear to ear, wearing the same khaki pants, jacket and brown shoes that he always had, with his hair freshly cut and his magnifying-lens glasses. He had been nearsighted since he was a little boy.

He told me the story. This Harvard-educated intellectual had not been responding in class because he couldn't see the blackboard, so the teacher had thought that he was mentally slow. His grandfather, a physician who later removed his tonsils on the kitchen table, didn't believe it. He insisted that Bryn's eyes be checked by a specialist and sure enough, the kid needed glasses. Problem solved. Now Bryn had a prescription for refrigerated eye drops to treat glaucoma; he had been using it for years. He never had anything more dramatic than that happen with his eyes.

This stretch of 9th Avenue was full of fun places to visit. We were just south of the General Theological Seminary, which had a beautiful courtyard of greenery inside its walls and spanned the entire city block all the way over to 10th Avenue. The building facing 9th Avenue had been sold and torn down, however, and a new building was going up. It would have apartments upstairs and stores on the street level.

A couple of years earlier, the Seminary had done something very interesting, and we had read about it in the news: they had drilled deep into the Earth's crust, to access some geothermal streams that now heated their buildings in the winter and cooled them in the summer. They had drilled 1,500 to 1,800 feet down, and had found, of all things, rubies. I don't know what they did with those, but it was certainly interesting, and a short-term source of conflict-free gemstones.

Looking north just across the street was a National Historic Landmark, a small, Federalist-era house where Clement Clarke Moore had supposedly written *A Visit from St. Nicholas*. (A park named for him was on 10th Avenue, on the same block.) Downstairs, on street level, was a French bistro called Le Grainne Café. It used to be called Le Gamin Café (which means street urchin, and made me think of the boy Gavroche in *Les Miserables* whenever I looked at the bistro). A chalkboard outside displayed the specials of the day.

This was the other of the restaurants that Bryn frequented, though not as often as Rafaella's. To tell the truth, I preferred Le Grainne Café, but the other place wasn't bad. I just lean toward all things French. Le Grainne had wooden floors and tables, late 19th century metal-patterned ceilings painted a dark green, and local artwork on the front walls, with early 20th century ads en Français for shows, wines, cigarettes and whatever else posted towards the back. A fabulous display of fresh flowers always graced the counter, over which busy chefs could be seen preparing moules, and omelettes, and crèpes.

My favorite seating area was on the left, with the half-booths of wood, because of the 1951 LaRousse French-English dictionary that was always resting on top of the booths, which stretched around the left corner. If I could get a seat over there, I would get it and look at it, learning more French words and inspecting the currency conversion pages at the beginning, fascinated by how low prices had been that year compared to the present.

Two more great restaurants, much more expensive ones, were immediately north of Le Grainne: Blossom, which was a vegan place that Bryn had invited me to the previous spring with his friend Rosie, and Bombay Talkie, an Indian place with custom-made, museum-quality oil paintings of scenes from Bollywood movies. Damon and I ate there once in the spring of 2008, and the food was well worth the cost. We sat in the window, up against a tall, narrow painting, and I was amazed that it had no Plexiglas to protect it. It had fingerprints and grease spots on the lower half. The other painting was a huge, long one of a song-and-dance scene.

North of that was the Korean-owned convenience store, Ha Ha Fresh, with the cat named after Michael Jackson, and on the northern corners of the following block, on either side of 9th Avenue, were the two diners that Bryn had eaten at when he was alone almost every night for decades: Moonstruck, and his all-time favorite, the Chelsea Square Diner, or the Greeks, as he called it.

The Slamming Door

The Greeks was staffed by mostly Mexican waiters, but also one Colombian who had taken some of Bryn's classes at the Henry George School. An old Greek man who owned the place would ring up the bill by the door, and free copies of *The Onion*, New York City's tongue-in-cheek newspaper, were in the entryway. A mixed collection of inexpensive stained-glass lamps hung all over the diner, which was dimly lit with floor-to-ceiling windows that wrapped around the seating areas that faced the street. There were round barstools and booths farther in, and Bryn had told us that he usually sat there when we weren't with him, but Damon and I had many meals with him over the years in the windows. Autographed photos of movie stars decorated the bar walls, and they had been there for a long time.

The placemats at the Greeks were a menu of wild drinks, which were sold mostly on weekends. New York City diners are typically open all night in this city that never sleeps, and Berta told me that she and her friends used to go to the Greeks and try as many of the drinks off of that placemat as they could. I was amazed; that would have made me sick after several sips. Those drinks were concoctions of hard liquor. They looked pretty though, with stripes of color such as blues, reds, greens, purples, and cream. Some had umbrellas, some had fruit added, but their names were their most interesting features, such as Sex on the Beach.

The food at this place, however, was not particularly healthy, and I had a suspicion that Bryn would have had a fighting chance at not getting cancer had he known more about food and nutrition and eaten regularly elsewhere. But he didn't know, and this was the place that felt like home

Chelsea, Shopping, and a Celebrity

to him after his divorce, where he knew the owners and the staff, and kept current on their lives and happy or sad events.

Overcooked, color-faded vegetables, heavy gravies, fried fish, and salads with iceberg lettuce were standard fare. Matzoh ball soup with chicken broth, fatty clam chowder, and sugary milk shakes were sold there, and an array of cakes revolved in the tall display case near the door. A fun collection of breads and crackers was always offered at the beginning of each lunch or dinner there, and we would always save the Melba toasts in our bags.

There was much more to the neighborhood than this. Coming out of Greeks and heading south, back to Bryn's place, we would pass a Vietnamese-Chinese place that was another favorite, followed by an Irish bar called Jake's Saloon (part of a chain), and where we all ate and drank many times while I was staying with Bryn that year.

Continuing on south, we passed a Rite Aid where I bought a night-light for Bryn's room – a dark blue plastic one with cut-outs of crescent moons and stars. That was about a week after I arrived. On the same block, almost back at Bryn's street, was an antique shop with high-priced wares, followed by Billy's Bakery with its wonderfully soft, moist cookies and colorfully-iced cupcakes and larger cakes, a high-end beauty salon owned by a wealthy gay man in our building, and a high-end florist shop on the corner.

We walked past this particular block many times together after eating at the Greeks, the Viet Grill, or Jake's Saloon.

Down the next block, past Rafaella's, was a Sikh take-out place called the Dil E Punjab Deli, where we could get a spicy vegetarian dinner of dal, chick peas and spinach over basmati rice for five dollars and delicious chai tea for a buck. The place was heavily patronized by Sikh taxi drivers who would park on the street right out front, filling a special taxi cab parking meter before coming in.

Inside, up above the counter, a video was always on. It was usually of a golden Sikh temple in India or a Bollywood movie. The men in there were always very polite, and I always told the elderly man in the cobalt blue or royal purple turban (he alternated) who waited on me that I loved his food. He would smile and thank me. Once I attempted to ask him about the construction outside, but he had real trouble communicating, so I stopped asking him about anything other than food after that. It was okay; the Sikh guys were used to a lone American woman coming in to buy some chai tea for a buck.

On the corner was a very fancy shop called The Three Tarts that sold tiny cookies, hot chocolate with alternating flavors such as chili pepper, green tea and coconut, and stuffed animals, dishes, stationery, and children's books. I got to know a couple of the employees who sold treats there because I stopped in for a 75-cent cookie fairly often.

However, when I went south on 9th Avenue, my destination was usually Chelsea Market. Past a couple of boutique shops along the way that sold French porcelain, linens and soaps, past the famous Maritime Building with its windows that resembled a ship's peepholes, across the avenue just north of 14th Street and inside the old building that used to house the Nabisco Cookie company was Chelsea Market.

Chelsea Market on 9th Avenue.

Chelsea, Shopping, and a Celebrity

Inside, the halls were made of gray stone, including the benches, which were uncomfortable, but at least they blended into the general décor. The artwork of professional photographers typically decorated the walls, changing with each season. About halfway down the hall, near the old industrial elevators and the rest rooms, was an amazing water fountain. This fountain was viewed either from one railing straight ahead or by leaning over from a curving one around the corner to the right. Both were made of iron.

A display case in the hallway of Chelsea Market, full of Nabisco cookie tins and other Nabisco artifacts.

The Slamming Door

Atop some of the straight, square newels were some anatomically correct human organs, also made of iron, including a heart and a liver. Looking down into the fountain was the waterfall effect of it, and coins could be tossed in. Unfortunately, it had recently been covered over with a plain wooden frame to increase the rate of coin tosses; these were to be donated for a program that would bring clean water to third world countries.

I would go there to buy fresh fish, fruits and vegetables, plus breads, rolls, brownies, and cookies. Bringing a plastic bag from Whole Foods to carry my purchases, I would set off with a list and come back ready to cook a delectable meal or two for myself and Damon whenever we stayed with Bryn. If I could coordinate it with him, I would cook for all three of us, and several times he enjoyed one of my fish and vegetable dinners, always with a different fish: catfish, Spanish mackerel, salmon, tuna, trout, halibut, salmon cakes, crab cakes, etc.

I got them at The Lobster Place, which was just past the water fountain. That place was a feast of the best, freshest fish, and offered species that I seldom found in Connecticut. It was a fish market that offered all sorts of fabulous fin fish and shellfish, plus sushi and fish sandwiches, and hot shellfish soups.

The Bowery Kitchen Supply shop entrance.

Chelsea, Shopping, and a Celebrity

Chelsea Market was full of gourmet food shops; Damon and I liked to eat some lobster bisque at a tall side table in the hall outside The Lobster Place, and then get some tea and cookies at either Amy's Bread or Sarabeth's Kitchen. In the summer, we liked to get gelato at the place near the Bowery Kitchen Supply store. I had bought 4 plates for Bryn from the hallway sale tables of that store once, covered with dust and filth. The storekeeper had refused to do any more than put them into a plastic bag. But inside were all sorts of gourmet kitchen supplies, including Staub and Le Creuset pots, everything one could need or want for cooking and serving Japanese and Chinese foods, Nordicware baking pans, and so on.

There was a milk bar in Chelsea Market that sold great yoghurt drinks, and I introduced Bryn to them when his stomach started bothering him a few months after I came to stay with him. He promptly got addicted to them, and I had to comb the area stores for our favorite flavors: strawberry and blackberry. The place offered milk, ice cream, malteds, and milkshakes as well.

Aside from The Lobster Place, the most exciting place in Chelsea Market, at least to a gourmet cook (me) was the Manhattan Fruit Exchange (a cash-only store). The Manhattan Fruit Exchange offered dried and fresh fruits, chocolates, coffees to weigh and grind, cheeses from all over the world, exotic and local mushrooms from places like France, Japan, and the U.S., fresh herbs and edible flowers, fresh fruits and vegetables, and fresh-squeezed juices that included orange and tangerine.

Chelsea, Shopping, and a Celebrity

In October, the display just outside stretched the length of the Exchange, which was fully visible through its floor-to-ceiling glass windows (nearly all of the shops had those windows). Elaborately carved pumpkins were perched among gourds on haystacks all along the windows.

At Christmastime, smack in the center of Chelsea Market, encrusted a double-arch from which an old clock hung, would be dark green plastic strands of little white lights. The smell of overheated plastic was a bit alarming at that time of year, as was the heat emanating from it all.

There used to be a huge florist shop on the left as one entered from 9th Avenue, complete with a fluffy gray cat and a short-haired black one that had died from drinking the plant-food-saturated water, poor thing. It was gone now, thanks to the downturn of the economy.

Chelsea Market had several bakeries, including a brownie shop called the Fat Witch Bakery, which displayed a fabulous dollhouse inhabited by a toy witch at Halloween, Amy's Bread, and Sarabeth's Kitchen. There was also a wonderful restaurant called The Green Table, which changed its menu each season according to whatever the local farms were selling to its chefs. Damon and I had never gotten around to eating there, but this was the year that I would go there three times.

Outside and down around the corner on 14th Street, towards 10th Avenue, were several over-the-top clothing stores marketing Chanel, Prada, Stella McCartney and other brand names in stores that resembled The Closet in *The Devil Wears Prada*. Once in a while, I would wander through, wondering how anyone could actually wear what was essentially a faddish work of art. One pull on the fabric and its value would be instantly diminished.

The Gansvoort Hotel was just south of these shops and Chelsea Market, with its pink-lit rooftop bar that overlooked the Hudson River on one side; it offered views of the Empire State Building on the other.

One street north of Chelsea Market, halfway to 10th Avenue, was a terrible grocery store called Western Beef. Damon had tried and tried to make me shop there because it was so cheap, but I just hated it. It represented everything about food that I hated: it specialized in meats, which I avoid eating, and I just refuse to eat beef; Rudy pronounced its fish to be unsafe. The fish was only cod or salmon and packed in bulk – too much for us to finish before it would rot, so no savings there. If a professional chef turned his nose up at that fish, so would I. The produce was all wilted in that place, and I eat a lot of fresh produce, so this place just didn't work for me.

There was other grocery stores that I shopped at often, however: Balducci's, a gourmet shop on 8th Avenue and 14th Street, which was housed in a palace of a former bank building, a Garden of Eden store on 6th Avenue and 23rd Street with beautiful pastries, and a small Whole Foods on 7th Avenue and 24th Street. Balducci's was for special occasions, and alas, it closed the next spring. While it lasted, it was another reliable source of the yoghurt drinks that Bryn liked.

But Whole Foods was a reliable place to go for fresh fruits and vegetables, more convenient than Chelsea Market, and it sold many things that I was able to entice Bryn to eat. I was fascinated by the lines that formed behind three backlit signs the colors of traffic lights, and always waited behind the red one, which was on the left and depicted a cluster of cherries. None of the Whole Foods stores in Connecticut used these devices, but all of the ones in Manhattan did. Also, if one forgot to bring a recycled plastic bag, a 99-cent charge would be added to the final bill at checkout.

But it was the bookstores of this area that really thrilled me when I wasn't after the food. I found a place on 10th Avenue one beautiful fall afternoon that specialized in art books. It was called 192 Books, and Bryn had given me a gift of some money – a hundred dollars, I think – to spend on something fun. He made it quite clear that he wanted to see evidence of some sort that I had used it for myself. I did not spend it immediately; I had to think about it for a few days. But after perusing the books in this shop, I ended up with one called *Chanel and Her World: Friends, Fashion and Fame* by Edmonde Charles-Roux for sixty dollars. Bryn was satisfied. I didn't rush to spend the rest, but he wasn't concerned.

Chelsea, Shopping, and a Celebrity

Meanwhile, I read the book from cover to cover, and studied the photographs; Coco Chanel was an interesting subject.

The famous Empire Diner was just one block up from the art book store, and Bryn had once taken me and Damon there for coffee one summer evening after dark. We had fun sitting on the sidewalk seating, ordering plain coffee with milk, while he got it black and laughed to the waiter as he explained that his fussy cousins wanted milk and not cream, and to please remember to leave his black, or something like that.

Chelsea Piers was just another block away from there, and it housed a health club with views of the Hudson River, a roller rink, berths for yachts, and so on. Across the promenade by the water, just under the overhang, was a series of huge black-and-white photographs with captions that detailed the history of the place. There was even one showing newsboys selling *Extra! Extra! Read all about it!* editions of 1912 papers announcing the sinking of the R.M.S. Titanic, though it was to have docked south of there, at Pier 54.

On 8th Avenue was a nail-grooming shop on the left/north as one exited Bryn's street, and after that was a standard, chain grocery store, where I shopped for basic supplies, and a hotel that was under construction or renovation – I wasn't sure which. An art exhibit graced the ground floor while this project was underway. Up the street on the next block were a T-Mobile store (where I could pay my cell phone bill), a Starbucks, a Jamba Juice shop, and across the street, Bryn's favorite pharmacy, called the New London Pharmacy.

The New London Pharmacy was just one of two places where he chose to get his prescriptions filled. It was like a fancy boutique with a pill dispensary in the back, light, with new pale wooden flooring, fancy soaps, lotions, shampoos and perfumes, and two cats who lived in the basement but were sometimes allowed upstairs. They were sisters, adopted by the store's owner from a shelter on Long Island, and their names were London and Paris. London was all black, and Paris was a tiger-striped cat.

Several nice restaurants were along the east side of 8th Avenue, including a Cuban place with tropical rainforest murals painted onto its walls, a seafood place that offered a variety of oysters, and so on.

On 18th Street, on the way to the post office there, I found a millinery shop run by a very nice woman who liked to chat with me and show me her wares, describing how she made them. She liked to talk about all sorts of things, and would ask me how Bryn was doing during the year that I stayed to take care of him. She told me that she was from Bolivia, and she kept her little Chihuahua dog in a bed under her worktable in the back room. He would get up and patrol the shop every so often. She also offered to put some brochures for my editing and calligraphy service in her window, which was very nice.

Chelsea, Shopping, and a Celebrity

I don't remember this woman's name, but I do remember her shop and hats. It was called Ellen Christine's Millinery, and her hats were worn at the Kentucky Derby and other places where it was customary to wear fabulous hats.

This beautiful pale blue hat probably went to a garden party or the Kentucky Derby later on.

That about covers the haunts of Chelsea; however, just north of Bryn's area, still in Chelsea, across from the Fashion Institute of Technology, lived Damon's aunts. A huge complex of brick apartment buildings was set between 8th and 9th Avenues, and Aunt Summer had lived in her place on 28th Street and 8th Avenue for decades. Aunt Johanna lived a couple of blocks south of her place, but she had only moved there a few years ago, from a place on West 57th Street.

Technically, the aunts were the best friends of Damon's mother, who had moved to Arizona sometime in the 1980s to follow her daughters (Damon had dropped out of communication with his relatives for about 12 years, only resuming contact just before going off to the Persian Gulf War). But we called them both aunt, and I had met them when Damon and I had gotten engaged.

Aunt Summer liked a place called East of Eighth – located on 23rd Street just east of 8th Avenue, of course – a bit too much for Bryn's taste. The problem with it was that she had selected it as a gathering place a few too many times, though it was really very nice, and the food was, for the most part, delicious. It was just mildly amusing one year to hear Bryn give a message to whomever was going to plan the next gathering with both aunts to make sure that it was at someplace other than East of Eighth.

The Slamming Door

Aunt Summer was an interesting person, a retired pianist (a recording artist) who had left home at age eighteen to get away from a crazy mother. Her mother had done her blond hair in pipe curls and encouraged her in her music studies until she competed at Carnegie Hall and came in second place. When she got home and said how she had done, her mother had shrieked that she had disappointed her. With that, Aunt Summer had dragged a mattress into an apartment that her father owned and informed him that she was moving in. Her father had left years earlier, to get away from her mother. Lovely story; she went on to support herself with her music, marry a guy about whom I know nothing, and get divorced.

Currently, Aunt Summer lived in her 8th floor apartment – a lot of 8's in her life, I noticed – and visited with her boyfriend, a tanned, white-haired, retired real estate developer named Fred who lived in Florida. When he stayed with her, he paid for almost nothing, the relatives had told me. I don't know whether he made up for it when she went to Florida, but they had added that he was verbally abusive to her. No one knew why she liked him.

Aunt Johanna was different; she sold Hummel dolls for a living, traveling to Hungary and Germany to do so, but was retired now. She had a boyfriend who lived on Long Island with his wife (who apparently did not want to divorce him for having a girlfriend). He had made money in the stock market and retired years ago. Aunt Johanna always smelled wonderfully of roses thanks to a special perfume that Aunt Summer bought for her every time she went to Florida. She bought a bottle for me too, but Damon didn't like the scent of roses on me, so I just saved it and never told Aunt Summer that. (I had admired the scent, which was why she got it for me.)

Several years ago, Aunt Summer had come over to see Bryn's apartment, and had confided to us that Aunt Johanna was divorced because her husband had wanted a ménage-a-trois and she had not. Well…good for her for getting away from that situation.

Aunt Johanna was a singer and actress in her free time, and she organized a series of short plays that we saw in the basement of her building in the spring of the year that I stayed with Bryn. It was very good, but I spent the whole time silently crying; I wasn't doing a good job of keeping calm and cheerful that evening. I don't know whether or not anyone noticed; I went with Bryn, Albert, June, and I think Alissa.

Damon visited me in Chelsea about a week after I arrived, staying with me in our old room at Bryn's place. He was going to send the recipe for ImmuneACCORD for me to make for Bryn soon after that, but for now he was going back to his co-inventor in Maryland to make a few more tweaks with the formulation. After that, it was on to the laboratory

Chelsea, Shopping, and a Celebrity

at the University of Connecticut at Storrs to do a series of experiments for the same reason. Publications were being prepared, and soon the co-inventor would have bottles of the stuff packaged...just not soon enough to add the mixture to Bryn's food while he was sick, I griped.

To prepare for this drink-making task, I had gone through Chelsea in the opposite direction, over to 6th Avenue between 18th and 19th Streets, to the huge Bed Bath & Beyond shop, armed with a 20% off coupon that I had brought from Connecticut. I got a basic Waring blender for Bryn's apartment and put it on the tally sheet. Even though it was originally intended for making the spice drink, which Damon said might help control the pain caused by inflammation associated with cancer, that wasn't all that I did with it...but more on that later.

Unfortunately, pharmaceuticals tend to mess with a person's sense of taste. This happens whether a person has cancer or a heart condition or asthma or whatever a collection of pills has been prescribed to manage. The result is that spices end up burning the person's mouth, and then they give up eating any spicy foods, losing the benefits of them. It's not very helpful, and it's frustrating that medications do so much harm rather than only good. They seem to be about side effects as much as about whatever slight benefit they offer.

Just listen to any television advertisement for a pharmaceutical product. Damon had pointed this out to me many times: after a hypnotic explanation of the drug's use and benefits, the voice goes on to rapidly list a litany of horrendous side effects, often including suicide and death from heart attack. Damon proudly told me that his nutraceutical formulations didn't have side effects – only benefits. But marketing them was tough...pharmaceutical companies had powerful lobbies to block any competition. So we continued to be broke – brilliant but uselessly so and broke – I hated it.

Damon was in town to meet with his associates at the New York Eye & Ear Infirmary on 2nd Avenue and 14th Street about both another immunotherapy and ImmuneACCORD, and to introduce the executive from the Indian spice company that supplied cinnamon, turmeric and whatever else for ImmuneACCORD to the ophthalmologist he was working with there.

I met them too, on a sunny afternoon, in the office suite that we now knew well. As I sat in the meeting listening to everyone and taking some notes and photos, my cell phone rang. It was Berta, calling to check on some arrangement for her father or for a trip out to dinner, I forget which. Damon was appalled that I had forgotten to turn the phone off. Berta apologized and got right off of the phone when she realized that I was in a meeting.

The Slamming Door

But the reason for keeping the damned thing on was related to my duty to Bryn. Once I went to stay with him, I kept my cell phone fully charged, turned on, and in my pants pocket at all times whenever I left the apartment. The idea was to be easy to reach, a huge adjustment for me. I hate phones, I hate to hear them ring and startle me (they really upset me when they ring even now), and so I was making a big change in policy by doing this.

The point was for Bryn to be able to call me about changes in plans, requests for purchases, or assistance with an emergency while I was out. It was to increase efficiency. Other relatives could call me too for the same reason. I only shut it off at night, and turned it back on when I got up. No need to run it at home; Bryn was in the next room, and could just call to me. That worked well until the last week and a half before I left.

Damon got over the awkwardness caused by the phone ringing quickly when I explained how I had lapsed by not shutting it off; I had never done that before, and we had attended plenty of meetings together. He knew I was there to help Bryn.

Our chances to meet at Bryn's place for the purpose of seeing each other while we were homeless were ending. We ate out together a couple of times, including at the family's favorite sushi place on 23rd Street just west of 8th Avenue called Daioh, and I cooked a nice dinner or two for him, but Damon was depressed. He would drink a couple of large beers – cheap ones, because he isn't too fussy about the taste – and fall asleep in front of the television.

Damon was (and is) a brilliant guy and for the most part was very nice to be married to. He was very accepting of my difficulties with anxiety, my quirks about food and noise, and complimentary of my writing and cooking and baking skills. We both loved museums and action movies, science fiction and historical dramas, and cats.

We had a nice visit for a few days, and then he was gone, back to work.

We would never give up on each other or our career aspirations; we saw no other choice.

There was one other feature of Chelsea worth mentioning: the actor Ethan Hawke lived on the same street as Bryn, in a townhouse that was painted slate-blue. He was divorced from Uma Thurman by then, and about to marry his next wife, the nanny with whom he had had a baby girl. We saw him coming and going from time to time.

I don't fawn over celebrities. I find it demeaning and pathetic. A celebrity is someone who has been lucky enough to have a lucrative

Chelsea, Shopping, and a Celebrity

career doing something that she or he loves to do. A celebrity is a person, just like anyone else. But my attitude is atypical.

One afternoon, I was walking with Berta and Matt in a light rain with my head down a bit, and my blue rain jacket on, hood up. Matt was walking a few paces ahead of us. I forget what I was telling Berta about; I just hate to have the flow of a story interrupted and ruined.

As we headed toward 9th Avenue, a noticed a little black-and-white border collie on a leash looking plaintively up at me. "What a nice dog!" I cooed at it, and kept on going. Without missing a beat, I went right on with my story.

Berta started tapping me frantically. "Clarisse!" she said a couple of times.

"What?!" I said, annoyed.

"That was Ethan Hawke's dog!" she said excitedly.

Berta does fawn over celebrities, though I had yet to learn the extent of it. She had also had several failed attempts to make conversation with this particular actor. The problem was having a valid reason for speaking to a complete stranger; usually, there isn't one. People just want to go about their business near their homes, and get in and out of cabs without being startled by someone they don't know.

Berta hadn't understood that in her eagerness to interact with a famous actor, and he had been cranky about it. I can't say that I blame him. Neither could Bryn; he thought that the guy wouldn't want to bother with his neighbors acting like fools every time he went in and out of his house or around the corner to get a jug of milk.

Well, this was just funny to the point of hilarious. I hadn't even looked up at the dog's owner; I had just gone on with my story, treating the famous actor like anyone else. He probably loved that. It was probably just what he wanted from the people who lived near him.

I looked up at Berta when she told me that it was his dog, then back in time to see Ethan Hawke standing at his front door with the key in one hand and the dog's leash in the other, looking at us to see what we would do. I burst out laughing. So did he.

And then I had turned around and resumed telling my story, whatever it was.

Chapter 7

At MoMA with Albert and June

One afternoon early in October – a Thursday – Albert invited me to come with him and June to the Museum of Modern Art, to view the Van Gogh exhibit. Bryn insisted that I go and have a good time. I did; we saw Van Gogh's *Starry Night* painting and several others, plus we read all about his life, career, brother, trouble with depression, and death. Despite the subject matter, we had a good time.

That was Bryn's policy and philosophy: everyone must have a good time, and they absolutely must not miss any opportunity to do so on his account. There really wasn't much chance of that happening yet, especially considering the fact that I had just gotten there, so I didn't worry about it. I went, and saw *Starry Night* and many other paintings, and read all about the artist and his life.

I also got to hang out with Albert and June. I had always liked them, and found them to be pleasant, fun people, especially Albert. June, I didn't know very well, but I looked forward to getting to know her a bit better…at least, as much as one could with a person who was suffering from Stage 2 Alzheimer's disease.

Seventeen years earlier, I had taken care of my great-aunt for a mere 2 weeks, during the summer after I had graduated from college. She had Alzheimer's disease, and was slated to enter a rest home immediately after that time. She just needed someone to watch her until the appointed time, at which my father and I drove her all the way from north central Connecticut to Saranac Lake, New York, where one of her brothers lived with his wife.

The experience of taking care of Aunt Sharon was unforgettable. This was a woman who had gone on a full scholarship to Barnard College at age sixteen and double-majored in history and Spanish. After that, she had lived on her own in Manhattan and worked as the lead secretary in an office with a team of secretaries, first for a period of twenty years for one boss, then for another thirty years for a member of Congress. That was Congressman Keogh, for whom the 401K retirement plan was named, and my aunt had the very first one of those.

She also took each of her nieces to Europe, and when they grew up, she took me once. Aunt Sharon had lived in the Stuyvesant apartments, and chose never to get married, though she did have a boyfriend before I knew her. She was and her youngest sister, my other great-aunt, loved the ballet; when my grandmother (their middle sister) and I would go to visit each summer, we spent the week touring the art museums and attending one ballet at Lincoln Center.

At MoMA with Albert and June

When I took care of my aunt, it was with a state of constant vigilance. I had to watch her without making it obvious, and make sure that she didn't go anywhere, like outside and off down the street. Once, she announced that her grandparents lived over the nearest hill and she was going to go visit them. I had to follow her and chat with her until she thought of something else.

Fortunately, this was when I was teaching myself to be a gourmet cook and baker with a book that my mother had given me, called *The Best of Gourmet 1991*. Aunt Sharon was another gourmet, and the house that my parents and I lived in was out in a rural area. The result was that she spent most of her time helping me in the kitchen, doing little tasks like cleaning and drying things. I got the food preparation done and kept track of her simultaneously. But it was stressful.

She asked me repeatedly if I was reading *Pride and Prejudice* because I put the book out on the table in front of us. I put it away. This was a brilliant, self-sufficient woman who was now reduced to going over and over the same idea with no way of knowing that she had already done so several times. And I had really enjoyed her before this happened to her, so I tried to continue where we had left off by getting her tell me about things that she knew. It was tricky; I didn't want to freak her out by letting her realize that something wasn't as she expected it to be.

Now I was around June, and it was the same problem all over again: a brilliant woman who had aced her way through two master's degrees, one in psychology and another in art, who had carefully stored her own personally selected trove of knowledge in her brain, was losing it piece by piece through no fault of her own. She was only 68 years old – young to have Alzheimer's disease. She and Albert never spoke of it; the subject was taboo around her.

The best way to respect her seemed to be to answer every question she asked without delay, so that she would always feel that she was in on everything, even if it meant giving her the same information over and over again.

Albert and June were inseparable, both retired, and perhaps 5 feet, 4 inches tall. Albert had once been taller, but osteoporosis and shortened him a bit. June's only health problem was Alzheimer's; otherwise, she would likely outlast her husband, who was sick with prostate cancer and had been for over fifteen years. They each wore med-alert bracelets; hers said "memory impaired" and his said something about epilepsy and being a caregiver to her.

They each dressed in preppy clothes ordered from L.L. Bean, all done by Albert. Past photographs of them revealed that June had dressed in those clothes anyway, so her husband was just reading the tags for sizes and continuing that. He ordered clothes for their daughter Alissa as

The Slamming Door

well, which had its good and bad points; they fit, and she wasn't particularly interested in clothes shopping, but they weren't the sort of outfits that would help her acquire a boyfriend.

But more on that later…

Albert and June made a cute couple, a similarly-dressed, similarly-coiffed, retired pair. They each had short, waved white hair, cut and styled by the same pricy woman every few weeks, except that June's coif was streaked and shaped more prettily than Albert's. They typically wore loafers, khaki pants, and polo shirts with cotton sweaters.

Now, Albert had the difficult situation of attempting to get June to acquiesce to joining an elderly day care program for Alzheimer's patients. It was somewhere in northern Manhattan, at a place where she might possibly go to live at some point, but it was prohibitively expensive to do so, and Albert intended to keep her at home with him for as long as possible.

At this place, the caregivers ran a group that used art therapy to occupy the patients. The people there were all older than June, and had come down with Alzheimer's at a relatively young age, so she felt out of place there. That, combined with the fact that she and Albert never actually spoke the name of her condition plus the fact that she was a retired giver of this very same form of art therapy made it nearly impossible to integrate her into the program.

June was insulted by it. She had taken care of public school students using these skills. Now she was expected to be on the receiving end of that same therapy, and it didn't sit well with her. I didn't blame her. Aging is demeaning and insulting; I could hardly endure it when I took my grandmother to a doctor's office and heard the nurses talking loudly to her and in tones meant for a small child, and had complained about it to the doctor.

June was finally persuaded to participate by the caregivers when they convinced her that she worked there with them, and got her to help administer the art therapy to the other patients. Poor June…her father had had Alzheimer's too, but not until he had been much older.

Albert would try to do some work on his laptop downstairs in the same building while June went to this workshop. He had some book project that he had agreed to do, transcribing recorded interviews, but he was so overtired from constantly entertaining and watching June that he couldn't accomplish much. He wanted to earn some more money, but he just couldn't do it anymore. To compensate, he would cash in some stocks and use that money.

One afternoon that fall, I had tried to distract June while Albert called the stockbroker from Bryn's kitchen. The volume on Albert's cell phone was up too high, and she heard the stockbroker remark, "Oh right,

At MoMA with Albert and June

you can't work because of your wife," whereupon Albert yanked the phone away from his ear, turned down the volume, and muttered, "Right," and then hurried on to his next sentence as I asked June brightly, "Want some green tea ice cream?"

That did it; June loved green tea ice cream, and so did I. We had it every time the family ate in a Japanese restaurant, and I managed to find it for sale in some local grocery stores.

So here I was in Manhattan, watching a series of outrages perpetrated by nature upon great people: bone cancer feasting upon Bryn, prostate cancer feasting upon Albert, and Alzheimer's disease stealing and chipping away at June's memory. I had even looked it up on Wikipedia; Alzheimer's really did work that way, by chipping away at the brain. It reminded me of computer bytes being corrupted and deleted, randomly and bit by bit.

About Albert and prostate cancer: he had had it since 1993, and studied the topic to the nth degree and made his decisions based on his efforts. He had also never kept his illness a secret. When you share a problem with your support network, such as family and friends, it usually has the effect of making it easier to cope with that problem.

Alas, Bryn did not operate that way. Albert told me the whole story over a delicious vegetarian dinner of butternut squash purée over pasta in the MoMA restaurant. It was appalling.

What Bryn did was, he conferred only with his doctor, a radiation oncologist at Beth Israel Hospital, discussed the proffered treatment only with Cassie, and then, after she and he agreed that he ought to go ahead with it, accepted it.

That idiot doctor treated Bryn for prostate cancer with 80 radioactive seeds, injected into his prostate over a 2-hour period and left there ever after. What the seeds do is they kill off the prostate cancer, then stay in the body forever after and mutate healthy cells into other cancer. So much for the "first do no harm" clause of the Hippocratic Oath. This quack had caused the harm would come later rather than first, but it was the same difference. That was in 2005.

I couldn't believe this when I heard it; satellites are powered by this crap! It does not belong inside the human body. I had done my law thesis on outer space law, so I knew this from my research.

Anyway, that's the story of how Bryn got bone cancer.

"I hate to say it," Albert confided to me, "but I really think that the poor guy is just a goner." Albert was really upset; Bryn was his best friend.

They were just 2 years apart in age (Bryn was older), and they had raised their daughters near each other, gone to camp together as teenagers, both attended the Hackley School as teenagers (though not

The Slamming Door

together – first Bryn did his junior and senior years there, then Albert), and sneaked into the Harvard Club on 44th Street in Manhattan to run up drinks on their father's tab (naughty boys) after Bryn turned eighteen and could order their drinks (it wasn't until the 1980s that states raised the drinking age to 21). They still socialized together as much as possible, going to movies and restaurants together, and they always looked forward to seeing each other.

Yet Bryn never spoke to Albert about having anything wrong with his health until he was doomed with bone cancer and realized that pretending to be okay would be neither feasible nor realistic. Albert was a bit stunned by this level of stubbornness and secretiveness.

When Bryn finally admitted to being sick, he acted as though it were a crime or a source of disgrace. He didn't want to ruin anyone's good time or upset anyone, and he didn't want to face anyone else's feelings of sadness or anxiety about him, regardless of whether or not that was realistic or fair. It was all thoroughly appalling.

I thought back to the previous spring when Tim Russert had died of a heart attack and Bryn had told all of us that he had gone to see his cardiologist to ask whether or not he too would die of a heart attack.

The doctor had said no, recommended more fresh fruit and vegetables, and that was it.

No; Bryn was going to die of something much worse, much more slowly, with less dignity and a lot more discomfort. True to the saying, life would suck, and then he would die.

Chapter 8

The Rock Star of the Henry George School

It was Berta who came up with this coolest of all possible monikers for her father.

It fit him perfectly.

He didn't dress like one, he didn't act like one, and he didn't look like one.

But he was one. Bryn was the rock star of the Henry George School.

Almost everyone there – the director, the faculty, the librarian, the staff, and all of the students – loved him. They loved his outgoing, friendly personality, his cheerful attitude, and his entertaining classes. He made learning fun.

The way he saw it, he had to do that, because classes were free and optional. Georgism was about something that employers did not seek on resumes: land taxes. Henry George was a 19th century political economist. Property owners preferred to have taxes on buildings, which depreciate over time, thus lowering their own costs.

But with land taxes, that wouldn't happen, and more revenue would be generated for all, funneled into municipal service. That would prevent at least two social ills: a concentration of wealth in a small percentage of the population, and the hoarding of that wealth away from everyone else, which would lock it away from any benefit to the majority of the population.

The curriculum runs about two years, tuition (but not books) is free, and once completed, the graduate is given a diploma. Anyone truly fascinated by it – anyone who shows a great aptitude for and love of the subject matter – may be invited to become a professor after all this. Bryn was one of these individuals; he finished in the early 1990s.

Henry George summed up his philosophy in his book *Progress and Poverty* in 1879. Here, direct from the school's website, are the main questions dealt with in its curriculum:

> *Why in spite of all the inventions, innovations and marvelous increases in productivity, do wages not increase? Why are so many people who are willing and able to work unable to exchange their labor for the products of other people's labor?*

The Henry George School was founded in 1932. It also had branches in Philadelphia, where the philosopher was from, and in San Francisco, but its headquarters was in New York City. It is located at on East 30th

The Slamming Door

Street between Lexington and Park Avenues, on the north side of the street. Its building looks like a townhouse from the outside, but inside it looks very much like a school, with gray office carpeting on the floors of all of the rooms, a concrete-stepped and metal-railed staircase, and an elevator just inside the reception room.

In the warmer months, it is really quite pleasant to approach the place and stay awhile. Trees and branches and vines grow out in front, and the glass door and floor-to-ceiling front windows can be reached either by a few steps on the left or by a ramp that goes first to the right and then to the left, depositing the visitor at the door. The secretary/receptionist must buzz each person in, and there is another glass door to the right. Inside, one signs a list with the time of arrival and sees wooden bookshelves behind the main desk full of Henry George's books.

The front entrance of the Henry George School on East 30th Street in Manhattan.

Proceeding straight through, past the elevator, past the stairwell on the left and the rest room to the right, is the room where I spent most of my visits to the school. It is painted off-white, and needs touching up, especially on the large blank area where slides and movies are projected. Every Saturday during the academic year, movies are shown on that wall. The fall that I arrived, it was a series of film noir movies, all in black-and-white.

The Rock Star of the Henry George School

This was the room where a huge collection of metal folding chairs was kept, and were always set up facing the wall on the left. Straight ahead were some glass doors that opened onto the back patio. In summer evenings, gatherings would spread out to that patio, and a beautiful view of Manhattan townhouses and back yards stretched around and above us, replete with trees and more vines.

Classes are offered in Spanish as well as in English, mostly taught by a physician from Honduras who cannot dare return to her native country. She spoke out for better health care for all and paid the price: exile.

Only those who wanted to learn about Georgism would become students there, unlike students at business and secretarial schools, who hoped to become more desirable to potential employers. So if the classes weren't fun, there was little point in teaching them.

Not all of the people in charge of the school understood the logic of this.

Bryn did, and he included guest speakers, movies, and other colorful teaching tools in his classes. He was flexible, coped with interruption well, and routinely got standing ovations when he was concluded a class meeting.

He was also a member of the board of trustees, which was like any other group of educated, opinionated elders: they had opposing points of views and agendas. Their meetings were closed of course, but he would tell me a few major points about what went on inside them.

The people who attend are mostly elderly, and many ask questions or make comments asking for information that will be revealed if they just wait for the speaker or movie get to that part, but they can't wait. They cough over lines and sniffle and comment to the person next to them that they should have arrived earlier and gotten a better seat…throughout each presentation.

Sigh…

Damon had been invited, by Bryn, to lecture there twice, once about his work on mustard lung studies, and again on his efforts to bring better health care training to the remote reaches of Iraqi Kurdistan, where he spent the winter of 2008.

I was invited to speak once also – and like Damon, by Bryn – about my time in Kuwait. We set up the laptop with the projector and I presented a carefully selected collection of photographs from the trip. It was very interesting, but I was constantly interrupted with questions about what it had to do with Henry George's philosophy, which flustered me.

Kuwait has nothing to with that and Bryn knew it; he just thought that it would be a great opportunity for his students to see what the place

The Slamming Door

was like. If only he or I had known to explain that from the outset. Still, I think that the audience got something useful and interesting out of the slide show.

The most amazing lecture and presentation I ever attended there was one that dealt with the Parker Brothers game *Monopoly* and its precursor, *The Landlord-Tenant Game.* That had been in 2007, and Damon had been there too. Parker Brothers had paid the woman who created it peanuts for the legal rights to it. She never got another penny, and they made millions of dollars by changing it to the Monopoly game, which is all about capitalism rather than land taxes…a familiar tale. The fun part of this was that the guy giving the lecture had laid out his entire collection of games – every version of it every manufactured.

His last name was Biddle and he taught at the Philadelphia branch of the Henry George School. He laid the antiques out all over the tables at the front of the room, and I took photos (lost, much to my dismay, when my old computer died). There was a round version on oilcloth, and even one from England that featured a fox, with animal characters named for early 20th century British politicians. We saw a century's worth of board games that evening.

Another lecture – one that we attended in the fall of 2008 – was given by a professor of sociology about a housing project in Chicago. It was a well-researched lecture with a gaping flaw: no consideration was given to the wishes and needs of African-Americans, who were the majority of the residents in the project. This hole in his research did not go over particularly well with a large segment of the listeners at the Henry George School that evening, because they too were African-Americans, and he could not answer their questions. I was surprised to see an intellectual in the early 21st century make a mistake like that, but there it was.

Damon visited that month, and attended this lecture. He only stayed for a few days, then returned to the Storrs campus of the University of Connecticut.

I missed being with my best friend and soul mate, and this was all I could hope for now. It wasn't much, because Bryn told me that he didn't want Damon there much, because Damon was too noisy, and Bryn reminded me that he couldn't deal with it because he was sick now and home much of the time.

I knew that, I said. And I assured him that Damon wouldn't be around much.

Then I told Damon this, repeating the conversation when we were alone together.

He wasn't thrilled, but couldn't blame Bryn.

The Rock Star of the Henry George School

Damon is loud – he's deaf in one ear from the war in Kuwait, and talks on his cell phone a lot at the top of his voice. It drives me crazy too. I hate noise, and have even cried from the stress if he talks for too long, which has induced him to go outside or just wrap things up.

So we continued to communicate by cell phone, e-mail, and sometimes by Skype, the Internet phone system based in Luxembourg. We each had accounts with it, and as long as we were both near a net-connected computer, we could talk for free. We wrote and talked to each other several times a day, which made the separation a little easier, and coordinating work and life's details simpler.

That left me alone with the Henry George professor, and I ended up serving as his research assistant, which I felt easily qualified to do for him. I had been a research assistant to professors in college and in law school, plus I had done plenty of my own research in order to complete my degrees. Bryn was glad to have me there to help him prepare; I could do a lot with a net-connected computer and a printer.

When Bryn wasn't preparing a lecture of his own, he loved to go out and attend those of his colleagues – other Henry George School professors.

Some lectures were given off site, and one chilly evening in December Bryn and I took a cab to St. Mark's Bowery Episcopal Church at 2nd Avenue and 10th Street so that he could hear Alfred Maserati, a wealthy businessman and Henry George School professor lecture about the economy. But the lectures scared me, and I left. No one minded.

I took off with a woman who had left her friend there to listen. We found a diner and ate a Scandinavian breakfast – something hot with raspberry sauce – in the evening. Then she showed me a specialty toy store, called Dinosaur Hill, where Bryn later had me buy Hanukah gifts via cell phone. It was another cold evening, and I had walked all the way across town, enjoying the trip. We found toys for Nicola and Aaron's 2 daughters, and also for Alena and Josh's 2 girls. Bryn was godfather to them all.

Why didn't I stay and listen to Alfie's lecture? Hearing how bad the economy was, and Alfie's analysis that my generation was to be lost to poverty (I had heard it at past lectures) was just too upsetting. I told him so before departing, how listening to that analysis just made me panic, thinking that Damon and I would never have enough money to live together in our own country, and that it wasn't because I didn't want to listen to Alfie personally. He nodded and said it was fine and he understood, and that was that. The important thing was that I had escorted Bryn, weak and frail as he had become from two rounds of chemotherapy, to a warm room with his friends to continue doing what he loved to do.

The Slamming Door

There was one other detail of Bryn's life with the Henry George School.

Usually, in the summer, Bryn would go with them all to Philadelphia to tour Henry George's home, visit his grave, and just have a good time visiting with whoever went on the trip. Some of the photos on his bedroom wall were from these trips. Bryn loved to be involved with whatever interested him, and to socialize with whomever else was interested in the same thing.

His many interests could sometimes intersect, and so his friends from the Mendelssohn Glee Club, a men's singing group on West 88th Street, and those from the United Nations, where he was involved in the I.U. – the International Union for Land Value Taxation – would meet and discuss their mutual interests at gatherings that he arranged.

Bryn had been taking singing lessons in the last year before he retired, and he had a lovely tenor voice. He lived his life to the fullest, taking advantage of any opportunity that came along to pursue an interest, be it a new one or an old one that work had kept his attention from until retirement. He would burst into song – typically wordless but never tuneless – singing out one long, lovely note: "Laaaaaa...." and it sounded great – on key, trilling, and practiced.

View of the bar area inside Zana's, also known as 30 at 30.

Zana's was often the place where social gatherings took place outside of the Henry George School. It was also known as 30 at 30 (because of its address: 30 East 30th Street). It was a dark, modern-décor place set off the main, ivory-marbled hallway of a hotel.

The restaurant is dark inside, with modern décor and a long half-booth on the right, and a bar at the back left. To get to the bathroom, one exits the restaurant through a door on the right behind the seating area, entering the adjacent hotel lobby, and goes around to the left. The cream-hued marble hall was shockingly bright after sitting in the darkened restaurant.

Henry George faculty were given a discount at Zana's because they were regular patrons, and the owners, who sat at one of the tables outside in warm weather, smiled and waved cheerfully to the professors as they approached. A pair of wood-framed French doors flanked the front door; those were opened up in the summer, and covered with huge awnings. Most of the seating was inside, with some booths on the right, but mostly round and square tables.

The place offered Italian cuisine, featuring thin-crusted pizzas, salads, a variety of pasta dishes that included a delicious dinner of pesto gnocchi, and seafood salads. A reasonably-priced selection of red and white wines by the glass is also available.

In the spring of 2008, before Bryn knew why he would be using a cane for the rest of his life, just after the newsman Tim Russert had abruptly died of a heart attack, Bryn suddenly changed his eating habits. One night at Zana's with me and Claus, the director of the Henry George School, Bryn ordered a beautiful seafood salad that evening, and we sat at a little square table by the French doors on the right, which were open to the warm breeze. The salad was made of three endives fanned out pretty and heaped with calamari, scallops, shrimp, octopus, tomato chunks, red onion, fresh herbs, and so on. But it was too late for a dietary course correction; the iceberg of death loomed straight ahead, and his heart was not what would do him in.

After I arrived that fall and settled in, after he knew that he was in fact doomed to die a rather different death, Bryn asked me to do something fun and interesting for him. He had a reasonable expectation of still being alive and cognizant of his surroundings, of still finding some enjoyment from life, by the following spring. At that time, it would have been 50 years since he had graduated from Harvard University.

For a long time, I had known that in the short bookcase to the right of the desk in Bryn's apartment was a thick, heavy, hard-cover, maroon book. It was full of glossy pages, each with a bio and photo of a member Harvard and Radcliffe's classes of 1959, and it had been printed to celebrate their 25th anniversary since graduation. The women's section followed the men's; Radcliffe had not yet merged with Harvard when Bryn attended and graduated.

The Slamming Door

I had looked at it from time to time, intrigued by the photo of Bryn as he had looked 24 years earlier and shortly before he had moved to that apartment. He had thick glasses that resembled magnifying lenses even then, darker hair, and the same wide, cheerful smile. I don't recall what the bio said, but I now realize that Bryn himself would have written it.

Now Harvard was preparing another maroon tome, one to celebrate the 50th anniversary.

With the advent of computers and the Internet, Harvard was taking full advantage of virtual conveniences and the efficiency that came with them. Everything was to be submitted in digital form via a special website that Bryn would have to create a profile and password for.

But Bryn was just barely computer literate, still intimidated by this medium.

Could I help with all this?

Of course; no problem...and I had even brought my digital camera and its cord with me, so preparing his photo would be easy enough also.

Terrific! He showed me something to the right of the desk, in front of the bookcases.

Atop the 2 sealed cardboard boxes that were full of Berta's possessions (packed by Cassie years ago, to the great ire of their owner) was a box of ivory stationery with Bryn's name, address and land-line phone number centered at the top of each sheet. It was nearly full, and he used it often as I stayed with him that year, usually to write notes to the pharmacists who handled his prescriptions, authorizing me to pick them up for him.

He got some of it out now and went to sit in his new blue chair and write his latest and greatest bio. As a Henry George School professor and retired city social worker, I expected it to be a cheerful, impressive thing, and I was not disappointed. Here is what he wrote:

Bryn Warne Otterman – 50th Anniversary Alumnus Biography

The last 25 years have been productive and very happy.

I returned to my first love, New York City's Department of Social Services. For years I schlepped around the mean streets of the Bronx, orchestrating a full panoply of social supports to keep some of our mentally ill fellow citizens secure in their homes.

Then followed years of administering a program in a welfare hotel where hundreds of homeless, mostly drug-addicted, AIDS patients might find some hope and stability.

For almost my whole life, I've been acutely aware of the socially created injustices and miseries that virtually define our world. What does one do, however, when Marxism fails, and Democratic liberalism proves to be one more fig leaf for monopoly and theft? In the early 1990's, I discovered a solution in the social philosophy of Henry George, and now devote much of my time to promulgating his ideas. I do this mostly by teaching at our school in Manhattan but also through involvement in various Georgist organizations, in some of which I hold office (see list).

My most exciting cultural activity is singing in the Mendelssohn Glee Club, a male chorus founded in 1866. Last April we sang a joint concert with the Harvard Glee Club, on tour for its 150th anniversary. Imagine my thrill to discover that I remembered the words to *Fair Harvard*!

My remaining years will be devoted to spreading the gospel of Henry George and to singing – two sides, really, of the same coin.

List of Activities and Organizations

New York City Department of Social Services:
1. Protective services for adults who are mentally ill and demented.
2. Administered a program in a welfare hotel for homeless, drug-addicted, AIDS patients.

Common Ground U.S.A. – Board of Directors
Representative of the International Union of Land Value Taxation, an NGO, to the U.N.'s Economic and Social Council (ECOSOC)
Robert Schalkenbach Foundation – Board of Directors
Henry George School of New York City – Trustee
Mendelssohn Glee Club

When he handed it to me, it was written in his neat but slightly illegible cursive handwriting, with the blue ink that I would get to know came from his favorite brand of pen, a uni-ball with a bold-nib. I bought a lot of these for him over the next year.

The Slamming Door

I typed it up as best I could, then printed the short piece and brought it in to him, explaining that I had been unable to read every last word, and so had guessed or left gaps where I couldn't decipher his handwriting. No problem; he checked it over, wrote the missing words on it legibly for me, and I re-did the whole thing, printing it up once again. Now it was right. Good; we had a Word file to work from.

Next, we had to take the photograph.

Bryn got his pale blue sport coat out of the closet, put it on, adjusted his polo shirt until he looked like he was going to teach a class, and then combed his hair. We looked about for a suitable backdrop and quickly agreed that the tall bookcases, filled with books, was what fit the bill. He stood in front of them and smiled, and I shot a couple of photos.

When that was done, I loaded them to the computer and clicked on each one for him to inspect. He was satisfied with the first one, so I labeled it and saved it.

Then began the nit-picky process of signing him up for the new website meant for alumni and alumnae: I had to create a password and then fill in page after page of data about Bryn.

He didn't want to hang around for all of that, so I did the basic stuff, writing down the password and security questions so that we wouldn't find ourselves locked out of the system after the first draft. When it got complicated, he came back out and chose what parts he wanted filled in; it wasn't all required, and he didn't want to fill in every last category.

There was a page for the bio that he had written, and I copy-pasted it in from the Word file. There was a way to load his new photo, and I did that. After that, the system informed us that all was well and that the alumni book people had what they needed from us. That was on October 15th, nearly a month after my arrival.

Great; Bryn would pay for his new maroon book, and it would arrive next spring.

We looked forward to seeing it.

Chapter 9

Alissa, Art Galleries, and June

Albert and June's only daughter Alissa was the polar opposite of Bryn's daughter.

Alissa was quiet to the point of near silence, thoughtful, studious, focused, not at all intrusive, sweet (an adjective I rarely use for anyone), and a writer. I had met her before, on the same day that I had met Berta in fact, and had liked her from the start.

She called her parents Dad and Momma, and spent most of her free time with them when she wasn't writing. Albert never inquired as to what she was writing; he thought that so much as a word out of him interfere with her creativity and stop the whole process. He only found out what Alissa wrote when she had a play reading. June was only vaguely aware of Alissa's writing now, except when something was completed and shown. Sadly, she would then forget about it.

Alissa's eyes, a pale blue-grey color, had an alert, scared expression. It didn't matter what she was looking at – it could be a person, a thing, or she could just be staring off into space, thinking – that look was always there. Quiet people usually have a lot on their minds, and although she was an only child with two sick parents, that didn't seem to be the whole story.

She had a secret. I made no effort to find it out; sooner or later things like that just come up, either in conversation or else through others when concealing becomes more trouble than sharing it. That happened shortly after one of several visits to Albert and June's place to watch the presidential election debates. We were watching Sarah Palin face off against Joe Biden, who despite being a bit of a clown was easily able to mop the floor with her, yet he graciously held back just a bit, to avoid seeming obnoxious.

Against this backdrop of relaxing entertainment, we – Bryn, Albert, June, Alissa, Berta, Dionne and I – gathered around the flat-screen TV with our Leffe beer and Brie and chatted. Somehow, the conversation turned to our college days. All of us had college degrees, so this wasn't surprising.

What set off the awkward moment, which included no pause in the conversation, was when it came up that Alissa had begun her college education at Wellesley College. "Really?" I responded, "My aunt went there; she is an art historian. How did you like it?"

Oddly, Berta and Dionne suddenly did their best to distract me and steer the conversation away from Wellesley. Alissa said that she had graduated from New York University. Puzzled, I said, "So you switched

The Slamming Door

schools? You missed Manhattan?" hoping that this would suffice as cooperative, clueless though I felt. I am not good with abrupt, unexplained transitions.

Alissa just said yes, and I gave up, still wondering what that was all about.

The conversation abruptly shifted to other things, such as the trip that Albert and June had gone on the summer before to France. Albert had wanted to spoil June while she could still understand that she was on a great vacation with him to her favorite foreign country, so they had gone to Paris and the south of France, touring the medieval fort town of Carcassonne. June happily got out her book on the place and showed it to me. Alzheimer's disease can be amazing that way, with moments of clarity and seeming like one's old self. June had always been rather quiet whenever I had seen her before, but now she seemed much more relaxed, open and animated now that I was constantly visiting with her.

When Berta and I left for the evening in a cab, she told me what the big secret was: Alissa had schizophrenia, and was on medication for it. It kept the voices in her head quiet, making her thoughts her own. Now I understood what that frightened, tense look in her eyes was about: she was constantly worried that those damned voices would speak and try to crowd out her own thoughts, and take control of her mind away from her. That explained the fearful expression in her eyes; she had a recurring problem that could arise at any moment.

Berta emphasized that this was a secret, and that they had all been trying to get me to drop the matter entirely. Now it made sense, all that odd behavior. I told her that I didn't understand what they were doing at the time, but tried to go along and transition on to something else. She nodded, and said that Alissa had left Wellesley and lived at home with her parents to finish her bachelor's degree, which of course she completed in four years.

But her parents were completely unhelpful about her condition. They had sent her to many doctors and even a hospital at one point to be evaluated, and been told that there was nothing wrong with her.

They had both told me about this one afternoon at Bryn's place as we all sat in his room.

I couldn't understand it; if Alissa had unbidden voices that randomly started chattering away in her mind, that wasn't nothing. She had gotten to the point where she knew herself well enough that she could sense when they might start to talk, and would rush to take the pills to shut them up and take back her own mind. Good for her.

Berta summed it up rather nicely when I told her about my confusion regarding her aunt and uncle. "Albert and June don't live in the state of New York; they live in a state called Denial."

Alissa, Art Galleries, and June

Isn't that just perfect, I thought to myself. At least Alissa had gotten her own doctor, and found a medical solution to her problem.

Alissa had also been sent to that New Hampshire camp, and hated it. Damon had both things in common with Alissa: same camp, same feeling (there were bullies). For some reason, Albert could not understand why. He and his brother had loved it, and been counselors there. So their mother, Margery, had also followed this pattern of away camp, college, and fulfilled hopes of graduate school. It was an expensive pattern, but it tends to lead to a great résumé. Clearly, I had married into a family that followed a pattern of child-rearing that was similar to that of my own. Yet only our dads and Berta liked camp.

I was quickly getting the sense that even though Alissa and I would have very limited time together, she and I had a lot in common, and a lot more in common that with Berta. I really liked Alissa, and admired her devotion to writing, editing, and her family, as well as her foreign language skills and listening skills. She was a keen observer of people, and it showed in her writing, which we would find out about when we heard her plays read.

In 2001, she had completed her master's degree in medieval European history at Columbia University. She had no loans from that, thanks to Albert having been willing and able to pay those costs. Having no loans after one's education seems like the most wonderful thing to me; I still have to pay some from law school.

Alissa spoke and read French and Italian fluently. She had studied history as well as those languages, having begun them in high school. She had lived in Florence, Italy with her parents for a year at one point, though I wasn't sure when that was – high school, college, after – and had also stayed with an Italian family for a summer during high school. She even delayed the switch to vegetarianism until after that summer, just to make the visit easier. Bryn had told me that, complete with an approving tone.

But after that, Alissa went vegetarian, and just in the past year or so had gone even farther with that: she was a raw foods vegan now. We all watched a pretty, thin woman on television explain how she prepared her food, making carrot juice and dehydrated fruits, and Alissa told us she was saving up for a particular dehydrator. The woman on television had never been able to get her weight down any other way, she said in the interview, and she looked great.

Alissa belonged to two book clubs, one that read in English and one that read in French, and we all hoped that she would meet a nice guy and find a boyfriend through this social interaction. Unfortunately, she only had a couple of false starts. She met a much older guy who ate a smelly

The Slamming Door

sausage meal in front of her, and some other guy who wasn't right for her either.

It was difficult; she had little spare time now for dating with a job and two sick parents plus a dog to help with, and she wanted to use a lot of that time for her writing. Her wardrobe needed work too, but she seemed unaware of or unconcerned by this fact. Albert had asked me and Berta had bought her an endless series of solid polo shirts from L.L. Bean.

Alissa wrote short stories, plays, and was revising a novel called *A Novel*. There was no way to guess its plot from that, and perhaps that was the point, but was that title already registered somewhere for some other book? Who knew…but I was determined to show her how to register her work with the U.S. Copyright Office for certificates. I had done it before, it was easy, it was inexpensive ($45 – now up to $50), and gave a writer peace of mind.

It was great to find out that she was a writer, because it meant that we had something creative in common; that, and we could understand French. Alissa understood it much better than I did, however, thanks to making it an academic discipline for so long. I left off with what I managed to learn in high school and from a couple of trips to France.

In the spring, I did manage to show her the entire copyright procedure and explain it in detail, even going so far as to prepare a couple of documents for her. But I don't know that she ever registered anything. Being a lawyer, I am old-fashioned and scrupulous about securing legal protection for my intellectual property. I want to be able to sell it and make money, after all.

She was doing great; she had a job as an editor somewhere very close to Bryn's apartment, which made visiting after work easy. The only caveat was that we not call her at work; she sat in a cubicle where she might be heard taking a personal call. Just wait until 5:30 and all would be well if we needed to call her. The job was to edit small advertisements for cheap, junk jewelry sold off of pages in the backs of tabloids, usually stuff that meant good luck or made other astrological promises and predictions. That was all; it was a job that paid bills.

Speaking of bills, Alissa was very, very lucky for another reason: she had an apartment in an exclusive location, in one of a pair of buildings on the northwest corner of Central Park. It was more like a condominium, because she had bought it with a mortgage.

Albert told me how that had been possible: when Alissa was 18, she had been riding in a cab in Manhattan when it had crashed. She had been slammed into the barrier between the front and back seats, smashing open the skin on her chin right to the bone. She had a deep scar there, not too noticeable thanks to a plastic surgeon, and I had seen some photos in

Alissa, Art Galleries, and June

her parents' album of her with a huge, white bandage on her chin. It must have taken a while to heal.

Albert had pitted the lawsuit against the party at fault, and they had won some money. I don't know how much money, but he had invested it in the stock market for her and increased it significantly. That was how the down payment on the apartment had been paid – using the money from the settlement or judgment or whatever outcome of that case.

That building had a lot of rules, though. No pets, no sublets, no nothing without approval from some committee of appointed residents. Alissa was in the process of getting permission to rent it out so she could go live with her parents and take care of her mother, who now needed constant supervision. She was there constantly, and once a week, usually Saturday, they would go out together and do something, such as see an independent film or an art exhibit.

They invited me to a few things with them while I was in Manhattan: a British movie called *Happy Go Lucky* (sometime in the late winter) and two art exhibits in SoHo in the fall. Those art exhibits were amazing.

The first one was a walking tour of seven galleries, led by a nice man who had left a tenured university position to lead art tours because he loved the work so much. We saw: 1. a color palette of human skin and cosmetic tones painted in huge blocks; 2. an installation exhibit of electrified black walls that lit up and shrieked alarms, meant to remind us of Homeland Security terror alerts; 3. my favorite of the tour, which reminded of my outer space environmental law paper, which was 2 rooms full of models of human air, sea, and space travel relics, our use of fossil fuels summed up in a vine-covered oil-drilling station, and a wall hanging showing Antarctica with no ice and snow covering; 4. photography and a video from Baghdad, Iraq, showing the misery of life under constant siege, including a man in agony with his kneecap blown off; 5. paintings and sculpture depicting gay teenage boys in the South, complete with makeup and sad expressions on their faces; 6. computer graphic projections of brilliantly-colored, constantly moving, poisonous flowers and a tree that went through four seasons of change over and over again; 7. a colorful sculpture exhibit made of stressed rubber in many colors, including a golden eagle, a cuckoo clock, and a sun dial.

We had a great time on that exhibit, except when I worried that June would forget not to touch the walls in the alarm hall – we had been warned that we would get an electric shock if we did so. I enjoyed the exhibits so much that I went home and wrote up a detailed description of them all, partly to show my friends and relatives, and partly because I wanted a record of it all.

The next time I was invited out with them, the art exhibit was even better, if that can be possible: it was a John Lennon art exhibit with his

The Slamming Door

songs playing on stereo speakers throughout the gallery. All of the artwork had been done when he and Yoko Ono were raising their son Sean; John liked to draw with his son. A huge black-ink drawing by the rock star was part of the advertisement. It's a famous self-portrait of the singer, with chin-length hair and round glasses.

The most fun part for me was watching June sing along with every song that we heard. She knew them all by heart; she was a Beatles and John Lennon fan, and suddenly she seemed not to have Alzheimer's. She just kept grinning and singing.

When we came outside, we walked around SoHo, passed a Chanel store, a MoMA store, and several sidewalk kiosks that were offering scarves, sunglasses, and other cheap junk. Alissa bought her mother a pair of sunglasses, which June added to her collection. Inside her red Vera Bradley back-pack were four more pairs; she loved sunglasses, and constantly inventoried them.

After that, we went to eat lunch at one of Alissa's favorite places. It was on the corner of Spring Street and Lafayette, and called Spring Street Natural. It offered fresh-squeezed juices, lemonades, organic dishes, yellowfin tuna sandwiches, turkey, chicken and vegetarian ones, hand-cut fries, and so on and on. It was a beautiful sunny day, too.

Chapter 10

Signing Up for the Process of Misery

It was time to get familiar with the Sloan-Kettering Cancer Center.

Because it still early in my stay with Bryn, and because the family had been taking me here, there and everywhere to show me a good time, I wondered what the grim part of my job would be. But none of us knew the answer to that yet; we had to make it up as we went along.

No one knows precisely how they want to proceed until they actually get sick.

What I had anticipated was going to each and every appointment with Bryn and keeping him company while he was in the throes of whatever barbaric, torturous "treatments" the oncologists had to offer, then cleaning whatever messes that made and concealing the evidence of the more personal and embarrassing ones, maintaining Bryn's wardrobe, and shopping for whatever foods I could get him to eat or drink.

It turned out that I had most of that right, except for the doctors' appointments.

Albert would be accompanying him to most of those, either with or without June in tow.

The reason was eminently logical: he had done so much research on prostate and other cancer that he was qualified to manage Bryn's records. Add to that the fact that Albert was Bryn's life-long best guy friend and it was obvious why this was just easier for Bryn.

It didn't bother me in the least. I was going to put in plenty of time taking care of him. I didn't want him to feel stuck with me, and I did want him to feel that he could control as much of what was happening to him as possible.

I just had one hope: that if he ever needed a prostate cancer doctor, he would want my mother's former boss and my friend, Dr. Leonardi, who was now at Sloan-Kettering. But right now, Bryn needed someone different, someone who specialized in bone cancer.

I offered to write to Leonardi and ask him who we ought to sign up with, and Bryn and Albert accepted. A day or so later, Leonardi wrote back with the names of two doctors, one male and one female. The woman, Dr. Moira-Lorie Callahan, was available much sooner, and Albert rushed to sign his brother up with her.

The reports about her were all good; she was competent, available, and really cared. Her staff had caught her many times hiding in corners and crying when she got the point where she realized that she couldn't save a patient's life. When I heard that, I was sold on hiring her.

The Slamming Door

Once the deed was done, arrangements were made for Bryn's treatments.

He had already been irradiated at the other hospital in August to no useful end, so Dr. Callahan planned to poison him three times over the next several months. Wonderful; that confirmed my suspicion that he would lose his beautiful, thick white hair.

I didn't actually see the hospital right away; that would wait until chemotherapy began.

Meanwhile, I looked up the doctor's profile on the Sloan-Kettering website and found her photo, a list of journal articles that she had authored, her education and other credentials, and her contact information, not that I expected to use it. (I did once, asking her about special cushions to make Bryn more comfortable, but she didn't reply. Later I realized that she wasn't allowed to, and eventually found some on my own that I would carry around to restaurants for Bryn to sit on. They helped a little, but sofas and soft seats were better than hard chairs.)

Next I found out that the hospital had two separate locations, which was a bit confusing.

There was the in-patient facility on East 68th Street between York and 1st Avenues, with the main entrance on York Avenue. The Urgent Care Center was one level up from the ground floor. Dr. Leonardi's office was just a couple of blocks west of there on 68th Street.

That wasn't all; Bryn would be getting his chemotherapy elsewhere, on 53rd Street across from the Lipstick Building on 3rd Avenue. We saw it out the windows every time we went there, on the 5th floor. This fact came up a bit later, but it still surprised me when I found out.

Since there wasn't much else to do after getting the confirmation that poison loomed in his near future, I busied myself with the apartment. What had been comfortable enough as a bachelor pad while Bryn was well suddenly needed to be thought through all over again, bit by bit, as he began to spend a lot more time at home. He had always used his apartment as a place to go in between social engagements. Now it was being accident-proofed as a permanent base of operations for him.

A couple of days after I arrived, Albert and June had come over for a visit when I heard a loud crash in Bryn's room. I went in and looked around for whatever had made that noise. Nothing immediately stood out. Then Bryn told me it was the black-and-white photo of the Empire State Building on his drop-leaf table; it was a large one in a nice frame, and it had never been properly hung up. It had suddenly slid off the back of his table, right next to him, with a bang. I took it out from behind the table and looked at it, then put it on the bed.

Next, I went to the kitchen, got the hammer and a large nail out from under the sink, and came back. Bryn looked alarmed; he said he didn't want it hung up over his bed to fall on him while he slept. Like I would pick a spot there! I looked around, determined, and chose the small gap between the foot of his bed and the bureau, lined the frame up, saw where to put the nail, and with a couple of bangs drove it into the wall. Then I hung the frame onto it and walked out.

That was that; the picture was securely in place for the rest of the time that Bryn was there. For my next project, I said nothing but went out into the sunny afternoon to the Staples store on 6th Avenue, two blocks directly east of there and then two blocks north. I came back with a set of six clear plastic drawers in a black plastic frame on wheels, some labels, black Sharpie pens, and tape.

The Slamming Door

Bryn had plenty of manila file folders at home. I dragged the whole thing upstairs and into my room and labeled each drawer. Then I gathered the little piles of Bryn's papers and extracted all bills, medical data, retirement, insurance, legal, and tax documents and stuffed the drawers with the appropriate items – all 6 categories. It was tight, but it was organized and out of the way. It was none of my business to actually read until I was asked to do so, so I stopped and proudly wheeled it over to Bryn's room.

He and Albert were impressed and exclaimed in amazement over how quickly I had cleared it all up. I explained the filing system, said I had not done any more than sort it all, and shoved it into the space under the Empire State Building frame, where it fit very neatly. There it stayed until late spring, when I was asked to do a more thorough job and completely prepare it all for the estate, for Albert to handle later.

Meanwhile, it sat there as a table for Bryn's little tray of pills.

He soon added a plastic box of more pills that he kept on the floor in front of the TV table, down out of sight. He kept his notes and current reading material on the old black stool next to the TV table. The notes were about the Henry George School and his illness.

As for all of Bryn's recreational mail – cards, letters, articles, packages – that went here, there, everywhere, but no longer on the floor. I kept it piled on his bureau and on the little table by his bed, and even under the drop-leaf table where he kept a collection of news clippings, old *New York Times* crossword puzzles that he had ripped out and saved to do later, glasses, political buttons, cigarette lighters and matches, coins, his I.U. card (draped over his table lamp), and his framed family photos.

He had several drawings from when Hilda was a little girl, a framed photo of himself with Albert and June out in the garden where Damon and I had our wedding, another of himself on a Henry George School trip with friends, a portrait of Diane in profile, and a beautiful one of himself in a tuxedo and Diane in her wedding gown heading down the aisle. On the back were several smaller photos from the same event, which had been held at Gramercy Park, both in an events hall near its gate and inside the private park itself.

Soon I had Bryn's room the way he liked it but neater, just as he had ordered.

Every day, I would make him a cup of coffee when we got up and tea in the evening when we came home for the night. One for him and one for me: Mandeeling Sumatra and Toasted Praline coffee, and then Earl Grey green tea or Chinese Oolong for him in the evening. I had many different teas that I collected at my own expense – no reason to list my favorites.

Signing Up for the Process of Misery

Dionne brought over some vile-tasting health teas for her father to try, but after a few gulps, he refused to have more. We didn't say anything to her about it; I just kept them in the kitchen with the rest of the teas, and I served him what he liked to drink.

The kitchen had two white wooden bookcases side by side opposite the stove and sink. The one on the right was full of food: spices and salts and peppers on top with 2 huge mugs full of kitchen tools and flatware, some honey and Bryn's Miralax jar; his collection of coffee mugs next

The Slamming Door

plus his many boxes of tea; large mugs on the bottom and boxes of pasta, rice, and plastic bags and rolls of tin foil and plastic wrap. Underneath were canned goods. The one on the left was full of dishes and glasses, and vases on the bottom shelf. On top of it was a toaster oven and a lamp, and I made room for the Warning blender next to the lamp on the right.

Under the window was the original ice closet, a door set low into the wall. I put some old junk, candle-holders and other odds and ends, out of the way in there. Above the stove and the shelves were some old diner signs offering cheap greasy spoon breakfasts, made of metal painting white with red and blue lettering.

The stove-oven was made of white metal with gas burners. The back left one didn't work. The sink was an awful old white one with two wells in it; the one on the right had a dish drainer in it. Above that were little pot holders and the tea and coffee gadgets that I had made a present of to Bryn in 2003, along with 2 fancy cereal bowls, in a wrapped box from Williams-Sonoma. The long-handled coffee scoop was our favorite; I've given those to lots of people.

Above all that was a cupboard that was full of Bryn's mother's best crystal and china, which I had seen but never touched. I just ignored it; it was too high to reach without a ladder and there was no reason to use any of it. Let someone else risk damaging it; it was safe up there.

A filing cabinet that I never looked through sat next to the fridge, which was ancient. The fridge was covered with magnets from Bryn's travels, and probably from Albert's as well. The magnets were from London, Paris, and New York City. A huge sticker that depicted a colorful fruit arrangement was stuck to the door at the top. The freezer was inside, and had a removable tray underneath. A door inside the fridge door opened into the freezer, which routinely iced up so much that there was hardly any room for food.

I had learned in 2005 to hammer the ice off, except for the top, where the freezing mechanism was. After getting most of the ice off and leaving the door wide open, the rest would just fall off and I could melt it in the sink by running hot water over it. It was kind of fun to do.

After setting up everything to our satisfaction, I found that there was nothing dramatic to do for Bryn for a while. He wasn't going to get horridly sick the moment that I had organized his environment, so we fell into a routine of Albert bringing him to doctors and me keeping the apartment neat, clean and well-stocked.

We went out in cabs almost everywhere; Bryn had pretty much stopped using the subways because he didn't have the energy to go down underground and back up again. I quickly became very familiar with New York City cabs, observing their new computer system, the Passenger Bill of Rights posted inside, the new credit card payment system. Bryn paid with a wad of cash from his pocket every time, however. He didn't like the news to blare, so I would hit the "Mute" option on the touch screen before he could shut it off. I liked to see the GPS display of where we were. Bryn didn't mind; we fell into our mutually agreed-upon cab-riding habits.

Soon we were doing other things, like planning for the presidential election, for Albert's birthday, for trips to the film noir series at the Henry George School, and for visits with the family to movies and restaurants. We went to the Angelika Theater and saw the movie about the WTO protests, *Battle in Seattle*, ate Japanese food at Daioh on West 23rd Street, and lounged around the apartment with Berta and Albert and June.

Other than trying to pack some fun into Bryn's schedule, he and I tried to prepare for his upcoming physical misery, the resulting messes, and to conceal the evidence. As his partner in concealment, I stood ready to get whatever he needed, determined not to mention it to others unless and until it became unavoidable. Even then, if he had any toileting accidents, I decided that I still wouldn't tell, but he never did. Perhaps we had prepared so well that he stopped worrying, and thus the threat of that was eliminated. Two things worried him: messes in his bed and chair, and having a portable, genteel place to puke.

That second item sounds like an oxymoron, but Bryn knew what he wanted: a bucket.

I went out to the local hardware store on 7th Avenue and looked for an attractive bucket, because I assumed that he would take it when he had to go out. He certainly thought that he might. It couldn't be a noisy metal one or an ugly, cumbersome one that would only draw yet more attention to him, I thought as I walked toward the store.

Luckily, I found one in a pretty royal blue color that was lightweight, small – perhaps a little more than a foot high and a foot wide – with a metal handle that had a plastic grip in the middle of it. I bought it and brought it home to show Bryn. Perfect; he would put it in a large plastic bag if he took it out anywhere with him.

Did we have any large, thick plastic bags? He thought not; he had never shopped much.

Not to worry, I told him; I had been doing lots of shopping at a variety of stores, and had saved all sorts of plastic bags on top of the fridge so that we would have our pick. So we had several thick, large, white ones from Bed, Bath & Beyond which were perfect for this.

I acquired those solving his other problem: protecting his bed and Lazy Boy chair.

He had sounded embarrassed when he told me that he was afraid he might have an accident in his bed or chair once chemotherapy began. Of

The Slamming Door

course he was worried about that, I thought. I hated to see him embarrassed, so I offered a fair exchange of an embarrassing secret, complete with the benefit of my female experience at concealing and disposing of the evidence.

Feminism had to be useful to this situation, I had reasoned. Feminism discourages embarrassment over menstruation. It does not encourage yakking on and on about bleeding at random moments, but when the subject needs to come up, shrinking from it as though it were shameful is what is discouraged. Now that training was helping Bryn.

I told him that when women menstruate, often the blood does not go to maxi pads and tampons and nowhere else…there can be leaks and messes, plus surprises when we aren't even expecting the bleeding to start. This compares neatly to chemotherapy-induced accidents.

Then I went to my room and got the thick pad of cloth that I put in my bed during that time of the month and showed it to him. He looked delighted by the knowledge that such things existed, and I couldn't blame him. I proposed to go out and buy him 2 or 3 of his own such thick cloths, and held up my remaining 20%-off coupons for Bed, Bath & Beyond.

Naturally, he wanted the cloths. He showed me what he had been doing thus far, because even without chemotherapy, he had wondered whether the radiation treatments from August would make him leak. He had put newspaper on his chair and then concealed it with a folded bath towel. Good effort, but not sufficient, we both agreed.

Off to 6th Avenue to get the cloths. With those unwrapped, we immediately went to work on his chair: newspaper first, a folded cloth, and then a folded bath towel to hide the fact that he had a cloth in there. The cloths were sold as crib liners, but obviously they had multiple applications. The spare one was saved for his bed, and he wanted it in there when the poisonous treatments started. I changed his sheets every two weeks, and the next chance I got, I put one in there. No sense waiting for an accident, I thought.

Bryn was delighted with those cloths; I dubbed them peace-of-mind cloths, and we told no one about them. They could be rotated without leaving him uncovered at any time. And the best part is that he never actually had an accident; I had told him that being completely prepared tends to eliminate accidents, like some inversion of Murphy's Law. That made him happy.

After Albert took him to meet his new oncologist, they came back as far as the Daioh Japanese restaurant on 23rd Street and called me to join them. I did, and found out that she had directed Bryn to drink something called Ensure, a high-calorie concoction sold at grocery and

Signing Up for the Process of Misery

drug stores in vanilla, chocolate, and strawberry. Albert bought a lot of it immediately.

Bryn flatly refused to ever drink the chocolate ones; no problem, the other flavors were acceptable to him, and preferably strawberry. I exchanged the chocolate ones for vanilla later.

Meanwhile, Damon's recipe for the tomato-based spice drink had arrived, and I went off to the Vitamin Shoppe at the corner of 8th and 23rd to get the ingredients. Also on the list were a bunch of vitamins to take along with it, the result of much research.

I came back with all of it plus a pill box and started setting it up, only to have Bryn refuse to take those unless and until his doctor approved it. Here was the first obstacle I saw to Bryn's survival: he would only use FDA-approved treatments chosen by his doctor. Nothing experimental, nothing illegal, even to relieve terrible pain…and he never changed his mind.

Elah had offered to procure some marijuana for him – he already smoked a pipe, so why not just put pot in it instead of tobacco? We also suggested that I could bake pot brownies, and I did some online research, saving a recipe and studying the technique – get the stems out, cook the pot down, and the eater gets high, feels no pain, and has an increased appetite. An increased appetite…that would be great! Cancer treatments tend to have the exact opposite effect.

But no…Bryn turned the pot offer down flat. This wasn't the state of California, and even though Elah was obviously a proven expert at successfully having her pot and smoking it too without legal repercussions, he wouldn't take the risk. The way he saw it, he would be putting others at various legal risks of arrest for acquisition and possession as well as himself, and he was opposed to that. Clearly, he didn't want me arrested for living with a pot smoker, or for baking with it….

So no medical marijuana was in his future. Drat.

I hadn't seen or smelled any of the stuff since my first-year college roommate had rolled joints in our room and smoked them – plus some ivory pipes of it – with her friends. I had sat and watched, but hadn't participated. Instead, I had promised myself to get up early on the day that we chose rooms for the next year and the next and the next so I could have a room of my own. I did it, too – no more roommates!

But back to Bryn and his plans to cope: I stocked up on tomato juice, jalapeno peppers, lemons, limes, and Ensure, and lined the kitchen floor with those containers (there wasn't much storage space beyond those bookcases). Bryn didn't care how cluttered it was in there; I was the one in there most of the time, and as long as Hilda removed the trash and recycling regularly, he thought it looked okay.

The Slamming Door

Once I had the new Waring blender in place and the ImmuneACCORD drink recipe with its ingredients ready, I started making it for Bryn every afternoon. A lot of measuring and cutting and blending was involved, but I like to work with fresh ingredients, so it was an enjoyable task. Bryn said that it tasted like a spicy Bloody Mary, and said that he was a good patient and would do whatever was recommended. But soon he got tired of that drink, and wondered whether any variation might be allowed. I called Frank, Damon's co-inventor, and was told that carrot juice would work just as well; the juice was just a vehicle for everything else.

This drink-making continued until shortly before chemotherapy began, at which point all spices burned his mouth. The pharmaceutical drugs that Bryn had begun to take had altered his taste buds. Damn…that same thing had happened to my maternal grandmother years ago. She was 94 years old, has never had cancer in her life, but takes all sorts of pills. Damon was sorry to hear of this, but not at all surprised. He had been insisting to Frank that unless and until the formulation was either encased into a gel capsule or microencapsulated into a tasteless powder, it would only help a limited number of people.

Each night, I would follow Bryn into the kitchen and stand there chatting with him, keeping him company, while he mixed some Miralax into a cup of water and drank it. I just didn't want him to trip and fall, so I had taken to watching him whenever he walked around the apartment. He would hang his cane over the edge of the kitchen sink while he did this, using a plastic spoon and a small white cup with a farm scene painted on the side, one of a set that he had inherited from his mother. Choosing the right cup was a ritual with him.

Bryn had quite a collection of mugs, each kept always in the same spot, and I am an expert at keeping mugs washed, dried, and put away in the exact same positions each and every time. It sounds like a stupid, obsessive-compulsive habit, but it was convenient. The mugs that he had collected from museums were off to the right, and were for guests. I had a McNulty's mug, a gray one, that I used for each and every cup of coffee or tea that I consumed and it stayed in front of those.

Bryn's favorite mugs were all on the middle shelf of the left bookcase. He had short glasses for juice there, too, and they were shaped like little mugs with handles. Albert said that his brother certainly was set in his ways, but so was I. I loved it (probably comforting to an Aspie). The mugs Bryn wanted to use most were those farm scene ones for the evening Miralax, a Barnes & Noble authors mug that I had given him in 2003, and a pair from Chinatown that Piper and Melissa had given him many years before. One was a bright, pastel green and the other was yellow, and they were covered with Chinese flowers and other designs,

Signing Up for the Process of Misery

and had matching lids that Bryn never used but kept in a dish beside them.

His beverage ritual was as follows: coffee in the morning, made fresh, but not finished, and he would sip more of the stuff cold as the day wore on, and then have another fresh cup at night. Sometimes he would just finish it cold the next day, too. He might also have tea at night, but not so often. He would also drink an entire small cup of Miralax at night, too. That was all before he got sick, and for some time after.

I learned this exact ritual and then followed along with any modifications because I was in charge of preparing and serving all of his drinks, with the exception of the Miralax, from then on. When he got too frail to get it himself, I brought him his cup of Miralax water also, but meanwhile, I took charge of presenting him with fresh, hot tea and coffee.

Here's a convenient secret for anyone, sick or not: hot drinks help with constipation, while cold ones hinder it. Bryn was having trouble with that, and I didn't tell him why I was giving him so many hot drinks. He just thought I was presenting better drinks, which was certainly part of the plan.

The changes were that he got coffee when he got up and tea at night, and I would insist on fresh stuff each time, saying it couldn't be that great cold. Why not enjoy the fresh stuff, he seemed to think, happily handing over the used cups. I gave him his coffee in the Barnes & Noble authors cup so often that he would ask for the Chinese ones sometimes, which I had thought of for tea, but at first he hardly drank tea. About four months or so into my time there, it was tea in the evenings and coffee when he woke up, so it evened out.

Years ago, he had taught me how to make coffee with no machine, and I was fascinated.

He had a particular pot that he would boil water in for tea and coffee. (I never allowed food to be cooked in it while I was there – it seemed gross, and might have affected the taste of the hot drinks.) It was old and slightly dented, with a black handle, and it had no lid.

Once the water was boiling, he would shut off the gas and pour it through a contraption that he had bought at McNulty's, which was placed over the coffee mug. I had seen them for sale there after he showed it to me: dark brown (or orange) plastic sieves that looked like the top parts of coffee machines. A paper filter was placed in it after wetting it down so that it wouldn't cave in as the water was poured. If it caved in, coffee grounds would run the wrong way and end up in the cup. The trick was to not pour too much water in and thus overflow the mug.

At least once each day I used Bryn's 2 sieves, one brown and one orange, to make our coffee. I did it both at the same time using the sieves

The Slamming Door

side by side. I would take that perfect Williams-Sonoma coffee scoop off of its hook, get the white bags of fine-ground coffee out of the fridge, and add one scoop of Mandeeling Sumatra to Bryn's filter and one of Toasted Praline to mine.

If we had a guest over, I would show the bags with the flavor names stamped on and have them choose. "Whatever is easiest," they would say at first, thinking that I would make a huge pot. "No, really, choosing whatever you would really prefer is easier," I would say, explaining how I made the coffee. They loved it. Some people even wanted my flavor.

One other intriguing detail about Bryn's coffee: his cardiologist had, several years earlier, dictated that he have a blend of half regular and half decaf. But taste and quality mattered to Bryn, so it was always from McNulty's. Once, a few years earlier before he had retired, he had run out of it and gotten some Columbian stuff at a grocery store. He didn't like it.

Since he was dying, I saw it as my mission in life to make sure that whatever food he could control would be what he wanted and liked. I made sure not to run out of anything ever.

As I watched the comings and goings of visitors to the apartment, I began to learn who would visit most and how to please them. Claus, the German director of the Henry George School, liked his coffee a particular way and I remembered how to make it. Albert and June were always over, and June liked green tea ice cream. Alissa spent a significant amount of time there too, and when summer came again, I got a vegan kind of sorbet that she would eat. It was raspberry, and had no milk in it. The freezer was lined with rows of frozen treats.

To top it all off, Bryn informed me that he was very particular about ice cream, and it was his favorite that kicked off the collection of gourmet goodies in the freezer. Only Hagan Daas ice cream was to be purchased – no other brand. And he wanted strawberry. Oh…okay, no problem. I was quietly amazed by this; back in Connecticut, I had been raised to shop for the sale brand of ice cream, and from there to get picky about the flavor. But this was what he wanted.

Bryn told me to also get whatever I liked, so I added Swiss chocolate almond to the mix, and eventually vanilla bean when I started making frozen concoctions for him – but more on that later. June's green tea ice cream was made by Hagen Daas; I couldn't find that flavor in any brand but that one. Alissa's vegan stuff, which I also loved, had to be another brand, but Bryn approved – stock up on something for guests was his directive.

The freezer resembled a gourmet grocery store, plus it contained some homemade soups and sauces from Dionne and even a few from

Signing Up for the Process of Misery

Bryn's ex-wife, who said she loved him in a phone call. Funny what people are moved to say when death looms near.

The fridge was full of Ensure drinks, tomato juice, milk, Tropicana calcium no-pulp orange juice (a quirk of both mine and Bryn's; I was amazed that we shared it!), fresh salad greens, fresh berries, cooked beets and other dishes that Rudy made for Bryn, and many other items. I kept extra-virgin olive oil in a large bottle on the floor by the window and a collection of vinegars for salads, plus pastas and dried soups, and later some canned soups and apple sauces.

I would cook at home a lot, only to be surprised by announcements that the family was all eating out. I never ate out so much in my life as when I was in New York City. It's expensive, but apparently a normal way of life for my in-laws. Not in Connecticut; we eat at home and cook most nights, and going to a restaurant is a treat. In Manhattan, it was one food adventure after another or else a matter of convenience and companionship.

As Berta kept saying, "In New York, we don't cook; we order – or eat out."

She took me to diners and taught me another favorite saying of hers when I wondered if I could get a particular item or have something on the menu modified slightly: "This is New York, baby. You can get whatever the fuck you want whenever the fuck you want it."

This bit of wisdom was imparted with a huge grin, so I grinned back.

She was the hostess, showing me the ropes in her hometown. If swearing for a joke was part of the game, I could say the line along with her. But then I would lapse into my usual, book-like way of speaking. I avoid high-faluting vocabulary words – using them routinely appears intellectually snobbish – but I speak with no up-talk in my tone, enunciating carefully, and with proper grammar. Texting and shorthand are anathemas to me. I must have seemed remote to her.

We found the Eros diner on 7th Avenue, and discovered that its food was much tastier and even a bit healthier – with better-quality ingredients – than the stuff offered by the Greeks, even though this place was Greek too. We immediately switched, and did our best to wean Bryn off of it so that when we ordered out, we could have that food.

Bryn got hooked quickly enough; he wanted spaghetti and meatballs, which astonished Berta at first, and the recipe from Eros tasted better to him. Curious, I asked him why he had insisted upon eating at the Greeks so much when the food cost the same at another place but was a lot better. It was the people at the Greeks, he said. He ate there to see them. But if he was ordering in, he wouldn't see them anyway, so switching made sense.

The Slamming Door

All of those diners offered matzo ball soup in chicken broth, another favorite of his.

Thus far, we were as prepared and acclimated to foods, shopping, routines, and set-ups as we could hope to be. We settled in to wait for the process of misery to get underway.

Actually, at first life felt the same as it always had with Bryn; we stayed up late, usually until 2 a.m., watched television, discussed whatever we were watching and reading with one another, talked politics a little, and slept late. Then we woke up and drank McNulty's coffee. We would get up before noon, not after, but that changed later, and fluctuated depending upon how Bryn was feeling or what appointments we had to go to.

The family relaxed a bit, happy that all was in order, and we went to see Bill Maher's new movie *Religulous*. It was excellent, well-researched and full of wry, agnostic humor; I loved it because religiousness has always bothered me a lot. Bryn felt disillusioned by Maher's derisive attitude toward people with different attitudes. Despite our attitudes, we all settled into a happy routine of self-enforced denial about the issues of death, dying, the afterlife, and loss...

...until the evening that Hilda and her friends came over to interview us about all this. They had borrowed some audio-visual equipment from their school for this purpose, and with a huge microphone suspended from a long black pole, held that over us as we took turns sitting in Bryn's Lazy Boy chair to be interviewed. Carolyn, Hilda's friend with long dark hair and rectangular glasses, was in charge of the equipment; Hilda had come up with the topic.

I talked about how the illness didn't feel very real yet, but that I expected it to do so once chemotherapy got underway. As for what Bryn said, I didn't hang around to listen; I was trying not to think about the future too much. Why bother? I already knew it was going to be awful.

We never saw the interview; Carolyn recorded over it by mistake and sheepishly confessed her error weeks later. She had to do the assignment over on another topic.

There was one other thing that was the same as always: Bryn had a maddening habit, his one and only maddening habit. I suppose everyone has at least one of those. He would wait until he thought that I was through with the bathroom for a while, then go in there and sit on the toilet with his pipe and newspaper for a very, very long time.

He had done that all his adult life.

Berta told me that when she lived with him, he did that and she used to get desperate to use the toilet, and would even run across the hall to Elah. Elah would always let her pee in her bathroom, but really, it shouldn't have gotten that bad. I had to do that once, and felt awkward about it. People should go into a bathroom, do their business, and get out of there.

The fact is that women's bladders are a quarter the size of men's, so we need regular access to a bathroom. That's just the way it is. I willed myself not to feel bad about needing the bathroom so much. When Damon and I stayed with him in the long, hot summer of 2005, Bryn used to wait until he thought we were asleep for the night, and then go in there. Of course I couldn't fall asleep until well past 2 a.m., lying awake needing the bathroom...

He soon realized that sometimes I would hand-wash a shirt or a pair of shorts and hang them up on the shower rung, so he refrained from bringing his pipe in there, not wanting to infuse the clothes with the scent of tobacco. He told me so.

For my part, I hated to hint that he was making me desperate for the bathroom, and avoided telling him so. It stopped after a while; he noticed the problem on his own. Bryn was a great guy; if he realized something was a problem, he would try to fix it.

There are a very few people whom I have ever made such an effort to get along with on such points as I did with Bryn. Most of the time, I would just say that I was having a problem and ask for a change. Not with Bryn; I wanted him to have things as he liked them as much as possible. It was a big deal for me to run anywhere to take care of anyone, to leave my comfort zone for any reason. Bryn had to be a beloved, important person to me, or I would have stayed in Connecticut.

Going to the lengths I did to help Bryn when he needed someone was quite a leap for me; I knew I was an antsy, nervous sort, but this was the year that Asperger's became a part of my conscious thoughts. I got the diagnosis in 2000, the doctor instructed me to focus on other things, and I pretty much forgot about it. Now it cropped up constantly, while I just felt confused by the way that it connected to my life, my habits, my quirks, and my job helping Bryn.

Life can be a comedy of accommodation sometimes.

Berta and I settled into a routine of meeting for dinner in the apartment.

I would shop for fish, vegetables, salad items, and cook. At first, Bryn ate with us. He hadn't started any chemotherapy yet, so he was able to eat whatever came along. He had no problem with us rushing back to be on time for *Bones*, *NCIS*, and whatever else, and Berta surprised me by wanting to watch them and getting to know and like the characters. I wondered what she liked to watch, but she didn't let on much until the spring. Thus far, I knew that she liked *Mad Men*, about an advertising firm in the early 1960s; her grandfather, Bryn's father, had worked in one.

The Slamming Door

She showed me a nice recipe for ginger salmon, but unfortunately, I don't remember how to make it. Fresh ginger was involved, and the oven. The oven was okay for cooking, just not baking. Cooking is an art, but baking is a science – inflexible except for decorating. So we could dare to guess at the temperature and things came out cooked but not burned. To tell the truth, I didn't feel any too good about cooking fish in there because of all the unknowns, so I mostly cooked it on the stove.

To prepare to use the oven, I had bought a gas lighter, a long, red contraption. Grocery stores sell them. I didn't know when or why I might use the oven, but I knew that the gas jets inside had to be turned on and lit, and I was afraid to stick my hand in there with a match. I also got a small baking pan – Bryn didn't have any of those – and a pair of blue oven mitts.

When the time came to actually cook in there, I was still nervous. Berta didn't scold me or mock me for that; she agreed that electric ovens felt less menacing. She talked me through it, and after that I was fine. I cooked a lot of roasted potatoes, carrots, and red and yellow onions tossed with olive oil and herbs over the winter, and she and Bryn liked them.

Berta's recipe for ginger salmon was delicious. We only made it once or twice for some reason, which is probably why I don't remember how to do it now. She said that it was her most requested recipe (by Matt). Bryn asked her, with a skeptical tone in his voice, whether she knew how to make anything else. She indignantly insisted that she did, but that this one was his favorite. I just stayed out of it. They knew I could cook lots of things with or without a recipe.

If we weren't making dinner at home, we were ordering it, or eating out with Albert, June and Alissa. Most of the time, we ate on the corner at Rafaella's. We ate there so often that we got to know two of the waitresses; they were from Poland and Romania, pretty and cheerful.

Just inside of Rafaella's, on either side, were long tables with a sofa against the front windows. Upholstered chairs flanked most of the tables, so they blended into the décor nicely. We always looked for an empty front table, so that Bryn could sit on the sofa. This was the one restaurant where he didn't need to bring any pillows in order to be comfortable, and we all liked the food; plenty of fish for June, vegetable puréed soups for me Berta, salads for Alissa, and a hummus plate that Bryn liked. Albert seemed to like the thin-crusted pizzas.

We settled into a pleasant routine of eating out together as a family. I had been worried that I would be perceived as "just some damned in-law," as I put it, disparaging myself to pre-empt any such attempts by others. But no; they never did that. I was made to feel welcome by all, and Berta seemed to look forward to hanging out with me.

Signing Up for the Process of Misery

I could see that she and I were very different, but I was determined to find common ground with her – without losing myself along the way. She took an attitude of almost mothering me, sort of mentoring me in an ongoing tour of New York City. As long as I enjoyed it, which I did for almost all of the time that I spent there, it was fun. I saw nothing amiss.

Nothing, that is, until one afternoon when I was at home alone.

Bryn had gone out with friends or with Albert to the doctor; I forget which. The point was, I was alone in the apartment. While I was in the bathroom, I heard the door open and close, some footsteps, the sound of large plastic bags hitting the floor softly, and then more footsteps.

Coming out into the living room, I peered around – no one. I looked in my room – no one. Next, the hall and the kitchen – still no one, but there were 2 huge bags from Bed, Bath & Beyond on the hall floor. That left only one more possibility, so I went back into Bryn's room and found Berta in his Lazy Boy chair, in front of his old ottoman that was covered with his papers, notes, and manila folders, clutching her BlackBerry and sobbing quietly.

I was a bit surprised; it was a weekday, and leaving work without notice or a sudden uproar of some sort seemed like something that her employers would not be understanding about. It turned out that she was on her lunch hour, so her visit was to be a short one.

"What happened?!" I asked, aghast. What could have made her start sobbing such heaving sobs so soon after arriving? She couldn't have been sobbing when she arrived.

"I looked in his notes here," she said, indicating the manila folder where Bryn kept handwritten notes on his illness, a thing that I never looked at. I was appalled, but kept my expression neutral; looking at such a thing seemed like watching someone go to the bathroom.

Well…too late, she had looked and was sobbing. "What did you find?" I asked, not really wanting to hear the answer.

"He has P-----'s disease," she sobbed. Of course I didn't know what that was, and why would I? She immediately continued, "It's ------- ----
-. It has nothing to with cancer; I looked it up on my BlackBerry. It's an old man's disease." Then she resumed sobbing.

Wonderful. She had snooped. I tried to forget these details; I'm still trying.

I didn't fully realize it at the time, but Berta was the sort of person who, if she wanted information and knew that its possessor would be unwilling to disclose it, would dig for it when she thought she could get at it unobserved. Nonetheless, I made a mental note to keep logged off of my e-mail whenever I wasn't going to be near the computer.

The Slamming Door

But back to the sobbing; presumably Berta had either mined that folder of all of its secrets, or decided that it was too upsetting to continue her illicit and warrantless discovery process.

Leaving the legalese-laced quips out, I said, "Come on, Berta. Stop looking; you're just upsetting yourself. Bryn would be mortified to think that you even knew this about his physical condition, and all that it accomplished was to upset you. Let's get out of here." I tugged at her arm, trying to get her out of his chair and away from the scene of the crime.

Fortunately, she acquiesced.

We went out into the living room, and she brought in the shopping bags; it was more nice stuff for her dad, and we put it away for him to use. She went back to Wall Street, and I tried to forget what she had learned and shared with me.

Unfortunately, I still remember it all to this day, but have not included it in this story. Those dashes will have to suffice. I'm quite sure that that's what Bryn would have wanted, and I hope that it's what she would ultimately want, too.

Chapter 11

The Page-Torn Salon for the Arts

On West 22nd Street, between 9th and 10th Avenues, was a brownstone house shared by an acting family, the children of the Broadway actress Geraldine Page and the Hollywood actor Rip Torn. It was a beautiful old building on the north side of the street.

Its official name was the Geraldine Page Salon for the Arts, but when I found out that Alissa was going to have one of her plays read there by professional actors – using printed copies of her work – it seemed like a lot more fun to advertise it as follows:

The Page-Torn Salon for the Arts…
…where no paper is damaged in the course of an evening.

Well, I thought it was funny, and no one objected when I said it. The entire operation was conceived of and run by Angelica Page Torn, who was their daughter and a professional actress herself, which was how I got the idea. Plays were read by acting coaches, famous and unknown actors and actresses, and member of the Page-Torn family.

Alissa had written a play called *Linwood and Sascha*, about a couple who lived on Martha's Vineyard. There was one other character, and that completed the cast. The Page-Torn Salon's mission was to take a play by an unknown, unpublished writer, assemble some actors – both famous and up-and-coming were acceptable – and read it in front of an audience.

The reading took place in the room that overlooked 22nd Street, one level up, against a backdrop of high, curtained windows as the cast sat on the old Victorian furniture: a sofa, several beautifully upholstered and carved chairs, and a coffee table. Ordinary folding chairs were lined up in rows facing that area, with one aisle left open down the center.

The audience sat with their backs to the little hallway that led to the stairwell, the back room, which was curtained off for the family's privacy, and a pair of extremely tiny bathrooms across from the stairs. Those rest rooms were for the audience, and they were so tiny that one had to scrunch one's arms up and carefully rotate toward the sink, then again to face the door and leave. But they were comfortable enough, with soap pumps and toilet paper.

The building had a staircase that led up to the front door on its right side, showing the basement level windows set into the sidewalk. The night we went there, in early October, a tiger-striped cat dashed in with us, disappearing up the staircase to the level with the reading room.

The Slamming Door

The staircase was a beautiful old varnished wooden one with white walls and antique furniture at the top and bottom. Upstairs was pretty; we saw 2 more cats, black ones, flitting about, and a marble-topped table against the stairwell wall, stocked with bottles of wine, cups, and plates full of slices of cheddar and Brie cheeses and grapes. There was another table across from that, between the rest rooms, with cookies and tea or coffee. A kitchen sink was in a dim alcove to the right of all that.

The reading room had a marble fireplace on the right, surrounded by bookcases full of books, and more on the left. Framed black-and-white photographs of Geraldine Page were hung here and there on the walls. She had been a beautiful woman when she was young. Another photograph of her, taken as an older woman, showed her smiling and looking thoughtfully off to the side; it leaned against the wall on the mantelpiece, to the right.

Angelica Page Torn was very nice. I realized that she was the one setting up the cheese and crackers before the reading started, and found myself standing silently next to her, so I told her that I had recently seen her father's movie *The Yearling* (1981) on television, and that it had been on a lot lately. I added that I was sorry that they had killed his character – he wasn't a threat to anyone, just upset. She seemed pleased, and

The Page-Torn Salon for the Arts

commented that oh, yes, she remembered, it was based on the book *Cross Creek* (by Marjorie Kinnan Rawlings – 1920s). She was in her forties, pretty with chin-length, straight blond hair that she wore tied back with a small scarf.

I had seen her in *The Sixth Sense* and thought she had done a good job of portraying a mother who was mentally ill with Münchausen Syndrome. I told her that I had enjoyed that movie and remembered her role in it, and she said "thank-you" to me.

That was about it; I had my wine and cheese and went to sit down. The little girl black cat ran in and out and I found out her name was Bear, but she wasn't as willing to be petted as the tiger-striped one. I found I was missing my own black-and-white male shorthair cat, Cookie. It would be months before I lived with a cat again, and before I saw him again.

Soon the play reading commenced; the actors who professionals, but unknown to me and to the others who were present. Bryn was there, Albert and June were there, of course the playwright was there, and being very quiet as usual, plus Berta. It was a Monday evening.

Alissa's play was a bit of a mystery to all of us. She was very tense and close-mouthed about it. I asked her the title – no information was forthcoming. "You'll see," was about it. Okay, we all said. It was 50 pages long, written in a month's time, but created in Alissa's mind over a period of 3 years. That counts as writing time, because she pretty much had the play ready in her mind when she typed it into a Word file. It was fabulous.

The reason why we had no idea about her work was that no one had ever read it before. Albert certainly could have done so; his career was spent writing cliff notes for publication, among other things, and he had a master's degree from someplace in Iowa in creative writing. But he had deliberately maintained a policy of never, ever, looking at his daughter's writing.

When I asked him why, he told me that he was afraid of discouraging her with his comments, of coloring her perception of her own work. He was convinced that the best thing he could do for her was to just stay out of it. As I got to know him and see how they interacted, I began to understand why he thought so. Albert had a strong personality, and Alissa was as quiet as a mouse. Any opinion that he expressed and she heard caused her to shrink from doing otherwise, even if she were secretly inclined to do so.

By this I don't mean that the topic of his opinions were irresponsible behavior; to the contrary. He didn't approve of shopping for groceries at Whole Foods, because it was a huge corporation. Alissa, despite being on a raw foods vegan diet, thus avoided the huge store 2 blocks away

The Slamming Door

from her parents' place even though it turned out to be the perfect place to get everything she needed. No wonder Albert wasn't about to open his mouth unless and until a room full of professionals praised his daughter's work. It was definitely the right way to go.

We were all thrilled to go and hear the play, and delighted once the reading got underway, because her senses of wit and humor and observation were shown in the lines. No one had had any idea about her talent or those other qualities until Monday evening. She was that quiet. She was fine now, but because she used to have trouble with changes to her environment, this was even more of a nice surprise.

The play was about Sascha, a famous poet who had won lots of awards for her work. She is staying for the summer at a cottage on Martha's Vineyard with her boyfriend Linwood, also a poet but not famous. Sascha is translating the poems of the Frenchwoman Simone Poulet. A college boy was invited to visit the couple.

So there were 2 actors and one actress, plus a guy who taught drama reading things that would be in the playbill if it were an actual Broadway production. He announced things like set descriptions, time of day/evening, and which act and scene we were watching. The play had 3 acts and several scenes in each one, and the length was just right.

Angelica Page Torn read the role of Sascha, and of course she was the best of the 3 performers. This reading helped us all to imagine the play as a professional production, and picture the set a bit plus understand how great it would be with the lines memorized rather than read. But all three actors read well, and no pages were torn or damaged in any way.

There was a discussion period afterwards, and an established playwright, a friend of the Page Torn family, an older woman in the back row, said that the play was perfect. Other people thought that Jake's presence in the story needed perhaps one more line, such as to say that this visit with the famous poet Sascha was also an internship for his resume, and Alissa seemed amenable to that idea.

My comment when the discussion period was opened up was, "Someone call an agent."

I stayed with Alissa and walked her to the subway entrance. I offered to show her how to copyright her work. Also, Alissa had not learned how to back up her work, so I offered to go to Staples with her to show her CDs and memory sticks, plus give her some lessons at a computer. She was interested in that, so I told her about books with agents and advice on how to write query letters. She was interested in that, too.

After that play reading, I could seriously imagine her becoming a famous playwright.

Chapter 12

Diane/Dionne - The Split Personality

Bryn older daughter, who was his adopted stepdaughter, was around for a couple of weeks in October before his chemotherapy was to start, and for another week or so afterward. She came to visit us, and to take me out for an evening. The motive was easy enough to surmise: she didn't know me very well, and was curious to observe me for a few hours now that I had moved in to take care of her father.

I had met her before; it was sometime after Damon and I were married, perhaps in 2002 – or maybe it was in December of 2001, when we were getting engaged. Whenever it was, Dionne was temporarily home from Milan, Italy, where she had lived for 16 years. We rode the subway with her then, and she had said that she thought she would probably never get married.

But she did, and I was glad, because she had sounded wistful and sorry when she had talked about the idea. I guess that happens to a lot of women; we worry about the unpleasant possibility of never getting married, never having a companion to be our best friend, and perhaps, if we want one, a fairy-tale wedding. Fortunately, it was merely a worry for Dionne.

Dionne was Elvira's daughter by her first husband, the heroin addict that Berta had told me about. Berta had added more to story, explaining that Dionne was so angry about him that when she had met him many years later – out of curiosity, I suppose – she had told him that he was just a sperm. He was dead now. He had worked as an artist in Los Angeles.

That wasn't all; Berta had told me how Elvira had been awarded sole custody of Dionne. When Dionne was a baby, after her parents' marriage ended, her biological father had sneaked into their home through a window and taken her from her crib. Elvira woke up and freaked out, called the police, and soon had her baby back. No wonder Dionne had no use for her him.

So Elvira had raised Dionne alone until she met Bryn. He was thrilled to get a daughter with the deal, and adopted her, giving her his last name, which she kept after her marriage. By that time, she had established her professional reputation as an artist, so changing it would have been foolish. What really mattered to Dionne was the pronunciation and spelling of her first name. I caught on to the spelling easily enough, but because Bryn, Albert and Berta kept referring to her as Diane, I never was able to pronounce it any other way.

The Slamming Door

Bryn told me that Elvira had been mean to Dionne while she was growing up. I never found out specifically what she had done, only that the nature of the abuse was verbal. That saying that words can't hurt a person is nonsense; words can do plenty of damage, and Dionne's self esteem had suffered under the constant pressure.

When I finally saw those of her paintings that hung in Elvira's apartment, I noticed one right away over the dining room table that was a self-portrait. It was done when Dionne was a 14-year-old girl. The image is one of a frowning, sad girl. There was also a mallard drake in the picture, but the sad girl was front and center. It was when I showed Bryn the photo I took of it that he told me that Elvira had treated her badly.

Berta had told me a story about a time when Dionne was 11 years old. Bryn had decided to take his stepdaughter to Washington, D.C., just the 2 of them, for a tour of all of the Smithsonian national museums. "Why?" Dionne had asked. "Because you're my daughter and I love you," he had replied. So they had gone and seen the art and had a good time.

Berta was the one who explained to me that her sister's real first name was not Dionne; it was Diane. So why did she insist upon changing it, and prettifying it in a French form, I had asked (not that French and pretty confused me – it was changing one's legal name that did that)?

It was like she had a split personality, Berta explained. Diane was the ugly girl that her mother had raised and spoken nastily to, while Dionne was the sophisticated artist who had lived off the tax grid in an artist community in Milan, Italy for 16 years. Dionne had friends who were either artists themselves, or wealthy collectors from the U.S. and Europe, or both.

That made sense; Dionne had fashioned a new persona for herself, one that boosted her self-esteem. I suppose that we all do that to some extent as we age, though many of us do it through education and acquiring various skills, and find sufficient satisfaction that way.

Not Dionne; she had graduated from Boston University with a bachelor's degree in art, and lived and traveled on her own at very little expense for her entire adult life, but it wasn't enough. She was fluent in French and Italian and could converse with Alissa at length in both languages, though Italian was her forte. She had gone to India and lived on a dollar a day with some friends, too. It didn't overcome her past angst, however.

Still, I thought she had done very well and turned out to be an interesting, if remote, personality. She didn't listen much. She gushed loudly as a matter of routine, and often lapsed into Italian, especially in a restaurant, asking for her meals in sentences laced with that language.

Diane/Dionne - The Split Personality

Dionne was tall and thin, the physical antithesis of her younger half-sister. She had reddish hair that was naturally frizzy; Berta told me that her sister hated her hair. Bryn also confided to me that his daughters had some African ancestors on their mother's side of the family, which explained the frizziness. That was interesting, because usually when someone hates their hair, they have something done about it.

Not Dionne; no straightening was ever done to her mane. Perhaps she would have considered it a betrayal of her ethnic background, but I suspect that she just didn't want the bother and expense of constantly straightening it. Dionne was very frugal, despite being well-informed on feminine grooming tips.

She usually wore her hair in a tight braid gathered at the nape of her neck, but sometimes she wore it loose. It was shoulder-length, and it set off her green eyes nicely. She had a wide grin with straight teeth, which she flashed often. Only her eyes seemed to be missing the enjoyment reflected in her smile; they looked worried rather than happy.

Her clothes were always interesting. Dionne wore vintage dresses from consignment shops, and she carried them off nicely. She also wore jeans and tee shirts on occasion, but mostly we all noticed her pretty dresses.

She was uncomfortable with her age as well as her hair; she and Berta were 9 years apart in age, yet Dionne insisted that she was only 45 years old. Of course we never contradicted her; if she wanted to maintain that fiction, it was her choice, and hardly an unusual one. She certainly looked younger than she actually was, thanks to diet and exercise.

Dionne belonged to a health club at Chelsea Pier that offered yoga classes as well as workouts, and several times, she offered me a chance to go over there each day for a week, but I prefer to walk briskly all over an interesting area, noting the scenes and people-watching. I walk fast, so this has always worked well for me, and it is much more enjoyable than making piles of dirty laundry at a gym and having to either shower in some strange place among other people or else go home a mess. So I had politely declined these invitations.

Another reason why Dionne was so thin was her diet. She did cleanses sometimes, and had told me so one evening in the summer of 2005 when she had come over to visit. Damon and I were there during that long hot summer. I remember that evening; it was after dark, hot and humid, and I was wearing a sleeveless shirt with my hair up in its matte gold clip. I have always had trouble with acne, though much less so since my teens, so I usually hate to show my skin, but I was just too uncomfortable, so I was in a sleeveless shirt. Now little red dots showed all over my forearms, and Dionne said, "Clarisse! What happened?!"

The Slamming Door

I was not thrilled to have her call attention to this. But I told what had happened. That was what prompted her to talk about the cleanses, and about eating all organic foods. Too late to give me unscarred, nice skin, I thought. Besides, I eat lots of fresh fruit and vegetables, and use extra-virgin (triple-pressed) olive oil, plus a lot of fish. What more could I do? "Eat all organic foods," came the reply. Forget it, I thought, unwilling to hunt through stores for that, paying more for my food, and certain that to do so would be unworkable. Logistically, I couldn't see it.

Berta had told me later that her sister's thin physique wasn't entirely the result of organic foods and cleanses. Often, she had not had the money to buy food, so she had eaten sparingly to stretch her budget. "Dionne has the discipline to just not eat," she added, saying that her sister carried this austerity over to her eating habits as a matter of choice even when she could afford more food. "I just can't stand to do that," Berta added. Poor Berta; being thin seemed like an unattainable goal for her. But back to her sister…

In October of 2004, Dionne had gotten married.

I had met her fiancé that spring during a visit to Bryn's place. It was a rainy day in May and Bryn had told me that he was an artist with an exhibit at a nearby gallery in Chelsea, so I had gone to meet him and see his art. Unfortunately, I had a cramped, painful back from sleeping on that awful futon in the guest room, and spent the day leaning heavily on my umbrella as if it were a cane, which it could double as. And I can't think clearly when I am in pain.

The place was just a few blocks away, and I had gone there alone, with the cane umbrella. Albert Hornsby was a tall, thin man, dark-haired but going bald in front and back, clean-shaven, and wearing jeans, comfortable shoes, and a plaid shirt. He looked like a model for a hunters' catalogue, I had thought.

His art was an odd amalgamation of Native American materials and Palestinian issues. Using huge bearskins as canvases, images of war-torn Palestine were projected onto each one. The point of the exhibition seemed to be that the European settlers of North American and the Jewish settlers of Palestine were both groups of thieves, which was quite true.

We discussed that issue and some others, though I felt stupid as I failed to think things through with my usual speed and dexterity due to the back pain. I came away angry with myself, and told Bryn about it later that evening. He assured me in soothing tones that I had not come across as mentally deficient, and that telling Albert Hornsby that my back hurt had in fact compensated for that, though I had worried over it a bit more nonetheless.

Later, I found out more about Albert Hornsby.

Diane/Dionne - The Split Personality

He was from a wealthy family in Colorado, with one brother; both parents lived out there, plus they had a gorgeous home in South Carolina. Dionne had done some decorating in that home in 2008, painting pillars and walls in it to resemble various grains of marble, a skill she had learned in Belgium during a semester in Brussels in the fall of 2007. She also went on to do some of that in an office building that Albert's brother was fixing up in Colorado in the winter of 2009.

Her husband had never had a job, but he had gone to college. After that, he was free to pursue his art, not in need of a steady income. He owned a ranch in Wyoming where he liked to go and stay and hunt for days at a time while camping alone with his horse, a pet he had owned for several years. Damon referred to him as The Hornsby, and thought of him as a limousine liberal, because he was a professed Democrat who had no practical understanding of the difficulties faced by most Democrats. I just found it convenient, because we already had an Albert in the family, Albert Otterman.

Albert Hornsby had also owned some property in Colorado for a while, but had sold in a couple of years earlier, perhaps in 2005 or 2006, and bought a brownstone house with the money later that year. It was $10 million, I was told. There was some urgency about finding and buying a piece of property before the fiscal year drew to a close; otherwise there would be heavy tax penalties on the proceeds of the Colorado sale.

The upshot was that he beat the deadline by shopping in the boroughs of New York City relentlessly until the hurdle was leaped. When all was said and done, he had a paid-for townhouse in Brooklyn, complete with a basement, ground floor, and two more floors. He and Dionne lived on the upper two stories while renting out the others to friends as apartments.

Their wedding had been a fairy tale evening at Gramercy Park in the fall of 2004, paid for by Bryn (and perhaps a bit by Elvira, though I can't be sure of that). Gramercy Park is a beautiful enclosed space surrounded by upscale apartment buildings that date from the early 20th century. The Park is surrounded by a black wrought-iron fence; inside is a lush, green garden of vines, shrubs, climbing and flowering plants, and other beautiful greenery, plus benches. Normally, only residents of the surrounding buildings may access it, but if one rents the events hall that is located on that square, it comes with access to the Park.

Dionne had thus enjoyed the use of Gramercy Park that evening, in addition to the reception hall. Damon and I missed it all due to our trip to Kuwait; he was already there, and I was in Connecticut with my parents, getting the cat's legal documents ready for the trip.

The Slamming Door

Bryn kept some photos from his daughter's wedding on the drop-leaf table next to his Lazy Boy chair. They were all in the same wooden frame, on both sides of it, which was propped by a little wooden slat in the back. The front showed Bryn in a black tuxedo walking Dionne down the aisle; she wore a plain, white, a-line dress with her hair up and carried a big bouquet of fall flowers. The back showed smaller photos, such as Dionne and her groom cutting the cake together, and Hilda and Bryn on a sofa together, looking a bit tired late in the party. Albert Hornsby had worn a Native American chief's style of headdress with his tuxedo, with a huge fan of feathers framing his face.

Albert and June Otterman had not been invited to Dionne's wedding. It would not have been a good idea; Elvira and Albert had fought during her divorce from Bryn. Alcohol and shoving had been involved, and there was also some tale of Elvira getting so irate that she had attempted to run Bryn down with her car in upstate New York. Lovely story; I could see why they kept apart, by choice at this point in time.

After I arrived in the fall of 2008 and learned what I could about Dionne, it quickly became apparent to me that she would be around only intermittently and not with us much when she was in town.

That was fine, and it made sense; she would go out to Wyoming when The Hornsby did, and to South Carolina to stay with the in-laws when he did, and also to Colorado. She had no driver's license, so she would have to stay put when they arrived.

She told me the tale of attempting to learn to drive. It was in Manhattan, and decades ago; the teacher had shouted at her, and had also taken her on the very first lesson to the nearest highway and expected her to just drive on it. No advice about doing this was offered. She had given up on the endeavor.

I was appalled; my teacher had spent hours with me on back country roads before approaching the highway, and my father had taken me to empty parking lots to rehearse parking and turns at very low risk before doing that. Under no circumstances would they have me drive in Hartford, Connecticut, let alone Manhattan. If we went there, he drove.

City driving…and learning…can have serious drawbacks. I didn't do it until years later, after Damon and I were married and I had had lots of experience on the road. It's okay now. I could understand why Dionne hadn't continued with the lessons.

Dionne planned to be in town for most of October and into November, at which time she would go to Wyoming with her husband, and then spend a little time in Colorado the next winter, making that office building look as though its walls were made of marble.

Diane/Dionne – The Split Personality

For now, she appeared one evening after a weekend spent with Berta and Matt at her mother's house upstate in Oneonta, New York. It was the same house that Damon remembered from when he was a teenager, on the same street as the one that he had lived in. Damon's branch of the family and Bryn's had both lived first in Manhattan and then in Oneonta, New York. Damon's journey there was a bit more roundabout, and he is still insulted by how Elvira viewed him as a teenager.

When Damon was little kid, he had lived first in Michigan while his father, a graduate of Harvard University, had completed his Ph.D. in psychology at the prestigious University of Michigan. From there, it was on to Ankara, Turkey where he taught at an American university for a few years, then back to Manhattan. Damon's parents divorced at this point; his father had reproduced 3 times before realizing that he did not wish to be a parent – damn him for that.

Damon, his mother and his sisters were left in New York City, near his maternal grandparents, while his father worked for the U.S. Air Force as a psychological profiler in Ethiopia, where he had died in a plane crash on Damon's 9th birthday…some birthday.

Damon came home to find men in military uniforms and Damon's Uncle Rex, who had also arrived to deliver the bad news…on his birthday. After that, my husband hated his birthday and didn't want to celebrate it. When he grew up, he found another reason to hate his birthday: he hated the aging process and any reminder of it. He promised himself to study for a Ph.D. and learn ways to thwart that process.

Not long after his father's death, his mother moved the family to a horrible area because she was getting no death benefits from the military, and had very little money. Her parents had an apartment in Morningside Heights, but they couldn't help her much. Her brother and his family lived in Michigan, and she saw little of them.

The area was on West 94th Street, and in a gang-ridden area. Damon, as the one white boy in a Puerto Rican neighborhood, learned to run very, very fast, and joined a gang called the Electric Coffin. He had one friend across the street who was not a gang member; his father was a partner in a law firm. I have eaten dinner in their townhouse with Damon, in the summer of 2005; their Glo-Glue drawings are still on the basement walls.

Henrietta, Damon's mother, was studying at Hofstra University for her Ph.D. in education during this time. Her graduation coincided with the death of an Otterman relative, a great-aunt or aunt of Bryn's, and Henrietta was left a significant amount of money. The deceased had felt sorry for her, Bryn and Damon had explained to me.

With that, Damon's family – including his maternal grandparents – decamped to Oneonta, New York. Using combined financial resources, they bought an Italianate-style house, painted white with black shutters, and moved in up the street from Bryn, Elvira, Dionne and Berta.

Bryn was working on his Ph.D. while teaching at State University College in Oneonta, Elvira was a schoolteacher. Damon told me that Elvira had warned her daughters to keep away from him, as if he might harm them, and that he would hate her forever for doing that. Damon wasn't a threat to others; he was a quiet, unhappy, and introverted teenager, and with good reason. He also had Asperger's, though no one could have diagnosed him with that until 1994.

Damon's grandparents occupied the first floor of the house, and Henrietta and her children took the upper story. The basement was shared, and Damon spent hours down there in a nest that he made for himself, petting his tiger-striped cat, Pinklepurr, and reading J.R.R. Tolkein's *The Lord of the Rings* trilogy over and over again. That house is now a synagogue; we found a photo of it online.

But that was then, and in the present, Dionne had just come back from there, meaning that she had spent the weekend in this familiar territory. Elvira had kept her old house there, and returned to it regularly, spending entire summers there, some fall and spring weekends, and then coming back to her apartment in Stuyvesant Town in Manhattan. She also went to Alabama to stay with her elderly mother in the house where she had grown up, but that was another story.

While there, Dionne and her sister had attended a fall fair of some sort, and visited the Farmers Museum in Cooperstown, New York. She had bought a corn broom, a flattened, straight thing on a stick with pale yellow bristles cut off straight on the bottom and rounded at the top, where they met the stick. As she intended to go straight home to the brownstone house in Brooklyn after this, she carried it with her.

When I told Damon about that later, he dubbed her The Wicked Witch of Everywhere. The moniker was so entertaining to us that it stuck, though we refrained from telling the rest of the family about it. We doubted that they would have been as amused by it as we were.

That evening, Dionne invited me out to a bar on the roof of the Gansvoort Hotel; it was Tuesday, the 7th of October. Berta had told me that this was how her sister got drinks and snacks: she would attend art exhibits and eat the food, making a nonchalant dinner out of each event while networking with artists and potential clients, or go to a bar and buy herself just one drink, them socialize with strangers who would share pitchers of drinks with her.

Intrigued but determined not to get drunk – just to observe as usual – I went with her. Bryn practically insisted that I go; he wanted us to have a chance to get to know each other.

Diane/Dionne - The Split Personality

We headed out into the mild, pleasant, clear evening. A full moon was rising, and the air was warm and comfortable. Dionne led me down 9th Avenue to the Gansevoort Hotel, which was just south of 14th Street in the West Village. I had seen the place before; its top glowed dark pink at night with the lights that emanated from within.

In we went, with Dionne carrying her broomstick, up an elevator to the top floor, and out into a huge indoor-outdoor bar. The place was furnished in a modern style with wood and metal panels and many low, wood-framed benches that coordinated with the décor. We walked through the indoor seating area, around to the right, then outside to the terrace, where Dionne found us a spot to sit on some more benches with cushions and a table. She put the broomstick under our bench.

A waiter came over and took our orders; we each got a beer. By this time I had been introduced to Leffe and Blue Moon beers by Albert and June, so I got one of those, probably Blue Moon. I knew that this would be all; I wanted to keep my wits about me, and Dionne couldn't afford to buy more than one drink for each of us.

While we were sitting on the outdoor terrace, we met a Swedish woman and her daughter. I was the one who spent most of my time talking with them; Dionne had connected with a large group of people to our left. That group was mostly of men in their thirties, but a couple of women were present too. The men had ordered a pitcher of some pale blue or green liquid. It looked like it had a flavor with a high alcoholic content. Dionne had some; I nursed my beer. That pastel-hued stuff looked as dangerous as Romulan ale to me, but I didn't comment about it.

The Swedish mother and daughter were fascinating to talk to. So this was how Dionne liked to unwind, I thought, watching her out of the corner of my eye. She warmed up to the men on the left, loud and bubbly but never inappropriate. I couldn't follow their conversation; it was mostly banter about things that I either couldn't quite hear or relate to.

I turned my attention to the Swedes, figuring that eventually Dionne would get curious and talk to them too. It happened as I expected, and we all had a good time. The mother and daughter had planned this trip together, just a week-long tour of Manhattan, since the previous year. During that time, the father had gotten sick with something – heart failure, I think – and died. He hadn't died suddenly, but shortly after a doctor's warning.

The mother and daughter, 2 beautiful blond women, had almost cancelled this trip. But then they had realized that the father would have found that to be foolish, so they went. When we met them, it was almost over; they had to leave the next day. The daughter worked in Paris, and the mother lived somewhere near Stockholm. She had a nice horse that she liked to ride. I asked them about the new Euro and she told me (most of my conversation was with the mother) that Sweden still used the krona. Then she surprised me by making a gift of one of those coins to me. I was delighted and said so; I collect foreign coins.

As we sat there, we all suddenly looked up to see that the sky was stunningly beautiful due to a phenomenon around the full moon. It was called a penumbra, and was formed by the haze in the atmosphere as the moonlight reflected off of it. It looked like a beautiful, flawless ring of light circling the full moon, and we all admired it. I called it by its name, eliciting a request for a full explanation. No one seemed at all off-put when I sounded like a professor…and astronomy isn't my field. I had fun.

When at last it was time to leave, Dionne and I headed back to 9th Avenue together. She was still carrying the broomstick. As we walked, she talked about organic foods, saying that she was going to bring over some homemade soups and sauces for her father and put them in the freezer before she went away. That sounded nice. I assured her that I knew and loved the Manhattan Fruit Exchange, which was where Dionne liked to buy most of her food. I was making a regular practice of bringing Bryn fresh apples and pears to eat from all of the best grocery stores, and she seemed greatly relieved to hear this.

She was going back on the subway in the dark, all the way to Brooklyn. The long commute by train or cab back to Brooklyn was no deterrent to her. Bryn kept trying to give her money for a cab whenever she visited, but she always turned him down, insisting that she would be perfectly safe. I would have been afraid to go between boroughs by subway or cab; despite several years of visits, I was still only calm and at home in lower Manhattan.

Two days after this was Dionne's birthday, so she and Bryn went out to dinner together down the street at Rafaella's. I took a photo of them on the sofa in the living room together when they returned; Dionne had her hair down and wore a dark green dress that dated from the 1960s; she looked nice, and Bryn did too. Chemotherapy wasn't until the next week.

Dionne was concerned about her father being warm enough when he inevitably lost his hair from the chemotherapy, and so was I. She and Berta had both told me that he couldn't wear a baseball cap, because Otterman heads were too big for those. My father has the same difficulty; when he goes fishing, he wears a different style hat, a loose fisherman's hat.

I mentioned this problem to Rudy, hoping that he would know what to do; he wore a cool black fedora hat sometimes. I said that I anticipated Bryn losing his hair and was worried about him walking in the sun with

Diane/Dionne – The Split Personality

nothing on his head...but that I had no idea how to go about buying a cool-looking hat. Then I told him that I was hoping he could help, because he was a cool guy who wore hats. He looked pleased and said, "I'm a guy, I wear hats, I'll handle it."

Soon enough, it was the weekend after chemotherapy had begun, and Rudy and Hilda went out and bought 2 beautiful new hats for Bryn. The hats were both in a huge, white cardboard box with a handle, a special kind of hatbox from the store where they had shopped.

One was a sailor hat, white knitted material with a bright blue stripe. The other was a gorgeous woven straw hat with a band around it of dark red and dark blue striped ribbon, plus a little feather in it.

He tried them both on and posed for photographs, grinning. Of course he looked fabulous, and he seemed to be enjoying the gifts. He didn't end up wearing those hats much, but they were quite perfect to look at. That box ended up propped for months on end outside Bryn's door, with the hats carefully packed in them.

Meanwhile, Dionne got him two plain, soft, woolen black hats that he wore constantly. At least she saw him using her gifts all through the colder months, until his hair grew back in.

Chapter 13

Misery Round One: Chemotherapy

Time did that annoying thing where it hurries up when you don't want it to, and soon Bryn and I were on our way to his third IV-drip of poison.

I didn't approve of this treatment, but refrained from saying so.

What was the point of poisoning him so that everything would taste awful, his beautiful thick white hair would all fall away, he would puke and puke and puke, and then die anyway?!

There were better weight loss plans.

Granted, he had belly fat and that puts one at risk for cancer, but as he already officially had the monstrous disease, it seemed like a moot point now.

The first day that he went, I stayed home and wrote this note to Dr. Leonardi, because my mother had been e-mailing me repeatedly about meeting him for dinner to catch up, hear how he liked his new job at Sloan-Kettering, and to tell him about taking care of Bryn, even though it was just companionship, household chores, and a little drink-serving thus far.

Hi - *I haven't forgotten about visiting with you.*

Tuesday, October 14, 2008 1:45 PM
From: "Clarisse N. Reynard"
To: "Vance P. Leonardi, M.D."

Hi Dr. Leonardi!

How are you?

I haven't forgotten about you.

Bryn is at his 1st chemotherapy session right now. As before, he doesn't want an entourage to go with him, so his brother Albert and sister-in-law June will meet him there. They are probably there now, because the poison drip session is scheduled for 2:15 p.m.

(June has to go because she is losing her memory and gets scared without Albert.)

Misery Round One: Chemotherapy

Bryn will have more poison doses tomorrow and Thursday, then 2 weeks off, and then repeat this pattern twice more.

He asked me to buy him a bucket in case he gets too nauseous, so that he may puke in as dignified a manner as possible. It's in a plastic bag. I saw him off in a cab, then came home again. We are hoping that he won't feel too horrible – and his doctor is allegedly giving him some pharmaceutical analgesic to deal with that.

Apparently, she believes that it will do the same job as pot brownies – another thing that I researched on the Internet – while being legal and of course providing revenue for pharmaceutical companies.

I am likely to work myself into a rotten mood over this quickly. I don't think that any of this will save Bryn – just make him bald, torture him, and kill him painfully. I am absolutely disgusted at how little the medical profession has to offer him. Bone cancer is the most painful, I have been told, and the most hopeless.

The really annoying aspect of all this is the fact that he may have gotten this problem as a side effect of a prostate cancer treatment that he had in December of 2005. He kept it a secret from the entire family. He had hormone therapy, then radiation, then 80 tiny radioactive balls injected into his prostate gland over a 2-hour period in December of 2005.

If he hadn't concealed the prostate cancer – which that treatment eradicated – we could have called you! I know you aren't a miracle worker, but you are the best.

But he just quietly and secretly worked with some other doctor and was told that osteosarcoma was a rare potential side effect. Now he has won its unwanted lottery.

I still want to visit with you, but this week seems bad – I don't know how rotten Bryn will feel tonight – we just can't guess or know until he comes home.

Please let me know when you would like to see me.

The Slamming Door

My cell phone number is (xxx) xxx-xxxx.

I would like to hang around for Bryn this week, but probably next week it would be okay to meet you. I don't mean to put you off – but then you know what I am doing, and you can tell that it's not meant that way. It's all about being available at crucial moments when Bryn needs me.

Say "Hi" to Kaitlyn for me – I hope your family is doing well.

Love,
Clarisse.

That was it; I thought no more about seeing Dr. Leonardi until later in the week.

For now, I was watching to see how Bryn's first course of chemotherapy would go, and how he would feel. Albert had gone with him to the first session, on Tuesday, so this was my first exposure to the Memorial Sloan-Kettering Cancer Center. I went to the Wednesday and Thursday poisonings.

We took a cab up to 3rd Avenue and 53rd Street, heading north on 3rd and then west on 53rd, and getting out across the street from the entrance. Our destination was on the southwest corner of the intersection, on 53rd Street. It seemed to be slightly off the beaten path, but then there really is no such thing in Midtown.

It's just that I would not have noticed the place had we not gone directly to it.

I was just following Bryn; he had found out exactly where he was going in advance when he met the doctor with Albert, and this was his third day of chemotherapy. Add to that the fact that he knew the city like the back of his hand and it was no wonder that I just followed him in, learning the route as we went.

I had given him Damon's ImmuneACCORD drink every day, and he now felt less pain. It was helping with inflammation. The previous Wednesday, after Albert had taken him to meet his oncologist, we had eaten lunch – Bryn, Albert, June and I – at Daioh, the sushi place around the corner, and Bryn actually sat down for most of the meal. Previously, it hurt too much and he would keep standing up. So the tumor was shrinking, I had thought. He didn't even have his cane when he met me on the street corner.

Now it was my turn to go with him and see the Sloan-Kettering Cancer Center. The place was beautiful, probably to take the patients'

Misery Round One: Chemotherapy

minds off of the fact that all of the effort that was to be expended on their behalf was likely for naught.

We walked straight back. On the right, I saw a huge, modern water fountain. It was a wall of black granite with water cascading down it. There was an odd-looking wall hanging behind the desk, a flat metallic sculpture, also dark. The walls were mostly beige, and some huge paintings hung in a row across from the elevators, which were just to the left of the desk and behind them.

Doormen stood around in uniforms, greeting people as they walked by but not doing anything more if the people seemed to know where they were going, which Bryn did.

We walked directly to the elevators, and then rode up to the 5th floor.

I didn't have my camera with me, but my old cell phone had recently died (the microphone had suddenly quit as I chatted with Damon), so I had a new metallic pink one with a little camera in it. It was my first one of that kind, and I decided to try it out. As a result, I have a small collection of photos from Bryn's first round of chemotherapy. He wasn't in them; they were just of the place.

He went there for 3 days in a row, a Tuesday, a Wednesday, and a Thursday, and I watched it all unfold, wondering unhappily when Bryn would feel miserable. The place was interesting, that was for sure, but then I tend to get morbidly fascinated with the macabre.

I hate horror movies – they are just pointless blood, gore and slashing – but the forensic dramas are different. In law school, in criminal law class, I found that without any effort at all, I could picture whatever disturbing fact pattern was presented. The greater the emotional impact of the subject matter, the easier it was to picture. That's probably why I could watch this horror unfold right in front of me, studying it. Besides, it was a little early to start panicking. Bryn wasn't going to die right away, and his appearance would change gradually, not abruptly.

We got out of the elevators and found ourselves facing a beautiful wooden wall with a counter set into it. A couple of bright pink orchid plants decorated the counter. It was an island in a huge room, I realized as we moved closer to it. This was the check-in point. Bryn walked up and announced himself.

I looked around. Farther down on the left, across from that desk, was a door that I eventually learned led to the doctors' offices. Back in the huge room where we were to spend a lot of our time waiting, I moved closer to the check-in desk and looked in. Several people – with pleasant-looking facial expressions – were working at computers, updating charts, noting arrivals and poison queues, and those were just the ones who were facing front.

The Slamming Door

The ones facing the other way were sitting down at a lower level, in chairs, each in a little alcove to give some illusion of privacy to the cancer patients facing them in the chairs on the opposite side. This was where appointments were made, but I found that out much later when Bryn was making them.

Misery Round One: Chemotherapy

It was hard to see what was going on past that point, due to the rock gardens, walls and plants just behind it. The walls were works of art, with cut-outs of morning-glory flowers in them. The flowers were in clusters here and there, like shadows set into them.

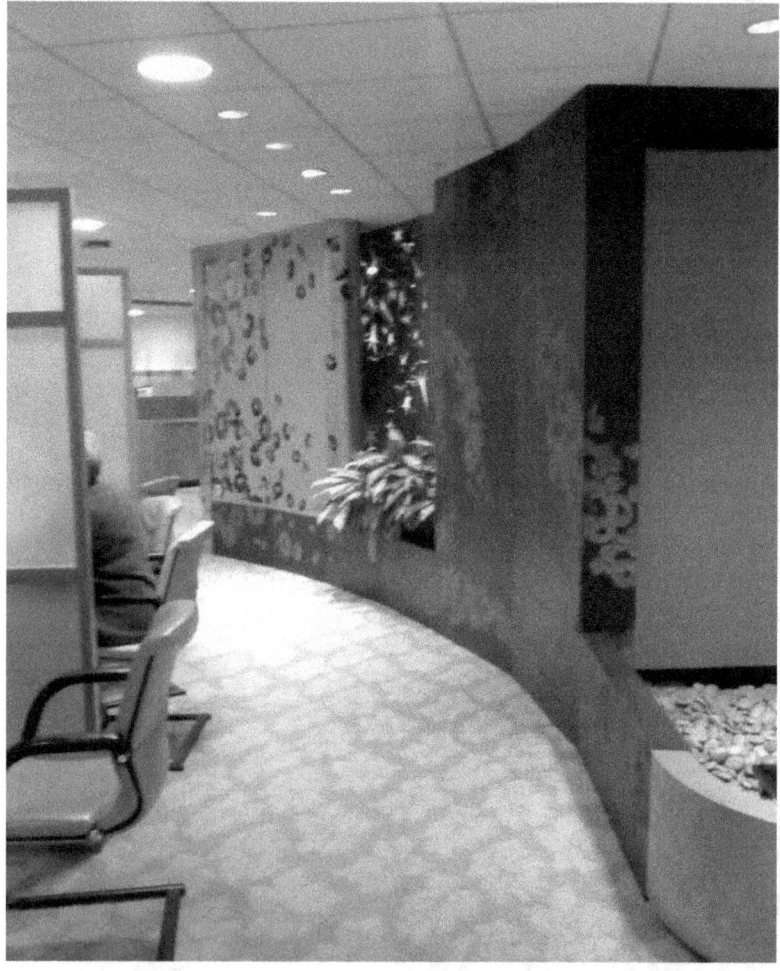

Bryn led me around like he had been there before, and that was when I guessed that he must have come here to meet Dr. Callahan with Albert. Her name was listed on the glass sign with a slew of other oncologist, under the sarcoma category.

The Slamming Door

We turned left from the wooden reception area, then right into what resembled a huge living room. Over to the far left was an area with complimentary coffee, tea, hot chocolate, and canned juices in the little refrigerator. We each tried some of the cappuccino; it was awful, but what else can one expect from a machine? The juices weren't very good either, but at least it was all included in the upcoming torture for the patients and torment for their accompanying relatives. Bryn and I immediately thought of looking elsewhere for beverages, but we made no further effort on this particular day. We were still getting familiar with this place.

Misery Round One: Chemotherapy

Turning to face the windows, we saw a small area with a large television set into the part of the wall that jutted out, sectioning off that part of the room from the rest. A set of doors was between the coffee area and that television area; they led to the chemotherapy alcoves.

With our backs to those doors, we faced the length of the room, with an expanse of windows to the left and the morning glories with the appointments desks behind them on the right. That long living room had sofas built in under the windows, more comfortable chairs grouped around them, and coffee tables everywhere. Copies of magazines – good ones, such as *Time* and *Newsweek* – and *The New York Times* littered the tables, along with people's beverages.

Bryn looked around, then made a beeline for the corner sofa all the way down at the other end. We settled in with our stuff and took out the reading materials that we had brought, including his copy of *The New York Times*. We noticed that the waiting room had lots of copies of that newspaper, though, probably left by other patients.

Before I settled in, I turned around and stared out the windows at the buildings nearby and the street below. We were facing 3rd Avenue. The really interesting building was the Lipstick Building diagonally across from us, on the northeast corner of the intersection. It was a series of ovals that gradually got smaller on the upper stories. The other buildings were just rectangular ones, not so memorable. I often found myself staring out the window at the Lipstick Building on future visits, just because its architecture was so unique and therefore interesting.

The Slamming Door

Not long after we sat down, a nurse came over to check on Bryn. The reason for doing that was to see where we were sitting so that she could find him when it was his turn to go in.

We had arrived in mid-morning, around 10:30 a.m., so Bryn guessed that his turn would come soon. He had no intention of arriving really early to do something unpleasant; now that he was retired, he was following his preference of going to bed at 2 a.m. and getting up at 10 a.m. – unless he had something to do. But if it was this awful, arriving at 8 a.m. would have made no sense, hence our leisurely arrival time. The time of a patient's arrival was entirely discretional, which made the process slightly easier to bear.

Misery Round One: Chemotherapy

No sense in hurrying up to be poisoned.

All too soon, it was his turn, and we swept up our stuff and followed the nurse.

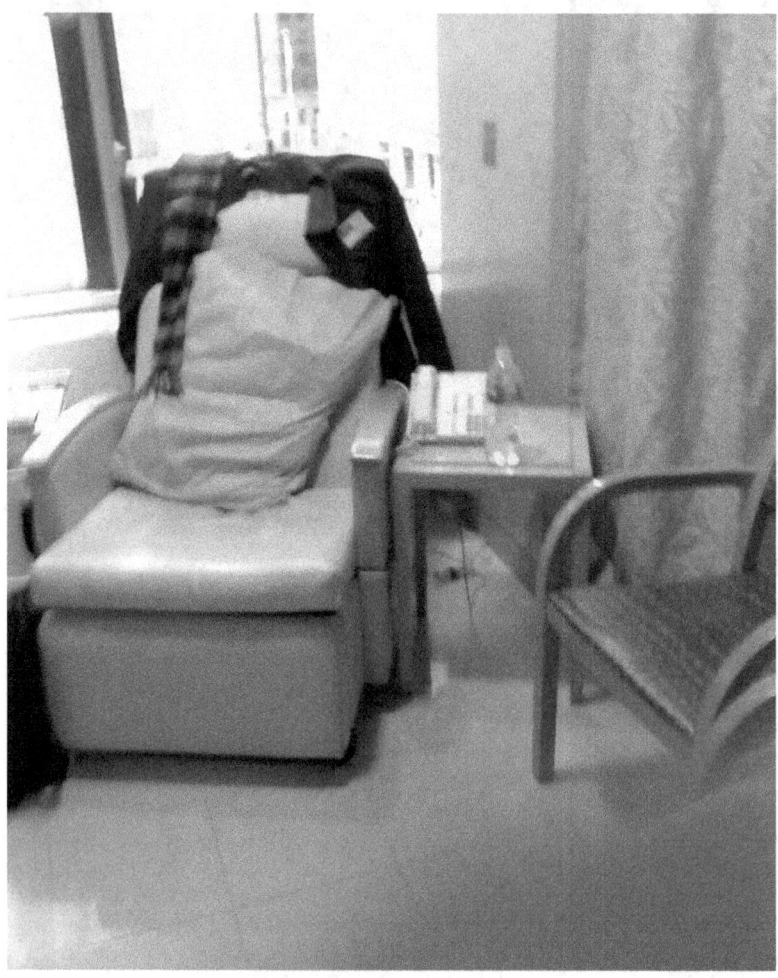

She led us to what we jokingly referred to as a corner suite. Really, it was just an alcove with windows on two sides, plants on the shelves, and the standard accoutrements of all the other alcoves: a television with a remote control for the patient, a computer with a rubber keyboard that could be rolled up (Matt Farrell used one in *Live Free or Die Hard*), a hospital version of a Lazy Boy chair with a little table next to it, a phone that was presumably for the patient's use, an IV stand on wheels, and a set of drawers loaded with medical supplies.

Bryn took off his jacket and put his black back-pack on the floor. He sat down and took out his newspaper. I noticed that a couple of upholstered armchairs were along the side by the curtains and settled myself and my stuff onto them. We waited to see what would happen next.

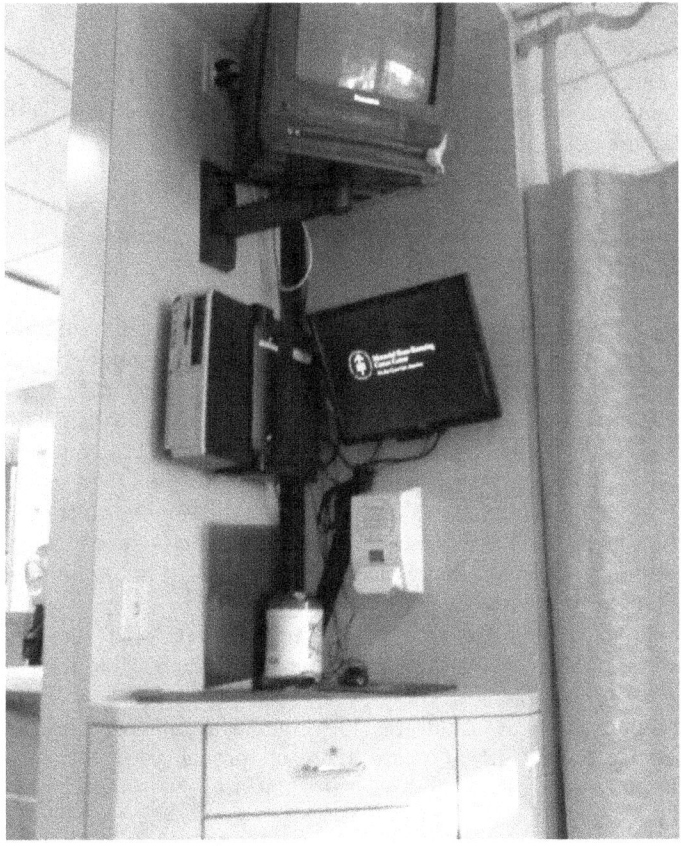

"They have to order the poison now," he told me, when I asked what the procedure was.

Soon it arrived; it was an IV bag of orange liquid. I looked glumly up at it. Here we go, I thought, that crap is going to drip into Bryn. An image of Dr. Callahan turning a fire hose of the stuff onto him sprung up in my mind.

Misery Round One: Chemotherapy

The nurses were very nice. None of them talked to Bryn as if he had suffered hearing loss due to age, or somehow morphed into a child, or had lost his considerable intelligence. They all wore blue scrubs and sneakers, and kept their hair tied up.

Bryn was poked with an IV needle, a tube was attached for the IV, and the little clear hose was connected to it. Soon the vile stuff was dripping into him. I didn't like it.

I got my book out.

Bryn checked out the television, and we both stared up at the screen as he scrolled through the channels. We learned what the choices were quickly enough, and we both liked world news and movie channels, so we anticipated and hour and a half of simultaneously being well-informed as the poison settled into his system.

He asked me for a drink of something – water, I think – and I found that there was another small fridge and a sink down the hall past more alcoves. The bathroom, a one-room one, was to the right of it. I came back with his drink and gave it to him.

At some point, a nurse took his order for lunch, which came with the treatment. Bryn could order off a menu from a nearby deli or diner, I forget which, and he invariably chose chicken soup and a sandwich. He didn't always eat much of it, preferring to wait and eat more at home. I had brought him some yoghurt from home after stuffing myself with breakfast minus the coffee, hoping to avoid needing the bathroom much.

After a while, the nurse changed the bag, and this time ran saline solution through it to Bryn; interesting. They were diluting the poisonous potion a bit. Finally, we were free to go. We left, out the same way as we had come in. A doorman hung around the front of the building, summoning cabs for patients as they came out.

We went home and I wondered when Bryn would start to feel awful. It was the first time he was getting chemotherapy, so I just didn't know what to expect.

He enlightened me; it wouldn't happen right away, and probably not until he had had at least 2 days' worth of poison, probably 3, and maybe not until the next day after it all. The real agony was supposedly going to come a few days after that.

Terrific; I got him tea and served his leftovers, and he calmly settled in front of his old television, which emitted a low buzzing sound, to watch MSNBC, CNN, and whatever else looked interesting. He was distracting himself by watching the economy melt down, which was a source of morbid fascination to him.

He seemed all right, so I went back to my room to read, feeling a bit lost and confused.

The Slamming Door

I didn't worry about that, though; there was no option but to watch and wait, and just be available when he needed something.

It was actually a fairly calm routine that first week, despite the fact that we were living a horror show in reality. I had been watching him since Tuesday, waiting for something to happen.

Nothing much happened those first few days, despite my expectations of instant misery.

Nothing, that is, until the morning after it all, on Friday.

Bryn woke me up a little after 10 o'clock, calling to me from just outside my door. I jumped up and opened it, and he was standing there. He said he woke up feeling weak and awful and wanted to go back to the hospital, so I hugged him and said that I would get dressed and find some breakfast at the hospital to save time.

That was what he was hoping to hear, so he let me go into the bathroom and get washed up. I rushed about getting dressed and putting on makeup, throwing my books together again for a return trip to what I thought was 53rd Street.

Bryn wasn't as fast as I expected about getting ready to go; I ended up with time to make both of our beds. I helped him pack his stuff in the back-pack, complete with his newspaper as we headed out. He didn't want anything to eat, which was no surprise.

I had my cell phone with me, of course, and he had his.

We got a cab and took off, and now I found out that we were heading for York Avenue and 68th Street, which was where the Urgent Care Center was. As the cab pulled up in front of the place, Bryn's cell phone rang. It was Cassie calling; he recognized her number.

But he was paying the fare and couldn't answer, so I did. I had never met her before, had never spoken to her before, and had only seen one profile photo of her on his bedroom wall. Cassie had long, wavy red hair and a complex about her appearance: in short, she labored under the delusion that she wasn't pretty.

She was pretty, but in any case, who cared right now; Bryn felt awful. I said hello, indentified myself, and explained why I was answering and that Bryn would get the phone in just a minute and I would talk to her until he did…all at once. I didn't rush the words, but it really was all at once.

Cassie's voice sounded rough, and I realized that it was a smoker's voice. She also sounded awfully tense.

Bryn took the phone a moment later and we staggered into the building together.

I wasn't paying much attention to his phone conversation; I was too busy grabbing the nearest wheelchair for him to collapse into and then

Misery Round One: Chemotherapy

going the way that the guard inside directed me; it was back past the escalators and into a little hallway with elevators.

But the reason for Cassie's call was that her husband Chip had just had a heart attack, and she was frantic and needed to tell Bryn, because that made her feel calmer. I could relate to that. Poor Cassie; Chip was in his eighties, retired, almost blind, and had just had cataract surgery a day or so earlier. Now this; it was one trauma and drama after another.

It wasn't until Bryn was settled for the day that he told me this.

For now, I drove the chair out of the elevators and down a series of halls that I would eventually know quite well. The halls went in a maze through the story that was just one level up from the street, and we passed a series of placards that detailed the entire history of radiology and the founding of the Sloan-Kettering Cancer Center, including one about the Nobel Prize winner Marie Curie, who discovered radium with her husband, Pierre. Their work had poisoned them. That's what this place had to offer: more damned poison.

Finally, I pulled up to the double doors that led into the Urgent Care Center and pressed a button to make them open. I rolled Bryn straight back there, not seeing the first desk on the right with the little waiting area, up to the one on the left in the center of a ring of alcoves. These alcoves didn't have Lazy Boy chairs – they had hospital beds.

"Fix him," I said to the first doctor or nurse who approached us. They all wore scrubs; I couldn't tell right away which they were.

Bryn was promptly settled into bed 19, around to the left, in a corner. His doctor was called, and the on-call interns took care of him all day. He was just having a bad reaction to the sudden introduction of poison to his system, which was what I had thought. He wasn't about to drop dead; he just felt awful.

I made sure he had whatever he wanted and then sat down to see what to do next.

He told me up front that he did not want to call anyone just yet, so I didn't do that either.

Soon, he told me to leave him there for a while, get myself breakfast, eat it, and then come back after that. He handed me some money for that. I took it and left. The nurses would handle things until I got back, at which point I would just sit there again.

A whiteboard hung on the wall as I left the area, just across from the nurses' desk, which was basically a huge island in the center of the alcoves. This entire area was windowless; it was in the center of the hospital floor.

Off I went, finding the cafeteria quickly enough, and eating a good breakfast complete with orange juice, though I forget what I had. The coffee looked lousy, so I wandered off to the gift shop, which was all the way back the other way, around the maze and at the top of the escalators near the door from the street.

That place had good coffee, and I found a 1937 birthday card for Bryn, which I bought and hid in my bag for later. There is a whole series of birthday cards that details everything of historical interest that happened in a particular year, and I was sure that Bryn would like it. His birthday wasn't until the 21st of November, but I like to shop early for events and holidays.

I looked around; the shop was cheerful, full of windows and natural light, and a little counter at one end with stools. Outside the shop, overlooking York Avenue on that same end of the floor, was a place with rows of upholstered chairs. I sat down and called Damon to tell him what was happening.

After that, I considered what to do next. Albert had been overtired from watching June and whatever else he had to do, so I suddenly made up my mind not to call him until at least noon. Let him sleep. If I called now, he would just rush to the hospital, and it wouldn't make any difference whether he arrived at 1 p.m. or right now; Bryn would still be in bed 19, with a nurse and an intern to work on him.

Albert and June had gone for Tuesday afternoon's chemotherapy, plus 2 appointments after that at 8:45a.m. on Wednesday and Thursday. I figured Albert could get more sleep before calling, because once I called, he would insist on coming to the hospital – and I guessed right. He brought June of course, because she couldn't be left alone at all, and took over.

After buying the coffee and card, I went back and sat with Bryn again. We read the news and our books and waited some more. Eventually, I went out and called Albert; there was no cell phone reception in the Urgent Care Center, which was no surprise at the center of a building.

Albert came right away of course, with June in tow. I was on the phone with Damon again when I saw them get off the escalator.

I caught up with them and led them to Bryn. June had her red Vera Bradley back-pack with her and kept looking in it. I hadn't yet caught on to the fact that she did this constantly; if something wasn't right with her handbag, she would fret and fret about it to Albert.

We settled around Bryn and I found a magazine that had been abandoned on the shelf next to the wall. Each cubicle contained a set of monitoring equipment over a hospital bed, plus at least two chairs, a shelf with drawers of medical supplies, a garbage can, and a button for the patient to push to summon a nurse. Bryn didn't bother pushing it much; he just asked me to go over to the nurses with his questions. It was only a couple of steps away.

Misery Round One: Chemotherapy

That magazine provided us a few minutes' entertainment. In the middle was a spread of pages containing an outline of the 48 contiguous states, white on black. A study had been conducted about each state, rating them on a list of characteristics, and Los Angeles came in very low for intelligence per person but very high for looks. Human migration patterns to the movie industry had to be the explanation, but no doubt that area had some geniuses and unattractive people living there. DNA can compete with migration, or compensate for it, or whatever.

When we weren't distracting ourselves with reading material, we kept checking on Bryn. He was trying to doze off in the afternoon, but a heart monitor above him kept beeping and waking him up. It was really obvious because his eyes popped open every time it went off. I offered to tell the nurses about it, but he said no, they needed that machine. Damn...no rest or relief for the miserable, I thought, staying in my seat.

I was careful not to show any sign of moving when he told me he didn't want something done; if I moved at the wrong moment, I thought he might worry that I was going to do something anyway after he said not to.

One thing he said not to do was to call either of his daughters. Albert and I both paid attention to that; Bryn had opened his eyes when he said it. He told us he didn't want them around all day; Dionne would have just talked nonstop incessantly in a loud voice about herbal teas and dire outcomes, and Berta would have gotten teary and thus driven her father crazy.

So I didn't call them. I couldn't have called Dionne if I had wanted to; I didn't have her cell phone number. As for Berta, she could find out later, after work. What was the point of telling her about this now, while she was expected to stay at the office for several more hours?

Eventually, I did call Elah, when it was later in the day and Bryn didn't object. At 4 p.m., after I had lunch with Albert and June, Berta called me. I updated her and she asked about coming there...so I said she should talk to Albert. I figured her uncle could be the one to flat out tell her not to come in. He did it nicely, and she seemed fine about it; she wouldn't come there. But he totally forgot to call Dionne, so there was trouble when she finally found out about this.

At some point that afternoon, I called Dr. Leonardi's office and explained that I was a friend of his, and asked them to take a message. I said that Bryn and Albert, the Otterman brothers, were both in the Urgent Care Center at bed 19, and that this would be a convenient chance to meet them both. All I was expecting was a brief visit of about 5 to 10 minutes.

The doctors studied on Bryn for a while, and ultimately concluded that they should worry that he might have pneumonia...or not...and they

The Slamming Door

decided to observe him all weekend because he had been off of his heart pills for a month. Wonderful, I thought – now he'll be stuck in a hospital room with noise, a roommate, and who knew what other unpleasantness.

Eventually, it was decided that I would take June home in a cab, and Alissa would meet us there. I did not know where we were going, so I was glad that Albert came outside with us, hailed a cab, and told the driver where to take us. From there, I figured I was good to go with the experience of taking care of my great-aunt Susan under my belt plus a cell phone; I could always call Alissa if anything went wrong.

But nothing did; she met us in front of the building, and we walked with her cousin Seth, who was visiting from Chicago on business and staying with June and Albert, to Zutto's, a Japanese restaurant nearby. It was an old favorite of Alissa's and June's. Its décor was rather dark, with nice wall hangings here and there.

Alissa got sushi with peanut and avocado, and did so every time I ever went out for Japanese food with her that year, which was fairly often. June got one of those also. I got something a bit more interesting, with fish in it as well as avocado, and Seth…got a doggie bag. Seth worked for a company that did $45,000-ads for physicians in publications like *The New York Times Magazine's Style* issue, and he showed me one. He sat down across from me and chatted a bit; he was in his early forties, liked to talk about careers and current events, and seemed nice enough, but something was bothering him.

At last we found out what it was, just when I began to wonder if my social skills were failing, though no odd quirky comments came to mind when I reviewed our conversation in my mind. The problem was his stomach! He had eaten some deli food for lunch, something from the Food Emporium, which was directly under Albert and June's place. He had thought that those asparagus spears were just grilled and wilted, but now he realized that they were…decaying.

Gross – and people call me spoiled and fussy sometimes! I rarely get sick because of food, however, so I won't change my habits. I'll just defend myself and keep on being fussy and careful. Poor Seth had to go home and moan in his bed. He was okay the next day.

The three of us remained, however, and we enjoyed some green tea ice cream, the first of many in Japanese restaurants with June. It became a happy-ending ritual with her and me and Alissa – and that was when I began to think of getting some to keep at Bryn's place for her.

After dinner, I took a cab home to Chelsea.

Dr. Leonardi had been in surgery all day, but he called me as I arrived home at 8 p.m. He had gotten my message at the end of the day and he was calling to invite me out for dinner on Monday evening. He also wanted to confirm Bryn's exact location before setting out to visit.

Misery Round One: Chemotherapy

After we hung up, he had gone to the Urgent Care Center, where Bryn and Albert were still waiting for Bryn to be admitted to the hospital. Albert told me on the phone later that he and Bryn were really pleased about that. Dr. Leonardi stayed just 5 minutes – the perfect length of time, Albert commented later – and both brothers really liked him and thought he was a "nice, caring doctor" – in other words, everything I had led them to expect.

Next, Bryn's land line phone rang. It was Dionne, and she had just found out that her father was in the hospital. She was off the wall, upset, and accusing me of preventing her from taking care of her father. "You've got to step back and let me take care of my father," she said.

Well…upset or not, I wasn't about to allow her to continue thinking that I was deliberately getting in her way. I told her that I didn't have her phone number, so I couldn't call her, and that Bryn had not wanted any calls made until later in the day, at which point Albert had arrived and I had left it all up to him. I concluded by telling her that 1. She should call her uncle to get the details about her father's condition and that 2. I wasn't trying to take possession of Bryn; if she wanted to come over and do something for him, I wouldn't stop her.

She calmed down and rang off politely enough; I found out later that when she got Albert on the phone, he had hung up on her. Meanwhile, Berta called me and I told her everything that had happened from when I woke up to our current phone conversation. She chatted happily enough for a while; at least she wasn't displeased with me.

So…Bryn's daughters were okay, just not thrilled, but then there was no reason to be; he was feeling too sick to stay home. Berta was the one who asked me to come and stay with him, and she was calm enough. Dionne, however, was off the wall, and Berta told me that she had lots of emotional problems including, but not limited to, abandonment issues.

Berta talked to me for a while, and told me all about why Dionne was the way she was, and said not to worry. Although I kept most of it to myself, I had visions of my relatives in Virginia during the time when my great-uncle was dying: Kumiko, Uncle Ron, and Julie and Gwenn. Uncle Ron was my maternal grandmother's older brother, a World War II flying ace and 3-star general in the U.S. Air Force, and he had 3 daughters, Gwenn and Julie by his first wife, and Kumiko, a Japanese woman whom he had adopted with his second wife, Aunt Winona (an Air Force colonel), whom I had known, when they were stationed in Japan after the war.

What I shared with Berta was that I saw some parallels: Kumiko/Clarisse; Julie/Dionne; Gwenn/Berta. I didn't tell her how nasty things had gotten, only that there had been some similar remarks from Julie to Kumiko about the caregiver (Kumiko) doing too much, just as

The Slamming Door

Dionne had accused me of doing. Well, we were not clones of them, but I told Berta that I saw a similarity here, including the fact that I was just doing what Bryn had told me to do. Berta appreciated the analogy but wasn't too worried about Dionne – and I figured that it wouldn't be quite like that situation anyway – they were other people. It all seemed fine here.

No one was dying just yet, and Bryn would come home and have more food and visits.

A little while later, I got to talk to Bryn again, and found out that he had a room all to himself. His appetite was gone, but he had no aches, no diarrhea or significant nausea, and he was told that his appetite would be back soon. Meanwhile, the hospital would keep him hydrated and okay until it returned. His appetite had waned on Wednesday evening, the second day of 3 days of 90-minutes worth of chemotherapy. The planned pattern was this: 3 days of chemotherapy, then 2 weeks off from it, times 3. After that, the doctor would look at the test results to see what it accomplished. The expectation for now was that during the 2-week breaks, he should be able to eat again and maybe go out to a movie.

Next, Bryn told me the full story about poor Cassie. She had had no idea what we were doing. Her husband Chip had cataract surgery yesterday (the other eye had never functioned, so he just got his sight back after years of near total blindness!). She thought he had a collapsed lung, and had rushed him to the hospital. It turned out that he had a heart attack instead, so he was back at the hospital. It sounded as though he would get over that – but this day had just been one uproar after another for her.

I told him that I hadn't heard her voice before that day, and that it had sounded harsh and raspy. He said that was because she smoked like a furnace. So I had guessed correctly about that. She was a social worker who also mentored teenage girls with horses in her free time. She ate a healthy vegetarian diet and cancelled it out by smoking...oh, well...

After we rang off, I settled in for the night with the movies and books, called Damon again, and hoped to find out more about Bryn the next day. What I wanted to know was: was the food any good, was he comfortable and able to get any sleep, and so on.

The next day, I spoke to Albert first, because he called me. He told me not to call until later in the afternoon because Bryn wasn't getting enough sleep, so I waited.

Albert was writing a book, or trying to, and had not been able to transcribe some interviews for the final chapter; they were all recorded. He planned to pay me to do that – and I can type fast. It never happened because he couldn't find the tapes, but it was a nice idea. He

Misery Round One: Chemotherapy

just needed them as Word files, and then he thought he could assemble the book while June was at that elderly day care place.

I would also soon do some work for Elah – mindless Internet stuff – and she was going to pay me to clean her apartment a bit, the kitchen mostly. Elah was short, a heavy smoker, tired, and overextended, so I would make a brief project of this while staying near Bryn. I started the cleaning job on Sunday afternoon, before Bryn came home.

The Internet work was for a real estate company that posted its listings over and over again several times a day. She was looking for someone else to do some of it so that she wouldn't be a prisoner to the work. The problem was that unless another person was found to help, she could barely function outside of that job, and that was no way to live.

I ended up trying it for a few weeks, but ultimately the company found someone else to fill in for Elah. As far as I could tell, I did what they wanted the way that they wanted me to, but I wasn't going to do it forever, because I wasn't going to live in the area after Bryn didn't need me anymore. No one ever told me anything else about it, so I have no option but to guess as to why it turned out this way. The interview had been weird; they had taken one look at my CV and pronounced me overqualified – as if there were an issue to me. I was after a little extra cash, not a career in online postings. But I really don't care; not spending more time doing that was not exactly something to get upset about.

Elah originally intended to have me clean her entire apartment, which was very dusty, but in the end she just had me scour her kitchen. For what turned out to be a mere forty dollars of pay (she really didn't have much money, so I didn't object), I scrubbed the kitchen sink, stove, walls, tall shelf with all of the machines on it, and the blue stained-glass lamp that hung over the table. It was utterly filthy in there from years of Rudy cooking and no one really thoroughly cleaning up, and I used up all of their steel wool pads to do it.

I definitely earned that money and then some. Cleaning has always seemed like fun to me, especially when I can really see the dirt. It just feels satisfying to make a noticeable difference. Hilda commented about how good it looked after the fact, too. Sometime later, I wondered why that kid wasn't doing the cleaning; I would have when I was a kid. I had chores, and the only ones I noticed Hilda doing were at Bryn's place, but I didn't dwell on that.

When it was later in the afternoon, I got a chance to talk to Bryn.

The news about the food was impressive: a chef worked for the hospital, and he would make anything a patient wanted. Each order was placed individually, like a home rather than a restaurant. Bryn ordered a chicken scaloppini dish and even though he couldn't eat more than half of it, he thought it was really good.

The Slamming Door

He surprised me by saying that he didn't want any visitors, it was so relaxing. He also said that he had called Berta and Albert and everyone else to tell them the same thing, so that they would know that this request came straight from him.

Huh...so I was home alone for the weekend, and he was perfectly satisfied with his situation; fine. I repainted my toenails a dark raspberry pink that afternoon, and then went to meet Albert, June and Alissa in TriBeCa. We went out for Chinese food and to see the new *W.* movie starring Josh Brolin. It was very good. The only problem was that Bryn was missing it; he had been interested in that one.

When I arrived, Seth was there and feeling much better. He told me that it was just food poisoning, and it was all over now. Good. I remember taking off my socks and looking at my pedicure and being upset that I would have to do part of it over again later (but I got it right). Seth had started to tease me, asking me so many silly questions that I had turned my gaze upon him and asked just as many back: Did he have a girlfriend? Yes. Did she have painted toenails? Yes. Then didn't he realize that such things would be thought of? That shut him up. He wasn't malicious, though. He had other plans for the evening, and left before we went out.

We walked to the restaurant, south on Greenwich Street and then west on Chambers, and when I looked at my Manhattan street map, I realized that we were right next to Battery Park City, and that I was looking at a huge outdoor sports arena that I had seen on *CSI:NY*. The place was all lit up with huge spotlights on a grassy field; I didn't pay attention to what sport the people on it were playing. The restaurant was down a narrow walkway right across from it, and the movie was just a few steps away from that.

While I was out with them, I found out that Dionne's husband, Albert Hornsby, was missing. (For purposes of avoiding confusion, I shall refer to him as The Hornsby from this point on.) The Hornsby had gone on one of his many overnight hunting camping trips with his pet horse, whom he had had for years. He almost always went alone, and he had done so this time. He was due back Friday evening, and hadn't returned, so Dionne was scared.

When we heard that, we immediately forgave her for acting so wild the previous evening.

We were a bit worried too; he could have been stuck down a ravine with a broken leg, with his horse staring over it at him, unable to help. Cell phone signals were nonexistent where he went, so Dionne was forced to just wait it out.

The Hornsby seemed like a difficult person to be married to.

A day or so later, it turned out that he was fine.

Misery Round One: Chemotherapy

The jerk swore up and down that he had told her he would be gone for a full week on this particular hunting excursion, not just a few days.

And people think that Damon is difficult to be married to!

I had a fun evening with Albert, June and Alissa. We came back, saw Tina Fey doing her parody of Sarah Palin on *Saturday Night Live!*, and laughed when it ended with Palin herself interrupting only to step in and shout "Live from New York, it's Saturday night!" I went home shortly after that.

The next day I started cleaning Elah's kitchen – Rudy's, really, since he did almost all of the cooking in that family – and enjoyed hearing Elah say that Rudy was a nice person to married to when it came to food because: 1. He cooked almost everything and 2. If she cooked and it didn't come out right, he would say nothing and just fix it, never criticizing her efforts. That sounded about right for a professional chef, and I had heard similar stories on TV from other women whose husbands were professional chefs.

Bryn came home the next day – with Albert – and I began to wonder whether I would soon be doing any serious work as a caregiver. That seems hilarious to me now.

He settled into his chair, I made coffee for him, and went across the hall to finish the cleaning job in Elah's kitchen. When I came back, I was satisfied except for the inside of the fridge, but Elah didn't care about that. It turned out that she didn't care so much about having me clean the rest of the apartment, or maybe she just didn't have the money for all that. She paid me and that was that.

Now I was back with Bryn again, so I got cleaned up and prepared to hang out with him and watch him without being too obvious about it. It was still very warm in Manhattan, and I was comfortable in shorts and a tee shirt with the windows open. Bryn still had his screens in, too.

He lasted one more night without much trouble, and then it hit.

When it did, his appetite took a hiatus.

My subconscious responded by creating an image of Bryn's appetite personified – a little mischievous-looking cartoon character in a tee shirt labeled "Bryn's Appetite" with pointy teeth and ears and a mischievous grin scampering out the door, cackling… It had annoying little pattering footsteps, and was about a foot tall.

I was a bit surprised that Bryn didn't feel the urge to throw up during that first round of medically induced torture. But he could barely eat his meals. I had expected that. It lasted for a few days, and then he started to eat again. He lost some weight, but not enough for new clothes.

Instead, he just couldn't eat much. His energy was nil, and he sat listlessly in his chair watching the news, reading, and wanting to sleep. I was glad he wasn't throwing up, but his hair did start to disappear. When enough of it fell away, he went out alone and had it buzzed off.

It was during this first round of misery that Bryn began to want oatmeal for breakfast, and I decided that I might as well join him with that. I would make a double batch for us whenever he felt up to eating it, and when I started, it seemed like a good idea to try slipping in as many healthy extras to the mixture as possible.

So, I added cinnamon, which Damon told me is great for preventing and even fighting cancer. It certainly tastes good, at least to me and to most people. Not to Bryn; this was when I found out that the Ottermans don't like cinnamon. Not Albert, not Bryn, not Berta…I didn't check on Alissa, but those were all of the Ottermans I could reasonably check on. Wow – I had never met anyone who didn't like that spice before.

Okay, so I stopped adding cinnamon. I'll be damned if I'll even try to force anyone to eat anything that they don't like. My mother never did it to me, and she never let my father enforce an "eat what's served or go hungry" policy, which is how his Depression-era parents had run his childhood. I was so lucky on that count that my mother was in charge of my food. I only had to take sincere tastes of everything to see what I really thought of each item, and that was that.

Next, I attempted to get Bryn to eat golden raisins and dried cranberries mixed into the oatmeal. That met with more success; I would mix a lot of them into the whole batch at first, because I like a lot of berries. It tasted delicious to me, but then no one had messed with my sense of taste.

I waited and watched to see how that would go over, ready to adjust the oatmeal if it didn't taste as enticing to Bryn as it did to me. His system was soon full of chemicals after all, so his taste buds were about to send him lots of infuriating and distressing false information, and he would trapped into acting on that information by either puking or giving up on food or switching to a very small list of things.

Sure enough, he told me that I kept surprising him, and that he didn't want so many berries in his oatmeal, just some, perhaps 5 or 6…a really small handful, he specified. After that, I added the berries after the whole batch was cooked and in the two Williams-Sonoma bowls, a lot for me and a small amount for him. That worked for him.

So that took care of his breakfast each day.

Bryn didn't want lunch per se; a snack in the afternoon of Ensure drinks and apples were all that he wanted. I could understand that; I almost never eat lunch myself (and my weight and nutrition are fine that way). With this illness, its treatments, and its effects, it was all he could do to eat and retain breakfast, afternoon calorie drinks, and dinner.

Misery Round One: Chemotherapy

He wouldn't accept any more spicy ImmuneACCORD drinks at this point, so I turned to the Ensure bottles. I would pour a mug full of the contents of one little bottle, alternating between the strawberry and vanilla ones. He didn't mind them, but they felt really filling to him.

The most memorable moment over those drinks came one evening when Berta was on her way out of the apartment. She paused at the door to say to me, as if giving me marching orders, "He should be drinking 4 Ensure a day."

Bryn and I looked at each other as if to say that this wasn't realistic; the most he could manage was 2 before he just got too full.

I replied, "If he drinks all that, he won't have room for his food – they're really filling."

That didn't satisfy her, so she went on about the doctor wanting to keep his weight up. It was weird, because he was standing right there.

To put an end to the conversation, and because Bryn was looking trapped and anxious, I said to her, "Berta, I am not going to torture your father with food."

With that, she let the matter drop, said good-night to us, and left.

She wasn't mad at me; she just wanted him to live longer.

As for me, I didn't want him to dread me. I was the one who was going to be there with him all the time, presenting food and drink. The last thing I wanted was for him to think that I was going to push it on him or bully him in any way, and I told him so once we were alone.

He looked relaxed when he heard that. Good.

But that left other meals; dinner was another story. He bravely forced himself to try to eat, but at first it was just too gross. The chemicals had so messed with his taste buds that it was all awful. He still was able to eat chicken soup with matzo balls, but everything else was a trial.

Rudy tried to help by making several things that he knew that Bryn liked: cooked beets, beef stew, meatballs in tomato sauce, cole slaw, and so on. It didn't work. I felt bad when the food went to waste, but that was par for the course with this illness.

Eventually, things calmed down and Bryn began to eat again though. He ate Rudy's food, he ate take-out food, and he ate some of what I cooked. It felt like the eye in a hurricane. I knew that after a brief period of lovely normalcy, the storm would be back with a vengeance.

Chapter 14

Dr. Leonardi Invites Me Out

For the past few weeks since I had arrived at Bryn's place, my mother had been e-mailing me about contacting Dr. Leonardi, her former boss, for a visit.

Dr. Leonardi was a family friend now. My mother had been his office nurse since my last year of college, just after she had completed her bachelor's degree at the University of Connecticut. She was already a fully qualified nurse by then, but she had wanted to finish her bachelor's degree before her daughter did, and she achieved that.

Then she got a job at Hartford Hospital's office building, working with Vance P. Leonardi, M.D., a Georgetown University-educated prostate cancer surgeon and urologist. He was very nice to work for, and she learned a lot. She also decided to take another licensing exam, one for a Certified Urology Registered Nurse (C.U.R.N.), and passed it.

For over 20 years, they worked together. Then Leonardi left for the Memorial Sloan-Kettering Cancer Center (M.S.K.C.C.) in Manhattan. My mother still had her job, but now she was a telephone triage nurse, directing patients in dire distress to immediate help.

Sloan-Kettering had been wooing Leonardi for quite some time, and he was getting bored in Hartford. It was time for a greater challenge. Of his 4 children, 3 were out of high school. The fourth, his only son, was in 9th grade; I had just seen him when we had picked apples at his house. The kid said that his local public high school offered Chinese, which intrigued me, because when I was a teenager, the choices were French, Spanish, and Latin almost everywhere.

Kaitlyn, Dr. Leonardi's wife, did not mind having her husband take the train to Manhattan every Sunday evening and return on Friday evenings. If one of her older daughters were available to watch her son, she would go to Manhattan to be with him. I supposed that soon the apartment he had found would be nicely furnished under that schedule. I liked Kaitlyn; she was a lovely, quiet, thin woman with long sandy, wavy hair and glasses. It was fun to talk with her. She and husband had attended my wedding, too.

After exchanging a couple of e-mails, I found myself invited to meet Leonardi at his office building at 6:30 p.m. on the Monday evening following Bryn's first 3-day stint of chemotherapy drips, October 20th.

Bryn was starting to feel the misery of it, quietly disinterested in food but still with a full head of hair. He just sat very still in his Lazy Boy chair in front of the television with news shows droning on and on, *The New York Times* in front of him, and looking a bit listless. I took that

Dr. Leonardi Invites Me Out

to mean that he was uncomfortable, but I really wasn't sure what to do for him. Asking too many questions just stressed him out, so I was left looking in on him from the hall, worried.

Dionne came over to sit with him in front of the TV that evening, arriving as it was time for me to go out. I was glad she came over for 2 reasons: 1. She had been upset the previous Friday when she felt left out of everything, so having her father to herself for a few hours would make her feel better; 2. She might just be able to get some food into him. I would find out what and how she did later and repeat her procedure, and then she could take credit for the idea.

I buzzed her into both doors at 5:30 p.m. She had keys, but didn't like to use them; they stuck in the door a bit. The day I had arrived, Berta had had even worse trouble, and her key had wound up broken off and jammed into the inner door's keyhole. The building had lots of bad keyhole stories, so this wasn't surprising.

Off I went with my street map of Manhattan, via subway, getting out at Lexington Avenue and 68th Street. Leonardi's office was directly east, at 2nd Avenue. I pulled out my pocket watch and checked the time; it was only 2 blocks away and I was a half-hour early. Now what? I ducked into a Coldwater Creek store and walked around, right on the same intersection as the subway exit. I found a sleeveless periwinkle blue shirt with a lacy edge on the bottom for $6.99 on the sale rack, which killed about 20 minutes.

Next, I headed east, hoping that I would be able to meet up with Dr. Leonardi without searching the building or finding that I was locked out while he stood inside, wondering where I was. Briskly walking east, I soon reached his tall, white building.

I had been there the Friday before, hoping to say hello, when Bryn had told me not to hang around all day, to go take a walk around the area in the nice weather. It was still fabulous out; sunny but not humid, breezy, and pleasant. I was even overheated from walking fast.

Dr. Leonardi's building was modern inside, beautifully updated, and inside the lobby was a balcony that overlooked a huge waiting room – which he shared with the other urologists in his building. His office was on an upper floor, I found out later.

As I approached, I realized that I had no reason to worry; there he was, standing just outside, chatting with another doctor. I assumed that the other tall, thin man with glasses was a doctor and Leonardi's colleague.

Funny; 2 tall, thin, bespectacled men, both oncologists who looked the part…but then, I knew where I was going and who I was meeting.

Dr. Leonardi saw me and smiled, greeted me, and introduced me to his colleague. Yes, it was another MSKCC doctor, one Jerry Feingold,

The Slamming Door

M.D., a specialist in testicular cancer, the one who had begged and begged Leonardi to leave Hartford Hospital and move to New York.

It was Feingold who suggested the restaurant, a tiny place called ZaZa's that Bryn seemed to vaguely remember. Feingold walked with us part of the way, then took off on his own, probably to go home for the night. But while he was with us, we talked about Bryn and how he had gotten sick with bone cancer.

I was sure that these doctors would be able to tell me something useful, because Bryn's problems had started with prostate cancer, and both of them worked with that problem, Leonardi more than Feingold. Sure enough, I learned a lot, and later shared it with Albert...and Bryn.

After describing the radioactive seed treatment that Bryn had gotten in 2005, complete with the story of becoming a radioactive hot spot at Rockefeller Plaza, the two oncologists seemed appalled. They both spoke disparagingly of it. I knew that Dr. Leonardi was the leading prostate cancer physician in the country, and now he told me that the radioactive seed treatment was a death sentence for Bryn, that it had killed him (in advance of his actual death), and that it had long since fallen into disfavor. Dr. Feingold backed him up vigorously.

In fact, Leonardi was amazed to hear that the radioactive seeds had been used.

Now I was really upset. Bryn's impending death suddenly sounded preventable.

He could have been alive for several more years with a chronic condition, albeit a creepy and disgusting one – cancer – but not imminently doomed, as he was now. Damnit! I thought, he could have lived to be 80 years old, just as he had said he wanted to, teaching at the Henry George School. That had been his retirement fantasy, now ruined.

We still had a couple more blocks to walk together, with Dr. Feingold, so I asked him some questions about his field. I told him that I knew of a guy in my graduating college class who, shortly thereafter, in his early twenties, had gotten testicular cancer and survived. I hadn't known him well, only that he was generally thought of as a very nice guy. My question was, how do you preserve a patient's quality of life without castrating the poor guy? Dr. Feingold said that in most cases, one testicle is okay and can be left.

Huh. I knew perfectly well that this meant that in the remaining cases, guys would end up 100 percent castrated. Damnit...that was for rapists, not nice guys! It's a punishment. It further backed up my statement at the beginning of this tale of woe that only nice people get cancer.

It also warned me that I could not spend much of my life hanging around with cancer patients and oncologists if I hoped to avoid being

Dr. Leonardi Invites Me Out

hopelessly angry and depressed. For Bryn, I would do it, but after that, I wanted a change of scene. The problem was that I don't like changes of scene – I wanted Bryn to live on and on, provided that he could enjoy life, because then there would be no change.

Berta was a wreck over all this, though she was able to act like a party girl most of the time, cheerful and giggly. Her father was her favorite parent, not that anyone had any trouble seeing why that was, and she wanted him to live forever. He wouldn't, and there was no way we could extend his life at this point, yet we had no idea how long he would live. The only thing I understood was that we could not make him last longer. He was an adult who had a right to choose his food until the end, regardless of the wishes of others. It was his life…and death.

I resigned myself to keeping him comfortable on his own terms as much as I could.

But for now, it was still early in the game. Bryn would easily last through the course of poison that his doctor had planned for him, so as imminent as death seemed, it wasn't immediate. We had time to contemplate it and time to spend with Bryn, and to enjoy his company.

I turned my attention back to Dr. Leonardi before his exchange about work and schedules with Feingold ended. My reverie wasn't noticeable to the two men as a result. Soon we were saying good-bye to the other doctor as he gestured at the now visible front door of the Italian restaurant. The restaurant was a tiny place, and the doors were wide open thanks to the lovely warm weather. It was a bit dark, but we sat in the window, with Leonardi facing into the place.

ZaZa's was Italian, and offered handmade pasta. We ate: one bowl each of asparagus soup with a potato base; a shared order of Portobello mushrooms with roasted tomatoes and salad greens; pasta with porcini mushrooms and truffle cream sauce (me); pasta with tomato and shrimp sauce (Leonardi); Merlot wine (me); some type of white wine, possibly Pinot Grigio (Leonardi); cappuccino and vanilla ice cream rolled in cocoa powder and hazelnuts (me); decaf espresso (Leonardi). The pasta was shaped like fettuccini but wider and flatter. Its name was not listed in the menu, and it seemed to be the only shape offered unless one ordered the ravioli.

Leonardi was a great listener, one who always acted like he was in absolutely no hurry no matter how much work was on his schedule and yet to be done. He had questions, and I answered them all. I told him how Damon and I were doing with our work, how it was to stay with Bryn and how he was doing thus far, and then started asking him some questions of my own. It was fun.

Then it was his turn. Dr. Leonardi answered my questions about his children's education, and his travel experiences. He hadn't traveled

The Slamming Door

much, but I could tell that his trips to China, France and Italy were educational and that he enjoyed them. He said that if he went traveling again, he would go back to Europe – South America didn't hold much interest for him, and he had had enough of China. He went all over it for 2 weeks, and saw quite a lot.

He also told me that the hospital had found his apartment for him, and that thus far, it hardly had any furniture in it. He didn't have any time to do anything about it, either. He had ordered some cheap, assembly-required things from IKEA and put them together so that he would have a bed to sleep in and a futon to sit on with the TV, but other than that, he spent little time in the place. It was off to the gym for a workout and a shower, then on the office each day.

I asked him about his kids. He said that having a boy was a new experience for him and his wife after having 3 daughters, because Vance Jr. allowed them to ask maybe three direct questions in each conversation before telling them to stop asking him questions. The girls always wanted to chat. Bryn later told me that that was just normal boy behavior. Leonardi and his wife seemed to realize that and would just stop asking questions when the kid demanded that they do that. As for his daughters, the third one was an undergraduate at Yale, the second was in medical school in Manhattan, while meant that he could see her sometimes during the week, and the oldest, the one who was fluent in Chinese and Mongolian, was between jobs now.

When at last the visit was over, we went our separate ways, Leonardi turning north and me west and then on south down Madison Avenue a ways. I didn't want to take the 6 line home; it had been scary at one point, with a sharp drop close by as I came out of the tunnels. I was going to the familiar area of Rockefeller Plaza to catch the E line home, viewing the upscale shop displays along the way.

When I got back to the apartment, Dionne was gone, but so was an apple. Dionne had sat next to Bryn in front of the TV and handed him slice after slice of the apple, making it seem like little bits to conquer rather than a whole apple; clever. The next day, Berta told me that she had also visited for a couple of hours, and that her father had eaten most of an apple, plus some beet soup that Dionne had made and brought over. Terrific! Bryn's appetite was on its way back, then. She added that Alissa had come by, too.

Still, it was shaky for the rest of the week, and I quickly found out that the smell of cooking made him nauseous. The only thing he could bear to smell was chicken soup, so I ended up getting it for him at the diner – still the old Greeks that he was used to – or letting Albert do that, if he was on his way over.

Dr. Leonardi Invites Me Out

My dinners that week were take-out food, furtively carried into my room and eaten in solitary confinement in front of the television. I carefully toted the empty containers to the kitchen and washed up before going near Bryn, so that he wouldn't smell the $5 Sikh food, or the bagel with smoked salmon. These meals came from places nearby, around the block.

The next week, when he felt a bit better, he complained of being constipated, bored with his food, and hungry. He added that he wanted something to eat that would help with all of that at once. I didn't realize that the drugs he was on would soon make eating spicy food impossible, but that hadn't happened yet anyway.

So I suggested the Sikh food, which he knew was right around the corner but had never tried. "$5 for enough food for both of us? Good; go get us some of that," he agreed. Off I went with five bucks, where I asked the nice elderly Sikh man in the cobalt blue turban to please microwave the lot, because we had no such oven. He smiled and did it.

We had a huge Styrofoam container of basmati rice topped with spicy spinach, spiced dal, and spiced chick peas. I also spent a dollar on the chai tea, just because it was so good, and happily toted it out. All of the other people in there were Indian males, but they smiled happily at me when I said, "I love your food."

I dished the food out into Bryn's wide, low bowls, old ones with red, blue and yellow tulips that Cassie had given him ages ago. We ate together in his room, which was standard for us unless I had a TV show,

The Slamming Door

or unless I had to keep food smells from reaching him. It felt nice to be sitting with him over a meal again.

He ate his share up – all of it.

So did I, but that wasn't remarkable.

A few minutes later, he went in and out of the bathroom, spending a lot less time in there than he normally did. He didn't bother to bring a newspaper with him, either.

Then he sat back in his chair and did something hilarious.

He looked skyward, stuck his tongue out in a small, straight stick, and said, "That cleaned me out!" and then laughed.

So it had worked. Spice, garlic, yoghurt – those are magic foods.

Sadly, cancer treatments turn one of those charms into torture.

Soon Bryn was using yoghurt to stay comfortable, though he had eaten Fage brand Greek yoghurt for years…just not regularly enough. I don't think he liked garlic much.

When I had returned from my visit with Dr. Leonardi, I had told him about that conversation about radioactive seeds.

"But that's how you get rid of the prostate cancer," he had protested.

The problem with that method of treatment was that it stayed in his system forever after and grew another kind of cancer – a worse kind. It meant that there was currently no way to win. I realized that the operative words with Bryn were "get rid of" – he hadn't wanted to manage cancer, he wanted that creepy parasite GONE from his system. I can't blame him for that; he saw bladder cancer destroy his nice mother. Margery had died in 1981, when Berta was 11.

I asked Bryn who this doctor was who had put those seeds into him – what was his name. He told me it was Darren Chacha. I listened, but I was so angry that I forgot and had to ask him again a few months later. Then I went to the computer and looked him up so that I wouldn't forget again, then made a Word file about him. He was a dark-haired man with a tie and lab coat, going bald a bit in the front, and he looked smug and well-off from his evil work. I hated him.

"He killed you," I said to Bryn when he first told me the guy's name. "Just because you will be alive for a while longer, that doesn't change the fact that he killed you."

Bryn nodded in agreement, and that was all that we said about that.

There was nothing else to add to it.

The next summer, in 2009, while Bryn was still alive, a doctor in Virginia who treated war veterans actually got called before the U.S. Senate to explain his irresponsible use of this same treatment…because he screwed it up and missed the target.

There was just no way to sell this idea any more. I saw the surgeon on television, getting interrogated by a bunch of male U.S. Senators, and

Dr. Leonardi Invites Me Out

they gave him a tense grilling, then banned him practicing medicine. Good; men with the power to stop him, horrified by his methods. If more women in the Senate could do the same thing to gynecology-oncologists, that would also do some good, though it seemed like a more remote possibility. Men usually get their problems addressed first.

The day after I got back from eating with Dr. Leonardi, I wrote to my mother to tell her about the visit, and in enough detail so that she would feel that I had told her enough to make it interesting. At last, she would be satisfied about this; she had asked me about it over and over until I had actually gone out on a visit with him.

That night I assembled Bryn's shower safety seat, which had sat in its box for a month. He asked me to do it, but wasn't really sure that it would be necessary yet. I knew that the idea was to have stuff ready before it was needed, not realize that it was needed and then rush to get it ready.

We went on like this for a couple of weeks, with Bryn getting over the worst of the effects of the chemotherapy and starting to see his friends again, before the boiler died.

The phone proved to be a challenge for me.

Phones have always stressed me out.

Bryn had so many friends that his just kept on ringing whenever he went out.

It drove me to distraction and tears after a few calls, which just kept coming.

I pulled the plug on it and breathed an immense sigh of relief.

He had a cell phone; if people really wanted to reach him, they could, unless he didn't want to be reached.

I had a cell phone; if Bryn needed to reach me, he would call.

Either way, pulling the plug on the land line cut down on the constant ringing; I couldn't relax and concentrate on anything with the constant interruptions.

I had to do work – editing – for Damon and for my own pay, and I couldn't focus on it with that obnoxious contraption constantly coming to life, demanding that I either try to tune it out (impossible!) or stop working, get up, and go into Bryn's room to answer it, talk nicely with someone, and write the down a message after answering a million tedious questions as to his whereabouts while wondering whether or not he even wanted me to disclose anything.

Add to all that the general societal expectation that a woman answering a phone will have a congenial tone in her voice that invites yet more chatter and natter, and I had a problem. I don't have that tone, and I don't ever wish to. I use polite enough words, but I don't sound inviting. I just want to get off the phone as fast as possible, unless I feel invited to chat.

Occasionally, if I knew something about the caller, I would chat a bit.

Otherwise, I wouldn't.

This is just another classic sign that I am an Aspie – we don't do phones well.

If Bryn left instructions not to pull the plug on his phone, I wouldn't, but he quickly found out – because I told him about this anxiety – that I hated the constant ringing. He didn't really need all those calls answered, and the land line had a recording service.

Then he started copying my phone management methods, which surprised and amused me. The reason was that he wanted to sleep in the mornings, just as I did, and people who didn't want to do that would call him every morning all morning.

What I would do was, I would shut off my cell phone late at night and charge it up, and then pull the plug on the charger until the next night, still leaving the cell phone turned off. Why? They get worn out if left on constantly, and so does the owner of the phone. I wanted to sleep.

Bryn listened to my method late one night when he complained about his phone waking him up in the morning, and promptly pulled his own plug and shut off his own cell phone. The next morning, he woke feeling wonderfully well-rested.

It was great for him, but when we turned on our phones again around noon, we each found several nervous messages from Albert and one from Berta. They had to get used to this, it seemed. We called them back and explained, and Albert immediately relaxed about it; he was run-down from taking care of June, so he understood perfectly. I don't know exactly how Berta felt about it, but she made no complaint once she knew what was going on.

Poor Albert; he would try to fall asleep, but June would keep him up until the middle of the night, constantly paying attention to her. She couldn't remember what time it was. Albert had made the error, Bryn informed me, of taking June out for breakfast across the street a couple of times, so now she would get up at 4:30 a.m., get dressed, and say she was going out for coffee and croissants. Then Albert had an awful time persuading her that the place was still closed and to please go back to bed. She would just sit there, looking at him, unable to settle back to sleep.

No wonder he had the urge to call his brother and chat.

And Bryn was by nature a night owl, just like me.

At least we were both the same in our general habits.

Dr. Leonardi Invites Me Out

The only difference was that Bryn was vastly more sociable than I was. I was stuck with social anxiety, especially over the telephone, plus I hated noise and interruptions. Part of it stemmed from the fact that I was born without an innate ability to read subtle nonverbal cues, so my mother had relentlessly coached me in social and telephone etiquette. I'm glad she did it, but she never stopped. She still did it, often ruining my punch lines, unable to tell that I had reached the punch line of a story, and thus not allowing me a congratulatory moment from the listeners.

It was worse with phone calls. She would be nearby and severely scold and criticize my entire conversation once I hung up, making me feel terrible. We did know that I had an autism spectrum condition to contend with; not that knowing might have changed her methods of coping with it. The upshot of this was that I hated phones, swore I would never work with them in any office, which would be infested with witnesses who could eavesdrop and criticize my efforts.

To this day, I furtively check to make sure that no one I know is around to critique my phone calls, and have conniptions if the phone rings.

This was clearly not what Berta wanted in a caregiver, and I could sense that before the subject ever arose, but I thought it was only fair that she know about it from the beginning, so I explained it all to her. She didn't sound thrilled, but didn't demand that I be like her either, constantly and cheerfully answering the phone.

Berta worked in an office as a floating secretary, answering phones in that congenial tone that I will never ever have all day, plus doing various other tasks by phone and computer, copying, filing, waiting on executives, and interacting in person with many people nonstop. Her desk was out in the open, among the witnesses I so dreaded. I could never do what she did.

Fortunately, I had been very determined about school and completed both of my degrees in the expected time frames, and then relentlessly built up other skills that made me overqualified for what she did. I had qualified myself out of that situation, for all the financial good that it did me. But at least it shielded me from offices. I had little other choice than to do unconventional work, to write, to edit, to teach community college, to tutor people, and to be a caregiver when the time came. It was what I could do correctly.

I'm a good teacher. I keep working with students until they understand, changing the words and methods until I get through to them, and don't get angry with them for not understanding things the first time they hear them, or in whatever way I first phrase them. I've had teachers who would just repeat the exact same words and phrases over and over again and then wonder why they failed to impart knowledge. That was the biggest lesson about teaching I ever learned about what not to do.

But I have to work with adults – no children.

I tutored Hilda a couple of times, but that's about it.

This year, she was off with her friends so much that I never did that. Bryn was frustrated with her; he said that she didn't study enough, and worried that she wouldn't get accepted to a good college when the time came. In the summer, Hilda took a college-level geoscience course, but she ignored my repeated offers of tutoring, despite the fact that I had taken a geoscience class in my first term of college. What was going on with that kid?

But I had plenty of other things to think about. Damon was always away, and sometimes that meant out of the country. I had to talk to him twice a day by phone or I would get too depressed and lonely. Bryn was getting worse and worse, so my time with him was growing shorter and shorter. I couldn't concentrate on any of my own work, and gradually I just gave up on the creative aspects of it, only doing typing jobs, calligraphy, and other work that only required rote copying.

I would have to wait until a different phase of my life to write. It wasn't until the spring that I settled into this realization, worrying that I was giving up. In fact, it was only a temporary surrender, and one of unknowable duration, but it bothered me anyway.

For now, in the early fall, I had not yet reached that conclusion, and began to take notes for *The Slamming Door*. The effort was intermittent and undertaken with Bryn's knowledge and without objection from him. He knew that I wasn't kidding about being a writer, and he voiced no objection to the idea of me writing the story of being his caregiver and companion.

It would be from my own point of view, not his, so his deepest thoughts would not be included. Perhaps that is why he did not object. I am not a telepath, so his secrets were safe with me. Instead, I would just understand and observe as much as I could, and I refused to snoop through Bryn's private papers. Anything he wanted to keep to himself, I stayed out of.

I wouldn't like it if someone read through my stuff without my knowledge and consent, and I wouldn't give consent to many people. If I wouldn't like it done to me, I certainly wouldn't do it to anyone else.

Bryn's private papers were all over the place, in what I thought of as his recreational mail, plus any legal and financial documents that existed. But there were more financial documents to find elsewhere in the apartment, I soon realized. More work to do later...

I had located, identified, and filed the ones on his bedroom floor without reading them: not the numbers on the financial papers, not the

Dr. Leonardi Invites Me Out

legal provisions, and not the cards and letters. They were his, no one else's.

Perhaps that was why he was content to have me there, and trusted me to be home alone with his things. He seemed to sense that I took the ethics of being a lawyer and the duties of care-giving and friendship so seriously that I would not snoop. So what if phones made me hysterical to the point of tears and I pulled the plug if I came with utter trustworthiness?

I could reach no other conclusion.

If other people were dissatisfied with me in the end, all that really mattered that Bryn was satisfied, and hopefully Albert, too. Albert assured me that he was in fact very satisfied with me as a caregiver to his brother, and did so again long after the fact, so I don't worry about it.

The weird thing about this was my own father's response when I told him about this. I thought he might have disagreed with my decision to pull the plug on that phone. When I described the situation to him, how it interfered with my efforts to do work, and how it stressed me out to the point of tears and a not-so-congenial tone of voice, he agreed with pulling the plug! Shut down the phone-answering service; it's a waste of my time. Now I realize that my father is an Aspie; it's hereditary, and I certainly didn't get it from my mother.

A lot of my angst about all this was clearly fueled by worries of not seeming flawless in my efforts on Bryn's behalf, even if that would have been impossible and ultimately self-destructive. Who cared what his daughter wanted every step of the way? If I had let such thoughts direct my every move, I would not have been able to function.

She asked me to do the caregiver duty because she couldn't be there to do it herself.

She couldn't be there because that would have meant quitting her job. No one would have been in favor of that; Bryn would have had a fit. She needed that job. She needed it to take care of herself, and her father would never have condoned quitting on his behalf. Add to that the fact that he didn't want her as his caregiver, and the whole idea just becomes a moot point.

He wanted me, and he intended to have me for as long as he possibly could keep me.

It was as though he could read me enough to see that although I was a nervous, quirky, intractable sort, he could tell that I was also ethical, careful, and a safe choice. His secrets were safe enough with me.

Yes, he would puke sometimes – cancer patients do that. That's not the kind of secret he needed shielded from the world.

What he needed to hide were his financial and legal details, his letters, and the details of his deteriorating medical condition. I filed and

The Slamming Door

organized them without reading them. I discouraged anyone other than his brother from looking into them. I aided and abetted with his efforts to circumvent embarrassing incidents.

In those ways, I acted like his lawyer, his sentry, his brick wall.

I knew I would eventually be resented for this.

I didn't care; I did it anyway. It was my duty.

And I promised myself not to accept abuse or criticism over it. Resent the adherence to his wishes, but shut up about it was – and still is – my attitude.

I had plenty to feel anxiety about.

That is the sort of person that I am: I anticipate the details of the future, and project my thoughts and worries into the future. My Aunt Joan says that I shouldn't do that, but I often can't stop myself. In this case, I seem to have accurately projected what could go wrong later. For now, I only spoke of it a little, telling Bryn and Albert that it was important to me not to be thought of or treated like "some damned in-law." I probably brought that up more than once.

They assured me that I was part of the family and said not to worry about that.

But even if they had a good attitude toward me, what would happen when they were gone? That was why I felt that a door was slamming on a part of my life that I loved. I loved those brothers; they were great friends to one another and to me.

Chapter 15

Computing - Even When It Didn't Compute

There are many ways that a computer simply will not compute.
The problems can range from technical difficulties with one's own equipment, to software glitches, to human error and human interference.
I had all of them.
It was only recently, within the past year or so as he had announced his retirement, that he had added the computer to his desk. Back in the long hot summer of 2005 when Damon and I had been staying with him, he had had none. Damon spent most of his time out at that table with our now defunct laptop that we had brought back from Kuwait. The thing was an Acer, and it lived for precisely one year before failing due to constant use and finally overheating. Laptops are a bit better now.
But Alissa had given Bryn a fairly decent computer that a friend had passed on to her, and he had gotten a printer to go with it, selected and set up by me. Damon had gone with us to the Staples store in Union Square to carry it; Bryn was using a cane in July, and we still thought it was an orthopedic problem. Ignorance can be bliss sometimes...
The machine had Windows XP and Microsoft Office 2000 loaded into it. Bryn placed it pretty much at my disposal, only occasionally attempting to use it to access his e-mail, and almost always with some degree of hand-holding by me. When this occurred, I would do my best not to hover in any obvious way while still making a point of being home and on alert, because he kept needing help.
Other than that, I used it constantly, with occasionally web-surfing by Albert or Berta.
The reasons for me to use the machine were:

1. Working to earn money as an editor;
2. Working to help Aaron, Damon's cousin-in-law who ran his own computer rescue and recovery service;
3. Taking notes for my writing projects;
4. Maintaining a reliable virtual encyclopedia;
5. Functioning as Bryn's research assistant;
6. Satisfying the random curiosity of anyone with a logistics or trivia question;
7. Keeping in touch with people for work and friendship;
8. Having a low-cost distraction available for times when I needed to keep an eye on Bryn without being obvious about it.

The Slamming Door

That last use entailed playing games on a free site called www.pogo.com – word games, balloon-popping and virtual mahjong – while sitting just around the corner from his room, with no ambient noise to keep from hearing him if he needed me. Towards the end of my time with him, I spent hours into the night like this, often until 4a.m. No one else was up then, so it was up to me to watch him.

But before that, it was more cheerful, except in the early days when it would crash.

After much fuss and hassle, I figured out how to beat those problems.

Like most computer difficulties, this drove me crazy until I got it under control, and I quickly became rather possessive of a machine that I did not actually own. However, for all intents and purposes, I seemed to have acquired an unwritten right to control this one's settings for the duration of my stay. It was not for my exclusive use, but it would make no sense to undo all of the settings at the cost of having a machine that worked as it should.

The family quickly learned what that meant, because everyone hates being harassed by a machine. How dare it not work like a slave without delay or annoyance?! At least, that's how we all feel about computers, even though the problem can usually be traced back to us.

In the early days with Bryn, and as I mentioned earlier, I began to write a rough draft of this tale of misery, but found that I couldn't concentrate on it while being a guest, a caregiver, a family member, and otherwise occupied. It would have to wait.

So it became a research and editing tool mostly, but a crucial one.

At first the computer worked well enough, and I did several jobs on it with no trouble. Aaron and I set up a system that enabled me to see the workings of his computer in his basement office at his home near Boston, and I did a typing job for Peter Freund.

Bryn got me that job by chance one Friday afternoon at lunch. Piper had gone out with him to Rafaella's and moaned that typing the bibliography for his latest sociology journal article would take him all weekend. When he heard that lament, Bryn said that I could do it, and it certainly wouldn't take me all weekend, so I earned $50. It took me a couple of hours in the evening, followed by a couple more after dinner – done. Piper was thrilled.

I thought I had the machine set up just so, with my collection of news articles, my writings, edit jobs, and so on. Then the stupid thing began to freeze up and throw away my work right in the middle of an edit.

This was particularly upsetting around Thanksgiving, when a Chinese graduate student at the University of Connecticut hired me to

Computing – Even When It Didn't Compute

help him get his Ph.D. applications ready for eight different schools. I would be putting the finishing touches on the personal statement, and the whole file would just vanish without a trace, leaving me only the version I had started with.

Bryn came out then, leaning heavily on his cane, about to chat about whatever he was reading, and instead found me bug-eyed and silent, heaving deep breaths in the front of the screen. I couldn't discuss interesting subjects like that. He thought I was mad at him, so I had to explain what had happened, and then he understood: it was the computer.

At first, I didn't know what could be causing the problem. I e-mailed the specs on the computer tower to my uncle, a computer expert, and he wrote back saying to get a specific kind of memory upgrade for it. I ordered the cards on NewEgg.com and unscrewed the side of the tower, popped them in, and figured that was that.

It wasn't; although I had installed the new hardware correctly and increased the memory to the fullest extent possible at my own expense – thus giving me a much greater proprietary interest in the computer – the problem persisted.

I thought about what had gone on with the computer in recent weeks. Since Bryn's return to the apartment, other people had spent time using the computer: Bryn, but he barely knew how to access his e-mail, and needed me to stand there with him showing him how to get at attached documents, so it couldn't have been anything he did; Berta, who checked her AOL e-mail and Facebook page, but she wasn't tinkering with the software; and Albert, who had downloaded various programs that he was convinced I would enjoy.

Aha…it was the stuff that Albert had added. The computer couldn't handle all that. As it was, I had just learned that AOL uses a ton of software, which necessitated shutting off all other applications whenever someone wanted to use that search engine.

Albert had added Google Earth, 1-Click something-or-other, and Answers.com. When I figured that out, I told Bryn what I had learned and that they were all optional…and the reasons why the machine was trashing my work. "Throw out that stuff," he said. Greatly relieved, I deleted all of those programs and like magic, I had control of the computer again.

The next day, Bryn told Albert never to ever download anything again onto that computer. He said that I needed it to be reliable for my work, and that was the end of the problem. But Albert now had a made-to-order button to push with me whenever he felt like teasing me. It was our little joke from then on; he would say, "I'm going to download some programs to the computer," and I would say "Stay away from my computer!"

The Slamming Door

And then he wouldn't download anything. He had his own laptop to set up exactly as he chose, and it was newer and more powerful. It could take whatever he dished out. He would still use Bryn's and my computer, but after all that trouble, he would just use it – no modifications.

It was wonderful when it stopped throwing my work away...

Back in Connecticut, I had a lovely new computer that I had just gotten at the end of January, a PC with Windows Vista. I still have it, wrote this story on it, and can't see what all the complaints were ever about. I love it. It can handle whatever I demand of it, and it's so pretty – it accepts National Geographic photographs as wallpaper for the desktop.

But back to computing in New York City; it was just a couple of weeks after I arrived that Bryn decided we should have a wonderful, super-fast, Time-Warner Cable Internet connection along with the television system, and I had set that up. Once the computer itself was reliable, I adjusted back to the prior Windows technology without missing a beat.

I also e-mailed my uncle to tell him that I had won the battle of the computer tower.

From there, I organized all of Aaron's client and personnel training folders and files, thus increasing his company's efficiency by a thrilling factor. He saw me doing that one afternoon after he had authorized it and called me, laughing. From his end, it just looked like some invisible person was rapidly clicking on and relabeling the folders, then moving around their Word and Excel files. I'm sure it looked funny; but he was delighted to finally have it done. He never realized how helpful it was to be organized until it was a reality.

The computer became my standard daytime spot, unless I was reading a book. But often I had some work to do out in the living room, and I always ate breakfast in front of it while reading the news online.

A lot of visiting with Bryn and Albert took place in front of that computer.

Bryn would be in his room reading his print copy of *The New York Times* while I read the same stuff online, and whatever either of us hit on as particularly significant got converted into a Word file for future reference. I would have loved to have been able to do that in law school, but the technology wasn't ready yet, at least not on my antiquated home computer.

The most interesting discussions between me and Bryn – and if he was there, Albert too – came out of all this newspaper reading. Bryn would often worry about the future of famous and respected newspapers because of online versions of them. I would counter with the fact that having vast swaths of forest chopped down daily – a nonrenewable resource – was a terrible thing. "But how with these newspapers survive?" he would ask me.

"They will survive online, if they are good enough, and the mediocre ones will fail. Survival of the fittest and of the forests too – at least, that is the hope." He would nod and agree that that would be all right; it wasn't like *The New York Times*, our favorite, was in any danger.

On the subject of environmental issues, something that was my shtick more than Bryn's, I should mention another article that we both paid special attention to. It was from my collection that I had brought in my pocket on that memory stick from Connecticut, which I continued in Manhattan. *The Hartford Courant* – the oldest newspaper in the country, but not one that I expect to survive the online purge – had published some stories of pharmaceuticals in the common water supply.

I printed them up and brought them in for Bryn to look at in his chair. He read them over carefully. That was another wonderful thing about him; if I had a news article that I found to important or just interesting, and gave it to him to read, he would really look at it, and enough to be able to discuss it intelligently. Few people outside of a university have ever taken such an interest in whatever I wanted to share, other than my husband. Albert would take a look too; the Otterman brothers were great fun that way.

The reason why I chose this particular set of stories was that Bryn had a lot of pills that doctors were trying out on him, only to switch to something else. Once someone possesses a bottle of pills, they can't be legally sold to anyone else, so the unused ones just go to waste. A lot of people had disposed of them by flushing them down toilets, perhaps to make sure that drug addicts couldn't get them, so now the water supply was contaminated with dissolved medicines.

Waste water treatment plants can only do so much to purify water and get it ready to release for drinking and bathing. These well-researched articles explained that the engineers simply could not remove the drugs in the water. People everywhere were ingesting small doses of antipsychotics, narcotics, barbiturates, and whatever else.

Bryn was appalled; he had never thought of that before. He was busy thinking about the economy, another worthy mental occupation, but this mattered too, so he swore not to flush any drugs. I didn't ask whether or not he had been doing so. I suspected from his expression and tone that he was feeling guilty, which meant that he might have done so in the past. Now I noticed that he disposed of them by putting the empty bottles in the recycling bin and the pills tossed and mixed deep down in the compost garbage.

The Slamming Door

It was funny; he had obviously gathered the old pills shortly after I gave him those stories and then gone into the kitchen when I wasn't in there to properly dispose of them.

Bryn was awesome.

The place where I sat in the afternoons and evenings was the center of my life in Bryn's apartment. He gave at least two lectures in the spring at the Henry George School, and I served as his research assistant, doing online searches for data relevant to his topics. When he said he had enough, I stopped, but assured him that I had saved all of it as Word files just in case he lost it. He was very happy with that. I also saved articles by his colleagues who taught at Columbia University and from *Counterpunch* magazine.

The table with the computer on it used to be Marlie Otterman's dining room table, and had a wall high of books on the left that Bryn had collected at random for years at various bookstores, including The Biography Bookshop of Bleecker Street in Greenwich Village, which was within easy walking distance and on the way to McNulty's on Christopher Street. Some books were upright and others stacked, simulating stones that had been placed in structurally strategic positions, minus the concrete. Somehow, it all held together.

The Biography Bookshop in Greenwich Village. It has since moved.

Both Bryn's friends and family found it rather hilarious, and called the pile The Fort. It was something that the aunts and Albert teased Bryn

Computing – Even When It Didn't Compute

about. In 2005, it was uneven on top, not yet complete, but by the fall of 2008, it was a perfect rectangle across the edge of the table.

The computer was in the center, and its tower was down on the floor to my right. An old, tall table lamp with a yellowed, slightly torn shade stood at the back right. The printer was just behind and to the right of the computer, and all of the cords connected to the long, thin surge protector on the floor. Above the table, dead center, was a wonderful painting of the Boston Symphony Orchestra; Bryn's mother used to go to concerts by this group. It was a caricature in color of each member from that time, in color.

To the right was a small bookcase, small in that it wasn't a tall one, but it had two sections of three shelves. On top were several interesting items: a Nazi sword that someone had inherited and then left to Bryn; a Ward family sword from the Civil War – Yankee side of the conflict (Bryn's mother's last name was Ward, and she was originally from Boston); an ornately decorated wooden box with mother-of-pearl inlay with a Mah Jong set inside that Bryn's mother used when she invited her friends over; a framed bill of lading from a suit for salvage in the early 19th century; old silver candlesticks; a Burger King hat from a kiddie party for Hilda.

The long, Art Deco sofa was against the adjoining wall. It was old, and its sea-green silk upholstery had been scratched to shreds on top by various family cats over the years. A green sheet covered it. The one window in the living room, which overlooked an alley and showed the side wall of the building, let in the only natural light. Looking out, one could see the kitchen window, Leelee's windows, and Hilda's family's kitchen and bedroom windows beyond. Straight down was concrete; it was the area past the basement garbage and boiler room. Trees in the back yards of other buildings were farther back, but none of us ever went there.

All of the furniture in the room had been made for the Otterman family a long time ago. Bryn and Albert had told me that when their parents had gotten married, their paternal grandmother, a widow, had announced that she was giving them a fully furnished house. They happily went off on their honeymoon, came home, and found that she had moved in with them. Surprise! But she didn't stay long; she got her own place after a little while, and there was no upset involved. They guessed that she didn't want to live with newlyweds after all.

That window was a nice, double-paned one. It had two panels side by side that worked as all the others did, by grasping the modern metal frame of the pane on the bottom and shoving it upwards. A screen would then be inserted, positioned, and pressed into place by pushing the pane onto it. That was it. Whenever I arrived to visit Bryn, usually with a few

The Slamming Door

months' interval between visits, the first thing I would do was clean all the windows – frames and all – thoroughly. The air pollution made them utterly filthy – black.

Bryn watched me that September as I did it, amazed at how gross it was. That window was open on top, and I had looked up at it, worried, so he just lifted his cane up and pushed it upwards, shutting it. So that was the trick; but I only opened them from the bottom after that.

The living room floor had some spots that had rotted away, but they were negligible. All of the slats in the wooden floor were narrow pieces of perhaps an inch across, but a few feet long. I saw a machine snapping new pieces into place the next spring when the place downstairs was gutted and redone; a nail went in here and there as the grooves were lined up. Bryn had wondered what that snapping sound was, and I had gone down to ask; it was fascinating.

But those wooden floors got really filthy, and I came to know the grains of wood well. Using a stick mop – a sponge on a stick that could be squeezed out – I would mop the entire apartment every few weeks, using the oval garbage can full of Pine Sol and water as I went.

Bryn hated cleaning, so while he was well enough to go out with Albert or with friends, I would do the cleaning whenever he was out, then wash up and relax. There was a ladder that folded up in the hallway, and I would climb up and dust the tops of the two tall bookcases next to the living room windows. There were a couple of porcelain statues up there, and a Persian musical instrument that Damon had brought back from Iran for Bryn a few years earlier.

The dust bunnies would show, and I would mop. The next day, the dirt would show on the soles of my bare feet, which amazed me. "I feel like I just cleaned, but a mere two days later, my feet are dirty from just walking around at home!" I said to Bryn once. "It's the air pollution; there's nothing you can do about it," he said. "I know you just cleaned; I smelled the lemon solutions. Don't worry about it."

There were just a few other things in the living room: a small tasseled rug under the windows on which a pale-pink painted, string-less guitar rested, and it was covered with writing. It was Berta's. A plant that Bryn had rescued from some trash on the street many years ago dangled its vines onto the guitar. Next to that, between the windows and the tall bookcases, was an antique rocking chair with its caned seat smashed through. Berta had it re-caned at great expense late that fall, and it came back looking beautiful.

Between the hall and my room was a table, another drop-leaf one like the one in Bryn's bedroom, only longer. It stretched all the way across that wall. On it was the only other lamp in the room, with a greenish, stained glass shade in wrought iron. I don't know whether it

Computing – Even When It Didn't Compute

was a Tiffany's original or something similar, but it was a beautiful antique. Back in 2005, it hadn't worked, and neither had the tall one on the desk. For $2.80 at a local hardware store, I had gotten each one fixed, leaving the shades at home and carrying the lamps up 8th Avenue.

When Bryn had come home from work, I had told him I had a surprise for him, and pulled the chain on the stained glass one. Ta-da! Light. Soon I had the other one done too. Bryn was delighted; he used to bring home backlogs of paperwork from his office and sit at the desk to catch up once his lights worked again. Some part inside where the light bulb went had gotten old and loose, and that was what was replaced for the lovely low price of just under three bucks.

The Tiffany-esque lamp was flanked by two small metal sculptures, a headless nude woman on the left, and a miniature replica of a defeated Gallic warrior on the right. The poor guy was flopped sadly on the ground with a loose rope around his neck, like a leash. He was naked, so the décor of the table was balanced; Gallic warriors had fought the Romans that way because they considered it a sign of bravery. He had thick wavy hair and a mustache, and he stared listlessly at the ground, as if he would never be happy again. He probably wasn't; the Romans carted their vanquished foes off as slaves.

There were a couple of wooden chairs lined up in front of the tall bookcases when I arrived as Bryn's caregiver that fall, and I don't remember them being there in previous years. I think they came from Matt's kitchen on Long Island when he and Berta got different ones. Soon Bryn's son-in-law found a matching pair on the street and there were four of them, though The Ringsby's addition wasn't as nice. Albert Otterman tried gluing it, but it just didn't work.

I sat at the desk on a white metal chair with huge blue cushion. It had always been there. When guests came over, I simply turned to face them on the sofa and chairs. I lived in that spot for half the day. It was the only place that I really wanted to sit if I were in the living room, partly out of a sense of personal territory, and partly out of a need to protect the computer.

I heard many stories from Albert about the family, plus whatever else, from that spot. He told me why Berta didn't like France and French things while sitting on the sofa one afternoon. Since I love all things French, I had been curious about this, and paid close attention.

It wasn't a long story. Berta had studied French in high school, but not with the avid interest that Alissa had, and not even with the love of it that I had. French sort of grew on me; learning to think in another language had not come easily, but visiting some nice people in the south of France had done the trick, and I began to really improve after that.

The Slamming Door

Albert and June were interested to know about my paternal grandparents' travels all over France, living in the Montmartre of Paris and touring the chateaux of the Loire Valley, and my own enjoyment of the Louvre and the Grand Palais museums, where I had seen the Mona Lisa and a series of Monet's impressionist paintings.

Not Berta…she had been what Albert called an Ugly American.

When I looked puzzled, he explained. Berta had held out a handful of coins in shops when it came time to pay for her purchases, offending the Parisian shopkeepers. Oh…that made sense. It put the burden of choosing the right amount of money on the shopkeeper; if there was any doubt later as to how much money she had offered, there could be an unpleasant exchange of words or worse. No wonder people had gotten upset. Berta had blamed the Parisians; the fact remained that a shopkeeper anywhere on the planet would have reacted that way.

What else had gone wrong?

Well, Albert said unhappily, Berta had gone there to visit a friend who was studying and living there, someone from high school, but she had embarrassed her friend with crass behavior, speaking English and being loud at social gatherings, and their friendship had broken up over it.

I didn't tell Berta what her uncle had said. But the next time we were sitting together – me in my chair and Berta on that same sofa – I had asked her about France. Her version was different, of course: she had gone to visit her sister. Maybe she went to stay with Dionne after things went sour with her friend.

Berta had been locked out in the rain, yelling "Dionne!" and the neighbors had woken up and yelled out their windows at her to be quiet. Fun time…Dionne had been in a rush and hadn't bothered to leave her sister with a key.

The final objection that Berta had to Paris was that a cab driver had shouted at her, "Quel arrondissement?!" and when she couldn't answer quickly in French ordered her out of his cab. I sympathized; some Parisians were irate and rude with foreigners who weren't fluent in their language, regardless of whether or not that was reasonable behavior.

But Berta more often than not would refuse to eat the Le Grainne Café, saying that she didn't like the French place. She seemed to like Le Pain Quotidien though, and she didn't know that it was Belgian. I shared my own stories of Paris and France with her, the good and the bad.

Not long after all that, I found a wonderful French coffee and sweet shop on West 23rd Street called Madeleine Patisserie. It sold Madeleine cookies, financiers (little round orange sponge cake cookies with mini chocolate chips), macarons, tartes, and café au lait. The kitchen was at the back, and it had a gorgeously decorated bathroom at the end of the hall to the left.

The sofas, chairs and table were all different and as comfortable as any from a living room at home. Customers bused their own tables, directed by a sign in English and in French.

The pictures on the wall included a huge upward-slanting view of the Eiffel Tower, some old French movie stars, and a wonderful image of Marie Antoinette saying "Let them eat chocolate croissants." That queen never said "Let them eat cake," however…that was just yellow journalism, selling newspapers, an invention of the 17th century.

I met a nice German girl there once, and asked her about the Parisian attitude toward visitors who spoke some French but weren't fluent. Why wasn't that good enough for them? American high schools offer French or Spanish, rarely German or Italian, and we seldom have anyone to practice our language skills with, so what do they expect?

She told me that it was insecurity on their part, and that other Europeans have the same problem, not just Parisians, despite the fact that they are the ones who get talked about for such nastiness most of all. Most Europeans only speak one language themselves. I don't remember

The Slamming Door

what Berta said when I passed that on to her, only that she was still disgusted with the French and didn't like them.

Not me; I would go back for another visit any time. It's their art, food, architecture, gardens and museums that I would want to see. France is where all that is beautiful comes from. I can put up with a few rude Parisians and hold out for the odd nice ones, and I have met some nice Parisians, so I know from experience that there are always some nice people and some awful ones wherever you go in the world.

Bryn agreed; he had been studying French and loved the food and the language, too.

Many times, I bought those financier cookies home to share with him, and he ate them happily until the next summer. We had fun for most of our year together, despite the bad times.

It was worth it, and so was he.

Chapter 16

Dead Boiler - To TriBeCa

Albert and June lived in a brick apartment complex not far from the World Trade Center site...just a few blocks north of it, in fact. The first time that I saw the place, it was late in September, and Bryn hadn't yet had any chemotherapy. We had ridden down to the corner of Greenwich Street and Jay in a cab. The seats of the cab and Bryn's back-pack, which he never left home without, were both black.

Bryn had spent the first week or so of my time with him urging me to learn how to recognize when I was being teased, and to learn to tease others. This was a recurring theme of my social life; how to spot teasing and join in. We eased out of the cab after Bryn paid the fare, Bryn first and me following. I assumed responsibility for maneuvering out with his backpack and my handbag, expecting him to just stay balanced with his cane and not worry about anything else. Suddenly, as the cab pulled away from the curb, he asked, "Did you bring my back-pack?"

"No, I left it in the cab," I responded, taking care to sound deadly serious.

He turned and gaped at me in horror. Because he had tachycardia, I had no intention of dragging a joke such as that one out for more than a split second. I pulled it forward from my shoulder, where it had been dangling behind my back. "I'm kidding! You said I should learn to tease people, and this was the best I could do."

He grinned at me and took his bag back.

We turned to face the building, and I noticed that a Food Emporium grocery store was on the ground floor, spanning the length of the left half of it. In the middle was a huge set of concrete steps that widened as it reached street level, with a metal pole down the center, that led up to a huge terrace. There was a parking garage between the stairs and grocery store.

Bryn led me up those steps, and we ended up on a garden-edged terrace that stretched across the apartment complex with a grammar school to the right, and more living spaces beyond it. The terrace floor was made of large squares of terra cotta tiles, like specially made bricks. We turned left to the doors there, which led from outside into a tiny foyer with two doors, one on the right – the neighboring apartment – and one straight ahead, which was Albert and June's place.

Barking began as soon as we opened that outer door; it was Pearlie, the Shetland Sheepdog that they had adopted late in 2001, after the disaster of 9/11, on Martha's Vineyard. She was beautiful – just like the Sheltie I had given my grandmother a couple of years before that: black,

The Slamming Door

brown and white. She came from a shelter there, and June had told me, years ago, that drug dealers had bred her just to sell her puppies, then abandoned her when no one wanted to buy the poor mother dog.

Thanks to that and some generally mean treatment, Pearlie was terrified of being yelled at when she first moved in with them. She wouldn't get onto their bed with them, and it took a lot of coaxing and assuring to convince her that she was wanted up there.

Consequently, Albert and June decided never to scold the dog no matter what she did wrong. Usually the only thing she did wrong was to bark incessantly and loudly until Bryn and I had had more than enough. Still, no one was allowed to object. Every time Pearlie heard the slightest sound, she burst into action, barking and racing either downstairs to the door or up the little flight of white steps that her owners had bought for the window between the kitchen and full bathroom, atop which was a hunter green oval dog bed from L.L. Bean.

On our first visit to this place, Albert greeted us cheerfully, and I found out about the ban on scolding Pearlie no matter how much noise she made. Bryn broke that rule when he couldn't stand it any longer.

The dog also knocked over her dinner, spilling it all over the parquet floor as she did so, whenever she heard the doorbell. Dog dinners were served in soup plates meant for human use, an unstable choice of canine dinnerware. Alissa got to clean that up every evening. She had taken to coming over each night, feeding her parents, and would soon move back into her old room on the third floor, which looked much as it had when she had been growing up there.

The three of them had moved in when Alissa was a little girl, perhaps when she was three years old. The place had a tiny room just past its front door, the purpose of which was to house the stairwell. Dog leashes and toys littered its floor. The floors throughout the unit were beautiful wooden parquet, and the stairs were varnished pieces of wood set into a metal frame, allowing for a clear view between each step as one ascended them. There were metal railings, and as an acrophobic, I was glad.

Up on the next level, the first thing I saw was a closet with sliding doors. To the right of that was a way into the kitchen with no door. The kitchen had a dishwasher, an unheard-of luxury at Bryn's place. The rubber-coated metal prongs on its lower tray were bent every which way; when I cleaned up after dinner, I bent them into their proper positions, which astonished and delighted Albert, Alissa, and June. They had left them like that for decades, putting up with the resulting difficulty in loading the machine. I was amazed by that, but kept quiet.

A full bathroom was across the hall from this kitchen, and the windows in that room, the kitchen, and where Pearlie's stairs led all looked out over the courtyard, where resident kids were played with Frisbees and skateboards. The bathroom was littered with tiny bits of old soap bars, half-used tubes of makeup and toothpaste, and whatever else. But it was clean; a cleaning woman came in every two weeks.

Coming out of the bathroom and going back the other way led to a huge living and dining room. A large, red, Persian carpet covered the floor. On the left was the sofa, coffee table, and June's artwork, both purchased and painted by her. Family photos were everywhere, too. I was pleased to have the chance to see it all. An abstract painting of birds against a dark grey background was over the television, a medium-sized flat-screen, on the wall to my left. CDs and DVDs were strewn in disarray on a table on the other side of the sofa, and some plants were on the opposite wall, which was made more of windows than wall.

To the right was a door to the long, narrow balcony. I went out with my camera and took some photos, trying to imagine the view as it was on 9/11. The balcony had some plants on it and a dead Christmas tree on its side. Albert said they had to get that out of there. I came back inside.

As I did, I saw a console piano against the wall on the left. It was a nice varnished wooden one with pretty carvings. I didn't ask who played, but suspected that June had. That was in the corner by the balcony door. To the right were some nice wooden bookcases, very solid-looking, and full of books on art and Europe. Albert and June had spent some time living in Florence, Italy with Alissa when she was a kid. But they had kept this place to come back to, and there were family photo albums that June showed me in there too. I saw images of their past pet cats and dogs, and the Martha's Vineyard house, and of the horse that June had ridden there. She loved horses, and had painted some pictures of them.

The dinner table was next to the bookcases, and there was another low bookcase on the wall next to them. The kitchen stove was right behind that wall. On the other small stretch of wall that separated the dining area from the kitchen was low set of drawers, covered with a disorganized collection of June's earrings. Albert was always buying her more junky pairs whenever they went out together in his desperation to keep her happy and occupied.

Vera Bradley bags, socks, sandals and shoes completed the detritus that June had absently strewn all over the place. The family photo albums showed a very different townhouse: June had kept things neat and orderly before Alzheimer's had started feasting on her brain's memory chips. I tried not to consciously focus on that damned thief of a disease; it outraged me too much to think of the care with which a person stores memories and organizes the physical aspects of their life only to have it be chipped away bit by bit.

The Slamming Door

That was the main floor of the unit. Upstairs were three bedrooms and a full bathroom, which had a dryer stacked atop a washing machine. Bryn later told me that this was an illegal setup, but of course we would never tell. Doing laundry in Manhattan is an expensive hassle without one's own machines. One either totes bags to and from a place that does it however they do it, or else one spends times guarding the clothes as they churn around for hours on end, reading a book. (Bryn and I used the Chinese-owned place down the street, which only accepted drop-offs. It was just 3 years earlier that I had been able to do it all myself, more cheaply, there.)

The bedrooms were strewn with more clothing, but I could see when I went up there that it was a lovely place to live. June's quilt on their big bed was pretty – pinks and purples and blues, I think, though I don't remember it well now. I wasn't up there for long or often. A beautiful framed photo of June as a young woman was in their room. Alissa's room looked like it was frozen in the 1970s, with a green bedspread over the neatly-made twin bed, and the desk and other furniture looked fine. There was no clutter in it, hardly any clothing, and no mess.

Her room faced the courtyard, as did the bathroom. Albert and June had a window overlooking the street, and so did Albert's clustered mausoleum of an office. Getting to his window to open the blinds looked like a discouraging task, so I never tried.

The family enjoyed all of this well-appointed, attractive space for the lovely cost of $700 per month, rent-controlled. The unit next door – same specs - was on the market for $3,400 per month, available only at full market price. My generation could forget about affording lower Manhattan, which was really the only area of New York City I would ever want to live in. No way was I about to commute from anywhere and then trudge home. If I were live in a city, it would be this one, but only on my own terms, terms of convincing enjoyment. I get attached to the history and specific sites of a place.

On a subsequent visit, though I forget precisely which one it was, Albert asked me if I could go upstairs to his office room and see if I could get his new photo printer hooked up properly to his laptop. This meant loading the disk of software that it came with onto the laptop, and so on. But first, another problem confronted me: the black hole that was his office.

What a mess! Clothing tossed here, there, and everywhere. Dust and unidentifiable debris all over his desk, which also had a side table extending from the left, facing the door and closet, piles of papers and paper clips and pens…it was one of the worst morasses that I had ever seen.

Dead Boiler - To TriBeCa

Alissa appeared once as I was sorting through it, delighted that someone was doing so, and commented that her mother's condition had nothing to do with the mess. Albert had always kept it like this. The only problems that could be linked to June's memory deterioration were the laundry that kept piling up and the earrings and sunglasses strewn downstairs and elsewhere.

I did a decent job of cleaning and clearing it up, clothes, pens, dirt, and all, and at last was able to settle down and work the computer problem. But the Internet snarled me up somehow at the last step – registering the software – and I went downstairs. Albert was pretty happy about it in spite of that, and grateful for the cleaning effort. All I had managed was a hole in the mess, however. At least the clothing got sorted, hung up, folded, and tossed out to the laundry pile.

The funniest part was the fact that I kept finding pairs of glasses here and there. Each and every pair was identical in appearance – heavy plastic tortoise-patterned round frames – but I suspected that the views through them would not be identical were Albert to actually put them each on and test them out. Still, he was glad that I had unearthed them all.

Downstairs, where the real visiting took place, we found that Albert had bought June's favorite Belgian beer, called Leffe, plus some red and white wine, Brie and bleu cheese, grapes, and crackers, and laid it all out on the coffee table for us. The news was on. We happily sat down and accepted some Leffe beer that evening in September.

This might have been the visit in which I learned that having beer and wine in one evening gives me a headache; in any case, I enjoyed everything I ate and drank. Albert learned that I can't eat bleu or other moldy cheese – an allergy that makes it difficult for me to breathe kicks in – and I suddenly felt appreciated and cared for when Bryn loudly scolded him when his brother forgot and offered it to me a second time. But I happily feasted on the Brie, skipping the floury edges, and enjoyed the beer.

My in-laws certainly consumed a lot of beer, I noticed. My own parents kept boxes of red and white wine in the house, and they bought awful beer – light beer in cans. Here, it was always bottled beer, and always something special. Any problems that the Otterman brothers and June had ever had with alcoholism were now forgotten; they had decided to still drink, but had made themselves stop at a certain point each day. It was under control.

Alissa didn't drink, though. She was bound and determined to lose some weight, even though she wasn't fat. She just wanted to be thin and pretty. She made a delicious salad, and I memorized her recipe: salad greens, sliced scallions, vine tomatoes, avocados (she excelled in

The Slamming Door

selecting these); a dressing of extra-virgin olive oil, Dijon mustard, and balsamic vinegar. Dinner was spaghetti and tomato sauce. Alissa couldn't cook well, yet the task of feeding her parents whenever they ate in had fallen to her, so she tried to cook.

Just two blocks south of this apartment complex was a brand new shopping area that looked like heaven to both Alissa and me: it had a Whole Foods store and a Barnes & Noble. But Albert disapproved of Whole Foods; it was driving the older, smaller, mom-and-pop and other foods stores nearby out of business.

Alissa was reticent to the point of absurdity about challenging him on this point: she even avoided the Whole Foods store, although it was the only place within reasonable distance that sold the things she needed to eat a healthy raw foods vegan diet. When I found this out, I scolded her. "You have to be able to get what you need. Your father doesn't have to shop there if he doesn't want to, but you have every right to go there if you want to."

It was in late October – 2 weeks after Bryn's first round of chemotherapy – that the ancient boiler in our building failed. The entire building was left with no heat or hot water for over three weeks, and just as the weather began to turn cold. Bryn decamped to TriBeCa and took up residence on Albert and June's leather sofa, putting up with Pearlie and her noise, and enjoying his brother's company, heat, and hot water. He had the downstairs bathroom to himself.

Meanwhile, I had learned in those first two evenings (before he left) how to make do without hot water: I warmed up several pot-fulls of water on the gas stove to wash my hair, then filled the tub the same way, but only a third full because it was such a production. As I was home alone, this wasn't a big deal. Bryn had spent a couple of evenings using the heated water, giving his blue bucket its first job as he took what he called a whore's bath over the bathroom sink, before deciding it was too cold to live in the apartment.

He had said that it seemed unsafe to him (because he was sick) to stay there, and I agreed with him. But I worried; would I be allowed to stay in Chelsea? Of course, he said. I relaxed. What a relief. I didn't' want to be stuck with the dog, and I had thought that he would stay in Alissa's room and me on that sofa. He didn't want to go all the way up to her room, and as it turned out, she was there a lot. So I got avoid a change of environment, and Bryn would not catch a cold. All was well in the land of the in-laws for now.

Piper and Melissa lent me some quilts to sleep under, and I was comfortable enough.

Next, the landlord sent Luis, the new superintendent, to every door with a clipboard and a space heater for each apartment as an apology for the problem. Meanwhile, Teo was kind enough to go down to the basement with Luis and show him everything he knew about the boiler, but it turned out to be broken, worn out, and completely used up. A new one was ordered, and we were all informed of the fact. It sucked, but that was that.

Bryn instructed me to accept a heater but not to overload the fuses.

Not knowing exactly how to avoid that, I promptly blew a couple of them out when I ran the hair dryer in my room while watching television and trying to warm the room up with the space heater.

Bryn sounded quite upset on the phone, scolded me, and told me to call Luis to look at the fuses. I did, and Luis showed me the array. It was ancient; 6 large red and blue round things in one box, and 2 more in another below that. No wonder the landlord had to refurbish units!

After a trip to the hardware store and some tinkering and testing, I had everything working perfectly again, and kept the heater off whenever I dried my hair. Berta said I shouldn't have told her father about the fuses, but I had to find out how to fix them. She also said that he was terrified of having a fire, and that when she was a teenager, he used to worry incessantly whenever she styled her hair. She had obviously expended some effort and hair care products on the elaborate waved and curled dos of the 1980s. I'm sure she looked gorgeous.

As long I don't resemble the 1970s, or the late 1960s, I tend to be pretty happy with the way I look. I have a theory about this: people tend to become attached to the styles of the time when they were teens, and I was a teen in the 1980s. I love those styles – beautiful waves and poufs of hair, hair parted only on the side, never in the middle (a hideous remnant of the previous, unattractive decade!).

Berta and I commiserated over this; she agreed with me about the virtues of 1980s styles and aesthetics – floral patterns, pockets in all of women's clothing, and so on. When the hair dryer incident blew over – which was quickly – we settled into a routine of going to Albert and June's place most evenings. As long as Bryn was staying there, that was our hangout. It was great fun, and I got to know them all and learn some more of the family history.

They didn't need me there all day long, so I would amuse myself with books or the computer or whatever work I might have in Chelsea, and perhaps go out exploring the area during the day. Albert had taken over Bryn's medical files, so I wasn't wanted at the doctor's appointments much. These few weeks were just...fun.

Bryn was enjoying his stay there, going out with Albert and June to eat breakfast and lunch in the cafés nearby, and glad to have a chance to see how his brother was coping with life as a caregiver to June. He told me all about it.

The Slamming Door

One afternoon, they all ate lunch at a place across the street, and when they were finished, June wanted to use the rest room. Albert escorted her back there, and then returned to the table to sit with Bryn and wait for her. Some time passed, and the men began to think that June should been back by then. Suspicious, Albert went back and found absolutely no one there.

Horrified, they paid the bill and rushed home. They were not surprised to find that June was pounding the door and in tears, confused.

Another thing that happened was that Albert got his medication seen to at last.

He needed to go to Martha's Vineyard and arrange to sell the house that he and June had there, which meant that he needed to put their car through emissions. When he drove it out of the garage to do just that, he promptly and literally ran into trouble: he nearly fainted at the wheel.

With effort, he managed to call Bryn, who was upstairs on the sofa with the news on and his cell phone handy. Bryn, as sick as he was, got his cane and ambled around the corner, which was as far as Albert had managed to drive. Bryn put the car in gear and drove it back to the garage under the apartment building. (Bryn had supported himself as a cab driver after his divorce, so he had kept his driver's license available all his adult life.)

That did it; Albert definitely had a problem. He was just too tired all of the time, and no one knew why. Alissa took a day off from work and brought him to the neurologist, who said that he should have come in a long time ago. Albert had epilepsy, and it had been years since his medication for that condition had been evaluated. It was time for an adjustment: less medicine!

Bryn told me the tale the next day, and expressed some anxiety that Albert wasn't any different on the different dosage. I wasn't concerned or surprised by that at all and shared what I knew: it would take 2 weeks for the half-life that the drugs had built up in Albert's system to wear off. After that, and he would be much better.

How did I know this? Well…Damon was one possibility, but actually, I had learned it from my mother. My mother the nurse had told me this. She was always teaching me interesting things about medicine. I can't help remembering them, but I would never have become a doctor or nurse. Seeing a photo of diseased tissue or a video of an operation freaks me out; I jump back and look away.

Bryn was pleased to hear that his brother would be fine soon, and sure enough, in just 2 more weeks, Albert was back to normal. He hadn't had a seizure in decades; the medication worked. He just needed to get his normal level of energy back.

That was about as much drama as we experienced during the few weeks that Bryn stayed with them. Other than that, June kept telling me that we had to get together, and that she wanted me to watch a DVD of Paul McCartney in Moscow with her. At some point, we did watch about an hour of it together.

Another night, Matt and Berta and Alissa were all there, and I volunteered to cook dinner for everyone. Alissa and June decided to come with me. I wondered what would happen next; whether they chose to come with me or not, I intended to shop in that Whole Foods store.

I brought my recycled plastic Whole Foods bags with me, but that didn't tip them off. Off we went into the darkness, and everything was fine until I tried to enter the sliding doors. Then June balked, saying, "I don't know if I want to do this." I said she didn't have to, but that I was definitely going in, and took another step inside. The place was fabulous, and new to me. We had Whole Foods back in Connecticut, but it was smaller. This place was enormous, and I felt like a kid in a candy shop. (I didn't know it yet, but there was an even bigger one in Union Square.)

Berta later told me that before June had any memory problems, she insisted on all organic stuff, like what Whole Foods offered. Unfortunately, she couldn't remember that, and parroted Albert's opinions now, oblivious to what was going on. June had decided to come with us to the store, and as I walked in and took a shopping cart, she turned around and said that she didn't want to do this and wanted to go home.

I looked back to see what Alissa would do, and she decided to take her mother home. Oh well…time to get on with it. I moved through the store, buying Cajun catfish, asparagus, salad greens and whatever else for Alissa's delicious recipe, and even tried to get the blueberry drops that Albert had been combing the area stores for, but it wasn't there. (I found it elsewhere later on.)

That wasn't all that Berta told me; while Alissa and I were gone, June kept asking, "Where are the girls?" to which Berta kept replying, "They're at the store." It just showed that Albert and Alissa needed to watch her constantly. They were devoted to her, so they were quite willing, but the rest of us wondered how they could handle the pressure.

When I was almost done shopping – and had gone to the store's upper level – Alissa suddenly caught up with me, slightly out of breath and looking delighted; she had rushed back and gone shopping! She was holding a basket full of things on her raw foods vegan diet, and informed me that she hadn't been able to find them anywhere else.

Well of course I felt triumphant, but kept my mouth shut and refrained from saying I told you so; what mattered was that she was in there, shopping. She wasn't going to get malnourished after all. When we went home, Albert loudly and pointedly said that he had never had any objection to anyone else shopping there if they needed something that Whole Foods had and no other store had; he just didn't want to shop there. Sigh...well, at least Alissa had gone in there; being quiet and reticent can delay things.

I unpacked my food and quickly got dinner going; Alissa made the salad and stashed her own purchases. The catfish came out good, but Bryn didn't feel like eating fish, and Berta said she didn't like catfish. I felt bad; but Bryn said that the chemicals were the problem and not to worry. As for Berta, it took me a while to notice that more often than not, she avoided eating fish. Matt, however, said that I had restored his faith in catfish; he liked it. I wondered what that meant, and he said that he had had catfish years ago. It must have been badly cooked, because he had thought he didn't like catfish at all. Now he just thought that someone was a bad cook.

Okay. At least I was having fun with this bunch. We played with the dog, ate dinner, watched presidential and vice presidential election debates, and just enjoyed the visits.

One night, I went out walking around the huge, sprawling terrace with Alissa and June and Pearlie, just to walk the dog and chat with them.

We went out, turned left past the preschool, went as far back as we could, and turned right. Apartment unit stretched to our right, and a huge indoor gym to our left. So that was how universities in urban areas dealt with athletic programs, I thought. We were looking in from the upper story windows, down at a huge basketball court of Manhattan Community College.

Alissa and June directed my attention in the opposite direction, across Greenwich Street, to the rooftop of a building over there. It was a loft with many panes of glass making up the roof, and the room was all lit up with a row of kitchen or living room spotlights. It was hard to see much detail from where we were. Alissa told me that Robert de Niro lived there. Oh – that explained why it was of interest.

Famous celebrities lived all over New York City, and to a historian who gets her kicks walking around and seeing famous sites, National Historic Landmarks, monuments, and the occasional museum (they're not free in Manhattan, so I don't go to many), this was an example of watching current history, which became another hobby for the duration.

But I don't like to get into the faces of famous people who are still alive, trying to go about their business. As I have said before, it feels strange. What do you say to a complete stranger? Why speak to them at all if you can't sound intelligent, and without a logical reason for doing so? I don't want to. I don't think Alissa or June wanted to do that either, and I was glad. We were just observing the apartment from a polite distance.

I once came around the corner in Chelsea from the grocery store after dark to find Ethan Hawke standing on our street and concentrating on text messages on his cell phone. His new baby girl was strapped to his chest. I knew it was him, but just kept walking; I didn't want to scare the guy while he was distracted and holding his baby. So what that he was famous?! When I got home and mentioned this to Bryn, he thoroughly approved.

It was during these few weeks that I learned a bit more about Alissa – from Berta. Alissa was just so quiet that I was never going to learn about her from conversation with her. One intriguing thing about Alissa that Berta told me was that Alissa had been nearly silent when she was a little girl, and that at family gatherings, she had communicated with people other than her parents entirely through Berta.

Elvira, Berta's mother, had always been rather miffed by that, but there was nothing to be done about it. They just had to wait for Alissa to grow out of that. Bryn commented at one point that he really liked Alissa, and was always interested in what she was doing with her life, but she would never really open up and talk to him either, and that disappointed him. Yet she visited him often while he was sick and increasingly confined to his apartment that year. He knew she cared about him.

One evening – a Saturday, I think – Berta insisted that both Alissa and I accompany her a few streets east of Albert and June's place, to attend a party. It was a sort of housewarming-combination-birthday party for a friend of hers.

I don't know how they met, but they got together from time to time. Berta's friend Tina was in finance, and had turned up in L.A. briefly while Berta lived there; they had encountered each other by chance in some upscale bar. Then they both moved back to New York City and met up again by chance in yet another bar, resuming their acquaintance.

Alissa and I agreed to go with her, leaving the parents in the TriBeCa apartment after dinner was over with and cleaned up. We walked a few blocks, and then turned right to enter a building that had once been offices, now converted to million-dollar apartments.

This was intriguing; Berta's friend had just bought the place, and if it cost over a million dollars, she must be very successful at her job, I thought to myself. I wondered what she did in the world of finance, and Berta told me that she worked as an investment banker on Wall Street, and that she had been raised in London. I didn't ask any more questions.

We all went up an elevator to the 5th or 6th floor, around a long, narrow hallway with torch-like wall sconces lighting the way, and to her friend's front door.

The Slamming Door

The place was all in light beige, with some marble in that hue in the bathroom. The room we entered seemed empty near the door; it was as if the owner hadn't yet decided what to do with that area. A small bookcase sat on the wall to the left, with family photos on it. It was when I looked at a photo of Tina and her brother standing with their parents that I knew they were Sikhs; their father wore a turban. This area had no windows.

Straight ahead, with a nice, wide window, was the living room, with two long sofas, one with its back to the front door and the other with its back to the dining room, which was just beyond the kitchen. The living room had a huge flat-screen television and a large, elaborate stereo with huge, tall, thin speakers that sat on the floor. That was to the left, and a gap in the wall between the living room and the empty room led to the bedrooms.

To the right was a pass-through to the kitchen, which was beautifully finished with granite countertops, a fancy new refrigerator, gas stove, oven, dishwasher, and microwave – the works. It was well-lit, too. To get into the kitchen one walked past the counter and made a U-turn through the living room and dining room. The kitchen was the brightest room in the place.

We were let in by Tina herself, who proved to be a short, heavy-set woman with shoulder-length hair tied back in a barrette and bangs, a pretty face, and a sleeveless top and knee-length skirt. I don't think she was more than five feet tall, perhaps less. So like Berta, she was very heavy but had a pretty face.

Tina was confident and constantly smiling. I don't know how happy she was, but she seemed to be having a good time for the whole evening. She was probably forty years old, but I didn't ask her age.

Her brother was there too. In contrast to his sister, he was very thin and wore frameless glasses, and he had a short haircut with no turban – but another Sikh guy, a friend of theirs, wore a beard and a black turban. The guests included lots of white people and some Indian people.

Alissa only stayed for a little while, perhaps less than an hour. She excused herself, saying she had some writing to do. We knew she would do that; she had warned us that she would. Good for her; she could escape from this social situation.

Unlike Alissa, who knew her way home from there and had a ready-made excuse, I was the guest of a guest (Berta), and had to make the best of it. It was a lovely party, but it soon got horribly noisy. None of the other guests seemed to mind that in the least, but I retreated as far from the source of the deafening noise as I could.

Tina had cranked up her expensive stereo system, and stood grinning happily in the center of her living room, dancing. People cheered and sang Happy Birthday to her, and I sang too. It was quite a while before the noise abated even a little, and I wondered about the neighbors. Wasn't this bothering them?

To disassociate myself from it without seeming rude, I went into the kitchen where several people were standing around chatting. The noise came straight through the pass-through and the open space where I had entered, but I busied myself with cleaning up anything and everything. It gave me something to do other than have trouble hearing what people said to me, and gave me a chance to tour the fabulous kitchen, which I really wanted to scrutinize.

The dishwasher was interesting; instead of a basket for the flatware, it had a tray that slid out of the top. It took me and a couple of other people a while to figure that out, and finally Tina wandered in and just confirmed our guess. The other appliances were beautiful stainless steel.

She served lots of delicious, healthy, catered food and fancy little desserts at her party. There were pulled, spiced chicken pieces on long sticks; grapes and fancy cheeses; strawberries; a huge platter of fruit; a tray of tiny chocolate mousse rounds and fruit tarts; another tray of small cakes; and plenty of beer and wine, which meant using Tina's long-stemmed wine glasses.

At one point, I noticed a huge, square, plain-framed painting on the wall to the right just outside of the kitchen. It depicted a few fish swirling around against a teal-blue background, with some red and gold here and there. Tina came over and told us that she had just bought it recently, and had it shipped here for this spot. It was nice; modern, colorful in this beige apartment, a focal point, and it set off her nondescript dining room table and chairs.

Later, I need to use the bathroom and got to explore the rest of the place. Tina's bedroom was well-lit, sparely and modernly furnished and decorated, and her bathroom had a modern shower that one simply walked into, shutting the glass door. Only a wall of glass enclosed it. It was just like something from one of Hollywood's latest, set-in-Manhattan movies.

Down the hall behind the unused front room was a laundry area that was not in a room, and before that were the guest room and bathroom where her brother was staying.

Tina's brother chatted with me and Berta and someone named Karen in the kitchen. As we talked, a recent story about bullying at a school in Brooklyn came up, one in which a group of bullies pulled a Sikh boy's turban off. I had heard about that; I commented that that was terrible; the poor kid probably had to run and wind his long hair and turban back up into place with those idiots chasing him and impeding his efforts.

The Slamming Door

Berta looked like she wanted to make me be quiet, but seemed to think better of it when Tina's brother smiled appreciatively at me; he seemed to enjoy the fact that knew something about other cultures than my own. Encouraged, I added that when I was in Kuwait, a friend of mine told me that she attended graduate school in Pittsburgh, and once, a guy had walked up to her and attempted to knock her scarf off her head. When confronted, he had said that he wanted to see if she had hair. Unbelievable; of course she had hair – and she didn't want him to see it – that's why she wore a scarf!

That was about the extent of my conversation, except to tell about myself – law degree, writing, editing, husband the scientist and Gulf War veteran, etc. Other than that, I lapsed into cleaning. I just couldn't stand around like Berta did, holding a drink and chatting about nothing in particular. I never could do that well; it feels dull, boring, and awkward, and sooner or later I say too much or else add something that doesn't fit into the flow of conversation.

The best I can do is say something interesting, and then just listen. But listening here was too difficult; the deafening noise made it hard to understand anything. It was frustrating.

As I cleaned everything up, Tina came in and thanked me, and her brother commented at one point "you're perfect," which was nice. I thought, if I'm so perfect, I would have lots of my own money from published books and Damon would have money from products on the market and we would be living together…but I just smiled and said nothing.

I was glad when Berta said we could get a cab and go, but also glad to have visited.

The next evening, we were back in Albert and June's apartment, eating Brie and watching news of the presidential election campaign. I loved it.

Chapter 17

Hallowe'en in Chelsea

I love Halloween.

As if that weren't enough to be enthusiastic about, Halloween in Chelsea was even greater fun than what I was used to in Connecticut. It was like a giant carnival, safe and full of happy, friendly people who also loved the holiday.

I was determined to see as many of them as I could. Normally I am not this sociable, nor do seek out the company of children, but this is the one exception to this aspect of my personality.

I don't care how this sounds: I'll never grow up, I'll never stop enjoying Halloween and seeing costumes, and I'll never let anyone tell me I should.

Damon and I met on Halloween in 1995 at a party for graduate students with food but no costumes. He was about to begin his Ph.D. studies, and I wasn't a law student yet; I was still in the process of applying. We were both dating other people, and I was working at the UConn Health Center Library. We became best friends almost immediately.

The freaky thing about this was that as I was chatting with everyone else, I saw Damon sitting alone, quietly on the sofa at the back of the room, watching me intently and listening, and a phrase flashed through my mind: "your future husband." What?! I had seen this guy walking around outside the Health Center before, but why would my mind shout this at me?

But it was true.

It took a while to happen, but it came true.

We both loved Halloween.

In Connecticut, I would answer my grandmother's door to give out candy and ask each kid what their costume was if it wasn't obvious, and give compliments on some. I would also wear my witch costume, a zodiac-patterned black cap with a satiny black witch hat.

If Damon were around, he would participate; one year he wore his outfit from a Saudi citizen, a white dishdashah, a beautiful wool bisht with silk threads and tassels woven onto the opening, and a guthra and ekal for a headdress. To top it off, he put a demilitarized, empty grenade that he kept for laughs – which usually was on a board that said "Complaints? Take a #" – and tied it onto his belt. He only did that once, but it was great fun. That was the same year that we saw a George W. Bush costume, complete with a mask; that was much scarier.

The Slamming Door

In New York, Damon and I would go out to eat, and he would buy me a dozen pink roses. Then we would go walking around Chelsea to see the costumes. Chelsea on Halloween brings out two phases of celebration: 1. The standard of kids and parents out trick-or-treating; 2. The gays and drag queens in their costumes. There was some overlap, which was great fun to see also. And of course, in the time leading up to Halloween, imaginative decorations appeared.

Halloween fell on a Friday in 2008. Bryn was still at Albert and June's place in TriBeCa; the boiler had only died a few days earlier. He was fine where he was. Albert had been saying to come on down and hang out with them all evening, every evening. But tonight I just didn't want to, because I didn't want to miss the fun of Halloween. I called them and told them so, and Bryn and Albert had no problem with that; they said to have fun. I was free to do as I wished.

The haunted dollhouse in the Fat Witch Bakery in Chelsea Market at Halloween.

A couple of times that evening, I called both Bryn and Damon, or perhaps Bryn called me to see what I was up to. I told him, and he seemed

Hallowe'en in Chelsea

to enjoy hearing about it. Damon said he missed me and he loved me, and I said it back.

It was the one night on which I had little interest in sitting in the apartment with a book and a movie, or using the Internet like an encyclopedia. Off I went, more than once, to see anything and everything.

If I haven't mentioned it before now, Chelsea was an area with a large concentration of gay residents, but it also had its fair share of families with children.

Bryn had mentioned to me that many gays were annoyed by the influx of straight, traditional couples and families to what they considered to be their own area, one where they were the majority rather than a persecuted, reviled minority. I could appreciate that point of view, but it seemed a bit paranoid and unrealistic at the same time. Everyone has to live somewhere.

As I spent more time in Chelsea, I realized that the gays who lived there seemed to have accepted the influx of traditional families, and that the newcomers had arrived with a good attitude: they chose to move to Chelsea knowing that lots of gay people lived there, so objecting to their presence would not be fair or reasonable. The gays had responded by relaxing and enjoying life in Chelsea, and Halloween showcased this.

In the hall outside the Manhattan Fruit Exchange in Chelsea Market at Halloween with carved and whole pumpkins.

The Slamming Door

Halloween had its usual customs, observed by both groups: decorations, costumes, and trick-or-treating. The result was some overlap of the two cultures that evening: kids out with parents until sundown, treated by many gay men doling out candy, followed by drag queens and other gays dressed up in fabulous costumes both before and after dark, with the ratio of gay and transsexual adults to children enjoying the holiday increasing as the evening wore on.

For about a month leading up to Halloween, I had been looking at the decorations in the neighborhood and enjoying them, taking photos and bringing them home to show Bryn and the others. Chelsea Market had outdone itself as usual with its carved pumpkins at the Manhattan Fruit Exchange and the witch dollhouse in the Fat Witch Bakery.

After dark, seen from straight across the street, this window-witch appeared to be flying over a harvest moon thanks to the yellow-orange globe-lamp that hung behind her.

Hallowe'en in Chelsea

Elsewhere, every street-level window seemed to have a display of tiny pumpkins. On our street, opposite us and down near 9th Avenue, a huge witch hung close in a window with a broomstick, a black hat and long black dress with long, scraggly black hair, framed by a huge globe of a light fixture in the dining room behind her. The effect after dark was of her flying over a full harvest moon – and I loved it.

Bryn thought it was pretty cool, too. So did the rest of the people I showed it to. I ended up e-mailing it to all of my friends and relatives. That digital camera was a lot of fun.

But on Halloween itself, I set out in the broad daylight of mid-afternoon to see the sights. I knew that there would be plenty of things going on, plenty of people wherever I went in costume, and plenty of decorations to photograph well before dark. And if I waited until dark, I could forget about the photography; my digital camera wouldn't get really good images at night.

I headed east, out of Chelsea, as far as 6th Avenue, then walked north a couple of blocks. Here and there, just as I had hoped, were people in costume walking around in the mild, warm weather. This really was a perfect Halloween.

The Slamming Door

Up ahead of me near 6th Avenue were a couple who were dressed as pirates. The woman's costume looked creative enough, but the man's seemed to overlap into his everyday life because of all of the tattoos that he had on his forearms. He posed for a photograph, looking happily rakish with his black outfit all patterned with huge, white skulls. He wore a black hat with a skull and crossbones on one side, complete with a red band across it. His beard and mustache looked like they had been glued on, a goatee with long mustaches hanging to each side.

He and his girlfriend were from Long Island, they told me, and they wanted sushi. I walked them to the Monster Sushi bar restaurant and found out that the man was a famous animal rescuer who worked mostly with cats. He and his colleagues – all volunteers – had been featured in an issue of *People* magazine, and he had it with him. Sure enough, there he was, clean shaven and tattooed with a bunch of similarly-decorated guys, each of whom held a cat.

I left him and his girlfriend at the sushi bar and roamed on through the area, thrilled that Halloween was off to a great start. Walking back via West 23rd Street, I paused at the Madeleine Patisserie for some financiers. I bought a cylindrical box of them and a hot chocolate to go, and then headed home again.

When I got back, Hilda and her friends were back, costumed and out front.

I took several photos, feeling almost in awe of Ophelia's handmade Marie Antoinette costume. It was gorgeous, and she had done it all herself. She even had a blond wig in the style that the unfortunate queen had worn at Versailles. This was a reine in her happy days as a teen at the palace, before she was hated by and terrified of her people. Ophelia had sewn a fabulous powder-blue gown, complete with a polonaise skirt, a laced bodice, and a white lace parasol.

Hilda's other friends also had nice costumes, including a Rosie the Riveter and Marilyn Monroe. Hilda herself intended to run upstairs and change; she had one costume for trick-or-treating, and another for the weekly run to *The Rocky Horror Picture Show* and the Halloween parade. Halloween was on a Friday, after all, and the kids weren't going to miss it. Hilda started out as a dancer in *A Chorus Line*, and was switching to Holly Golightly of *Breakfast at Tiffany's*. She even had a cigarette holder to carry as a prop, not that she smoked.

The kids looked a bit exasperated by my enthusiasm over their costumes, but agreed to meet me upstairs in Bryn's apartment for the other photo. I knew I wanted the photos, and had no doubt that Bryn would be thrilled to have them as well. I was not mistaken.

Hallowe'en in Chelsea

With the cookies put away and the photos on the computer, I headed out once again to photograph yard decorations. The next street up, 22nd, proved to be a haven of fun, with fake cobwebs strung on most of the trees, jack o'lanterns on every set of steps, and other things dangling here and there. There were giant arachnids, giant and smaller-sized bats, skeletons, gravestones, ghosts, mummies, random devils, an odd Frankenstein monster, more witches, ravens, and a skeleton with glowing red eyes that sat up and laid down in its coffin.

The Slamming Door

Hallowe'en in Chelsea

When I was finished touring the neighborhood, I went home again to save all of the photos on the computer and check in with Bryn by phone. Bryn was delighted to hear about the fun I was having, a trait of his which always fascinated me. He was off doing his own thing but wanted to hear all about special details in other people's lives. I told him I had gotten lots of photos for him, and he was happy.

Also, I made sure to say that I had dropped off the bags of Halloween candy that he had asked me to buy for the Ecuadoran family next door. We planned to give those kids some holiday-specific treats for as long as we were roommates. The kids seemed pleased and surprised when I knocked and presented the chocoholic loot; they didn't even have to treat-or-treat for it.

The Slamming Door

By the time I was finished with all of this, it was getting dark out; time for some serious trick-or-treating. I went back to 22nd Street, certain that it would be worth my while. I was right; families with little kids in costume were there. The most memorable thing that I saw was a gay couple giving out treats.

Both of the men were dressed the same, in long black pants with short-sleeved black tee shirts and extremely short hair. One stood on the steps of their brownstone building, just behind the wrought-iron fence, giving the candy away. The other was lying down in an open coffin with his arms crossed over his chest. He kept sitting up very slowly, opening his eyes as he did so with a deadpan expression on his face, then closing them as he lay back just as slowly.

After that, it was time to see about dinner, so I headed out again, determined to make a special occasion of it even if I was spending the holiday alone. The Empire Diner on 10th Avenue seemed like a promising idea, so I headed west in the dark, encountering lots of parents with small children as I went. It was almost eight o'clock now.

When I got there, I realized that the menu wasn't that exciting, but I decided to stay anyway. I ordered the chicken and some chips with guacamole, plus some raspberry lambic (Belgian) beer when I noticed that it was available. I sat at the bar admiring the Halloween costumes on the wait staff. The best one was the drag queen waiter who was dressed as Marilyn Monroe – he looked so authentic, and more convincing than Hilda's friend, who was a redhead.

Hallowe'en in Chelsea

This guy had blown up two small pink balloons to fill out the front of his white dress, his blond wig looked absolutely perfect, and his makeup was predictably flawless. He was wonderfully cheerful and friendly, too, clearly enjoying himself.

A couple with a little girl came in and the Marilyn Monroe waiter talked to her. He squatted down and complimented her costume, but I don't remember what hers was thanks to the impressive display that the drag queen put on. As I watched, I found myself musing about what lies the heterosexual parents might tell their daughter to explain the man dressed as a woman. Whatever they planned to say, they saved it for later on. The encounter went nicely.

I ate about half of my order, finished the beer, and headed home to watch the Halloween episodes of my favorite television shows and then heat up bath and shampoo water in pots on the stove again. I was so delighted with the festivities that I didn't mind the inconvenience.

Chapter 18

Obama! Obama! Obama!

Election night was spent mostly at Albert and June's place in TriBeCa, a little bit in a cab, and lastly in Chelsea. Before that, I spent the day in Chelsea, at the apartment, waiting to see if the heat and hot water would come back on.

Bryn and I had both voted by absentee ballot long before then.

I had ordered my absentee ballot before I even knew that I was going to stay with Bryn, when I didn't know that he was sick. The reason was that I had no car with which to go to the polling station, so I had called the registrar of voters in my town and been told that it was no problem – I could have an absentee ballot. All I had to do to get it was call for an application, fill it out and send it back, and I would receive an absentee ballot. After that, I could prepare the ballot according to the instructions and send it back at any time.

The application arrived and I sent it off right away; I'm not the sort of person to waver about a decision, and once made, I'm not the sort to second-guess or regret one. Why procrastinate? So I had gotten on with it.

The ballot went to my house in Bloomfield after I went to Bryn's place; my mother sent it on to me. Ironically, I was now really out of town for the election, even though when I had ordered the thing, I had been contemplating a much shorter distance to the polling station. Now I really needed an absentee ballot! I voted for Obama with it immediately, and that was that.

All his life, Bryn had voted by going to the polling station, waiting in line, and placing his vote. Suddenly, he didn't think he would have the physical stamina to do that. When I suggested an absentee ballot, he stared at me for a moment, uncertain, and so I pointed out that illness and infirmity met the legal requirements to qualify for an absentee ballot. He was really pleased when he realized that, and announced happily that he would get one and vote for Nader.

Cool – well, not the part about voting for Nader, but that Bryn was going to vote and no illness would prevent that. I had met Ralph Nader when Damon and I spent six months in the Washington, D.C. area in 2003. Damon was there to write a grant application at George Washington University, and we saw Nader speak at the National Press Club, and met him at his office once. (The grant was about a study of war veterans, so Nader was interested in it.)

Ralph Nader is a hero for getting seat belts to be a standard feature of motor vehicles, and for advocating that vehicle shapes not have pointy

Cassie Visits – I Like Her

wing-like projections, the purpose being to drastically reduce the number of injuries from auto crashes. But that and his other public advocacy work is enough right there.

The problem I saw with voting for Nader and anyone else who commands a rather small percentage of the overall vote in a race for the presidential office is that this just takes away votes from the ones with a real chance of winning in a close tally. Nader is partially responsible for us having been stuck with George W. Bush for two terms, and W. was the worst president in U.S. history. When someone like Ralph Nader runs, it seems more like ego gratification than anything else, and it should be about public service more than anything else.

But that is just my opinion, and I didn't tell Bryn any of that. Why spoil his fun? It was his vote anyway. So I just enjoyed seeing him delight in being able to participate in the political process in spite of his illness after having briefly worried that he might not be able to. An absentee ballot is such a simple end run around that problem.

So that was that; we were both free to enjoy the election as observers.

There was such optimism about Obama; as a lawyer, a pro-choicer, and a Democrat, he seemed like the best choice for the job. But no one seemed to be realistically looking at the task before him: cleaning up such a monumental mess left over from the previous administration that he would likely make only a small dent in it before 4 years had elapsed.

That mess was the economy. Obama was going to get blamed for not completely fixing it. People would not look his efforts in a reasonable light; their problems and angst over those problems would cause them to lose patience with him, even though he would do his best and apply great ideas. People would forget that Congress blocks change in order to stay in office, delaying decisions with filibusters and debates and whatever else.

An image of a political cartoon came to mind – one that, I am sorry to say, never appeared in any newspaper that I came across, despite a lot of reading. It was entirely my idea. The image was of a gargantuan heap of manure, complete with emanations of stench. The heap had a label on it – "The Economy" – and next to it, tiny, would be Obama with his shirt sleeves rolled up, on his hands and knees, working away with the biggest scrub brush that he could hold. He was making negligible headway at cleaning it up.

But the only solution was to vote for him and turn him loose on the mess. If we didn't start cleaning it up, we would never be finished. I suppose that is true of the environment as well, even though we refused to consider the solution: regulation and control of human reproduction. There were just too many of us for the planet to support now, not enough resources left, and we were using them up with reckless abandon like parasites. But we wouldn't stop; to even say this is taboo, not that such a consideration would ever stop me from doing so.

At least America is a society in which we can speak taboo opinions without retribution.

Here's another one: reproduction is the ultimate act of selfishness.

It does not guarantee that your offspring will take care of you when you are old, or that you will have children whom you would want doing that for you. Look at Bryn – he didn't have or want that. He once told me, years earlier, that if he had it do over again, he would not have reproduced. The reason he gave had nothing to with Berta herself; it was that he considered the world to be overpopulated, so why add more people to it? He would just adopt a little girl instead. It sounded reasonable. But he could afford private school, camp and college for her.

If you cannot give your children all that you had and better, meaning lessons in art, music, language, math, history, writing and a competitive college degree, then you are dumping an insurmountable problem upon them. Too many people have had the same idea: their children must be educated to the point of qualifying to work in the middle class tier and live at the middle class level. But there isn't room for all of us to do that.

Nevertheless, anything short of that is now considered beneath most of the American population, and beneath a certain percentage of immigrants too. Who will do the other work that fuels this nation – that fuels any nation? And what work will the rest of us do, those of us who are supposed to have been groomed for something better? There is less and less of it now, and although we see what kind of work we should be doing – greening the nation – we don't yet know how to go about it.

We needed to simultaneously rearrange our collective finances, energy use, energy supplies, and work methods. No wonder Obama was in for so much trouble. Bryn agreed.

But people were caught up in the excitement, and wanted to party about the hope that he inspired. They would not look for audacity right away, but when they got around to it, he was going to be in for a brick wall of disappointed expectations.

When I thought about the Republican ticket, I was more disgusted and annoyed than usual. McCain was blatantly anti-choice and so was Sarah Palin, his running mate. Her teenage daughter Bristol was pregnant, and sat holding hands with Levi Johnston, her boyfriend. It was obvious that he didn't love her, and I doubted that he would stick around much past the election.

As if that weren't appalling enough, I had done some online research about McCain, beyond the basic checking of his stance on abortion, the environment, and the economy. What I wanted to know about was the

Cassie Visits – I Like Her

way he interacted with women. Something wasn't quite right there. Why had he divorced his first wife, the one who had waited for him while he was a prisoner of war in Vietnam, strung up by two broken arms and tortured?

So he was a war hero, one who had refused a chance to go home when his identity as the son and grandson of famous U.S. Navy officers had been made known to his captors, and thus been stuck as a prisoner for 5 miserable years. That alone did not justify voting for him.

What I found was that his first wife had been a beautiful, tall brunette swimsuit model. They adopted a couple of kids and had one other one before McCain was lost in Vietnam in 1967. Then, on Christmas Eve of 1969, his wife was injured in a terrible car accident while driving in icy conditions. 23 operations later she was full of pins in her smashed legs and pelvis, and not so statuesque. She told her husband nothing of this in her letters to him, stoically suffering at home on her own to spare him any further anxiety in captivity.

And what was her reward for this? When he came home and saw that she was no longer a beauty, he stopped caring about her. He had affairs, and by 1980 they were divorced, but not before he had a replacement for her lined up: another beauty queen.

This one was a blond bombshell who had been named Best Dressed Senior in high school, gone on to become a rodeo beauty queen, and then joined a sorority in college, where she studied to be a special education teacher. To top it all off, she was an heiress to a huge beer company fortune. So that was what did it for McCain: beauty above all else, and now he had named the governor of Alaska, a former beauty queen herself, as his running mate.

It was like he was saying to the women voters, "Look! Here's a woman on my ticket! I'm with you!" even though he wasn't; he was anti-choice, and a detailed search of his dealings with his wives had revealed not only affairs, but worse yet, beatings. He had beaten Cindy Lou, his blond second wife. No way was he getting my vote, that was for sure.

Regardless of all that, it was time to focus on the election and just enjoy it. There is only so much that worrying about the future can accomplish, so we enjoyed the present. Funny how taking care of a sick and dying and favorite relative can persuade you to enjoy the person and time with them while it is still possible to do so. So whatever I could enjoy that year, I did.

I did it because there seemed to be no other sane option. Once the time was gone, that was it; it was over, couldn't be repeated, and there was no point in regretting it. So I would just do the best that I could, knowing that somehow, when it was all over, someone would find fault with something about me and my methods or who knew what. I didn't

The Slamming Door

care. Caring would only induce extra misery for no reason. It would be like second-guessing the future.

Not knowing what might go wrong until it already had, I decided that if critics wanted my job done differently, then they should have found a way to do my job or else shut up. Meanwhile, I did the best that I could, checking with Bryn almost daily to see if he was happy with my performance. Who cared how the others felt in the end? It was his death, not theirs.

As luck would have it, the evening of the election was a great success.

Before I left, I dutifully waited all day to see if the boiler would be fixed, making sure not to call the superintendent more than once or twice. The poor guy was no doubt overly stressed out as it was with worry over this, harassed with calls about it both from tenants and the landlord, plus it was election day. I finally called him around 5 o'clock and found out that the power company had not shown up yet.

Poor Luis; I asked him whether or not he had voted yet, and how far away from his polling station he lived. He said he lived right down the street, but that he hadn't gotten a chance to go vote yet and his wife had called him to say that the line was stretched around the street.

"If they haven't come yet, they're not coming today," I told him. "Go vote. You are entitled to go out and vote." He said he would go now. I rang off feeling disgusted but pleased with myself for talking him into concerning himself with his own political voice.

Then I called Bryn and reported all this. He listened, approved, and then told me to get a cab and come on down to TriBeCa for the evening, so I did. Happy in the knowledge that our votes were safely in and we could avoid the uproar while watching from a comfortable living room, we settled in.

Alissa was there too, but Berta was out on Long Island with Matt. Matt had just completed his citizenship requirements in time for the election, and was excited to go out and vote. He wanted Berta to go with him and walk him through the process so that nothing went wrong with his vote. We all thought it was pretty cool to say the least.

Dionne arrived shortly after I did, entering with great fanfare and enthusiasm. She had her hair down for a change, instead of in its usual ponytail with long braid, and was wearing a wild-looking gold jacket with a boa that appeared to be made of baby ostrich feathers. But that wasn't the main attraction of her attire.

She flashed the jacket open and proudly displayed her black tee shirt, which read, in rounded, blockish gold lettering: "Hot Mamma for Obama!"

Cassie Visits – I Like Her

There was a round of approval from us all, and then she sat down in the circle of chairs that Albert had grouped around the coffee table. We all ate our dinner there, watching the pundits analyze the results over and over again as they rolled in.

Albert's birthday was two nights later, but for some reason, we gave him his presents while we watched; he enjoyed everything. I had also bought a little gift for Bryn: one tiny cheesecake with strawberries and a kiwi fruit slice on top (at Whole Foods – the new one near Albert and June's place). He smiled, thanked me, and saved it for later.

I had gotten Albert 2 magnets and a card - the card is one of those people cards I like to give, but it shows a Lewis Carroll character, the Mad Hatter. The magnets said "Attention: Chien Bizarre" and "If the Economy's so Good, How Come I'm So Broke?" – because Albert liked French language things and he and June have a dog, and because he and Bryn moan about the economy a lot. Bryn approved both magnets with a huge grin, and Damon approved them over the phone, so I guessed that they would be well-received; they were.

A little while into the election-watching, Dionne began to be loud and ridiculous again, to the point that I asked her how much wine she had drunk...thanks to too many remarks about hoping that Republicans would get assassinated. I told her she could go to jail for that even if she didn't mean any of it, because it wasn't protected speech, but she kept it up. No danger – we were just at home with the family. At least her tee shirt was funny.

She was entertaining for some of it, putting on southern accents. I really couldn't blame her for getting so excited over Obama, because I had been told several stories about her background. Her Alabama grandmother had been treated badly for having a black ancestor...and her mother was turned away from the roller-skating rink there when she was a teenager. The mother and grandmother looked lily-white, but the racists in the neighborhood knew about the black ancestor, whoever it was, so Dionne and Berta and their mother and grandmother were bitter about the rude and unequal treatment that it got them.

I stayed for quite a while, until around 11 o'clock, but the thought of heating up the water again for my bath and shampoo made me want to go home before the election was officially declared in favor of one candidate or the other. There seemed to be little danger of the air-headed beauty queen-and-wife-beater team winning; the results were almost all in by then.

June and Alissa stuffed a $20-bill into my pocket because I cleaned ALL dishes yet again. I felt a bit bad, but they actually forced it into my pocket and hugged me. I think it was meant for food and expenses. Bryn, though aware of that gift, appeared with $12 more for a cab, and insisted

The Slamming Door

that I take it. Then Albert stood at the curb with me until a cab came along. A nice older Sikh guy drove me, and told me that he was applying for U.S. citizenship, and that he loved the place on 9th Avenue where all the Sikh cabbies get their dinners. I told him that I loved it too, but wished that it sold mango lassi. He thought that was great...and agreed with me.

As we entered the Chelsea neighborhood, the cab driver slowed to a crawl because 8th Avenue was packed with people – crowds of them. They were all smiling, cheering, waving, and shouting "Obama! Obama! Obama!"

Even though the outcome of the election tallies was obvious, I needed to hear it for myself. And even though I was closing fast on my very own television with which to confirm it, I opened my window, grinned, and shouted out, "Is it official? Did he win?"

People answered gleefully that he had, smiling and waving. I gave the thumbs up and closed the window partway. It was a pleasant, warm evening and I enjoyed the breeze.

When the cab rolled up in front of the apartment building, I paid and got out, happy.

Upstairs, the heat and hot water was not on yet, even though it was now legal to turn it on, so I turned on the TV and started heating up the water again.

I took my time, e-mailing Damon.

The next night, I called my Aunt Johanna (I too had an Aunt Johanna, but a blood aunt), found out that she was happy about the outcome, and then she HAD to go to sleep early. Nothing new there; she and my father have always preferred to be morning people, rising at 4 a.m. and going to bed at 8 or 9 p.m. But she is so different from her brother, always sweet and cheerful.

On Albert's actual birthday, we decided to celebrate again...or for real, depending upon one's point of view. I went to Balducci's on 14th Street and 8th Avenue, the one in the former bank building that looked like a palace for money, and ordered his cake. Albert liked chocolate, but wasn't supposed to have too much dessert, so I bought their last 6-inch one. It looked absolutely delectable – rich, dark chocolate with ganache and cocoa powder around the side, plus white and dark chocolate shavings on top. I paid for it and arranged to have "Happy Birthday Albert!" written in green letters around the shavings.

So we all had a nice time, eating dinner together, drinking wine and Leffe beer, and watching him blow out the candles on his cake. I got several nice photographs of his party.

The stupid heat and hot water was turned on at the end of the week.

Cassie Visits – I Like Her

When I found out what had happened and told Bryn, he groaned, but wasn't really surprised. Karen Carter was what had happened. She had called the gas company and lied to them on Monday, claiming to work for the mayor's office and swearing that it was not yet safe to turn on the new boiler. So despite the fact that the computer readouts in their trucks said to go ahead and turn it on, the men had not. We couldn't really blame them for it, but it was infuriating. (This was the same time period in which she stole the poor superintendent's clipboard from him, too.) On Wednesday, the landlord and his daughter got wind of all this and straightened it out personally, and by Friday we were back in business.

But Bryn lingered a bit longer in TriBeCa, enjoying it there with his brother, and not in any hurry to go through the hassle of relocating. I was starting to miss him in the apartment, even though I saw him often. It was just weird late at night not to be able to wander in and check on what he was watching or reading and then go back to whatever I was enjoying.

Cassie planned to visit for a few hours on Thursday, at Albert and June's place, so they planned to go out during that time. I was expected to come over and meet Cassie, and hoped to get a photo of her if I was lucky. But then I planned to leave; I didn't want to hang around much. She would be driving 2 hours, visiting, and then driving back for another 2 hours.

Albert told me that Cassie was very nice, but manipulative…for having two guys and with the full knowledge of her husband. He and June thought it was terrible, that Bryn shouldn't do this, etc., but added that 30 years is 30 years, so that was the way it was. Albert said not to worry – Cassie would be pleasant to me, and that she was grateful that I was taking care of Bryn. She couldn't take proper care of two guys who were geographically separated anyway.

I wasn't particularly worried about it at all – just really curious to meet her. What kind of a demeanor went with that gruff voice that I had heard over the phone? Well, I knew that it was just a smoker's voice, but I couldn't help wondering about that a lot.

Regardless, after being in the Islamic world where men routinely had more than one woman in their lives, I secretly thought it was really cool that this woman had more than one man in her life. Since both of them knew and accepted the situation, I did too.

There. I had said it to myself. I enjoyed the smashing of a double-standard immensely.

Aside from that aspect of the enjoyment, I took comfort in the fact that because no one was lying to anyone or sneaking around, this was something that I could talk about with the same tone of satisfaction. I had actually done so in years past, and to some male Kuwaitis – Muslim men who sneaked around and lied to and cheated on their wives. No Muslim

The Slamming Door

woman wants a co-wife, regardless of what the Quran allows. My friend Massoumeh Parsi had even said so.

Telling those men about Cassie had been great fun.

Cassie Visits – I Like Her

Chapter 19

Cassie Visits – I Like Her

So after hearing about her for years, after admiring her, I met Cassie in TriBeCa.

After all that time, it was great to finally converse with her face-to-face.

Her long, wavy red hair was barely streaked with white, she had very few wrinkles, wore no makeup, and looked pretty much just like the few photographs that Bryn possessed of her. Cassie had barely aged since those photos in Bryn's room had been taken over a decade earlier. She looked a lot younger than I knew she actually was, despite the smoking. For someone who was the love of his life, she certainly hadn't allowed him to possess very many images of her.

It turned out that she was so convinced that she was unattractive that she wouldn't allow me to shoot so much as one photo of her. I was bewildered and disappointed, but made no protest other than to disagree with her opinion of her appearance.

And I sincerely disagreed.

Cassie was decidedly pretty.

She was not a beauty, but she was not plain, either.

But as we had just met, I was not going to be able to take any photos, or to make any progress with understanding her attitude, so I gave up and just told her that she seemed most definitely pretty to me. She smiled and seemed quite pleased by that.

When I arrived, it was late in the morning, and the visiting nurse had just left. Albert and June had received her once before, and holed themselves upstairs in their bedroom with the dog again, only to have Pearlie escape repeatedly and bark incessantly. I was glad to have missed it.

Then Cassie had arrived, and I found her sitting on the end of the sofa holding Bryn's hand. It was their 30-year anniversary of having met in some bar in Greenwich Village, in 1978. Cassie had been newly engaged to Chip, a much older professor of English literature. She was 63, Bryn was now near 71, and Chip was in his early 80s. I was fascinated just contemplating all this, but of course said nothing about it.

I liked the way that Cassie looked at me and spoke. She looked me straight in the eye, never holding her chin slightly upwards, and without a trace of condescension in her voice. All that I sensed from her was total and utter acceptance of me as I was. I was happy to return the sentiment. I look at and speak to people that way, too whenever I can.

The Slamming Door

We could do that, and because this was all too rare for me, I was really pleased with it.

It was different from when I spoke with Berta, who always seemed to be instructing me in some way about things that barely mattered, if at all, such as how to order food or interact with complete strangers. The food-ordering was fun, but I didn't like the other.

Interactions with Cassie were very similar to those with Alissa. Alissa stared a lot, but seemed anxious about her own issues, never concerned that I might somehow embarrass her by being myself. I could almost but not quite connect with Alissa, and I genuinely liked her.

Cassie another story; Cassie and I seemed to connect right away.

But that is not to say that this was the start of a rewarding and fulfilling friendship.

There was almost no time and very little opportunity for that.

It was a sad thing to say, but geography and circumstances automatically precluded that.

What we would have would be an instant understanding and acceptance, and a friendship of limited but sincere enjoyment, whenever, wherever and however we did in fact interact.

That would have to do.

Hours later, when Cassie was gone and I was back there with Bryn, he told me that she had liked me instantly and very much.

Excellent; the feeling had been mutual. I told him so.

However, since Berta had always loathed her, partly for being in what had been her mother's place and partly for being the way that she was – with a personality that differed markedly from Berta's plus being her father's beloved girlfriend – I sensed some foreboding.

Oh well…whatever this foretold, we wouldn't have to deal with it for a while.

That afternoon, Bryn and Cassie went across the street after a little while, to eat lunch at a café alone together. I had other things to do, so I left, too. Among them was the picking-up of Albert's chocoholic birthday cake.

I thought about Cassie some more. She was an artist who had graduated from the Parsons School in Manhattan, but now she worked upstate as a social worker with teenage girls from families with problems. She combined that with her hobby, which was that she loved horses. She owned a brown male with a white stripe down his nose named Louis, and helped out at the horse barn with all of the animals who were quartered there, bringing the girls to help out, too.

Bryn had lots of fond memories of visiting Louis and singing to him with his lovely tenor voice. Louis loved it. I could just picture all this; the photos of Cassie riding Louis and grooming Louis helped with that.

Cassie Visits – I Like Her

All I had to do was add other images – memories, really – of Bryn singing, and the picture was complete. That mental composite was a great image.

The Slamming Door

Chapter 20

TV and Take-Out

After another few days of visiting Bryn in TriBeCa with our boiler fixed and operating, I asked him when he was coming back, and said that I missed him. He gave me a startled look, like he hadn't thought that through, and a few days later, he was back. I think he liked being back in his own place, in his own room, with a bed and no dog barking or jumping on him. It had to be much more comfortable.

Evenings at home tended to be spent watching favorite shows while eating dinner.

That was part of the charm of having a television in both rooms and being able to visit during commercials; we missed nothing, not the plot of a season's worth of entertainment, not each other opinions about anything; nothing. It was fun for all of us as long as Bryn's stomach felt quiet, and even better when he had an appetite.

Why were we eating in front of the TV? It was fun, and there was nowhere else.

I knew that it was healthier and encouraged better social graces to sit upright in chair around a dinner table. Even Hilda's family had a dinner table – it was in their kitchen, shoved up against the wall, and they sat around at mealtimes, eating.

The problem was that the apartment had no dinner table, because that piece of furniture had been designated a desk. The table had once upon a time been used for its intended purpose, back when Bryn and Albert's mother had been alive. She had had a dining room complete with formal china, etched crystal, silverware, and linens – the works.

When she died, Bryn acquired most of her home furnishings. Elvira had kept most of their things in the divorce, and Albert and June had their own, including some nice things from her own mother, and so it was decided that it was fair and reasonable for Bryn to get her dinnerware, bookcases, a lot of her artwork, sofa, dinner table, and bedroom furniture. But he shoved the dinner table up against the wall on the other side of his bedroom and piled it high with books. So it became a desk.

As I spent more time at that desk, I began to notice boxes of stationery, old checkbooks, paper clips, an empty cigar box, blank CDs, old tapes, a nice black-and-white photo of an eighteen-year-old, normal-sized, beautiful Berta, and various buttons from political movements and campaigns. It was the detritus of a lifetime of interests collected at random on a work area.

So...that was why we ate in front of the televisions, violating social graces while attempting to honor them as best we could. Who cared? We

TV and Take-Out

were having fun while living through a sad and stressful situation, so we went ahead and did it. We ate out so much – at tables while sitting properly in chairs – that it wasn't ruining our sense of social contract.

Often, Berta would arrive before it was time to eat or watch TV, so we would sit in Bryn's room and talk. That was when we would hear more about what her job was like. That fall, she had her yearly evaluation, or performance review, or whatever it was called at Deutsche Bank. The review consisted of going into a conference room and having her day-to-day efforts and demeanor analyzed.

She described it as a session in which her supervisors faced her like the adversaries that they were across a table, listing everything she had done while finding it all fine, then picking at something and saying that she needed to work on it. Why do this, I wondered, if she was performing her duties up to par, which it certainly sounded like she was?

No review was allowed to be perfect, was the reply.

I was appalled. This explanation meant that underlings always had to be beaten down as a matter of policy in the corporate world. The same was true of the retail world; my own experience backed that up. It was something that I had never been willing or able to accept.

There was more to it, however, and the only way I could make sense of this situation – the one called being an employee – was to keep on observing Berta. This was about the same time that I was starting to look up what it meant to have Asperger's online, which I did very tentatively, because I hate to psychoanalyze myself. I just find that so depressing that I avoid it.

But I have Asperger's; I am an Aspie. There is nothing wrong that, though.

It would take me the rest of the year observing Berta to figure her out, but I finally managed it. Stories that she told us revealed that she was the leader of her clique in high school, and she was a natural at navigating social situations. By that I mean that she intuitively understood how to manipulate her way through…as long as the other players were NTs.

An NT has neuro-typical brain patterns. People with Asperger's are the different ones.

That seemed to be the root of my problem: I wasn't an NT, so I couldn't read her without studying her. And I don't like feeling as though I'm not in on something while everyone else is, so I made the effort. It was so much more work to understand what most other people intuitively and therefore instantly understood, but I was determined to get where they were.

The Slamming Door

I listened to the tale of the performance review silently, but later reiterated what I had said to Bryn in times past: Berta's life at work seemed horridly depressing.

Her job was to make reservations for her bosses at 5-star hotels and restaurants around the world while going nowhere herself. That alone would have made me feel awful, not that I would ever have wanted to travel with any of those people.

Add to it the performance review and the social interactions that made up her entire day at work – with heavy phone contact and the requirement for what to me suggests intensely obsequious behavior, and I felt…extremely depressed. To tell the whole truth, I felt suicidal when I contemplated actually applying for a job in any corporate environment.

I was rapidly coming to the realization that I was not capable of functioning in very many work environments. It was something that would be nearly impossible to explain to most people, and only became comprehensible to me after I returned to Connecticut and read in depth about Asperger's. Already, experience had taught me that most people – the NTs of the world – did not accept this about others. If we could not do what they did and accept a life like theirs, they deemed Aspies lazy and said we had a chip on our shoulders. That has never sat well with me.

Here I was with an impressive, even enviable CV, and I wondered what I was qualified to do to earn money. I knew what I wanted to do – write and publish books, and edit those of others – but knowing that was a far cry from having access to an opportunity to make money doing so.

Bryn's response to my assessment that Berta's job was depressing was the same as it had been before: it was wonderful that Berta had her job, and no one else was going to support her.

I couldn't disagree. She needed the income from it, and perhaps it was a useful way for her to spend the day. Perhaps it kept her out of trouble. Perhaps…never mind – that covered it.

Her salary was a puzzle to me. How much did she take in each year? Was it $50,000? Or was it $80,000? I heard each of these figures at least once, and found them each to be confusing. How could her efforts be that lucrative? My mother, an office nurse, made roughly $45,000 each year. How could a floating secretary – one with no particular boss – make more money?

Maybe it was because she was in Manhattan, and the employees needed more money to cope with high living costs there. No…that was insane. Why else would I find so many stories about Manhattan apartments occupied by 3 or 4 single people who weren't related, all to cover high rent costs? Was Deutsche Bank so well off and so generous? That didn't make sense either.

TV and Take-Out

The only stories that added up to me were the accounts – from Berta, of course – describing the bonuses and salaries of the top executives. Those individuals had multiple McMansions, time-shares, sports cars, stocks and whatever else struck their fancies.

Berta seemed to have lots of money for whatever she needed or wanted, but then when it's not your life and you don't know everything about a person, such illusions can be quite convincing. Still, I wondered how she could save any money for the future while paying her mother half the rent for a 2-bedroom apartment at Stuyvesant Town, rent on a storage unit that contained whatever of her possessions she could not keep at her mother's apartment, endless restaurant and take-out meals, shopping at mid-to-low-end stores, and occasional travel to places like California. Bryn told me he thought she spent too much money.

Maybe she had nothing left over to save.

Well…it was her life, her money, and I wasn't going to ask for more information.

I kept my confusion to myself.

If I could just make sense of how she survived in a corporate environment that would help a lot in my effort to understand how most people functioned. My mother and Damon had both tried to explain things to me in their own ways, but watching Berta told me much more, and made the situation clearer.

My mother the NT had shared plenty of office stories, but I still felt clueless and confused by her life and her ability to function in such an environment.

Damon – my husband, whom I now understood to be an Aspie like me – had told me about the 3 Bs: brownnose your superiors, browbeat your subordinates, and back-stab your peers. But that wasn't enough information; I needed to be able to mentally visit the corporate world, not quite like a fly on the wall, but more like a telepath who could inhabit a participant's mind unnoticed. Since much of our evening conversation that fall involved Berta's office, there was plenty of data on the topic to silently crunch.

Berta's stories about work and Bryn's explanations told me more than I had ever been able to learn about such things in the past. It was morbid fascination combined with a desperate effort to understand what made me different, and (for now) feeling helpless about my own ability to earn a living. Why couldn't I do it?

The real question was: why couldn't I do it in the sort of environment that was found almost everywhere?

The ability to function in the sort of work environment that can be found almost everywhere means that one can find and keep work in a wider range of places and situations. Asperger's effectively narrowed the playing field for me, and did so to a considerable degree.

It made me feel scared and depressed, even though I wouldn't have traded my mind and brain patterns, nor my perception of life and human interactions, for anything.

I have never wished to blend in, fit in, or assimilate.

Resistance is not futile, and it feels like the only path open to me.

It's harder, but it's what I can make a success of.

My life feels harder, narrower, and yet more exciting than what most people get.

An added bonus of Asperger's is having my own schedule, and being able to avoid crowds and therefore many time-consuming inconveniences.

I have traveled, I have gone out and about when most people are confined to a 9-to-5 work schedule, and have seen and learned things that most people don't have the time or the opportunity to be exposed to or contemplate.

Whether or not they care about doing so is another question, but my past conversations with other people suggest to me that they do care, they do feel the lack of variety and excitement, and they do envy me.

I hope so; there has to be some compensation for the fear and lack of ability to function in most income-producing situations. And I still need to find my own unique income-producing situation. Fitting in is out; I must make a success of being odd.

At some point that year, Berta remarked to me that I made a success of everything I do.

But lately I found myself defining success as making money, and enough of it to earn a living, and so I disagreed with her. Damon was in a state of permanent depression and anxiety over that same definition. He was a famous scientist with an enviable CV but no money.

What the hell did it take to fix that?!

Marketing his ideas was one idea, but how to do that? His business partner didn't seem to be particularly adept at it, and neither did he. Maybe things just take a terribly long time, but then again maybe not. How long is too long? With minimal start-up funds, it could be like climbing Mount Everest, but failure was not an option.

Damnit. So I found myself eking by, living with Bryn as a caregiver, knowing that he was giving me a temporary rescue from being shut up in my home in Connecticut with my parents. He knew what he was doing and had said so at the beginning. But he needed me and liked having me there; I wasn't just being rescued for nothing. He was actually getting something out of this arrangement.

The trade-off was that I couldn't see my husband much anymore.

TV and Take-Out

Bryn's place had ceased to be a meeting place for us, except at holidays and for my anniversary, and then I found myself assuring Bryn that Damon would be gone in a couple of days. I did this in advance, almost apologetically, but never actually apologizing because to do so would have galled me.

This condition was what made me resolve never to ever be a caregiver for a stranger.

Bryn asked me about the idea once, and I told him that no, I would only do this for someone whom I loved, a relative, but never a stranger. A stranger would not want me to have my husband around at all, and I was unwilling to sign on for that. And older people often look very angry when they are just thinking, and even though their thoughts are usually unrelated to the caregiver, I would become frantic that I was in fact the subject of my employer's thoughts, and get upset and anxious. No; only for Bryn would I be a caregiver, or for some other relative. I knew Bryn, so I knew his expressions, and I knew that he wasn't angry with me when he looked like that. He was just thinking, and it was not all about me. I didn't want it to be.

He nodded, accepting my explanation.

Again, the field of income-producing possibilities appeared to narrow.

I was so sick of feeling that way: anxious, limited, afraid of life, and stuck.

Such a serious mindset for TV and take-out…and TV and take-out was such fun.

I had to lose myself in the fun of it to keep from obsessing about all this, and to maintain an appearance of calmness and amiability around my in-laws. I think I did a decent job of it most of the time. Only when Berta would quiz me about how I would cope with Damon's potential failure to make a living in the United States would that effort come undone.

Then I would truthfully tell her that I would rather be dead if that happened, and might actually kill myself rather than put up with it. She would get upset when I said that, and say "Don't upset me while my father is dying," or object to losing her friend after getting to know me. Well, she was the one who brought that depressing subject up, I thought to myself, looking at her in dismay and annoyance.

I just couldn't imagine that she would care whether I continued to exist or not, or really want to be my friend forever. Hanging around just to make her happy was not much of a motivator to put up with an unacceptable outcome. And Damon always away with no money to stay in my own country was exactly that: an unacceptable outcome. Life on any terms, even miserable ones, is just not worth it to me.

The Slamming Door

I am younger than everyone in my family and don't like kids. If I can't be happy, I don't see much point in sticking around on any terms, regardless of how glum they are. I'm not religious, I don't believe in hell after life, and I do believe in life as hell. Plus I have no patience with people who lecture to me about how I ought to feel, how I ought to perceive the world and life, and how I ought to live. I will go with my own judgments, thank you very much.

So it was back to watching the crime shows that I liked so much.

What I really liked about them was the interaction between the characters. They were like old friends who would not suddenly turn around and tell me that I was not fulfilling some sort of social contact to their satisfaction. There was that, and the shows that I chose typically contained one oddball character who stood out in some way yet was accepted by the others like family.

Add to this the fact that each show told an interesting story while imparting new and intriguing facts to the viewer in a memorable way, and I could feel relaxed and excited just knowing that a new episode was about to come on.

Bryn was very accepting of this, not that I explained it to him in such depth. He just thought I should be able to see my shows, and not be sorry to have missed them. It was no strain on anyone's schedule or anyone else's pleasure, and he would ask about my favorite shows. Were they on tonight? Was I missing any of them? Did I get to see them? Had I enjoyed them? Interesting...he wanted me to have my idea of fun. It was utterly impossible not to feel relaxed around him and to love him. He had a couple that he liked, too: *The L Word* and *The No. 1 Ladies Detective Agency*. But those were on much later at night.

Berta and I would get settled before the shows started, with our dinners on plates and our glasses of water ready, and Bryn's meal laid out in his room while he watched news of the economy, which he couldn't expect us to rush in to watch. They bored Berta and terrified me.

Some nights I cooked, and many nights Berta would get us all take-out food. It was probably about evenly divided between the two possibilities, and on weekends there would be trips out to restaurants with Matt and Albert and June and Alissa. As a result, I learned to shop for only small amounts of food to cook at home, nothing much bought ahead, because we wouldn't have time to eat it before it rotted. So, even when Bryn had his appetite, we couldn't keep up with all of the food that we had.

At one point, to help her lose weight, Berta signed up with an expensive service that delivered meals to her, one that cost her $300 on weekdays for all lunches and dinners. I'm not sure she was eating

TV and Take-Out

breakfast though, which I had learned a long time ago was a mistake. Just giving your stomach something to do when you first get up activates your metabolism, which is what makes you lose weight.

Once, she had fish with little curled slices of fennel around it. I could smell it; fennel makes me sick with its licorice-like scent and taste, sick to the point of nausea. Berta tried a bit of it and said she didn't like it. Then, oddly, she kept trying more of it, grimacing and wincing as she chewed. Still, she didn't like it.

Watching someone try to ingest something unpleasant is doubly nauseating if I dislike it too, and I said, "Stop! That's disturbing!" so she stopped at last. A couple of weeks later, she gave up on the service, saying that it cost too much. She never exercised anyway, so it wasn't doing her any good. 300 pounds is an awful lot to lose. I never watch those weight-loss reality shows, but the ads do reveal that exercise is a significant part of the process.

Anyway, she would show up with her dinner in little black rectangular plastic boxes, so I would just worry about cooking for me and Bryn, or cooking for myself and ordering him more spaghetti and meatballs if his digestive system was still menacing him. At that point, he could accept the scent of food cooking, even if his appetite hadn't yet returned to normal.

When he felt like that, he could only tolerate very specific things, so cooking got tricky. Rob kept leaving the same foods over and over again, which helped, except that a lot of it kept going to waste: cole slaw, cooked beets, meatballs with tomato sauce, and occasionally some melon slices. The only thing I would consider eating was the melon, but I just saved it all for Bryn, hoping he could eat it.

Other than that, Bryn was feeling amazingly comfortable between chemotherapy rounds, so Berta and I just enjoyed it. It meant that his personality was the same as ever, and he could enjoy the TV and the visits with us, which was great. Since he didn't want to watch what we were watching, so we would check on him during the commercials, which coincided.

Meanwhile, just as with *Bones*, Berta got hooked on the characters in *Criminal Minds* and *NCIS* as I explained them to her. She liked the overweight computer witch on *Criminal Minds* who wore wild, cheerful colors to work, and wondered about Abby, the Goth girl on *NCIS* who was the forensics expert; she had a CV full of journal articles like Damon's.

Why, Berta asked, were these women allowed to dress with such individuality?

Of course she would ask that, coming from such a socially homogenous corporate job.

The Slamming Door

I was glad she asked, because that was precisely what I enjoyed about their characters. The answer is that those women were geniuses at what they did, and the price of having them work with the teams and be able to calmly concentrate on their work was to leave them alone about such trivial matters. It fascinated me endlessly that the law enforcement bosses were wise enough not to mess with them, and even loved them as they were.

The only time I had ever seen a boss foolishly mess with one of them was when the Director of NCIS was a beautiful, conventional redhead who didn't interact with the Goth forensics expert much. She instituted a dress code, which proved the point: Gibbs, the team leader, found Abby in tears, uncomfortable in a lavender skirt suit, and unable to focus on her work. That ended that silliness. Abby was back in her Goth get-up by her next scene.

I love seeing such human interest situations because they show the oddball in a group of mostly conventional people being accepted as she is. As *she* is – there are lots of women with high I.Q.s in these shows. Their personalities and skills are at an impressively high level, too, and they are respected as they are, and enjoy being part of a diverse group.

Now that I understand Asperger's, I realize that my enjoyment of these shows is all about my pet fantasy: success, acceptance, respect and friendship for an Aspie woman among the many NTs that populate the world. I don't need a psychiatrist; I can psychoanalyze myself.

Berta listened silently and nodded, then got absorbed in the plot lines. After a few episodes, she asked me why I liked all these crime shows, which typically included horrible things happening to people. It was a familiar question. I told her that I liked murder mysteries, and puzzling out their facts and details. I liked the interaction of the characters who worked together to solve the mysteries most of all. *Law & Order* couldn't give me that; it was all law, with very few chase scenes, and almost no fact-gathering and analyzing, which was my favorite part of the story. No sense watching something that lacks my favorite part of the puzzle.

Odd coming from someone with a law degree, she said.

Not really, I replied. When I was in law school, the facts that made the case were what I had always cared about most. If they didn't add up, I saw no justification for arguing in favor of them anyway. I realize that that is precisely what many lawyers are expected to do, but I just can't do it. It seems wrong. No wonder I don't practice, and no wonder one of my professors said that he didn't think I could, and no wonder I never felt bad about that. I didn't know that all of these conditions were the markers of being an Aspie at that time.

TV and Take-Out

We talked about something else another evening, something that was equally fascinating.

It was about homework assignments from our pasts in which we had accurately predicted something that later came to pass in reality. We had each done this, me in college for a women's studies paper, and Berta in high school for some science homework essay. I had something like that once in the 8th grade, but it was just a list. Anyway, we had fun telling each other what we had predicted.

My prediction came in the form of a paper in which I gave myself the role of research scientist for a pharmaceutical corporation. I wrote it like a journal entry in my diary. The company I worked for was collecting plants from the fast-disappearing Amazon rain forest to save in its greenhouses. The purpose behind this effort was to save rare species of medicine-bearing plants before deforestation made them all extinct.

As the fictitious scientist, I was searching among the salvaged and preserved plants for a cure for cancer. Alas, all that I had found thus far, completely by accident, damnit, was something that cured impotence in men. In short, I had predicted Viagra, Cialis and Levitra years before the fact. How annoying; no cancer cure.

At least I got an "A" for that paper.

Berta's story was a bit different.

She had predicted shopping on the Internet before the Internet existed, describing with perfect accuracy the point-and-click method of selecting and purchasing items. The teacher gave her a failing grade for that, calling it ridiculous and unlikely ever to happen.

Amazing...the fool ought to have been fired for that, I responded. The idea was clever!

Why did she do this, anyway, I couldn't resist asking?

She didn't like Berta's mother, came the reply.

I should have asked when this assignment came along...was it before she went to the Emma Willard School in Troy, New York, or after? I would never know, but if it was at that expensive, private boarding school that her father paid for, somehow that would have made it sound all the more appalling. There was all there was to that, but it was intriguing to think about.

At least Berta and I were having a good time with the TV and take-out.

Chapter 21

Asperger's, Bones, and Me...Not That I Knew

I had rarely felt acceptance from someone on the scale that I felt it with Bryn. Added to that was the fact that, even with my life-long history of looking up to older people, I was uniquely impressed with him. The less obsessed with authority and the more accepting of me as I was, the more I loved an older person. I suspect now that this is because I have Asperger's.

So Asperger's was another thing that would play out over the next 11 months.

Aspies may be neurologically different from most people, but we aren't an alien species.

I had mentioned to Berta that I had it sometime after settling in.

"You do not have Asperger's!" she said, with a disingenuous smile and looking startled.

"Yes I do," I said, a bit annoyed. "I was diagnosed when I was 30, a year after I finished law school, by a psychiatrist. She focused much more on the effects of it, and didn't explain what it is, but she definitely said that I have it. That's why I can relate to your experience with those pills for anxiety and depression; I had those until they made me fat, then I quit taking them."

Berta regarded me quietly for a moment, then stopped arguing the point with me. It's hard to argue the facts of someone else's past and psychological makeup with them. She carried a BlackBerry with her. I still don't know whether or not it really was for work, or just a toy that she liked to have in order to stay constantly connected to the World Wide Web. In any case, she Googled Asperger's Syndrome shortly thereafter and suddenly became the resident expert on the topic. That annoyed me; it was my condition, not hers.

I don't like to psychoanalyze myself. It's upsetting and just intensifies feelings of anxiety. So I hadn't learned what Asperger's was beyond that it had something to do with autism. At this point in time, I had never researched Asperger's Syndrome. But this was the experience that would change that.

Immediately, I promised myself to look up something about it on the Internet myself, and when this unhappy time was over, to read a whole book about it, preferably by someone who had Asperger's Syndrome (I had no intention of reading some condescending tome by a neurotypical-brained psychiatrist).

Somehow, I had completed my entire formal education through the graduate level without the diagnosis, and gotten by socially by being a

Asperger's, Bones, and Me...Not That I Knew

loner and by using rote memorization – coached in large part by my mother. Neither of us knew about Asperger's; we just coped.

It wasn't our fault. The diagnosis, as it turns out, didn't hit the English-speaking world's psychiatry books until 1994, 14 years after the death of the Austrian physician Dr. Hans Asperger, and so it is not surprising that 6 more years passed before I got mine. I now realize that having Asperger's means that I don't have software for social skills; instead, I store them in my brain as data. Either the formula fits a situation, and it goes reasonably well, or it doesn't, and I come away from it stressed, seeking reassurances and advice. There is no other option but to cope in this way, but then I wouldn't have it any other way. I don't want to be neurotypical.

Of course, I didn't know any of this while I was in New York City taking care of Bryn. I learned it right after I came home to Connecticut by (how else?) reading a book. It was written by a male Aspie, Michael John Carley, the head of G.R.A.S.P. – the Global and Regional Asperger's Syndrome Partnership – which is based (where else?) in Manhattan.

Predictably, it turned out that one of its support groups was held just a few blocks north of where Bryn's apartment was, which I discovered via the organization's website. There were none near me in Connecticut. C'est la vie…

I think that the reason I like to people-watch is that I can't figure other people out unless I observe them for a very long time, and even then it's really difficult for me. I prefer books; they outline the characters and then develop them, and I can read and understand the people in them at my own pace. With living people, especially NTs, it just takes such a long time, if I ever get it.

The fact of the matter is, I don't want to be an NT. I want to be what I am, an Aspie.

When I look puzzled and try to understand a situation, it's not because I want to join in and be like the others. I just want to do what I am trying to do, which is understand what's going on. When you understand something, that's power, and power gives a person options. I want the option of either cooperating with or nixing a situation and understanding why I am doing that and what the ramifications of doing that are. And so I keep trying to figure people out. It's fun, even if I can't always succeed at it.

Would I have preferred to go through school knowing I had Asperger's?

Interesting question…my answer is, not if knowing would have prevented me from achieving everything that I have, including, but not limited to, my law degree.

The Slamming Door

It might have, and I see enough news reports on the subject of children with the condition to feel some concern about that. Better to end up like Mozart, Thomas Jefferson, Jane Austen, and Virginia Woolf (except for the suicide part) than to not complete school and write! They all had Asperger's, it turns out, and they all went down in history as great thinkers and achievers – without the diagnosis.

Having gotten this far, and having amassed a lovely curriculum vitae, I didn't see why I couldn't just continue and do well at this point. I still don't. And I like being the way I am. My life is unconventional. Forget a standard, 9-to-5 job in a cubicle with a lengthy commute.

That is a recipe for failure or even disaster for me; I just couldn't last long and do well socially. The work wouldn't be a problem; it would be the office politics and background noise that would kill it for me.

So never mind that; I will write and do whatever odd things crop up in life.

I've learned my lesson; working at any job on a regular schedule, with the exception of teaching at a community college, has not ended well. (I have coped until I could leave gracefully, so my CV looks okay.) Oddly, I have some friends from almost every one of my past jobs, but I left many of them upset, feeling bad about relations with the boss. Usually, this would be a boss who demanded obsequiousness, also known as obvious shows of obedience to authority.

I worked as a historic interpreter – that's a tour guide with pay – at authors' house museums. That only ended when I left to go to law school, but not officially until my good friend who ran the visitor center was treated badly. That was an irregular job – odd hours, lots of individual creativity required – but still a retail job with treacherous pitfalls awaiting me. People-pleasing is dangerous for Aspies. I like that word, Aspie. It's better than using the doctor's last name every time I refer to it, and I like its passive-aggressive undertones.

Pleasing Berta would be tricky, and I knew that ultimately, she would be extremely displeased – no, make that upset and enraged – by me, and that I in turn would hold that against her. But that was off in the future. I was here to do what Bryn wanted, not what anyone else wanted. This was his death, not hers. The fact that I sensed that she just didn't understand that and had no interest in doing so was another matter, and one for later…as much later as possible.

Authority figures…I only give them respect after observing them and concluding that they deserve it as people. Perhaps that's why I did well teaching at the college level, working in a museum, and also in graduate libraries. That and the fact that no children used those libraries…children are stressful to me.

Asperger's, Bones, and Me...Not That I Knew

Children and teenagers call people old (I hate that intensely!) and they make constant noise. Low-level noise drives me crazy, just as office noises do, and loud noises depress or alarm me. It's all part of being an Aspie, and just as inescapable. As I mentioned earlier, the sustained noise of children shrieking is depressing and stressful to me, and the playground across the street from my window at Bryn's place produced this sound, which I tuned out by sleeping through it.

It was funny how the subject of Asperger's came up, and even funnier that I saw no connection at the time between that and a show that I love to watch: the television series *Bones*.

Bones is about a woman with Asperger's who is a genius at the top of her field as a forensic anthropologist, and who solves crimes with her expertise. She has limited social skills that are all the result of rote memorization after consulting neurotypical people she can trust: her friends. The show never, ever comes right out and says that Bones is an Aspie. But after learning about Asperger's, I can see the markers of the condition practically stamped all over her.

What's more, I love it. I think Bones is cool, and I thought so all along.

The way that she interacts with children, expecting them to think logically regardless of their inclinations, her literal interpretations and rattling off of facts, and her ability to love her friends all make me love that character.

I have a lot in common with Bones: we are both well-educated women, articulate, talented at what we do, and we can't read nonverbal cues. I too rely on rote memorization for my every social skill. I too stare steadily and eschew the insincere facial expressions that NTs seem to favor above precise words when they want to communicate something. I speak in flat tones, emphasizing logic over emotion, and a bit louder than most people, too.

Berta knew that I liked that show, and that it was my favorite one of all, so she had gotten me a book before I arrived. It was by Kathy Reichs. The *Bones* series is based on her novels. I was delighted, and read it in a few days. I read fast. I thanked Berta, and she and I made plans to watch the show together; she happened to like it too.

Berta did not know why I loved that show, however.

The funny thing about Asperger's was that when I finally did look up just a little bit about it, I understood myself. I am different from the majority of the human population because my brain patterns are different from theirs. I stand out from the crowd. What's more, this has always pleased rather than upset me. Fitting in never held any appeal for me, because the very last thing that I have ever wanted was to blend into a crowd. I want to be extraordinary.

The Slamming Door

Of course, a good kind of extraordinary is work – serious work. I have always done what I could about that, studying hard, cultivating interests and skills, and achieving whatever I can in my areas of interest. My CV (curriculum vitae) is something to be proud of now.

Berta, in contrast, seemed to be the epitome of wanting to fit into the crowd.

I don't think she understood that being different was not a drawback to me. She kept trying to coach me in ways that would enable me to fit in. Because I work by memorizing social skills, following the theory that knowing the rules enables one to intelligently break them, I let her do this. The trouble with Asperger's, however, is that often I can't help breaking the rules. You don't fix Asperger's; you live with it. And I'm not broken just because I'm different.

As the time in New York City wore on, Berta would point out things here and there about me – getting upset at phones and the sudden noises they make, needing to stick with the same seat for an entire restaurant visit, and with my back to the wall – as indicators of Asperger's.

At first, I was intrigued. As I said, I have always been unique, and have never been sorry about it. I have never, ever wanted to just fit in, blend in, and be ordinary. To be ordinary would be, to me, to be nothing special or memorable. Now that I understand what it means to be an Aspie, I am proud of it. Accepting myself as such was as natural as breathing.

Perhaps she eventually realized this about me.

I don't think that sat well with Berta, but I really never cared.

Maybe it bothered her that I am as secure with myself as I am.

Well…I couldn't spend the time learning about Asperger's in Manhattan while I was upset, scared, and taking care of Bryn. I was very anxious about how the future would be without him alive, and how everything would change for the worse without him in the world. I was also nervous about how his illness would go. I didn't want to disappoint him as a caregiver, and I was afraid to see him die, which I knew he would do slowly, like someone hanging onto a precipice, unwilling to let go even though the fall to his death was unavoidable.

So reading about what it meant to be an Aspie would have to wait; for now, I could only do a half-assed job of learning via the Internet.

I love the Internet; it's a virtual encyclopedia. Forget stuff like Facebook and social networking; I don't want to leave my digital fingerprint all over the World Wide Web. I just want access to a learning tool that is constantly available.

Sometime over the fall and winter, I got curious enough to look it up. It didn't take me long to find a few helpful sites, and soon I was also e-mailing some of what I had found to Cassie. The best thing was a checklist that covered childhood, adolescence, and adulthood.

It wasn't necessary to have each and every one of the items on that list in common with it; most would suffice. Here they are:

- Not picking up on subtle, nonverbal cues, such as facial expressions;
- Disliking any change in routine;
- Appearing to lack empathy; note that an appearance is not the same thing as actually lacking empathy!
- Taking jokes literally;
- Speaking in flat tones, being too loud, and using formal vocabulary;
- Having very specific interests and lecturing on and on about them;
- Having delayed motor development, such as riding a bike (that was me!)
- Trouble coping with sensory stimuli such as smells or sounds.

That's the childhood checklist. I never learned to ride a bike, hate disgusting odors to this day, couldn't stand the sound of sniffling (still can't, in fact), and spent every recess pacing the perimeter of the playground, away from the loud, sustained screeching of my classmates.

Unlike Cassie and Damon, I had been formally diagnosed with the condition, but I suspected that they both had it as well. When I went over that list with Damon, he was amazed; he fit almost all of the criteria to a tee!

The funniest part of discovering what it was to be an Aspie was sharing it with Cassie. She read through the checklist via e-mail and promptly concluded that she too had Asperger's. I agreed with her; by that time I had met her and talked with her several times. Her stories of childhood and interests – such as playing hookey from school at age 8 to watch the McCarthy hearings – added up nicely.

When Bryn heard that, he seemed to feel like a light went on for him also. Suddenly, his preference for my company and Cassie's made sense: he liked Aspie women. He liked girls and women in general, but he liked intelligent, thoughtful ones who listened most of all.

Later, when I did have a chance to thoroughly research Asperger's, I found that condescending NTs call it a disorder, while Aspies call it a condition. That wasn't all; little girls with the condition seem like the perfect, quiet children, studying silently in a corner, or just sitting quietly, causing absolutely no trouble. In fact, that is how most of us fail to get diagnosed with the condition for a long time, and end up living in ignorance of it altogether.

The teenager part of the checklist said that we don't fit in, and don't care about following social norms or conventional patterns of behavior. That's still true of me, and it's true of Damon too. As a teen, I never cared about peer pressure, and was happily immune to it.

The adult part of it said that we can learn social skills and cues – through rote memorization; every Aspie I have since discussed this with had agreed with me on this point – and that our attentiveness to detail and ability to focus and concentrate makes us excel at university level education. I don't know about excelling, but I certainly loved it, finished it all on time, and studied whatever interested me.

Berta hated details, couldn't listen for long, and liked to keep the television on constantly. I like to turn it off and read and write and concentrate. Daytime television seems banal and dull to me, so I watch it in the evening, when the crime shows and movies are on. This was a potential obstacle to interacting successfully with her long-term, but not a problem just yet.

Some other things about being an Aspie:

- We stare. Usually it just means that we are concentrating on whatever someone is saying to us, paying rapt or polite (or both) attention. It also happens because we don't blink much, and we never do long, slow blinks fraught with any meaning (frankly, that annoys me…a lot!). Instead, we just do it to keep our eyes moist, annoyed even to have to bother with that distraction.
- We seem unemotional or childishly unaware of other people's emotions, but it's nothing more than the appearance of that. What is actually going on is that we are quite capable of empathizing with others when they are in distress, but often only after they tell us that they are upset. Once we know, the most noticeable expression that we tend to show is a widening of our eyes. Look for that in an Aspie when seeking signs of empathy.
- We don't get caught up in a group mentality – more evidence of immunity to peer pressure. We don't scream or cry at rock concerts, if we even attend them, and we tend to just quietly observe groups of people who are having a wild, fun time at a night club or other group activity.
- We have some sort of social anxiety. My mother coached me on social skills even though we didn't know what was stopping me from innately sensing my way to acquiring them.

- We startle easily. I often still hide when I hear someone coming, and I jump a mile when I don't and the person is suddenly right next to me.
- We are such individuals that we are not team players, don't like team sports, and don't do well in office or other corporate work environments. It's best if we just work quietly and independently, away from phones and the sounds of others.
- Many of us – including me – are very particular about food, focusing on texture, smell, and taste. We are often labeled fussy and spoiled due to our inflexibility about this.

All this adds up to us seeming thoroughly anti-social and superior to others. Then we are amazed that people take us that way, when we aren't thinking any such thing about them. We are just thinking about whatever we are thinking. We're not broken, or wrong; we're just different.

The staring and near-silent observing that I do as a matter of habit is like breathing to me. But I think that it freaked both Berta and Hilda out. They didn't know with absolute certainty what I was thinking about them or anything else unless I told them, and I often didn't tell. Sometimes I would tell, and when I did, it was with honesty – probably disturbing honesty. I don't know how to lie. As Mark Twain said, "If you tell the truth, you don't have to remember anything." Lying is too difficult, and too much work. One lie leads to another, and another.

Another thing that I do, and that wasn't particularly significant until later in Bryn's illness, is that I keep my door shut. I can't relax and I certainly can't fall asleep with it open. This goes back my entire life. I am hypersensitive to every little sound, and if I think that someone might just come in – which they certainly will if a door is open – I become a nervous wreck.

I grew up with a father who had a very short fuse (anger management problems), so keeping my door shut and locked became a reflex to life in general, though it didn't always preempt subsequent problems with him. Still, keeping that door shut – wherever I have been – has kept me sane, calm, and functional.

The door to my room at Bryn's place was an ancient one. It had glass panels from top to bottom, but they had long since been painted ivory along with the rest of the apartment, and some had probably been replaced with wooden squares along the way. The knob had fallen apart a couple of years before I moved in; it had been there in 2005, when Damon I had been there, and we had once been locked out of our room because it had twisted the wrong way as we shut it. Now it just had a hook-lock inside. To top it all off, there was an inch of space between the bottom of the door and the jamb, so if Bryn were to call out to me,

The Slamming Door

hearing him would be no problem with it shut until he completely lost his voice. After that, nothing would help.

I knew that this door hang-up made me different. There was more, of course; whenever someone appears silently close to me and then makes their presence known, either by speaking or another sound, I jump a mile and give a slight shriek – but not a really loud one. Bryn found that out almost immediately. I couldn't help it, even though I tried.

Add to this the fact that I walk quietly, not stomping, and I don't trod heavily across the floor, and I no doubt come across as a bit creepy, suddenly appearing in silence, staring, not blinking a lot, not emoting as I talk, only emphasizing bits of whatever I am saying as if reading from a book, and listening expressionlessly when others are speaking.

Most people don't like the different ones. They find us scary, and they neither understand nor care why that is. No wonder I anticipated trouble with Berta. I just couldn't understand how until it was over.

As for me, I am always drawn to the different ones, because I am a different one. My favorite *Star Trek* character was always Spock, and half-human, half-Vulcan, highly intelligent, well-educated, odd-person-out…and the epitome of an Aspie. He was quiet, he was expressionless, and he was an observer. Kirk was cute and fun to watch as an action hero, but Spock was hot. Most people go for Kirk, not Spock, and I knew it. But I didn't mention this.

One other thing about Berta stood out to me: her boyfriend, Matt, was a quiet and thoughtful type of guy who liked to learn things. He liked to read history books – serious, heavy topics – and would listen intently to historical lecture tours. She couldn't stand it, and would make him leave. Matt would have loved to go to college. What a nice guy…but what was he doing with her?

It was like she was following her mother's mating pattern: first a guy with a drug problem, then one who liked beer (Matt enjoyed drinking!) without hurting anyone, and who wanted to study quietly.

Damon was like that, and very interested in everything that he did. But he was also like a real-life Spock: studious, quiet, and different. I could not have married anyone else, and getting married was so important to me. However, I would not go to Iraqi Kurdistan with him, or live in Eastern Europe or in a Muslim country. No…Kuwait had been an adventure, a one-time thing.

We had issues, but I was still glad that Damon was my husband, and proud of him, even if I never got to enjoy much time with him, and we were always strapped for an income. And Damon was proud of being an Aspie, too. As he put it, it's a biomarker for a high I.Q. Who wouldn't want a high I.Q.?

Asperger's, Bones, and Me...Not That I Knew

Another observation I have about Asperger's is this: it makes the human species stronger to have a minority of its total with different neural patterns that those of its majority. Whenever a group is all the same – all male, all white, all straight, all Christian, all whatever – that is a weakness. It is a weakness because the group's thinking becomes lazy and sloppy. Aspies make the human species stronger.

Have you ever noticed that every crack team has a socially awkward genius? There's the Aspie. The team won't proceed without her or him – it can't. We gather and crunch the data, and we do it best. Without one of us, the others grope in the dark and make fatal mistakes.

I love it.

Chapter 22

Damon Visits

Damon visited from Friday, November 14th, 2008, to Sunday, and then returned to Storrs. He brought my suitcase full of winter things that my mother had packed with him. I had sent my mother a list via e-mail, and she had dutifully assembled it all. Then she and my father had ridden to the university campus and handed it off to Damon.

Damon was so angry with them for banning him from the house – forever – that he didn't even speak to them. He just nodded, never looked at them, took the suitcase, and wheeled it away. My mother told me about it over the phone later. At least I was set to stay with Bryn a lot longer, with all seasons' worth of clothing. I didn't want to talk to my mother much now.

Frankly, I was so angry with her that when she told me what a weird and socially unacceptable guy my husband seemed to be to her, I blew her off. I didn't ring off; I just wouldn't agree with her. She was the one who had dismissed him first. She was the one who had made every stay at the house in Bloomfield so stressful, always mad at my husband for eating the wrong thing at the wrong time or falling asleep on the sofa. She made him a nervous wreck.

Now that I understand the profile of an Aspie, I can see what was going on.

Aspies can't take that kind of stress, or adjust to it, so we just refuse.

The problem was that although their own daughter was an Aspie and my parents would always love and accept me as I was no matter what, they wouldn't accept it from a son-in-law. For that, I would not forgive them.

I silently predicted trouble with certain on my own in-laws in the future over such things, though never with Bryn. No, Bryn would never cause such upset.

Damon arrived via some sort of Chinese-run bus service that let him off in – where else – Chinatown for the nice low cost of $15. It only ran at certain times, but he had hit it just right. He had been sleeping on the laboratory floor with a blanket and pillow that I had bought for him. When he went back there, it was with an old air mattress of Albert's that he noticed in the closet in my room. Albert said he was welcome to it. At least he would be more comfortable.

Damon was willing to endure the worst physical hardships to get ahead – secret showers in basement labs, sleeping on hard floors, and eating scavenged food from functions – but as yet it hadn't yielded a permanent, continuous income. It depressed me, and it depressed him too.

He would be returning to Storrs for 6 weeks of lab experiments on ImmuneACCORD, which had been trademarked. Chuck, the scientist whose lab he was affiliated with, had always done a lot with this sort of thing, and so he was happy to get some journal articles out of this.

As yet, ImmuneACCORD was still just a recipe for the spice drink that would serve as a vehicle for his immunotherapeutic formula. It wasn't prepared for marketing, so no ready-made samples existed. I would have to mix it up myself.

Damon was with me long enough to see everyone. We also found time to eat at a place called Dr. Jekyll and Mr. Hyde: a Restaurant and Social Club for Explorers and Mad Scientists. It was hokey but fun – average food but lots of spooky stuff. The bar stools rose and fell, surprising patrons. The rest rooms were hidden behind fake bookcases. To find the women's room, I had to look for book titles involving women; same with the men's room.

At some point when we were about to go out – the family as a group, that is – Berta sat on the sofa putting on an extra coating of makeup and commenting about the fact that I made no money for long periods of time from my editing business, and that for someone who was a feminist, I wasn't doing a very good job.

And at this point in the story, it should be obvious that my effort to like her and to get along with her was just that: an effort.

I know that the paradigm of a feminist is typically thought of as a woman who makes money at her profession, and enough of it to pay for her own existence. Never mind that I had gone traveling when I had the opportunity and that it was career-related because I got a book out of the experience. Never mind that I was no good for the sort of environment that Berta was coping with quite well, which was a corporate office. Never mind that I had anxiety and panicked whenever I had to move. Never mind that I don't approve of being so intractably a feminist that I might end up divorced. That happens to lots of feminists, and I don't like it.

It's always so nice when someone makes a nasty, jabbing judgmental remark about someone else's life based on incomplete data. Well, no it's not, but that was sarcasm.

I could have gone to town on her, but I kept my mouth shut.

The only promise I made to myself then was that if she ever got openly abusive toward me I wouldn't put up with it. The whole situation would probably blow up then, but at least I would come away with my self-respect intact, and that would be the most important thing. It would probably also be the best that I could hope for.

But that was off in the distance.

For now, I just pointed out that I wasn't about to sacrifice being with Damon or traveling when I could so that I could have steady employment in some office, where I would not do well and would just be miserable. She could do well there, I said to her, I couldn't, and I didn't care.

She dropped it, we went out and ate dinner, and didn't dwell on that further.

And I reminded myself that money wasn't the only part of feminism. Virginia Woolf lived with her husband, who earned most of their money, and wrote in her own room. She was just one example of many feminists who made a name for themselves professionally. There have been lots of them who did not even have to worry about making money, women who were not wealthy but had people in their lives whose job it was to earn a living. I wanted to be like them, married and living in my own country with my husband. It was a problem that was constantly on my mind, earning money.

Part of me was just angry that Damon hadn't yet taken care of this and as a result we couldn't live together. I hated hearing other people's remarks about it. Even Bryn had told me once, knowing that I wanted to

Damon Visits

distinguish myself as a writer and thus with my own career, that earning a living was my husband's responsibility, not mine.

Lovely…and galling, since it wasn't a faît accompli as yet.

It angered me to think that I might have to do all of that myself. If I managed it, it would be a miracle, and of course I would be proud of myself, but I had some reasons aside from the charged issue of feminism for wanting Damon to earn the bulk of our living. If he did that, we could tell all of those who had ever suggested that we couldn't live our lives on our own terms and make a success of ourselves that they were wrong. Plus I would feel more attracted to him, and proud of him. If he didn't, he wouldn't be doing a single thing in our marriage that anyone, including a feminist, would expect of him. We wanted his family to see him successful.

And damnit, I wanted him to do those things. I wanted my husband. I didn't want him to become a moot point. If that happened, even though I would stay married to him – he was, after all, my best friend – I would feel out of the club of married people and into the pool of what I saw as losers – people who were not in emotionally successful and financially functional relationships. And I wanted to be in that club. I always had, all my life.

I don't give a damn who disapproves of that. I want to have my life and live it happily, too. And my definition of happy is married with no children, and with enough money to enjoy it.

As long as Damon was visiting, he decided that he might as well enjoy the movie channels that Time-Warner offered a couple of times. One evening, *The Office* was on. Damon despised corporate culture, so he sympathized with the main character and his friends. Even though I felt the exact same way, I had already seen that movie, so I wandered in to see how Bryn was doing.

"What's Damon watching?" Bryn asked.

"*Office Space*. They're killing the fax machine; it had it coming," I said.

Bryn gave one of his signature silent roars of laughter. He knew that movie, and he loved that scene best; *Office Space* was one of his favorite comedies. Damon loved it, too.

I was frustrated at having to have my husband visit for such a short time, not because of any resentment at Bryn for wanting a quiet place to himself, but because it meant another sign of failure. Damon had no place

The Slamming Door

to call his own, and we were only together because Bryn was being nice by having us both there.

Yet Bryn never once objected to Damon's career choices. He listened patiently and with interest whenever I talked about Damon's efforts, cheered when Damon had won a prize at the university for his mustard lung research, and often asked how his work was going. He even respected Damon's expertise, asking for Damon to explain all the technical details of his medical reports, which Damon gladly did.

Bryn really couldn't say anything, because he had deliberately avoided corporate culture like the plague that it is, running in the opposite direction of Wall Street and big banks in favor of personal visits with the city's poor and to classrooms.

Once, I had asked Bryn how he felt about having me around.

"You're quiet as a mouse; I love having you here," he replied.

Huh. At least if he had to have a caregiver in his home 24/7, I fit the bill.

I knew I loved living with him, and for the same reason. He was quiet, too.

While I stayed with Bryn, we watched a lot of movies together. On weekends, I was more willing to keep my television on, and of course in the evenings I would put it on for my favorite forensic crime dramas. If I saw a politician or economist on Letterman's show, I would tell him and he would usually tune in to see how the discussion was going.

But I hate soap operas with their circular plots, and talk shows and reality shows.

That was perfect for Bryn; he seemed to enjoy living with a person who wanted to learn something new when she watched a movie or show, and we would talk about whatever we had just seen, or repeat the jokes to each other (that was me more often than him).

Damon was very glad that I was there. As long as I was with Bryn, he felt quite happy and relaxed about my sanity. I was in a calm place, Damon could tell himself. At least if Damon couldn't give us a home, I was someplace with a nice person. At least I wasn't with my parents.

This was also about when I began to shop for a hat – an elegant, to-wear outside hat.

When I began to do so, I met the woman who ran the millinery shop on 18th Street, Ellen Christine's. I wish I could remember her name, but I do recall that she told me she was originally from Bolivia. She was in her fifties and wore her dark hair up in a bun or down long with a barrette at the top. She was often in high heels, and never in sandals, unlike me in warm weather with my Teva sandals. She was very serious and very nice, nice enough to let me photograph some of her hand-made hats just for my own interest, and to talk a bit about her craft.

She showed me how the little cocktail hats stayed on the wearer's head, pulling out the concealed elastic straps or explaining about hatpins. Some of them were quite exquisite, with black feathers curving dramatically upwards, while others were wonderfully fanciful, such as a gray felt one with a bit of white fur thrusting up out of it. It was constructed to resemble a giant teacup and saucer of milk at the Mad Hatter's tea party in Wonderland.

She introduced me to her little dog, a Chihuahua, I think. He slept in a round pouf of a bed under her work table in the back room, directly across from the wide-open door. She talked to him like he was a person, just as I have always done with each of my cats. He was silent unless someone entered the shop; then he would jump up and run out to see who it was, barking a little. Ms. Ellen Christine would tell him to be quiet, and he would then mind his own business.

Sometimes, over the next several months, I would see them both out together in the neighborhood, or they would see me. Once, the milliner told me that she had seen me talking on my cell phone to Damon on a beautiful sunny afternoon, and that she had told her dog that they would not interrupt me; that was cute.

When summer came, she told me that she made many of the hats that were worn to the horse races at the Kentucky Derby, and to garden parties or events in Britain, where women still wore hats often. That was when I admired the hats that seemed to be made out of light, transparent canvas, which were all in the most beautiful, delicious shades of pastels.

The Slamming Door

Many of them had flowers attached, or loops of the same canvas material sculpted like ribbons.

I must have looked at hats in every shop in the area, both high-end, medium-range and low-end thrift stores, but I never had any intention of spending any more than perhaps $50 for my hat. In the end, I just gave up on the shops and surfed the Internet, and found the most perfect specimen that way.

Soon it arrived, and I was in hat-heaven with the thing. It was all black, a rounded felt thing with an upturned, curving brim and a huge, black velvet ribbon wound around and around and finally tied in an elaborate bow. It went nicely with my J.Jill wool swing-coat, which was a raspberry pink; I had found the coat on sale the previous winter and worried about the accessories later. I didn't want any other colors involved; one was enough. A little while later I found a black scarf and gloves and was all set.

I e-mailed the photo of it from the website to Damon, and he thought it was great...so great, that he began to tease and act silly and threaten to wear it.

He did things like that, just to be funny. He was no cross-dresser; he just liked to carry a situation as far as he can for maximum effect, trying to see just how many comments and protests he could elicit from his audience.

I can appreciate that; I even envy his ability to do that.

Chapter 23

Misery Round Two: More Poison

The Friday before Bryn's second round of chemotherapy, he told me that he wanted to go out and see the latest James Bond flick, *Quantum of Solace*, and eat dinner in a restaurant somewhere nearby. Good idea; now that we knew the pattern of misery, it seemed like a good idea to go out and have fun before the cycle started all over again.

There was a prescription to pick up at the New London Pharmacy, plus a bit of other shopping to do, so I planned to get the movie tickets early and bring them home. Buying movie tickets in Manhattan has to be done earlier than in the suburbs.

Accordingly, I dropped off the prescriptions, showing the pharmacists Bryn's note (on his stationery) authorizing me to get the medicines for him, then went around the corner to the movie theater on West 23rd Street.

It was only a little after 4 p.m., so I figured I was plenty early enough.

I was wrong.

All sold out, the guy in the ticket booth told me.

Really...

For once, I actually got mad and decided to fight this.

I politely asked to see the manager, and was told to look for her inside.

In I went, determined to come out with the tickets for the show that started after 6 o'clock. I asked for the manager at the desk, which was just inside on the left.

She came forward and listened.

I told her that I had come over 2 hours ahead of time to buy the tickets, and that it should have been early enough to actually acquire them. What was the problem? I demanded to know.

Well, obviously, it was that it wasn't early enough.

Hmm...I wasn't about to just give up and go home. Bryn only had this weekend to have fun before the next round of misery got underway.

Suddenly, I decided to tell this woman exactly what his situation was and to insist that she cough up the tickets, though I put it all nicely enough.

So, I explained that Bryn had bone cancer, that next Tuesday was the beginning of his next round of chemotherapy, and that it meant that this was the last weekend that he could expect to feel well enough to have fun. Accordingly, he absolutely had to have the tickets to *Quantum of*

The Slamming Door

Solace tonight. I added that he wanted to attend the 6:30 p.m. showing of it.

But I didn't stop there.

I went on to describe what a wonderful, nice, unselfish guy he was, detailing his career as a social worker for homeless people and AIDS patients. I concluded with the insistence that since Bryn had taken great care of other people in this city for years, it was now time for this city to entertain him.

"Now I know that you have more tickets," I continued, "because movie theaters always have some that they hold back, just in case. Lots of businesses function that way. I want you to sell me 2 of them." With that, I calmly stared her down.

It didn't take much staring; I had made my case. She sold me 2 tickets.

Then she told me to show up about 20 minutes early, because seats would fill up fast.

I thanked her, and promised that Bryn was really sick and would appear with a cane.

That was probably unnecessary, but I don't believe in lying to someone to get what I want...mostly because I just can't do it. I can't lie. Guilt probably takes over, and I feel utterly unconvincing, so I just never do it.

I headed home with the tickets and Bryn's prescription, which was waiting for me at the New London Pharmacy around the corner.

When I got there and unloaded all purchases, pills, tickets, and whatever else, I confessed to Bryn – albeit unapologetically – how I had gotten the movie tickets. I added the manager's warning to show up 20 minutes early.

He looked at me for a moment, stunned, but just accepted the tickets and my actions.

What was the point of scolding me for being so determined that he have the fun he wanted when he wanted it? There was none. He knew he had an unknown and limited amount of time in which to enjoy himself.

We ended up going to the movie first, and then to an Italian place that I hadn't noticed before. It was next to the Daioh Sushi place across 8th Avenue, and called Patsy's Restaurant. I had mushroom ravioli, and he had – what else – spaghetti and meatballs. The food was delicious.

And that was that. He liked the movie, he enjoyed his dinner without a trace of nausea, and the evening was a success. I felt absurdly pleased with myself over the whole thing, but kept my mouth shut about it until Berta stopped by again.

Then I couldn't resist telling her the whole story.

Misery Round Two: More Poison

She listened, and then said, "That is the funniest story I've heard in a long time."

Huh. Validation. Well…I hadn't really expected to get scolded for ensuring fun.

Early in the afternoon of this second round of chemotherapy, I found a computer out in the waiting area that was available for patients and relatives to use. It was a Windows PC, Internet capable, and I was able to access my e-mail. I signed in and checked everything, then wrote to Dr. Leonardi to tell him how it was going. I had his new Sloan-Kettering e-mail address, given to me by my mother. She was keeping him informed about his Hartford patients with it.

When I was done, I made sure to sign out of my e-mail account, and then I went back to Bryn's corner office to see what was happening. He was fine, channel-surfing on his television.

It was during this second round that we discovered the Café Europa, which was on East 53rd Street, just to the left out the door of the building. They had hazelnut coffee, which thrilled me, and good Colombian coffee that Bryn liked. He would ask for some just after we got settled into the huge waiting room with the morning-glory metalwork. We both refused to ingest so much as another gulp of the free but awful-tasting coffee at Sloan-Kettering.

I was getting used to the place, I realized.

Sometimes we would chat with the people who waited with us, but most of the time we would just get out *The New York Times* (Bryn) and a novel or autobiography (me) and read. Bryn kept choosing seats on the back right corner sofa by the windows.

I was reading an account by a woman doctor, a Pakistani Muslim who was trained in Manhattan in the late 1990s and was unable to get a green card to stay longer…so she had taken a job in Saudi Arabia. It was fascinating. The moment she had arrived, her passport had been handed off to the driver from the hospital she was to work at; women could not retain custody of their own passports in that country. She had cried on 9/11, and been outraged when some Saudi women ordered cake. The Saudi hospital administrator had reprimanded them for doing that.

Sometimes we would chat with other patients and their families; we met a family from New Jersey who drove all the way in for treatments at the Sloan-Kettering Clinic. It was a sick father, the mother, and their 2 adult sons. They all ran a family business together.

The sons complained about a movie that Bryn and I and the others had all gone out to see together, though I don't remember now whether it was *Milk*, *Battle for Seattle*, or another one. They hadn't liked learning

The Slamming Door

something; they only went out to the movies to be entertained. I found this incomprehensible, but Bryn didn't. At least I kept my comments to a minimum, but Bryn knew how odd it all felt to me. It was fun, being with someone who understood that and was bemused by it.

That same week, while he still felt okay, Bryn wanted me to take him out for walks in the warm sunshine during this time, so I did that. He thought he wasn't moving enough, and it was a beautiful day. The idea was to get some exercise before it got too difficult.

Rita Matthews was running her bedbug campaign at this time, and tried to entrap us both into a lengthy plea for our attendance.

Bryn just walked off as I stood there, feeling stuck, until I noticed that he off down the street alone, moving steadily away on the sidewalk. I said good-bye, interrupting her but not caring whether or not she felt offended, taking off fast as I said that I had to stick with Bryn.

When I caught up to him, he said, "That is a very selfish woman," and left it at that.

I took his word for it.

She soon proved it, stopping me in the halls to demand that I attend a tenants' meeting at some other address, and to show me the notice that she was about to put up about it.

I told her I wouldn't be there, and that I was not legally authorized to participate anyway because I was technically a guest of Bryn's and not a permanent, legal resident. No way was I about to let on that I received mail and packages there; she might have tried to argue that I could, and I wanted nothing to do with her nonsense or Rita Matthews herself.

After that, I became adept at avoiding her, and we didn't have much occasion to speak. She never asked about Bryn's health, even though she could see that someone was wrong with him, and lots of people in the building knew what it was. Maybe she didn't know; people tended to avoid her because she was so pushy.

Another pair of issues that cropped up came from Dionne: she kept inviting me to go exercise at Chelsea Pier – over and over again – but I just didn't see it fitting into my schedule, and I just didn't want to go. I just politely put it off, saying that I couldn't fit it in.

The other topic she kept returning to was organic foods, with those awful-tasting herbal teas that revolted Bryn. He had tried them each once, then quit. He only wanted stuff that tasted good, and I didn't blame him. If I were the one dying and therefore only going to be able to taste

Misery Round Two: More Poison

things of any kind for a little while longer, I would be determined to make it count too.

It felt strange to realize that even though we were sadly going through a terrible time known as the process of death and dying, it wouldn't be miserable every moment. It was more like long stretches of calmness with a bit of fun and visits with the family thrown in here and there, punctuated by bouts of agony for Bryn and terrifying upsets for me.

Realizing this was probably what made me realize that I could take it.

This happened during that week after the next round of chemotherapy, as the misery associated with the poison in his system set in. Then the puking began, with a complete lack of interest in eating. Bryn would grab his bucket and sit with it, then lose whatever he had just eaten. It sucked. I stroked his upper back and shoulders, more out of sympathy than anything else, and let him bolt for the bathroom to puke some more and flush the contents of his bucket.

He looked so apologetic and was so determined to flush his own mess that I hastened to assure him that I thought of him as a couth, genteel guy who sought to hide anything that might possibly be construed as disgusting – but that I would clean up whatever he couldn't keep up with nonetheless, not to worry…and he seemed to relax and feel better when I said that.

He seemed so tense when things got gross, as though he was ashamed of it and apologizing silently, which was why I had said that. I didn't want him to be stressed out about anything more than the effects of the poison in his system. It hadn't been this bad the first time, but now that he had lots of poison in his system, he was getting a taste of the misery that we had expected with chemotherapy.

The only thing I could do for him during these rounds of misery was to rub his back as he puked into his bucket, look glum because I felt that way, and let him do whatever he insisted on doing on his own and then do whatever he asked me to do.

Poor Bryn; this misery wasn't his fault. It was just the only thing that the medical profession was willing to offer him. It infuriated me though; poisoning a person throughout their body doesn't seem like a rational way to attack a parasitic disease. What that does is it poisons more than the parasite, and weakens the person, thus decreasing the body's ability to fight the parasite. The best that the doctors could offer was pathetic and barbaric.

The Slamming Door

It disturbed me to think that in a few years, a better treatment – a less torturous, less disfiguring, and more effective one – might exist, but too late for Bryn to benefit by it.

Then I tried to think of something else.

The puking happened for two or three nights in a row, late, after people stopped visiting, calling, and otherwise seeking conversations with him. That was when I was home alone with him, and when I just sat there with him, ready to do whatever he needed me to do.

He was so determined to clean up after himself that it seemed to me that what he really wanted from me was company, so that he wouldn't be alone and scared with the misery. I was glad to give him that. I was also glad when he let me wash his bucket with Soft Scrub; it made me feel like an active caregiver.

Eventually, he decided that he could lie down and rest, and I took my shower. It was late at night by then, after both comedy shows, which I hadn't watched. Then we went to bed, and he had his night light on, his bucket nearby, and me with my door propped open across the hall.

I hated having that door open, but it is a testament to my level of comfort with Bryn that I agreed to this without a word. He did not know that I hated to have it open until months later; I was determined to try to leave it open for as long as I could go without saying anything at all. I propped it with a box so that I could keep it from swinging wide open but would be able to whip it out of my way in a hurry.

Despite the open door, nothing happened to him at night once he settled down to sleep. He would puke, and then he would be okay until the next night. Then the wave of nausea passed, and he found that he could eat again, but also that things tasted like chemicals. That was when we both decided that my door didn't need to be open all night.

I figured I could repeat this again for each round of chemotherapy; keep the door propped open until he didn't feel the need for any more, then hook it shut again. Leah and other people tended to wander through during the mornings; they had keys to the apartment. If I couldn't wake up thinking that I was effectively invisible to them all, I would be a nervous wreck. I could just picture it; people would start peering in at me, and I wasn't about to invite that.

It was also during this second round of misery that I found out that Bryn had a stash of anti-nausea pills. Why hadn't he told me about this wonderful tool before? He probably hadn't thought about it. He was so secretive about bodily functions, unhappy when he had to admit that he needed certain items from the pharmacy. I would just calmly note the specifications of each thing and write it down, determined to get the shopping errands just right.

Misery Round Two: More Poison

As for the anti-nausea pills, I found out about them in a rather frustrating way: he puked one up and told me so in a sad tone. It was nearly 2 a.m.

"You have anti-nausea pills?" I asked. "I didn't know those existed."

"Yeah," he said. "But the doctor told me that they only work for the first couple of days."

I said nothing at that point. But I was angry; the stupid medical profession couldn't get rid of the cancer that it had given him, it couldn't keep him comfortable and in a state of physical dignity, and it even tortured him in some twisted attempt to save its own face.

The puking continued, and I felt awful. There seemed to be little or even nothing that I could do to help him relax, to keep any nutrition down, or to otherwise feel at ease.

I hadn't wanted to do what I did next. I was still so angry with my mother for banning my husband from the house. But at 2 a.m., I called her up and woke her.

She answered right away.

When she asked what was the matter, I got right to the point. "Bryn just puked up his anti-nausea pill," I told her. Why beat around the bush when you wake someone up? "Is there anything that would make him more comfortable, anything that would be easier to keep down?"

She recommended buying him some Gatorade, chicken bouillon cubes, and Jell-O. I could cook some rice and make some chicken broth, have him drink the Gatorade and eat the Jell-O, and he would most likely have no trouble keeping those things down or eating them.

I was annoyed at myself that I didn't already have that stuff in the kitchen, but rushed to put it on the list for the next day. Bryn heard me calling her and writing it down. He was so miserable that he didn't scold me for waking her up. He knew that she was a prostate cancer nurse, and that I was on the phone to get great advice.

The next day I stocked up on all of those things and cooked the rice and broth. Bryn couldn't eat the whole serving, but he got about half of it down before he just felt too full. At least he was keeping what he ate down. He ate some Jell-O too. I had been careful to get only red Jell-O, a pack of strawberry and raspberry. I figured if I hated the green, yellow and orange flavors, he would too. He said I had chosen correctly.

I also went to Chelsea Market, to the Manhattan Fruit Exchange, and bought Bryn some fabulous apples (2 kinds) plus a fancy Asian pear that was shaped like an apple, but he could only eat part of each one before he just couldn't continue. He had stopped throwing up by then, but his appetite was nil. Still, seeing him eat that healthy, fresh food and keep it down felt like a reason to silently celebrate.

The Slamming Door

Kasey also had a good suggestion: ginger tea. She told Bryn it would help keep his stomach calm, so I went out and bought a box of Twining's ginger tea and started serving it every afternoon, right after the coffee that he still asked for. He said it helped. This became a part of the routine as long as his stomach threatened him with nausea, and bit beyond that.

Another week or so of not cooking my own food, and of spiriting my meals into my room to eat them in front of the television alone so that Bryn wouldn't smell any of it, ensued. As long as I kept the TV on while I ate, I stayed calm. Of course, I never tried eating in silence. Eating dinner alone with no TV on made me anxious. If I had someone to sit and talk with, I didn't need the TV on. But I didn't; Bryn was sick and I had to keep my food away from him.

I knew that it would be different later, when the nausea let go of him. Then I could take my plate into his room and chat as I ate, if we wanted to watch the same thing or nothing at all. When Berta wasn't visiting, I sometimes liked to do that.

Until then, the misery gripped him.

I tried not to talk about it much, or food in general.

The slightest suggestion or mention of it would get him going.

Albert came over and meant to be sympathetic and friendly, but he just said everything that could possibly set his brother off again, puking. The problem was that he mentioned food: food that Bryn might like, food that he and June had eaten, or food in some other context.

Bryn warned him not to do it, but Albert just talked on, oblivious, until his poor brother – and best friend – abruptly grabbed his bucket and puked into it again.

Finally, Albert understood and found something else to talk about.

I wondered why he didn't get it; Albert had had prostate cancer for 15 years by then.

Maybe he just hadn't had that much chemotherapy for it.

Oh, well.

I left them to it, and a little while later served Bryn some more Jell-O without saying anything about it. He ate it.

Meanwhile, I thought about my own direct, blunt way of speaking. It shows when I write. If someone throws up, I say that they puked. I really, really don't like the word "vomit" so I just don't use it. And I get annoyed if anyone tries to verbally or otherwise edit my word choices.

Wait until someone dies…the phrase "passed away" isn't just one that I dislike. It infuriates me. It glosses over a harsh, inescapable reality. I absolutely refuse to use it.

My grandmother was dead; she had died of lung cancer when I was 17. She had hung on until I got home from my first term of college, because she was so excited that I was going. She had grown up in the

Misery Round Two: More Poison

Great Depression, aced everything in high school, and been accepted to Cornell University with no funds for tuition. So she had not attended college.

Bryn was going to die, not pass away.

To me, the only time that such a phrase even fits is if someone who is much older than Bryn was dies in their sleep in comfort, unaware that death was even coming; that, and with no long, drawn-out illness to torture them or rob them of their dignity. That, to me, is passing away.

Every other kind of death deserves to be called dying.

Chapter 24

Bryn's Last Birthday Party

It sounds awful to say that someone's birthday was their last, but I knew it was his last.

I knew it just as I had known it when my grandmother was dying of lung cancer and we threw a great party for her, even though she lived for nearly another year. She died just 25 days before her 72nd birthday, and we were celebrating Bryn's 71st on November 21, 2008.

It had to be experience that was informing my judgment about this; he would have more fun before the party that he called life was over, but not a full year's worth.

I hate knowing stuff like this.

That makes no difference, of course. Sometimes, we just know things, and how we feel about knowing them changes nothing.

Regardless of all that emotional baggage, it was time to plan some fun.

Berta wanted a strawberry cake frosted with coconut for her father; she said he liked strawberry best. I knew that from his ice cream orders, and kept a large container of Hagen Daas strawberry ice cream in the freezer at all times. The coconut was probably just something that she thought would be exciting and special.

She said to order it around the corner at Billy's Bakery on 9th Avenue and that she would pay for it, so I went over there a couple of days ahead of time to place the order. No strawberry cake! They didn't offer it. I even asked, just to make sure. But they had white cake with coconut frosting, so I signed up for that and decided to buy fresh strawberries, cut them all up by hand, and serve them on the side.

That took care of that. Bryn said he was looking forward to it.

The day before the fact, Rudy asked me to come over and help him figure out how much food to make. He insisted upon making all of it, and was planning spaghetti, meatballs, red sauce, beets, etc. In short, everything Bryn liked.

When I heard that, I wondered what Alissa was going to do. Starve seemed like a nasty expectation. I don't approve of the attitude that people should just be willing and able to eat absolutely anything whether or not they can actually can just to be polite.

Of course, telling a religious Hindu, Jew or Muslim to eat pork goes over like a screen door in a submarine. So does telling a Christian during Lent to eat chocolate cake at a party. So does telling a vegetarian that they are spoiled and unreasonable. Food allergies…oh, who cares?! I told Rudy about Alissa's raw food diet and that I would add salad to the

Bryn's Last Birthday Party

spread, and get it ready myself, following her recipe. He raised no objection.

Then he wanted me to calculate how many people would actually be there and come up with a number. I sat there, next to his desk by the piano, wedged in against Hilda's area (I can't call it a room), thinking out loud.

There would be: Bryn, me, Berta, not Matt for some unknown reason, Hilda, Rudy, Elah, Alissa, June, Albert, Dionne, Melissa, Piper...that was it.

Rudy rudely interrupted me, telling me that he didn't care to know who was coming and whether or not they would eat the meat – though he did agree not to mix it into the sauce or pasta – just come up with a number.

I couldn't do it, though. This was the first time I had tried to tally up the number of guests. I told him so. I got flustered and muttered it all again, this time trying to count. He interrupted again until I told him to just wait a minute and let me do it, that I reverse numbers when I count silently – I have dyslexia with numbers, and does my aunt. Finally he stopped bothering me and shut up. There – 12 people, I finally was able to tell him.

After that, I went home. I wanted to get away from him. He was always very quiet and unsmiling, sometimes interesting to talk to because he was intellectually curious, but this was the first time that I had seen him be blatantly unpleasant.

I described the encounter to Bryn, and he said not to worry about it.

So I went back to planning.

Oddly, despite the fact that Bryn had just been poisoned with Round Two of chemotherapy the previous week, he felt well enough to be looking forward to all of this. He had been warned by the oncologist that she had used a different recipe – a very slight difference, really – and that as this was the second dose, he might feel lousy at Thanksgiving time.

Oh, great...that would ruin his chances of enjoying the holiday, I thought in disgust.

But that would be next week. This week was his 71st birthday party.

I forced my mood back to the fun of this week.

The day of his birthday, I went out to the florist shop on 8th Avenue and 22nd Street, the one where the little female black cat lived. She was a shy, shorthaired creature who hid a lot, but she would let me grab her and pet her occasionally, and I had some photos of her. Her name was Juliet, and she had a bed hidden under the green painted risers, where she had raised her 2 black kittens the previous Christmas. The fluffy, cuddly, black male cat, Romeo, her mate, had died of liver cancer earlier that fall. I was upset when I heard it; Bryn had seen him sitting outside and

The Slamming Door

watched as he let me pick him up and pet him. I never told Bryn what had happened to him.

The Greek family who ran the place was very nice; they had had their florist shop here for decades. Their prices were low compared with the upscale competitors in the neighborhood that seemed to cater to restaurants, business lobbies and the sort of weddings that appeared in bridal magazines. I got to know them a little and told them about Bryn's illness.

I had decided to surprise Bryn with a bouquet of flowers from this shop, and to say that it was from both me and Berta. After looking around for a few minutes, I chose a white Easter lily and a bird-of-paradise stalk with a beautiful blue-and-orange blossom poking out like a bird's plumage.

The Greek lady wrapped it for me in plastic with a nice pair of blue and orange ribbons around it while I talked to Juliet, who ran behind the counter to munch on dry cat food.

It was early in the afternoon, so I went straight home to present Bryn with the flowers.

He was delighted, but then he was always pleased with whatever people gave him.

Bryn's Last Birthday Party

Next, I decided to give him his present rather than wait for all of the noise of the party when I would be too busy to enjoy his reaction. He agreed with that idea and opened it.

It was a mug from the Unemployed Philosopher's Guild, a global warming one. It looked like a map of the world in blue and green, complete with topographical detail. When hot liquid was poured into it, the sea level rose 30 feet or so, submerging a significant portion of the continents and drowning many islands.

We were both fascinated by it, so I made his tea in it and rushed to present it in before the heat did its thing with the paint job. Manhattan

The Slamming Door

disappeared, which disturbed us, as did Florida, a lot of France, Malaysia, and many other places that we were fond of.

Well, it wasn't happening right away, but we vowed to continue recycling diligently.

With that, I unpacked his flowers and put them into a tall, clear, cylindrical vase with the ribbons tied around it. Then I put it onto the front hall table with a card that he had received from Claus and the other Henry George people.

At that point, it was time to go out and get the other things: cake, strawberries, and salad items. I checked for napkins and plastic ware, and then realized that it didn't matter; Elah was going to bring over some of her stuff. Combined with ours, it would be enough. The only thing we needed was the dessert, raw foods and some party candles.

I told Bryn what I had to do next and he said to go ahead.

I did the grocery shopping first, unpacked it all, and then went right out to get the cake.

Time was running shorter and shorter, but I didn't feel rushed. There was enough time left to get it all ready. I started cutting up the berries and salad things.

Alissa arrived and I told her about Rudy's catering plan and the fact that I was worried that she wouldn't have anything she could eat, explaining that I was preparing her delicious salad recipe as I cut up tomatoes, avocados and scallions and tossed them with salad greens, Dijon mustard and extra-virgin olive oil.

She was delighted, and quietly said so as she effusively protested that I didn't have to do any of that, and that it was a lot of trouble. She obviously appreciated it, but felt uncomfortable about the effort being made because of her. I told her that I wanted this food too, because Rudy's stuff was too much meat for me also. She relaxed when she heard that.

Elah and Rudy soon appeared with the rest of the food and dishes and flatware, to which I laid out neatly. We set it all up on the stove like a buffet table, and soon the party was ready to start. Guests started arriving, Piper and Melissa from upstairs, Albert and June soon after, and Berta and Dionne soon after that.

Hilda came and ate and went. I took photos, but she wasn't in them. She left too soon.

Someone had arrived with a bouquet of a dozen red roses, some greens and baby's breath; at some point that evening I put them into another vase on the front hall table. I moved the other flowers into Bryn's room and put them on his side table. The mug stayed out in the living room, opposite a new photo of Hilda. In it, she had a new short hairstyle with pink and blond dye in the front and on top, and natural brunette color in the back. Bryn was a bit taken aback by it, but told her she looked nice when she proudly presented the photo.

Dionne was just back from Colorado or Wyoming, and her husband would follow the next week. He was still enjoying himself out on the ranch with the horse. He seemed awfully set in his ways on often completely off on his own despite being married with lots of money and time. He was free to be with his wife a lot, but he didn't make a point of being with her.

We all ate on chairs in the living room, with Bryn getting up and going into his room when Cassie called, then returning after that. She always called him at the same time, morning and evening.

When it was time for the cake, all of the dinner food was cleared up with Elah's and Alissa's help, washed, dried and put away, with Bryn's leftovers saved for him. It was good, including Rudy's pasta.

With the stove cleared – it was the only work area, with its flat, white-painted areas on either side of the 4 burners – I proceeded to lay out the cake and berries with a stack of plates and forks. There was a huge, wide, serrated knife that I normally considered too floppy to be a safe choice for cutting vegetables, but it would be okay for slicing and serving the cake.

Berta and I put the candles in and she lit them with the gas stove lighter; I took her picture doing that, plus some of just the cake and

The Slamming Door

berries side by side on the stove. It was pretty; some of the coconut sprinkles were toasted, which was a nice effect. We sang Happy Birthday and watched as Bryn blew the candles out; then I brought it back to the kitchen.

I got called away to check on Bryn or a guest or something, and Berta went into the kitchen and began serving the cake. The next thing I knew, someone was presented with an oversized slice that no one wanted to accept.

I took that plate and immediately returned to the kitchen, where Berta stood over the cake, brandishing that knife over it, and said "All right Berta, give me the cutter. This piece is too big; no one wants it."

She handed the huge knife over and left, but didn't seem perturbed. I cut the slice into 2 smaller ones and went to work on the rest, until all of us had a piece with a pile of strawberry slices on the side. Soon all of the guests were happy, eating it and chatting. Bryn said it was just what he wanted, so I was happy too. It tasted great, and I hoped he could taste it properly.

That was pretty much it.

Bryn enjoyed himself, the guests had fun, and everything tasted great.

Happy Birthday to Bryn, who loved life and had planned on a decade-long retirement doing what he enjoyed: singing the tenor voice parts in the Mendelssohn Glee Club, teaching at the Henry George School and editing a book by some Georgist author, and participating in the International Union for Land-Value Taxation, an N.G.O. (non-governmental organization) at the United Nations.

Instead, he had just celebrated his last birthday party. What a rip-off.

I suppose that I should be writing that we should be grateful for the time we have on earth, or some such trite nonsense, but that is all that it would be: nonsense. I just don't buy it.

He deserved those extra 10 years of fun, and I am still angry that he didn't get them.

Chapter 25

Thanksgiving in a Brooklyn Brownstone

Legend has it that a cook's mood affects the results that come out of her kitchen.

A sad cook's food tastes like a disappointment and can transmit that mood to the people who eat her food; an angry, embittered cook can pass that on through bad-tasting, sour, burnt, or greasy food; a lustful cook, such as the one in *Like Water for Chocolate* whose lover was given away to her sister, can rub that feeling off on her food, as the chef in it did when she added rose petals to the entrée; a happy cook makes the best food of all. Professional chefs who become decorated successes must be happy, because their food always gets rave reviews.

I must have been an anxious pastry chef that season, away from a familiar kitchen, using an oven in what had been advertised as a hostile environment. I hope my results tasted good to the others. They tasted okay to me, minus the pie crust. That was a crappy, store-bought, premade one. Actually, it was 2 of them, because I made 2 pies; the crusts were sold in sets of two.

Mood isn't the only ingredient that affects taste – ingredients count for a lot, too.

At least I could control the filling, which was what mattered most of all. I would use my Grandma Rénard's recipe, with my own mix of spices plus pumpkin purée with some eggs, cream and milk. I would get the ingredients at my own expense at the grocery store around the corner.

Why was I doing this?

Dionne was hosting Thanksgiving in the brownstone building in Brooklyn.

I wanted to contribute something to the meal, so I volunteered to make 2 pumpkin pies a couple of weeks before the fact.

That meant a trip across town with my supplies and recipe to use Elvira's oven.

Berta arranged it; she knew that baking requires an oven with temperature controls and legible numbers on them, and that Bryn's oven lacked that essential feature.

I e-mailed my mother to ask for my grandmother's pumpkin pie recipe – no other would do. She got my little red book with the handwritten recipes and typed it up, and I was all set. Since then, I have put many of my recipes into Word files and saved them on memory sticks. That's good planning, but not really good enough; I should finish the collection.

The Slamming Door

But back to the story...before I actually went to bake any pies, something else happened.

Elvira's friend fell and cracked her ribs, which meant that she couldn't go to a Broadway show that Elvira had bought tickets for. It was *Hairspray,* and each ticket cost $111. Harvey Fierstein was in a lead role as the mother, Edna Turnblad. Such tickets are hard to get, expensive, and lead to great enjoyment, so wasting them was out of the question.

To solve that problem, Elvira gave Berta and me her tickets as a gift.

To thank her – both for that and for the use of her stove – I brought her a beautiful bouquet of flowers from the florist shop with the nice little black cat. It included a pink Easter lily and a blue iris, tied with a pink ribbon. It wasn't much, but it was nice, and I hoped that she felt thanked.

I knew that Elvira was very difficult to live with, but until I experienced it, I knew that I would not really understand what that meant.

"Guess who called me up and said that she loves me?" Bryn had asked me and Albert recently. It was Elvira. Funny how people say good things when life does its worst; it seemed that Elvira still felt some affection for Bryn.

She had also sent Bryn a tall jar of honey from a farm near her house in Oneonta, and so whenever I made tea for him for months on end, I stuck a long-handled spoon into it to add some of that honey to the steaming cup. He enjoyed it.

I had seen Berta's mother's place several weeks earlier, before getting a cab back to Bryn's place after 1 a.m. – it was like my Great-Aunt Sharon's place – in the same complex of apartments in Stuyvesant Village. Elvira had just returned, either from her house in Oneonta, in upstate New York or from Alabama, where she often visited Berta and Dionne's grandmother, who lived in her same old white house with the porch in front and a shotgun.

The 2 fluffy cats, Cinders, a grey female, and Zulu, an orange male, had let me cuddle them. The living room was full of paintings by Dionne (despite the fact that, as Berta informed me, their mother routinely told her that she wasn't a real artist...what an insane thing to say!) and books, including 2 whole sections of gourmet cookbooks. That area was intriguing; I paused to scan the titles until Berta continued the tour in hushed tones. Elvira was asleep in her room.

The kitchen was very well-equipped too, and I was surprised to note that Elvira had dishes exactly like my aunt's – the same Wedgewood pattern, called Edme. Berta and Dionne's room had 2 twin beds arranged at different angles, and Matt was staying over; he was reading on Dionne's bed under the window. We were all very quiet so as not to wake Elvira.

Thanksgiving in a Brooklyn Brownstone

At that time, I wished I could have seen a photo of her, but the place had none. Dionne's paintings hung over the dining room table. Berta unhappily told me that Elvira liked to get up early and play the piano in the living room, heedless of the fact that Berta was exhausted after a week of getting up early to ride the subway to the office and wanted to sleep in on Saturdays.

That reminded me of life as a teenager, when my father had selfishly and thoughtlessly placed a table saw in the basement directly under my bed, and then run it every Saturday morning at 8 a.m. He liked to do carpentry work. I was exhausted from less than 6 hours of sleep each night during the school terms; I had to complete the homework before bed.

Berta and I nodded in mutual agreement, hating not having sufficient control over our sleeping conditions. I couldn't help but feel convinced that my generation could, by and large, forget about affording control over our own homes. That standard of living took a level of income that our broken economy would not allow for us. I tried not to think about it, because if I did, I might start getting angry, depressed, and even fantasizing about killing myself.

I had my own problems, not just the ones connected with the imminent and most unwelcome loss of Bryn.

But that was not the only reason why it was a distracted holiday week.

Bryn was feeling lousy again, not puking incessantly but still unable to really enjoy food or endure the smell of much of it. It was like a vague, lingering feeling of gastric unease that had stolen his appetite. That little cartoon appetite demon I had imagined had stolen his ability to eat and enjoy food, and it seemed to have done so with glee. No doubt, in my anger over this, I was imputing malice and emotions to what was in reality a cold, indifferent condition…but indifference can be the worst attitude.

That was one thing, but another change was that by now, Bryn had lost both his beautiful white hair and all of the belly fat plus any other fat that he had, and was constantly feeling shaky and tired.

He would fall asleep with his favorite ball-point pen in his hand as he worked on the crossword puzzle, and the pen would make a huge ink blot on his oversized Dockers pants. Both pairs were now ruined, but he wouldn't allow me to get him new ones that fit. I kept serving tea, coffee, Jell-O, and chicken bouillon with rice. I also found some instant chicken noodle soups that Bryn really liked.

Aside from that, he and I instituted a new policy at shower time: He would leave the door about an inch ajar, and I would sit at the computer playing word games. The point was to be close enough to run and help

The Slamming Door

if he showed the slightest sign of flagging in there. The faucet and shower head were in the center. He wasn't feeling as confident taking showers anymore.

So I would lay out his pajamas, socks and underwear, check his towels each time he was going to take a shower – which was every night, late – and wash the bathtub for him. He just didn't get around to taking his shower any earlier, and would often comment that we both ought to get going earlier, which would help for about a week. Then we would be late again, with him in there around half past midnight and me after the late shows.

I ran *The Late Show with David Letterman* while he bathed, which in Manhattan was immediately followed by *The Late Late Show with Craig Ferguson* (back in Connecticut, the tedious tabloid show *Entertainment Tonight* ran in between them; this was much nicer). As the comics told their jokes, I would listen from my post at the computer, and if they were funny enough, I would go up to the bathroom door and repeat them for Bryn. He laughed every time.

The point of this was to have something better to say than "How's it going in there?" every few minutes. What I was really doing was checking on him to make sure that he was okay. We found this system to be free from embarrassment for both of us. If I did ask that dead giveaway of a question, Bryn would say, "All is well." We kept this up for months on end, until the beginning of summer. It surprised me how long we were able to continue this way.

He was still getting some visits from the nurses at home, and now we had a form that one of them had left, and that Bryn had asked me to photocopy. The pill sheet, I called it. I hadn't copied it; one look at it had made it abundantly clear that doing so would use up the printer's black toner in no time. So I had made a Word file with a grid and filled it out with his medications, pointing out that I could just edit it as time went on.

Bryn thought that was terrific; he didn't have to fill the whole sheet out every day. He just had to check off that he had taken his pills. I kept him well supplied with a stack of them. I don't know whether or not he showed them to his doctors, but I'm sure that they would have liked what they saw if he had. We felt very efficient over the whole thing.

That was about all that was new when it was time to think about Thanksgiving.

That, and the fact that Bryn announced that he didn't feel well enough to go.

What a glum announcement it was; the previous year, he had been able to go up to Cassie and Chip's place with Albert, June and Alissa and eat everything in sight. Also, his birthday had happened to fall the day

Thanksgiving in a Brooklyn Brownstone

before. Last year, I had sent him a birthday package from Harry & David's, of Anjou pears and Havarti cheese. I was worried that he might not notice it and take it in, so I had called him, and he told me that they took it with them to Cassie's place. Good.

This year he would be at home all day, with Leah to check on him during the time that I was out at the Thanksgiving dinner party. I had hesitated about going, but I had hardly gotten a few words of that out before he absolutely refused to hear it. I gave up; I had promised the pies, and Bryn wouldn't accept the idea of me missing the holiday celebration on his account. He insisted that he would be okay, and said he would like a taste of my pie brought back later.

Fine.

There really wasn't any other suitable response. This sucked, but we all expected this to suck. Life sucks when someone is in the process of dying. We would just have to feel bad that a man who loved life would miss a good time and that he would have to stay home. If he felt nauseated, all that food would just make him miserable and embarrass him during the social gathering. Staying home was obviously the easiest way for him to spend the holiday.

Meanwhile, we had a show to attend.

It had been a Friday evening, the one before Thanksgiving, when Berta and I had gone to see *Hairspray*, and I had gone to wait for her at the theater. I was wearing my raspberry pink coat with the fabulous new black hat. She had promised to wear her hat that night so she could show it to me.

I waited until she appeared, knowing that she had to wait until she could leave work on Wall Street, then ride the subway all the way to up to the Times Square area. It was cold, but I was okay with my hat, gloves and scarf. I paced around, looking at the foyer inside and then standing around outside, puzzling over the show's advertisements, which were plastered on the walls of the building.

I didn't know what this show was about, and had never actually watched the movie version of it on cable television. John Travolta just looked too repulsive in drag to me. As it turned out, Harvey Fierstein looked cool in drag, and I enjoyed the musical.

Berta showed up after a little while. By then, I had studied the posters across the street as well, which advertised a show starring Jeremy Piven. I was glad when the wait was over; there wasn't much else to look at, and almost no one was around, so people-watching was impossible.

Berta marched up to me in a huge white winter coat of boiled wool and a pretty teal-green hat with a narrow felt bow of the same material on one side. I admired it; the color and style flattered her. She pointed out that it was one of the few kinds of hats she could wear, because

The Slamming Door

Oatman heads were too big for most hats. Like her father, she told me, she could not wear a baseball-style cap.

Really? I had something in common with her, I thought, glad to have something to share. My father and I both had large heads that required bigger hats, too. There just wasn't much that Berta and I had in common, so whenever something cropped up, I tended to grasp at it with pleasure – I was absolutely determined to get along well with her. I had to do this for as long as possible so that I could keep my promise to Bryn.

At this point, I only had a vague, subconscious feeling that Berta and I were not destined for lifelong friendship. I did not consciously realize that things might not turn out okay, but I know that I simply did not allow my thoughts to go in that direction. I needed to ignore as many unpleasant possible outcomes as I could so that I could concentrate on getting along with whomever came into regular contact with me for as long as possible.

I tend to keep quietly to myself most of the time and just people-watch, even among relatives. I did this among my in-laws, too. I can't help it; when things got noisy or boisterous, I would just clam up and watch. I didn't want to join in, I didn't know how, and I really didn't wish to. Dinner and a show was the perfect way to pass an evening. My discomfort with most social situations could thus be masked to some extent…not that Berta had seen that.

Anyone who is on notice about an autism spectrum condition and who clearly has innate social skills would be onto such things. I guess I just didn't care about concealing it; it is far more work to not tell and thus have to keep inventing silly excuses and lies than to just tell. And it brings to mind one of my favorite Mark Twain quotes about lying: "If you tell the truth, you don't have to remember anything."

I love not having to remember any extra rubbish.

Social skills software in one's brain takes up a lot of room – room that I would rather devote to learning things that I consider to be interesting. So I learned whatever I absolutely had to, and then stopped worrying when I realized that that is the best I will ever be able to do on that count. I must juggle whatever skills I have acquired through rote memorization.

Berta took the typical attitude of attempting to coach me from time to time.

For the most part, this wasn't a problem.

It was too early for the show, so we ate Mexican food around the corner before going back to the theater. When the show ended, I left one of Damon's business cards for Harvey Fierstein, hoping to help sell ImmuneACCORD while doubting that he would ever hear from the

Thanksgiving in a Brooklyn Brownstone

famous celebrity. I wrote a note on the back explaining about the spice mixture. Nothing ventured, nothing gained.

Berta bought some plastic cups at the concessions stand with the musical's name all over them, one for her and one for me. I asked her why she was buying this plastic stuff, and she said, "Because I'm cheesy like that."

Okay...I thanked her for mine, took it home, and washed it after she had consumed the soda inside that I would never drink. It sat on the bureau in my room until my stay was over. I'm a pack-rat; I keep mementos of my whole life and take care of them.

The next Tuesday, I went out to get the ingredients for the pie.

Bryn was okay, eating the chicken broth concoction with basmati rice in it and Jell-O.

On Wednesday, it was time to go over to Elvira's place and make the pies.

Bryn was all set for the evening; I forget whether Albert and June were going to eat with him or whether Elah and Rudy would feed him, but it was taken care of. I packed my stuff in the Whole Foods plastic bags – recipe, pie shells, and ingredients – and headed out the door.

Next stop: the Greek family's florist shop. I bought Elvira that thank-you bouquet of flowers. She could have given anyone else that expensive show ticket, but she had given it to me and I had enjoyed it. Now I was going to take over her kitchen for a few hours. No way was I going without a gift.

Once that was ready, I took off, using the bus as Berta had instructed. I walked down to 14th Street and rode east, until I was right across the street from where she lived. Berta was standing outside at the curb, waiting for me, because Stuyvesant Village is a maze of red brick buildings and trees, like a park of sorts strewn with towers of apartments at odd angles.

We went in, and again I had the nostalgic sensation that I was on my way to see my great-aunt Sharon Barnes. But Aunt Sharon had lived on the opposite side of the complex, on East 20th Street. Still, the hallways and elevator and mailboxes looked the same.

Elvira even lived on the 8th floor of her building, just as Aunt Sharon had.

In we went, and I found myself in that living and dining area in daylight, looking at the sad teenage self-portrait of Dionne again, the wall of books topped by the eleven blue-patterned plates that Berta's Otterman grandmother had given her, and the houseplants and piano by the window. Cinders and Zulu appeared.

I put the stuff down on the dining room table, took off my Merrill shoes, heavy black suede things with thick, comfortable rubber soles,

The Slamming Door

placed them in an out-of-the-way spot, and began to unpack the pie things on the kitchen counter. Berta started showing me where everything was: mixing bowls, whisk, spatulas, measuring tools, etc. I got to work.

Elvira came out then, and I stopped to introduce myself, thank her for the use of her kitchen, and give her the flowers. She was tall, with a pretty, somewhat waved, thick hairdo that was dyed a honey blond color, brown eyes, nicely shaped brows, and a slight limp. She saw my shoes and commented that she had a pair like them, a slightly different style, but the same brand.

I said that that was nice, and that I had an even nicer pair of black shoes that I would wear to the party tomorrow.

"Oh, are you saying that there is something wrong with my shoes?" she asked.

Damned if I could see what I had said wrong, I thought to myself. Aloud, I said, "No. Elvira, are trying to start some sort of argument? I heard about you," hoping that she would drop it. Berta had warned me that her mother loved to pick fights with people at random over nothing, and I knew that I wouldn't be able to spar with a champion if I engaged with her.

Thankfully, Elvira let the matter drop. I hoped she wouldn't stick it to Berta later.

The pies weren't much work; I was just slightly nervous at being in a strange kitchen to make them. Elvira came back out briefly to say that she would make some miniature cheese rolls and a side dish later, but that she was going out to the big Whole Foods store at Union Square to get a few things first. She left, and I mixed up the pumpkin pie filling.

Soon I had both pie shells filled plus an old round Corningware dish with handle, a porcelain frying pan. I arranged them in the oven to bake and set the timer. It would take an hour and a half, I told Berta, who had hung around to chat as I worked.

That left us some time to kill, so we went into her bedroom and relaxed.

I had seen it before, but this time we sat in it and visited, so I noticed a lot more.

She turned on her TV, invited me to sit on her bed, and started showing me things.

Berta began with her computer, an Apple desktop. It reminded me of the ones that Miranda's 2 assistants had used in *The Devil Wears Prada*, because it was all about pretty pictures. What about writing on it? I asked, curious. It didn't have Word, Berta told me.

I refrained from saying how odd that seemed. She had enough of an income to buy a beautiful personal computer, but hadn't bothered to buy basic software for it. She had a viewing program, though; she showed me her résumé, a one-page thing that she had paid someone a hundred dollars to make, with unlimited corrections. She e-mailed it to me.

I had never worked on anything like it. I had edited the CV of my aunt, an artist and art teacher, and done one for my mother, a nurse. Theirs weren't densely packed with text, and they went on for at least a couple of pages. I couldn't help it; I was fascinated to see what a run-of-the-mill cubicle-dweller resume looked like, even though I knew that Berta's desk wasn't surrounded by any cubicle. That wasn't the point; she had a very standard job.

The visit went on in the apartment as the pies baked, until they came out of the oven. Next, Berta went through her lotions and cosmetics, which were on the tall bureau to the right just inside the room. Cinders sat crouched in front of me, purring. I petted her nonstop, enjoying being with a cat after two months away from Cookie.

Berta told me that when she got ready for work in the morning, she would let Cinders smell each lotion, unscrewing the caps and holding the containers under the fluffy gray cat's nose for her. If the cat made a face and turned away, she wouldn't put that lotion on. It was their morning ritual. She demonstrated it for me; it was cute.

I paused to smell some of Berta's things, and suddenly Cinders put her paw on my leg and stared up at my face intently. "What is she trying to tell me?" I asked.

She was telling me to keep petting her, Berta told me.

I laughed and resumed immediately.

We had fun doing nothing until the timer went off, and then I took everything out of the oven, happy to be getting out of the way in time for Elvira, who appeared as I did so, content after her shopping trip. I got some trivets and put it all on the dining room table so that Elvira could have the countertops to work on. She was about to do her cooking projects.

Elvira said not to worry about the pies – she would leave them to cool like they had to, and Berta and I could put them away later. We were going out to eat dinner nearby. Elvira was full of comments about the crowds at Whole Foods, and of outrage at one customer who had broken the seal on a spice jar right in front of her, smelled the contents, and then put it back on the shelf. Elvira had scolded her for making it unsuitable for sale; I agreed with her, disgusted. After that exchange, Berta and I left. I was glad to get away without any trouble with Elvira.

We walked directly south and settled on a place with Cajun or southern-style food, where we had sweet potato fries, trout with lime juice, and other goodies. I thanked Berta for all of the restaurant outings, commenting that we had been out very often, far more often than I was used to, and said that I appreciated it.

"Oh, I'm expecting a lot later on, when this is over," she said with a smile.

I must have looked oddly at her, because I wondered then about what was to happen later on. Obviously, "later on" meant when her father was dead and the care-giving role was over, but what was I going to do after that? Go home to Connecticut? I was mad at my parents for banishing my husband. I didn't want to go back there. Go somewhere with Damon? That was contingent upon an income for us to live on in our own country. Too many unknowns...

With no clue as what the future held, I just moved on; I smiled and we ate our dinners.

Berta finished hers; I got a doggie bag. Those ought to be called kitty bags when people order fish, I thought to myself. We went back to her place to stow the pies in the fridge; Elvira had very nicely promised to pack them up tomorrow and bring them to the party for me. Taking them all the way back to Bryn's apartment would have been absurd; I was to meet Berta and her mother at their place on the way to Brooklyn.

We put the pies in the fridge, and suddenly decided to eat the extra custard together.

We got through two-thirds of it before we realized how much was there, and gave up. We saved it for Elvira, who was nowhere in sight. The place smelled like singed Gruyère cheese, though. She had made her contributions to the party already.

I went home for the night, and e-mailed Desta, who would be riding with us the next day. Phone numbers, addresses, e-mails, all of it – she didn't have that information, and Bryn had just told me that someone ought to coordinate contact information with her. I even programmed her cell phone number into my phone.

The next day, I got ready to go early, and dressed nicely with my black flats, black knee-highs, long black skirt with pockets, and a comfortable raspberry pink sweater-blouse. Then I kissed Bryn good-bye and went out with Berta and Matt in the SUV.

The SUV was capable of holding seven people in comfort, and would be doing that today. For now, I rode in the back seat – one row behind Berta and Matt. We went to get Desta first. She lived with her mother somewhere on East 20th Street, in the exact same path that my Aunt Sharon had lived in. Ms. Abraha was in Antigua, however, and would not be joining us.

I called Desta; she found us and got in. Then we rode around the perimeter of the complex to meet Elvira. Berta went to get her, and she

Thanksgiving in a Brooklyn Brownstone

came out with the bags full of food, which Matt helped arrange in the very back of the vehicle, opening up the back door to do so.

That wasn't all; Desta and I were now shifted carefully to the very back, which accommodated 2 people. We found ourselves barricaded in. Until we arrived at our destination, we could not get out. The regular back seat held 3 people, so our only way out was blocked. I didn't mind.

Elvira settled in and we went to get 2 of her friends, which fascinated me. There was Carlotta, a wealthy widow who actually owned a house in Greenwich Village off 6th Avenue. It was brick, and I could see the front hall wallpaper from the street. It was an ugly black-and-white pattern, but that was all that I could see. Her husband had been a successful stockbroker on Wall Street, Berta remarked as her mother helped Carlotta to the vehicle. So that was how she managed it; I had a hard time imagining how anyone in my generation could expect to be so lucky.

The next person we picked up was a very frail woman, a pretty Greek lady named Olympia. She had a walker, so Matt helped her get settled and then stowed it in the back with the food. While Elvira was out getting Olympia, Carlotta told us that Olympia was very upset because her relatives were forcing her out of that apartment and into some sort of assisted living facility. I felt awful; I know we will all age, but I am upset by the thought of being an old woman, alone, and stuck in a place like that. I didn't blame Olympia for not going quietly.

Now we were off, headed for Brooklyn; the streets were oddly quiet and without traffic for a major metropolis such as New York City. I guessed it was because all of the hurrying, fast-walking inhabitants were off work today, busying themselves with visiting and eating. I found myself staring and staring at the area, fascinated by both the route and the quiet.

Soon we were in Dionne and The Hornsby's neighborhood, and suddenly we were pulling up to their tall brownstone building. It was a nice, clear day, and the trees were bare of leaves. It was easy to see everything in detail.

The building was three stories tall, and when Desta and I were released from captivity in the back of the vehicle, I asked what I could carry. But Matt and Berta and Elvira had grabbed it all, so I took out my camera and shot some photographs of the house as the others walked in, then rushed to catch up.

I was curious to see this place. The Hornsby had bought it in somewhat of a rush a couple of years earlier for approximately $10 million. Added to that was the fact that I had never seen the inside of one of these buildings, so I figured that at the very least it would be a memorable visit. I already knew what Dionne and her husband were like;

The Slamming Door

she was flighty and hard to connect with, and he was remote and aloof, very conventional in his manners to the point of being formulaic. Whatever his true self was like, he kept it thoroughly masked.

So I would study their surroundings and infer whatever I could from that. As usual, I was making few hypotheses and drawing even fewer conclusions, preferring to just gather data and see where it led me.

I followed the others in and found myself looking at a stairwell with white plastered and painted walls, and a staircase made of dark, varnished wood. There wasn't a lot of light in there, just what came through the windows through the open door and from the half-circle window above the front door.

There was a door to the left that was closed; we were told that it was an apartment, and that the tenant was away for the holiday, which was no surprise. Shortly after we were settled inside, I found out that one of the guests was the tenant of the basement apartment and Dionne's friend. She and I shared a first name and a love of cats.

All of the desserts had been stowed in her fridge upon arrival, but I hadn't been involved. So it was hours later that I met her cat, Mischa, a beautiful, short-haired male whose gray-and-white tuxedo fur felt like suede. I met him when several of us went down there to retrieve the desserts, of which mine were only part of a tempting array. The cat was lonely, and came up to me, mewing. I picked him up and kissed him and petted him, and he purred...loudly.

But for now we all marched upstairs, and were told to go directly to the room just to the left of the top of the staircase, which was the bedroom. We put our coats in there on the bed, and I looked through my small Whole Foods bag for my camera again. The place certainly smelled like Thanksgiving, we noticed, inhaling the aroma of the turkey roasting.

Dionne and The Hornsby's bedroom was well-lit by two tall windows that showed the back yard and the backs of the neighboring buildings. Inside was a comfortable double bed with an ugly leopard-print covering on it, an antique bureau-bookcase that belonged to Dionne, and some other bookcases. All of the furniture in there was made of an attractive dark wood, probably cherry. Some Native American weavings were draped over the bookcase near the windows. There was also a beautiful carved, white marble fireplace.

The next stop was the bathroom, which was wedged between the bedroom and the staircase. It was all in white, and sparsely but comfortably furnished. Dionne's Chanel No. 5 perfume was displayed in the white cabinet opposite the sink.

Coming out of the bathroom, I had a direct view of the front windows straight ahead, with the staircase to the left and the dining room on the right. Another carved white marble fireplace was in the center of that wall. Dionne had set up two tables, one with a lacy white cloth and the other in slate blue, and arranged some gourds, hand-made birds with feathers and candlesticks on each one. It looked inviting and pretty.

Walking toward the kitchen, I glanced back and saw an enormous, floor-to-ceiling-sized work of art leaning up against the wall opposite the windows. It was a portrait of a smiling black man, close-up and done in mosaic tile. He seemed to wearing a sports team uniform in green with some blue here and there. Someone told me it was Pelé, the Brazilian soccer player.

I was really interested in seeing the kitchen, however, and continued on to the front of the room to greet Dionne and have a look around. Kitchens are my favorite parts of houses, especially if they are well-equipped, and Dionne's was. She had a gas stove and plenty of cookware that appeared to have come from gourmet kitchen supply shops such as Williams-Sonoma and other, similar stores; I saw a large oval Le Creuset pot, a porcelain cow creamer, and an espresso machine.

Dionne, wearing another vintage 1960s dress in dark reds, greens, black and beige, was busy pulling the turkey out of the oven, so I just said "Hi" and kept to the perimeter of the room, observing. I had once cooked and served an entire Thanksgiving meal, and was used to cleaning an entire house each year to prepare for the holiday, plus making lots of side dishes and pumpkin pie, so I wasn't about to distract her from her task. When she wasn't balancing anything heated or heavy, I complimented her on the kitchen. Elvira was helping her set up the food.

There was one other piece of artwork that caught my attention, a kaleidoscope view of snowy owls that was framed in black on the short stretch of wall by the kitchen. The Hornsby appeared and told me it was a gift from a friend of theirs.

So there he was, The Hornsby: dressed in a dark blue polo shirt with a dark pants suit, leather shoes, and his usual expensive-looking but ugly metal wristwatch, tall and thin with a slightly condescending expression on his face. He directed me and the others to the staircase, up into the loft, where the party was getting underway.

That was when I realized that he and Dionne occupied the upper two floors of this building. Front to back, they enjoyed plenty of light, with the best advantage being on the top floor. As I emerged into the loft, I noticed that Dionne's easel and painting supplies were in a corner towards the front windows, and The Hornsby's desk and computer at the back. There was a very small television opposite the desk, and a stereo with a music collection near the painting supplies. A couple of skylights lit the stairwell. A banner of flags in various colors saying Peace in a

The Slamming Door

litany of languages was draped between them. This was where they did their artwork.

But not today; today, the loft was a living room. In the center of the room, facing the railing for the stairs, was an L-shaped sofa with a brown abstract pattern next to an ancient coal stove (no longer in service). On the wall above the sofa, was one of The Hornsby's old art exhibits, from the gallery where I had met him in the spring of 2003. It was a buffalo skin stretched over a wooden frame with some writing about Palestine on it. A glass coffee table faced the sofa, and some wooden chairs had been pulled up to the other side of it.

The sofas were almost fully occupied, and the coffee table was laden with small votive candles and hors d'oeuvres. There were four women whom I did know, and I met them now. There was Carla, the basement tenant and a German translator (she was American); a Swedish artist named Malin; an Austrian artist named Magrit; and a Russian woman, an aging blond bombshell named Natalia. Someone – Berta, I think – told me later that Natalia supported herself by working as a high-class call girl.

Natalia arrived wearing jeans and a black tee shirt with a sparkly heart on it, and later changed into a tightly-fitted, thigh-length, sleeveless, sequined black dress with a high neck and long black boots. She had long, thick, straight hair with bangs, and it was probably dyed. I never got a chance to chat with her because I fell into conversation with Malin and Magrit, and ended up sitting with them and the other Carla, Claus and Desta at the slate blue table for six.

Elvira, Carlotta, and Olympia were in the chairs with Matt and Berta and Natalia, all grouped around the coffee table. The artists, translator, and Desta were on the sofa, and Malin shifted to invite me to sit on it next to her, under the artwork. I was delighted, and I had a perfect view of the entire room, with my back to the wall. Dionne sat down with us for a few minutes.

Claus appeared a couple of minutes later, handsomely outfitted in a tuxedo with a red bow tie. He was the most dressed-up person present, overdressed even, but he carried it off beautifully. He loved it when several women – including me – told him that he looked great.

Berta was on the chair next to me, and she showed me the Gruyère cheese puffs that her mother had made the night before. Elvira piped up that Colette had fed them to her lovers. I would have to look Colette up later, I told myself silently as I bit into one. It tasted burnt. I choked it down without showing it, wondering about Elvira's mood as she had prepared them.

Next, Berta poured me a glass of wine and showed me something quite fascinating: a corkscrew that Dionne had said was hand-crafted in

1820. Berta held it out and I shot a few photographs of it. It was black metal, with a shaft down the center surrounded by a coil of metal that looked like a spring. A cork was in it, surrounded by the coil of black metal.

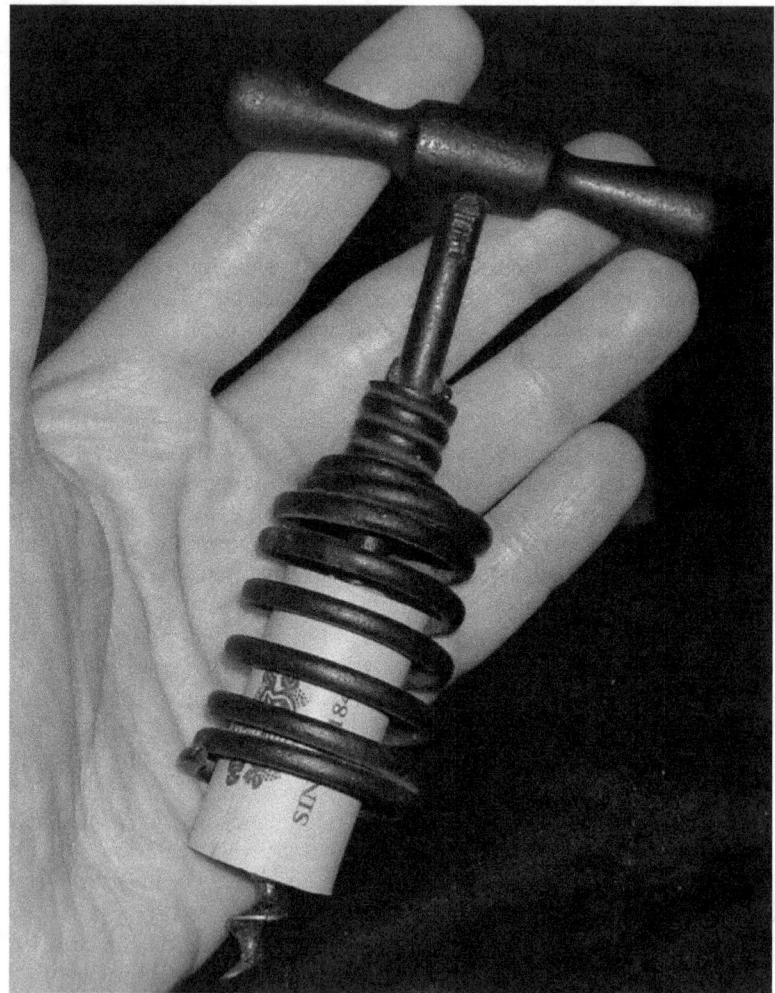

Corkscrew made in 1820 – with a cork in it.

After a little while, I got up to see the rest of the room. Heading toward the back, where The Hornsby's things were, I saw more of his Native American-Palestinian artwork over the desk. It was a black-and-white photo of spent artillery shells lining a street in Palestine. A Karl

The Slamming Door

Marx portrait sat in the corner. Turning around the other way, I noticed a row of thick glass panes set into the hardwood floor right behind the sofa; it showed the white lacy tablecloth directly below.

I needed to use the bathroom again, so I went back downstairs. The toilet wouldn't flush. I came out and looked for The Hornsby; he was upstairs in the loft. How was I going to get his attention? "Houston, we have a problem," I said, and he looked up at me immediately. I told him what was wrong. He disappeared and fixed it.

But I wanted to walk around a bit, so I headed back downstairs. Dionne didn't need my help in the kitchen – I had offered and she said she was all set – so I wandered down to the ground floor. Matt was there, standing on the front steps in the fresh air.

Matt was such a nice, quiet guy that he too must have decided that he needed a break from the constant noise that socializing makes. He didn't smoke; he just wanted quiet. He greeted me cheerfully and when he saw that I had my camera, insisted that I photograph the lock on the large door that sealed off the upstairs quarters. It was a functioning antique, a huge, gray, heavy thing that said *The Fox Police Lock Co. – New York*.

Dinner was delicious. Dionne served it buffet-style after The Hornsby carved the turkey to bits and presented them in two huge tinfoil containers, with the side dishes off to one side and the plates on the other. Some people ended up eating on the tall stools by the windows; there were at least 14 of us at the party.

I sat facing the front windows, near the owl art. The table behind me was far louder than ours, and more crowded. I didn't pay attention to what was going on there. The conversation where I sat was pleasant and not too loud or boisterous for me, and I didn't feel pressured to say too much, though I did talk about my work and tell how Bryn was doing.

At some point during the party, I called Bryn on my cell phone to check on him. He was okay, watching television in his chair. I passed the phone around to various people, including Claus and Desta, and when I got it back, he told me not to hurry back, to just ride with the others when the party was over. He insisted that he was feeling well enough to wait until I got back, and not uncomfortable.

Frankly, I was relieved I would not have to go out alone in the dark in Brooklyn and figure out how to get back by subway. I was afraid to walk around in an unfamiliar area. Dionne did it all the time, but she knew exactly where she was going.

Bryn probably knew that and didn't want me to try it either.

When it was time for dessert, the turkey was cleared out of the way and the pies and other things were laid out on the counter. In addition to my pumpkin ones, there was a teardrop-shaped mango mouse, an apple pie, and an entertaining, demented-looking fruit plate made by Natalia.

She had taken a cantaloupe melon, poked it all over with toothpicks, and then stuck strawberries stem-wise on them all, strawberries which had been cut with criss-cross slices. In those strawberries went raspberries and blueberries. It looked freaky, like a lump that had sprouted a crop of delicious red-and-blue shapes.

I had some of the berries, of course, a slice of pumpkin pie, and a little of the mango mousse. The Hornsby insisted upon cutting and serving it from the end opposite the little raspberry, even though I asked if I could have it, so I just raided the raspberries off of the lump.

After a while, I got out the camera again. Natalia had changed into her sequined dress, and she struck an inexplicable pose when I raised the camera. A little wooden block with a painting of Jesus on it was sitting on the table in front of her, and she suddenly held it up as though she were in a showroom displaying merchandise, complete with a broad salesgirl smile. I was nonplussed, but shot the photo without comment.

Next, I found Berta standing by the upper staircase. She posed with me for a photo, then shot one of me with Desta. We were all similarly dressed, in dark skirts with pretty colored blouses, and holding glasses of wine.

Berta went over to the other staircase and pointed out something interesting.

The Slamming Door

It was a rare species of mid-western antlered rabbit...mounted on the wall at the top of the stairs to the dining area. Was The Hornsby making art out of the victims of his hunting trips? Maybe, considering many of the decorations, but not this one; this one was a commonly available joke sold in stores locally, called a jackelope.

The party continued until a couple of hours after dark, with much laughing, talking, eating and drinking of dessert and coffee.

The jackelope in the stairwell.

Eventually, we all headed back out to the SUV where Matt proceeded to ensconce me and Desta into those back seats and settle Elvira and her friends in the long back seat together. Soon we were on our way back to Manhattan. The streets were now dark but with no more traffic than we had seen earlier in the day.

It took a while to drop everyone off, but at last I was back with Bryn, followed by Berta and Matt. For once, parking on the street was easy; Matt could come upstairs and take his time. We found Bryn exactly where we expected to see him, in his chair with the TV on.

I showed him the plate that Dionne had prepared, with some of absolutely everything from dinner, plus a slice of my pumpkin pie. I didn't see any other desserts on it; mine was probably the only one not bought in a store.

Bryn asked for an extremely tiny taste of each item, pie too – just a little bit.

He wasn't ready to seriously eat. What he wanted to do was to get his ticket punched for Thanksgiving by tasting one taste of turkey, cranberry sauce, and pie. That was all he could bear to do, but it mattered to him. Clearly, he needed to feel like he had experienced the holiday.

Berta stayed a few minutes, then left with Matt. She could see that her father was low on energy, and Matt wanted to stretch out and relax. He was sitting politely on Bryn's bed, using the long brown pillows like a sofa, waiting until it was time to go.

I don't remember whether they were staying at Elvira's place or on Long Island.

When they were gone, Bryn surprised me by asking what Berta had eaten at the party.

What he meant was, how much had she eaten, and how many helpings of each item?

Bryn did that a lot. He would either comment to me when we both returned from a social gathering that included his daughter – "Did you see what/how much Berta ate?" – or he would ask me what I had seen her eat if he didn't go out with us.

I told him that I had sat with my back to her, and not paid any attention.

I was not conducting covert ops to spy on Berta and then report on her intake volume every time we went out anywhere...not that I added that. All I said was that I had not paid any attention.

Bryn let the matter drop.

Then I told him in great detail about the party – the arrangement of tables, food, hors d'oeuvres, wine, dessert, coffee – and about the nice people I had met and chatted with. I also told him about the lovely cat, Mischa.

He enjoyed that.

Chapter 26

The Big Apple Circus

In December, Berta invited me to go with her to something called The Big Apple Circus. I had never heard of it. When she told me that it was in a tent on the Lincoln Center grounds every year, I was surprised. She got the tickets at work; it was one of the many perks of her job.

"Yeah, it's really there. I go every year. Come with me this year," she insisted.

On the evening of the circus, I left early and went to the bagel shop on 8th Avenue between 22nd and 23rd Streets. I got a smoked salmon bagel – they had a long list of smoked salmon choices – and a bottle of water, plus some chips. I was sure that nothing at the circus would seem healthy, and I didn't want to be stuck eating fat, salt and sugar. I could have some popcorn to be polite, I decided.

Then I headed over to Lincoln Center, walking up the middle of the square, facing all three of the buildings – ballet, opera and symphony halls.

A huge banner was draped across the Metropolitan Opera building, announcing that Mozart's *The Magic Flute* was playing through December, a truncated version for children, in English. It had already started.

And here I was, heading for what seemed to be…a kiddie circus. Hordes of little kids – toddlers and kids under the age of 10 – were being led towards a huge white tent that loomed to the left of the opera house.

What had I agreed to?!

Too late now…

Before continuing on to the circus tent and looking for Berta, I had to get this out of my system. I took out my cell phone and called Damon at the lab in Connecticut. I described the scene in front of me, lamenting the fact that such a wonderful example of art and culture stood before me, but that my destination was clearly one of utter banality.

Of course I got the sympathy I sought.

Damon had had a similar experience long before I knew him at this same place. Back in the 1980s, when he was a research scientist for Dr. Jane Setlow at Brookhaven National Laboratory, he had fallen hopelessly in love with a beautiful blond nurse named Jen. Jane Setlow, wanting to be nice to Damon, had given him a pair of tickets to Mozart's *Don Giovanni* at Lincoln Center.

Jen quickly proved less desirable as Damon got to know her; she was bored by the opera and insisted upon leaving during the

The Big Apple Circus

intermission. Damon never got to see the whole opera, which was a disappointment, and when Jane Setlow found out, he felt awful about it.

So that was it for Jen, which was lucky for me. Now Damon was married to someone who would never, ever want to walk out on an opera, especially one by Wolfgang Amadeus Mozart. Unless the performers were incompetent, I would be thrilled to attend one.

Damon chatted with me for a few minutes, heard the whole lament, and we rang off. Reluctantly, I turned left and faced the huge, white tent.

I approached the gate and saw Berta grinning and waving to me. She handed me a huge ticket and I followed her in. "What's that?" she asked as we went into the tent, looking at the bag I carried.

"It's a bagel with smoked salmon. I didn't want to rely on junk food for dinner, so I brought this. I'm looking forward to popcorn, though."

She looked a bit surprised, but nodded and got a huge, long hot dog and slathered it with ketchup and mustard from red and yellow squirt bottles, plus a lemonade, pink cotton candy, and popcorn. "We can share this," she said, handing me the popcorn and pink sticky stuff. Then she ordered me a lemonade. "Don't worry, it's all part of the ticket," she added. "You can get as much as you want – take some candy bars!"

"Are you sure?"

"Yes! I do this every year – well, I did before I went to L.A., and I did it again last year."

"Oh." I took a couple of Hershey bars and the lemonade. It came in a huge, gaudy, plastic cup with a straw attachment that bent up and down. The top was transparent, fluorescent green, and the cup itself had the Grandma clown painted onto it.

"The cup is a souvenir. I've got several of them," she told me.

Lovely; I smiled and said I would keep mine too.

A clown – male, but dressed like an old woman – waved us in. It turned out that he was the Circus's signature character, the Grandma Clown. Red and yellow decorations were everywhere, and a concessions stand was straight ahead, just before a right turn that led into the seating area.

Hilda showed up a minute later. She looked awful; her hair was chopped in short, stick-like stands that were parted in the middle and hanging stiffly around her face, and was dyed blond. The effect was like straw. Hilda wasn't a pretty girl as it was, but her trips to the salon made her look worse with each visit. I didn't understand it. Berta gave her a ticket, and soon they both had huge, long, greasy hot dogs, popcorn, soda, and a cloud of pink cotton candy for Hilda.

We went in and took our seats, which gave us a decent view of the ring, halfway up and a third of the way around the ring from the performers' entrance. I was in the middle.

The Slamming Door

Berta asked me where my camera was.

"I left it at home; I didn't feel like bringing it," I replied.

"Clarisse, you're fired!" she protested, giving me a big grin.

So she was disappointed, but that was all. I may have Asperger's, but it was easy for me to spot teasing and disappointment in that comment. I was glad to have left the camera home, though; it was all little kid-oriented entertainment, and the flash might have startled the performers. Cameras and live entertainment don't mix.

Hilda started eating her junk food, and I took out my dinner. She looked askance at me as I ate my different food, but I didn't care. The kid had a history of making unwise food choices. I just watched the show; her opinion didn't matter to me.

Soon Hilda and Berta were chatting across me, and I was left out of the conversation. It was a scene that had been repeated many times throughout my life whenever I belonged with a group but didn't fit into it.

The show started, and I wondered about the trapeze artists. Perhaps there would be some death-defying feats. I liked the idea as long as there would be a net. But when the time came for acrobats, they didn't go up very high at all; in fact, the men merely carried the women around the ring while the women twirled around a few times.

There was a dog act, but that wasn't remarkable. The dogs didn't seem to do anything too fascinating or difficult, and they were mostly little toy breeds. And so it went.

I watched the kids around me, bewildered. Their parents kept grinning at them and encouraging them to clap and smile. I recalled being a child with no difficulty; this would not have impressed me then, and it seemed utterly inane now. But then, I was a strange child, only impressed by a good story or something that I could learn – a bit of science, art or history.

What was particularly unpleasant was the constant touching of my legs and shoulders by sticky little hands – and no doubt germ-coated as well – as the toddlers balanced against everyone and everything that they came in contact with. Their parents did nothing about it.

I had been inadvertently and unknowingly lured into this situation. I just had to get through the rest of the evening, I told myself, and then I wouldn't come back if I was paid to.

As we sat there, with the inane circus act going on interminably in front of us and with toddler kids ambling and brushing all around and against us, I asked Berta why she liked this.

She turned to me with a big grin and said something that put her interest in this dull spectacle into abrupt and stark perspective.

"I want a baby."

The Big Apple Circus

I looked at her very seriously, keeping my expression as deadpan as possible. Frankly, I was appalled. Another baby in the world – on top of all these around us….and from a woman who seemed utterly unfit to be a parent, from what I knew about her thus far.

A moment later, I found my voice again.

"A baby?!" I said, without raising the volume of my reply. The tone had conveyed my disapproval as it was. "But the world is overpopulated. There aren't enough resources for everyone to enjoy a happy, comfortable, and interesting life."

Her reply was as thoughtless as it was instantaneous: "But I don't care about everybody else," she said with a careless giggle and a huge grin, "I just care about me, me, me."

I made no reply. There was just no suitable response to that.

She was easily the most selfish and self-absorbed individual that I had ever met.

She was also what was contributing – in a species-wide movement – to the problem of human overpopulation: a short-term thinker. Short-term thinkers place their present comfort and enjoyment ahead of and to the exclusion of future concerns, often to the detriment of those who come after them. No wonder past empires have collapsed.

At least she had the one redeeming virtue of being honest about it.

I was disgusted, but pushed the thought of her reproducing out of my mind. She wasn't yet married, and she was nearly forty years old, so I felt no urgency about an actual child being added to the situation. We went back to watching the show.

My thoughts wandered, as they do whenever I am bored. I thought about my grandmother; her stepmother, a beautiful Irish-American woman from Boston, and she had had some female cousins who were trapeze artists in the Ringling Brothers Circus.

On what happened to be D-Day, June 6, 1944, my grandmother had attended that circus with her husband and stepmother in Hartford, Connecticut. They had brought my uncle Roddy, who was a toddler, but my mother was still too little to attend, and my great-grandfather had stayed home to babysit so that his wife could see her cousins perform in the circus.

Nana had told me that that was the day of the disastrous fire; the tent was made of oilcloth – highly flammable material. The Roget-Conroy family wasn't very far up in the bleachers, and they had a great view of the band. Suddenly, Great-Nana's cousins noticed that the tent was on fire and directed the band to play some music, hoping to calm people.

A boy with a pocket-knife had been outside, and had gone around the tent, cutting slits here and there for people to run out of – emergency exits. He probably saved a lot of lives that way. My family got out quickly, and so did the cousins, but driving away was not possible for a while. They sat in their car and watched the mayhem, having no other choice. A lion in a cage was wheeled past; the straw was partly in flames, and he was terrified, pacing up and down and roaring. Someone threw water on it to put out the flames.

That was it; that was all that Nana had told me, but it was enough, and it was much more interesting that what I was watching now. I had been to circus acts before, and they had been much more death-defying and interesting than this one. I even rode a circus elephant when I was six years old, and enjoyed it…silently.

Were the organizers afraid of inducing nightmares in the children? Why was this so dull? When I was little, lion taming acts and high-wire feats – I mean really high, not this lame presentation – would not have terrified me. They would have thrilled and fascinated me. But I did say that I was an odd child, not like most others.

When at last it was over, we all walked out and found a photographer by the exit. Berta had us pose together, and a few days later, she e-mailed the result to me. There we all were, with me in the middle, Berta in her huge white winter coat with her rectangular glasses and brown Ugg boots on the left, and Hilda with her straw-like travesty of a coif on the right.

We wandered into the symphony hall of Lincoln Center to use the rest room, and then continued on out to the front of the complex, where we hailed a cab for Hilda and sent her home. She had homework to do.

Next, I suggested that Berta and I go do something else together. I didn't want her to know what I really thought of the circus. We walked to a record and poster shop on Broadway, where we had some fun browsing for *Wonder Woman* and Stevie Nicks paraphernalia. I didn't buy anything, but I definitely had fun.

I was glad that we did that, because I would have to spend leisure time with Berta on a daily basis for the foreseeable future. We needed to find some forms of enjoyment in common. Eventually, we had seen enough and hailed a cab after Berta bought an old Stevie Nicks poster. She let me out at 21st Street, and rode on to Stuyvesant Town alone.

When I got home, I told Bryn all about it, and even mentioned the circus fire of 1944. He asked about Hilda, and I said that we had sent her home in a cab to do her homework. He nodded with approval, and I made him a cup of tea, either China Oolong or Lapsang Souchong.

I also washed the lemonade out of that fluorescent green cup and dried it off; there was no way that I would drink any more of its sickly sweet contents. Perhaps I was a food snob, and perhaps I was no longer able to tolerate high levels of sugar.

After that, I made myself a cup of tea – with milk but no sugar.

The Big Apple Circus

Sometime that fall, after Dionne had returned from Colorado and Wyoming, she had come into my room for part of her visit and seen that I was still living out of my suitcase, which was lying on the floor in front of the bureau. Above it, on the dresser to the right, were my other things – makeup, toiletries, etc.

"Why aren't you using the bureau drawers?" she asked me.

I told her it was because they were full of Maggie's things. Maggie had visited that fall, but she was living in Florida. She was also about to have a kidney transplant, marry a much older man (perhaps 30 years older), and go back to school while raising the daughter whom she had left school to give birth to out of wedlock. She couldn't take any of her things away at that time. So there they were, over 4 years after she had abandoned them, filling up the bureau on the right, plus much of the closet. We had an address to send them to, but that was it.

Berta had not been ready to go through the old clothes yet. Maggie had said to just drop them off at the Goodwill place; that she couldn't fit into them anymore. But which things were hers and which were Berta's? I wasn't about to have a problem with Berta over this, so I hadn't moved my things into the drawers.

Dionne didn't agree. "You should take Maggie's things out of those drawers and put yours in," she told me.

A couple of days later, I did it. I was amazed to see how little there was in them.

With that, Berta was at last interested in sorting through the old clothes.

Soon we had the giant, shiny, orange laundry bag out of the closet. It was stuffed to the point of bursting, full of Maggie's things plus some old possessions of Berta's. No wonder I had waited for her to do this. As for the things in the top two, smaller drawers of the bureau, which weren't clothing, I boxed them up and wrote the address that Maggie had left on them. Unfortunately, the stupid things sat in the back corner of the front hall for several months more.

Berta kept a few items, but the rest was arranged in large plastic recycling bags and slated for departure. When it was over, I had reclaimed the floor of the closet for my own use. I stacked my suitcase in there, a couple of other items. It was nice to have more room to move about.

Later that same month, Berta and I went out to eat together at the Royal Siam restaurant, a Thai place nearby on 8th Avenue; Bryn was off doing something with his Henry George School friends.

The Slamming Door

As we sat eating our dinners, Berta asked me how I felt about Damon traveling to Iraqi Kurdistan, Kuwait, and Hungary.

"I hate it; he's never home, and I won't go back to the Middle East, or move to Eastern Europe, or otherwise not live in my own country. If I have to wait and wait, I will. I want to live in my own country, and I need to. I can't write somewhere else. That trip to Kuwait was a fascinating adventure, but once was enough in an Islamic country."

"Then you shouldn't have married him."

I stared at her. What the hell?! Of course I should have married him. He was my soul mate. I told her that he was my best friend, so no one else would do, but I was really annoyed. There was no way to know before I married him that he would keep going elsewhere and not be able to just do all of his work in the United States, and anyway, he was way more interesting than some guy who just got a job and a mortgage and then watched team sports on television.

The conversation moved on to Berta's life.

Had she had any other serious boyfriends before Mike?

Well, yes, as a matter of fact, she had. He was a guy she knew when she was in her 20s, and she pointed out some old photos of him to me later that evening when we were back at home. The guy was of medium height, medium build, going a bit bald, with dark brown hair and eyes. He wore tee shirts, shorts and sneakers in the photos. He looked nondescript, but by then I had heard all about him at dinner.

They broke up because he had a problem with drugs.

Interesting...her mother's first husband had been a heroin addict.

What really shocked me was what came next. Berta said that if her ex-boyfriend hadn't gotten married to someone else after getting clean, she would have left Mike and gone back to him. I stared at again, unsure what to say at first. Why would she ever want that guy again after he had had a problem with drugs?! Mike was so much nicer...and cuter, judging by the photo.

I told her my opinion about Mike being a better, more reliable choice, but I doubt it had any great effect. It didn't matter; Mike was available by default.

It didn't seem like a great bargain for him, but at least he could enjoy ignorance.

At least, without knowing any better, or any more about it, I could think so.

As Bryn began to feel a bit better, he ate more and went out more. There were still some doctor's appointments to go to, and Albert insisted upon being the one to go with him, so I stayed home. I saw these all-day

The Big Apple Circus

or half-day trips as opportunities to clean the apartment and change Bryn's sheets, a luxury that he had often forgotten for much longer periods of time when he lived on his own.

On one of these afternoons, I had just found a piece of paper, perhaps one of those inserts that come with magazines, that had fallen onto the floor next to Bryn's chair, on the far side where it had gone unnoticed until it was affixed to the floor by some spilled water, when the Bryn's land-line phone rang.

I had just poured some water onto it and gotten the chisel from under the kitchen sink a moment earlier, and was scraping at it when I picked up. It was Kasey. "They're gone for hours; I'm cleaning the whole place!" I said into the phone.

She laughed; Bryn had told me that her house was absolutely spotless at all times.

I told her Bryn's itinerary and she must have called him on his cell phone.

In early December, Bryn surprised me and Alissa by inviting us out with him to the Henry George School faculty and staff Christmas party. I don't know why he didn't invite either of his daughters; they were both around, and probably available.

I think he wanted to invite Alissa somewhere, because he hadn't been able to spend much time with her as long as he had known her. But that wasn't anyone's fault, and she knew that he admired her and was proud of her. She was an accomplished writer, fluent in French and Italian, well-read, well-educated, and very nice.

It was her shyness and introverted personality that held her back from bonding more with her uncle, that was all. They both knew it. We all knew it. It didn't matter; each of them was well aware of the other's high regard.

As for me, I assumed that Bryn just wanted me to escort him to the party, take photographs, and enjoy the event. He had already complimented me by wanting me as his caregiver and trusting me with his errands – ATM card, prescriptions, unpleasant details that were the routine secrets of being terminally ill, etc. – so I didn't wonder why I was going.

The party was to be held at Marchi's Italian Restaurant, within walking distance of the Henry George School. The other faculty members whom I had eaten and visited with at 30 at 30 for years would all be there, plus some spouses.

But the evening of the party, Alissa couldn't come with us. She had a cold.

The Slamming Door

We were disappointed, but all we could say was that we hoped she felt all better in time to enjoy Christmas. There was nothing else to say. It was just bad luck. Alissa refused to expose her uncle's compromised immune system to her cold, which made sense.

I had forbidden my body to catch so much as a cough while taking care of Bryn, and for some reason, my luck held during all of those months with him. There was that, plus the rigid routine I followed of drinking orange juice every single day, eating fresh berries, and sleeping enough. That was probably the real reason why I never caught anything contagious.

So Bryn and I got dressed up in our best formal dinner jackets that night, which was early in December, and went to the party ourselves. It was a rainy night, and of course after dark when we found ourselves walking from a brief rendez-vous at the school to Marchi's.

As we walked, I worried about Bryn being out in the rain, but he insisted that he could handle the short walk under the umbrella with me. I clutched his arm anyway, watching him amble along at a decent pace with his cane. Well, he had been saying that he should walk more.

He was fine. We arrived at the restaurant, and the atmosphere was dark, somber, and lit up with cheerful little white Christmas lights everywhere. It was the décor that made it seem somber; dark reds and wood paneling dominated.

An Italian-American waiter appeared to collect our coats and umbrellas. I looked around, puzzled, wondering why the place was so quiet. The Henry George people seemed to be the only customers. After a little while, I found out that we were the only customers. The place was reserved for a private party – us – so that was why.

Soon we found ourselves greeting Claus and Keisha and the others, and I met some members of the Board of Trustees whom I had never seen before but heard of often when Bryn described them. It was fun.

First we went out to the bar, beyond the dining area, where Claus greeted me as usual with a kiss on the cheek. Bryn wandered off to one side, chatting merrily with some other people. He was already having a great time. I did too, chatting with Claus and Alfred Mazerati; where was Alfred's wife, I wondered? I had only seen her once, a few years ago at 30 at 30, and rarely heard about her, but he wore a wedding ring, just like Claus did. Claus's wife lived in Florida, I knew; but Alfred seemed happy enough, so I didn't worry about it.

Next, we were told to adjourn to the dining room because the meal was ready.

Interesting; we were in a restaurant, but the food was all ready. I wondered what sort of agenda this place had. Was the meal catered

The Big Apple Circus

somehow? Why did we not order food? Well, I would watch and see what happened.

Bryn looked for me at this point, knowing that I was unsure of the agenda. He brought me out to a table on the right, motioned me to a seat on the end of a table that seated 6 people, and took a seat to my right but with someone else in between us. That was fine; the point of a party is to talk to people you don't see every day.

To my left was a nice Asian-American lady from Connecticut, possibly Vietnamese. I suspected that she had married a former Vietnam War soldier and moved to the United States but didn't ask. Her husband sat next to her, across from Bryn; he was a trustee. I liked him.

Now Bryn explained the agenda to me, as the waiter started bringing appetizers to the table: Marchi's Italian Restaurant simply made the exact same meal every single night for each and every party that signed up to eat there. It was a traditional Italian meal, formal. Later, when I mentioned it to Leah, she told me the same thing, and that she had eaten there once, too.

Well, that cleared that up. I watched, fascinated, recalling Italian Christmas Eve fish dinner parties with handmade pasta dishes and cannolis and wine and dish after dish after delicious homemade dish. Rose and Tally, my parents' friends, put one on every year and invited us each year that I was in college. They also attended my wedding, but had since died.

Marchi's dinner party had different items, but the presentation reminded me of Rose and Tally's parties anyway. The first thing that the waiter brought out was a plate of raw winter vegetables and fresh melon. We all ate some of it, passing the dish around and choosing whatever we wanted. I saw a huge fennel bulb cradling most of the other items and didn't touch it, but after a little while people started asking what it was.

"It's fennel, a bulb-like vegetable related to dill and chervil, which are herbs, and to a spice called anise. It has a vague taste of licorice," I said.

Curious, Bryn reached out and cut off a small bit and tasted it. "Yep, it does," he said.

It was nice – very nice – to see that Bryn felt well enough to experiment with food.

But I could see that he didn't particularly like fennel. No one else wanted any. Licorice has always sickened me, so I was glad it was at the opposite end of the table. The waiter came back soon after that with salads, and not long after took away all evidence of the first course.

Next came lasagna, followed by deep-fried fish, cold beets (Bryn was happy with those!), and string beans in oil and vinegar. That took care of courses two and three.

The Slamming Door

For the fourth course, two entrées were offered: roast chicken and veal, plus a heap of cooked fresh mushrooms and more tossed salad. I ate some of everything but the veal.

The fifth course was dessert, which included an enormous, beautiful bowl of peaches, oranges, bananas, pears and apples. Cheese was presented to go with the still life image before us. That wasn't all: we also enjoyed a lemon fritter with two names, crema fritta and cristoli, deep-fried twists of sweet batter dusted with powdered sugar. Coffee and milk were provided.

When it was over, Bryn was a bit tired, but happy.

I knew that he would have to sleep and do almost nothing for the next couple of days to recover, but neither of us would have missed the party. Bryn only had a limited and unknown amount of time left in which to party, so if resting and laying low after a social event was what it took to enjoy one properly, he was ready to accept that.

So was I; I expected it.

My role was as his enabler – to enable him to have as much fun as possible.

Chapter 27

Bryn Throws a Party at the Hahvahd Club

Once he was past his second round of misery, it was the middle of December. The doctor informed Bryn that she didn't want to spoil Christmas for him by poisoning again so soon, so she was going to wait. I liked this doctor; she seemed to appreciate the need for quality of life as much as quantity, despite the fact that poison was the best that she had to offer him.

With that, we realized that we were in for a month or so of pure fun and enjoyment, even if Bryn was feeling a bit weaker than he was used to feeling. We settled into planning on making the absolute most of it that we possibly could. Damon was coming, Vianne was coming, Alena and her family were coming, and I actually made hotel reservations for Christmas Eve and Christmas night so that Damon and I could go off and be alone together. Bryn approved, too.

Other than that, we intended to participate in everything that the rest of the family was doing. Meanwhile, I concluded my Christmas shopping for the relatives in Connecticut and mailed them home, wrapped and ready. The only items that I needed help with were the L'Occitane products that I had acquired before leaving but never wrapped; half for my mother and half for my Aunt Johanna. I called my father at an appointed time and talked him through putting the stuff into two pretty boxes provided by the company – done.

During the same span of time, I had been shopping for the New York relatives, stashing things in my room to wrap up, including some toys for Nicola and Aaron's daughters that I would mail to them in time for Hanukah. Bryn was their godfather, so I also bought them stuffed animals on his behalf, wrapped them, and sent them after his cards were written. It was fun.

Getting the stuffed animals had been taken care of shortly after Bryn had gone to that Henry George lecture by Alfie Mazerati in the Bowery. I went back to that wonderful toy store called Dinosaur Hill, which sold rare and beautiful stuffed animals, puppets, learning toys, puzzles, and so on. He wanted 4 toys, one each for Nicola's daughters, and one each for Alena's.

We had agreed on a plan: I would walk across town to it, then call him on my cell phone and describe the toys as I looked around. It was a freezing cold afternoon, but I had my chic black hat on, a scarf, gloves, and my winter coat. This was good exercise, and it was fun.

When I arrived, I didn't call immediately; instead, I found the woman in charge and explained my plan. She agreed to help, and I got

The Slamming Door

Bryn on the phone. I walked around describing things in great detail, and he told me what he did and did not like. The store had some fabulous monsters from Maurice Sendak's *Where the Wild Things Are*, but he didn't want monsters, which was understandable.

Bryn liked the realistically rendered animals. When the shopping was done, he had a gorgeous rabbit that was made in Germany, a cute panda bear, and 2 others that I don't remember now. Soon the shopping was done and I was walking back home, pausing to talk to strangers with dogs as usual. I love to do that – pet the dogs, and then leave the shovels and bags to someone else. It was after dark, but still early, and there were lots of people around.

When I got back and showed him the toys, Bryn was delighted. I laid out each one on his bed to face him as he sat in his chair holding court over the room. He admired each one, and then I started to wrap the ones that had to be mailed to Massachusetts, to Nicola's girls. The others could wait; Alena would bring her kids to see us all in person. Bryn preferred that; he procrastinated on writing his cards, which was characteristic of him. Not me…I was in a hurry to finish all shopping, wrapping, everything, and just have it sitting, ready to give away.

Bryn did get on with something else, though: gifts for his doctor and her nurse practitioner. He wanted fancy boxes of Godiva chocolate for them. I had gone out to Rockefeller Plaza one dark afternoon, both for fun and this errand, staying until past sundown (Bryn was fine at home for a few hours) and shopped. I wandered around the Anthropologie store, the French bookstore called Librairie de France, and the Metropolitan Museum of Art store.

Bryn Throws a Party at the Hahvahd Club

The Slamming Door

While I was at it, I found a small Godiva chocolate shop, one that had concrete floors and makeshift walls. It was temporary, just for the holidays, and just north of Rockefeller Plaza. I bought the candy and called Bryn to say that the deed was done. He would see the medicine women the next day, so I had been determined to get their gifts in order without delay.

Meanwhile, Albert was constantly out with June, trying to keep her entertained. She didn't like the elderly day care place for Alzheimer's patients, so he was unable to work. He took her out for any reason he could think of, or that she could think of. They ate out for lunch often, and they shopped. Soon, she had yet more cheap hoop earrings, and Albert exhausted himself searching for just the right underwear for her, poor guy. His wife had always handled such details for the two of them, and now their roles were abruptly reversed with no time to prepare.

One afternoon, he came over with a bag of men's sweaters. He had gone on a shopping spree and gotten carried away, so now he wanted to give them away. He insisted that I check for any that might fit Damon, and I found one huge, soft dark blue one. But there were more. I called Rudy over to try on a brown one that looked his size. He put it on and said, "This is a great sweater," and that took care of that. Bryn got the other one, a very soft dark grey one.

A little while later, I gave Puma, Elah's cat, a new toy. Elah was home but busy, so I left after a couple of minutes. But then a nice e-mail came back from her, saying thank you and commenting on how nice it was that Rudy got a sweater. That wasn't all; Hilda came over with an odd garment on: a red flannel blanket with sleeves, tied to her waist. It was called a Snuggie. Elah had bought a bright blue one for Bryn also, and I took a photo of them together. It was mid-December by then.

Christmas and Hanukah shopping was pretty much over by then, with gifts for all of my Connecticut relatives gone, Vianne's ready for her visit, and gifts for the New York clan ready. The only things I needed were toys for Alena's girls. I found them at an outdoor market in Union Square that Berta had mentioned: Silly Puppets. They looked a lot like the Muppets of Sesame Street, but less expensive, about half the size of Muppets, and without wires. Instead, the user put her hand up inside them. I found a fairy princess and a girl with a rose-patterned dress. I would give Lillian the roses; her older sister usually got all of those, thanks to her middle name.

But the biggest hurrah of the season was being planned by our family saint.

Bryn wanted to proceed with a yearly tradition: his brunch party for family and friends at the Harvard Club on East 44th Street in Manhattan.

Bryn Throws a Party at the Hahvahd Club

This year, it fell on a Sunday, on the Winter Solstice, December 21st. I had been there several times before with him, and enjoyed it.

He was very excited about it; apparently he did it every year, and he sensed that this one was his last winter holiday party there. He put lots of thought and planning into it. Berta mentioned to him that I could do calligraphy, so he asked if I could make place cards. Definitely, I said, and went out to the Da Vinci Art Supply store for felt-tip calligraphy pens and place cards.

There would be 3 tables for our party, he told me, and went to work plotting who would sit with whom, imagining who would make the best dining companions for one another. He got a bit obsessed over this aspect of the planning. I didn't worry about it; that would have no effect on the calligraphy, and I was quite willing to sit wherever he told me to sit. He worked it out on some scrap paper, and then gave me the list:

1. Bryn Warne Otterman, M.S.
2. Clarisse Nicole Rénard, J.D.
3. Damon Drake Hardy, Ph.D.
4. Vianne Hardy Halloran, M.A.
5. Alena Hardy Lipinsky, M.B.A.
6. Josh Lipinsky, M.D.
7. Roselyn Elin Lipinsky
8. Lillian Hannah Lipinsky
9. Aunt Summer Lindsey
10. Berta Otterman
11. Matt Dylan
12. Toby Maddox
13. Dionne Otterman
14. Albert Hornsby
15. Albert F. Otterman, M.A.
16. June Otterman, M.A., M.F.A.
17. Alissa Rand Otterman, M.A.
18. Hilda Mae Ranger Stone
19. Carolyn
20. Ophelia
21. Kandi Kramer, M.F.A.
22. Kandi Hamilton, M.S.W.

The cards came out nice, with a lovely black script in the Chancery Italic alphabet, on a plain ivory background, and folded in half neatly. With the exceptions of the 2 Alberts and the 2 Kandis, when I made the place cards, I just used first names.

Toby Maddox was Bryn's friend from work, now retired, who had worked at a desk as his supervisor. Poor Toby had hated that job, wishing that his NBC newscaster position had never been cut. Toby was in his late seventies, and he attended lectures at the Henry George School other social events with Bryn. He wore an eye-patch after a botched cataract surgery had left him with a detached retina. He and I had a cute thing going in which I would supply him with a new patch each Halloween, bought at a costume store. He loved the pirate packaging.

The Slamming Door

Bryn wasn't careful when he was teaching me who was who at first because it was just the two of us at home with no witnesses to hear how he phrased it: Black Kandi and Jewish Kandi. That really didn't help me to remember who was who, because it was awkward. My brain tends to hit the "delete" button when something is said that can't be repeated.

I told him that this wasn't good; it could become a habit and then he might end up saying it when we were out somewhere and could be overheard. Was there some other characteristic about each one of them that would help me remember them, as going by last names had clearly failed to do the trick?

Yes – he told me what they did for careers, and how he knew them: Kandi Kramer (a.k.a. Jewish Kandi) was an art teacher who had been educated at the Parsons School, a branch of the New School, and would bring Bryn rice pudding on almost every visit to the apartment. Those visits began after his chemotherapy rounds. Kandi Hamilton (a.k.a. Black Kandi) was a social worker that Bryn knew from his last city job.

He had actually met Kandi the art teacher in the early 1980s when they had both been selling sets of Encyclopedia Britannica. They had kept up their friendship since then. Kandi the social worker he knew from work; I remembered her from the photos taken at his retirement party. Problem solved.

We finished the place card project quickly, with me presenting them all and laying them out in front of him on his bed again. At first, there were 4 more for Alena and her husband and daughters, but then Bryn found out that their plane wouldn't get in until after the party, so it was just 18 of us. I put the cards in the order that he wanted for each table, stacked the 3 groups of 6 up, and sealed them into a zip-lock bag. When we left for the party, I would take my digital camera and the cards, plus a bag with my formal shoes. I would wear boots in the winter slush.

A week and a half before the big day, I followed Bryn into the kitchen to chat with him nonchalantly as he got his Miralax and drank it by the sink. What I was really up to was making sure that he didn't trip and fall. But I enjoyed the chance to chat with him, and looked forward to this nightly ritual, which usually took place at eleven o'clock.

As he stood there by the sink, with his cane hooked onto the rim, I suddenly looked him over, and recalled our last trip to the Harvard Club, which had been early the previous July. Bryn had worried me nearly to tears over my attire, specifically my black leather sandals, only to discover that every woman in the place was wearing black leather sandals and mine were the prettiest of them all.

Now his attire needed some attention.

Up until this point, he had forbidden me to do anything about it. He had been losing weight so rapidly that he had assumed that there was no

Bryn Throws a Party at the Hahvahd Club

point in shopping for new clothes until he stopped shrinking, and so I had agreed to wait.

But now was done shrinking, at least for his pants size, and that was what mattered right now. He possessed 2 pairs of beige Dockers pants, and one belts. Both pairs of pants now ballooned out around him, and the left hip of each had a huge blue ink blot due to his tendency to nod off over *The New York Times* crossword puzzle with an open uni-ball pen in his hand.

That wasn't all.

As I looked at him, I noticed that he had tucked his polo shirt and checkered, multi-colored sweater into his pants to hold them up, and cinched the lot together with his old belt, which had a huge crack next to the hole where it used to buckle, now unused, plus a shaggy hole where he had poked a new one – from the inside of the belt – to accommodate his smaller waist.

There he stood with his black woolen hat on, this atrocious outfit, and white socks.

I brought up the question of his attire. "It really is time for new pants now," I insisted, "and I know that I'm supposed to get them at Dave's Pants on 6th Avenue," I added.

He looked up at me, nonplussed.

I went on, reveling in the serendipitous opportunity for a comedic moment. "I mean, look at you – you've got a hole poked into your belt, showing the frayed edges of the leather, and not only your shirt but also your sweater tucked into huge pants with an ink blot on each pair – you can't go to the Hahvahd Club looking like that!"

With that, he bent over slightly, plastic white spoon in his right hand and little white ceramic cup in his left, peered down at his outfit with a brief surveying glance, and then looked up at me with a big grin. His outfit was appalling and he knew it. It hadn't mattered until now, when we had to get him ready to enter that famous sanctum.

I knew he cared about the presentation he made there, so I knew he would agree to this.

The only problem was size; what size was he now? It was vastly more preferable to go into the store knowing what I was looking for, so I could just come back with it and consider the task accomplished, over and done with. Neither Bryn nor I liked to bother with returns and exchanges if we could avoid it.

"I know that my inseam is 29 inches," he told me, "and that won't have changed, but the waist size is the thing we need to check."

I had brought my sewing kit from Connecticut; at the bottom of the bag was a tape measure, rolled up tiny. That was one possibility. Another, even better one, suddenly occurred to me, however.

The Slamming Door

"I have been saving a new pair of pants for Damon," I told him. "He's been exercising at the UConn gym, and has lost some weight. You could try them on to see if the waist fits, just to give us an idea. His inseam in an inch longer than yours, however, so I will still have to shop, whatever this tells us."

Great idea; he tried the pants on and they fit – waist size 38, down from…44. Wow.

Nasty thing, that cancer diet, and fast, too.

Most diets make the person put the weight back on once they go off of them, but we knew that this change was permanent. Bryn liked it, though. He had been unable to get the excess weight off for a few years, and now he said he was the same size that he had been as a teenager. Hmm…at least there was some benefit from all that misery.

I bought him two new pairs of Dockers pants the next afternoon; one beige and one olive green. He had forbidden navy blue, black, or white, and requested that both be beige, but I was lucky to find just one pair and had no more time to search. Then I went up the street to T.J. Maxx and bought a new belt for him. It was reversible, too.

Bryn was skeptical of the olive green pair of pants when I got home, but a day or so later announced that he liked it better than the beige, and intended to wear that pair to the Harvard Club. I was intrigued when Albert dropped by with June and commented that Bryn had worn beige pants for his entire life, and only beige. This was a noteworthy change. And I thought I was set in my ways about clothing!

It was true: Bryn had practically worn a uniform of sorts for his entire adult life. Polo shirts or Oxford shirts, depending on the occasion, beige pants with pockets that could double for either everyday or formal wear if a jacket and tie were added, white socks, brown shoes, and if he had to rent a tuxedo for a random social event, so be it.

So easy, with minimal effort, shopping, searching, or maintenance…so unlike what I had to do, which was coordinate colors and search for pockets in everything or else get them installed, if I liked a dress that much. I could see why Bryn had worn a "uniform": it was easy.

Bryn showed me a beautiful blazer that he intended to wear; it was the same one that he had worn to Marchi's Italian Restaurant for the Henry George School Christmas party, the one that Alissa had missed when she caught a cold. It was from Claus, German-made, and all grey with no lapels. It hung straight in the front, with carved buttons and a short collar that stood up. He also had a Christmas tie that Vianne had given him the year before.

My outfit was ready too, and was more trouble: I had a beautiful jacket from Coldwater Creek that looked like a piece of pink tapestry

Bryn Throws a Party at the Hahvahd Club

with blue iris blossoms here and there on it. Like Bryn's jacket, its collar stood up straight; it closed with an invisible zipper. I would wear a soft black skirt (alas, no pockets, which really bothered me!), black knee-highs, black shoes, and a dark pink, soft shirt.

Thus prepared, I awaited Damon's arrival, which was to be the evening before. His suit, tie and blue shirt were ready; he knew he would have to wear them to the Harvard Club, or else face the seldom-seen wrath of Bryn. That wrath was really more of a vague rumor than a reality. Bryn was just so easy-going, and there was no way anyone would consider upsetting him by dressing down when he was hosting a party there.

Meanwhile, Bryn's friend Nils from the Mendelssohn Glee Club stopped by with recordings of past concerts by the group. He heard about Damon's past military experience and hoped to meet him, but it was clear that our schedules over the holidays would not mesh. Still, it was fun to see another one of Bryn's friends and observe him. He was very nice, a tall, white-haired man with no glasses, and very cheerful.

Before the relatives arrived, Bryn told me something else: he had found out that Alena's older daughter Roselyn, who was now 9 years old, was having trouble with depression, and that she had recently held her breath on a long car ride until she passed out. Alena and Josh had had to pull over and check her while her little sister watched. After that incident, Alena took the poor kid to a psychiatrist for some prescriptions. I hoped she wouldn't get fat from them like I had.

I was appalled – not only could the pills make her gain weight, but they could also dull her mental functions. That was what had happened to me, and when I quit taking them, I went back to normal…at least, what was normal for me. But this kid was doomed to the negative effects, because Alena was a firm believer in medication. She had suggested some of it for me on occasion, and would do so again when she found another opportunity.

Alena had suggested it to my mother in years past, sometime after I had quit taking the pills and shrank back down to my normal, healthy size and resumed writing. My mother had refused to get involved; I was upset about life in general and worried about Damon, as he was off somewhere again trying with great difficulty to earn a living.

Damn conventional, corporate-minded, conformist Alena. Functioning among most people in most situations was easy for her, and as a result she was the wealthy head of a small corporation in New Mexico that funded the kiosks in shopping malls, and other small businesses. Bryn had a cool Polaroid photo of her shaking hands with Hillary Rodham Clinton from when she was the First Lady. Alena's job was admirable, but her personality wasn't.

The Slamming Door

Alena was hard to talk to face-to-face because she used formulaic phrases to distance herself from revealing anything emotionally or otherwise significant, and unreachable by phone. She preferred to make appointments to call other people, which was what we had started doing when we got cell phones…at last, effectively shutting down her way of controlling things.

Bryn, however, could be trusted to listen to things as both a retired social worker and the family saint. Damon and I liked to call him that. I also thought of him as the glue of the family, because he seemed to hold it all together just by being there. It was effortless for him. He made everyone feel at ease, both about sharing secrets with him, and about life in general.

When I realized that Alena wouldn't make it in time for the Harvard Club party, I was glad. Without her personality in that mix, it would be a much more relaxed and friendly party. There would be no one who would stop talking, look at me as though I shouldn't have spoken and wasn't wanted in a conversation, and that would be great. But I told no one this.

Alena had done that to me there once, and I hadn't forgotten about it. If someone is sitting right across the table from you at a fancy dinner, it's not nice for you and the person next to you to try to have a private conversation apart from her. Even I know that; NTs can be very rude to Aspies. I had long ago given up trying to be friends with her.

Vianne, however, was a different story. For one thing, she had similar problems communicating with her own sister. Vianne loved to go and visit her nieces, and Alena would take advantage of the free baby-sitting that this led to by buying her sister plane tickets and then going away with her husband, Josh, while Vianne came to stay. But Josh would initiate the discussion about each visit, making the first contact by phone.

Next, Alena would call back to say, "Are you coming?" So it went, until Vianne arrived.

Alena excelled at putting people at a distance, and she was coming to stay at Aunt Summer's place with her kids and husband, and with Vianne. Aunt Summer would go stay at Aunt Johanna's place while Vianne and the girls used the fold-out sofa bed.

No matter how it worked out, we would still have a couple of visits with Alena.

Damon felt the same stress that I did, and usually coped with it by being loud and wild with his nieces. Alena seemed to enjoy that. So we hoped that there would be fewer opportunities for her to say that she couldn't understand how he could have a Ph.D. yet be at the bottom of the economic ladder, or some such thing. She had once, when he stayed

Bryn Throws a Party at the Hahvahd Club

with her because of a lecture he was giving in Albuquerque, told him not to let me hold him back, which infuriated him.

When the visits got noisy and wild, I got quieter and quieter, waiting for the uproar to end. I hate noise. I would just watch and avoid drawing much attention to myself. Suffice it to say that I was not excited about this, but I was ready with the stupid Silly Puppets.

Josh was nice enough, but I didn't trust him because he doted on Alena as much as Damon doted on me, and he had money and resources at his disposal to lavish on her, which meant that she got to live with her husband. I hated to be around happy, economically solvent people as it was, and Alena just seemed too smug about her entire situation to be likeable.

Her daughters were another story. Roselyn had never thanked me for a gift until she was 7 years old, at which point I thought, Alena must have taught her that. Lillian, however, thanked me the first time I saw her at an age when she could talk, and she smiled and chatted with me. I liked her. The cold stares of her sister alarmed me, despite my dutiful gift-giving and pleasant greetings. But now that I knew that Roselyn was depressed, I felt empathy for her; however, understanding her situation and feeling bad about it would not translate into being able to help.

I put it out of my mind until we would actually see each other.

We still had to experience the party at the Harvard Club.

There were lots of pleasant memories of the place. Bryn had invited us there for dinner in the summer of 2005, and despite the fact that Alena had been present, we had had a great time. The food was terrific, of course – dinners mean ordering off of a menu, and Bryn was always a generous host – and he took us on a tour of the premises, explaining the rules and customs of the place, and showing us each room.

No photography was allowed in the dining room, but it was allowed out in the bar, in the smoking room where no one smokes any more (that room must be a relic of past times), and in the huge sitting room to the right of the dining room. All were paneled with beautiful dark wood, and the dining and sitting rooms have huge windows that face East 45th Street at the back. We had saw the wall hangings in the sitting room: there were several French tapestries that depict medieval hunting scenes, and Teddy Roosevelt's elephant head.

A copy of Teddy Roosevelt's White House portrait hung just below the library balcony, to the right as one entered from the old smoking room. The artist who did that reproduction had been forced to apply to Harvard University several times by his parents, who wanted him to live a conventional life. He kept failing the entrance exam until they gave up and let him be a painter. Because of that story, which was on a small

The Slamming Door

placard next to the portrait, it was my favorite. Bryn had told me that it was his favorite too, and for the same reason.

For the winter holidays, a huge Christmas tree was always set up in the sitting room.

It was two stories high, covered with red and gold ornaments and garlands and white lights, and hollow inside. I didn't know it until late in the party, but Hilda had a tradition of climbing inside it with her friends and sitting there to chat. I stuck my digital camera between the branches and took a couple of photos of them for Bryn. Hilda was wearing spiky heeled shoes and a revealing dress, which looked oddly out of place in this palace for academia, and she didn't looked pleased when I stuck the camera through the structure, but Bryn wanted the photos.

The morning of the party was a bit hectic in the apartment with all three of us getting ready to go. Bryn wanted to leave early with me so that we could set up the place cards; I hadn't realized that he was planning on doing it that way. He wanted Damon to go in a separate cab with Hilda and her friends. I got ready quickly enough, got the place cards, camera, and bag with nice shoes and prepared to dash out with him.

Just as he was about to take off, all dressed up in his beautiful new pants, belt, and German jacket, he accidentally knocked his yellow Chinese mug from Piper and Melissa onto the floor and smashed it. He had it for a couple of decades. Damon and I felt sorry for him. I picked

Bryn Throws a Party at the Hahvahd Club

up the pieces and checked, but there was no spilled liquid to wipe up; Bryn had drunk it up before he knocked the cup over.

I made a mental note to buy him a replacement as an extra Christmas gift. Chinatown was one of the places we were going on our own. But for now I said nothing; it would be a surprise, and hopefully make him feel better. At least he still had the matching green one…

The dimly-lit back room of the Harvard Club on East 44th Street in Manhattan with the giant Christmas tree lit up.

The Slamming Door

We took off in a cab together, into the snowy, sleety morning at 10:30 a.m., and into the club entrance where Bryn announced himself. We were allowed into the dining room to lay out the place cards. I hung up our coats and stashed my beautiful hat on a shelf; Bryn had worn his favorite soft black woolen one from Dionne. I put that up there, too.

Bryn took the cards from me in groups, carefully laying each one where he wanted them, and pronounced himself satisfied and ready to party. Soon the others started to arrive.

We had a great time at the Harvard Club, and posed for lots of photographs as a family in front of that giant Christmas tree, plus in the bar. I got a great one of just Bryn, grinning in his grey jacket and Christmas tie, and another or Albert, who wore his own Christmas tie – also a gift from Vianne the previous year.

June seemed to have fun; she sat across from me with Alissa on the end, opposite Bryn. We were at the middle table. The brunch was buffet-style, with an omelet bar, croissants and raspberry jam, smoked salmon, smoked trout, shrimp, and other fish delicacies, a waffle area, bacon, sausages, roast beef, vegetables, and assorted gourmet tarts, cakes and cookies, plus fresh-squeezed orange juice and coffee or tea. We all got stuffed, of course.

But there was place card mutiny almost right away: when people started to arrive, Berta decided that she wanted to sit next to her boyfriend. I wasn't looking, but suddenly Damon and Vianne joined in the mutiny of musical chairs and I found Vianne transferred from Berta's side to mine, and Damon over there.

Well…I was happy to sit next to Vianne. Damon explained that he didn't want me to watch him eat, but his ulterior motive was to bag extra smoked salmon off of his plate to take home. Sigh. He had learned that in Virginia from my Japanese cousin, Kazuko, who had routinely arrived at the Westfield International Conference Center, a place with brunch parties comparable to this spread, for my great-uncle's birthday parties with a secret supply of zip-lock bags in her purse, also for smoked salmon.

Wonderful; leave me out of it, I thought. Bryn looked upset at the mutiny, and I hastened to assure him that I had had nothing to do with any of it. I think he believed me, but it took him a few minutes to get over it, and he complained about it a bit more, later that evening, when it was all over. He knew that his daughter had been the instigator.

As for Damon's raids on the food, Albert disapproved and told me so, even asking why I hadn't stopped him. He sounded like he thought I had control over Damon's actions. I explained that I had no control over Damon's behavior, and referred him directly to Damon, and so Albert gave up. My husband's relatives knew what they were dealing with.

Bryn Throws a Party at the Hahvahd Club

When Damon was a little boy, no one could control his behavior. "It's time to go visit the psychiatrist again," was all that his poor mother would say when he did something outrageous, which was often. At this point, I think that Asperger's Syndrome was the driving force behind his mindset and a lot of his behavior, though his departed father gets a good share of the blame too. Damn Damon's father for not wanting his kids and not realizing it until he already had them! I had told Damon and Vianne that this was my view on the matter, and Vianne had just nodded.

Other that the smoked salmon raid and Berta's mutiny, a great time was had by all. I still have the collection of photographs from the party to look at. One of them was taken on the way out as Damon borrowed Ophelia's red hat, which had a bow and a feather, put it on, and posed with a psychotic grin under a wild boar's head that was mounted right across from the coat racks.

That night, I gave Bryn a Winter Solstice gift: *The A to Z Crossword Puzzle Dictionary*. Both of my grandmothers had been addicted to it, and my Grandma Rénard had been a New Yorker who did *The New York Times Crossword* with it. Bryn was very pleased to have one. I had another gift for him for Christmas, and grouped it with everyone else's for him to take to Dionne's place on that day.

Earlier in the month, during Hanukah, I had given gifts to Elah and Hilda. For Elah, I found a mug by the Unemployed Philosophers' Guild – all in Yiddish. She loved it, and then she had surprised me with a beautiful antique hat-pin. It was decorated with white porcelain beads painted with pink and blue roses. She looked delighted when I showed it to her, poked into my hat on the side opposite the bow. It's still there.

For Hilda, I got a CD of yet another musical, though I don't remember which one it was now. She said thank-you, but other than that, I don't recall any great effusions of delight. It didn't matter; a CD of a musical was my standard holiday gift to her, and she typically memorized the songs and sang them beautifully, on key, with her soprano voice. At least it always pleased Bryn.

The next few days were busy; we had Alena and Josh and the girls and Vianne, Albert and June and Alissa, and me and Damon in the apartment the next afternoon. Bryn had fun; we gave Roselyn and Lillian their stuffed animals and Silly Puppets, and took lots of photos of the girls playing with them. Damon played with my black velvet hat, wearing it and posing with Lillian, and Alena put hers back on, a plainer but similarly styled black hat. I sat quietly on a chair in Bryn's room against the wall, waiting for the loudest moments to calm down.

I just hate loudness, no matter who is making the noise. It stresses me out, I don't know how to respond, and I can't join in. Whenever a group of people shriek loudly, cheering something on, I just withdraw into myself and silently observe. The group could be teenagers or college students shrieking at a rock concert or ball game – it makes no difference. The sound of my nieces screaming with Damon egging them on and acting crazy to entertain them had the same effect on me; no doubt I seemed unhappy. It's just the way it is with me; Aspie and quiet.

So I sat quietly and tensely in the wooden chair by the door in Bryn's room after taking some photographs and politely noticing everything that happened during the visit: gifts being unwrapped and delighted over; French cookies being offered to the little girls and others, also by me; posing for photos and shooting them. If it seemed that I was participating in various holiday rituals in order to visibly demonstrate involvement and enjoyment, it was true. That was the part that I could find pleasure in, not the noise.

The next visit was easier.

The next night, we went to Aunt Summer's apartment and ate something strange that Damon explained to me when we got home: Jewish Chinese food. It had all of the taste and uniqueness and good qualities of normal Chinese food removed. He said that *The New York Times* had explained it in an article that week, but I couldn't find it online. The aunts had ordered take-out from a place that they were used to. I was getting sick at that point, and wondered whether I had caught a bug from Damon. Later, we figured it out: Damon's salmon had not been refrigerated quickly enough, and when he ate some the next day, it made him really sick. I had one bite the afternoon before the aunts' party, so the digestive torture was starting for me then.

Damon had eaten the lot of it the afternoon that Alena and the gang came over. I had one piece. That evening, he got sick, while I just had one fast bout of misery. I was fine after one trip to the bathroom in Le Gamin Café. I thought that was it, because the next day I felt fine while Damon was sick with puking and diarrhea all night and then a fever the next day. I gave him chicken broth soup, made from Knorr bouillon cubes.

No such luck; I was in for another tough time after having carefully budgeted and planned for a romantic getaway with Damon. Instead, I was miserable for Christmas Eve, okay for Christmas Day, then sick again during Christmas night and the day after. We still had fun, but it would have been much better if I hadn't been sick. We left in the evening, after dark, when I was able to leave the bathroom.

I realized that it was from the salmon and stopped worrying that either of us might infect Bryn with anything, but I was so annoyed. I was also a bit nervous about going away anywhere and leaving him home alone. He sensed this – I must have given him some anxious, appraising looks – and said firmly, "Don't worry about me!"

Bryn Throws a Party at the Hahvahd Club

So I went. Damon told me later that he called to check on things and found out that Bryn had hailed a cab on his own and gone over to Aunt Summer's place to see the little girls on Christmas Day, so at least he was okay and had had a good time. Everyone went to Dionne's place for Christmas dinner, including Albert and June; Elvira was with her mother in Alabama. Damon and I called on Christmas Night during dinner and chatted with them all for a few minutes.

I had rented a hotel room for us in SoHo for 2 nights on Hotels.com, and had gotten a good deal. Damon was delighted with the place when he saw it, thrilled when I added that a small gym downstairs was part of the deal, and even happier when the staff lent us a small refrigerator. We definitely got our money's worth: I had great baths with L'Occitane products, and he used the gym – all for $160 per night. The inside of our door said that the rooms cost $299 per night at the very cheapest; the struggling economy was no doubt driving prices down.

We got settled and soon headed out to find a Chinese restaurant that would offer Peking Duck, which Damon was absolutely determined to eat for Christmas Eve dinner. After a quick walk a couple of blocks southeast, to Chinatown, we found the famous Peking Duck House.

We put our name in and were told that it would be at least 45 minutes before we would be seated; the place didn't take reservations. So we went out and got a new Chinese mug for Bryn. It was green with Chinese characters all over it. He liked it, and promptly enjoyed some Lapsang Souchong tea in it the evening after Christmas, when I presented it.

When we returned to the restaurant, the wait time was up and we got a table in the middle. There was a view of the host's podium, and we could see the waiters coming and going with hot dishes. Some sizzled as they arrived, including ours. We had the Peking Duck, of course, and steamed sea bass. Our fortunes were pretty good, so I saved them. I ate very little, but enjoyed some of everything.

After dinner, we returned to the hotel. It was great to be in a room alone with my husband and a tub to use with no feeling that I had to hurry out of it. I had a great bath with a L'Occitane rose bath pebble in the hot water. Damon was pleased that I was enjoying it, and we watched TV for a while before falling asleep. We were just a couple of floors up, overlooking Lafayette Street. The bed was comfortable, and the curtains let in no light.

The next morning, Damon enjoyed the exercise machines. I slept, and worried that my troubles from the bad salmon weren't over. Fortunately, I was able to enjoy my birthday. When I woke up, Damon wanted to open presents, so we did. There were some from our Iranian friends, Massoumeh (my co-author and memoir subject) and Afshin

The Slamming Door

(Damon's scientific colleague). Afshin had also brought pastries from Iran with almonds and pistachios and honey.

The best gift was from Damon: he had asked Aunt Summer to get him 2 tickets to the matinee of Mozart's *The Magic Flute* at Lincoln Center for New Year's Eve. The show was set for 1 p.m., in English, abridged and for kids, but we didn't care. It was going to be fun. This was just the coolest thing that Damon could have done. I knew I would be fine by then.

I had some clothes for Damon, and a couple of books, including Lemony Snicket's *The Lump of Coal*. He loved it, and read through it right away, laughing about the story and enjoying the illustrations. I usually gave him something like that for Christmas – a dark, bizarre tale with great drawings included.

After we looked at the gifts, we went out to Little Italy for breakfast via Canal Street, then crossed south into Chinatown to go exploring in the sunshine. Damon wasn't particular about what he ate, unlike me; he was just determined to eat in Little Italy. I wanted to have coffee and juice and something breakfast-like. We found a place that fit the bill a couple a streets over form the hotel. It was dark and staffed by one Italian-American guy who had to do all of the table-waiting himself. I wondered what fun he would be able to have for Christmas as I ate a chocolate-dipped cannoli; Damon had a calzone. We both had orange juice and cappuccinos.

From there, we crossed the street and got the exploration underway. Damon had been talking about this for weeks; he had gone through Chinatown in May of 2001 with Vianne, then walked around at the South Street Seaport with her after that; he was celebrating the completion of his Ph.D. then. Now he wanted to go back there with me.

Chinatown smelled awful to me in many places, like dried and salted fish products, but interesting in others, like dehydrated, sweetened fruits that I had never heard of, let alone tried. We looked at all the weird stuff there and Damon bought some. One item that he did not buy was a bird's nest in a jar. It was yellow, in sauce, and cost between $35 and $70. The Chinese woman who ran the shop told us that it really was a bird's nest.

We saw some beautiful dolls dressed like the concubines of China's imperial court, fans, carved jade, and more mugs. We didn't buy any of it; we just wanted to window-shop. We met a great tomcat next in a knick-knack shop with Chinese dolls and tea sets. He was a wonderful tiger-striped fellow with white paws; he came out, smiled at us, and meowed a greeting. I picked him up and cuddled him, and he purred and smiled at us some more. The Chinese woman whose cat he was delighted that we liked him. We talked to him a lot and then put him down and left.

Bryn Throws a Party at the Hahvahd Club

There were some outdoor markets that we shopped at: I had forgotten my sunglasses and the day was very bright, so I bought a pair, plus I saw a huge, royal-blue scarf with red and yellow tulips on it and bought it for Massoumeh's birthday. She had told me that the word for tulip in Persian/Farsi is "laleh" and I wanted to send it to her. Her birthday was just 4 days after mine. Damon thought the scarf was perfect, too.

After we had seen all of Chinatown, I wanted to continue on a historic walking tour of lower Manhattan. Damon agreed to it; we planned to walk to the South Street Seaport anyway, and he loved hearing me talk about history. I had studied the area near Wall Street and wanted to show him the historic sites there.

We walked south, past the New York City state and federal courthouses (they are right next to each other, and appear on *Law and Order*), with their familiar palatial steps and carvings, then on past the statue of Benjamin Franklin across from the mayor's office and City Hall.

City Hall, across the street from the mayor's office.

The Slamming Door

The mayor's office, which cannot be approached past a gate on the side.

We kept going, with me playing the tour guide, past St. Paul's Chapel on Broadway, the back graveyard of which is across from the World Trade Center site. St. Paul's Chapel was closed, but I had been in there several times. It is where the volunteers rested and got massages as they sifted through the rubble at Ground Zero of the World Trade Center wreckage. George Washington had a pew there and gave his inaugural address there; when D.C. was still under construction, our national government was in N.Y.C.

Saint Paul's Chapel on Broadway.

Bryn Throws a Party at the Hahvahd Club

George Washington's pew in Saint Paul's Chapel, preserved as a museum exhibit.

All around the inside of Saint Paul's Chapel, on the perimeter, are mementos of the rescuers and rescue operation that took place after the September 11, 2001 attacks on the World Trade Center, which was just across the chapel's backyard and street behind it. This one was of patches from firefighters and police officers.

The Slamming Door

Continuing on down Broadway, we looked at the historic notations in the sidewalk about which world leaders had been there and when – mostly from the 1950s to the late 1970s. John Glenn and Olympic athletes, male and female, were also listed, as well as the British and Dutch Queens, Shah Mohammad Reza of Iran, and so on.

We continued on down Broadway to Trinity Church, where we sat in a pew looking at the stained glass windows, then outside to see the red-painted metal sculpture of the Sycamore tree root, called *Trinity Root*; It was made by a Pennsylvania artist, who took the original root of a Sycamore tree home with him to copy, to commemorate the tree that the 9/11 blast threw from the backyard of St. Paul's Church to the Trinity Church yard.

This tree used to be in the back yard of St. Paul's Chapel up the street, but when the Twin Towers came down, the force generated uprooted this magnificent old tree and threw it to the spot where this artwork now stands. After the artist was finished making this replica, the tree was taken back to St. Paul's Chapel graveyard and buried there. I'll bet the sextons never anticipated digging a grave for a tree.

Alexander Hamilton, the first Secretary of the Treasury and creator of that office and Cabinet post, is buried there with his wife. Vice President Aaron Burr shot him in a duel in 1804 and killed him, leaving his widow with 8 kids and no way to make money (early 19th century women had a terrible time making ends meet if their husbands died). If you stand near their graves, laughter from another ghost can be heard.

Bryn Throws a Party at the Hahvahd Club

No one knows who the ghost is or what the joke is, but I have heard it too.

The graveyard was closed, so I couldn't show Damon where Alexander Hamilton was buried with his wife, or have him hear the ghost that laughs. Damon could see ghosts, so I was disappointed to have to skip that. Trinity Church faces Wall Street, so we went that way to see the plaque that describes the Dutch wall of horizontal planks that stood from 1653 to 1699. We walked east past the New York Stock Exchange (NYSE), its Christmas tree, and Federal Hall with its giant black metal statue of George Washington out front. That building was our nation's capitol building until the one in D.C. was far enough along to move everything out of Manhattan.

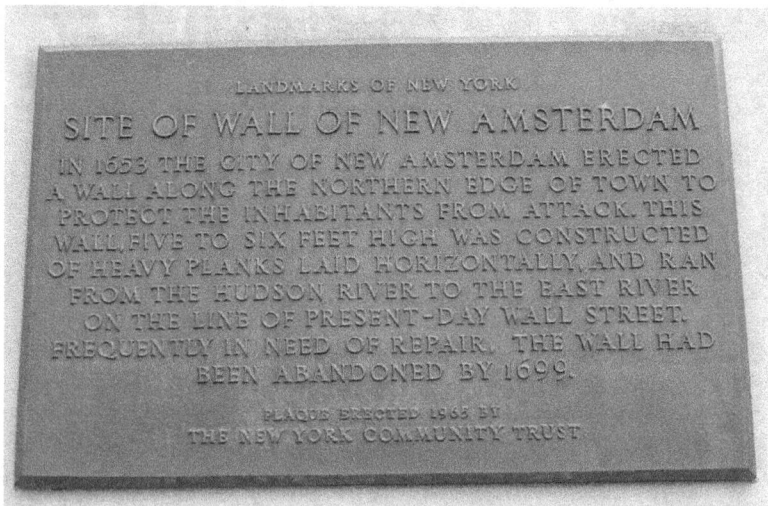

The Slamming Door

Federal Hall Memorial with the bronze statue of George Washington at the top of its steps. He conducted his entire presidency here, because the Executive Mansion was under construction.

Bryn Throws a Party at the Hahvahd Club

The New York Stock Exchange or, as I think of it, the National Casino, where the House always wins.

Across from the national casino (a.k.a. the N.Y.S.E.) was the J.P. Morgan building, a bank built in 1913. It looked like a mansion, and it was built as such when skyscrapers were going up around it. J.P. Morgan didn't care that he was putting up a structure that didn't blend with the surroundings; he just wanted to be next door to his money. He was one of the owners of the White Star Line, which owned the Titanic. A cart blew up in front of this building in 1920, and the pock marks in its marble steps were still there.

J.P. Morgan's mansion, directly across from the New York Stock Exchange.

The Slamming Door

Wall Street had more to see, so we kept walking and saw Tiffany's – it was a new branch – and another branch of La Maison du Chocolat, both closed, of course, and then Deutsche Bank, where Berta worked. She had told me that she hated it. Damon and I said again that she worked for the Nazis, but these particular executives were Americans. Just as in *The Devil Wears Prada*, Berta had to go down to the cafeteria, get her food, and eat it at her desk. No time to exercise or make good food choices. It even looked like Nazi architecture – but I had left my camera at Bryn's, not wanting to deal with it on my birthday. It was a monstrously tall, cold edifice of brown marble, with grilled windows on the 5th floor, looking like a tower of doom.

Tiffany's on Wall Street.

After that, we walked as far as the last street before the shore, Water Street, turned north, and went to Fulton Street, where we saw the Titanic Memorial – in the form of a light house that used to serve as a beacon for ships coming to Manhattan – and Fulton Market and South Street Seaport. Fulton Market had changed since 1984 when my Grandma Rénard took me there. Now it was like an upscale mall, in what looked like a historic village of Federalist-era buildings, with mid-scale stores. They were closed, but I wasn't interested. We went into the South Street Seaport…and right back out. There was a gas smell in there, so we had to leave. We paced around on the wharf looking at the East River for a while until the problem was resolved, and then sat in the upper level drinking coffee and looking out until dusk. We could see the Statue of Liberty from there, which I hadn't expected to see from that angle, but was just visible.

After the sun set, we walked up Fulton Street to the subway and went uptown for our 6:30 p.m. reservation at Marseille, a French-Moroccan restaurant. I didn't want to be stuck on my birthday without reservations in a big city. The menu was prix fixe, so after I got a Belgian raspberry beer, we shared a goose and black truffle risotto, and a pureed soup of apple and chestnut with spiced maple. Next came duck with pistachio sauce and some sort of savory puff pastry, and smoked trout with lentils and pearl onions that had been soaked in red wine. I had a Buche de Noël log slice for dessert – a Yule log with raspberry mousse and chocolate ganache – and I saved the rest in the hotel's fridge. Damon got mixed berries with Chantilly crème.

A nice Jewish couple sat next to us and told us about their Christmas movie marathon: 2 movies on Christmas Eve, and 3 on Christmas Day. We compared notes on what shows we had seen or wanted to see; it was fun. I had a Jewish friend in Connecticut who made a tradition of doing the exact same thing every year on Christmas Day, when there wasn't much else to do.

Unfortunately, I woke up sick again in the middle of the night, and couldn't face traipsing around Chinatown smelling odd smells while feeling like that. The infuriating part of it was that everything just stayed in limbo. That's all I'm willing to say to describe it. Damon and I went to an Au Bon Pain on Broadway, where I took forever to eat a late breakfast. We saw a lot of tourists who seemed to be from France in there, and other international tourists trolling the sales in Broadway's shops as we walked back to the hotel.

We packed our things and checked out, then sat down to rest for a while. I kept hoping to feel better, and being near the rest room was soothing. Eventually, I felt ready to go back to Bryn's place. As we sat there, a huge group of French tourists arrived with their handler.

She checked them in and they stood around talking. The group was mostly families of 4, parents with teenagers, and some couples. None of them spoke English. I wanted to talk to them and practice my French skills a bit, but was at a loss for an excuse until I glanced at the magazine that Damon was reading.

He had the pages open to a huge article about how Tina Fey had parodied and impersonated Sarah Palin, and its angle was that she had

The Slamming Door

helped prevent Palin from becoming the Vice President of the United States. The title was great: "Fey Accompli" – a play on the French words for "a done deed," which are "Faît Accompli" – so I read it out loud with a laugh.

That got attracted the tourists' attention. I grabbed the magazine from Damon and showed them the article and explained. With that, I was chatting with people in French, which always gave Damon a thrill. The tour group was from Paris, and they were very nice. They did not know who Sarah Palin was, which I found encouraging for our nation's image elsewhere. The French people were nice, and I asked them what they intended to do and see on their vacation. They wanted to visit museums. I told them that most of the museums were closed on Mondays, and pointed out whichever ones I could think of. They thanked me, and soon I was ready to leave.

We took a cab home, and I gave Bryn his mug and made tea for him, serving it in the gift. Bryn said that he had a good time at his daughter's house for Christmas dinner. Then I found out that there had been a mix-up with the gifts, and his was still in the apartment. Drat; I gave it to him and he opened it up. It was *The New York Times Coffee Break Crosswords*. He startled me when he saw the title by letting out a huge, loud, whoop of delight.

I jumped, but then realized what a hit the gift was and was thrilled.

So that was our Christmas, and it was fun.

That left thank-you notes to write to my relatives in Connecticut, which was odd to do while not knowing what people had given me, but I did it anyway. In the few days between Christmas and New Year's Eve, Damon and I went out to see the movie about the failed assassination plot on Hitler, *Valkyrie*. It was pretty good, and Damon liked hearing Wagner's *Ride of the Valkyries*.

For New Year's Eve, Damon took me to the Metropolitan Opera at Lincoln Center to enjoy the Mozart opera, *The Magic Flute*. It was as wonderful as I had expected it to be, complete with fabulous sets full of Masonic symbols, beautiful costumes, makeup and lighting, and of course the orchestra and singers were thrilling to hear. We had a perfect afternoon.

Perfect, despite the late arrival of the family who sat in front of us.

I was amazed that the ushers allowed anyone in after the performance began, but they did. The family included parents, a little girl and boy, and grandparents, including a grandfather with beautiful, thick, snowy-white hair and glasses. He tinkered with his cell phone, texting for a moment after they all sat down.

Bryn Throws a Party at the Hahvahd Club

We were seated in the mezzanine, off to the left, in seats that slanted toward the stage. The late arrivals didn't block our view at all, but the bustle of them entering and sitting down was a bit distracting, and it caused Damon to look at them for a moment.

Suddenly, he gestured toward the father and said, in a stage whisper, "Hey, I know who that guy is; he was on the news. He's in the mafia!"

Without missing a beat, I hissed back, "Will you shut up?! This is a date! I don't care who he is; I don't want anyone to get whacked!"

Damon didn't open his mouth again.

I was annoyed. Here I was on a dream date with my husband, only to have him threaten to get himself murdered. Fortunately, nothing happened, not even during the intermission when the alleged mobster might have had an opportunity to knock someone off.

We settled in to enjoy *The Magic Flute*, watching the Queen of the Night attempt to manipulative everyone around her, only to remain Queen of nothing but the Night. I had never seen a production of any opera before; previously, it had been movies only that fueled my interest and enjoyment, plus recordings. My father preferred symphonies for some reason, while I wanted a story to go with the music. No wonder I liked the orchestra scores of movies so much.

The audience was wonderfully quiet and attentive throughout this production which, though in English to appeal to children, was a completely different world from the Big Apple Circus next door. Here, children were encouraged to take the adults' lead in their behavior, learning the etiquette of attending a formal opera. Children were present, but silent. I loved it; this was the fine art appreciation that my great-aunts had raised me with.

When the performance ended, we walked out with the crowd, stopped at the rest rooms while also taking time to admire the artwork nearby, then went up the grand curving, red carpeted staircase, into the snowfall that was blanketing the city that afternoon. We went to the Time-Warner Mall on Columbus Circle, then south across West 58th Street for a hot chocolate in a Starbucks. It was a perfect end to a perfect afternoon.

There was one more family event to enjoy before Damon's holiday visit ended and he went back to the lab in Connecticut: a belated birthday party for me. Bryn was feeling quite well enough to be in on it all, so it was perfect. Damon, Bryn, Albert, June, Alissa, Berta and Matt all spent an evening with me.

First we attended a showing of *Slumdog Millionaire*, a movie which we had all been wanting to see, and it was excellent – so enjoyable, in

The Slamming Door

fact, that I used some of the Christmas-birthday money from Bryn to get the soundtrack a few days later. That was another detail: Bryn had given me a gift of $500 and said to me with a severe expression on his face that it was all for me, not Damon, and to just put it separate from our shared money. Interesting; I took that to mean that he didn't want me to use it to pay routine bills. I would listen to it when he wasn't home, as the stereo was in his room. I didn't listen to music very often while I was with Bryn.

After the movie, we all went to the Daioh Sushi restaurant on West 23rd Street, just a short walk away from the Loew's Cineplex just across 8th Avenue. Bryn ordered a big dinner and ate at least half of it; June and Alissa and I got green tea ice cream; Damon and I had sushi, and Albert and Bryn and Berta were all in a fine mood.

Albert and June and Alissa had a great book for me: it was about Dewey Readmore Books, a fluffy yellow cat who had been adopted by the head librarian in Spencer, Iowa. Albert had written me a lovely note inside the cover, and the story was wonderful, despite having a tear-jerker of an ending. That's the trouble with lovely pet stories; they take one through the entire life – and death – of the wonderful animal. But it was cat book. They had given me a gift that they knew I would love.

Chapter 28

Misery Round Three: The Final Set

The title of this chapter sounds like a sports commentary, and I don't even like team sports. But that is what the doctor's attempts at tackling Bryn's bone cancer felt like.

January 13th, 14th, and 15th made up the last and most intense week-long dose of poison.

There would be more, but not in sets of three. From then on, it was just once a month. The doctor had decided that 3 blasts in one week would just kill Bryn faster, and the whole point was to put the brakes on the process of death, not speed it up.

The month thus kicked off with a couple of weeks' reprieve, during which time Damon had returned to his laboratory.

Then the time was up, and the torture resumed.

The beatings shall continue until morale improves…the torture shall continue until the cancer abates…the stupid sayings shall continue until we see that life will still suck…

Albert insisted upon accompanying Bryn to the hospital for this round of poison. Fine; I busied myself with stocking up on whatever Bryn might possibly need while he recovered from the nasty stuff he was about to have drained into his veins, wondering for the millionth time why the oncologists couldn't do any better than poison not only the disease but the patient as well.

This meant walking around the city in the cold, which wasn't all that cold. I kept my cell phone on, and checked it periodically. If I used the subway system at all, I checked voicemail for messages. On the third day, I found a message from Albert, but it wasn't about Bryn.

It was about Captain Sully Sullenberger, or to be more precise, U.S. Airways Flight 1549, which had been dealt a bird-strike by some geese and gone down in the Hudson River. "It's just a tragedy," Albert's message said.

"A tragedy?!" I thought to myself. "I'll wait until I hear of at least one human death before I agree with that," and went home to turn on the news.

Nope – not one death. Just a really cool-headed landing and inspection of his plane by Captain Sullenberger to make sure everyone was out, then a quick rescue by nearby boat crews. It was all rather awesome, and I was a bit sorry to have been in the center of the island and thus seen nothing firsthand. Dionne had seen the plane float right past her as she worked out at the Chelsea Pier health club, or during a yoga class. It was thrilling just to be near the scene, though.

The Slamming Door

The day after the 3rd round of chemotherapy, I found myself preparing a hot bowl of soup for Bryn. It was chicken and rice soup from Whole Foods, and he had asked me to buy it. I kept putting some in the pan and taking it out, putting a bit more back, then taking some of that out, until I was finally satisfied. How much would or could Bryn actually eat, I wondered glumly, without that little cartoon monster cackling and scampering off?

Not much. He didn't like it because it contained lots of solid foods, very little broth, no noodles (rice instead), and tasted rather different. Well of course it did – that instant stuff was high in sodium and low in calories and nutrition. But…that's what he liked, and what was easy for him to eat. We couldn't blame him for that…

This had immediately followed a trip to the hospital for a shot of Neulasta, which was meant to increase Bryn's white blood cell count, followed by a brief stop on the way home to see the cardiologist about shortness of breath, which was attributed to the large amount of saline solution that had built up a temporary but necessary excess of fluid in his body. It was part of the chemotherapy treatment.

So we settled into a familiar and unwanted pattern of waning appetite and small meals of cereal with banana or instant chicken noodle soup. Berta began calling to ask what he was eating, and when I provided full details, she would push for more food. Knowing full well that this was impossible, I didn't bother arguing with her. I just kept letting Bryn decide how much to eat.

We had all week to hash this out. So would Bryn, as he fought to eat, keep food down, and fend off endless annoying and unsolicited suggestions. I wasn't about to bother him with 20,000 ideas. Imagine if I were on receiving end of said suggestions, I would tell myself. Imagine if I couldn't get away from the person making the damned suggestions, thanks to a lack of energy after what doctors and nurses have dubbed treatment – really a travesty of a treatment, because it's just a lot of poison – and I felt too nauseated to eat much.

If that were me, I would just feel cornered, trapped, angry, and more nauseated.

I would blow up at everyone.

No, I wasn't going to be the one to pester him to eat, eat, eat, so that he could then puke, puke, puke. Let someone he wasn't living with do that. At least he could conclude the phone call – in whatever manner he wished – and think about whatever he wished.

Misery Round Three: The Final Set

Naturally, Berta continued to visit almost daily.

The previous year, I had seen that Matt gave Berta some jewelry for Christmas, as he had the year before that. Always, these things became evident after the fact, not before, and as I had been away on the actual day, it was after the fact that I was shown the evidence. It was mildly entertaining to see what he gave her each year, as it is with any girlfriend, I suppose.

Going in chronological order, for Christmas of 2007, it was a "right-hand" ring. What that meant was something that I hadn't given any thought to before: a ring with a highly-desired gemstone (or more than one) set into it, to be worn on a woman's right hand on her ring finger, opposite the finger where an engagement and wedding ring would go.

Matt's gift to Berta was set in white gold with several (3? 4? 5?) spans set randomly with tiny round white diamonds. She seemed to really like it, and wore it constantly for a couple of years. I knew that she secretly wished for a left-hand ring – also known as an engagement ring – but as yet, one did not seem to be forthcoming.

For Christmas of 2008, Matt gave her a pair of earrings that matched the right-hand ring.

Those were also well-received, but as with most women, Berta alternated among her collection of ear decorations. No one found this remarkable, not Matt, not me, not anyone. It was normal and routine. But she did wear them often, and accord them special prominence in her collection by wearing them for formal occasions.

But for Christmas of 2009, he gave her something that was not so well-received.

I don't even recall precisely what it was, because I never actually saw it.

What I did see that was new after that holiday season on Berta was a hideous white plastic wristwatch with a hot pink digital display. This nonplussed me; why would she want one of those? She already owned a stainless steel wristwatch with a rectangular dial – with an hour, minute and maybe even a second hand – which, she had told me, was her favorite style of watch. She had always worn that style, she told me, since she began wearing wristwatches.

This came up when I first arrived and she asked about my watch.

Like her father, I hated to have ANYTHING on my wrists, especially a watch.

I think I even told her about our conversation about wristwatches, which took place years earlier when Bryn and I were first getting to know each other. It took place because I had happened to notice that Bryn didn't wear a watch on his wrist either.

The Slamming Door

I had said, "I think wristwatches are hideously ugly, no matter how expensive or well-made; it's a machine strapped to one's wrist. I'd rather have my beautiful pocket watch and make sure that all of my clothes come with pockets for my keys, so that I will never get locked out of my home."

"I couldn't agree with you more on all points," Bryn had replied.

I got a kick out of that.

The pocket watches that I had carried were always beautiful to look at, and reminded me of my history studies. The latest one, bought because the previous one had been failing, was from Damon and had been made in Venice, Italy (at least, the back had); it was a multi-colored millefiori pattern of Murano glass...much better than some ugly wristwatch.

Which brings me back to Berta's latest acquisition: What, I asked her, had Matt given her for Christmas this year?

It seemed that the right question was more like: what hadn't he given her this year?

She had wanted an engagement ring, and he hadn't given her one.

Apparently, Berta felt that they had been dating long enough that they ought to be getting engaged by now. And apparently, Matt didn't feel the same way...not that he wished to discontinue dating, but he wasn't about to propose, either.

What a mess.

So what about the gift? What was it? I asked, still curious. Might as well get the whole story rather than continue to wonder about it, I thought.

"It was a pair of diamond earrings," she told me, "tiny little round stones."

"That sounds nice," I said, "so where are they?"

"It wasn't what I wanted, so I returned them and got this watch," she replied, and explained that this was a sport watch. She wore it for the rest of the time that I was in New York.

Huh. So she was willing to wear an exchanged gift that was patently unromantic to look at as a daily reminder to Matt that it was technically from him and a sign that his not-engagement ring gift had been rejected.

Would he get the message? If so, would that impress him or motivate him to propose?

With that odor and stain of negativity, it seemed unlikely.

Damon had proposed to me on my birthday in 2001, right in front of my family. He had wrapped the ring in a bag that came with a bottle of champagne and a little Teddy bear from the jewelry store that we had visited together. Grinning, he had asked, "Do you want that?" when I at

Misery Round Three: The Final Set

last extracted the ring from the bottom of the bag. He gave me the box it came in later.

But my ring was exactly what I wanted, and Damon had made sure of that. We had gone to the jewelry store weeks earlier together, where he had said, gesturing at the sales clerk, "Tell her what you want."

I wanted a pink sapphire heart on yellow gold.

The sales girl immediately attempted to sell us something different, which didn't work and annoyed us both, then summoned a colleague, a nice Iranian man whose relatives back in Tehran were all jewelers. That was funny; he immediately started talking about how to get us what we were looking for: order the spare parts and assemble them. Stores do that.

But what about Berta's fairy tale; what would be her ideal wedding story? I asked her about it, knowing that Bryn wished that Matt would marry her and that he liked Matt. We all liked Matt. Berta and I were in my room, watching television. I wasn't about to ask such questions with her father present – too much pressure. This was supposed to be fun.

City Hall in blue jeans would satisfy her, Berta informed me.

I was surprised. No white wedding gown?

Well, maybe...and if she were to have one, she would like the strapless kind, plain down the entire front, floor-length, perhaps with the slightest train and flared in the back. At last – I had an image in my mind of Berta as a bride. That was all that I had wanted.

It was a rather dull image, unremarkable to contemplate, but at least it showed me what Berta found attractive. That style of dress is, to me, the epitome of ordinary. There is nothing unique about it. It is a blend-into-the-crowd style of wedding gown.

Bryn had told me long ago – back when he wasn't sick – what the holdup was about Berta and Matt's potential wedding. It was Berta's weight. Matt saw no reason to get married unless they were going to have a child, and since he doubted that any child Berta had would be healthy due to her weight, he saw no reason to risk it – hence their terminally dating status.

And that was why Berta wore that ugly white plastic wrist watch with the pink digital display, the one that she who was well beyond any likelihood of serious exercise called a sport watch. What an oxymoron...a morbidly obese person with a sport watch.

Bryn knew that Berta had returned and exchanged Matt's gift; she had told him so.

Other than finding that out, it seemed pointless on many levels to discuss it with him.

The Slamming Door

On one of the days that we went to the 53rd Street clinic for a 2-hour session of saline solution, to rehydrate Bryn, he also had an appointment with the nurse practitioner and the doctor. That also happened to be the day that Barak Obama was sworn in as President.

Somehow, I was determined to observe as much as possible of both events, though no more of Bryn's appointment than he wanted me to. For some reason, he either wanted me there for part of his appointment, or didn't mind me being there. So I went in with him and met the nurse practitioner.

She was a nice woman, middle aged, white, pretty, pleasant, and she knew her job.

So this was the woman I had gotten a fancy box of Godiva chocolates for at Christmastime. Her and the doctor...whom I had met during the previous round of poison, when she came in flexed Bryn's right leg, getting a sense of the waning mobility in his hip.

I liked that doctor, because I had found out that she often cried when she got to the point in a patient's care where she couldn't help any more.

But today we were seeing the nurse, and she came in with Bryn's case file.

He sat there and asked her something that didn't surprise me, even though I had seen *The Bucket List* and remembered how Morgan Freeman looked when the doctor told him his best guesstimate of how much longer he had to live.

"Can you tell me roughly how much longer I have to live, and how this will go?" Bryn asked her. He looked as calm as ever, but interested in her response. He also looked as though he actually expected her to know the answer.

But how could she? That would take a crystal ball, I thought to myself. Well, let her explain it to him, I thought. He'll believe it if she says it. I waited and listened as she explained that each patient's illness is so unique and so specific, depending upon a long list of factors such as one's health over the course of an entire lifetime, activities conducted, treatments given, severity of the disease at the time that the doctor meets a person, and so on, that there is just no way to accurately predict how much longer Bryn had to live. Everyone's story differed.

He nodded, accepting that. I think I had been waiting for this interchange for months.

After that moment of significance, the visit got a bit dull as details of scans and charts and lab tests were discussed, and my mind wandered as I worried that I would miss seeing Obama sworn in. There was a large television out in the waiting area, and I wanted to watch.

Bryn knew that, and we both knew that the most important part of the meeting in here was over. After confronting the issue of how much

Misery Round Three: The Final Set

time he had left, the rest seemed like routine nitpicking that we found somewhat incomprehensible. All I needed to do was track the pill sheet changes; I couldn't decipher the scientific minutia.

Damon had gone over it all with Bryn at Christmas, looking over the medical data in detail and then explaining what he could to Bryn late one evening. I had walked in and out, restless and unable to contribute anything. Damon hadn't realized that Bryn was such a night owl – like me – that he would have to do this in the evening. Damon was a morning person. But Bryn found this discussion easier to face late at night.

On this particular morning, it was late – almost noon – when I began to fidget and glance at the door. Bryn, concerned as ever that someone in his family might be missing out on a good time, said "Go!" when I thought of walking out during the nurse's discussion. So I went. Bryn planned on seeing the inauguration himself, once we were moved to a cubicle.

A small crowd was grouped around the television, patients, relatives, and MSKCC employees. Some were standing, some sitting, and some in wheelchairs. I found a spot by the double doors that led to the chemotherapy cubicles and stood with my back against the wall.

First, we enjoyed a brief concert of a new piece by John Williams, *Air and Simple Gifts* (which evoked Aaron Copeland's *Appalachian Spring*). It was performed by Yo-Yo Ma on the cello, Itzak Perlman on the violin, Gabriela Montero on piano and Anthony McGill on clarinet.

We all enjoyed watching as Obama was sworn in. Michelle, the incoming First Lady, wore a fabulous yellow suit and gloves, and I liked the fact that we were getting another attorney in that spot. It made American woman look great, having an education professional for a First Lady, and I was certain that she would do something useful while her husband worked in the Oval Office.

Next came a poetry reading by Yale Professor Elizabeth Alexander.

There was one brief but hilarious distraction during the poetry reading, however: Bryn. He came out of the consultation room carrying all of our stuff – our coats, reading material, his bucket concealed in a plastic bag, and my beautiful, decidedly feminine hat...on his head, over his own wool hat. He was grinning at me, from ear to ear, inviting a response, which was promptly forthcoming from me. I laughed, grinned, and pointed, and said "There's my cousin, wearing my hat!" for the benefit of the people around me.

When he had enjoyed the satisfaction of grins and snickers all around, Bryn quietly came over to me and told me to stay there and keep watching, that he was going to sit down, so I took my stuff back, including the hat.

The Slamming Door

We were left standing there for a few minutes longer, when we were invited into the back to settle into one of the curtained cubicles for his treatment. Meanwhile, we all cheered with undisguised glee as we watched W. get out of town. That came right after a benediction was given by the Reverend Joseph E. Lowery; at long last, we could see the Bushes and Cheneys depart. All eyes seemed quite happy to see the helicopter fly farther and farther into the distance as the television cameras panned around the crowd of spectators in front of the Capitol.

It occurred to me that among this group, there were probably quite a few Democrats who disagreed with just about every decision that Dubya Bush had made as Chief Executive. I had found him to be a never-ending embarrassment, and felt that our nation's legal and governmental system was at last proving itself to be intact as Obama took over.

This inauguration just felt better, like our nation's dignity and honor was returning.

But enough political commentary; this mattered to me and I knew that Bryn approved of it too, but that he would continue to analyze and criticize every economic decision taken without interruption nonetheless. That was just what he did; the economy mesmerized him and mattered to him that much, but it didn't affect his future.

What affected his future was what was happening here at the clinic.

He knew it, and he knew that the reasons why I could sit calmly with him and hold his hand while he got sicker and sicker were that: 1. I had promised to keep him company through this misery and not run; 2. That I could do it because we weren't at the actual moment of his death; 3. That because it wasn't all over yet, this felt less frightening to me than listening to the details about the economy, which felt like a heavy, ominous foreboding about my own future.

Often, as I thought about the economy and Bryn's illness, I felt as though my time to be calm and to enjoy being alive would end with his life.

Bryn was the old pro at emotional intelligence, while I was still just an apprentice.

Bryn had nothing further to fear from the economy, while I did.

Bryn could wish the economy and the rest of us well and study it with detached interest.

The rest of us had to live with the consequences of the financial, environmental, legal and moral waste and damage that the outgoing administration had inflicted upon it and us.

No wonder I felt like celebrating this changing of the Presidents.

Once we were settled into our cubicle, I decided to make a quick run to the Europa Café before tuning in to the inauguration again. Shortly I was back with my hazelnut coffee and a snack of yoghurt and granola,

Misery Round Three: The Final Set

and tea for Bryn. His lunch arrived – more of his favorite food, chicken soup. I tuned into the inaugural festivities again. Almost every channel was devoted to following the politicians' every move.

I got a kick out seeing Hillary Rodham Clinton, a plethora of past presidents and vice presidents, senators, Nancy Pelosi, and more intros by Diane Feinstein of California, who was serving as the Mistress of Ceremonies for all of the inaugural functions.

Then I left to check the Internet – there was a public computer out in the waiting area – because I wanted to see the fashions of one Isabelle Toledo, whose work Michelle Obama was wearing, and read about the lunch menu (seafood stew followed by duck and pheasant with sour cherry sauce and molasses sweet potatoes concluded with apple cinnamon sponge cake). With my curiosity thus satisfied, I headed back in.

When I got back, I found that I had missed something: Senator Ted Kennedy had had a seizure during the luncheon and been hauled away on a stretcher. He was able to speak a little, his friends and colleagues informed the ever-inquisitive reporters. Drat; I had missed it. I kept listening to toasts and speeches and observing the wait staff and lunch attendees.

That was when Bryn and I became unpleasantly aware of the person who was just settling into the next cubicle. Female, rich and self-entitled, and close in age to me (I heard her birthday: March 21, 1971. This was the standard security question that the hospital staff used to confirm that they were in fact treating the correct patient with the correct, matching prescription of poison.). After feeling briefly horrified when I registered the fact that a woman who was a year younger than myself had cancer, I went through a quick spectrum of thought and emotion.

I felt bad that her pretty, frosted, streaked hair was going to fall out.

I hoped that she would recover from this illness.

Then, as I heard her settle in, briefly acknowledging the nurses and other hospital staff, I realized that I had gone to private school with girls just like her, and that she would have frozen me out if I had so much as spoken to her. My energies were better spent on Bryn, who had chosen to share his illness and time with me. I didn't know this girl; I wasn't about to invest much emotion in someone whom I would most likely never see again after today.

Still, I was curious enough to arrange to catch a glimpse of her: long, salon-streaked brown hair, a designer cloth folded for use as a hair-band, and black clothing – pants, coat, etc. She had a cell phone and immediately began to chat away on it about fund raising activities and well-known personalities (at least in her own world, which didn't sound at all familiar to us).

The Slamming Door

She was likely a well-connected, wealthy person within the Manhattan area. That was enough information to satisfy our passing interest before we lost interest and resumed staring intently at the television above our cubicle's entryway.

Bryn let me flip around the channels and enjoy myself, alternating between reading his newspaper and falling asleep when he wasn't drinking tea or eating soup. He didn't mind me being glued to the TV – I usually disdained daytime television, but this was special – and he wanted to see this, too.

Suddenly, I became aware of an annoying noise from the next cubicle: a rather loudly expressed and insistent demand that the nurse get the television next door turned down. She meant ours, of course; it wasn't hard to figure that out. Her strident tones roused Bryn, who cast a disapproving glance at the curtain between us.

I know I am a bit deaf, but I wasn't blasting the sound on that thing! I had checked the number on the sound indicator as I had set it, and listened to the levels of sound both on the set and around me. However, I wasn't about to run the sound so quietly that I wouldn't be able to understand what the people on television were saying.

A nurse came in and asked that it be turned down, so I did that…minimally.

Then I realized that I had a channel on that included loud background noise, including the reverberations of many people talking in the rotunda of the Capitol building, where the luncheon had just been held. I flipped around to find one that contained the same scenes but without that noise – easy enough – and resumed listening to everything that was said.

A few minutes later, the loud woman next door was heard to say, "I'm a patient too!" and ask the nurse to go back and ask us to turn it down. How manipulative, I thought. Clearly, she would not be satisfied unless those around her were forced to keep their televisions inaudible to her, which would also mean inaudible to them…to us. My sympathy for her was rapidly waning.

The nurse very obediently trotted back in and ignored us when I said that I would turn it down myself with the remote control. She turned it down manually, and too much, so I just put it right back the moment she was gone – to level 24, which was not that high. Bryn said nothing, but nodded when I worked the remote after the nurse walked out. This was ridiculous.

I went to high school with girls like her – rich, spoiled, and speaking in mellifluous and slightly strident tones of television English. No way would I let a spoiled woman in my own age group, sick or not, bully me out of hearing what I wanted to hear…especially as a parade of her

Misery Round Three: The Final Set

friends and colleagues trooped in and proceeded to hold loud conversations, oblivious to the wishes of patients at least two cubicles away from her own to doze in their chairs. That would not be possible while the self-entitled were visiting...

She never turned her television on the entire time.

As Bryn and I got ready to leave, I called Damon on my cell phone and told him that I had something to tell, but would have to wait until I got a bit farther away. Bryn took his time getting ready to leave, so Damon's curiosity grew as I put him off while asking about his next experiment. I made sure not to shout our conversation, just to show Ms. Next Door how to speak in a shared hospital space (not that it would make the slightest impression on her). At last we were a few paces down and I told all. Damon predictably said that he would have said something directly to her.

Bryn, meanwhile, said nothing about it until we were in a cab heading home, for the simple reasons that my cell phone call ended just as we were boarding the elevator, and we had to wait until the cab was moving to converse further.

He agreed with me: she was spoiled and self-entitled. That was gratifying. "She probably voted for McCain," he added. Still, that's no excuse for trying to stop others around her from listening to Obama's inauguration and festivities.

I thought about it more later. A brat is a brat, whether she has cancer or not. But...it made me angry to think of a young and attractive person being eaten at by cancer – and poisoned in order to stop that disgusting parasite from feasting on her. Judging from the way she looked, she was at the beginning of her misery.

That full head of hair as long as mine, salon-streaked to chic perfection, adorned with a designer scarf, would soon be changed. The beautiful hair would be gone, and that scarf would cease to be a decorative effect as it would suddenly be a means of concealing a horrifying lack of hair. There would be no mistaking her for a Muslim woman who wished to hide her hair...not that any non-Muslim, Western woman would ever want that thought to cross anyone's mind. No...she would look like a cancer patient soon, thin, pale, with jowls, and perhaps a lack of eyebrow hair would give her away.

As I had watched Bryn lose his thick snowy white head of hair – Bryn never had so much as a receding hairline or a bald spot – I often mused that it would all seem worse on a woman. It is just not acceptable to us not to have hair. We define our femininity by the possession of a full head of hair. Bitchy though this girl was, I got angry as I thought of the outrage about to be visited upon her; cancer was going to steal her hair and her attractiveness.

The Slamming Door

Damnit, I thought, this cancer treatment had better work so that she lives long enough to restore her appearance with another full head of long hair. My sense of innate solidarity with other women was coming back to me the more I thought about this, and I just couldn't stop. Wigs just weren't good enough, I continued. I am terrified of this disease and its ability to steal attractiveness. It was so strange to sincerely want a bitchy stranger to recover and live, but I did.

But back to Bryn…on the way home, he mentioned that he didn't think that he would be spending much time doing what he loved, which was teaching at the Henry George School, or going to Desmond's Tavern around the corner from it with his colleagues. Unfortunately, I was starting to believe him, as he was able to attend only a few functions associated with that school. I am not the sort of person to naysay such things when I know perfectly well that I would just be uttering nonsensical platitudes that don't offer any real solace.

Bullshit insults intelligence, so why utter it? Bryn and any other terminally ill person would spot that in an instant. Instead, I cast about for something pleasant to say that had something to do with that school. I mentioned Claus Heider, the German guy who served as Director of the Manhattan branch of the school. Bryn liked him a lot. I asked when Claus might visit us again. Bryn seemed to perk up just a little bit when I brought up the idea, and suggested maybe inviting him to stop by this weekend.

I asked about getting Claus's phone number. That's when I found out that Claus had no cell phone, and at home only a land line with no answering machine. He usually didn't go home until 11 p.m. (in Queens), so people just got in touch with him by calling the school. I made a mental note to program the school's phone number into my cell phone later, and did so.

But what would I say? What time to call? It would seem a bit odd, calling this guy up, until I explained the reason. What if he became alarmed at receiving my call? What if thought Bryn's health had landed him in the hospital or worse? Or – Claus was the same age as my husband – no, this was getting ridiculous. I would just have to call him at work in the middle of an afternoon and say why. I had the rest of the week, and I imagined that this weekend would be a good time for the visit. Bryn ought to be ready for a visit by then. I had seen this pattern of recovery twice before, after all. But he had already lost every last bit of fat…

I reminded myself not to panic – just keep him hydrated with juice, interesting teas, bananas, soup…and then he would eat more when his taste buds could enjoy normal sensations and his stomach felt more cooperative. Next week that would happen, right? I sure hoped so…

Misery Round Three: The Final Set

Late in the afternoon, probably after returning from the college he taught at in Montclair, New Jersey, Piper stopped by. Bryn told me he could only deal with 10 minutes' worth of visiting, because he was vomiting a bit, and that he had warned Piper.

So when Piper knocked, I opened the door slowly and deliberately, and in a grave tone asked him: "Do you solemnly swear to visit for only 10 minutes?" He grinned – it was inauguration day, after all – and he swore to do that.

Then I asked him about his accident in San Francisco, falling on his gargantuan backpack and hurting his liver or kidney or whatever the hard object in the pack had hit. "How did you know about that?!" he howled, seemingly outraged. I looked at him like he was crazy and said, "Melissa told us – she was worried about you!" Oh...he looked calm and seemed to understand the whole thing when I said that.

We chatted for a moment more, and he went in to see Bryn. True to his word, he departed after a short chat. Bryn told me that Piper could be quite clueless, but if you came right out and told him how something must be, it worked. Melissa, who was only half-clueless, often directed Piper's behavior. It all reminded me a bit of me and Damon, though I like to think that we are a bit less clueless. Still, I suspected that like me and my husband, Piper and Melissa were Aspies, and that that was why it was easier for me to communicate with them.

Nothing too interesting happened the next day – I went out walking in the afternoon, and bought a dinner dish for Pearlie, Albert and June's Sheltie dog, which they received when I came home. They were visiting Bryn. Albert was quite pleased, and said that she would eat out of it that evening. June looked happy also.

I chatted with them for a while, and then Albert stood up to get his coat. That's when I noticed that he was shedding hair all over his navy blue sweater. The all-day chemotherapy treatments at Cornell's hospital were already robbing him! He still looked the same, but since he had announced a couple of weeks earlier that he was in this awful year-long clinical trial for prostate cancer and getting 8-hour stretches of poison, I was upset to think of what was in store.

I started brushing off the silvery strands rather roughly (sticks to wool!) and Bryn said, "Hey, not on my floor!" But I noticed that he was grinning. I wasn't too concerned. Soon I would be mopping the dust off of every floor in the apartment, which I did every few weeks. Bryn's place had never been so clean...

Bryn had a Henry George School Trustee emergency on Thursday, so I brought him to a Trustees meeting. We had a great plan, which was for me to go with him to the school in a cab, leave him there with both

The Slamming Door

of our cell phones turned on as usual, and go walking around the neighborhood.

I left him off at the school, black book-bag, bucket and all, and chatted with Astrid, the elegant secretary/receptionist for a few minutes before leaving. As we chatted, I plotted my route, because Bryn needed me to get cash for him from an ATM.

I was determined to get it from an ATM maintained by his bank, and thus avoid incurring a fee, which surprised him. He used a bank that didn't have offices or machines in very many places – perhaps only in Manhattan and a few surrounding towns. (I like big banks, with branches wherever I go so I won't incur fees.) Bryn had always used whatever convenience store ATM was closest; I was amazed that he hadn't suffered identity theft.

The route thus chosen, I took off. 12 streets north and I was soon done, already wishing I could give Bryn back his ATM card, the cash, and the receipt. I feel ill at ease carrying someone else's financial secrets and loot around and can't wait to give it all back; not a bad trait. I kept the stuff carefully concealed in my pocket, reasonably confident that a thief would neither notice or nor come in contact with me. I was staying in an affluent, well-patrolled area: 5th Avenue. Park and Madison Avenues were okay, too.

A Victorian Christmas window display at the Lord & Taylor department store.

Misery Round Three: The Final Set

Heading south, I went into the flagship store of Lord & Taylor and started browsing, wondering whether or not I would find a use for some Christmas money from my grandmother. I needed some socks and had been looking at nightgowns for a few weeks, without finding one worth buying. This ought to keep me busy for an hour or so, I guessed.

That turned out to be right; I found what I was looking for, and even had time to get coupons and apply them to the sales before Bryn called. While I wandered the store, Albert and June called me from a cab just to say "Hi" and see what Bryn and I were up to. I told them what we were doing. I always told June whatever she wanted to know however many times it took, because if I were stricken with Alzheimer's disease, I wouldn't want to be treated like a child or not feel like I was in on things.

As I was going down the escalators – and there were 8 floors in that store – Bryn called. He was so reasonable about how long things took, or what other people might be doing or wish to do! He suggested 20 minutes, and I said that to be completely honest, we should just imagine how long it would actually take me to go down all the escalators, hail a cab, and get over to the school. He rang off sounding perfectly satisfied about it all.

It actually took a bit of walking and 2 attempts to find a cabbie who would take us, but I found one on Park Avenue. Competing for available cabs with the shoppers on 5th Avenue was a losing battle, so I just started walking east. The first guy who stopped said he would have to drive all the way over to 6th Avenue (odd – 5th goes south!), so I figured he didn't know what he was doing and got out immediately. The next guy asked if I was going on his way, so I told him my plan. He said it was kind of on his way, so he would take us. Great; I got in.

When the cab pulled up in front of the school, I whipped out my cell phone and called Bryn. No answer. He must be in the elevator. I called the school, and watched as Sigrid answered the phone at her desk. She said he was just getting out of the elevator. I said I was in a cab right out front. Bryn came out slowly, with Claus carrying his bag and his faculty mail.

This was perfect. No more wondering how to call him and plead for a visit without Bryn overhearing me and thinking I sounded grim about his prognosis or some such glum thought.

"Claus! Come visit us!" I called out, grabbing the bags and throwing them in behind me. He said perhaps he could come by this weekend, if Bryn was feeling up to it. Bryn said he thought he would. I was looking forward to making coffee for Claus and seeing him sitting on Bryn's bed up against the long pillows. I could just picture the scene: Claus putting the mug on the rolling plastic filing cabinet, his hat off and on the front hall table, and chatting with Bryn for an hour or so, telling him that the

The Slamming Door

Henry George School was lost without him, or some such ego-gratifying thing.

Bryn was getting a macabre sense of humor about the nausea involved in these "treatments" – as I found at odd moments. In the cab on the way home, he asked me something about a coupon I was holding. I started to look at the fine print and stopped. Reading makes me motion sick in just about every conveyance except for airplanes, and I said so. Bryn grinned and offered to lend me his bucket. I laughed it up with him.

Berta came over that evening. Actually, I met her at a subway stop, and we went out for Japanese food first – it was too early to serve Bryn's dinner. We went home after that, stopping to buy some ice cream that she really wanted (Swiss chocolate almond Hagen Daas) and then rushed in time for a 2-hour, double dose of my favorite crime show, *Bones*.

She kept asking me to somehow make her father eat more food than he wished, and to stuff himself even if he puked, because at least he would keep 20 percent of it down anyway.

I didn't say anything; I just dished out his dinner and heated it, serving it a few minutes before our show began. No way was I going to torture him.

He only ate a little bit before sending it all away – chicken, mashed potatoes, and macaroni with cheese. It was demoralizing, but it also just wasn't his fault. I threw it out.

We watched our show and chatted during the commercials. Berta was pleased that I had OCD (obsessive compulsive disorder) too, because I channeled that energy into cleaning and organizing the area around me. The area included the entire apartment.

When this subject came up, she told me that Bryn had OCD too – and that it manifested itself in different ways. He used to keep a pile of newspapers on top of the refrigerator for recycling, and she found out that he would never throw out the one on the bottom. He just wanted to see how old it got!

Oh no, I said – I threw them ALL out when I came here and took over the chores. It turned out that he didn't care now.

It certainly was fun to hear all these stories about Bryn's personality and to get to know him better and better. I loved it – it was great entertainment.

On the Friday afternoon after the inauguration, we went through some more of that nonsense on the phone with Berta, with me telling her that I refused to torture her father with food, until Bryn put his hand out and asked for the phone back. I gladly gave it back to him, letting him tell his daughter not to insist, or whatever diplomatic way he put it.

Misery Round Three: The Final Set

He had done rather well, I thought. When I went into his room for the first time that day, he had said that he had some good news: he wanted to go eat pancakes at *Rafaella's*, the restaurant on the corner of 9th Avenue. Great! I got ready.

Poor Bryn. He walked so slowly, and explained later (no prompting) that when he wasn't eating, he just didn't move. He sat in his chair, he walked slowly, he didn't walk much, etc. School was in session, but not recess or gym, so the street was ours as we walked. No cars, no kids playing, no noise from the playground.

We got to the restaurant, and we were in luck: the table with the one-armed sofa to the right of the door was empty. I pulled the white oval marble table out of the way and Bryn sat down. The missing arm was in the corner, out of the way. I headed for the throne-like chair against the wall, and prepared to sit down where I could preside over the table (that's how it would look, anyway).

The arm almost came off the throne, and I laughed. Bryn grinned. We got settled, stashing the bucket (in another Bed, Bath & Beyond bag) down in the corner out of sight. I looked around. The artwork had been changed. It was all beautiful oil paintings, unframed, of white iris flowers at the back, and a vase of pink and white and yellow ones over the dessert case. The previous set of work was a bit racy – one abstract pornographic couple of stick people over the dessert case had hung there for four months…but we had fun noting the changes.

I tried the Moroccan breakfast: couscous with strawberries, bananas, blueberries, walnuts, and raisins, served with hot milk on the side. After I had put my order in, Bryn told me he had had that several times and that it was really good. A quiet girl from Romania was our waitress, and she was new, but she did a perfectly good job.

Bryn got pancakes with fruit on the side, fussing over the syrup, wanting either real maple syrup (not corn syrup – the fake crap that some places try to pass off in order to save money) or else butter. We each got coffee, plus a drink of juice for me and ginger ale for him.

He didn't like the ginger ale – nothing tasted right unless it was the familiar brands. I promised to go out and get more Schwepps plain ginger ale later.

He ate quite bit of one 4-inch pancake, opting for the butter, plus almost all of the fruit. That was because I started spearing the fruit and holding it out to him on the fork, and he accepted it. Then I unearthed the rest of his pancake and cut it up. He almost finished it.

The waitress watched from the dessert bar, along with another girl who was a few years older, who had steamed the milk for my food. We were eating breakfast at 1 p.m., but so what – Bryn was eating. A man eating along near the dessert case watched me feeding my cousin, but I

The Slamming Door

just stared back at him, disinterested. He was an older guy with glasses, reading and eating, and had probably figured out that Bryn didn't feel well.

The only other customers in the place were three women at the other oval table, discussing a wedding and showing photos of bridal gowns on an I-Phone.

Bryn and I asked the waitress where she was from, and she told us: Romania.

When she was gone, Bryn told me about a serendipitous thing that had happened a few years ago. That restaurant near the Henry George School, 30 at 30th Street, had a Romanian waitress who spoke fluent English. It turned out, when Andrew Mazzone (the wealthy businessman who teaches at the school) asked her about her background, that she was a Romanian attorney.

Romania was such a poor country that, even though she was admitted to the bar, she couldn't make a living there. European attorneys typically studied for years, reading law and attending lectures without interacting with their professors – only watching them march in, lecture, and march out again – then took an exam. If they passed, they would apprentice in a law office for a few more years…for free. But not everyone can get this necessary internship. It requires influence and personal connections. Families must be able to support adult attorneys until this time is up, and then it's time to seek employment.

But there was none of that for this attorney. So she came to the United States, where she was working as a waitress, with full qualifications in Romania, plus access to whatever she would need in the European Union for clients that she didn't have.

And along comes Alfred Mazerati with his patents and in need of someone like her!

She worked out beautifully, he later told Bryn. Pretty cool…

Bryn also asked this young Romanian girl, who clearly needed a tutor if she were to improve her English language skills, about our friend the blond Polish waitress. Yes, the girl said, she still worked there. She would get married in February, but the girl could not tell us whether or not she would continue to work at *Rafaella's*. I asked whether or not she any reason to think not, and she didn't. Likely she would still be there the next time we ate dinner there.

By the time Bryn announced that he was finished eating and couldn't eat any more, he had consumed what seemed like a decent amount considering the fact that his stomach was being so uncooperative. I pointed out that his hands still had tremors, and he held them out straight to look, but the tremors had decreased considerably. We got ready to go.

Misery Round Three: The Final Set

Bryn walked home faster than he walked to the restaurant, then said he felt so good that he wanted me to go out in the sunshine and walk around and enjoy myself. How long would I go out? Maybe an hour, I said, not wanting to sound like I was planning a huge absence. I didn't think I ought to disappear for too long. "Stay out longer!" he demanded.

I ran a couple of errands first, getting milk, ginger ale, and whatever else, then serving tea and ginger ale and one Ensure drink (strawberry, his favorite flavor) before heading out.

Damon called me once I was good and far away from home, wanting help getting cash with no access code and no I.D. (I still couldn't believe he managed to lose his passport last May! He though it got thrown out by mistake.). I told him to go to the bank with his VA card and ask for help...and to get a new passport SOON.

We rang off and I got on with enjoying my afternoon out alone. After wandering through Greenwich Village for a while, staring around at beautiful houses that likely dated back to the Federalist Period and wishing that Damon and I could afford to buy one, I got some coffee at McNulty's coffee shop. Bryn's coffee supply was holding steady while his tastes buds continued to inform him that his favorite flavor, Mandeeling Sumatra, tasted funny.

I window-shopped my way back, stopping at the famous Biography Bookshop on Bleecker Street. There was a book that Bryn wanted, and I found it there: *The Big Spenders: The Story of the Rich Rich, the Grandees of America and the Magnificoes, and How They Spent Their Fortunes* by Lucius Beebe. With one of the shop's thick, unmarked, dark brown plastic bags in hand, I headed up 8th Avenue.

Next, I stopped at the *House of Cards* to find a Valentine's Day card for Damon.

I chose the card, and then stood reading the political and other magnets until I saw one that said "Lawyers Prohibited – Prosecutors Will Be Violated." I joked to the guy behind the counter that I guessed I had better leave. We chatted about my qualifications for a few minutes, and I told him that I wrote and edited and tutored rather than practicing law.

When I mentioned that my parents had given me a sweatshirt (during law school) with Shakespeare quotes all over it, including "The first thing we do let's kill all the lawyers," he tried to recall which play that was from. It turned out that he was taking a Shakespeare class, and wanted a tutor! I gave him my card, said I was available afternoons and evenings, and that I had to work around caring for my elderly cousin who has bone cancer (rather than give someone false expectations of a normal life and unlimited availability).

Then he told me about a woman he knew who had bone cancer. Diagnosed late, dead in 3 months, and he had taken her dog in. I got all the details, started to feel fear that Bryn would die soon and I would be out of here and back with my parents and never again be able to call him up or look forward to getting away to visit him…then reminded myself that everyone was different and that Bryn is not in such bad shape.

He had a bit more time, I told myself, until I heard more details.

The doctor actually thought it was worth bothering with all this misery, after all. The scans came back with the desired result: stabilization. The cancer hadn't progressed further. Of course, new cancer had appeared in his upper left lung, but it wasn't growing. It had probably appeared while she was meeting him and setting up the first round of chemotherapy.

She would give him some more, much lighter doses and then scan him again.

Misery Round Three: The Final Set

I tried to think of it all that way. Everyone was different, every case comes out differently, Bryn would get over this latest round of chemotherapy and soon go out to dinner with the family and to see movies, etc. I sure hoped so...

But that evening, he puked up his dinner of one fried egg and a small amount of macaroni and cheese...though it seemed that he had only eaten half of both. Damnit...I cleaned the bottom shelf of the fridge and found, to my delight, lots of strawberry and raspberry Jell-O. That would give him some electrolytes and keep his blood sugar up, which would mean less dizziness. I served a couple of those before bedtime.

As he ate them, he told me that Piper and Melissa would likely be stopping by the next day before going out walking and window-shopping through some carefully selected neighborhood in Manhattan. That was a favorite weekend activity of theirs. They didn't spend much money, but that wasn't the point of the activity; they just liked to see different things.

I said that I intended to beat Melissa to the punch before she could lie on Bryn's pillows. My plan was simply to use a particular bath towel – it was dark green with some writing embroidered onto one end and in perfect condition – one that neither of us ever used. I called it the Melissa Guard, and Bryn gave one of his silent roars of laughter, looking up at the ceiling with his head thrown back, grinning and shaking with mirth. It lasted ten seconds.

Bryn hated to have ANYONE lie down on his pillows, and asked that I change the pillowcase if that happened. Melissa happened to be the only visitor who did this. She had a back problem, so she flopped on her side and sat with her hair all over the pillow, chatting. And Bryn absolutely refused to say anything to her about it, no matter how revolted he was by it – and he was most definitely revolted by it.

He was entitled – everyone has their quirks, and I happened to share this one. I always told visitors to stay off of my pillow. That was the difference between me and him: I had no problem telling people what my spatial boundaries are, and I required them not to be offended.

Bryn thought that they wouldn't show up until the afternoon, which meant that I would have plenty of time to spread the dark green bath towel over the pillows.

It didn't work out that way. I slept late (in part because I stayed up long enough to tuck Bryn in and make sure he had taken all of his pills correctly) and didn't want to see or speak to anyone until I had been in and out of the bathroom to do normal things: use the toilet, wash my face, and brush my teeth.

Quite reasonable.

The only way to avoid seeing or speaking to people was to dash in there, which was easier when it was just me and Bryn. He had quite

The Slamming Door

cleverly caught on to my wish, and I mentioned this to him, eliciting yet another knowing grin. So when Piper and Melissa showed up at 11:15 a.m., he let them in and they talked quietly. What nice people, not being loud!

As soon as they were gone, I came out with my bed made, dressed, etc., and dashed into the bathroom. When I emerged, Bryn was in his room with the quilt thrown over the bed and the green towel across the pillows! He was triumphant about having managed to put it down before Melissa sat on the bed.

Then he told me something interesting: Melissa had sat where I had thought she ought to sit all along: against the long cushions on the side of the bed that is up against the wall, like a makeshift sofa. Maybe she got the silent hint.

I gleefully made the bed properly, straightening it all out to perfection, and folded the green towel away in the corner for the next time. Bryn and I were rather pleased with this system; we planned to keep it ready for every visit by Melissa. It was the perfect solution.

Berta had been planning a great surprise for him, and would bring it later on Saturday afternoon: a new HDTV television, one that could have his DVD player plugged into it. Currently, he had a 15-year-old color television that she bought, but it was small and it buzzed loudly. Time for a new one; it could connect to the cable box and the outlet, but that was it. So the DVD player that Claus had given him last year was useless. Bryn had just the television, the newspaper, magazines, books, and some visitors now, so this was important.

My mother had suggested contributing to the cost of a television a while ago, but no one else had been thinking about this, so the idea had fallen by the wayside. Claus was the only other person to bring it up, and Bryn had promptly told him not to do it.

That was the problem: telling him what you were planning would only result in being told by him not to go through with it. The only thing that worked was a lovely surprise, so that was Berta's strategy. She and Matt would be stopping by with the surprise later that afternoon.

I knew about it days before, but said nothing. If you said anything, he would just protest: "Don't buy me anything!" So Bryn knew nothing about it until it was at the door, and then he was thrilled. It turned out that when Berta bought the old one, it was his first color television. Same attitude back then: perfectly happy with his black-and-white one, but thrilled over the vibrant colors once he had its successor.

She came in innocently, as though just to visit, and whispered to me that Matt was bringing it upstairs from the car as we spoke. Then she

Misery Round Three: The Final Set

went into her father's room to chat. Bryn didn't suspect a thing until Matt brought it in: a Sanyo brand 26-inch, HDTV LCD. Hours of fussing and hooking up ensued, until it was just so. It was the perfect surprise.

Right after the new television was positioned, I had cleaned the table for the new TV and the mopping the floor around it. But then that wasn't good enough, and I ended up mopping and dusting the entire apartment later that evening. I did that every few weeks, when I could see the dust on the floor. It got thick and obvious, and I enjoyed seeing the lines of Pine-Sol water appear as I outlined each room and then moved the sponge-mop in the middle of each room every few weeks. I was satisfied with the place after that.

After the cursory cleaning of the TV table, Albert and June dropped by, and as I sat with the instructions and remote controls, studying the new electronic arrangement, Albert kept asking curious questions and taking the instructions away just as I started to understand how it worked.

I finally had to tell Albert that I was secretly (yeah right – not so secretly once I said what I was thinking!) waiting for everyone to go home and then I would figure out how to work the new setup. To figure it out, I needed all the remotes plus all the instructions, and time to sit and peruse them while pointing and clicking.

Bryn could see that, and suddenly told his brother it was time to go home. It was; it was late, and there was nothing more to do in the normal pattern of socializing; even I, the Aspie girl, could sense that. I was getting stressed out by the effort to decipher the new TV instructions with all this interference, but I wouldn't say anything more direct about it.

Albert liked to figure technical stuff out, but I was the one who needed to do that, because at midnight when Bryn needed help working the new setup, I would be the available person to ask, and no one else. Albert took June and their stuff and left, without feeling at all annoyed.

He was as easy-going as his brother, and always caught on without getting upset.

Soon I had it hooked up properly, connected to the cable television box and to the DVD player from Claus. The old TV went under the little round table in the front hall, tucked out of the way until it could be put out at the curb on garbage day.

So at last, Bryn was enjoying his new television.

Meanwhile, Bryn thought it was cool that I was writing his story, especially since Cassie had suggested that he write this story, but he told her that it just wasn't his style to write about his own illness.

The Slamming Door

After I had completely cleaned the apartment – which I did when everyone had gone home and the television was understood by both Bryn and me – and it was mopped and dusted to spotlessness, I took an early bath. Then I ordered an Indian take-out dinner to be delivered, and heated up what Bryn wanted: baked beans and instant chicken soup.

His urge to puke was diminishing, but not entirely gone.

But as if that weren't enough to deal with, he woke up with his heart racing and had to take an extra pill. Usually, he took one at night for his tachycardia condition, but the cardiologist had said to take another if this happened on a weekend (like that Sunday) when he wasn't available. So Bryn did that, his heartbeat slowed down, and we planned to visit Dr. Hossein A---on Monday at 1 p.m.

This is just another indication of why I couldn't just get a job outside of the apartment. Sometimes, people would ask me why I didn't get one while I was in the city…until they realized why I was there.

So I took Elah's and Berta's advice and advertised on Craigslist.org, offering my editing services in one ad and calligraphy in another. The account was free, so why not? I couldn't pay for advertising – no money. I checked the prices of other, far away services so that I could set my own rates in case anyone actually contacted me.

Aunt Joan Orlov was in a play that afternoon, and we had planned to go see her in it, but we didn't because of the accelerated heartbeat problem. The play was on all weekend in Harlem, and she was quite good (no surprise – she had been doing this all her life!) according to Albert, who took a cab and went with June to see her act in it.

We had another crowd in Bryn's room that afternoon. Berta and Matt came back, and Matt fell asleep on Bryn's bed – but not on his pillows. I got him an extra one. Then Albert and June showed up to tell about the play. Then Rudy dropped by, letting himself in with the key that the Strayer-Block family had, and chatted for a few minutes.

He told us about Hilda's new boyfriend, who played the French horn and had sloppy-looking long hair (just my point of view about guys with long hair). Then I told him that Hilda hadn't visited all weekend, and that she knew I had a gift for her and a cupcake. Rudy said he would send her over.

Sure enough, Hilda appeared – boyfriend in tow – and liked the gift, which was a set of hairpins with little red rhinestone dragonfly decorations. She couldn't do much else with her hair, she informed me (Really? I would never have guessed that shaggy dyed blond bangs and short brown hair couldn't be put in ponytails or braided or whatever…). I asked Riley, the boyfriend, how long he had played the French horn. The reply: 8 years. That is one of the toughest instruments to learn, I happened to know, so he must be a decent player. He smiled politely.

Misery Round Three: The Final Set

I gave Hilda a package of 2 cupcakes from the Magnolia Bakery – both of them. It looked too cute not to, and I didn't need all that dessert. Bryn was delighted – he said that the teenagers would love them.

I had bought them on Friday when I was out walking through Greenwich Village. That place left stacks of boxes for either 2 or 12 cupcakes in the window area, so customers could just put cakes in and then pay. It was the first time I had actually bought anything there, because the cakes were usually more about frosting than taste, or so I imagined from their appearance and the fact that the place had fans that blew sugary smells onto the passersby outside. That would mean that anyone eating them would notice a strong taste of food coloring chemicals.

Soon I found myself in a funk, depressed and thinking intently about the future, the present, and about all of the things that induced anxiety and depressed in my life. I often thought that nothing that I wanted to do would be possible thanks to the economy and to Damon's lack of financial success in his career. Without that, we were where we were now were: homeless.

Granted, we had relatives to stay with, but separately. As a couple, we were homeless.

I went out on Sunday afternoon and thought about it some more, hoping that the fresh air would help. It did and it didn't, but it was the best I could do.

Walking around Greenwich Village usually alternately thrilled and depressed me.

It thrilled me because of the beautiful old Federalist-era buildings. I wanted to live in one.

It depressed me because I didn't see how that can be afforded, and my thoughts started to return to discussions with Albert about wanting to live there. He had told me to just forget it, that prices had shot up too much and I would have either to settle for unsafe and ugly northern Manhattan, or else live in some other borough of New York City and take the train into Greenwich Village.

I knew I would never do that. I would have to actually live in the area to really enjoy it, or I would feel like it was just an out-of-reach tease just by living elsewhere yet nearby. Who wanted to do their routine pharmacy and grocery shopping in some other area and then lug the stuff home?! Not I, and I suspect not many others, if anyone. I'm a writer; it's not like I could commute regularly. Either I lived there and enjoyed the area or the whole idea was moot.

The Slamming Door

Albert and Bryn had enjoyed Manhattan, living in the most desirable spots, but I felt angry and deprived whenever I thought about the likelihood that I would never be able to do so myself, which was what I really wanted. I wanted to get a place in Greenwich Village with Damon, where cars were unnecessary, everything good was within walking distance, and I could work that bit of regular exercise into my routine just by necessity. Going to a gym would still be something I would want to do (yoga, machines, etc.), but walking as transportation is great for people. I couldn't do that in the suburbs, where everything was spread out.

So I got anxious and depressed as I thought that I could just forget it, and worried that I would just end up back with my parents forever, stranded, never living with Damon again.

I was mad at them.

They had told me over the phone that they actually paid a psychiatrist to tell them (last April) that Damon would never make any money – at least, not enough to pay for us to live on our own. It made me feel suicidal – both the nagging anxiety that such a thing might turn out to be so, and/or the fact that they would do that in the first place. My parents were so good at inducing anxiety and depression, and then calling their attitudes and actions maturity and realism. I called it unhealthy – so much negativity that my mind left little room for focusing on other thoughts and activities, such as writing books that might actually earn me some money.

So that was my dream, anyway: living in a paid-for, beautiful, Federalist-era home in Greenwich Village on some QUIET side-street (there were lots of them!) with Damon and a female cat named Hermione. He could do his immunology work at the New York Eye and Ear Infirmary, I could edit, write, and cook and bake, and walk in what felt like a safe enough area, and we could walk around together in the evenings looking for restaurants to try while holding hands. No wonder I couldn't watch reports on the economy; I already understood quite clearly that the time when couples without a really high income could just get a place in Greenwich Village and expect to enjoy it for decades was over.

I felt frantic at the thought that our idea of a nice life together would just never happen, or that I would get gray, dried-up and wrinkled before it did. Or that Damon would.

I wanted Damon.

That was another source of anxiety. He was fascinating and fun and loved cats and New York and had nice relatives who liked me…but they were getting old and probably dying off and Damon was 14 and a half years older than me and I didn't ever want to live as a widow.

Misery Round Three: The Final Set

I had tried to fall in love with someone close in age to me, but it just didn't happen, and I think Damon is just the coolest guy anyway, so I wanted him, and maybe age is no indicator of who will live longer because there is no crystal ball to crunch the combination of data: DNA, family history, individual health history and risk factors for illness, chances for some freak accident, etc. But I wanted to die first, when I was old but without looking ugly – hence the fight against the aging process. No wonder Damon saw me as his soul mate.

For Damon, the fight against the aging process was aimed at living for a few centuries or more. We obsessed about the same things, but he carried the ideas to more pronounced extreme than I did.

For me, the fight is against being made unattractive by the aging process. That is just the worst thing that aging can do to a person – not kill them, but make the person ugly. I must continue to look attractive as I age.

I am vain and unapologetic about it. I would do whatever it took to keep my skin from looking terrible. But at some point, plastic surgery would probably be necessary, depending up what cropped up.

Maybe I should call Damon, I thought; that always made me feel better.

Calling Damon DID make me feel better, but that would only last until the next crisis.

Despite encouraging me to go out and walk around, Bryn was dehydrated on Sunday, plus he ending up having that tachycardia episode. On Monday afternoon, when we went to see the cardiologist, he ordered Bryn to call Sloan-Kettering and arrange for an intravenous drip of more electrolyte fluids.

After that call was made, Bryn proceeded to drive me crazy on Monday evening and into the night with odd behavior. His behavior made me think that some new and disturbing health crisis was brewing, which of course it was.

He didn't want dinner for a long time. He drank some of those awful Ensure drinks, but was eating absolutely no solid food. He had been giving up on attempts to eat even small bowls of cereal for days. I hated the weeks immediately following chemotherapy, on the anorexia/bulimia diet. I ate my dinner in bits and pieces alone in my room, where he wouldn't smell anything. At least the puking seemed to be over with, not that I truly dared to believe it.

In the evening, I discovered that there was an editing chore to do for Massoumeh's sister, Zahra, who wanted to come back from Tehran now that her English was allegedly improved. As I sat at the computer trying

The Slamming Door

to do the job, Bryn found a loud, violent movie on television that enthralled him for over 2 hours – screaming, crashing, yelling, etc. I could barely think. I kept asking him what he was watching, but he just explained a bit and continued to watch it. Still, he didn't want his dinner.

Finally, it ended, and Bryn came out into the living room. He started checking the heater, which I never touched unless he requested that I do so, and telling me about that blasted movie. As he talked on about it, somehow oblivious to the fact that I was trying to work, the bug in the Microsoft Word program on that computer resurfaced and threw away my work. I said so, and got that sickened look of horror that I get when I have no choice but to start all over again. Bryn caught on and stopped trying to talk when I said I didn't want to talk, that the computer had just eaten my work. He was so understanding about that, even when something was up.

I worked until 1 a.m. – another couple of hours – and sent it off to Massoumeh and Zahra. Suitably thankful notes followed the next day, and that was that. Meanwhile, this was when I found out what was wrong with the computer: the unnecessary programs that Albert had downloaded. I deleted them, and Bryn told his brother not to do it ever again. What a relief.

At 1 a.m., Bryn asked for his dinner – just more chicken noodle soup. Was I going to have dinner, he asked me? I stared at him incredulously, then told him that it was one a.m., that I had eaten hours ago, and that I would give him his dinner as soon as it was ready. Okay. But Bryn, I found myself asking, what is going on with you this evening? You're driving me crazy by acting rather oddly, I told him, and wondered why he had spent the evening this way, listing each odd activity. He just wasn't hungry, he admitted.

I fed him and he ate about three-quarters of the soup. He went to bed a while later, and then I took my bath and shampooed my hair and went to bed. I did not fall asleep until 3:30 a.m., which was quite late...or early, depending upon one's point of view. Not good.

At almost 7 a.m., I heard Bryn call me: "Clarisse!" I jumped out of bed, not exactly astonished that something was wrong.

There he was, partly dressed, with the right half of his tongue all swollen, talking with a slurred aspect to his speech. He had called the hospital and they had said to go there. Great – and to top it all off, he looked bluish-white.

I rushed and got ready to go in less than 10 minutes – bathroom, face washed, teeth brushed, makeup, earrings, warm outfit (snow and cold expected) – and we headed out. I grabbed his newspaper in the foyer and realized that it was so early that the street was not yet blocked off for school. Perfect: almost immediately, I had a cab stopped for us.

Misery Round Three: The Final Set

Bryn caught up with me and climbed in, asking me what I was doing instead of jumping in and just waiting for me to follow. Stuffing his newspaper into his book-bag, I replied. Off we went, and I tried chatting with him with some success. I wanted him to stay awake.

When we arrived at 68th Street and York Avenue, the cab driver let us out on the right-hand side of the Avenue, which meant that we would have to walk across. Bryn suddenly seemed to have a lack of energy and gripped my hand tightly all the way across. The traffic let us go, slowing down for the red light, aware that this was a hospital entrance.

I wanted a wheelchair after that shaky stagger across the street, during which a pair of elegantly dressed and coiffed women had quickly gotten out of our way when they saw how unsteadily Bryn was moving.

The guard at the desk jumped up and got us one quickly, rushing to replace the one I had grabbed for some reason; there was something wrong with it, I guessed. He directed us to the elevator and up. I knew where we were going – it was the same Urgent Care Center that we had gone to back in October, right after Bryn's first round of chemotherapy poison.

I wheeled him there, with Bryn asking me if I was going the right way, assuring him that I knew where to go. And I did. The wooden doors opened automatically for us (some sensor must have been aware of our arrival), and I pushed the chair up to the desk, and said, "Fix him!" to the nurses, who were expecting us.

A nice gay Asian male nurse named Kenny took us to bed 13 – lucky 13. I am superstitious, so I was a bit annoyed. The last time we had been there, Bryn got a nice benign number: 19. I thought of Dr. Leonardi's social visit, paid to just Bryn and Albert in the evening after the rest of the family had gone home. We settled into our assigned area.

I waited to see what preliminary things would be done, then asked Bryn if I might go to the cafeteria to eat breakfast, and if so, what I might bring back for him. Of course I could go, he said, and gave me a twenty, insisting that I stay and eat. (I was thinking that a big breakfast would help me get through a long day with only 3 and a half hours' worth of sleep – and I was right, as it turned out.)

He wanted coffee, which he never drank, and I took off to eat a toasted raisin bagel with cream cheese plus a small plate of bacon and scrambled eggs. Unhealthy, but all this insight into cancer was strengthening my resolve to come down with heart problems INSTEAD of cancer…anything to die with all of my hair, looking pretty, with no disgusting internal parasite eating away at me, making my breath sickly sweet (though Bryn didn't have that as yet, but my grandmother had gotten that). I also had fresh-squeezed orange juice and coffee with milk,

The Slamming Door

which I drank last, wondering whether or not it would backfire on so little sleep.

I returned to the Urgent Care Center with some strawberry Jell-O and coffee for Bryn.

He was rigged up to a vital signs monitor, comprised of multiple stick-on cords, plus a heart monitor, and an intra-venous combination drip of saline and magnesium, followed by another one of saline and potassium. He still thought we would be going to 53rd Street next for our 11:15 a.m. appointment, but I doubted it. This place could do for him what the other one had been scheduled to do.

Sure enough, it did, and an on-call doctor, a Vietnamese-American guy, came in to explain to Bryn what was wrong (that we didn't already know about) and tell him what would be done about it. We liked him too, and I liked him even more later on when I left my business card at the desk for the file. The doctor saw the *QueenBeeEdit* card and asked, "Could you edit my life?" I laughed, then left the area to get a cell phone signal and call Albert.

The magnesium burned Bryn, so Nurse Kenny pinched the line to slow it down a bit, which eased the burning sensation. It turned Bryn's tongue orange for a couple of hours, but his tongue deflated and returned to its normal shape. The potassium didn't do anything odd.

Next, they intended to take him upstairs to an overnight bed, and give him 2 pints of blood, they announced, because, as the doctor had explained, his bone marrow had been killed. I began to have horrified thoughts of Bryn needing an unobtainable bone marrow transplant, but before I could voice any of them, the doctor added that the transfusion would regenerate the bone marrow. Oh…good. Albert had arrived by then.

We waited and Bryn slept until the bed on the 12th floor was ready, and then they disconnected him and prepared for the trek upstairs. I watched how it was done: a transport technician (job description in a fancy name) arrived. She started to move Bryn's bed, but got snagged by the heart monitor. I tracked down Nurse Kenny again to disconnect everything. He rushed in from seeing another patient, cheerful but not thrilled that he had been told that everyone else was ready to move, and got everything in order.

We headed out, and took the elevator.

The last time that Bryn stayed in that hospital overnight, he had his own room, and slept for the entire weekend, eating custom-cooked meals.

This time he had a roommate – a quiet guy over in the corner with a shock of hair (!) who was talking on a phone in low tones about household bills. Later on, after I had left for the evening, the roommate

Misery Round Three: The Final Set

had woken up from a nap, delirious and confused. Bryn told me he had walked over to him and reassured him that everything was fine, and he was just reacting to his medications. The guy had calmed down.

There was also a tall desk just inside the room, by the door. Alas, it turned out to be a nurses' away station. All night, Bryn told me, they kept coming in and out to take notes on it. It was not a restful hospital stay.

Bryn asked me to get him some water, so I wandered down the hall, looking for a place to get it from. I found a kitchen that the patients could use, and was suddenly face-to-face with a woman who looked to be about my own age. She was tall and thin, with glasses, dark eyebrows and lashes, and a covering over her head that resembled a shower-cap. There were some older patients, but this one shook me up the most. I waited until they had what they wanted, got the cup of water, and went back to Bryn's room.

It was Tuesday, and I realized that Albert was getting that horrid chemotherapy clinical trial across the street at Cornell's university hospital. Bryn wanted me to leave, so I went across the street, to the northeast block, diagonally across from Sloan-Kettering.

After asking around, I found Albert. He was sitting in what looked like an office waiting room with some other people, reading *The New York Times*. This place was rather different from Sloan-Kettering; it was like a doctor's office rather than a series of living room sofas, all stiff little chairs with thin wooden arms.

I didn't stay too long; Albert was fine, Alissa had taken the day off to be with June, and we couldn't talk to loudly in there. Albert hadn't had his dose of poison yet, but he reassured me that it wasn't going to be as strong as what Bryn was getting, and that he wouldn't lose his hair. He was right; ultimately, his hair just thinned out a bit, but that was all. He still had it.

After Bryn came home – he just spent one night away – his pain pills had been changed, which meant a trip to the pharmacy. I noticed that it was now upgraded from a form of codeine to one of morphine. Berta and I set out to get it after I served water, coffee, and ginger ale.

We had to wait a bit, so we tried to see the black cat, London, but she kept running away. The Greek women who ran the place (beautiful thin women with long, wavy black hair and finely sculpted eyebrows in black pants and tight black shirts) seemed annoyed at us. I didn't care. I couldn't have a cat, the apartment would die with Bryn, I was getting nervous about him, and imagining a hurried, pressured process of packing up that apartment as the evil landlord chased the family out so that he could start charging non-rent-controlled fees.

The Slamming Door

Berta suggested that we eat at the Thai restaurant next door, and wondered – should we get take-out, or sit down? Sit down, I said. She seemed to be getting more and more upset, perhaps with some tears threatening, so we couldn't go back yet. The pain pills wouldn't be needed until bedtime anyway, and Bryn was fine in his chair for now.

We went in and chatted for over an hour about her father, her mother, her boyfriend, everything. And we chatted about my mother. My mother had refused to even look at Damon's ImmuneACCORD website. She didn't like him anymore. ImmuneACCORD was going into the University of Connecticut Dairy Bar's ice cream at some point, complete with the logo on the boxes, and in honor of the work being done in Chuck's lab. But she didn't want to hear about it, Damon was always going to be making some money soon and then never did, and so on and on.

Berta's mother induced stress in many ways just as my own mother did. They just nagged and brought out the most stressful, depressing moods rather than offering any useful or emotionally intelligent advice. It was ironic, considering the fact that my mother was the one who had introduced me to the concept of emotional intelligence in the first place. She advocated it but exercised none of it. Instead, we operated with emotional stupidity. It was about this time that I just stopped talking with her much at all, though later on I just flat out told my mother that I refused to be banned from talking about my own husband, and that I expected her to refrain from saying anything negative when I mentioned him. That helped, but was off in the future.

Berta encouraged me to explain about life with my parents, but as usual demanded that I give a short version with no details. She hated details, she said, and she had ADD, she reminded me. For once, I wouldn't let her dictate how I tell a story. I said she was making it all too stressful, that I didn't care if she only took in certain points, because she would inevitably ask me to fill them in later when she was ready to think about it all again, and that it was much easier to tell without her adding rules of telling. She started laughing, realizing what sort of effect she was having on me, and acquiesced.

I told my story, and she could see why I hated being back at home with my parents, cat or no cat. She wondered if I could get another situation, a job this time, as a caregiver to another elderly person in Manhattan, after Bryn didn't need me any more (my euphemism of choice for death, I suppose). No way, I told her. I could never do this for a stranger, and feel like a servant. Every time the person looked like she or he were brooding, I would be convinced that it was about me, some sense of displeasure over whatever I was doing or not doing for them…no way. I had even mentioned all this to Bryn of my own accord,

Misery Round Three: The Final Set

I told her, and he understood – I could only do all this for a relative whom I loved and got along well with. Besides, I couldn't have Damon visit me, so don't even bring that up again. She understood and dropped the subject.

Next she told me that Matt was making her unhappy, but that she would like to continue with him as long as her father was alive so that he would think that she had a nice guy. She began to cry at that point. Matt's behavior reminded me of my last boyfriend before Damon, an Indian dentist who found endless fault with me – I ruined food, he claimed (what was he referring to?! I am a gourmet cook and baker!), I should be working 80 hours a week in a law firm, he didn't like cats and said "Die cat, die," to my wonderful pet Charcoal Cat…and Matt was haranguing Berta about her weight while she was under extreme stress about her father.

As she cried and talked, I told her that she couldn't go home yet. We would chat until she was calmer, then go back to see Bryn and watch crime shows or movies until we were certain that Elvira would be asleep. Then she could go home and relax. The last thing Berta needed was to go home and find Dorothy calling her a fat pig.

We watched *Juno* until we thought it was late enough – Berta hadn't seen it yet.

Bryn and I barely slept through the night. He just wasn't able to relax all night and rest.

I couldn't relax knowing that he wasn't staying in bed asleep, so I gave up and watched a silly movie called *Knocked Up*. At the rate I was going, I would soon have seen every silly, interesting, romantic, dramatic, and action-adventure movie available, except for horror movies – only the ones about Hannibal the Cannibal held any appeal for me. He was fascinating character.

The next afternoon, some new books that Bryn and I had ordered both arrived, which we enjoyed, but he didn't eat all day. I served everything he wanted: cereal, half a banana, coffee, ginger ale, and Ensure drink…and he only ingested those last 2 items. His appetite was missing in action again.

Albert and June stopped by. June had actually enjoyed the Alzheimer's care place! And Albert had been given a place to write! At last – some problems seemed to be under control. Albert brought us each a cupcake from Billy's Bakery (around the corner on 9th Avenue), but Bryn doesn't want his as yet. Damnit…I wanted his appetite back NOW.

Berta arrive a little while later to watch television and possibly bully me to force more food and liquids down her father's throat. She called his behavior "being an asshole" when he wouldn't eat much, so I told her

The Slamming Door

that I was guessing that this translated as being stubborn while not feeling well enough to force it as she fretted about it. She said that I had it right.

She brought some new underwear for Bryn that was too small (he hadn't shrunk THAT much), and we went out to do errands before going out walking and to eat somewhere together. It was just routine stuff like mailing letters, getting laundry back, and buying Bryn some prunes. He ate four of them – a whopping bowl full of 4 little prunes. I wanted his damned appetite back NOW. Not that the little cartoon demon I of my imagination gave a shit...

Berta had an idea: sneak Pedialyte into his water bottle. We did it, and Bryn drank quite a bit without missing a beat. Then we I took off when he had what he wanted for the time being. As usual, the parting remark was, "Have a wonderful time!" Nice Bryn.

We headed straight for the souvenir shop *Reminiscence* to exchange a gift that I had bought for Berta as a surprise, to cheer her up. To our great delight, Tony the Tiger was sitting on top of a glass case just a few paces inside to the right. He was a beautiful, enormous, wide and green-eyed panther of a cat with white feet and paws, a white stomach, and a tiger-striped back and tail and mask. One ear had a slight rip in it from his early days before the shop owner took him in. Something about his demeanor suggested a real tiger – he was a huge, strong, lumbering, majestic animal, but quietly friendly. He seemed to understand people rather well, and was quite tolerant of cat lovers who wanted to cuddle him.

We cuddled him and cooed over him to our heart's content, and the shop employee made no move to stop us. It felt great. Tony the Tiger Cat just stared at us as though we must be on crack or something – especially at me, since I was the one holding him. I simply explained to him that we loved cats but that I couldn't have one right now, so that was why I was metaphorically drinking my fill and then some of cat therapy. He endured it without objection, while seeming a bit incredulous nonetheless. I liked him.

Berta browsed while I checked for another *Wonder Woman* mug – no luck. We had hoped to exchange the one that I had surprised her with for another when we found a slight flaw in it under the packaging. I looked around and found a pocket mirror for just a buck more than the mug cost, a rectangular thing with a red background and Wonder Woman on it. I made the exchange, paid the difference, and presented it. It was the perfect thing: exactly what she needed. Berta had told me that she loved to collect *Wonder Woman* souvenirs a few evenings earlier.

We left and strolled around West 23rd Street, in and out of various shops, looking at brass drawer handles in Home Depot, shoes in other stores, etc. Then we turned south and started looking for a place to eat.

Misery Round Three: The Final Set

The Cajun place was too loud – too bad. The Indian place was in the wrong direction – just as well, I had eaten Indian take-out several times lately. We settled on a Greek diner called the Eros Diner. I had pumpkin pancakes – breakfast for dinner. She had matzoh ball soup, a tuna melt and sweet potato fries. We ate some of each other's food – 40 percent of her fries for one of my 3 pancakes.

Damon called early on, just as Berta's matzoh ball soup arrived. He insisted that I inform her that someone had castrated a matzoh so that she could have that soup. She laughed.

We chatted for a while, enjoying our food, and then went home.

Bryn was okay, and he mentioned that we would be going back to 53rd Street and 3rd Avenue tomorrow for an 11 a.m. appointment with Dr. Callahan and a re-hydration session. Good, I said. I set my alarm for 9:45 a.m.

Berta stayed a while longer. I mentioned to her father that she was feeling like a traitor about something at work – a woman was to be fired...well, laid off really because they couldn't afford her any more...next Wednesday. Berta knew, but the bosses didn't know she knew, and she was feeling particularly bad about it all because she would be expected to summon this unfortunate woman while pretending not to know why, and tell her to go to the conference room on some other floor.

The laying off would be done there, and then a guard would escort her out of the building after someone else was dispatched to retrieve her coat, boots/shoes, handbag, etc. – whatever she would need just to walk out in public. Her other possessions would be boxed and shipped later, thus requiring her former co-workers to inspect all of her personal things as they packed them up. This process would also afford them the opportunity to acquire her stapler, her headache pills, etc. She would only get back whatever they chose to send back.

What was the reason for this insult to injury? Fear by the corporation that she might return to her computer, steal corporate secrets, and hurt the offending corporation that was so callously depriving her of employment just before bonus time by selling their information.

Berta was plotting to have an imaginary doctor's appointment to run out to at 11 a.m. that morning so that someone else would have to be the traitor and not her.

Bryn listened, smiled, and said, "You have to do it," meaning stay and betray this woman. He didn't mean it in a nasty way, just that there was no real escape because a hasty and timed departure such as she was plotting would come across as a tip-off that she knew what the bosses were up to.

How horrible. This whole story only strengthened my resolve to stay the hell out of offices and corporate environments. Apparently, this

The Slamming Door

woman was a good worker who had done a good and even better than good job…but they had to cut expenses. It was the economy. But the way that these places canned people was humiliating, and I have no intention of allowing one of them to do it to me. Better to be miserable in ways that I was already used to coping with than add this indignity to my list of experiences.

The next morning came, and Bryn and I headed out. We got a cab on 9th Avenue, and Bryn was in good enough shape to walk out to the other side of 9th and stand until a cab pulled up, then walk calmly and steadily into the hospital out-patient building.

He was much better than he had been on Wednesday, but still felt rather crappy with little appetite. He did eat his chicken noodle soup, but not Jell-O, which I gone out to buy for him. Nurse Karen was very pleased about Berta's plan to add Pedialyte to his water cup, which he had noticed the night before – something tasted a bit oily. The nurse insisted that this was exactly what he needed to be doing, that it was better than water, and so on.

It had been a pretty depressing afternoon, overhearing the nurse in the next alcove trying to find a vein to puncture for the next I.V. for whomever she was treating. She gave up and went to get another nurse to try. And Bryn…Nurse Karen said he was so dehydrated that she had trouble doing that for him also. She recommended something more permanent, something that would be installed in his chest after he was sedated.

I listened, then asked her: "Is this the same as what Morgan Freeman's character got in *The Bucket List*?" Yes, she said – that is exactly it. That thing bled in the movie when he was all dressed up in a fancy restaurant, I pointed out. She had never heard of that happening with these things. I said I supposed that the scriptwriters just needed a bit of drama in the dialogue, then. She agreed; we didn't have to worry about it actually happening to Bryn.

But it was depressing and disturbing when he grinned and says, "I look like a drug addict – look at my track-marks!" and held out his bruised arms. Poor human pin-cushion…no wonder the nurse talked about rigging up this reusable contraption.

When we came home, I put some in his individual-size water bottle (he kept a leftover commercial plastic bottle and continually had me refill it in order to track how much water he drank): half water and half Pedialyte. He agreed to keep drinking it that way for now.

Next, I did the errands, only to be fooled by disorganized pharmacy workers. They told me to come back in 40 minutes for his anti-fungal pills (his tongue was getting a disturbing white fuzz, a side-effect of chemotherapy!). When I got back, they told me: "We called Mr.

Misery Round Three: The Final Set

Otterman. We won't have the pills until tomorrow. If you come back after noon, we'll have them."

I wasn't happy, but I went home after dallying in some shops just to browse, chatting dispiritedly with the shop workers about it. They commiserated with me quite nicely.

I brought my calligraphy supplies out – just purchased while waiting for the 40 minutes to pass – and began to plot out my advertisement samples. I would make them this weekend, scan them, and have them to e-mail to potential customers as attachments. Bryn thought the text sample that I prepared – to copy from with the calligraphy pen – looked great.

I fed him Brie cheese with crackers, and he ate a couple of them with small bits of cheese – very small bits. I ate some with him, glumly realizing that I was eating at least four times as much as he was. Something was upside down here – a woman eating more than a man, and I am a regular-sized woman, so this was a grim thing to observe.

As we ate, Damon called me and I asked Bryn if it would be okay for him to visit overnight the next Saturday evening. This was what Damon had just found out that he could do – just that afternoon – because his Iranian colleague, AliAkbar, would be driving to Manhattan and back and staying with people elsewhere in the city.

Bryn wondered to me if I had known about this for a while and not asked him. I was a bit annoyed, but concealed it. I had not known; I don't know how to put stuff off like that. Bryn said that he didn't know how he would feel that weekend, but okay, the answer was yes. I relayed this to Damon, every word, and added that he could only stay for a night, and that was that. In the end, the whole trip was cancelled; neither of them came to New York City.

If I worked for some stranger doing what I do for Bryn, I could not have my husband visit like this. If I needed to use the bathroom, or have a professional life beyond being the servant to some stranger who needed a live-in companion, there would be no allowance for or understanding of that. I had mentioned all of these considerations over the phone to Berta that afternoon as I sat with Bryn during his I.V. treatment; the blasted subject had come up again.

After we ate the cheese, I cleaned everything up and returned to the computer to vent about something. I vented my frustration with Bryn about a particular issue in a letter to Dr. Leonardi, the leading urology and oncology expert in the nation, because he is my friend, my family's friend, and my mother's former boss. Here it is:

Hi Dr. Leonardi!

The Slamming Door

How are you?

Bryn has been feeling lousy all week, dehydrated, so we had him re-hydrated twice with saline solution and other fluids. His appetite reappears when that happens, but he can't seem to drink enough liquid on his own to maintain the appetite. He has agreed to drink Pedialyte instead of water, plus he has fruity yoghurt drinks and Ensure and ginger ale.

But that's not what led to this particular letter. I just want to rant about something:

He needs a urologist, he informed me this morning, as we went for the latest saline solution.

It has been my secret hope all along that you would end up as his urologist, because you are the best.

Well, I can just forget it.

He doesn't want you, even knowing and believing that you are the best and nicest, because...we know you!

I am just so infuriated over the absurdity of it all and the disappointment that I had to write to you about it and rant. Secret hope dashed. He'd rather have that stupid quack who gave him those radioactive seeds than you, apparently. Albert did say that he is stubborn.

I think I'm actually angry at him. And I am quite sure that he has never before induced this emotion in me.

So I was forced to tell Dr. Callahan today that he doesn't want you, because you are our friend, because we know you, etc. Bryn had me remind him of his request for a urologist recommendation for her, with that caveat. By the time I brought it up, he had forgotten all about needing a urologist, but wanted the recommendation as soon as I reminded him...

The nurse informed us that the computer just announces who is the most available MSKCC doctor in whatever field needed, with caseload capacity...then we can say that we don't want so-

Misery Round Three: The Final Set

and-so...damnit. I know you have room - you're new! You told me all this.

This is stupid...you are legally forbidden to tell us ANYTHING about ANY patient – like their secrets – doctor-patient confidentiality, it's called. But he just doesn't care.

So that's about it - waiting for his taste buds to work properly and his appetite to return.

At least the puking phase appears to be over...I hope.

Sincerely and Disgustedly,
Clarisse.

It felt good to type it out and send it. I just didn't care that this was Bryn's illness and death (though his heart condition still could pre-empt the bone cancer). And I'm sure he didn't care how others feel – he just wanted it his way. I would. But I suddenly wanted something about it my way – as in, with him alive longer, longer, longer – so I was feeling frustrated.

People who love sick people are selfish like that...and unapologetic about it.

At last I was reacting to an aspect of this situation the way that Berta did, but about doctor choices rather than food choices and quantities. But I tried to push it out of my mind; Bryn wasn't going to choose Leonardi. My entire therapy for this consisted of that e-mail.

This is why writing about that woman who was slated to be fired next week and then telling Damon by sharing this story with him was just so damned satisfying. It was of desperate importance to me to be able to tell Damon everything. He was my best friend and soul mate, and nothing else was keeping me sane. I knew that I needed something good to read – not for knowledge, which was what I usually went for – but for fun and escape. I still needed to find it.

It was the middle of the night – either Friday night or early Saturday morning, depending upon one's point of view – January 30, 2009, and Cassie called while he was in the bathroom – 2 a.m., to be precise. She laughed as she told me that they had a long history of this particular coincidence: her calling him at precisely the wrong moment, when he can't talk.

We chatted until he was ready to come out.

Quite some time before that, Bryn had told me that I could tell interested friends and acquaintances and relatives and so on – interested parties – how he was doing. This included a basic summary. Nothing would make much sense without one.

That night he changed his mind suddenly – or perhaps he forgot, conveniently, while feeling upset. I had mentioned to Cassie that he wanted a urologist, and that I was quite upset that he didn't want Dr. Leonardi. I told her why he didn't: because Leonardi was our friend, someone we knew. She too found that odd and nonsensical. He ought to want him, she went on, said that was no reason. Of course I agreed and told her so, but added that there was no point in making a fuss to him – he knew, because I had immediately told him, that it had long been a secret hope of mine that Leonardi could become one of his doctors – but to fuss would be pointless.

She conceded that point. Bryn took the phone.

I resumed typing this story.

Suddenly he finished his phone call, came out into the living room heading for the kitchen, turned, and complained in an angry, resentful tone, why did I have to tell Cassie that he needed to see a urologist?!

I couldn't believe it. Immediately, I defended myself by reminding him of the rules that he had laid out at the beginning. I kept the volume and tone of my voice low enough, and after a moment, Bryn went into the kitchen.

I was extremely upset over this.

Granted, he felt trapped and that he had lost control over his life.

Also granted was the fact that he had intended to conceal this illness despite the logistical impossibility of doing so – hopping around on a cane saying "Ow, ow, ow!" is a bit of a give-away that one has a serious health problem. Nevertheless, he had intended to do that until he realized that it just wouldn't work.

Now he was resentful of the fact that information is leaking out like a cereal box with a hole in it, trailing details all over his territory.

Then there was the fact that I had no sense of shame over telling what I could have sworn was authorized. I also reminded him, just before he went into the kitchen in a huff, that I did have another piece of secret information that he shared with me while in the hospital the other day, and that I was just not telling – not to others, and not in this tale of misery.

No changing the rules, I thought as I typed. No scolding, berating, nothing. I would not be told off, not even if someone wanted to do it – you want my help, don't yell at me or get mad at me. I not only can't

Misery Round Three: The Final Set

take it, I won't. I refuse to "learn a lesson" about it, feel shame, guilt, whatever. I was doing the best I could, and being nice.

Antisocial of me, isn't it? Well, that's too damned bad. I just didn't care. Life is all about not being told off for me, and always has been. I go to great lengths to avoid being chewed out, and bitterly resent it if anyone does in fact decide to tell me off anyway. No excuses and no attempts at justification will impress me – not illness, not forgetfulness, not stress.

Other people aren't the only ones who are miserable. I was trapped in my circumstances, with no financial way out of them. That, and I had a long list of memories of being told that I hadn't handled some interpersonal situation just right at various times in my life, and I had decided that I just wouldn't put up with any more of it. If anyone other than Bryn tried to scold me or otherwise tell me off for any reason during this illness and death, I promised myself silently that I would not be as conciliatory or tolerant of it as I was with Bryn.

As it turned out, Bryn lived for quite a while longer, but didn't get mad again.

Bryn felt cheated, trapped, and a loss of control. I got that – it wasn't exactly hard to figure out and understand. And I had made it a constant policy to imagine how I would feel if it were me sick with cancer and then do whatever pleased him.

But I would not acquiesce to being yelled at or scolded for any reason.

I was not my maternal grandmother, the professional home care nurse who would just go into another room and ignore her charge (some wealthy and spoiled and cranky woman named Mrs. Campbell whom she took care of for several years just before retiring) until the brat realized that she had overdone it...no. Nana was still alive in Connecticut, retired.

No...this was my nice cousin, who was no brat – just a scared guy who was being cheated out of his retirement by some radioactive crap that was still sitting in his prostate, continuing to inflict damage.

When Bryn returned to his Lazy Boy chair, I hasten to assure him that no one was plotting against him, and that no one – not me, not anyone else – was maliciously leaking information with the intent to destroy his sense of privacy. He simply wanted something that had become utterly elusive since getting sick: privacy.

It could no longer realistically or logistically be had. The family could offer him just so much of that and then the level that he truly desired became unattainable.

Bryn suddenly looked up at me, miserable, but with comprehension that I wasn't guilty of any breach of promise, and that I was still his best friend. We were back on happy terms again. We even hugged, and then

The Slamming Door

I went back to the computer so he could stare at the TV and try to focus on something, anything, else.

And then there was Damon: you want mean, just read on…

He assured me that if he ever got a diagnosis of cancer, he would just blow his own head off rather than endure the slightest indignity or freakiness associated with the damned disease. He'd have none of it, thank you very much. No needles, no chemotherapy poisoning, and certainly no loss of privacy.

That meant that he was planning to just suddenly cease to exist without the slightest warning whatsoever to his wife. He would leave me a widow, and in shock.

He had damned well better outlive me. He owed it to me after all of the miserable time apart with no money that we had been stuck with. I often worried that the moment we became solvent enough to have a home together, he would get sick and die, and we would never have our life together – no romance, no sex, no cat, no walking and talking and sitting and being together. I felt cheated right now, damn it – never mind later.

I hated my life.

Back to my active fantasy life, then, and lots of sleep. Those things kept me sane, just as good books and movies did. Paying attention to my life could drive me over the edge.

If this family wanted me functional and of use as a caregiver – and I knew that I was better than some hired stranger bankrupting Bryn while being less trustworthy with money, security, food, personal interactions, and so on – there must be no scolding for saying or doing some random thing that I could not have guessed would bother any of them…or for sleeping.

I did tell Bryn when tucking him in that this place was one that I thought of as home.

It was emotionally soothing there on many levels…just not while being scolded while in fear of a sudden end concluding with abrupt and callous eviction by a mercenary landlord…that was not exactly a soothing thought.

At least Damon has assured me that he would promptly drop everything to help pack the place up and empty it rather than just leave it to the rest of us…packing always made me hyperventilate – that was an anxiety problem of mine.

He had also promised to threaten the landlord in some other odd way to prolong our stay here…a bluff, but one that actually sounds like it might work. Complete with an unchanged rental fee. Damon was crazy and determined.

I loved Damon. He was a rule-breaker. He had damned well better outlive me – I had no interest in learning to be without him. I wanted him

Misery Round Three: The Final Set

my whole life – and had been obsessed with the idea of him before we ever met, and determined to have a nice best friend of a husband to lean on emotionally while being leaned on back – and now I had him.

That made the thought of not having him quite terrifying. He traveled to Iran and Iraqi Kurdistan, to lots of dangerous places, and taken all sorts of chances. I hated it. I wanted him here, solvent and with me. And I wanted to travel to safe and fascinating places with him and only him on romantic and intellectually intriguing places. And I wanted to have a cat with him.

Watching Bryn slowly die was like being told over and over again that life would do its best to tease and disappoint and upset us.

Chapter 29

Twilight...and Milkshake Time

I wanted Damon.
But he had to be away, and I had to be where I was.
So I welcomed any distraction that I could get from that thought.
On the last night in January, Berta invited me out for the evening – with a great itinerary for a Saturday night: we would eat at Le Pain Quotidien, and then see the new vampire movie, *Twilight*. She had read the book, and really wanted to see it.
It was written by a Mormon woman and with posters plastered in every subway car I had ridden in for the past four months. Apparently, the story was hot, despite the utter lack of sex scenes, a forbidden item for an unmarried couple in a tale written by a Mormon. I was intrigued, but other than that, had paid little attention to the latest craze.
I am quite capable of getting caught up in a popular culture phenomenon, but it must possess certain qualities, not the least of which is a plot that I find engaging and can get lost in. If it offers a compelling escape from reality, it works for me.
The delay had been that Berta wanted to read the book first, and then see the movie. Reading took her a long time, what with having an office job to commute to and fighting Attention Deficit Disorder, but she was interested, so she read it.
At last, she was ready, though I still didn't see what the hype was all about. I figured I would have to see the movie to feel the effect of the general enthusiasm about it. Sure enough, that was what happened: I watched Edward and Bella meet, watched her figure out that he was a vampire, saw them fall in love, saw him save her from a crazed tracker, and I was hooked.
I did several errands for Bryn and told him about the invitation. Before I went out for the errand run, he said, as usual, "Have a wonderful time." I felt sorry for him, cooped up. I asked him why he always said to have a wonderful time when I told him I was just doing mundane stuff like errands, and he said that it was because he wanted me to have a wonderful time. Okay...I could believe that. I didn't add that the timing seemed a bit off – that line would be perfect as I headed out to a movie or some other fun activity, but not to the pharmacy or ATM.
He was in a good mood, and had a parade of visitors that afternoon, including Toby Maddox, his old friend from work, who brought a photo of his 3 grandsons. He showed me, and I asked what their names were. The kids all appeared to under 10 years old – not an age I would want to meet, but I could present a passable appearance of mild interest by asking

about names and ages. I did not think to ask about hobbies. Fortunately, Albert and June and Alissa were there as well, so I could escape to see June and joke with her a bit, and talk to Alissa.

June was sitting on the sofa with a fish and chips lunch that Albert had bought for her, using a chair pulled up in front of her as a table – the usual method here. She seemed to be enjoying herself, except that she began to complain about the huge bun that was included, which she wouldn't eat. I noticed that the window was open slightly, overlooking the back alley behind the apartment building, grinned, and threw the bun out for the pigeons. June loved that. She also shared lots of her fries with me, ate only half the meal, and eventually got up and went looking for Albert. I packed up the lunch and put it in the fridge. I could eat it the next day…nice, unhealthy, recreational, fun lunch. No wonder June was so thin…that, and trips to the gym.

Alissa was going to join me and Berta for dinner, and I was glad. She didn't want to see the movie – she wanted to go home and get more writing done as usual, and do more reading for her French and English language book clubs. I wished I could get to know her more, but we had few opportunities to hang out together, and she was very quiet. We set off together in the cold.

I did my best as we walked to the restaurant. What was new with her? She proceeded to tell me how her mother was adapting to the elderly day care place for Alzheimer's patients. She added that her father was able to get some writing done there, and that soon a room would be available for him to sit in with his laptop so that he could write.

That's great, I said, but what was new with *her*? She began to talk about her writing and book clubs. That was more like it. What languages did she speak besides English and French? Just Italian, she replied. That's enough, I said cheerfully. She sounded modest, no doubt by polite design, but her abilities were impressive.

I told her that I wished we could visit more, etc., and that I worried about her not having time to date, though I could see that her writing career was well in hand. I added that my Aunt Johanna Rénard had given me a great piece of advice, which led to me realizing that Damon was the one for me: "You need to find someone who likes what you like and dislikes what you dislike."

We talked and walked, with me doing the bulk of the talking. Alissa wanted to stop at a bank to use the ATM, so we went to a couple of places until we found one that would work (her card wouldn't let us into the first place – something was wrong with the mechanism there).

Then we met Berta in the Belgian franchise, the same one where she and I had eaten on that first Sunday in September. We had a great, healthy, delicious dinner with café au laits and chamomile tea, and fun chatting, for about an hour. When we were finished, we headed south on 7th Avenue. Alissa went down into the 14th Street subway and we went to the movie, taking a bus in the bitter cold across 14th Street.

I called Bryn to say where we were, and then shut off my cell phone as we stood in the ticket line. I always did this just before going in to watch a movie, because cell phones ought to be off in there, but this also meant being out of communication with him for while. Bryn promised to drink more Ensure and said he had eaten half an apple. Great. We went up a couple of flights to the theater, stopping to use the bathroom, where the attendant raved about my hat. Hats.com, I told her – this was fun, it kept happening!

The movie was great – so great that we when we went to The Strand, the famous discount bookstore two blocks south of the theatre – where I bought the book. It was then that I realized that it was only the first of four books of the same length. Eureka…more tales. I flipped through the first book, feeling like I had just found the most delicious treat that I wouldn't be able to stop eating or drinking until it was gone, but better than a food or drink – because I could just read it again and feel just as good!

Berta was amused to see me in such a state, and to see my glee upon finding that there were more books to look forward to. I only bought the first one for now, but I commented on how great the price was. "I'll hold out for The Strand the next time I want a particular book," I told her.

"Always hold out for The Strand," she replied.

I would – as long as I had no coupons for Borders or Barnes & Noble. I'll shop wherever the prices are right, or wherever I can actually find what I am looking for. The Strand certainly offered a great variety of books that the others didn't, I was happy to discover on future visits. Sometimes it was limited and one had to either buy what it had or move on, though. Just like shopping for anything else, one could not expect to rely on just one store.

The prices were making me feel spoiled – I wanted to move to lower Manhattan! The usual feeling I got when enjoying Manhattan and mentally comparing suburban bookstores and prices was pressing in on me. I was out of my padded cell – I didn't want to go back. Even suburbia felt like a cell, unless one began to miss being on green grass.

That didn't happen too often to be a problem.

It was bitterly cold out. I was glad to have my pink coat and new velvet-ribboned hat on. The hat still felt new and wonderful after three months, probably because it was perfect for the city, chic, black and covering my head against the chill. Manhattan felt horridly bone-chilling in the winter; it was the long streets that allowed for the winds of the East and Hudson Rivers to blast across the island. They felt as though they were going straight through me sometimes.

Vianne called me as we were getting ready to leave the store. We talked to her for a while. She and Ron and both dogs were fine, and she wanted to call Bryn tomorrow. Would it be okay? What time should she call him? Yes, and in the afternoon on the land line, I answered. Berta added that he couldn't hear well on the cell phone, and always wanted to end calls quickly.

We walked around Union Square shops a bit, bought some things in Whole Foods – the huge one that had been so crowded a few weeks ago that I had left without buying anything – and headed home. Berta told me that she had had a similar claustrophobic experience in that store, and that she had asked a security guard to escort her out.

I hated crowds, and avoided them by doing errands at off-peak times.

When I got home that night, it was so bitterly cold that I was glad to get inside.

I checked on Bryn, got us both settled for the night, flopped on the bed in front of the movie channels, and opened the new *Twilight* book. Once I started reading, I knew that I had found the escape – the mental drug – that I had been wishing for.

It would be a few months before I was ready to put these stories down again and look at other things, to return to non-fiction books, biographies, and other educational tomes aimed at boosting my knowledge of women's studies, Middle Eastern studies, and whatever other historical disciplines struck my interest. I knew it and I just didn't care. I needed this.

For now, all I cared to do was escape into Forks, Washington and think about a vampire who cared for nothing but being with his quiet, beautiful, physically awkward girlfriend who loved to read great novels. I was convinced that Bella had at least a touch of Asperger's, and entranced by Edward's devotion to her.

At last...a way to forget my problems and my life for a while.

Of course, I still enjoyed the sights and sounds of Manhattan whenever I went out, and I loved living in Chelsea. I loved seeing gay people and straight people co-exist. Connecticut was not as open-minded as a college campus or a big city, and I had missed that.

Add to that the fact that Bryn had told me that he had watched over the years as first the area became mostly populated by gays, and then straight people began to move into the area in larger numbers until it was almost evenly mixed. The gays had been upset at first, feeling that they were missing out on having their own area, he had told me. But they adjusted, and it was fine. I just enjoyed seeing signs of mutual acceptance wherever I went. I hadn't thought about this since Halloween, but he mentioned it again in conversation.

Part of the attraction no doubt came from memories of my stay in Kuwait, where a Kuwaiti friend of ours once burst out with "That's disgusting!" when Damon and I mentioned that the same gay waiter had served us food at Souq Sharq several times, and then asked precisely where to find him. I had replied that I absolutely would not help him find that guy and make him miserable, or perhaps get him deported (he was a foreign worker). Our friend dropped the subject, but the incident had sent my thoughts straight to Chelsea with a nostalgic longing.

It was endless fun to me to see people and their pets out and about, and I took many photos with my digital camera, which I then saved and shared with Bryn on his computer and my memory sticks. Everything that I was accumulating while I stayed with Bryn – news articles, writing efforts, photographs – went to his hard drive and my 2 memory sticks.

One of those things did not get recorded as a photograph, unfortunately, so I just wrote it into my files to remember that way. It was something amusing that I saw on the way home, up 8th Avenue, one night: It was a man with a pug dog on a leash.

The dog was outfitted in a plain, smooth, shiny, black, very, very Chelsea leather jacket.

The dog looked so serious – deep in thought, oblivious to how absurd it looked.

It was such a great image – and just another reason why I loved it in Chelsea.

I told Bryn about it the next afternoon. I felt bad that I was often his window to such images, because he wasn't up going out whenever he wished, but then I realized that no story about a funny sight would be even worse, and I told him what I saw in my wanderings.

Happily, he wanted to go out walking that day – it was only 45 degrees out, so why not.

His friend Kandi, who taught art classes at a junior high school, was coming over to burn copies of CDs – which would take a long time. Bryn had no concept of how much time this would take, and what a huge distraction it would be. It was an entire set of *New Yorker* cartoons! He had a beautiful big book of them with a matching set of CDs.

Why was this frustrating me?

I still had to make calligraphy samples to scan and put online with my ad for that service, and I kept getting requests to do this, that, and some other damned thing. I wanted some time to be left alone to do the artwork! To do it, I needed dry hands, a calm mood, the desk, and no one trying to talk to me. That meant no one forgetting that I was concentrating and suddenly coming out and, oblivious to the fact that I was working, starting to talk! I would just write what I heard and ruin the materials if that happened. I knew this from experience.

I tactfully told Bryn all this when he brought his soup dish back to the kitchen. "Bryn, I have been putting off explaining to you what is involved in doing calligraphy for pay. And some fussy things are involved." He perked up and listened, and let me explain it. I couldn't be ruining expensive materials provided by clients because of distractions.

He was supportive of the idea of me working and trying to make money. And I was absolutely determined to do it at that desk. I wanted to be available to him, and have no boss to worry about aside from myself. It seemed like the best way to fulfill my promise to him while also coping with all of the endlessly helpful suggestions that one gets from one's relatives when one has no formal employment. Whether wanted or not, people kept making them…no wonder I was obsessed with writing. It would be great to get my work published, though I had doubts that even that would stop the suggestions from coming.

Damon called me as I was writing, joking about the pug dog image. I told him I was working on the calligraphy. He said that he liked it when I was working, and I said I knew, and I realized that he tended to get off the phone fast if I said that I wanted to work. He would just stopped clowning around and go. I loved Damon – supportive of my efforts, whatever they were.

Kandi arrived, and Bryn loomed silently over the desk. I only had half of the demo page of calligraphy ready, and had been forced to start over after ruining a capital "N" with a bad pen stroke. I looked up and told them that I needed to be alone with what I was doing a while longer. He very nicely took Kandi to his room to talk.

I finished after another 10 minutes or so, scanned the page, and saved it carefully.

With that, breathing a sigh of relief, I sent it into cyberspace, e-mailing all 3 potential clients plus Damon, who immediately promised to save it to his own memory sticks. I breathed a sigh of relief. Although I fully intended to write more beautiful samples, including poetry, quotes, an envelope address and a website link, I had what I needed most: the alphabet and a sentence that used all lower case letters: "The quick brown fox jumps over the lazy dog." I could solicit calligraphy jobs with this. I also saved the original parchment just in case of some unforeseen (they usually are!) mishap and document loss.

Meanwhile, Berta arrived during the scanning. I showed her what I was doing. She sat down on the sofa with the book of *New Yorker* cartoons, letting me finish up.

The Slamming Door

Soon I was done; I called Bryn and Kandi – ready to do the next job.

Kandi came out and powered up her laptop, an Apple, and a field of purple allium flowers appeared – wallpaper. I showed the disks that I was going to use.

Berta stayed on the sofa for a few minutes more, and then went to watch the television in my room. It took Kandi and me a while to familiarize ourselves with what needed to be done, but soon we understood the job. The problem was that Kandi wasn't completely used to her laptop; she had just bought it 6 months ago and was still learning about it. As for me, I was a Windows person, but I could usually figure things out if left to just click around the system, looking at things and assessing them.

After a short while, I was into the groove of the project with neat labels for everything, plus the how-to files, and putting them in the right places. Kandi also had a memory stick to save things onto, and I put the entire new folder of cartoons on that too. Midway into it, she realized that hovering and asking 20 questions was slowing it down and went back to chat with Bryn. Kandi was nice, and she needed these cartoons for her students. She clearly understood how people learn and think. She told me that she had realized that I needed to think it through quietly.

I could hear Bryn saying that I was a genius with computer and technical things as he stayed out of the way, sitting in his blue easy chair. That felt good. The task seemed simple enough, especially considering that I had saved these same cartoons to the old, defunct laptop that Damon and I had owned 3 years ago, and still had them on CDs, safe in a box in Connecticut.

When it was done, I cleaned Kandi's computer up for her (filthy!) and we packed it all up. She was as happy as could be with that and the free images, and so was I. Next, we all headed out to Rafaella's on the corner. Bryn felt like walking outside, and like buying dinner for everyone. Now he was getting his wish, walking just enough not to overdo it, with a purpose at the end of it. Albert and June would meet us there; they were taking a cab from TriBeCa.

When we came outside, we met the woman with the huge English Mastiff puppy named Harlem, who just a little over a year old. The dog was really friendly, despite a marked resemblance to the Hound of the Baskervilles. Bryn agreed: nice dog, and looked like he had leapt from the story's pages.

I walked on ahead a bit, rushed inside, and found, to my great delight, that the tables on either side of the front door – the ones with cushy sofas – were both empty. That meant that Bryn could have his pick and sit on the sofa behind the door. I threw my coat down onto it quick,

Twilight...and Milkshake Time

and grinned and gestured at the sofa through the window as he approached. He smiled, pleased, and settled onto the sofa.

Dinner was fun; Albert and June arrived shortly after our orders were placed. We all ate – including Bryn. This was a big deal; for the first time since his latest round of chemotherapy, he ate most of a large meal that included a starch: couscous. It was the Moroccan Breakfast, the one with strawberries, bananas, blueberries, dark raisins, walnuts, and steamed milk. And he had tea. I was thrilled. He seemed to enjoy it, and there was no sign that he might puke it up. Life might just be good for while.

June was lively, too. She liked the Middle Eastern rock music that was playing (that's all that they ever played there – in a restaurant with an Italian name!) and started grinning and swaying in her seat. We all cheered her on for a minute.

Bryn was tired going back, though. I caught up with him as he walked back, anxious to get home and get the walk over with. He said that he felt cold. I said it was much better than yesterday, when bare hands were painful, but if he felt cold, he felt cold.

We said good-bye to Kandi, and the five of us went right back.

As we walked, a truck raced by at an alarming speed, outraging June (who looked great this evening – perfect hair, long hot pink coat, and bright blue beret hat) and disgusting the rest of us. I urged her and Bryn to get away from the road and onto the sidewalk. They did.

The rest of the evening was fairly quiet. Bryn needed to decompress a bit, so Albert and June couldn't stay long. June kept complaining about being too hot, which bothered Bryn. I didn't notice this right away. It wasn't her fault; she couldn't remember from one moment to the next that she was driving someone else crazy.

I was watching her with Albert in the restaurant. I worried a bit – granted, I had my own problems, but I could worry about them too if I wanted to! She kissed Albert, he teased her, and so on. I hoped that his cancer treatments would keep him around for years and years, so that she wouldn't have to rely on only strangers to take care of her on a daily basis. I reminded myself that Albert didn't have radioactive seeds working against him. Thus reassured, I stopped obsessing for the time being.

As June and Albert took their leave, I came out to say good-night. June liked me a lot, and she suddenly surprised me by hugging me tightly, kissing me, and smiling.

After they left, I saw that she had forgotten her periwinkle blue L.L.Bean sweater. I called them, but Albert checked with her and they decided to just go home. They could get it next time, which would very likely turn out to be tomorrow.

The Slamming Door

Then it was just Berta and me with Bryn...until Hilda came over.

Poor Hilda. She was 15 years old, and her father, the one who pushed for the pregnancy 15 years ago, had ordered her to leave the apartment. Berta and I were outraged. Rudy and Elah had a rent-controlled apartment, a one-bedroom, so Hilda's room was also the living room and desk area. A set of blinds created a visual partition with no sound barrier. She had no room with a door to close. Elah was quite happy to have a daughter, despite not being eager to reproduce at the time. But now Rudy wanted childhood completed so that he could have that outer room to himself, or so I imagined, judging by the nonsense that he pulled from time to time.

I gave Hilda some ice cream and an Edward Gorey book, *The Gashleycrumb Tinies*, and we let her stay until she thought that her father would be pleasant enough when she went home.

My eyes needed a bit of a rest thanks to wearing glasses all day. I had thrown out my disposable contact lenses the night before, and would put in a new pair tomorrow. Glasses made me dizzy, disoriented, and uncertain on stairs. Damon thought my round/oval tortoise-patterned, wire-rimmed glasses looked sexy on me, but I needed to see and balance well, so too bad. He wasn't there to see the stupid glasses anyway. At least I had a boy who made passes at me when I wore glasses, despite that stupid warning I used to hear as a kid.

The next day was pretty good, except that I got up late because I couldn't see the clock without putting my eyes four inches in front of it. I finally did so at what proved to be 1 p.m. when I heard Elah come in. This produced remarks that it's like living with a teenager when I came into Bryn's room, dressed in shorts and a thin shirt with earrings and my glasses on, and my own bed made. I immediately made Bryn's bed. I just couldn't win when I couldn't see. When my contacts were in, I always got out of bed sooner, sure that it was time to do so. Sigh...

As I made the bed (which I could do in about 60 seconds flat), I let Elah in on the joke that Damon and I like to make, which was that he stopped growing emotionally at age 9 and I stopped at age 15 – so it is sort of accurate that Bryn lives with a teenager (a computer-savvy, calligrapher-writer-editor-lawyer who can cook, teenager). Well...I didn't want to age anyway.

Elah chatted a bit, telling us a few other mundane things, but one stood out: she lost a box of family heirloom dishes in 1987 when moving from 14th Street (then a crime-ridden area with drug addicts, prostitutes, and other miscreants) to this street. Someone must have grabbed it in the shuffle of loading boxes into the van – some stranger. She didn't miss it

Twilight...and Milkshake Time

until a month or so later, because unpacking takes a while. Great...that's just something else to watch out for when moving anywhere in N.Y.C.

Bryn's appetite really seemed to be returning. He ate prunes, a grapefruit, come cereal with bran in it, coffee, Ensure, a strawberry yoghurt drink, a small amount of baked beans with avocado, Rudy's homemade chicken broth, and said that soon he would also have some of the rice pudding that Kandi brought yesterday. I joked to him that the little appetite demon was gone, and that soon he would likely want to go to the movies. I didn't know what movie, but a movie. He looked pleased at the idea, and like he actually believed it would happen soon.

Bryn was definitely feeling a bit better at this point; with his third round of chemotherapy over with, he was past the worst throes of agony that it induced. Now the doctor planned to ease off a bit and let him get his strength back. He was eating again, and the smell of food wasn't bothering him, so I had resumed cooking in the apartment.

In one of my many visits to the area's grocery stores, I had come across a kind of bottled water that was fruit flavored, called SoNu. It came in several varieties, and they seemed to perk Bryn up. He had never really taken to the Pedialyte, and a couple of bottles of the stuff sat ignored in the fridge. Now this fruit water was a regular item on the grocery list. It looked like gourmet, luxury food. His favorites were the strawberry-cranberry and the lemon-tangerine, which I found out by bringing him every single flavor to try.

Each time I went to Whole Foods, I took 2 of their recycled grocery bags, made of soft plastic in bright colorful patterns. If I didn't (and I never forgot to bring them), the store would charge me 99 cents per flimsy brown paper bag. I would wait in line, always behind the cherry symbol (red – there is also a yellow fruit and a green one, only in big city stores with huge long lines, not in the suburbs – I was being such an Aspie whenever I shopped there!). Then I would lug the heavy bags home, getting a workout in the bargain. This routine felt soothing somehow.

Once he was addicted to that water, Bryn kept two bottles down on the floor by his chair, hidden on the left. One would be the real thing; the other was from the tap, for taking his pills. Berta wanted him to drink only bottled water, but he had other ideas. I just kept buying what he wanted.

He wanted macaroni and cheese, apples, chicken soup, strawberry Ensure, Hagen Daas strawberry ice cream, roast chicken, hummus and pita bread from Rafaella's, and when he felt well enough to eat out, who knew what he would order. But I knew it would be gourmet food.

Our culture seems to instill a sense of guilt for gravitating toward gourmet food.

The Slamming Door

I have always ignored this while combining my determination to access that wonderful, healthy, delectable diet with gourmet cooking and baking skills. All it really means is fresh fruits and vegetables, lots of fish and chicken, and natural recipes prepared from scratch.

The guilt heaped on the regimen's enthusiasts is due to the cost.

Having food that is not processed and that takes time to prepare costs time and money.

Yet this is how people used to eat before the industrial age changed agriculture. Well...that's part of the story. Thanks to industrialization in food production, we can have all this wonderful fresh food year-round rather than only when particular items are in season.

But if I wanted to make Bryn last as long as possible, it seemed like a good bet.

He wasn't going to eat any more food of any kind than whatever felt comfortable. Overeating was just not an option because it felt uncomfortable. And as I had said to Berta, I was not going to push him to eat.

Presenting apples and pears wasn't getting the job done, but it was still a good snack option. That was gourmet, and Whole Foods had endless varieties of apples year-round.

Whenever Bryn got spaghetti and meatballs, I knew that it wasn't particularly good for him, but if he craved it, that was that. Who was I to say anything? I wasn't dying. And I enjoyed sweet potato fries with grilled Muenster Jack cheese, avocado, and bacon on whole wheat sandwiches when Berta and I ate out at the Eros Diner. We had tried the place one evening and decided that we liked its food much better than what could be had at the Greeks' diner.

We would bring Bryn the matzoh ball soup and, if he felt like eating it, spaghetti and meatballs from there after eating in. He said that he liked it better than the food from the Greeks' diner on 9th Avenue. I asked why he had eaten there so often if the food wasn't that great, and he replied that it was because of the staff; he had gotten to know them and liked to eat with them.

But, he added, if he wasn't seeing them while he ate, he might as well have food from the Eros Diner. He might as well have what tasted better.

So I found myself offering him a mixed bag of gourmet and comfort food, which worked out to giving him whatever he wanted. Why not? I would want that level of control over my food if I were him. It was just good to see him eating again with enthusiasm, enjoying his food.

I even started working on the manuscript for this tale of misery again. I couldn't do it while I was feeling too sad, scared or upset, but once I felt calm again, I found that writing was a calming, soothing way to spend my time. It kept my mood steady that way.

But it couldn't last; there was too much going on in there, with too many people passing through. After catching up with a mere summary of events, I had to put the project aside again. It felt like a lazy way to function, but I couldn't focus on it properly while fetching drinks for people or hearing them moving about the apartment. I would just have to rely on my memory.

Not really a problem; I have an excellent memory.

Bryn and I would just have to enjoy more time together, visiting, reading, watching movies, and then receiving visitors when they appeared. When that happened, I would often disappear if they weren't relatives, and sometimes even if they were. Open the door, greet the guests, let them in, serve the coffee, and disappear. That way, no one would start asking me to leave them alone to talk. I loved to preempt that because I hated to be asked to leave, because that just proved that I didn't know when to go. And I didn't know, so I just tried to beat that by taking off abruptly.

Sometimes, Bryn would warn me in advance that he and the guests would want to talk alone. But if that didn't happen, I would leave them alone anyway; better than being told to go.

I didn't really want to stick around anyway; I had books and the computer to keep myself occupied. I wasn't emotionally dependent upon being included and staying the room to listen to every conversation.

I was glad to have my own things to do.

Winter in Manhattan was a new experience for me; I had never been in the city in the dead of winter, when it snowed heavily and often. In Connecticut, I just stayed in a lot when that happened, watching the white stuff accumulate and seeing how pretty it looks, feeling so glad that to be writer who didn't have to join the traffic jams and threats to my car during storms.

It was around this time that we noticed that two or three of the movie channels weren't working, so I called Time-Warner Cable and spoke to a representative about that. It was funny; I complained about it, saying, "What am I supposed to do, watch sports?! I hate sports. I have to stay home because I'm taking care of my cousin, so I want to watch things that I actually like."

I had gotten rather adept at negotiating politely with vendors over the years, thanks to telephone and Internet sales rather than face-to-face retail. Shopping remotely is easier and more fun that way. The man on the other end of the line promptly offered to give us a free month of several extra movie channels to make up for the weekend that three of them hadn't worked.

The Slamming Door

After accepting his offer and concluding the call, I went in and told Bryn about it.

He grinned and gave me the thumbs up, then picked up his remote control to have a look at which ones we would be enjoying. Bryn liked the odd football game, but movies were more valuable to him. He liked a good story as much as I did. I showed him the whole list, and he smiled as he scanned it, eagerly anticipating several movies when he saw the titles listed.

Several times, we found ourselves with the same one on each television, which prompted me to shut mine off and watch with him, flopped on his bed while he sat in his Lazy-Boy chair.

Another day, I went through the old stuff on the table where the computer was, sorting through the junk, making more room to move, and organizing stuff like paper clips and old business cards. While I was at it, I found something: old photographs from the 1960s.

One of them was a neat surprise: Bryn's wedding photo with Elvira in her long white gown, and Albert and June standing next to them, all dressed up. It was in color, and it offered a chance to see what they had all looked like before the aging process caught up with them.

The shot was a small, square one with a white border, showing the 4 of them in a dark, wood-paneled church. I hadn't known that Bryn and Elvira had had a real, formal wedding. Albert and June hadn't; they had lived together until June got pregnant, at which point his mother had marched them down to City Hall with Bryn in tow as a witness for a rushed civil ceremony.

Elvira looked the slightest bit taller than Bryn in the photo, probably due to high-heeled shoes. Her hair was dark brown, as were her eyes. Bryn was dressed up in a tuxedo with dark-framed glasses and grinning broadly.

Albert was straighter, thinner, and darker; in fact, his hair was a dark brown. June looked at it and said to me, "Wasn't he handsome?" with a smile. He was. She was looking very serious as she stood next to him, turned to one side and up against him, with her blond hair long and coiffed elegantly into a bun, and a chic, powder blue and white satin dress with horizontal stripes, cut very straight. The year had to have been either 1968 or 1969.

The other photo was the same size, and showed 6 people eating at a table. Bryn said it was the same one that the computer was now on, and that it was in his mother's old house in Yonkers. Oh yeah; he had inherited most of her furniture. The people were Bryn, Albert, Elvira, Marlie, and a couple that they all knew through Elvira. The husband was a doctor; I forget what specialty – either ophthalmology or endocrinology – and had some African-American ancestry, though it

Twilight...and Milkshake Time

wasn't obvious. Funny how this was so significant, but in the 1960s, it was.

When Bryn mentioned that, at first I wondered why that mattered until I recalled that if Elvira was the connection, it meant that he was a southerner from the era of those despicable Jim Crow laws. Even the slightest trace of African ancestry would have doomed a person to second-class status for life back then.

I looked at the photo some more. Bryn and Berta had inherited Marlie's facial structure, especially in the nose and brow. But Elvira was intriguing to look at, too. She looked like a brown-haired, straight-haired, version of Dionne. Funny how one of her daughters came out looking like herself, and the other came other resembling Bryn. Genetics were fun to consider that way. Elvira had been lucky enough to get straight hair, but unlucky enough to be subjected to a second-class school system. I couldn't blame her for resenting that forever.

It was early in February that we had what felt like an actual snow day. The snow came down in fine and heavy flakes, alternating, all day. I loved it. Snow days made me feel like a little kid, with a happy promise that I could stay in with books. That is what I did that day.

Someone stole Bryn's copy of *The New York Times*, so I called it in for a reimbursement, and Piper Firman was so nice as to go out to buy a replacement. He even pointed out that he bought it, being careful not to expose Bryn to any extra germs (Piper got his own newspapers from trash bins, Bryn told me later, even though he could well afford to buy them.).

Bryn was feeling much better. He took a shower in the middle of the afternoon, before Albert and June arrived for a visit, and his appetite was convincingly back. He ate a lot...but I was also focused on another kind of fun: Alissa's new hat.

She didn't know about it yet, but Bryn, Albert, June, and Berta all knew.

I had bought it for her online, from www.hats.com, and even found a coupon code on another website. It was soft, collapsible, with a brim folded upwards, round, and made of burgundy red velvet cloth. It had 3 cloth roses with green leaves decorating the front, and had been delivered that afternoon.

It was a complete secret. I showed it to her parents while they were here, and then wrapped it in pretty pink paper. The only problem foreseen, one that couldn't be confirmed until Alissa actually tried the hat on, was size. It was offered only as a one-size-fits-all product, so I had taken a risk. Albert pointed out that Alissa had the "Otterman head" – a large hat size.

Then Albert said that he would buy it off of me for June if this didn't work out. I told him, despite attempts to pay for half of it if Alissa kept it, that he could only pay if June got it.

I wanted quiet Alissa to have a social life – as in dating. She did have fun with her French and English book clubs, and did go out to eat with vegetarians and club members, but she had no boyfriend. Also, it was cold out. She had been wearing nothing on her head but the hood attached to her black down coat in this freeze.

She wrote to me when I asked her about hats that she wasn't stylish like me. She thought that my hat looked great on me, but that she didn't wear hats. Yeah…well, let her try it out. I was not as stylish as she imagined. She and I both had mothers who were more fashionable and chic than we were ourselves, so I thought it would be fun to go ahead and give this a chance. Berta thought Alissa would love the hat.

Hilda and her Russian-American friend Nikolai stopped by and took away ALL of the garbage and recycling. And she told us what her father's bad behavior this weekend was all about: her report card. He had anticipated that it wouldn't be good, so he had made her miserable in advance. Then it arrived, and he looked at it. It was better than he had assumed, so he said nothing, apparently chagrined into silence. The nerve of him! Elah just said that he had made a big fuss over nothing; that it had all worked out fine.

What a rotten thing to do. He had been terrible, ordering Hilda out of the apartment and embarrassing her in front of her boyfriend. Riley had given her an engagement ring. They were both 15 years old; who knew how that would turn out.

For dinner, Bryn and I ordered from the Greek diner (the Chelsea Square Restaurant). He got pasticcio (Greek lasagna: cheese, pasta, meat, peas, carrots), and I got a Muenster cheese omelet. And then he ate more than a quarter of his dinner, plus all of his matzoh ball soup minus the two matzoh balls. I told him that someone castrated a matzoh so that he could have those, but that then they didn't eat them. He seemed amused. He only left them because he got full.

Later, he wanted strawberry ice cream, and he ate it all.

I gleefully commented that the little appetite demon had left.

Next fun event to plan for: the movies!

Or maybe something else fun…he was talking about going to Cassie's place in Goshen the weekend after this one. I pointed out that that was Valentine's Day weekend (it would fall on a Saturday). He said that that might just mean that Damon and I would be alone!

Twilight...and Milkshake Time

Damon was coming here that weekend, he had told me – definitely. He didn't care that the bus ticket would cost a bit more – he was coming! We would see a movie and eat out. Insert partying emoticon here.

So it was back to reading *Twilight*, I guessed, and feeling good for a while.

It seemed that we could have more of Bryn and enjoy it too.

At some point during the cold weather, Bryn had asked me for some legal advice.

Berta was present; it was just the three of us sitting in his room that afternoon.

He was thinking about the details of his will, and he wanted to leave some money for Hilda so that she could attend culture events until she was 21 years old. He had always supplied funds for this, and he wanted to continue that for a few more years after he died. He planned to set aside $25,000 for that purpose, and leave Berta in charge of it.

The question he had for me was, should he just designate that in his will, or set it up as a trust? What would be the risks benefits of either method?

I knew what to tell him without much thought; it helped to know something about the people involved. Rudy had made his one abortive attempt at starting a gourmet restaurant, only to have it fail when he couldn't get a liquor license by opening day. He might want to start a catering business at some point.

Explaining my thinking to Bryn with Berta listening, I said that a trust was definitely the way to go. The reason was obvious: with every promised good intention of giving the money back at some unnamed future time, Rudy would manage to get a hold of that money if it weren't legally tied up and protected as a trust fund. If the catering venture didn't work out, the money would be lost. If it were protected as a trust, the intent of the donor could not be thwarted.

That was it – that was my advice.

Bryn seemed to buy it, and Berta said nothing. She just nodded like it made the most perfect logical sense, which I knew that it did. I had taken the trusts and estates course at my law school. Although I didn't remember many specifics off the top of my head, the overall lessons of caution when dealing with human nature had stuck. The course had served its purpose, it seemed.

We didn't think about this much again until the spring, when Bryn and Albert went to see their childhood friend, the attorney, and actually make the will. They had it witnessed at that time as well; they told me that the other attorneys in the office just came in and did that, and then signed on the appointed lines.

So that was that.

We had plenty of other things to think about in the meantime.

Bryn's lovely ability to enjoy life was back, and he was eating and having some fun.

He went out with some friends from his 8th grade class one night – and with Dionne, who had just returned from Savannah, Georgia, and from Colorado. The friend had just completed – and sent a copy to Bryn – a 10-year book project. It was a history of Mormons in the United States, from Brigham Young to the present. Bryn hadn't seen the author for a few years because he lived in Boston. He invited Dionne to come along, and came home in a great mood, absolutely delighted with his older daughter's conversational skills. That was nice.

Dionne's in-laws were very wealthy, and had homes in both Georgia and Colorado While she had stayed with them in Savannah, she did some amazing decorative artwork in their mansion, painting pillars and a bathroom to look like marble. It was something she had learned the previous winter in Belgium. She did several kinds of marble, and took photos with her digital camera to show us all – before and after shots. They looked amazing; if she hadn't told us it was paint, I would have wondered what quarry it all came from.

We all admired the photos when she and Bryn came back.

Berta and I watched *Bones* until they came home. Before that, we had gone out to dinner.

I was feeling quite pleased with everything, and part of it was because Damon had called and agreed to deal with the taxes this year – so I was going to be free of that! I told Berta about this, and she did not understand why filling out forms...and figuring out what to put in the forms...would make me a basket case.

For the past several years, I had been forced to handle the taxes because Damon was busy working, and because he couldn't understand why someone with a law degree couldn't do it.

He understood now.

Reason One: A law degree is NO preparation for filing tax forms. All we get for tax education is a class with cases to read and lectures to take notes from, with a multiple-choice exam at the end. There is absolutely NO training in preparing tax forms. Our professor was very entertaining with his cardboard box of course exhibits, but that did not prepare us for tax forms.

Twilight...and Milkshake Time

Reason Two: Anxiety gripped me like a vise when I tried to do the taxes. I saw static and hyperventilated. The mere thought of figuring the taxes out terrified me – how was I possibly going to get it right? I had to have the right forms for some very complicated self-employment taxes. And copying them over to make a nice, neat copy made me a nervous wreck. I found myself worrying frantically about how to pay what we owed or getting audited.

For the past few years, thanks to Damon not having all of the necessary papers ready for me to work with, we had often been stuck filing late forms to postpone everything. Once, we even filed more than one year's worth at a time, because we had just gotten married and I found that Damon had some complex stocks sales to compute. We asked our friend Mack to help us; he had taken a course in tax preparation, and loved to do this torturous task.

Mack thought out loud about how he calculated everything; the constant talking was as upsetting as the topic. He made errors in computations and had me start over in the middle of hand-copying. At that point, I would start crying. Or he would check the stock market, freak out about his assets, and run off. He went to the library and came back hours later.

So Damon was handling it this year – the torture session with Mack, and the papers. We didn't put his name on the forms as the preparer – we just took responsibility and signed. If the I.R.S. sent us a demand for a little bit more money, we just paid it. Some years we didn't owe a cent, because we earned no money. I hated it; it just scared me so much every year to think about our lives, reduced to numbers on paper, knowing that our social security contributions were nil.

What I wanted was to be able to afford an accountant to do it all for us – but that would take a few hundred non-existent bucks. Damon would present me with the papers to sign this year, after enduring Yakkety Mack. We usually paid Mack with gourmet food. I couldn't do that this year, and I certainly couldn't have Mack anywhere near Bryn, stressing him out. Damon would have to deal with it all so that Bryn could be blissfully unaware of it as it was happening. Damon had promised, and I just felt so relieved. I would send Mack fifty dollars this year.

Aside from that, I was busy helping my favorite editing client and co-author, Massoumeh Parsi, Ph.D. and outspoken reformist member of the 6th Iranian Islamic Parliament, get her green card application materials in order. At last, she had decided to just bite the bullet, pay lots of fees to an immigration attorney, and arrange to stay in the United States. She couldn't go home to Iran; activists were typically arrested and held in Evin Prison indefinitely. The next task was to do yet another edit of her curriculum vitae. I really liked doing that; I was her original

The Slamming Door

editor of that document, which had been unformatted and hard to read the first time I saw it.

Meanwhile, the *Twilight* series of vampire novels was utterly and delectably addictive. When I finished the first one, I had walked all the way back to The Strand and bought *New Moon*, which was the second one. It didn't take me long to devour it. I read fast.

After that, I had walked up to Madison Square Garden on 8th Avenue, where there was a Borders Books & Music store over Penn Station, and bought the remaining two, *Eclipse* and *Breaking Dawn*, plus the music that went with the first movie, using a gift card that my mother had sent for Christmas. Then I was all set; I settled into a groove of escaping into the world of Forks, Washington over and over again.

Cold or not, I couldn't wait to get those books. Reading this series reminded me of how absorbed I was by the *Harry Potter* stories. These stories didn't have anywhere near as much detail as J.K. Rowling's epic tale, but I didn't care.

Even though I could see flaws here and there and had gotten out a pen to fix some missed edits (in black, so the copy looked as it should have been), I found that the story made for the perfect escape I had been longing for. I was so upset about Bryn and the lack of money for a life with Damon that I wanted a good, long story with engaging characters to forget myself with.

Bryn thought it was hilarious; he said that now he knew that all I needed to keep occupied and enthralled was a good vampire. He didn't realize that the thrill wasn't just Edward.

Bella was fascinating, and I felt an affinity with her. She wasn't into clothes, and neither was I. We each liked a few nice items, and then just wore them over and over. We would much rather have a good book than anything else, we were loners, we were physically awkward, and it all added up to wondering whether or not she might have Asperger's...though I doubt that Stephenie Meyer planned it that way.

Regardless, reading the stories was like sucking up the most delicious, perfect, memorably and simultaneously sweet-and-tart freshly-squeezed orange juice; I remember every detail with no effort, because I am enjoying it so much. That orange juice metaphor is my favorite one for describing how I read when I really love a work of fiction.

This has been my experience many times, whether I was learning about something that I really loved to know all about – outer space law, women's studies, American women's herstory, Middle Eastern women – or reading fiction, such as *Star Trek*, *The Lord of the Rings*, or the *Harry Potter* series. I was so glad it was happening again, now, while I was so unhappy.

Twilight...and Milkshake Time

Hilda asked whether she could borrow one of my *Twilight* books for her boyfriend; I didn't promise one way or the other. I didn't want to let any of these books go. I just read them over and over again, because I could read fast and I still needed the escape that they offered.

When I had my next chance to talk to Berta face to face, I told her this.

She told me that I was under no obligation to lend those books out and to just forget about it and not feel guilty about keeping them. Case closed; I would do just that. It seemed crazy, but I didn't care.

Hilda had been in for another visit with Bryn that week, one in which she stood in front of him but didn't settle in to chat for very long. He asked her how she had liked the *Twilight* movie, aware that she had – along with the rest of her peers – read the book first.

"Oh! My! God!" she answered, "It was so bad," and then proceeded to just go off on it like it was the most flawed piece of entertainment ever, not that she had seen enough movies in her short life to know that. Bryn and I just let her rant until it faded out, which it did shortly.

But I was privately annoyed. Who had died and made her the arbiter of what was cool?!

Teenagers, whether that meant today's teenagers or my peers when I was a teenager, had always annoyed me by acting this way. I like what I like and don't appreciate any suggestion that if someone liked a thing that another person wasn't impressed by, then that someone was a fool.

Comparing a movie production with a book fascinated me; things must sometimes be cut or their sequence rearranged to cope with the time constraints of movies. Not so with a book. Aside from that, enjoying both was just fun; I am a visual person, and a book only goes so far in bringing a story to life, but a book has the advantage of offering much more detail and depth.

If I weren't so nervous about the present and the future, I would have moved on and read other stuff, but I just couldn't right now. *Twilight* was still the perfect tranquilizer.

Bryn had just met with his doctor that morning about the next round of poisoning (I thought of it as chemotherapy with quotations around the word "therapy"), which would be a simpler recipe. The doctor said that a stabilization has been achieved – insert partying emoticon here – and that the next round would begin on Tuesday, February 17th.

So...there would be more chemotherapy, I thought unhappily. The doctor had decided that she shouldn't just stop using it altogether. But lighter doses would be a lot easier to endure.

All of this meant that there would be no more late-night puking and nausea at the mere whiff or sight of a plate of food. Bryn would be able to eat meals during the next rounds of chemotherapy. How exciting…even though he was broken, he would live a bit longer and he might actually enjoy a lot of it.

Albert went with him to hear all about it, with June in tow. He would be getting his next dose at Cornell University's Hospital on that same day. He was so cheerful about it all! He still insisted on being the one to go to the doctor with Bryn this time because he had been studying up on chemotherapy for years, so he knew a lot about it, and wanted to keep track of the changes in his brother's treatment.

They called me from Rafaella's on the corner around noon, wanting me to meet them, so I did. That was how I heard all about this. It was fun chatting with Albert about law school, teaching, working for a thorazine-infused nut-job of an attorney, and working at Williams-Sonoma.

On the way back, we saw a mail-cart on the street, seemingly abandoned. Albert quietly said to me, "Let's take this guy's mail cart." Of course he didn't mean it. The postal worker was just coming back out of the building it was in front of.

No sooner did he say this than June came up to me, clutched my arm, and said, "We should take some letters out of this mail cart!" with a mischievous gleam in her eye.

That was hilarious – I laughed and pointed out what they had just said, each without noticing that other was saying it! I caught up to Bryn, who was just a few paces ahead, and told him that his siblings were trouble-makers – had he heard what they were just suggesting?!

He had, and he laughed.

I left them all at the door and took off to run errands, which I finished before they left Bryn's room; very efficient. With that accomplished, I settled in front of the computer to write the anecdote up. It was a lovely Friday afternoon, so writing felt like a pleasant escape.

Too bad I couldn't do it more often.

One cold evening, Bryn went to see a different doctor – perhaps an endocrinologist, though I dutifully paid little attention – and he brought me with him. On the way back, he wanted to stop for take-out at a place called the 2nd Avenue Deli, which was near the Henry George School but relocated from 2nd Avenue. He liked it, and hadn't been there in quite a while.

We went in and he ordered matzoh ball soup after the briefest glances over the menu, then handed it to me and sat waiting on the front benches. He wasn't very hungry; he just wanted that. The place reeked of cabbage, pickled foods, liverwurst, boiled meats…in short, everything I hated. The fun part of it was seeing an item on the menu entitled *Instant Heart Attack*.

Twilight...and Milkshake Time

So...this was the unhealthy diet that Bryn had liked, the one that, combined with the Greeks' diner, had contributed to his vulnerability to cancer. I didn't realize it yet, but fussiness about food is a big issue with Aspies, and I tend toward healthy food choices. Added to that was the fact that I was now terrified of this diet not only because it had always been the sort of food that had to be choked down, but also because I was convinced that eating it would make a person die a death by cancer. I stared at that menu for several minutes, not saying anything.

I couldn't find anything on it that I could eat, and Bryn picked up on that.

To my surprise and delight, he said we could just get me something off of one of the take-out menus we had at home. Of course this was his reaction; he had been revolted by certain food smells repeatedly with each round of chemotherapy-inflicted misery. He knew to an extreme extent how I felt.

I got vegetarian Indian food that night – okra, basmati rice, dahl, and mango lassi.

It was during this time – still in the cold weather – that Berta decided to get some lovely, furry winter slippers for her father. She had free shipping with an L.L. Bean credit card and could have stuff sent either to work or, if it wasn't for herself, to Bryn's place.

When the box arrived, they proved to be the really great kind with pale brown nubuck leather on the outside and soft creamy fleece on the inside. They even had rubber soles. I opened them up on Berta's instructions and checked them against the invoice; no problem. Then I showed them to Bryn.

Bad news: he didn't like them.

Sure, they were the very best, but they were too heavy, thick and hot to wear.

He promised to handle any awkwardness about this with his daughter, and I went online to look for alternatives now that I knew what he didn't like. L.L. Bean only had more of the same...which had been great all my life in Connecticut, where houses tend to be cold.

But here in Manhattan, the apartment felt like summer in winter. The heat was included in the rent, and came from old-fashioned heaters – metal ones that banged a bit when started up. I could understand why Bryn didn't want the warmest slippers on the market.

Switching to Lands' End, I quickly found the perfect thing and showed Bryn. It was more nubuck on the sides and soles, but no rubber soles and no fleecy insides. The soles on these were a bit thicker than the sides, but that was all. The tops came in a thick felt or flannel, in various

The Slamming Door

colors. I ordered Bryn a navy blue pair. They arrived a few days later and he took to wearing them constantly, except when he went out.

His feet had swollen slightly, and he had given up wearing his dark brown leather shoes, the ones that I had seen him with since I had met him; he now wore pale blue canvas slip-ons that he had worn when since just before his diagnosis, in the summer. He must have worn brown leather shoes almost daily for his entire adult life, judging by the photos in the picture frames on his bedroom wall. There was one frame that accommodated several images, all clearly from the 1970s. Bryn and Albert were both there with their daughters, who were playing together.

Berta looked exuberant, even boisterous, while Alissa looked cautious and quiet.

As the winter wore on and started to warm up slightly, Albert developed a habit of showing up in the middle of the afternoon without June (he left her at the Alzheimer's care group). We would hear the door open and close, and then a loud shout: "It's milkshake time!"

Bryn and I would look at each other, startled at first, but after the first couple of times we got used to it. Albert was buying the milkshakes at the dreaded Greek diner, chocolate for me, vanilla for himself, and strawberry for his brother. Bryn loved strawberry best.

The milkshakes were dreadfully, uncomfortably, sickly-sweet.

Eventually, I found out what went into them when I walked by and asked at the bar: ice cream, milk, and a heap of sugar. The flavor of the ice cream determined the flavor of the shake. There wasn't much measuring going on, either. The man behind the counter just tossed in the ingredients, put the cover on, and ran the blender.

I was appalled. Cancer thrives on sugar. Albert was just trying to stuff his brother with more calories, but in the bargain he was loading Bryn's system up with the wrong thing.

I wondered what I could do about it; the chocolate milkshakes were a thoughtful treat from Albert, but after the first few, I had told Bryn that I found them sickening and couldn't face any more of them. I also felt bad telling Albert this, because it was so nice of him to bring them, so Bryn did it for me. He was so adept at phrasing such things that Albert wasn't at all offended.

What could I do about Bryn's milkshakes, though? He found them to be quite a bit sweeter than he would like, too. I thought about it some more.

There was that Waring blender that I had gotten when I first arrived; it hadn't seen much duty since the spicy tomato and carrot juice drinks, just before Bryn signed on with the osteo-oncologist.

Twilight...and Milkshake Time

And then there was me, with my gourmet cooking and baking skills. I could create recipes, and had a proven track record of delicious ones. I would create a milkshake recipe with less sugar in it.

It was really quite easy, once I sat down alone and brooded over it for a few minutes. The trick was to realize that ice cream already contained sugar; there was no need to add any more. I told Bryn my idea, and he was eager to try it out, so I bought the ingredients and proceeded with my recipe, which was as follows:

Clarisse's Berry Milkshake

2 cups fresh cut strawberries, raspberries,
blackberries or a combination of those
2 scoops Hagen Daas vanilla bean ice cream
2 cups low fat milk

Put all ingredients together in a blender on the high setting until pink.

Serve.

Makes 2 servings.

It looked beautiful as I made it, and at every phase. The berries were so pretty all laid out on the cutting board, nice red strawberries. I started with Bryn's favorite berry; it was only later that we got adventurous, trying other combinations of berries. (Once, we tried it with blueberries mixed in, but neither of us liked it that much, and so we didn't have it that way again.) The ingredients looked lovely in the blender, layered together just before I put the lid on and ran the motor: berries, ice cream, and then milk poured over it all.

The result was a bit thick and creamy, and it was delicious.

It wasn't overly sweet, and we all knew what we were consuming.

Albert stopped buying milkshakes, and I stole his announcing line. He didn't care; he loved the recipe too, and joined us with it many afternoons.

Whereas the diner's milkshakes had arrived in clear plastic cups with lids and straws poking through them, my concoction was served in large mugs. That probably cut down on the quantity of liquid that we were all consuming, but Bryn got pretty full from it anyway.

The Barnes & Noble authors mug that I had given him became his milkshake mug.

The Slamming Door

I used my McNulty's mug, and Albert had the MoMA one. He went there a lot with June, so it seemed fitting. We spent many a cozy winter's afternoon in Bryn's room enjoying the strawberry and other berry milkshakes.

But I was just foolish enough to tell the whole truth about mundane things to people.

I told Berta all about this, thinking that she would be pleased that I was doing something that was a bit of work each afternoon to stuff her father with some tasty and nutritious calories.

She did seem pleased, but suggested, "Put Ensure in instead of milk."

Hmm. I had no objection to the idea of tampering with the recipe, but would Bryn go along with it? He had become hypersensitive to every taste and would not accept surprises or changes to his diet...not unless the doctor directed something. He had quit the Pedialyte, too.

I ran the idea by him, figuring that since he was dying anyway, he might as well have as much control over his food as possible. It's what I would want if I were dying. I must have reasoned my care-giving actions with that mantra a million times while I was there.

His response was terse and succinct: "No."

Fine with me; I just kept making the milkshakes with all natural, regular ingredients.

I shopped for the ingredients mostly right around the corner at the grocery store on 8th Avenue, and one afternoon I got a wonderful surprise: a glimpse of a little cat, a shorthaired black-and-white one, running across the back of the store, by the refrigerator units at the back.

C.P. liked to sneak upstairs during the store's open hours, which is how we met. I caught her under the egg shelves.

Twilight...and Milkshake Time

Thrilled, I rushed back there to get a closer look, and managed to stop the cat under the eggs and grab it. It was so silky and friendly! I carried it up front to ask about it. The staff thought it was a boy, though it turned out to be a girl later on when they took it to the vet for its shots. They were going to keep it for rodent control, and because it was such a nice cat.

Her name was C.P., which stood for City Produce. She had stowed away in a truck with that name, and arrived in the late winter. The story was amusing: Bananas, good. Oranges, check. Kitten, oh wow! Let's keep it! When I had the chance, I brought Berta to see the kitten, and it was a good thing that there was something cute to distract her with.

She called back later in the afternoon after suggesting the Ensure, and I told her that I had run her idea about altering the milkshakes by her father, and he had said no. Silence on the other end of the line. I moved on to other things quickly, such as the idea of meeting this new grocery store cat. She was in, of course. The next time she came over, we went to see that kitten.

After dark, when the store was closed, the kitten was allowed the run of the store.

The Slamming Door

I supposed that there was just no chance of pleasing Berta with each and every move that I made, but then I was really here to please Bryn and to give him as comfortable and easy a death process as I could.

So be it: I would concentrate on making Bryn happy.

If someone was angry at me for the decisions that I made later on, I would just hold that anger against them. That was how I would steel myself against any onslaught of negativity.

I was the one who was there with Bryn, having to make decisions on a day-to-day basis.

If other people – whoever they turned out to be – disagreed with them, then they should have quit whatever they were doing and taken my job over. If they didn't do that, then too bad.

But Bryn wanted it to be me with him, taking care of him.

I was on his side about the decisions he made; whatever he wanted, I would deliver.

It wasn't as though he would last any longer if I fought him on any point.

We had no crystal ball, no way to know how long he would live, how long he would enjoy living before life became a state of physical misery and humiliation, and so the wisest course seemed to be to just keep him as happy as possible.

I was miserable a lot of the time.

I wanted to be able to afford to live with my husband in the United States, and he was sleeping on a laboratory floor to do experiments. I saw no end in sight to it. I saw no sign of financial security. When I read or watched the news, I saw no indication that there was a job for him to get let alone one that would last long enough to justify the investment of moving all of our household possessions anywhere.

The only things that helped were the milkshakes and the *Twilight* books.

Chapter 30

Valentine's Day Visit

Valentine's Day came on a weekend. Bryn left with Cassie on Thursday, and Damon arrived on Friday. He left before Bryn returned on Sunday, because the bus left at noon, so there was no chance for them to see each other, not even for a few minutes. I'm sure that that was fine with Bryn; he said many times that he couldn't handle overnight guests because he was sick, and sounded upset at the mere idea.

When the visit was over, I had a lovely collection of Valentine's Day trophies – the perfect love card from Damon, a dozen roses, plus other cards from Aunt Joan, my father and Cookie Cat, my mother (who put a one hundred dollar bill in hers), and Cassie. Cassie also gave me a rose and a cute gift.

Damon and I saw *Gran Torino* on Friday and then went for Dim Sum, something we had not been able to do over Christmas thanks to the galloping gastrointestinal virus that we both had. I had found the restaurant then, but we couldn't enjoy it. It was in Chinatown, on East Broadway and Catherine Street, called Dim Sum Go-Go. The food was interesting, though it was hard to avoid finding pork in almost everything.

The most entertaining moment was when Damon told me that he was sure that the man at the large round table just a few feet away from us was a famous actor. I looked, and agreed – but I couldn't remember his name or which movie or show he had been in until later, when I could get at the Internet. Sure enough, it came to me then: Will Patton of *No Way Out*, *The Punisher*, *Armageddon*, and others. He was sitting with a mixed group who did not appear to be actors; they were most likely his agent and some other behind-the-scenes colleagues. We left him alone.

On Valentine's Day, a Saturday, we saw *Defiance* and ate at a great place on Broadway called *Punch Bar and Grill*. It was named for the Italian Renaissance puppet character. Everything tasted wonderful, and I had some hard apple cider called Antoinette with my dinner. (I have always liked Marie Antoinette's aesthetics, so that was a fun idea. Plus, it was libel rather than truth that she said "Let them eat cake." She never said such a rotten thing.)

The food was amazing, and I enjoyed sitting with Damon in a back booth with a view straight down to the front of the restaurant. Outside, visible through the floor-to-ceiling front windows, was a huge, cast-iron mobile that depicted Punch. Around us were some couples, but also a few groups of women who clearly had no dates for the holiday, so they

The Slamming Door

had decided to all go out together and give each other cute little gifts. We often people-watched as we ate.

On the way home, Damon stopped and bought me that beautiful bouquet of a dozen red roses with baby's breath, fussing carefully until he had chosen the best one. We were at one of Manhattan's many small convenience stores with an outdoor array of floral arrangements.

Unfortunately, I was in a depressed mood. I didn't know when or if Damon and I would ever be financially solvent and independent, and therefore living together in the United States on a permanent basis. It was all I cared about, but I had no clear sense of the future. I just did not do a good job of enjoying the visit with my husband. It couldn't have helped that I knew that when we got home, he would just roll over and fall asleep as we watched a movie together.

Bryn had been asking if something was wrong with me. I just told him that I was feeling a bit morose over the uncertainty about when I would see Damon again. Bryn had also asked, at a pub where we ate on Sunday afternoon/evening, about any news of Damon making money. I didn't have any clear news about it. I told him so, then added, with some slowness to do so, that I had actually gotten quite morose (that was when I used the word) over that, and failed to properly enjoy the visit. With that, he apologized for bringing it up. I tried to entertain him over dinner by telling him all about growing up in Enfield, Connecticut, complete with stories about all the families that I grew up visiting with there. He enjoyed that.

It hadn't helped that immediately after his departure on Thursday, a day that I would have to myself, I came down with my period, a painful, cramp-ridden misery of a one. I had been sick to my stomach all week from it, and it hadn't even started yet. Terrific – pain and blood for Valentine's Day. Of course, the saint had died in a bloody and painful way, but that's not how anyone hopes to spend that holiday.

I did manage to clean the entire apartment, take a quick shower, and haul the laundry down to the cleaners before it started. Then I felt awful – an additional kind of awful to go with the week-long stomachache – just when I had intended to enjoy the *Twilight* series of vampire novels in peace. Just perfect, I thought. But at least I had managed to do the cleaning when Bryn wasn't around, which was ideal.

I kept my cell phone off that weekend, wanting to try to forget about life. With Bryn at Cassie's place, that was fine. I knew that Damon and I would only partially relax and enjoy the weekend, due to our perpetual lack of confidence in the future. We were incapable of normal romantic feelings while we lacked money, which meant security and calmness to us. Damon was even less capable of feeling romantic than I was, and

Valentine's Day Visit

because of that, I was in a constant state of gloom, because what I wanted most was exactly what I couldn't have.

All this reminded me of something that Elah had said a few weeks earlier: she used to get really worried about everything, but not anymore. Somehow, everything always worked out.

I hoped that would be true for us.

Meanwhile, I just lived in my mind. It was interesting in there, and I kept filling it with fascinating things, just as the dean of my school, William Smith College, advised us all to do in her welcoming speech when we first matriculated. I was endlessly good at doing that, reading history, women's studies, fiction, humor, Middle Eastern women's studies, you name it...art, fashion history (as long as the designer was a woman – that made it women's studies).

When Bryn came home, he had something for me from Cassie: a stone heart with a cat's paw print etched into one side of it. It was cute, and very nice of her. He had one from her, as well, plus a card. That was the first time that he asked how my weekend visit had gone, and I had to say that I had not done a very good job of enjoying it, and had not succeeded in focusing just on the weekend itself.

He didn't look too happy to hear it, but at least he cared.

Soon after Bryn came home, he was back on chemotherapy – but just one poison, not a mixture. And it was just one day's worth. Dionne took him to 3rd Avenue and 53rd Street on the appointed morning, diagonally across from the Lipstick Building (a graduated skyscraper of ovals). Toby Maddox was there when I arrived to carry out a "changing of the guard" as Bryn dubbed it. Dionne had somewhere else to go that evening.

Dr. Callahan was there, just checking in, and I asked her what to expect, telling her that for the previous three rounds the misery Bryn had suffered a lot from puking and not eating throughout the following week. She looked at me – I have a very direct, unflinching stare when I deal with doctors or other experts – and replied that there should be no ill effects, and then warned Bryn to force himself to eat.

There was no scolding of either one of us from her, I noticed. I won't put up with any of that from anyone. We were already miserable enough as it was. If she couldn't cure him and keep him feeling wonderful all the time, she had nothing to scold about.

He was tired from the treatment that night, but he ate dinner. Soon he was getting sleepy, after having swallowed all of his pills. I did errands for him that afternoon, and that was about it.

As I settled onto my bed with the *Twilight* books again, I noticed that I was on the second one, *New Moon*, in which Edward leaves and Bella is terribly depressed. My life was a parallel of that story right now.

The Slamming Door

I supposed I would just retreat into the world of fiction and my interesting mind next. Life just didn't hold much attraction for me, so I would live in worlds that did until I liked life again.

I used to like it. That was around the time that I was getting married, when I was so happy that the people around me must have wondered whether or not I might be on some drug other than just happiness at living out my own version of a fairy tale.

Odd...I knew then that the marriage that presents the image of following the pattern of a fairy tale day is often tough, but even then I had a sense that mine would be even more so, and that money would be a huge factor. Yet I went ahead anyway, convinced that this was to be expected, and that after a lot of terrible trouble, perhaps a decade's worth, life would improve.

Why not? Abigail Adams, the second First Lady of the United States, endured similar disappointments. John Adams was away for over three years as an ambassador first to France and then to the Netherlands, and he wrote her no letters. She was miserable, but it all worked out in the end.

I tried to keep that in mind as Damon was away and I read about lovelorn vampires.

Chapter 31

A Double Birthday Party

Matt and his niece Sorcha shared a birthday most years, and had their own every four years. This was because Sorcha's birthday fell on Leap Year, and his was March 1st. Berta decided to throw them a fancy birthday party over lunch at a restaurant on Broadway called Craftbar.

She sent out an invitation via e-mail. It said that the party would be held at 2 p.m. on Sunday, March 1st, at 900 Broadway. The group was to consist of her, Matt, Sorcha, Dionne, Bryn, me, and Alissa. Albert and June were busy selling their house on Martha's Vineyard, so they would not attend the party.

When I got the invitation, I immediately started thinking about gifts. So did Berta, as her messages indicated. She asked me to get some specific gourmet goodies at Le Pain Quotidien and have them be from me, and wanted to give me back the money. Her note said that she didn't want me to feel forced to buy stuff as she knew that I had limited funds.

I wrote back immediately; I said that I did not feel forced to buy gifts for nice people who had been very pleasant to me and whom I sincerely liked. Also, the idea of her selecting and paying for stuff that was to be from me was unappealing, I added. I am good at selecting things, and doing so shows evidence of my thought processes.

Matt and Sorcha were both intellectually curious people, so books would be the perfect gifts. Bryn agreed; I would do our shopping at The Biography Bookshop in Greenwich Village. Matt wished he had had the opportunity to attend college and loved history and historic house museums; Sorcha had a Ph.D. in neuroscience. I was sure I could find them some good ones.

I wrote to Berta, saying that I would do my own shopping, plus get the hazelnut butter and red raspberry jams that she had asked for. She certainly couldn't go; the place closed at 6 p.m., which was when she would emerge from her job. Yes, she could pay me back for that stuff, but it would be from her. Her next note had suggested that I look at scarves for Sorcha in some store – she referred to a "curiosity shop" – that I only vaguely remembered; I wasn't into that.

She might have meant House of Cards, that cool shop with the magnets, puppets of authors, composers and other intellectuals, cards, and animal skeletons, but I planned to get books. Berta had mentioned that Matt liked biography books. After enough note-passing on the topic, I headed out to get cards, gift wrappings, Belgian goodies, and Bryn's prescriptions. Those things were all fairly close by; I could get them, bring them all home, and then go on the longer walk into Greenwich Village for the books.

Soon I was done with that errand, making Bryn's soup for lunch and e-mailing Berta yet again, telling her how he was doing and that I would go out for the books after that.

Bryn was satisfied with the cards I brought back, which were from the store on 8th Avenue called Rainbows & Triangles. He liked that one, and so did I; everything didn't have to be from House of Cards, much as we all liked the place.

I duly reported it all – there were gift wrappings from The Container Store on 6th Avenue, Belgian goodies from 7th Avenue, cards and a prescription from 8th Avenue, a bill for Berta from this for $55.17, itemized, and her father was comfortable in his chair with everything he desired.

The wrought-iron statue called *The Family* in the park on Bleecker Street and Hudson Street.

It was a lovely, mild, slightly overcast afternoon, and I headed back out again with my cell phone on. Down 8th Avenue until it became Hudson Street, past House of Cards, onto Bleecker Street, and there, on the corner of Abingdon Square Park, across from the wrought iron statue

A Double Birthday Party

called *The Family*, was The Biography Bookshop. On the opposite corner was a branch of The Magnolia Bakery, with its usual long lines of people and machines wafting sickly sweet, sugary frosting smells onto the passersby.

After browsing the shop carefully and gathering four books, one for both Matt and Sorcha from me and Bryn each, I had a small pile ready. The only frustrating part of this was the fact that I couldn't get Berta on the phone to make sure that I was buying the right book for Matt; it was about the Revolutionary War, a hardcover one with a battle scene on the cover. Bryn answered his phone, though, and approved what I had picked out to be from him. I bought the stuff, went home, showed him everything, and wrapped it up.

Often, Bryn would dally when there were cards to write, but as we only had one more day, he got on with it fairly soon. I did everything all at once, including the cute bags with tissue paper sticking up and out for the gourmet goodies. All set for the party, I could forget about it until it was time to leave for it – which was just the way I liked it.

Sunday rolled around and Bryn and I got a cab; he wasn't up to walking the three wide city blocks east, but he was in fine form to enjoy a party. He wore his soft black wool hat from Dionne, olive green Dockers, and a sweater. By this point, Berta and Cassie and I had replaced a lot of his clothes, and not just the pants and belts. Berta and I had sifted through everything, bagged up the outsized stuff off for the Salvation Army on 8th Avenue, and I had lugged it down there. Bryn now had lovely new wardrobe of dark blue and dark green shirts and sweaters. His old polo shirts were fine, though.

When we got to the appointed spot, I looked around in dismay. Where was this place? New York City's buildings were forever being renovated and so many of them typically had scaffolding and dark, boxy awnings covering them at street level. We couldn't see the sign for Craftbar. Bryn had his cane, a beautiful wooden one with a top shaped like a Spanish language sueño, one that Cassie's father had used. I wanted him off his feet and settled as fast as possible.

Not to worry; Bryn spotted the sign in the shadows as I rushed about, flustered. I hurried back over to him and we calmly walked into the restaurant.

Berta and Matt were already in there with Sorcha, and Alissa and Dionne appeared almost as soon as we did. Soon we were all settled in the middle of the dining room at a big round table, smiling and comfortable. I was between Berta and Alissa, with Bryn on my right to Alissa's other side. Matt was next to Berta, of course, then Dionne and Sorcha. Gifts were piled in the center of the table.

The Slamming Door

But we didn't turn our attention to those until later in the party. For now, we looked around at the modern décor, the dim lighting, and I heard the songs of Coldplay in the background. I had just learned some of those, and decided that I really liked them.

Berta insisted that we each get an interesting drink, preferably alcoholic, plus an appetizer and an entrée, so we did. She had ordered a special cake, so that took care of dessert. We had some imaginative, delicious things: chickpea fries with black olive aioli (Alissa's); pecorino fondue with acacia honey, hazelnuts, and pepperoncini (mine); salad of fresh greens, radish, shallot, and pine nuts (Bryn's); orechiette with fennel sausage, oven-roasted tomato and ricotta salata (Berta's); pecorino-stuffed risotto balls and fried oysters with cucumber and old bay aioli (mine); fried eggs with fingerling potatoes, cippolini onions, and bacon (Bryn's); rabbit ballotine with morello cherries and pine nuts (Dionne's); skate with fingerling potatoes and sauce gribiche (Matt's). There were other dishes, but this list is quite long enough.

When Matt saw skate on the menu, he paused over it, wondering what it was.

I told him that it was a miniature ray fish and that Damon had tried it the previous 4th of July at a French restaurant, and he had really liked it. Sold; Matt really enjoyed it too.

There was also a delicious drink that I tried, a flute of blackberry champagne.

A Double Birthday Party

The cake was a beautiful devil's food cake with hazelnut buttercream frosting and hazelnut brittle shards for decoration plus, of course, the words *Happy Birthday Matthew and Sorcha* written in chocolate on top. It was absolutely delectable.

About halfway through the first course, a tall black man in his late twenties or early thirties walked up to our table, greeted Sorcha, and put a large glass fishbowl on the table in front of her – with one large, beautiful goldfish in it – wished her a happy birthday, and walked out.

We all sat there staring at it, stunned. How was she supposed to carry that home?!

And how was she supposed to properly care for such a time-consuming pet?! Fish require expensive habitats and a lot of cleaning and temperature regulation, or they die quickly. It was like, Happy Birthday, here's a problem for you. Sorcha announced that she would take it down the street to Petco after the party and see what was involved; if it was too much, she would return it and get the money. Good plan. She worked in a laboratory at the Rockefeller Institute; she had no time to spend on this.

Alissa was as quiet as ever, but she was smiling and enjoying her vegetarian dishes.

Berta was in her element, leading the festivities and clearly enjoying herself.

Matt felt bad when he opened my gift; he had already read it. Berta told me later that he was really upset that he had already read it, because I had chosen so well; it was a book that had really enjoyed. She quoted him as having said that the gift was given "from my heart." I took that to mean that I prefer to research a person before selecting a gift, especially if I have a good opinion of them. Matt was equally pleased with the next book.

All of the other books that Bryn and I presented went over well, however. Sorcha liked them; we had books that related to her interest in neuroscience, and she had not read them before. Berta gave her something pretty to wear, a scarf like the one that she had suggested in the e-mail, and they both were thrilled with the goodies from Le Pain Quotidien.

When the party was over, Bryn decided to go home, and as Berta and Matt wanted to go with him, I took off with Dionne and Sorcha to the Petco store at Union Square to see about returning the goldfish. It was just a few blocks south of Craftbar, right down Broadway.

Dionne was in a loud, bubbly, exuberant mood as usual, and wearing a tall, furry, Russian-style hat. She and Sorcha chatted merrily together as we walked down Broadway; I was left out of the conversation, but I was used to it and so walked on ahead, ignoring that. Being left out of a large percentage of conversations was just something that Aspies had to live with; although Dionne had done that to me before, I knew Sorcha didn't mean anything rude by it.

The fish section of Petco was downstairs, so down we went, where we saw the standard wall of fish tanks full of aquatic pets for sale and a counter next to it with two or three clerks. Dionne and Sorcha walked around and looked at everything. I walked right up the first clerk who wasn't with other customers and spoke to him.

The man looked at me with an expression of strong disapproval as I outlined the situation, prefacing it with the abrupt, unannounced and downright odd arrival of the goldfish. It was obvious that he agreed with me about surprising someone with the gift of a pet, especially without checking first to see if the recipient could handle the amount of care required for it.

I found Sorcha and Dionne and told them that this clerk now knew the whole story, and left them to it. Sure enough, to keep her gift alive, Sorcha would have had to spend another hundred dollars on a different tank, gravel, food, and a machine that would keep the water clean – a net for removing debris wouldn't be sufficient. She returned the fish and the bowl, only to find that the store had an undesirable return policy: a gift receipt was all she could get.

How ridiculous – she didn't have any other pets. What was she supposed to do, give her gift away to friends in the form of pet supplies and toys? Apparently; I guessed that my history book for Matt wasn't such a failure after all. It hadn't caused any real trouble.

Later that evening, I went through all of the photographs I had taken during the meal. There were plenty; people smiling and posing together, the appetizers and entrées, and the cake, plus the gifts and that stupid goldfish. I e-mailed them around to the partygoers as usual.

It had been fun; a good time was definitely had by all.

Chapter 32

At Desmond's Tavern Again After All

At one point, during Bryn's third round of chemotherapy, we had been returning from the Sloan-Kettering Cancer Center in a cab when it rolled past a bar that he had enjoyed many fun times in with his Henry George School crowd.

It was that Irish bar called Desmond's Tavern, and it was on Park Avenue.

As we went by, Bryn had looked up at it and remarked, sounding sad about it, that he supposed that he wouldn't have any more visits to that place.

I had another one of my Aspie moments then, feeling empathy – profound this time – for him without a change of expression on my face. Having no idea as to what to say that would be sincere and truly helpful, I simply promised myself and him – silently – that he would go back there at least one more time with his Henry George friends.

I am a very determined person, so I began to watch for the perfect opportunity for that.

A few weeks later, after Bryn felt a bit better and we had attended a showing of yet another black-and-white film noir at the school, I insisted that we go. Claus, Toby, and Piper Firman came with us. Piper had to leave after one beer, but who cared; Bryn was there again.

This was just a few days before Saint Patrick's Day, so seeing the bar's customary, year-round décor of paper shamrocks on the walls and the digital countdown-until-St. Patty's Day clock on the wall next to our table provided the perfect ambience. Matt had mentioned that in Ireland, there was no hype about St. Patrick's Day. It was just something used as an excuse to make money here in the United States.

We got Blue Moon beers – pints – and settled in for a couple of hours.

This was nothing that I would have had any interest in doing if not to please Bryn, but as I knew it mattered to him and he loved it, I was bound and determined that it happen. I settled in to spend the next couple of hours or so chatting with these guys, a thing which I found plenty of enjoyment in. Talking with intellectual men comes naturally to me, so I felt completely at ease.

My only problem was that there was no food with the beer, and Bryn wanted to share another pint with me, so I got drunk. When we went home, I had to go to sleep…urgently. A migraine suddenly threatened. I shouldn't have let Bryn talk me into that; one had been perfect.

At Desmond's Tavern Again After All

When I woke up 2 hours later and went in to check on Bryn, he was sitting in his chair, with his pipe and books. He knew exactly what had happened to me without being told, and thought it was hilarious.

Oh well...at least he had gone back there again.

Chapter 33

Blood Transfusion...with Toby Talking Boner Pills

Dr. Callahan decided that Bryn needed a blood transfusion just to build his strength up, so we went to the 53rd Street location, prepared to sit in a curtained alcove for hours on end.

Toby met us there and stayed with us for the entire time. He arrived part of the way though it all, after Bryn was ensconced in the chair and the IV of blood was hooked up.

We settled in with the newspapers and books that we had brought, and at one point, I went out and got some coffee for myself and for Toby; the nurses had brought Bryn whatever he wanted. We were there to keep him company while 2 pints of blood slowly dripped into him over a period of about 4 hours. It seemed like an easy enough job; all we had to do was hang out with him, chat, and stay in a good mood, and then I would ride home with him in a cab.

No problem, right? Everything was fine until about halfway through the first bag of blood, when Toby started musing about boner pills. Specifically, he discussed the pros and cons of each one that was currently on the market, how they worked, and then commented on the ads.

The gist of the comparison was that a boner pill would either cause a priapism and send the user rushing to the emergency room, or else it would stay in the guy's system until like magic, at just the right moment, when no one but his wife is home, he can benefit from it. Toby made great fun of each promise.

It went on and on, so without even looking up from my book, I said:

"Yeah, I know those ads. The one for Viagra has that "Viva Viagra" song; the one for Cialis shows a couple naked but in separate bathtubs outdoors; the one for Levitra uses a lot of sports imagery; they all end with a litany of dire side effects that can result from each one; and you're obsessed with them."

"I've seen that bathtub ad," Toby remarked. "It doesn't make much sense."

"No. Those separate tubs will be a bit inconvenient when the boner pill starts working," I agreed. "It seems as though the advertisers didn't think the logistics through on that one."

Toby loved that but, alas, wasn't done discussing boner pills.

I forget what else he said, but he kept on referring to them by name, and comparing the ads, even though I didn't see what more I could do with that.

Blood Transfusion...with Toby Talking Boner Pills

After a moment, a song from *The Prairie Home Companion* movie came back to mind:

> *Bad jokes, oh I love 'em,*
> *Bad jokes, can't get enough of 'em.*
>
> *Did you hear about the stolen shipment of Viagra?*
> *Yeah; police are on the lookout for hardened criminals.*
>
> *Bad jokes, oh I love 'em,*
> *Bad jokes, can't get enough of 'em.*

Toby loved that, and continued beating the subject to a stiff metaphor of itself.

He was like an adolescent boy who had deliberately gotten tongue-tied only to find that no one had told him to shut up. What was I supposed to do, tell a guy who was forty years older than me to change the subject? I wasn't uncomfortable, but it did seem that enough was enough.

I don't get embarrassed when it is someone else who is behaving badly.

Actually, I thought it was a bit funny, and had been amusing myself by wondering what the people in the next cubicle made of us. I knew that they were there, Bryn knew that they were there, Toby seemed oblivious to the fact that they were there, and I kept glancing pointedly at the curtain and back at Bryn.

I was waiting to see what he would do about this, but it took a while for him take action.

Finally, Bryn demanded a change of subject. "Toby, this really isn't a polite subject for a semi-public place. The people in the next section can hear us, you know."

I put my two cents in. "Yeah, you're providing prolonged, great entertainment for them."

Bryn nodded vigorously in agreement; giggling could be heard from the other side of their curtain. Toby agreed to stop at last.

Then I had a thought. "It sounds like you need to get out more if you're so focused on those pills. Isn't there any place near where you live that you could chat with some women your age? Maybe a diner or a book club?"

He looked at me for a moment, then said that there was a woman who ate in the diner near his apartment, but he hadn't talked to her. She usually read while she ate.

The Slamming Door

"Well, go talk to her."

He said he would. Then Bryn got to talking with him about current events and the economy, and I read my book.

Hours later, at home, I told Bryn that I had been thinking, "He's your friend and he's your age; you get him to stop."

Bryn grinned; he agreed with that.

Chapter 34

Mommy Visits

On April 8th, a Wednesday, my mother came to Manhattan to visit us.

She had Wednesdays off from her job as an office telephone triage nurse.

She took the train in for the day, and we proceeded to work our way through a previously arranged agenda, one that we had worked out via e-mail. She met me at Bryn's place, and as I was rushing about in the bathroom to get ready, she appeared. I could hear her talking to Bryn.

I hurried to come out and greet her, and she was smiling and pleasant.

It was weird to see her again after six and a half months away from her; all that time I had been emotionally distant from her after she had told me that she didn't want Damon in the house any more without supervision, and never overnight. I didn't care why; I was mad at her. No matter what I did (not that I did anything truly terrible), she still wanted me, but not him, and I couldn't accept that about her. It went against my ideas about what family meant. It also ruined my life-long image of having a husband with me at every family gathering.

Now she was there, standing in Bryn's Spartan living room for a visit. She had brought me a few of my spring clothes, some things I had mentioned in the e-mails, just a small amount that was easy to carry on the train. We had until about 4:30 p.m. before she would go see Dr. Leonardi in his new office. She hadn't been there yet, and he had been there for nearly a year.

The first thing we did was go out to lunch with Bryn at Le Grainne Café.

When it was over, we walked him home and then went exploring so that I could show her all of my usual haunts and anything else she wished to see that was somewhat close by. Bryn felt fine, so we took our time and she saw quite a bit.

We started with Chelsea Market, so that she could see all of its food shops, its one kitchen supply shop with a gelato bar, and the black granite benches and wrought iron organs on the waterfall railings. Next, I took her around the corner to the high-end boutique shops, one of which reminded me of The Closet in the novel *The Devil Wears Prada*. She was fascinated and delighted, and when we came out, she wanted to go somewhere else farther away: to an Eileen Fisher store. I looked at the paper she had torn out of one of its catalogues – all phone numbers, so I called one and asked where they were located.

The Slamming Door

My mother couldn't walk at fast paces like I did, especially in the pretty shoes she liked to wear, so I hailed a cab. She watched as I held up two fingers close together, and said she was impressed at what a seasoned New Yorker I had become. I said I was just copying my great-aunt Eleanore, who had shown me this when I was in my late teens. It seemed to me that my success was nothing impressive, and could be attributed to my long brown hair held back by sunglasses.

We went to 5th Avenue in the cab and got out in front of the store. She looked around, went into a dressing room, and bought a couple of things for herself. Then I took her out to see other stores; there was a Vera Bradley store, a Fishs Eddy store that she had never seen (the Alice in Wonderland and Wizard of Oz dishes were fun to look at), and there were the vintage clothing shops on West 23rd Street. She loved those; she often shopped in thrift stores and consignment shops in Connecticut. We even saw Tony the Tiger in the Reminiscences store.

She wanted to see Bryn one more time before getting a cab and taking off, so we took a cab back there. My mother wasn't in shape; she couldn't deal with the walk back, she told me. I suppose it seemed odd to me because tramping all over large areas of the city on foot had become second nature to me. It was also good exercise, something I could just build into my routine, I told her. She approved; she just couldn't manage it on a one-day visit.

Bryn was happy to see her one more time and chatted with her happily about what we had seen, then told me to go back out with her for the next cab-hailing, and that he was still perfectly okay at home alone. He was sitting in his blue Lazy-Boy chair with the window open in the sunshine, reading his books and watching the news channels.

So I did it; I hailed my mother one more cab on 8th Avenue, and made sure that she and the driver knew exactly where to go. East 68th Street between 1st and 2nd Avenues – and off they went. That was that; it was a good visit.

A long time later, after I was home again in Connecticut, my mother told me something.

While we were still in Le Grainne Café, after we had eaten and I had gone into the rest room, Bryn had told her that he preferred to have me stay with him and take care of him, not his daughters. My mother had wondered why he felt that way, and asked him about it.

His reply was that Dionne was just too busy and away too much, and he didn't want Berta to come stay with him, even though it could have been fit into her routine. Her Wall Street secretarial job was just a subway ride away, after all. But he didn't want her with him.

Mommy Visits

"I feel committed to her because she's my daughter, but I don't like her!" he said.

My mother was a bit startled, and Bryn admitted that it was terrible, but it was also true.

Wow. She was his own daughter and he didn't like her...

There wasn't much more that could be said about that.

A few days before my mother's visit, I had run an errand for Berta and Alissa. I had gone back to a pottery shop in TriBeCa called Color Me Mine and retrieved our painted pieces so that they wouldn't have to bother. We had all gone there the previous week and had a good time painting things. Berta had wanted to do this, and to hang out as a group, so Alissa and I had gone along with it. Berta had also paid for the pottery.

She had painted a platter a pale turquoise blue with word stencils that read "Believe," "Hope" and two other uplifting words. As for me and Alissa, we had not editorialized ours: Alissa had painted an Asian-style food bowl that came with chopsticks dark blue with some red spots, and I had painted a pitcher periwinkle blue with a pink heart on either side. I found time to drop Alissa's bowl on the way home; when I came back, I showed the stuff to Bryn.

"What's this "Believe" and "Dream" stuff about?" he asked me.

"I don't know – just some fun, fanciful words that Berta liked," I said.

He just grunted and shrugged, so I wrapped it all up in its paper and put it away for her. He liked the pitcher well enough; it looked useful. I think I might have put some flowers in it at some point that spring. My mother liked it when she saw it in my room.

Damon looked at the photo of the pitcher I sent to him and asked why we had done this at all. "To make Berta happy," I had replied. I had painted pottery when I was a kid, and again a few years before I got married to give a gift to my artist aunt. It was a water dish for her cat that was shaped like a cat, and I did an underwater scene inside. What could I say? It was fun.

In May, my parents went on their annual trip to Florida.

When they returned, a package arrived in the mail for Bryn from my mother. It was three different flavors of pipe tobacco for him to try that she had found while shopping in Florida. He said that they were some sort of unusual flavors, and that he liked them. When he smoked one of them, its scent reminded me of bitter chocolate.

The Slamming Door

He kept them in their little clear, plastic bags with the labels stuck on them down on the floor by his chair and puffed away happily, trying them all and then going back for more rounds. His corn-cob pipes were now steadily in use, throughout that spring, now that the tortures of chemotherapy were over with.

Bryn's sense of taste was back. He drank coffee, green Earl Grey tea, red wine, you name it, and he ate some of whatever he wanted without feeling nauseated. It was great, even though it meant that the doctor had changed her strategy to just keeping him comfortable.

We all took advantage of it while it lasted, enjoying restaurants, movies, and whatever else struck the fancies of each of us. We were having as much fun as we could while we could. Bryn was having a lovely time, living each day as if he didn't trust the good times to continue.

None of us did.

Chapter 35

La Chatte Nikita

Nikita came to stay with us when Berta and Matt went to California for a week late in April. Maybe their trip was longer; perhaps 2 weeks. I don't remember. I do remember that the cat arrived days ahead of time in the interest of efficiency.

She came early so that they wouldn't have any trouble making their flight on time, and ended up staying for the rest of Bryn's life because we just enjoyed having a cat around so much. Bryn loved her, and would let her get away with all sorts of naughtiness.

This was the man who had been so upset when his own cats had died that he had never gotten any more of them. He only inherited Gracie by default, when Berta moved to California, and when she died, he had figured that that would be it for him with a cat of his own.

Then he got sick, Nikita needed a place to stay, and we all figured why not? This is fun.

Berta had adopted her in California from a shelter that she had volunteered at for a while.

I knew that she had moved away without her pet cat only to adopt another one. Gracie had been pleasant enough, another fluffy female, and I had never asked why Berta didn't bring her. Perhaps the logistics of finding a place to stay in the beginning with a pet cat were too difficult to navigate. Hotels don't like to admit cats and risk having the rooms shredded.

That left Berta catless in L.A. – not a desirable condition. She met Nikita when she was a 3-month-old kitten in a cage at the shelter. The kitten, a fluffy black-and-white tuxedo female, had put her paw out to touch Berta and yowled like she was saying "Take me!"

Berta loved that sort of aggressive behavior, and said "Wrap her up!"

The other people at the shelter had asked, "Are you sure?"

She said yes.

They told her that no animal could leave the place without being spayed or neutered regardless of how young it was. Berta agreed to these terms, the deed was done, the vaccinations were administered, and she took the kitten home.

She named her Nikita because of a television show that was on at the time, *La Femme Nikita*, about a French ninja chick who was very aggressive, beating her foes up as she did her secret law enforcement work. I knew that story from a 1990 movie that had been on cable TV.

The Slamming Door

The name suited this cat to a tee; she was, as Berta advertised her, a little bitch.

I came to think of her as La Chatte Nikita because of that, patterning it after the TV character. But I liked her in spite of her nastiness because she was a cat. Nikita had good reason to be a cranky, cantankerous creature, however, because shortly after Berta had gotten her home from the shelter, the poor kitten had a terrible health crisis: her stitches popped. No one knows exactly why, how or when that happened, but one evening, Berta returned to find her guts hanging out of the incision. It sounded horrific and I'm sure that it was.

Back to the vet…but the vet's office was closed at that hour, so Berta had to take Nikita to an emergency vet. Emergency vets charge a lot more than the ones who are open for regular office hours. This one cleaned out Berta's entire savings at the time, which consisted of $2,000.

The stitches were re-sewn, an I.V. drip was attached to the kitten's arm, and Berta was told that she would have to nurse her back to health by keeping her close until the incision healed. The spaying surgery had been botched or done too early in Nikita's life or both.

Naturally, Berta rose to the occasion; she loved cats. She kept Nikita in a cardboard box under her desk at work, checking her constantly. The I.V. bag was changed often and the kitten was carefully fed and watered. After a while, she was completely healed.

But she never would allow anyone to brush her fur thoroughly, especially on her belly. That area stayed in knots, all matted up, permanently. No one could possibly blame her for that.

Her nails were another issue entirely; they had to be clipped.

I had a good pair of cat nail clippers that looked like short scissors, all metal with black rubber around the finger holes. Bryn remembered how easily I had trimmed Gracie's nails whenever Damon and I had visited him in the past; now I would have to groom Nikita's nails.

Everyone has to have manicures and pedicures, I commented dryly, but Nikita kicked up a terrific fuss. She snarled, growled, and even shrieked.

What the hell?! After a while, I realized that Berta had completely spoiled her; there was no other explanation. When Bryn protested my policy of enforced and therefore forced kitty manicures, I reminded him that because he could get a nasty scratch if this cat got angry and took a swipe at him…which she typically did when he tried to reclaim his own blankets. After that, I turned up the TV, shut my door, and sat on the little brat cat to groom her.

I had had cats all my life, and had trimmed their nails without fuss every time.

La Chatte Nikita

There was Charcoal, the short-haired male, black with a white spot on his throat. He was an outdoor cat and a hunter. When we moved, he stayed in...which made him very angry when he realized that he had become an indoor cat. I trimmed his nails and he let me. But he was always a lovable, cuddly boy.

Then there was Cookie Cat, a short-haired male with random black-and-white markings. He was always indoors. He let me trim his nails, too. I left him when I got married, and my mother bought a strange nail-clipping device that frightened him. When I returned to my parents as Damon traveled, I found it and heard all about it. I dubbed the gadget the Dick Cheney clipper because by the time it was maneuvered into position, the cat was hysterical from observing it.

Why prolong the agony?! I got out the black rubber-covered scissors and asked my parents how they could have failed to locate them. My mother just couldn't find them. My father said to throw out the Dick Cheney clipper. I did. Peace of mind was restored to the poor cat.

And then there was that short-haired female calico Kuwaiti cat, Scheherazade. Cute little black and orange and white calico cat in a harlequin suit that also looked like Desert Storm fatigues, I used to say to her. She was the cat that Damon had adopted on Failaka Island just after the Kuwait War had ended. She was playing with a cluster munition and starving – there wasn't much left to hunt there.

Scheherazade resisted arrest and grooming at first, but not for long. She sensed that I wouldn't take no for an answer, and I had those clippers that got the deed over with quickly. I held her in my lap, paws and feet facing outwards, and clipped them all efficiently while cooing at her that she was a nice cat.

Easy; Damon was impressed.

But Nikita would have none of it.

This was a problem because Bryn could not afford to get scratched. Cancer patients can get infected easily and die faster than cancer on its own will kill them if a cat scratches them. I had to keep this little brat cat's nails clipped, and that was all that there was too it.

Bryn had a fit whenever the cat started shrieking, though.

At first, I would do the deed whenever he was out with someone else. But after a while, that was not possible. So in later months, I would wait until we had no visitors, make sure that he was watching an interesting television show, turn on my TV also, and lock myself up with Nikita. The TV sounds gave me some cover.

Then I coaxed her into the center of the room, sat on her just heavily enough to pin her in place, and clipped all ten nails on her paws. The ones on her feet were sometimes a lost cause, but I usually managed to keep them short, too.

The Slamming Door

That was one aspect of cat care.

Others included litter box cleaning, food, water, beds, toys, and…interpersonal relations with La Chatte Nikita. This last issue was sometimes a point of contention.

When I coo at and talk to a cat, I tend to be a bit loud.

Also, I am bossy. I won't allow a cat to stick its face into my food.

Nikita was 9 years old when she came to stay with us, so I was amazed that she considered it to be her Goddess-given right to do this. Then I found out why: Berta always let her stick her face into anything she was eating.

This was new to me as I had always raised my cats to keep out of humans' food.

I had no interest in letting Nikita stick her face into mine.

Berta wasn't offended; she just laughed and watched me carry Nikita out of my room the first time that the cat attempted to do this. I had just served dinner to everyone – Bryn had his in his room, and Berta and I were eating on the bed with our plates in front of the TV shows.

Up jumped the cat, and I was just returning with my glass of water in time to see her try to lick the sauce that was around the fish and potatoes.

Outraged, I picked her up from behind and carried her, gripped comfortably under her shoulders and around her chest, into Bryn's room where I plunked her down onto his nice, soft bed. She yowled in protest and outrage.

I told him why I had done this, and he just nodded. Then I came back to my dinner, where Berta explained her cat's behavior, laughing.

Terrific; I had to tell her that I wouldn't allow that, and that I had never done so before.

This was after the trip to California. Perhaps Bryn and I ate out too often during her absence for either of us this to have come up earlier. In any case, we knew all about them now.

But my loud greetings were new to Nikita, and Bryn told me that I was scaring her as I said hello to her and that she was beautiful. How odd…no other cat had been startled by my voice before. Damon and I are both loud when we address cats. Sometimes I coo quietly at them, but only when the animal trusts me and vice versa. I wasn't about to stick my face close to La Chatte Nikita. I may love cats, but I'm not foolish.

Having her around was great fun nonetheless.

Having a cat in the apartment meant being its caregiver, and I had plenty of experience at that. Soon I knew every pet supply shop in the area. Petco and other big-box outlets were not nearby; the closest one of those was at the northwest corner of Union Square. So I shopped closer to home.

La Chatte Nikita

At first, I used the old litter box, a disposable grey plastic one full of litter that had sat there for over a year, since the last time that Bryn had cat-sat for Nikita before he got sick. I hadn't removed it because Nikita had visited for one evening the previous fall (that was the night that I met her, as Berta was on her way elsewhere with the cat and Matt in tow). Also, the thought of Bryn's place never having a cat in it again had depressed me.

That fall evening, Berta, Matt, Dionne and The Hornsby were all there when I arrived after dark. I don't remember where I had been; probably the local grocery stores. I was so pleased to meet Nikita that I took several photographs of her and posed her on my bed for some of them, calling out that I would come in and see them all after meeting the cat.

"No offense, but I have met all of you, and I haven't met her yet!" I called to them.

They all laughed and said none taken.

Little did I know that Berta would decide to permanently lend out her cat to us so that her father could enjoy Nikita for the rest of his life. When she did, she told me, "Clarisse, you dream of having a cat in here is about to come true!"

I was pleased when I heard the details. It was only later that our cat-lease was extended.

Then I was even more pleased.

So I got the cat a permanent, small plastic litter box, deodorizing litter box bags, litter, and Arm & Hammer litter deodorizer. Next, I got some canned food for her – Wellness brand, which is the good stuff – and eventually some new dishes as presents for Berta. They were just three bucks at T.J. Maxx. Berta was pleased, and took them to Long Island for Matt's house to use when the cat eventually returned there.

The cat soon got used to my loud voice whenever I fed her breakfast and dinner in the kitchen, telling her that she was a good cat and a beautiful little girl. I kept up a steady stream of this natter each time, and the cat enjoyed the food.

The whole thing was a ruse designed to get the cat's eye medicine, a gel in a spray can from the vet, to go down with just a spoonful of wet cat food – sugar to a cat. It worked.

Nikita also began to understand that I meant to be friendly toward her despite my loudness because I know how to smile at cats: this is done with one's eyes slitted and thus barely open. It's hard to see that way, but it's worth it. Staring with wide open eyes is viewed as intense anger by cats. One must communicate with cats on their terms, not human terms.

She even smiled back at me after a while.

The Slamming Door

People and cats are all different, and so we each take some getting used to.

And with that, we had a cat with us.

Soon we were back to focusing on other things, with the cat fitting seamlessly into our routines. Well, seamlessly except for the comedy and mishaps that are commonly associated with having a pet.

One night, Bryn was packing to go visit Kasey, laying everything neatly out on his bed before loading it into his black backpack. He liked to do his own packing, and I kept him well supplied with clean clothing from weekly runs down the street to the laundromat and toiletries from regular runs around the corner and two blocks of 8th Avenue to the New London Pharmacy, so he was easily able to get ready on his own.

Or so we thought…

He came in to my room suddenly to say that the cat had jumped onto his bed and pierced open his zip-lock bag of Miralax with her nails. (She was still giving me a hard time about grooming; we hadn't reached an accord on this yet.) White Miralax powder was all over the quilt. Wonderful, I thought…and told her, "Naughty cat."

I went in there and pulled the rubbish bin up to the bed, moving everything else out of my way. Then I lifted the quilt in sections, shaking it until the powder was all together, and finally dumped it into the plastic-lined basket; done.

We prepared another bag of Miralax and immediately put it into Bryn's book-bag.

That cat supposedly loved men more than women, despite having a woman for her main human companion. However, before the cat moved in with us, she had been home alone an awful lot with just Matt on weeknights.

Nikita had taken to climbing into bed with him as he slept and purring under the covers with him, until he told Berta that he was amazed by how attached to her he had become. Knowing that, I couldn't help but be surprised when they got back from California, came over to visit, and the cat smacked Matt on his arm, hard. Maybe she was mad at him for being away.

He replied in deadpan, calm tones with his musical Irish accent: "It's nice to see that you haven't changed one bit, Nikita."

Meanwhile, Berta had no particular reaction when I detailed all of the things that I had done to take good care of her pet. "The only

La Chatte Nikita

requirement for taking care of someone's pet is that it be alive when the person returns," she replied.

"That seems to be setting the bar awfully low," I commented, but left it at that.

I had seen Nikita in Matt's house in Hicksville, Long Island in early March, when I went out there on the train for a day. Nikita was under a mattress, up inside it, in the guest room. Berta showed me where she was and held up the box spring while I dragged the little beastie out.

Bryn had insisted that I go there at least once; he had gone once, too. I left from Penn Station, ate chocolate chip pancakes at a diner with Berta and Matt, saw Matt's house in Hicksville, rode around to see some the famous DNA campus at Cold Springs Harbor and some boutique shops in the same town, went to T.J. Maxx with Berta and got a new pink quilt (she bought a copy of *New Moon* there that evening), and we all ate at a lovely Indian dinner with them before coming back again on the train. I didn't want to stay overnight.

But I was glad to have seen the cat. Nikita was friendly enough then, staring at us in surprise once we extracted her. Berta had showed me the whole house, pointing out the cat's favorite places and habits as we looked around.

Berta had told me how she would have to get up in the middle of the night to keep Nikita company while she went downstairs to eat some dry cat food in the kitchen. I had never heard of such a thing. I have been known to get up late at night and serve a bit of canned food to a cat, but never to stay up and watch it be eaten, especially barefoot in cold weather. Berta also showed me how she would coax the cat up the stairs afterwards, one step at a time.

Now the cat was elsewhere, and she slept in Bryn's room every night.

One night in the spring, I came out of the bathroom after my shower and caught Bryn catering to the cat a bit absurdly: he was lying on top of his bed, which was still flawlessly made up in daytime mode at 2:30 a.m. (we both stayed up too late most nights), not getting under his covers because he didn't want to disturb the cat!

He was just stretched out around her in his red polo shirt and navy blue pajama pants, waiting for her to move. I walked right in, picked up that cat, and tucked him in, scolding him. He was sick – and thus well within his rights to move the cat and then settle her back into a comfortable position, which is what I did.

The Slamming Door

He was amused, and went along with that.

But before I moved either one of them, I shot a couple of photos of them together, just because it was so funny. Then I shot some more once they were tucked in. The cat wasn't even upset about being repositioned.

I e-mailed them to Albert, thinking that he would be amused, but his brother looked so thin and his hair was stubble, like a crew cut now that it was growing back in, so Albert found the images to be more depressing than funny.

Oh well...I guess I was getting too used to the gradual changes in Bryn's appearance.

The shock only seemed to register with me when I looked at older photographs from years past. When I saw how heavy he used to be, and how much thick white hair he used to have, then I was unnerved by the disease and enraged at it yet again. I had been trying not to focus on the upsetting aspects of it for a while. Sooner or later, I wouldn't be able to do that, I knew.

Bryn had commented to me that he was now back to the same shape and size as when he was a teenager, working as a camp counselor. He even showed me an old photograph in black and white of all of the camp counselors lined up in rows together, outside. Albert was in it too. There they were, teenagers with crew cuts in white polo shirts and shorts, with thick glasses on Bryn just like always.

Vianne sent me a musical card when she found out that the cat had moved in. "Meow, meow, meow, meow..." it sang, just like in the *Meow Mix* commercial. I opened it up and let it play for Nikita. She stared at it, mesmerized, then got bored. Oh well; I liked it.

Not long after that, I got the cat a present: a pale green, fleece, ring-pillow bed.

Petco was selling them for $9.99, with a dollar off if you had a customer card. I did.

The cat was thrilled with it. We put it onto a pile of old, folded quilts and blankets that Bryn didn't care about in the corner, right under the air conditioner. She spent hours curled up there, sleeping deeply.

When she was awake, she would often loll on Bryn's bed.

Soon I had quite a photo gallery of Nikita images to share with Bryn and Berta.

When summer came, Nikita took to alternating between her ring pillow bed and Bryn's Lazy Boy chair, sometimes fighting with him for possession of the seat. But mostly she would loll between his knees, long and furry, during the day. He loved it.

Late in the summer, after some family gathering in which Aunt Joan Orlov had left a large, glossy, paper shopping bag with rope-like strings (quite fancy), I found Bryn playing a game with the cat at 2 a.m. He was trying to coax the cat into the bag.

It took him a while, but finally she was part of the way in it. I helped her get settled and then sent the 5 or so images to Aunt Johanna Orlov. There was no reply, which made me feel silly. Odd…I would have thought that she would have been amused by the photographs.

On July 18, 2009, Berta came over and announced that it was Nikita's 9th birthday.

She intended to throw the cat a birthday party.

Fascinating…I had never known the birthdays of any of my cats, and so I had never done this for a cat before. Come to think of it, my parents probably would have stopped me, thinking that it was crazy and excessive.

But not here – no one was stopping us, and I was all for this celebration!

It was fun. We sang to her, and she looked at us like we'd lost our minds, but we didn't care; we just finished the song. Bryn watched us from his Lazy Boy chair and grinned at all of us. He seemed to find nothing odd about any of this.

Next, we went out to two pet stores to buy Nikita some new toys, and then to the grocery store to get some people food, beer, and smoked salmon to share with her. Berta told me that she did this every year. Mystery solved; Bryn was already used to the idea, and would never object to anyone else's idea of a good time.

We came home and I cooked up the food, got both Bryn and Berta to eat quite a bit of fresh melon – watermelon and cantaloupe melon, which were Bryn's favorites – and Berta also got some papaya. She loved that, and ate quite a bit of it. I'm allergic to it…a couple of bites and I'm gasping for air. No problem; I got some raspberries.

After we all ate dinner, I put the smoked salmon on a plate with some goat cheese and a bowl of crackers, plus a couple of forks. (Bryn didn't want any, but he had eaten a good dinner, so that didn't matter.) I also brought out a small bowl. Then I carried it all into Bryn's room, singing *Happy Birthday, Dear Nikita Cat* yet again.

The Slamming Door

This time she woke up from her bed and looked really interested – like she had caught on to what all this was about. She should have by then: we had just given her 4 new toys before dinner. She got up from her bed and came right over to me.

Berta look puzzled at the array and wondered what I was up to – the whole plate looked too much like people food. It was; I handed her the little bowl and told her that it was for bits of smoked salmon for the cat. Perfect – that was just what she wanted. She took some of the fish, ripped it to little shreds, and put it in the bowl on the floor. The cat was thrilled.

Bryn sat there grinning from ear to ear, watching it all.

When it was all done, the cat had her picture taken in her ring pillow bed, surrounded by a collection of new toys. She looked at bit overwhelmed but pleased as well. I thought we had just given her an absurd number of toys, but the deed was done.

There was no birthday cake – only smoked salmon. This was, after all, a cat's party.

Matt arrived a little while later and was goaded by Berta into wishing the cat a happy birthday, which he graciously did. Bryn wondered what he made of all this, so Matt said that he had wished Nikita a happy birthday for several years in a row now, and that he was used to it.

That was the first cat birthday party that I ever attended or participated in.

And people call me a crazy cat lady…

Chapter 36

Enjoying Life Until He Can't

Once the doctor decided to just stop poisoning Bryn and let him enjoy whatever time he had left before he couldn't walk and talk and live somewhat independently and with some feeling of enjoyment, he decided to throw himself into all of those things. He partied a lot more.

He went out to lunch with friends, lectured at the Henry George School, visited Cassie and Chip at their house in Goshen, New York – which meant that she would drive him there and back again – and did whatever else struck his fancy. Sometimes that just meant going out to eat with me in tow, along for the meal and conversation. He didn't always leave with a plan, so I would just follow him, going wherever he went.

In April, Bryn suddenly announced that he was going to visit Cassie, something that had hadn't done since before he found out he had bone cancer. There just hadn't been any time for that with all the treatments. Now he felt pretty good, and he wanted to go back there. He would be gone for a weekend, leaving me home alone in the apartment.

To tell the truth, I loved being home alone in a Manhattan apartment. Who wouldn't?

This happened several times that spring, sometimes for a week, but usually just for a weekend. On this particular weekend, right after he had left, Hilda came in to see me and make a request. Could I – would I – please leave on Sunday afternoon, all afternoon, and let her and her boyfriend be in my room?

That was the entire request. The rest was left up to inference; the kid wanted to be alone with her boyfriend so that they could have sex. She had to be kidding me, was my first thought. Then I thought, of course she isn't.

"No." I said with finality in my tone. The way I was raised – and I happen to agree with the way that I was raised on this point – you don't enable teenagers to have sex. Instead, you actively impede their ability to do so.

Add to that the fact that my sex life with Damon was pretty much nonexistent thanks to stress and constant time apart, and I was really annoyed that she would even ask me this. If I wasn't having sex in there, and I was a married adult, then I certainly wasn't going to vacate the premises so that she could. I felt infuriated, but of course didn't say any of this aloud.

"Pleeeeaaaassse?" Hilda begged.

The Slamming Door

Now I was getting really annoyed at her. I expect and require that when I say no, all requests cease. I don't like children, I don't have the slightest patience with a refusal to accept a no, and I have no interest in impassioned requests that I change my mind. Just take the no, shut up, and move on...and if moving means getting lost, so much the better.

I'm sure that this was a significant factor in why the kid ended up disliking me, but I just don't care. There is just no justification for her dislike. The hell with this. "No," was enough of a response. I gave no reasons, and shared no opinions on the matter with her. I may have added that it was my room, my place to come back to and be quiet in, but that was about it.

She gave up, left, and I watched movies and read books in that room that afternoon.

I told Berta about it, because the whole incident just felt awkward. I told her that I realized that Hilda had no room of her own, but even if she had, I doubted that her parents would have gone along with having boys in there for make-out sessions.

Berta agreed with my refusal to grant the request. As to the lack of her own space, her only comment on Hilda's situation was, "It is what it is." She also asked me not to mention the incident to Bryn, so I kept it a secret.

So I had the whole place to myself, and listened to my *Twilight* soundtrack and movie score on Bryn's little Bose stereo in peace. I never used it when he was home, except to dust it. I also watched my *Twilight* DVD, which had just become available, on the set-up in his room instead of on the computer. Usually, I would watch it out there at the desk, and then almost have a heart attack of my own when he suddenly came out and asked me what I was up to...a typical Aspie reaction to have when deep in concentration and oblivious to one's surroundings.

Bryn came back from his weekend with a funny cat story, which made it easier to claim that nothing remarkable had happened. He had woken up with Cassie's old gray girl cat on his chest, sitting there, staring at him until he opened his eyes. Then: "Meowww!" He got up.

Sometimes, Bryn would be in the mood to chat and tell me things.

One afternoon, he told me that Alena had never intended to have children; she was content to just be married and to work as a C.E.O. I was amazed, and told him why: Vianne's husband Ron had once told me that Alena didn't like me, because she could tell that I didn't like babies and little children.

So if she hadn't planned on having any, I couldn't help but be a bit surprised to hear it. I also thought that she had a hell of nerve to dislike me over something that she had been talked into doing after planning not to do it. It didn't matter to me that she was glad to have her daughters now that she had them; she was holding a basic element of my personality against me.

Bryn listened, accepting the fair exchange of just-between-us information. Then he told me that Alena had acquiesced to Josh's mother, who had made quite an issue of them having kids. The reason behind this was that Josh was the only son in his family, and so no one else had any chance of passing on the family surname.

Really? More absurdity; a woman, one whose own name was hidden as a maiden name, enabled someone else's last name to be perpetuated through the passing on of DNA. I remarked that her objective was a failure; both results were female, and since Alena had Lupus and was now well over forty (46, in fact, at that point in time), it was now unreasonable to expect her to make any further effort to perpetuate the unattractive last name of Lipinsky.

Bryn gave a short laugh of irony at that.

Bryn got new glasses on April 15th, a Wednesday. They had been ordered on the previous Thursday, the 9th.

He had surprised me by saying that he wanted me to go along with him when he ordered them to help him pick the frames out, and tell him what I thought looked good on him. Cool; I could do that. I have a great aesthetic sense. It was easy enough; we ended up with some rounded, oval frames that had a tortoise pattern to them. They weren't exactly like Albert's, but they looked good on Bryn. (Albert never did this; he just got the same attractive thing over and over again for decades. I love it when people do that.)

Albert and June were with us. June looked at sunglasses as usual (she was fascinated by them), and Albert ended up buying her a red-framed pair for a few hundred dollars. Wow…I couldn't imagine spending that much on sunglasses. She just added it to the collection that she habitually carried around in her backpack…5 or 6 pairs.

Sometime that day, Bryn and I had talked while he sat in his chair at home about glasses and vision problems, and I realized something interesting about him. He was so nearsighted, and had been that way since he was a little kid, that he did not observe visual details.

He did not know what color my eyes were.

It always fascinated me when I realized not only what it was about a person that jumped out at me but also why a thing was so. Because he was not capable of spotting minute details, he simply did not, and did not miss them.

The Slamming Door

"My eyes are a light, hazel brown," I told him, "and yours are blue-green," I added.

He asked me to lean in close and let him see, and for once memorized that detail about my appearance. I was definitely fascinated as I tried to imagine what his view of the world was like. He could see my long, brown hair, and the fact that I typically wore black pants or shorts and pink or blue or white tops. And I'll just bet that that was the extent of the detail that he recorded about me, just enough for recognition. Perhaps knowing the sound of my voice was part of his method.

So Bryn had gone all his life like this, unable to notice minute details. He had just accepted that about himself as his glasses gradually strengthened to the power of magnifying lenses, and at the same time been very accepting of the people around him.

For better or for worse, he could not see flaws or details, so he overlooked them.

I look at a person's face, the shape of their eyes, nose, mouth, eyebrows, etc. I listen to their voice, but have trouble matching it up on the phone later. And I notice how a person dresses, and certain habits. No wonder I am so critical; my contact lenses allow me to see every detail. I miss almost nothing because the lenses are right on my eyeballs, leaving no angle uncovered, which is what glasses do on the periphery. I even insist upon this, because I feel as though I am missing something crucial without them.

Different perspectives fascinate me, and this explanation of them was one in itself.

Sometime later, I discussed this exchange with Damon, still intrigued.

It wasn't until the summer, when I found some old photos of Bryn and Albert as little boys, including one of them side by side in matching suits – shorts, blazers, and white shirts – that something else came up about powers of observation. I had just sent it via Skype to Damon.

He couldn't tell which kid was which, but I could: Albert had the more attractive and expressive, larger eyes, while Bryn had very small ones. Bryn wasn't wearing glasses yet, which was interesting because the photo really showed the differences in their eyes.

I pointed the details out to Damon, and he said that my brain came with facial recognition software. That was hilarious, and no doubt true. We just loved the way that he said it; it reflected our mutual preference for forensics shows.

Bryn looked nice in his glasses.

Actually, he looked better to me with them than without them, due to the shocking change wrought by his illness. His face looked odd under

Enjoying Life Until He Can't

the glasses, like a thin mask, a shadow of the large, round grin that I had been used to.

There was something else that Bryn decided to do now that he could taste and enjoy whatever struck his fancy: he instituted a thorough and determined search for some tins of his favorite flavor of pipe tobacco.

He had kept the tins on his window sill for years by the corncob pipes, some pale yellow, some pale blue, and I hadn't noticed what else. But he was just about out of what he really wanted, and even though he liked the surprises from my mother, he wanted more of the same old thing. I couldn't blame him; what would it do, kill him? That was a moot point now.

The irony of my attitude was not lost on me as I aided and abetted his search once I realized that he couldn't find any, not in Greenwich Village on the same street as the famous Stonewall Bar, nor on the corner pharmacy of 7th Avenue Christopher Street as I followed him in, clueless. The second place was so small it was triangular in shape, with large identical red signs on either side of the entrance. It looked like it had been there for at least my entire life, and I was born the year of the riot that kicked off the Gay Rights Movement.

The Slamming Door

We were out with Albert and June on a nice, balmy day and Bryn just suddenly started stumping into tobacco shop after tobacco shop. We all followed, staring around at the displays.

It was ironic because I had convinced my own paternal grandmother to quit smoking at age 12, and now I was enabling Bryn to continue smoking. But the cause of his death was already known in advance, and it wasn't lung cancer, so I figured he might as well have whatever he wanted.

We had just eaten at a place called Riviera on 7th Avenue and 4th Street, where we sat in hot, bright sunlight that bothered June and sold appalling food. We ate there because it had once been pleasant in the long distant past when Bryn and Albert had eaten there before, but the menu was heavy on leather-like ham, sausage, while fruits and vegetables were almost non-existent.

The tobacco search yielded nothing.

When we got home and Bryn settled into his chair again, I asked him exactly what he had been looking for, and he showed me the nearly empty or totally empty tins, a small collection of perhaps 3 round containers.

I studied them, then carried them out to the computer, wondering whether or not I might find a way to just order them from cyberspace. If so, that would be great; Bryn could have the stuff and not traipse all over town looking for it and tiring himself out.

The stuff in the light blue tin was called Dunhill Early Morning Mixture. The kind in the pale yellow one was Dunhill Mixture 965. It was late April in 2009 at this point, and I hoped to stock up. Bad news; every site said that the stuff was discontinued. Terrific…I was determined to spoil Bryn during whatever time he had left, and the market wasn't cooperating.

With no time to waste on not finding it, I called the 1-800 number for one of the companies and quickly found myself on the phone with a raspy-voiced man, a telephone representative. I explained what I was looking for, and he confirmed that it had recently been discontinued by the British company that made the stuff.

Damn.

I paused for a moment, considering what to do next, with the raspy-voiced man still on the line. Then I did what I usually do: I told him all about my current situation – that I was taking care of my wonderful dying older cousin who loved that tobacco. I remarked that judging by the sound of his voice, he seemed like someone who used and knew pipe tobacco.

He admitted that I had guessed correctly, and was suddenly very friendly and helpful when I concluded my tale with the question: how was I supposed to spoil this nice, deserving guy (Bryn) without this pipe tobacco?

Well, the answer came, in several months it would likely be back on the market. The company was just reorganizing the operations.

"Well," I said, "that will mostly likely not be fast enough to benefit my cousin."

With that, the man directed my attention to another blend that was packaged similarly and tasted almost the same. It was made with this problem in mind, of satisfying customers who liked the Dunhill recipe. I thanked him, checked with Bryn, and ordered some of each flavor. Amazingly, when it arrived, Bryn said that it tasted almost exactly the same and that he was delighted with it.

Was he sure it was sufficiently similar and thrilling?

Yes, he insisted. It really was what he wanted.

I had to believe him, even though I was always suspicious that he might just be trying to be easy about things. He knew this product. Weighing his easygoing nature against his current behavior – he was smiling and puffing so contentedly on his pipe – I decided to believe him.

So it seemed that I had managed to spoil him on this particular point.

Okay…if I wasn't cooking much for him thanks to all of the restaurant visits that he made with friends and family, at least I had given

The Slamming Door

him ersatz Dunhill pipe tobacco, authentic McNulty's Sumatra coffee, Twinings tea and Taylor & Harrogate tea, homemade strawberry milkshakes, and whatever reading materials and toiletries struck his fancy.

Fine. I could keep that up and not allow any of his supplies to run out.

One afternoon, Bryn's friend from the Mendelssohn Glee Club reappeared. It seemed that he and Bryn had plans to eat out at some mid-scale French restaurant in the Upper East Side, and his friend kind of knew where they were going, but not quite.

Well, what was the name of it? I asked, curious and hoping to help out.

I don't remember what it turned out to be at this late date, but I looked it up on Google maps and found it. Of course, Bryn called out to me not to bother as I punched it into the site, thinking it was a lot of trouble as usual, but the information was up on the screen almost as fast as he could say that. So he relaxed and asked for the menu as long as I was at it.

Great…I printed up the prix fixe one that they wanted, plus a little map showing them which street corner. Why not? Bryn was leaning heavily on a cane, and I didn't want him wasting an ounce of energy that could better be expended on fun.

The guest was impressed and went on and on for a minute or so about that. I didn't see what was so amazing, but then I had more computer skills than they did, so that must have been why. I also tend to stare in amazement, silently, when people gush at me with compliments, regardless of how justified they are. Still, I had fun helping out.

At some point that month, in a cab with Albert and me, Bryn commented about me and Desta. "Desta and Clarisse have their whole lives ahead of them," he said.

I thought about that. I was 39, and she was either 40 or a couple of years older. The approximate guesstimate of her age was sufficient. Technically, and I couldn't help but think about the matter that way, our lives were roughly half over.

Perhaps not; perhaps we had yet to reach the halfway point. No one knows precisely how much time they have, and most people don't want that information. But for all I knew, as long as I continued to abhor tobacco, drink only moderately and eat a healthy diet (and such foods did ease my anxiety), I could easily live into my nineties. It was just a fact of my family history and personal habits – any other outcome would most likely be due to an accident or bio-weapon.

No, I was in for a long, quite possibly lonely and depressing life, damnit.

As for Desta, who knew? She was still working on her Ph.D. in anthropology.

But Bryn spoke with a tone of envy, wanting the retirement that he had dreamed of and now would never get: ten more years in which to teach at the Henry George School, smoke his corn-cob pipe, drink red wine or beer depending upon the social situation, eat in restaurants, and visit Cassie while enjoying Manhattan. He wanted to live until he was eighty years old, just as he had planned on doing.

As for me, I had doubts about living so long.

Not doubts that it would actually happen – they were doubts about liking it.

Life was backwards for us. He loved life and wasn't going to have much more of it, and I found lots of things not to love about life but would most likely have much more of it.

Damnit.

I wanted not to fear life.

I wanted to live with my husband in the United States – in some area where I would feel happy and interested in my surroundings and safe and able to do what I liked – and have a cat.

It just seemed like such a pie in the sky, that life, and I wanted it anyway. Anything other than that seemed like a punishment, a waste of my time, and even a trap.

It was about this time that we all went to see – Bryn too – *Revolutionary Road*. There was often a slightly gray, overcast sky throughout, and an ominous background sound of thunder rolling in the distance. The woman in that story did not like the cookie-cutter life that Americans are taught to like and want, and she had it: a house in the suburbs with a husband who went to work in a corporate office and a couple of kids. I could relate to not wanting the formula.

Most people like that, it seems, but she didn't. She wanted an outside-the-box life, perhaps one in Paris, but elsewhere would be acceptable too, as long as it wasn't the usual, expected thing. She was never going to get what she wanted. She tried acting, but wasn't talented. "She really had nothing to offer," Bryn remarked afterward.

That was true. But I felt sorry for her anyway.

I told myself to cheer up, that I did have something to offer and that my husband was not a cookie-cutter, formulaic kind of guy. He lived a very outside-the-box life, and so did I. I could write and observe and

The Slamming Door

travel and have many changes of scene. I was not stuck with the same old boring existence for my whole life.

But we had no money and couldn't afford to be together, and Albert would occasionally comment, "I know how he could get money: get a job."

Nice idea, Albert, I thought, but the jobs are drying up and disappearing, being downsized in the economic bust that you and Bryn watch so avidly in the news or spend hours reading about and discussing. Nice of you, a retired person with money, to suggest that. Nice of you, a blood relative of Damon who knows that he fits no standard profile, to think that such a thing would work out well for him, and be a long-term solution. Most employers don't want Aspies.

Even for the typical American male that is no longer an option.

Get a job, indeed. You can't get a job that lasts for your whole career any more. You can't get a full-time one with retirement and health benefits. No corporation is willing to pay for those any longer; they all want temps who can't command any benefits. The only solution is to make one's own money, even if you can't, or even if it takes years and you have to live on scraps in the meantime or with relatives until they resent you or get fed up with you.

My parents were fed up with Damon, not that his letter saying that he had never liked them had helped, and not that his inability to eat food at prescribed times and save dinner leftovers and not eat them for breakfast or lunch had helped.

His own relatives were fed up with him, too. Were they fed up with me?

My parents kept taking me back, unwilling to ever throw me out.

My in-laws wanted my help with the horrific process of Bryn's death, and so did he.

Whenever and wherever I stayed, I cleaned things and kept everything neat and organized, and I cooked. Damon could not offer that. I was very quiet, too. Damon, deaf in one ear, shouted his phone calls. It stressed them all out, including me.

So I had a place to go – more than one – while my husband's choices were shrinking.

And Bryn wanted more life.

Of course he did; he had a good life. He had his own apartment in lower Manhattan, a place where he loved to be. He had an income to live off of. He was a very sociable guy with lots of friends. He had things he liked to do and was good at. He had it all sorted and figured out.

And it did him no good; he couldn't have it. There was his cake, right in front of him, and he couldn't have it.

I had no cake for the future.

I felt as though I had no future; Bryn and the life I enjoyed with him, talking to him about whatever worried me, discussing our intellectual interests and activities, walking around Manhattan, all that was shrinking in front of me.

So what that I had over half of my life left to live?! I had a lot of trouble believing that I would enjoy it. There was no cake and I saw none on the menu in the time after Bryn.

His words depressed me to silence. My whole life ahead of me: that sounded like a judge pronouncing a sentence rather than an optimist looking at the bright side. I wanted Damon, and I wanted to be able to look forward to things.

The last time I had done so was while planning my perfection of a fairy tale wedding.

It was wonderful – sights, sounds, smells, tastes, the works – and I was in a euphoric high for the entire year leading up to it, plus for a little while afterward. Since then, anxiety had set in as I had stopped the fattening, mind-numbing pills and found that Damon's efforts met with corporate swindlers and roadblocks at nearly every turn and writing was put off into the future.

When would I have time and a computer at my sole disposal to write, and when would I calm down enough to do so? And then I would have to find an agent once I drafted a whole book…plus I would need to keep on writing after I wrote that Kuwait book.

What else would I write? *The Slamming Door*, of course, but I realized that I would have to wait for other reasons than logistics. For one, all events associated with Bryn's dying and death would have to be over with and some more time passed to put it all into perspective, at least a little bit. For another, I would be upset about it.

Better to wait a bit after getting settled elsewhere. But I didn't want to get settled elsewhere. Where the hell would that be?! I felt quite sure that I couldn't go back to my parents; they didn't want my husband around. They would take me, but I didn't like the idea.

Silly of me, I now know. That was exactly where I would be able to work while I let my husband pursue his goal of getting us a permanent, continuous income. His efforts required constant travel and away time, and I needed to stay put and write. Traveling with him would just reduce me to a useless, anxious burden. There was no point in joining him as a dead-weight. Better to do my own thing until things were better for us. I just hated it, though.

Well…I had no plans to go anywhere else. I was convinced that I had nowhere else to go. And Bryn still needed and wanted me around, and I had promised to stay as long as he did. I wasn't going anywhere just yet. But I was getting more depressed, and more anxious.

Bryn had taught me emotional intelligence, and I was learning its limits.

They were proving to be longer than I had expected.

Somehow, they were getting me through the long stretches of nothingness, the times in which Bryn was uncomfortable but still there, and obviously going to be there for a while longer. Those times were times of loneliness, anxiety, quiet, and much inactivity.

I had my books, and some CDs that I would only listen to when Bryn went away alone to visit Cassie. Sometimes I would use the computer to play movies when he was home, but then I would have to wear the headphones and not hear him, which worried me. What if he fell? So I did that less and less. I had seen the *Twilight* movie several times anyway.

Bryn was starting to have more and more trouble getting comfortable.

He would toss and turn around in his bed, trying to find a position that wouldn't cause his side to hurt. I thought it was the hip joint that was bothering him, the Ground Zero point for his bone cancer, but no, it turned out to be his rib cage on the right side.

How did that start to bother him? I thought (to myself) that the cancer had migrated there.

Bryn's theory was that he had wrenched his side muscles one afternoon adjusting his window to put the screen in when the spring weather started. I remembered that afternoon.

He had almost gotten the 8-inch-high screen into place and then had to call me and ask me to put it in properly. I climbed in close to the window behind his chair to do so. Bryn got up while I did it; it was impossible to maneuver the window unless I was standing up close to it.

He had tried to lean over and position the screen, something that I couldn't manage either. I had to be standing right next to that window, and I always climbed into position before working on the screen. Why hadn't he just called me to do the whole thing? He had thought he could just do it, that it wouldn't be that difficult, and so on. So that was likely the root of his problem; the slightest twist and he couldn't bounce back from it. He never really did.

When he first told me that his side hurt, I stood there for a moment, thinking. What were the options to make him more comfortable? This wasn't anything that qualified as a dire emergency, so it was up to me to think of something.

Drugs? He had all of the legal ones that he could get, which included methadone at that point. It was around that time that he had expressed amazement that the purpose of methadone was to control pain; as a social worker, he had seen drug addicts given that stuff as they were weaned off of morphine. Now he was getting it as a prelude to morphine. I was amazed that he had never realized what methadone was for and said so; but then, I read a lot, and on a variety of topics. Bryn stuck to the same ones, it seemed.

Pot? No…he wouldn't take any illegal drugs, though his reasons were never fully shared with any of us. I suspect that he just didn't want to get his caregivers in any trouble, plus marijuana wasn't legal for cancer patients in the state of New York. That still just seems wrong to me, as it had before Bryn ever got sick.

It looked as though the only option was a heating pad, which helped me every month with cramps. As I stood there, watching him toss and turn, I must have looked like a staring, expressionless, idiot savant for perhaps the millionth time in my life, but that didn't concern me. I was thinking about what I could realistically do for him, then and the next day.

So, I bought him a heating pad of his own after he tried mine for an evening and night. It seemed more hygienic that way, and when I got my period again I would just need mine back. But it didn't help much.

Bryn was afraid to run the stupid thing, convinced that he would short out a circuit in the old walls and cause a fire and burn down the building. He kept it on low like I showed him and never laid down on it, but he would only use it while awake and in his chair.

No wonder it did him little good; to really let a heating pad help, it is necessary to fall asleep and thus completely relax with it up against the sore spot. I explained that the heating pad shuts itself off after a while, so the danger of fire is managed that way, but no – he wouldn't try it. The pain continued.

Albert was over for a visit when I discussed this with Bryn, so we had an audience.

Bryn looked wryly at his brother, smiled, and said, "Clarisse believes in electricity."

Of course I believed in it! It warms me up, it keeps me comfortable, and it restores comfort when I have aches and pains. Why not avail oneself of it? It beats discomfort. But Bryn wasn't buying it. He was only teasing me, and his problems were worse than mere aches and pains; probably the heating pad wouldn't fix this.

I began to suspect that my first idea had been right: cancer creeping up to his rib cage.

But what did I really know?! I just hated to watch Bryn try to settle into his bed for the night, twisting this way and that to no avail. "Can't get any relief," he said, trying over and over again to get comfortable.

The Slamming Door

He would shift the long pillows around, lie on his left side, lie on his back, and then get up after a few hours of being in the bed.

In just a few more weeks, he told me that he could only sleep for a few hours lying down and then he had to get up and sit in his chair. Then he would sleep in the bed again. Then in the chair. Then it was time to be up for the day and he would look at the news.

That took us through the spring.

We didn't do much of anything for Easter that year, other than give some candy to the Ecuadoran kids next door. It was so different from the spring of a few years ago, when Aunt Johanna Orlov had thrown a Seder – the first one I had ever attended – and I studied for it by reading a Haggadah the night before. This time we just forgot about spring celebrations.

But I still wandered the streets of Manhattan on sunny afternoons with my camera, noticing the flowers that appeared: lilacs, irises, crocuses, daffodils, hyacinths, pansies, roses, morning glories (oddly, I found a few in the afternoons), wisteria, and so on. There was a lovely garden right next door to the House of Cards on Hudson Street that never failed to be beautiful.

One trait of mine that never ceased to leave Bryn looking a bit stunned was the fact that I rushed to complete each and every errand that arose as soon as I possibly could. This meant that no prescription had time to sit unfilled once I became aware of it, and that any other item needed or wanted by Bryn would go unbought for long. I just considered it unacceptable to risk running out of any of his pills, especially the ones meant for pain management.

When he commented upon this, I just said, "Are you kidding? I'm Ms. Do-It-Immediately, whatever "it" is." So…he got used to it, which is what I was aiming for. I kept up the pace. When all of your errands and chores are done, you have time to do whatever you want.

That, I explained to him, was why I kept the apartment mopped and the dishes washed, dried and put away, and all of the prescriptions and groceries bought before things ran out. At one point, when the weather was starting to really warm up that spring and we started keeping the windows open and the screens in, I commented to Bryn about the mopping.

"I don't get it; I just mopped two days ago, and I thought there would be no problem with walking around barefoot at home. But look at the soles of my feet – they're brown with dirt!"

Enjoying Life Until He Can't

"It's the city air; the pollution just comes in. I know you cleaned this place well."

Oh well…at least I was getting a tangible environmental lesson out of it. Back in Connecticut, I walked around barefoot on wall-to-wall carpeting in the summer, and my feet never looked like that. It was the big city versus the suburbs. I didn't care, as long as Bryn knew that I was cleaning regularly. He was home so often that he was starting to see it more. He saw me mopping his room a few times, and said he liked the fresh lemon scent that it left; good.

One lovely, somewhat warmer afternoon, Bryn decided to out to eat in the East Village, not near home. He wandered around the neighborhood just south of Union Square, on University Place near The New School, looking at menu after menu and scoping out the dining rooms of various Italian restaurants.

We sat in one, but he wasn't comfortable; there was a draft of chilly air coming at him. Out we went again, back down the street, until he decided on a darker but warmer place that Tony Soprano would have felt at ease in either with his family or for a meeting with the guys. We settled into the front window seating area of the Italian place, a semi-formal restaurant.

As we sat over a delicious meal of asparagus soup, rolls, garlic, red wine and gnocchi with basil pesto, Bryn told me that he was worried about me, specifically my future and financial well-being (I had no expectation of him leaving me any money – he wasn't wealthy, and I wasn't taking care of him for an inheritance. I wanted to spend time with him.), and my happiness.

That just depressed me. "You can't do anything to save me, Bryn," I said miserably.

He looked very unhappy about that, and didn't contradict me.

My hopes were pinned on Damon's science making money and my own writing, and that was before I had drafted any full-length book manuscripts. I was full of ideas for several of those, and I had an excellent memory for details, but had no time to record them. It would have to wait, and the waiting was terrifying. I couldn't work on them while I was busy and scared.

Bryn continued to read avidly, which was what he had always done.

That meant that he bought new books, despite his extensive collection. He sent me shopping for them, and I brought back titles that he specifically wanted or whatever looked like it would interest him. It was exactly what I did with my own books, meaning that the chances of reading their entire contents within a few months while also socializing and running errands with friends were nil. Neither of us cared; we just enjoyed the books.

We would look at each other's books, too. I loved the exchange. We would run through the table of contents, the cover illustrations, whatever other illustrations, the publisher's data page with its Library of Congress and ISBN information, and read the book jacket and reviews. Then we would give it back. Bryn and I weren't actually going to read each other's books from cover to cover; we just liked to know about them.

One title that he sent me after – to the Barnes & Noble branch on 5th Avenue, the one associated with N.Y.U. – had a cool title: *Weapons of Mass Instruction* by John Taylor Gatto. I found it, of course, and was intrigued by the topic. The book jacket said: "John Taylor Gatto's *Weapons of Mass Instruction* focuses on mechanisms of familiar schooling which cripple imagination, discourage critical thinking, and create a false view of learning as a by-product of rote-memorization drills." It was a well-reasoned bashing of inside-the-box education.

Yet another book, one that I bought at The Biography Bookshop in Greenwich Village, was called *Fool's Gold: How the Bold Dream of a Small Tribe at J.P. Morgan Was Corrupted by Wall Street Greed and Unleashed a Catastrophe* by Gillian Tett. It was something Bryn wanted, and one glance told me that it was like flypaper to a political economist. Bryn snapped it up happily. I didn't look at it, though. It reminded me of Camille Valmont, the lady down the street with 2 Italian Spinone dogs, who had lost her Wall Street job in the Bear Stearns collapse.

Enjoying Life Until He Can't

Once the weather had warmed up pleasantly, but before it was at all hot out, Aunt Johanna Orlov invited us – me, Bryn, Albert, June and Alissa – to see her act in a play in the basement of her building. She and Aunt Sunny were involved in it together, of course. They went to plays as volunteer ushers often, so that they could garner as many free tickets to as many plays as possible. It was clever of them.

Damon and I had been to a couple of plays courtesy of Aunt Summer's ingenuity, in 2005. One of them was lovely – odd, but interesting. Another was so upsetting that we suddenly cried and left, explaining to the puzzled ushers (Aunt Summer wasn't there) that it had nothing to do the quality of the performance. The problem was the subject matter of the play; it was all about despair, poverty, mental illness, and an utter lack of hope for the future. It scared us.

Aunt Summer didn't send us to any more plays after that, except when we asked her to help us get tickets. That was only once, however, due the expense, when we had seen Mozart's opera *The Magic Flute* on New Year's Eve. When we had seen *Wicked* in 2005, we had done that on our own, at the Gershwin Theater's box office.

This clock from *Wicked* is in the lobby of the Gershwin Theater.

The Slamming Door

This is what people see after watching *Wicked*. It's the perfect way to snap us out of Oz.

Well, now we were going to see Aunt Johanna and a group of other elderly residents from the apartment complex that both she and Aunt Sunny lived in perform in a montage of short plays. There was a cost for the tickets, which Aunt Sunny sat collecting in the basement hallway.

I greeted her; I was carrying a bag with Bryn's seat cushion, and she greeted me back.

Then I headed into the room where the show would take place to get seats. They were all folding chairs, so Bryn would most likely be uncomfortable after a while and squirm in his seat, even with the cushions. The previous week, I had rushed back to the apartment as he watched Rob play with his classical music group at Chelsea Market just to get the cushion. It was a standard piece of equipment now, wherever we went.

A couple of screens made up a makeshift backstage, though we could see people entering and exiting to the right (stage left). We just ignored that. The point was to have some fun.

The trouble with that idea was that I couldn't do it. I began to cry during the show, and hid it as best I could, using the Kleenex that I always kept folded up in my right pocket. I was sitting all the way to the right, so I think I got away with it. But I was a bit annoyed in the end that no one noticed. Either that, or they deliberately ignored it, either because they didn't give a damn or because they thought that I didn't want it noticed. I'll never know.

The plays were funny, at least. I remember the second one the most clearly. An old man starred. His character had been in some show in the building, he told the audience, and his elderly women neighbors thought he was hot stuff, so they all asked him to visit them, wanting a date with him. His line was hilarious: "So what could I do? I visited them all."

Aunt Johanna Orlov, for her part, spoke loudly, with perfect diction, emoting her roles flawlessly. She was exuberant, she gestured grandly, and I really don't remember much more than that. The point of seeing her act was that we observed how good she was.

Enjoying Life Until He Can't

The downside of it was when I remembered that acting, as much as she loved it and excelled at it, was not her main career. She had supported herself by selling Hummel dolls, those little German porcelain figures of children in lederhosen and pinafores. The job had led to travel in Germany and Hungary. It was about supporting herself rather than loving what she did.

That was the case with most people, and no matter how realistic and practical that fact of life was, it never failed to anger me. It meant that only a few, either lucky and random or elect and successful through nepotism, talented or not, who got to do what they loved for a living.

A long time before any of this happened, I did something nice for a girl I met at the Mark Twain and Harriet Beecher Stowe House Museums. The girl was in her late teens, a pretty brunette with a sweet temperament, and she walked with a cane.

She was in the Big Sister – Little Sister program in the area, as a little sister to one of the other historic interpreters, and because of that she had been hired to work in the museum gift shop. Her name was Kirsten.

When I asked my colleague why such a young girl needed a cane, she told me: Kirsten had grown up in a poor family in Bristol, and with no mother, so she was malnourished. Her father couldn't afford enough milk for her, and couldn't pay enough attention to her to watch her diet. As if that weren't enough, she had been in a car crash. That was why she used a cane; her bones were permanently damaged by the combined calcium deficiency and injury.

I chatted with Kirsten during breaks, curious to see what she was like, and because I would do that with every person in my small workplace. She was a lovely girl who liked Tim Burton movies, particularly *The Nightmare Before Christmas*, and Emily Dickinson's poetry.

Her one wish in life, she told me, was to see Emily Dickinson's house before she died.

Kirsten invited me to visit her at home in Bristol one hot summer evening, and I drove out there. Sure enough, she lived with her father, older brother, her brother's girlfriend, and their baby. The father had a low-paying job, quietly drank beer, and sat in the living room. No one seemed to be a threat to Kirsten's safety; she just didn't have a happy, high-quality life.

Kirsten's room was all her own, at least. She happily showed me her little figurine of Jack Skellington, her favorite character from the Tim

The Slamming Door

Burton movie, a gift from my co-worker. Then she opened her upstairs window in the multi-family apartment building, trying to let a breeze in.

Emily Dickinson's was in Amherst, Massachusetts. Also, I had a car. There was no reason why I couldn't make her wish come true.

Kirsten was amazed and delighted when I told her what I had in mind, and we made the drive on a beautiful sunny afternoon. The tour was lovely; the guide knew the author's history well, the house was beautifully restored and maintained, and we learned how shy and introverted Emily Dickinson was, and how happy she was to live right next door to her married brother.

And that was it. I took Kirsten home, and the deed was done.

I know why I did it, too. I did it because I knew that I would not keep in touch with her and therefore I would not find out what became of her, and that this was by my own choice. To do so, I thought, would have been too depressing. So I fulfilled this wish of hers instead.

It was odd to remember this while I was taking care of Bryn, but I realized that I had been enabling fun for someone else who, like him, seemed in danger of missing out on something that made life worth living.

If I can prevent that from happening, I always want to.

Occasionally, not too often but often enough to be a problem, while sitting in Bryn's room for a visit, June would comment that Berta had gotten so fat that she couldn't stand it. This was usually after Bryn mentioned that Berta was coming over right after work.

After we all looked uncomfortable, the moment would pass. Albert would wait until they were out in the living to tell June not to say that around Bryn, because he already knew that his daughter was too fat, but that he didn't like hearing about it because she was his daughter.

It was an exercise in futility, and June, with her small bones and thin physique, and small appetite and willingness to exercise, would just do it again a few weeks later.

One night, at 1 a.m., I gave Bryn a cup of strawberry Ensure to drink. He sat with it in his chair, drinking it slowly. I left him to it because he didn't like to be stared at. But he was sleepy thanks to the pain medication, and he dozed off. Suddenly I heard a thump, and went back in there to find a long pink puddle. Bryn was abruptly fully awake; he felt bad about the mess.

Enjoying Life Until He Can't

"It's okay," I said. "I'll just clean it up. Hang on; I'm going to put on my old clothes, tie up my hair, and get the mop. If I don't do this right away, it will stink."

Bryn just nodded. Before I left, I pulled the green quilt off the bed; it had been hit.

I came back quickly with the mop, its sponge soaked, and started swiping at the pool of pink. There was enough of it that I had to keep going into the bathroom and running the long stick into the tub to clean out the Ensure. Bryn watched me from his chair, then realized that he would have to get up before I needed to say anything. Some of the pink pool was under his chair.

He went out to sit on the sofa, which was older than he was. Its springs didn't offer much cushion any more. I felt sorry for him and hurried to finish cleaning. He apologized for the mess.

"Oh, don't worry about it, Bryn. You are the nicest possible sick person that anyone could take care of, and this mess is not your fault. It's not your fault because you're sick. You could get excused from pretty much anything because you're sick."

He smiled sweetly at me for that comment. I went back into his room to finish up.

As I dragged the chair off to the side, I saw yet another little pool of pink underneath, and realized that the footrest of it was hit. I rushed to get a wet sponge; more trips back and forth. That led me to explain what had happened to the chair. I like to explain delays when people are waiting and watching, especially if they are so nice.

That was it; soon he was settled again.

The next day, everyone came over. It didn't take Berta long to ask where the quilt was. "Your father fell asleep holding a cup of strawberry Ensure, so it's down the street at the laundry. I'll be back tomorrow," I replied.

And that was that.

But Bryn surprised and intrigued me with something else: he had never realized, in all of his time as a social worker, that methadone was a pain-management drug. Albert looked surprised, too. He knew all about cancer treatments after researching it so much.

"Really?" I asked him, startled. "I read about drug addicts in a fiction book once; the reason why clinics give them monitored doses of methadone is to help them cope with withdrawal pains. The pains are so bad that they would just give up and take illegal drugs again without it."

Bryn gave one of his nods with eyebrows slightly raised, indicating that he had absorbed the new information. He was cool about learning new things, open to the experience, and curious. That never changed.

Chapter 37

Helping Alissa

Alissa was in the process of moving out of her apartment at the northwest corner of Central Park, with its exclusive location and exclusive rules about renting the units out. She had gone back to her old room in TriBeCa to stay with her parents and help take care of her mother, who now required constant attention, but her furniture and papers were still in her apartment.

She wanted to lease out the unit and thus avoid having to come up with rent for a place that, for all practical purposes, she wasn't using anymore. Easier said than done; she had to get permission for this. One couldn't simply do as one pleased with one's own property there. So much for the simplicity of ownership; not in Manhattan, where property was visibly connected to that of others' property by walls rather than abutting on lines that were only seen on a deed.

After much ado, the committee in charge of permissions in her building had conferred its blessing on her to rent the one bedroom, 1st floor unit out. Now it had to be made ready.

I volunteered to help, offering to help clean the place and to do whatever else needed to be done. Alissa still had to sort through her papers, shredding, recycling, and crossing out indications of her identity with a black Sharpie pen, and so on. It remained to be seen just what she needed done until we actually arrived.

Meanwhile, I managed to see *The Reader* with her one weekend before she was actually ready to proceed with the cleanup job. We had a nice evening; that movie was exactly the sort of thing that we both enjoyed, and Kate Winslet and Ralph Fiennes were excellent in it. When it was over, Alissa and I went to Le Grainne Café for hot drinks and a chance to chat. That was a rare chance to converse with her; she was just so quiet, reserved, tense, and usually busy.

That was when and where I finally told her that I knew about the pills she took, because she said that she had forgotten to bring them and was afraid that if she didn't get home and take them soon, she would have a problem. I knew that this meant that the voices in her head would begin to talk, and that her thoughts would not be her own.

It was obvious that Alissa was ashamed of this. I had to confess to knowing what was going on at that point, which was that I knew about it. It's just not fair to possess information about someone and not let them know about it. Aside from that, I pointed out to her that it seemed that she was ashamed of a thing that was not her fault.

Helping Alissa

She looked at me for a moment, taking that in, and nodded. With that, I added that a fair exchange – at least, as even a one as I could offer – was in order. I shared my secrets with her then: depression, anxiety, Asperger's, medication for mood problems, weight gain, quitting the pills in order to be thin and able to write, and so on. I emphasized that I knew enough to keep our secrets a secret, and not tell everyone I met, not that I knew anyone to tell.

It seems funny to be writing this down, because it is meant for readers whom I do not know, but since this is a roman à clef with fake names for everyone in it (except for famous people, of course, like Angelica Page Torn and her dad!), my promise seems to be intact.

With that, we went out to hail her a cab, and one appeared almost immediately because it was mild Sunday evening. We hugged good-bye, and Alissa was off to TriBeCa, to get her pills and do some more writing. I walked the half block home to Bryn, who was waiting in his Lazy Boy chair and puffing contently away on his pipe in front of the latest episode of Charlie Rose's show. I was never going to get used to the idea of him not being there like that.

Despite the nice visit, Alissa showed very little sign of getting on with the cleanup job.

Just as I was wondering when it would actually take place, it was scheduled for the week before her next play was to be read at the Page-Torn Salon for the Arts. Bryn went out to the Moonstruck Diner with us for brunch before we went to Alissa's apartment. The plan was for him to go home on foot after we ate while Alissa and I took a cab north. We were on a tight schedule, because after the cleaning, Alissa and I were to go to the Page-Torn Salon to listen to someone else's play. That would mean coming all the way back that very evening.

I asked why we were doing this, not that I had any objection to going.

"Because Alissa must be seen to show some interest in the general operation of the place beyond her own work," Bryn informed me.

"Oh. That makes sense," I replied.

We said no more about that, and ate our brunches.

Whenever there is cleaning to do – even sight unseen – I tend to fidget and show obvious signs of itching to get my hands on the task. I just like to see dirt and disorder disappear due to my own efforts. I don't want to make a career of being a cleaning lady; it's just that whether it is

The Slamming Door

paperwork, editing, organizing, and removal of actual dirt, I derive a sense of satisfaction from bringing order to chaos.

I also like the variety it brings, and the chance to observe other human beings.

Everyone's mess is different. Albert's was several identical pairs of round, plastic-rimmed, tortoise-patterned glasses buried here and there in the detritus of papers, pens, rubber bands, paper clips, staples, and dust. Bryn's was papers and stamps and photographs hidden and forgotten all over his apartment. Damon's had been a lifetime's collection of old pens that I had tested on a pad of paper until all the drained ones were out with the recycling.

What would I find at Alissa's place?

Alissa's place proved to be a one-bedroom apartment with a full bathroom, a living-dining room, and a kitchen that needed a serious cleaning. An old desktop computer sat in the darkened living room by the curtained window, covered with dust. Alissa said it didn't work very well and that she wrote on her laptop. Clothes and used towels were strewn around the bedroom, but it was the kitchen and bathroom caught my interest; they needed a scrubbing out.

I couldn't have worked on or in the living room if I had wanted to; Alissa still had to shred and black-ink scads of junk mail. She settled in after we made a quick run to a nearby store that sold cleaning supplies and garbage bags. So I went to work on the kitchen as she sat on the living room floor, working on the piles of paper.

The kitchen didn't have much food in it, which was good, and understandable considering the fact that she was living with her parents again. None of them seemed to expend much energy on housekeeping; Albert used a cleaning lady to keep the dirt at bay.

Alissa used neither a cleaning lady nor her own time, of which she had none anyway.

Upon arrival, we had gone to the lobby downstairs to get the mail – Alissa used a key to open a small metal box in a wall of such boxes, which looked a lot like a U.S. Post Office – and to wash a few clothes in the expanses of a laundry room right below her unit. She lived on what was called, in European fashion, the first floor, while the street level was called the ground floor.

But back to the kitchen...the kitchen was filthy, and easily noticeable. It was a thin sheen on the counters, stove, oven, fridge and microwave oven. It was sticky, dusty, and the result of past spills and a rushed schedule. And that was what made cleaning necessary: you can't show a dirty apartment to potential tenants unless and until the layer of dirt is stripped off.

Helping Alissa

I went to work, finding whatever I needed for the most part. At one point, Alissa looked at what I was doing and decided to go out and buy some things to help me along – sponges with scratchy sides, Soft Scrub, etc. – but mostly I just kept going, stripping down to my tee shirt and underwear since there was no one else to see me and I would have to save those clothes for the Page-Torn Salon that evening. There would be no time to go home and change.

After about an hour and a half, the kitchen was more or less clean.

And I needed to visit the bathroom.

The bathroom…needed a brisk cleaning just to make myself comfortable.

I relieved myself, and then dove in. This proved to be much harder work than the kitchen, and there were things of Alissa's still in the vanity cabinet. I was very careful with it all, losing nothing. All pairs of earrings and cosmetics were kept together.

But the tub and shower needed a tough scrubbing out, as did the toilet, sink, counter, and floor. I worked up a sweat in the process. For someone who hates to generate laundry while outside of her home, this was a bit of a nuisance, especially since it meant that I might not look or smell good for the next event on our agenda.

This was not good; by now, I had locked myself into the bathroom and hung my underwear on the door's hook to save it. It was the perfect place to barricade myself, considering my minor predicament. What could possibly go wrong? I was in possession of a medium-sized and clean towel, I had soap and deodorant in there, the only other person around was another woman my age, and I was locked in a bathroom. So I took a quick shower after it was cleaned.

But the stupid tub wouldn't drain when all was said and done.

Alissa brought me some bleach, which did the trick for the most part.

After that, time was running out, so I moved on. My make-up wasn't perfect, but the eyeliner and rouge were still decent. I got dressed and studied myself for a moment. It was okay; I looked socially acceptable for the evening's activity.

I came out and found that Alissa was still at it; the amount of junk paper that she had had to go through was unbelievable. Some of it was old personal paper – drafts of writing – but most of it was junk mail that she had tossed aside to look at later.

That was a mystery to me; why put that off only to have a huge job of it like this?

I always shredded or otherwise destroyed my junk mail as it arrived, and organized the bills and recreational mail too. Each day, I had to do this, but at least I knew what I had and had no extra rubbish taking up valuable space. It was over with before it had time to accumulate.

The Slamming Door

Alissa looked at what I had done and realized the extent of the filth that had been removed. I was just glad that she had let me at it, undisturbed, for as long as it took me to clean it all. I hate to start something and be held back. That has happened to me before.

"I'm so ashamed," she said more than once.

I didn't get it – what was there to be ashamed of?!

Then I realized that I would have to say that out loud if she was going to feel okay about all this and understand that she had nothing to apologize for. What are friends and family for, anyway, but to do stuff like this?

"You have nothing to be ashamed of."

She looked at me like I had to be kidding, so I went on – not that I had intended to leave it at that – to assure her: "You are hardly ever here because you have moved back in with your sick parents and have a job. Taking care of them and the dog takes up so much of your time and attention that you have barely enough time to do what you love most, which is to write, so you expend your free time on that, which you should. You have no time left for this, and you have a right to let something insignificant go undone in order to keep your sanity. So you have absolutely nothing to be ashamed of."

At last, she smiled, accepting this.

"There's that, plus I had fun cleaning because I could see the dirt disappearing, and I always love to see the difference and know that I am making a significant, helpful improvement. I didn't know what I would find here, but I have wanted to do this for you for a couple of months now, since we first discussed this."

Now she actually laughed happily, and smiled some more.

With that, we cleared up the remains of what we had been doing, bagging up papers, tossing used clothing and towels into the hamper in the bedroom, and Alissa said that she and her father would remove it all later, and donate the old clothes. She never wore them anymore; she had what she liked in TriBeCa. These were all but forgotten.

The job looked unfinished, but the meter was ticking relentlessly and our time was up.

We made it to the play on time, greeted Ms. Page Torn, and sat politely through the entire reading. I saved a digital copy of the announcement, but to tell the whole truth, I don't remember a word that was read that evening. I was just being polite; it wasn't Alissa's work.

The announcement included Alissa's play as well as a couple of others, which was what made me want to keep it. When I look back at it now, I see that it was based on a Russian novel. I have never read any Russian novels. I can name them for crossword puzzles, but that's it.

Helping Alissa

To be even more honest, I was just attending this one the way that one takes a distribution requirement course that one has absolutely no interest in – but must sit through it in order to get to the subject matter that one really wants.

In this case, it was Alissa's work.

And Alissa's work was all that I had hoped for: fun to take in, and stimulating.

A couple of days later, Albert saw me and insisted upon paying me sixty dollars.

I tried to say that I hadn't been expecting to paid, that I had just wanted to help, but he insisted on it, and said that I had certainly earned it. So I gave up protesting and took it; I had worked up quite a sweat and eradicated a lot of dirt, after all.

All things considered, I felt pretty good about the whole episode.

Chapter 38

"Rip Torn Gave Me the Clap!" - and Other Stories

It was time to attend the reading of Alissa's play. We went back to the Page-Torn Salon for the Arts on April 5th, 2009, a Sunday evening, to hear it. Once again, no paper was damaged in the course of the evening, and a good time was had by all.

But Bryn had a story that he loved to tell every now and then…including now.

At some point many years ago, he had attended a party during which an irate woman had informed him that Rip Torn had given her the clap. I never heard when this happened, or what kind of venereal disease it was, or the outcome. Hopefully, the woman was cured by her doctor and that was that.

The upshot of this was that Bryn derived great amusement from relating this anecdote in social gatherings henceforth. Normally a couth and genteel man, he persisted in taking great delight in the telling of this rather short tale. It was incongruous with the rest of his personality, I thought, but after hearing something once, I tend not to have much of a reaction to hearing it again…or again and again. I even find it mildly funny.

However, what happened that evening at the Page-Torn Salon was funnier.

We arrived at the place, I saw him settled into a seat, and headed out to use the bathroom and get tea and cookies. When I came out to get the tea, there was Angelica Page Torn, the hostess and Rip Torn's daughter, saying that her father was in the building somewhere and would be reading one of the roles.

With that, I thought to myself, "I just know that Bryn is in the reading room right now, telling that story." I rushed in there just in time to hear him say: "Rip Torn gave me the clap!"

I hurried over to him and said: "Bryn, you might not want to be heard telling that story tonight. Rip Torn is HERE, and he's going to read one of the roles."

With that, Bryn immediately turned around and sat down in his seat, grinning like a naughty schoolboy. It was cute. But then I told him not to get too nervous, as Rip Torn wasn't in the room yet. He was just somewhere in the building, and would join us soon.

Bryn looked at me with a rueful grin, then calmly resumed chatting merrily with Desta.

As for me, I suddenly realized with satisfaction that it isn't always the person on the autism spectrum who makes a faux pas. And my

"Rip Torn Gave Me the Clap!" – and Other Stories

favorite person hadn't actually made one because I had stopped him in time.

But about Alissa's play…

We had started the evening off by meeting for dinner at Le Grainne Café. That was fun, complete with glasses of wine, always a part of a meal with this family, and delicious food. After that, we all ambled at a leisurely pace up the one block to West 22nd Street, up the steps of the tall brownstone building, up the staircase to the second level, and into the reading room.

Rip Torn (in hat) with another actor shortly before the play reading began.

Bryn had headed for his usual position on the right, started up his conversation with Desta moments later, and Albert and June settled into

The Slamming Door

seats on the left. It was an exact repeat of the reading that Alissa had enjoyed the previous fall, except for the fact that this audience was larger. That was certainly welcome, to say the least.

Alissa's writing teacher was there; she knew Albert from graduate school in Iowa.

Rip Torn read the role of a senile gardener, which was the smallest role of them all, reserving the larger ones for less-known actors. He was funny, and Alissa had inserted some clever *Harry Potter* references that showed the character's shaky grip on reality.

Unlike last fall's shorter play, this one was far more complex, with twice as many characters and twists to its plot. Like last fall's play, this one showed a keen sense of observation and awareness of the human condition. Other than that, I don't want to reveal much. That's Alissa's job, when she gets around to copyrighting and marketing her work.

I promised to show her how to copyright her work, which we did over the next week or so. But that night, the focus was on accolades and feting after the reading.

It started with a discussion, which Alissa was invited to take part in. She was motioned to the antique sofa, where she sat quietly and happily surrounded by the cast and Angelica Page Torn discussing how she had written this play.

Her method was that she typically spent a year or more thinking of a play in precise and minute detail, characters, plot, setting, pace, twists and all, and then a month or two writing it all down and tweaking it to perfection. That sounded familiar; I do that too.

Alissa was not interested in television shows or popular movies or popular culture. She liked Indie films and period pieces and rather cerebral works. She was just the sort of person who would seem intimidating if she weren't so down to earth and sweet.

I like a rough edge to my entertainment – nothing that is pure horror, though. That's for people with abandonment issues. Gore and guts with no complex plot seems senseless and upsetting to me, but some violence and toughness is welcome. And I like television and science fiction, but no nationally televised talent shows aimed at bringing fame and fortune to just anyone, regardless of ability or imagination.

Not Alissa. Alissa was all about talent, imagination, and quiet.

It was one of the things that impressed me about her.

I think Bryn was a bit in awe of her, and perhaps even a bit envious of his brother for having such an intellectually rigorous and talented daughter. His own daughter was all about popular culture and dreadful talent shows, shopping at malls and outlet stores on weekends, and she barely picked up a book. Yet Berta showed up and cheered her cousin on with enthusiasm.

"Rip Torn Gave Me the Clap!" – and Other Stories

I had no doubt that Berta was able to follow and comprehend what was going on in her cousin's plays; she had the education and background for that. It just wasn't her thing, but if a social situation called for her to pay attention to it for an evening, she could do that.

We all went out for beers and snacks after the presentation and discussion, just one block up and across 9th Avenue at Jake's Saloon, an Irish-American chain of pubs with locations here and there around Manhattan.

Lately, we seemed to be going there often for dinner with Bryn, Albert and June, and sometimes Claus or Berta and Matt. Now we went there with the whole gang, including the star of the evening, Alissa, and some Henry George School professors. Claus was there this evening, and had spent several minutes chatting up Rip Torn after the discussion broke up.

I took lots of photographs to share with the entire family plus any friends or distant relatives who might be interested. It was fun shooting image after image, but Rip Torn must have thought I was from some horrid tabloid and trying to humiliate him yet again about who knew what. He looked at me in horror for a moment after I got a candid shot of him chatting with Claus. As for me, I didn't know what to say; "it's for the family" probably wouldn't have put his mind at ease. He didn't come with us to the pub; it was just Alissa's family and friends.

In any case, I had fun sending the photographs around later that evening, with the tag line: "Page Torn Salon – where no paper is damaged in the course of the evening." People who got the e-mails enjoyed them, and wrote nice notes back.

A great evening was had by all, and soon we were back to our usual routines.

Another evening, Dionne was with us.

The whole gang of us went up two blocks via 9th Avenue, around the corner to 23rd Street, and into an Italian restaurant – Patsy's – the same one that Bryn had led me to the night that I had bought the James Bond movie tickets the previous fall.

It was fun, and the food was very good.

I don't remember why we went, not that we needed a reason, but Dionne was in fine form, talking loudly and vivaciously in an Italian accent, which she tended to do when she was in a good mood. Alissa spoke to her in much quieter tones, but also in Italian.

That was fine until Dionne spoke to the waiters in Italian; they were all Mexican.

We all tried to get her to stop that, to no avail.

The Slamming Door

"Spanish is similar to Italian – they understand me!" she said.

"No, they don't," was the chorus that replied to her.

Hours later, when we were home again – Bryn, me, Albert and June – Bryn asked if we had noticed that. "Dionne was really pissing me off this evening," he told us, a rare use of profanity for him.

Yes, we had noticed, and tried to just ignore it. But it was interesting.

One of Bryn's favorite routines was reading *The New York Times* each day with anyone who would discuss it with him. That could be me, or Claus, or Desta, or Albert. Most often it was me or Albert, with emphasis on different stories.

They read it on hard copy – contributing to the shocking and appalling deaths of millions of trees – while I read it online.

One afternoon, Bryn and Albert came across something that extolled a wonderful old-time invention: printed newspapers. "You read it, and when you're done with it, you throw it away!" Bryn said, reading aloud with a grin. With that, both of the Otterman boys grinned at me, looking insufferably pleased with themselves as they laughed over it.

I just stood there and stared at them with stony-faced disapproval for a moment, until they calmed down. Then I pointed out that their method of reading the news was terrible for the environment and not sustainable. "Only someone like Bryn, who can't sit comfortably in a desk chair reading it off of a computer, should be allowed to read *The New York Times* the old-fashioned way, using all this paper every day."

Bryn sobered right up, agreeing with me about that inescapable truth, but worrying, "What is going to happen to all of these news publications? How are they going to survive if everything goes online?"

"They aren't all going to survive. They will all have to start charging for online access, and only the ones that are any good will survive. Darwin's law will apply to news sources. It will be the best thing for the quality of the work and for the quality of our natural environment."

He looked at me seriously again, and then nodded, agreeing.

It would be a significant change, and one that he would not have to adapt to, but it had to happen. Bryn was really cool that way; if a change was good for society as a whole, and for the planet, he would not resist it or try to block it.

I loved having such discussions with him, and this one was typical of the ones we had.

Chapter 39

Distractions: Letterman and the Morgan Library

Bryn was determined to give some more lectures at the Henry George School.

He and Desta were scheduled to teach a course together, and sick or not, he wanted to do as much of it as possible, because he loved it so much.

But I still had a phobia of listening to lectures on the economy, and if I had actually sat down in the room just to keep track of Bryn, I would have paid attention, and then spiraled into an anxious mental state, most likely to be followed by a panic attack.

No way was I about to do that; I had to keep calm and not upset Bryn.

He understood and didn't blame me. I had explained this problem to him a long time ago, before he even got sick, so he wasn't offended in the least. I didn't bring it up again, even though I thought of it often.

To prepare for each lecture, however, he needed my help as a research assistant, and I was delighted to do that for him. Gathering data didn't mean I had to actually read its content, only to skim it, to make sure that it was relevant to the topic.

But researching the topics that Bryn needed to read up on was fun. Armed with both a law degree and the Internet, I quickly satisfied him every time with several pages of data. It was even fun; I enjoyed learning about corporate law, the American Monetary Fund, *Puck* magazine, various law cases and seeing whatever his colleagues had just published in *Counterpunch*.

Another night, while Berta was still away, Bryn was out late unexpectedly.

It was nice to have a cat to sit with while I made call after call to locate him and decide what to do next, then wait until it was time to act.

The day had started out normally enough.

Bryn had gotten back into his work at the Henry George School since the doctor had stopped poisoning him, attending trustee meetings and giving the occasional lecture. My job consisted of helping him to prepare for the lectures, making sure that he arrived on time for both the lectures and the trustee meetings, and then picking him up on time when they were over.

I wasn't allowed in the trustee meetings; those were supposed to be secret.

The Slamming Door

So it seemed like a nice afternoon early in May when Bryn asked me to drop him off at the Henry George School for a trustees' meeting and come back in a few hours. He put a few things into his back-pack – the day's copy of *The New York Times*, a few school documents, a bottle of fruit-flavored water – and off we went to get a cab ride to East 30th Street.

What could go wrong?

Plenty...but not right away, of course, and not early enough to tip me off.

As I left him off at the school, Bryn suddenly handed me a twenty-dollar-bill.

"This is much more than I need for a little orange juice, coffee, and a pastry," I said. "what do you want me to do with the rest – any errands?"

"Play with it!" he said with a grin, and got out.

Okay...I would, I decided.

Happily oblivious to any possible or impending problem, I decided to walk around the corner and up Madison Avenue to the Morgan Library & Museum, founded by Pierpont Morgan in 1906, and made public in 1924 by his son, John Pierpont Morgan, Jr., which I had wanted to see for a long time but never gotten around to. In fact, this was the only museum that I went to on my own; I was there to be available to Bryn, after all. I only went to this one because I could count on his trustees' meeting to keep him busy.

I kept my cell phone on and in my pocket as usual. Being in Manhattan, I could count on excellent signal service wherever I went, so I didn't worry that Bryn would have the slightest problem reaching me if he chose to try.

The museum was beautiful, with a huge, modern, wood-paneled gallery of artwork to look at, and then the $12 exhibit beyond it. That part of the building dated from the turn of the 20th century, when the financier had lived there.

His study was part of the museum; it was made up of imported medieval treasures from Europe and the Middle East. Pierpont Morgan had sat there in his spare time and read ancient, original texts – sacred calligraphy scripted into beautiful rare books. All around him were tapestries, statues, paintings, and chest-high bookcases made of ornate, inlaid wood with metal cage doors on them.

Coming out of there and into the hall that led to the library, one found white marble everywhere with some geometric shapes of red and pink and purple and gray marble in the floor, and pillars of various grains of more marble topped with carved Corinthian columns. Above those, in the atrium of the hallway, were frescos every which way that one turned.

Distractions: Letterman and the Morgan Library

The frescos depicted scenes of people in Roman costumes, thrones, worshippers, and clouds. Above those were some mosaic tile depictions of minor Greek and Roman gods and goddesses.

As one passed through this hall, looking left, there was a view into the librarian's office. Today, the Morgan Library no doubt has a small army of librarians, but this office is part of the exhibit, as it was for Bella da Costa Greene, the woman he hired during his lifetime to oversee and manage his collection. Naturally, with a slew of wealthy donors maintaining and upgrading the premises, the collection had grown, but what I was viewing represented what Morgan collected in his lifetime. Ms. da Costa Greene oversaw the use of that collection by carefully screened researchers.

The office was beautiful, full of books, with a carved wooden desk, white marble, and it too had plenty of books in it. The desk was off to the left, facing to the right. The room seemed to be well-lit without being either dim or bright.

Continuing on into the library itself, I found three levels of bookshelves, the upper two of which were on balconies that wrapped entirely around the room, even above the doorway that I had just walked through. The room was carpeted, and there was a cushioned bench in the middle. On either side, under glass, some medieval European texts were spread out for perusal. They were low enough for a woman in a wheelchair to comfortably roll up to and read, I observed.

But, I wondered, how did one get at the books on the two balconies?

A few more people walked in and stared upwards, also with puzzled expressions on their faces. In the corner, standing quietly in his museum guard's uniform, stood a black man in his thirties. He had apparently been waiting for enough visitors to gather in just such a state of mind, because now he spoke up. He told us to peer through the corner shelves on the left.

We did, and saw a brightly-lit, white marble, winding staircase behind the bookshelves. The railings were made of brass, and were of an ornate, curlicued design. No one was in there. But the guard explained further; this segment of the bookcase could be swung out, as could the ones directly above it. That was how one went up to the other levels and got at those books.

When I had seen it all, I went back out into the modern section of the building, used the rest room, and visited the shop. It was a heaven of books, toys, knick-knacks, magnets, and interesting ties and scarves that related to the museum's subject matter, and it was spread out over two rooms, with enormous coffee-table books on table after table. The second room was like a wood-paneled study, except that the books were for sale.

The Slamming Door

I chatted with the shop employees, and bought one book. It detailed the design, construction, and history of the place, describing Morgan, his librarian, and the new library facilities in the modern areas of the building that I wouldn't be seeing that day. I especially liked the political cartoon in it of Morgan holding a huge magnet, which he pointed at Europe and the Middle East, sucking antiquities out of those regions.

It was a lovely afternoon, and I was sure that Bryn would enjoy hearing about it later.

At the appointed time, I returned to the school.

No Bryn.

I called him several times after 6 p.m. – when I thought he would be done with that meeting – and his stupid cell phone voice mailbox was too full to take a message! I walked all through the building, not seeing him anywhere, and then started asking questions.

People knew who I was and that I was his caregiver, but most of them had no idea why he had left the building without contacting me. This seemed rather odd. I walked around some more, and finally found Claus. He left his class to talk to me, which was very nice of him.

Claus knew why Bryn had left, and promptly shared it with me.

What a relief…it was nothing terrible, and nothing personal…to me.

Instead, it was personal to Bryn. He had hemorrhoids. When I finally found this out – by talking to him on the phone – I could see why had hadn't just told me about it earlier. What man wants to tell a woman that?! Come to think of it, who wants to tell that to anyone? But it had gotten to a point that it was causing an inordinate amount of worry, so he told me.

Claus had only known that Bryn had gotten a call on his cell phone during the meeting, at 5 p.m., and left. Huh…3 hours into a dull meeting about school policy. Bryn had arrived in time for it to start at 2 o'clock. Now it was after 6, and I was just finding out about this.

When I talked to Bryn, he told me that he had been waiting for the hospital to call him and tell him either to come in or not to come in. When the call came and they said yes, he was relieved just to get away from the meeting; it was getting seriously tedious. He told me why.

The President of the board of trustees was a small-minded lawyer who interfered with teaching methods for the sole purpose of throwing his weight around. The guy didn't know much about teaching, and the school was tuition-free and for adults who chose to learn about the economy and alternative ways to run the economy; they didn't have to attend at all.

But this fool wanted to ban movies from the curriculum. Add to that the minor detail that Bryn and Claus were teaching a class on

Distractions: Letterman and the Morgan Library

documentaries, and this lawyer seemed even more irrational. How can one teach such a class without showing any actual movies?!

So Bryn was happy to get away from him for a while and think about future strategy.

He would solve that problem later.

Using my cell phone had gotten me nowhere, so I found all this out by going home, looking up the number for the Urgent Care Center of the Memorial Sloan-Kettering Cancer Center (MSKCC), and calling it from the land line there.

Sure enough, Bryn was there. The people there gave him the message, and he called me back on the land line. He wondered why I hadn't answered it all afternoon; he had tried calling it, assuming that I would have gone back to the apartment. But I had stayed out and gone back to the school to get him.

Bryn was sorry that I had wandered around for so long, confused and without any information. He had gone directly to the hospital in a cab – no doubt feeling uncomfortable – and forgotten to call me. Once he was settled there, in the center of the building and rigged up to an array of machines, he couldn't contact me via cell phone. There was no cell phone signal there.

No wonder I had to give up and go home.

Bryn had called me on his land line - after the nurses told him I had called them - and wondered why I hadn't answered the phone here all afternoon. I told him that I hadn't come home. He didn't mind that, just wanted to know/understand why no answer. Mystery solved.

We decided that I would just stay home and watch television and eat, and that he would call me if and when he was being let out of there. The hospital hadn't yet decided whether or not to keep him all night. They would give him a prescription for this latest problem, but meanwhile, they wanted to do a CT scan and look for more internal masses of cancer, just in case.

It sucked, but it was nothing to have a panic attack over or to feel gloom and doom about.

Accordingly, I ate, watched *Bones*, e-mailed my Aunt Johanna Rénard with the latest news of Bryn, New York City, and other goings on, and relaxed. I also called Cassie, and she told me that this problem had been brewing for a while. She seemed glad that he was finally getting it addressed. At least he had told her about it.

At midnight, he called me – he was free to go, and CT scans had found that there were no other nasty bits of cancer growing. He told me to stay put, that he would come home in a cab, he said, as if we hadn't discussed it earlier.

The Slamming Door

"You can't come home alone in a cab after being at the hospital all night!" I protested. "Stay there – I'll get a cab and come get you."

"Okay."

As fast as I could get my handbag and shoes on, I was out the door. It was a nice night out, and soon I found a cab. I didn't even have far to go before I found one. The cab was being driven by a nice man from Ghana, and he did the whole ride – round trip, from Bryn's door to Sloan-Kettering on York Avenue and back again.

I chatted with him the whole way, telling him all about Bryn, that he was sick, that I was his cousin-in-law and taking care of him, how cool and interesting Bryn was, how much fun we had staying together, and so on.

The man seemed genuinely pleased to hear about it all, perhaps because he was from a culture in which families took great care of one another. Some comment he made suggested that. It was a lovely, mild evening, and we rode along with the windows partly open.

I called Bryn just as we were about to turn the corner so that he wouldn't have to spend much time on his feet. It worked out perfectly. "There he is," I said to the cab driver as I saw Bryn come out with his cane, holding his cell phone up to his ear as we talked to each other.

Bryn was moving along at a fairly brisk pace, too. His hair was just starting to grow back in, and I was beginning to believe that the doctor would not poison it away ever again. He had his black backpack with him, and his dark blue jacket on. He looked okay.

He got in, with me fussing a bit until he was situated properly, and we were off.

I quieted down at that point, letting Bryn and the cab driver do much more of the talking. Bryn knew that I had gotten this cab right in front of our building, so he didn't worry about explaining the route to this driver.

When we arrived, I gave him fresh water, fresh McNulty's coffee, and chicken soup. He had eaten half a tuna fish sandwich at the hospital, so he wasn't particularly hungry. He also enjoyed being greeted by the cat when he got back. Nikita loved men, it seemed.

With Bryn back and settled in for the night, I e-mailed Cassie, Albert, Damon, and my Aunt Johanna to let them know of the outcome. Bryn was okay, comfortable, and not worried. We were all quite happy and calm; nothing was going to change for a while longer.

It was during this somewhat relaxed time – the calm before the storm, I suppose it felt like – that both Berta and I began to find time to do some things that we liked to do. We each did them on our own.

Distractions: Letterman and the Morgan Library

For Berta, it was to wait in huge long lines with many other fans of Stevie Nicks and Lynda Carter to see these lucky celebrities who had been able to have lucrative and fun careers. She asked me if I would like to come with her to see the actress who had played Wonder Woman (Carter), but I said no thank you.

I was a bit nonplussed that anyone would stand in line for hours on end after working in an office all day long. Wasn't she tired? Berta usually complained of being tired. But she seemed to find new energy when an opportunity arose to meet a famous person that she liked.

So off she went.

She had gone to see Stevie Nicks, her favorite rock star, sometime during the winter, or perhaps the previous fall (I forget which). Now she was going again. When she returned to the apartment to tell us about it – either later that night or perhaps the next evening – she said that she had cried when her turn came at last.

She *cried*?! Of course I kept my expressions as neutral and deadpan as I possibly could. But why cry, I wondered? And I was curious enough to contemplate the idea. Maybe she was crying because meeting a celebrity was the closest that she could ever hope to come to a break from her rather ordinary and mundane existence, which she seemed to loathe. That had to be it.

Still, these fandom excursions told me something else: if I wanted someone with whom to share a tale of an encounter with any famous person, Berta would willingly oblige me.

I had to be careful though; she had made much of my reports of seeing Ethan Hawke on this very street. But what was I supposed to do if I saw him? Not mentioning it later seemed a bit like someone was spoiling the fun, but I wasn't, as Berta had announced to the family, obsessed with him. Instead, I was rather pleased with myself for treating the actor as much as possible like a human being who lived nearby and just happened to be famous.

How else could I treat him? The guy lived down the street from us, but we all knew damned well exactly who he was. It was unavoidable. There are just some bits of information that one can't help knowing, especially if one has seen an actor a really good movie; you just remember that person because the movie was such a good story, like *Gattaca* and *Dead Poets Society*.

After Natasha Richardson died from that freak skiing accident, Bryn paid attention because her mother, Vanessa Redgrave, was a Georgist. He had me look up information on her because there was a chance that she might visit the Henry George School. Ethan Hawke attended the funeral for her daughter, he lived on our street...and noticing his comings and goings seemed normal and routine to us all.

The Slamming Door

But Berta took it a bit far...she and I and Bryn were slowly walking east on our street one afternoon as Hawke and his 11-year-old son were headed west. I was telling some anecdote when Berta interrupted, "Clarisse – look!" and there he was.

"So what?!" I said, impatiently. What did she expect me to do, stop talking and gawk at the guy?! What an idiotic way to behave!

Bryn agreed; he told Berta to leave him alone, that the guy was out with his son and to just let him go on about his business. He didn't need to have people stopping to stare at him every few paces.

He was likely returning from the funeral at that time; the photos on the Internet of Natasha Richardson and Liam Neeson's friends included Ethan Hawke, and he was in the exact same outfit. I saw them the next day when Bryn asked me to look up the information on her mother. In the end, Redgrave didn't go to the school. How could she? She was upset, no doubt too upset to think about Georgism. She must have changed her schedule.

There was another day when I dropped Bryn off at the Henry George School to give a lecture, intending to collect him at the end. I had done the research with him the night before, looking up everything and anything that he required on the Internet, printing it out, saving it for later, and checking with Bryn to see if it was what he needed. By the time he had 10 sheets of paper, he said he was all set; he had to read through it, after all. That wasn't all; he was making great use of his new flat-screen TV and DVD hookup to prepare. On Tuesday afternoons, I would set up the machine to play the week's movie so that he and Desta were both prepared.

I did this for him at least twice, perhaps three times, so that he could jointly teach a class with Desta that he was enjoying very much. It was the one that involved documentaries and movies that the students loved. How could anyone find fault with this curriculum, one that was part of a program that cost the students nothing?

Bryn would lecture like the rock star that he was, providing infotainment and thus tricking his students into learning a great deal by making it fun, and then come home in a great mood. It sounded like a great plan.

But I couldn't face hearing about economics; I was still too anxious about my own future.

And Bryn didn't mind. He knew I was scared and uncertain because I had told him.

It was far better to just provide him with full disclosure and honesty than to let him imagine that I found his topic dull. No – he was

Distractions: Letterman and the Morgan Library

fascinating and fun to listen to. It wasn't his fault at all; I was just scared of what the information made me think about. The next generation wasn't going to do well – it was going to be lost to poverty – just as Alfred's lecture had warned us last winter. I couldn't bear to hear about that again.

So I took off, cell phone turned on and in my pocket as usual, with my digital camera.

I decided to walk around the area where the school was, browsing in a rare book shop, wandering through a vintage clothing shop, and so on. But then my phone rang, and my plan changed. It was Berta; she wanted to attend her father's lecture and take him home herself.

Excellent; she would be there when I returned a little while afterwards.

What would I do with my sudden gift of free time to explore?

Leave my usual stomping grounds! I could wander farther away from the school since I didn't have to come back later. I headed for Times Square on foot, up Broadway. It should be interesting, I thought to myself, as Mayor Bloomberg had just instituted his experiment there, making it forbidden to motor traffic.

The Slamming Door

It was; there were green lawn chairs in the middle of the street and people enjoying the lack of cars and buses, walking every which way, unafraid of getting run over. A German couple, tourists, paused to ask me to photograph them with their own camera. I did it, then walked them to the TKTS booth to take their chances on whatever shows the stand was offering seats for.

A store on Broadway near 50th Street, one called Backstage Memories, sold books of music to all of the famous Broadway musicals, tee shirts, mugs, magnets, and so on and on. I went in there and found a heavy book on *Wicked*, the musical about what happened in the Land of Oz before Dorothy and Toto arrived. After thinking it over, I bought it, realizing that I would likely not have such an opportunity again. I had been in there before and left without it before.

Damon and I had gone to see *Wicked* in August of 2005 together. My father had even paid for the cost of one of those tickets, and I loved it. I had a CD of the music, and we had been lucky enough to see the show with the original Broadway cast. Yes, I was glad to get this book.

I walked up the street to the Ed Sullivan Theater. Raising my digital camera, I shot some photos; alas, when our old laptop had died late in 2005, it had lost some wonderful images of Rupert Jee, the man who ran the Hello Deli around the corner on West 53rd Street. He had smiled and waved to me one afternoon as I went by and paused to get his picture.

Distractions: Letterman and the Morgan Library

Watching *The Late Show with David Letterman* was a nightly ritual with me; in Connecticut, it made me feel more connected with Manhattan. In Manhattan, it was just great fun to see what the comic had been up to that day. I understood what I was watching a lot better after having walked around the island so much.

Once, the entire Late Show staff and Letterman had been ordered outside by the fire chief when an air conditioner caught fire. It might have been that summer; Letterman ordered the camera crew to film whatever it could. He liked to keep that theater in a state of constant chill, so it was no wonder that an air conditioner failed and caused so much trouble.

As I paced around, I suddenly got a surprise: Letterman himself was coming out!

He was wearing sneakers, socks, cargo shorts, a tee shirt, and a fleece jacket. With him was a man in a suit – his driver – and a woman I had never seen before. Out front, parked on the street, was a black sedan with dark tinted windows – his ride.

I rushed to get my stupid, slow camera ready in the gray, overcast afternoon.

Unfortunately, Letterman kept facing a crowd of middle-aged tourists who were approaching in the opposite direction, heading south on Broadway. I took a few photographs anyway; it was better than nothing.

The Slamming Door

But it wasn't great, and I called Berta as I walked home to lament the lame photos. Just as I had predicted to myself, she was sincerely sympathetic. I knew I could count on her to be interested in watching a celebrity. In this instance, I didn't feel guilty about hovering near a famous person; he was still in the public eye, just outside his workplace.

When I got home, Bryn was delighted with his performance and acclaim from that evening, which had come in the form of a standing ovation.

Unfortunately, he paid for it for the next day and a half. He was wiped out from the exertion and had to sleep a lot and sit quietly. I wondered why it was so bad – silently – as I took care of him, bringing him whatever he needed so that he could move as little as possible.

Then he told me what he had done that had so thoroughly worn him out: he had delivered the lecture while standing, just as he always had. I couldn't believe it, and gaped at him for a moment. "They all know you're sick – it's not a secret. Couldn't you do your lectures from a chair and get the same applause and thrill out of it all?" I couldn't help asking.

He immediately said that he could and that next time, he would. He was sure he would be able to do another one before the course ended. And he did.

But his biggest regret about being terminally ill, he often said, was that he would not be around to see what happened to the economy. Since the W. Bush administration had looted and crashed it – never mind that a lot of the impacts from the act of crashing it would be felt after that administration was long gone – he was intensely curious to see how it would go.

Bryn wanted to see how bad it would get, what would be done about it, how long a recovery would take, what form it would take, how the nation would adapt in order to recover, and so on.

And his curiosity would go unsatisfied.

Chapter 40

Leila, and an Air Conditioner

The topics of this chapter are unrelated; however, they did happen close together.

Sometime in early May, I forget exactly when, Berta spent a long time on the phone with a friend while sitting on the sofa. I was working at the computer as usual, but I was intrigued by the conversation. Berta was strenuously urging her friend to dump her cheating boyfriend.

When she rang off, I asked her to tell me about her friend.

It turned out that her friend was Iranian, but a secular person, from the Pahlavi Era. I wondered whether she had lived in Iran during the time of the last reigning Pahlavi shah, or during the Islamic Revolution, or after – or even all three – but Berta had never asked.

Could I meet her?

"Wow – I didn't realize that you would be interested," Berta replied. "Okay."

And so a fun new acquaintance began.

I overlooked the fact that Berta had forgotten about my book-writing project with a former member of Iran's parliament; she wasn't good at listening, and the project was on hold. It was too much to expect Berta to remember me mentioning all of the reading I had done to teach myself Iranian history, Iranian women's studies, and to learn about Massoumeh's career.

Leila came over the next evening to meet both Bryn and me. Berta brought her straight from work; it turned out that that was how they knew each other. Berta had started on the same floor as Leila, but had to move elsewhere when her boss retired and his replacement brought in his own secretary. That left Berta as a floater on another floor.

Leila was a swarthy, black-haired, dark-eyed woman with a chunky physique. She was not fat, but her body type was not the "fashionable ideal" either. That explained, at least to me, how Berta had hit it off with her. Overweight people tend to find others like them. Berta's face was prettier than Leila's, too, which did not escape my notice. Female jealousy is often a factor in a woman's choice of friendships. Damon occasionally reminded me of this when I wondered why certain women were unfriendly. I guess it takes an outsider – a man in this case – to see it.

But Leila wasn't ugly, either. She was plain. She groomed herself nicely, wore a pretty color of lipstick, and a lot of black. Her hair was straight and grown down to her shoulders with bangs, and up in a barrette. She was clearly a Pahlavi expatriate. By that, I mean that she was thoroughly Westernized. The Pahlavi dynasty had emphasized and favored such things.

I was immediately curious to learn about her life, and when she was done chatting with Bryn, I proceeded with my questions while Berta observed. I watched Berta out of the corner of my eye, observing her also. She was getting new insight into my expertise; I wasn't just a quiet care-giver. Now she could see the evidence of my education and interests, and self-discipline to constantly build on it. She kept her expressions neutral, or so I thought, but I can't read people's expressions when they are subtle. Maybe she was shaken up and jealous. I couldn't tell.

In any case, Leila was lovely to get to know.

She was a cheerful, friendly person, and she readily told me about her life. She had been born in Utah because her father, an engineer, was working there. She had two older sisters, and one of them had been educated at a boarding school in Switzerland. Leila herself had lived in Utah for the first several years of her life, which was why she spoke flawless American English.

When she was nine years old – and we were all the same age, her, me and Berta – her parents had moved the family back to Tehran, the capital of Iran. Lucky her, I commented wryly: just in time for the Islamic Revolution.

Indeed, she was not happy about that. Nominally, they were Muslims, but they were utterly and completely secular about it, happy with their ways, unhappy at being forced to veil, and it was an unpleasant time. Leila's older sisters were out of the country by then, and their parents kept them away. Better not to inflict Islamization on all three of their daughters.

"So you were stuck wearing the veil for a while?" I asked, knowing how she felt about it. I would not have phrased the question that way to a religious Muslim, but Leila obviously felt put upon over the issue.

"Yes," she replied. "I had to wear a scarf and a manteau," meaning that long, loose, and usually black, brown, gray or blue rain-jacket sort of covering, which is typically worn with long pants. The Ayatollah Khomeini demanded that women wear the veil on April 1st of 1979, and then went further when he made the veil compulsory for all women in 1983, decreeing that not wearing it would be treated as a criminal offense, with violators subject to up to 74 lashes, 2 months in prison, a fine, or any combination of the above.

"When did you get to leave Iran?"

Leila, and an Air Conditioner

"When I was thirteen," she told me. That meant that she experienced life under that monstrous veiling edict. I wish I remembered how they all got out, but I just don't. Perhaps her American citizenship helped; she had been born a U.S. citizen, the knowledge of which was no doubt a comfort to her after 1979. It must have been hard to grow up in a free and secular society and then experience life under the mullahs.

The family returned to the United States, her father found more engineering work, and Leila happily shed the veil and continued her education. She was not at all religious, and despised Islam now for all that it had wrought in Iran.

When it came time for college, she completed it without delay, though I forget now where and what she studied. That is probably because her graduate studies were so interesting to hear about: she had gotten her Master of Public Health degree in Caen, France, on the northern coast, and she had studied for her graduate degree entirely in French. She coached me carefully on the pronunciation of the city's name: "cahn" was the phonetic version, not to be confused with Cannes, which was on the Mediterranean coast and pronounced like canned food. That was where the French version of the Oscars was held each year, the award being called the Palme d'Or – the hand of gold.

She could still remember quite a bit of the language, she told us, but it was fading a little now. Her Persian language skills were still there too, but not perfect, she replied when I asked about that. Leila asked me about my work with Massoumeh Parsi, and said that she did not know as much as I did about the current structure of Iran's government.

At some point, I asked about her horrible and now ex-boyfriend. Why had she wasted time on such a jerk, I wondered? Her answer was interesting: she hadn't wanted to get married when she was younger, which was what her father had urged her to do. She wanted to be free to date, have sex, and do her own thing, and get married when she was older. So the answer was that not wanting to be tied down had led to a series of throw-aways rather than finding one keeper. Fishing for guys as a sport rather than as a necessity was her choice.

Berta and I glanced at each other when this information came up; we wanted keepers.

Then it was my turn: Leila wanted to hear my entire curriculum vitae, it seemed, so I told her the story of my professional life. At one point, Asperger's came up in the conversation. It might have been me, or it might have been Berta that mentioned it, but it came up when I lapsed into a lengthy, detailed response to one of her questions.

It was actually quite funny, because the term "professor" had cropped up, when I said that I had actually been called professor for one of my jobs, when I was an adjunct at a community college teaching law

The Slamming Door

and computer use. "Professor Rénard," she said, smiling and trying to get a word in. I paused for her to say more at that point.

We were quite fascinated with one another, and pleased to meet.

Berta looked like she was the odd woman out; it was a rare experience for me not to be the odd one out. That could happen when a visit was about intellectual skills rather than social skills. No wonder it was a rare and memorable occasion for me.

Leila became a part of our evening social calendar over the next couple of months.

When that happened, I reverted, for the most part, to being the odd woman out.

That was to be expected; Leila and Berta were old friends and I was new on the scene.

It was early June by this time, and getting hot out.

Just a couple of Sundays earlier, while Bryn had been at Cassie's, Berta and Matt had surprised me by calling to say that they were coming over to install an air conditioner in my room. Wow – I wondered what had motivated Berta to do this. She spent regular evenings in there and didn't tolerate the heat well; perhaps she assumed that I needed to be cool also.

Actually, I coped with the heat better than most. It was Damon who was in seventh heaven over having that machine installed when he came to visit for our anniversary. Most summer nights, I loved being able to sleep in the heat with just a sheet over me. I have always loved to warm. In the winter, I wear socks and slippers at all times. I hate the cold.

Still, it was a very nice thing to do.

I was out shopping for cleaning supplies when Berta called me, so I came home and got settled, put on my old shorts and a ratty tee shirt, and was ready when they arrived. It was a cleaning day for me; I had mopped, dusted, changed Bryn's sheets, put out new towels, and scrubbed the whole bathroom. Next, I went after the windows, determined to have them spotless by the time Matt went to work with his tools.

Just in time, I finished up in my room. The path to the window on the right was cleared, and the window spotless. I used a lot of Windex and removed cakes of brown dirt from inside every window molding. When Matt took over in there, I adjourned to Bryn's room, where Matt had installed a new air conditioner three years earlier. Berta had bought that one, too, and even though I had been in the apartment, there had been no chance to scrub that window at the time.

Now I intended to make up for that; Matt could check the window afterward. The upper inside pane of that window – the one on the right

Leila, and an Air Conditioner

of a pair that was side by side – was caked with brown pipe smoke. Bryn had built it up over the past three decades, and cleaning it had never been possible because in order to keep the air conditioner in that window, the upper pane had to be permanently positioned to hold it in place.

Outside, on the part of the air conditioner that jutted out over the street, was a used stick of deodorant that some tenant above us had dropped a couple of years ago. It had been inaccessible but annoying to look at all this time. I was going to clean it ALL.

Berta followed me into her father's room to watch me work. I asked her to spot me on the ladder as I scrubbed first the left window, which could be released inwards, dropping down to chest level for washing. When I finished that, I needed her help; I couldn't get the pane of the right window down the same way with the air conditioner there.

When I released the upper pane, we both watched the air conditioner anxiously, but it stayed put. I grabbed the old deodorant bottle and threw it into Bryn's trash can, and we cheered gleefully, laughing and giggling. It felt like a minor triumph. Then I scrubbed the whole window – both sides of the lower panes of glass and the inside of the upper one – and put it all back.

Or so I thought.

Matt came in just then to announce that the installation in my room was complete, stopped in mid-sentence when he saw the air conditioner in Bryn's room, and looked horrified. Apparently, it wasn't quite right.

I told him not to yell at me, and that I had timed this cleaning for his presence here so that he could check my work. He calmed down, adjusted the air conditioner just so, and all was well. He wasn't quite through clearing up the tools and packaging in my room, though, and he wanted to look over the instructions for the new machine, so he disappeared again.

With that, I went to work on the rest of the windows in the apartment, which included two in the living room and one in the kitchen. I was having a great time now that I had figured out how to release the catch on the lower panes; Bryn had told me that Cassie used to do this. Every time I had ever visited Bryn in warm weather, I had washed his windows, but never the outsides. Now I could do that.

As I worked, my cell phone rang. It was Bryn, calling just to say "Hi" and to see how I was doing. I happily told him about the air conditioner in my room, and the window cleaning, complete with the useful discovery of how to operate that catch.

He was thrilled – so thrilled that he raved on and on about it for at least a minute.

The Slamming Door

Two more things happened that month: Bryn climbed up into the linen closet by the bathroom and retrieved something old and important, and Berta at last got something done that she had discussed since the previous fall, which was that she got the old living room rocking chair re-caned. It was a beautiful, carved, varnished wooden antique, and the seat was smashed through. I couldn't remember it having ever been intact, and it was a family heirloom.

As for Bryn's artifact, it was a set of vinyl records that dated back to his high school years. He and Albert each had fond memories of their years at the Hackley School in Tarrytown, New York. It was an all-boys college preparatory school then, though it had since gone co-ed. Recently, Bryn and Albert had found an article about their history teacher; he had died, and he had been at the school for over fifty years. The man was friendly and immensely popular, the kind of history teaching who made learning the subject matter great fun.

That must have been a factor in Bryn's decision to get out his old records. They were recordings of himself and his classmates, singing in the school's two groups, the Octet and the Glee Club. It reminded me of my all-girls high school; there was a glee club and a group called Take Nine. Bryn was lucky in that he had a wonderful tenor voice, so there were two solos by him on the records – one in each group.

Now Bryn wanted to have the contents of the records transferred to CDs.

Accordingly, I researched the possibilities online and presented him with my findings.

He was serious about this, and we were all intrigued; we wanted to hear him singing as a teenager, but no one had a record player anymore. Berta found a place on Long Island that would do the job faster and for a bit less, and took the set away. In less than a week, it was all on CD.

Could I make labels for the twenty copies that had been provided?

Sure thing, I said, and trotted off to Staples to get jewel cases for them and stick-on labels that could be put through the printer and then applied to the top sides of each disc. Soon I was hard at work on the computer yet again, figuring out spacing and printing specs.

I made a label that could be slid into the lids of the jewel cases so that the recipients could read the titles of each song and who sang them all, plus the round ones that adhered to the discs. That was the trickiest part, but after wasting a couple of them, I had it right. It wasn't long before I was able to present the lot to Bryn, who was delighted. He was now immortalized as a teenage soul music singer.

He started giving out a few discs right away, but only a few. He didn't yet know who would get them all. I wanted one, but said nothing

Leila, and an Air Conditioner

about it for now; there was an original for making more copies if necessary, and it had been marked carefully as such.

Berta started inviting me and Leila out for evening excursions, and Bryn insisted that I go out with them and have a good time. He still thought I didn't get out enough. It was true; I could be anywhere – a quiet suburban home or an engaging big city – and I would still stay home an awful lot, reading, writing, and watching shows and movies on television. I did go out for movies on occasion, but not enough to seem like I was having lots of fun, apparently.

For our first excursion, Bryn happened to be away again. That meant that there was no need to even think about rushing back, so I wandered the area of SoHo with them from early evening to well after dark, by which time it had been raining for a few hours.

It was a Friday evening, and Berta had asked me to meet them at an upscale shop that offered modern kitchen and bath items, all specially designed, many of wood, and looking like they ought to be in the Guggenheim Museum than in anyone's home.

The draw to this place was an architect-turned-pastry chef, who was showcasing his creations for anyone who cared to try them. The point of the demonstration was to provide examples of architecturally constructed desserts; each recipe resembled a modern building. They tasted good, and there were free drinks also.

I arrived exactly on time, wearing my Teva sandals, black linen pants, and a comfortable but dressy blouse. With all of the walking I did in Manhattan, I insisted upon wearing those shoes. Leila arrived first, and commented on them; they contrasted with the rest of my attire. Oh well – I wasn't going to change my mind about them. Unlike most women, I don't like to go shoe-shopping. I defended myself handily enough. Leila was wearing flat-soled, slipper-like shoes, something that would be perfect for the environment she had just come from.

Berta arrived soon after, wearing a pale-hued version of the same style. We laughed about it and went in...after Berta said that I looked like a total tourist with my tall, narrow copy of *Manhattan: Block by Block* sticking out of the back pocket of my Vera Bradley bag. Leila agreed. I said I didn't care, that I loved having that map with me everywhere I went. They gave up, and we turned our attention to the next event.

The place was moderately crowded, and we tried some of everything, but we didn't chat with the chef; he was just too busy. It was too bad, because I had done lots of pastry and dessert-creating at home. It would have been fun to talk to him.

The Slamming Door

When it was over, we headed out and soon found a fancy soap shop, one of those places that cut slabs of handmade soap into bars after the customer made a selection. There was a sink off to one side, so that we could wash our hands and try scent after scent. Berta and Leila got into what looked to me like an absurdly serious discussion with the nice gay sales associate while I stood off to one side and watched, getting bored. It was just soap – who cared what spa benefit each flavor offered?! It wasn't like we could hope to remember it all later.

But I kept quiet. I may not respond well to what most people get a thrill out of, but I know enough not to make unsolicited announcements about how boring I find certain things. Soon the Chinese water torture ended and we were back outside, putting up our umbrellas.

As we moved along, Berta informed us that she knew of a corporate event in the area, and that she wanted us to go to it. I recognized the area; there was a Chanel store along this route, and a MoMA store. They were closed now because it was after 8 p.m. It was getting dark, and the rain was really coming down. I was glad not to be wearing better shoes.

Suddenly Berta stopped; she had found it. It was a corporate event put on by the Nespresso company. It was the sort of party that required an invite, but Berta wasn't about to let that stop her. Leila protested, but Berta was brazen and shameless. She was fascinating to watch as she calmly and audaciously walked right up to the hostess, who was standing at the lectern just inside the door on right, and explained that she had misplaced her invitation. Could she please look at her list and find us?

The hostess diligently searched her records while Leila and I withdrew to the shadows. We couldn't look. What was Berta planning to say when her name inevitably failed to be on the list? Would she just lie and claim to be someone else, someone who was on the list?

I don't know what she said to her in the end, but she got us in.

Doubtful but up for a minor adventure, Leila and I followed her inside. At least I would have a great story to tell Damon later on, I told myself. He loved outrageous tales such as this one. Whatever we were in for, it looked like a new experience.

It was; we had walked into a surreal situation that resembled a modern art museum and a fashion show for gourmet coffee machines all in one. Portraits of famous celebrities covered the walls, and each one was both enormous and composed entirely of Nespresso coffee pods of all colors glued onto a huge black square.

That was a clever if wasteful way to showcase the product. Nespresso coffee comes in many flavors, and each cup is made by inserting a small pod of coffee into a machine that pierces its aluminum foil to reach the finely ground coffee inside. Hot water is then filtered through it and into a waiting cup below. Once this phase of the process

Leila, and an Air Conditioner

is complete, the pod, foil and all, is thrown away. A side attachment is included with many Nespresso machines – the company offers both coffee pods and machines – so that one may also have foamed milk in the drink.

The whole process is so over-the-top luxurious as to be damaging to the environment.

How did I know this much detail about it? Williams-Sonoma and Sur la Table offered those machines for sale, and they offered free samples. I had offered and been offered many a cup of the luxury drinks complete with foamed milk both as a sales associate and as a customer. But no one at this event needed to know how I had acquired what was common knowledge.

Berta ushered us as far back into the space as possible, handing me and Leila each a fancy, thick paper shopping bag with rope handles and the company's logo on it. Inside were some brochures. We found a small counter on the right, and stood there. It had more brochures, and Berta stuffed some into our bags.

There was a team of wait staff walking around with trays of gourmet goodies, and they weren't all desserts. Many were delectable treats that could, if consumed in large enough quantities, constitute a small dinner. We all proceeded to make use of them accordingly. There were crab cakes with a remoulade sauce, grilled cheese toasts, smoked salmon, and several other great things. At the very back was, not surprisingly, a Nespresso bar offering free latte, cappuccino, espresso, and so on.

Leila and Berta lapsed into chatting about our surroundings and whatever else they could think of while watching the proceedings; I wandered over to the coffee bar to get a cup of cappuccino. The woman working the machine presented it in a porcelain cup and saucer complete with the ubiquitous Nespresso logo on them, jazzed it up with foamed milk, laid one wrapped square of Nespresso dark chocolate on the saucer, and gestured to the shakers of cocoa and cinnamon on the counter to the left.

This was fun. I shook on some of each topping, carried it over to the others and stood with them, less interested in conversation and more absorbed with savoring the drink and gourmet goodies. That was always how I enjoyed restaurants, cafés, and other food-and-drink-focused social events. And that was fine, because Berta was in her element, explaining our surroundings to us both.

Leila and I listened as she pointed out a woman at the front of the space, standing near the windows, being interviewed with bright lights. She had long, thick, slightly waved red hair, heavy makeup, and high heels on. She was shorter than Berta but appeared to weigh the same as Berta, and she exuded confidence as she fielded questions. Berta told us

The Slamming Door

that she was a billionaire fundraiser but that she couldn't recall her name. Interesting; we just nodded and listened.

When I went to use the rest room, I encountered a tall, large-boned and somewhat overweight man with thick, straight white hair; he was wearing a navy blue, pinstriped suit and a beautiful tie. He was obviously a CEO for Nespresso, or some corporate bigwig. He was nodding and smiling, and he benevolently put his hand on my back to help guide me along as I headed toward the bathrooms. I was glad for the background music and chatter; it meant that he wouldn't try to engage me in conversation. What would I have said?

Granted, I could be fun and interesting to talk to, but when deception was part of the game, I didn't want to dig myself in too deep. I wanted to leave that to Berta. She was certainly doing a lovely job of it; the next coup that she pulled off was to snare us each a corporate gift, which we gently lowered into our bags: there was a mesh bag that contained 2 sets of espresso cups, saucers and spoons emblazoned, of course, with the Nespresso logo, and one box each of individually wrapped wafers of milk and dark chocolate, also with the logo. I would give my grandmother the milk chocolate one for her birthday, I decided then and there.

At last Berta felt that we had seen it all, and we walked back out into the rainy evening and up Broadway. I breathed easier knowing that there was nothing to worry about, and was even pleased with the outcome.

She walked north until I spotted a bookstore that I hadn't heard of before: the Shakespeare & Co. Booksellers on Broadway and

Leila, and an Air Conditioner

Washington Square. The place was full of wooden bookshelves and tables, carpeted in green, and a lovely female cat named Agnes wandered among the displays. She let me cuddle her.

We all wandered around, looking at books and enjoying the cat.

As we did so, I came across a book that I wanted to give to Bryn; it was called *The Street Book: An Encyclopedia of Manhattan's Street Names and Their Origins* by Henry Moscow. I showed it to Berta and asked her what she thought. She approved wholeheartedly.

I browsed some more and then stopped because I had found a huge book of old maps, reproduced from London, Paris, and many other places. I didn't want to get interested in buying anything else, even though Damon would doubtless approve of this addition to our collection.

Almost as soon as I sat down on the floor to look at my new books and pet Agnes, my phone rang. It was Bryn, calling to see how I was doing. Not mentioning the book I had found for him (I wanted to surprise him with it when he returned), I chatted with him for a few minutes before putting Berta on the phone with him. He was having a good time and feeling okay.

That concluded our visit for the evening, until the next one with Leila.

The Slamming Door

Chapter 41

About His Papers…

Sometime in April or May, I forget exactly when, Berta sat on the living room sofa and informed me that she wanted to keep any bit of paper found in the apartment with her father's handwriting on it.

She didn't say why, and she didn't need to.

The reason was quite obvious: she wanted keepsakes, and she wanted to be able to read anything and everything that he had written when he was alive after he was dead.

I could just picture her doing that, crying quietly and sniffling over each item, then getting too upset to continue, dropping the piece of paper, and sobbing uncontrollably. She was going to drive Mike and whoever else lived with her crazy by doing that.

Then again, maybe not: if I found out that Bryn didn't want his papers read after he died, I would make sure that they were all gone.

I had a sneaking suspicion that he wouldn't want her to have or read his written material.

And I knew that she liked to read other people's personal, most private things whenever she got the chance, having seen her do just that with Maggie's old stuff. When it was just those letters from a prisoner to that former occupant of the guest room, I hadn't wasted much energy fretting about it. But Bryn was another story: I cared about his wishes, and I knew him well enough to have a sense as to what they were. And I was there to do whatever Bryn wanted.

But I like to confirm things rather than proceed on assumptions.

So I did just that.

At the time of this demand (that was couched in the terms of a request), I had told Berta that she had to understand that if I came across anything that the lawyer would need to settle the estate, I certainly couldn't give her that. She raised no objection to that. It was logical and unavoidable that those things would have to be handed over.

But the personal papers – which I came to refer to as recreational mail, plus notes, research, and other data – those were different.

Accordingly, I simply nodded and at this point in the conversation and let the matter drop, having committed myself neither to saving the stuff for her nor refusing to do so. I knew that there would be trouble from her over this later, but that would be later. Later would be awful, but I was content to ignore that thought for now and focus on less upsetting thoughts.

Bryn was still coherent, lucid, and even enjoying life, visiting his girlfriend at her house in upstate New York on his own. He knew exactly what was going on around him, and was well able to make his own decisions. There was no reason to escalate the slightest hint of conflict at this point in time.

There was a simple way to discover what his wishes were: I told Bryn an anecdote about Bess Truman as a litmus test for understanding his wishes, and explained Berta's request.

Here is the tale…

Long after his presidency, Harry S. and Bess Truman were back at their home in Independence, Missouri, living out their retirement together.

One day, Harry walked in on Bess in the living room to find her standing over the lit fireplace, burning their old love letters.

"Bess!" he exclaimed, "What are you doing?!"

"Oh, it's okay," she replied, "I've memorized them."

"But Bess – think of history!" Harry protested.

"I have," she said, and tossed the last pile into the flames.

That's it. She didn't want anyone to read her personal, private correspondence after she was dead. Those letters were hers, and hers alone.

I agreed with her. Damon and I had some things that I would definitely want to destroy rather than have anyone poring over and commenting upon, analyzing and critiquing. Maybe I would deliberately leave some things to be read, and selectively destroy others.

But back to Bryn…I explained why I was telling him this tale, and repeated Berta's "request" to me about his own papers.

He was, as I had anticipated, appalled, and said that he didn't want her to have the papers.

"So you want me to get rid of them, and not save them for her?"

"Yes – absolutely; make them go away."

"Okay then, I will. And I won't read through them as I do it; I'll just make sure that they fall into the category in question, and into the recycling bag they shall go."

"Thank you," he said, giving me a grateful, relieved glance.

It was certainly a special experience to be trusted by a dying person.

The Slamming Door

Out went the papers, but not until halfway through July, when Bryn was ready. Until then, they sat around him, comforting and familiar, in piles on his bureau and under the table next to his chair.

I had always had a suspicion that Berta would eventually hate me. Now I knew why she would hate me. Well, I wouldn't consciously recognize this before I actually had to face that. But something else nagged at me...something looming in the near future: Berta had promised to have a complete and utter mental breakdown when her father died.

It was one thing to say that she was sure that she wouldn't be able to cope with the loss emotionally when it actually hit, but quite another to promise to freak out. I said nothing when she told me this, which was about the same time that she mentioned the disposition of her father's papers.

As usual, I just silently contemplated what that would mean, and who would bear the brunt of the outbursts, upsets, and whatever else.

It occurred to me that the person who would feel the brunt of all that would be me.

As it was, I was very depressed about both my own life circumstances and future, and the imminent, looming loss of Bryn. Not having any answers about living with Damon on our own, as in when and where, was high on the list of anxieties. The thought that I didn't know what would come next after my time with Bryn just scared me. Sometimes, when Berta and I were out walking together – usually to or from a diner – I would tell her so.

She would only say, "Don't upset me while my father is dying."

At other times, she would say that I would just have to accept an unacceptable future. Whenever she said that, it meant that Damon and I might never manage to earn a living and be together in our own country. I was very afraid of that. In fact, I was simply unwilling to live that scenario, and if I felt forced into that with no other options, suicide suddenly seemed like an attractive option. I'm just the sort of person who is unwilling to put up with anything other than the achievement of my goals. I'm not the only one, but I know that I'm in the minority.

My friend in Connecticut, Mrs. Biani, had had no interest in anything other than a retirement with her husband, but she had been denied that when he died just five months after retiring from the family auto-body and towing business that he had started. The expression on her face indicated that to her, life just wasn't worth living when her daughter suggested that she baby-sit the grandkids 24/7, and I could relate. She wanted Mr. Biani, and no one else. Mr. Biani was a very nice husband to her; he was worth the emotional energy she put into him. She died of a broken heart a few years later.

Uncle Damon Dies...on Damon's Birthday

Well, Berta didn't like that, or care how I felt about it, or have the slightest interest in my point of view. Of course, what else could I expect from someone who had squandered her dreams of achieving the sort of college credentials necessary to work in the field of her choice, and then accepted that her own life would never be particularly fun or interesting?

Her response, when I told her how I really felt, was always, "Don't say that! I don't want to get attached to you and then lose my friend. Don't upset my while my father is dying."

The result was that I was convinced that she only cared about her own emotional state. She just couldn't bring herself to say anything soothing that might make me feel better. She would demand that I guard her allegedly fragile emotional state while disregarding mine. That didn't sit well with me.

I began to pull away from her emotionally.

For months, I had been determined to be friends with her. I have always had the idea that relatives and in-laws have a duty to like each other and become friends, so I had done my best to do exactly that. We were thrown together due to awful circumstances, so I had been convinced that becoming good friends with her was the best thing to do. Now I wasn't so sure of that.

She was selfish and so was I, but in completely different ways.

She was selfish in a useless, consumer-like way, wanting the standard life of marriage, babies, a house, and if the price was a dull and slavish job devoid of real meaning, so be it.

I was selfish in a different way, seeking self-fulfillment and a meaningful career with constant opportunities to learn new and useful things while enjoying a marriage to a man who did the same and sharing a cat with him.

Add to our brands of selfishness the fact that she had attention deficit disorder and I had Asperger's, and we had a recipe for conflict, discord, and eventual disaster. I could concentrate and hated noise; she could not focus on anything for long and loved loud, startling events and sustained noise. It was clear that we were polar opposites.

Well, that was just perfect; I had been morbidly curious to get to know and understand her, and I had gotten my wish. That happened a lot, usually whenever I went away from home and had any kind of adventure: I learned a lot of new things, many of which I found I didn't like, but I never regretted learning them.

The upshot of this learning curve was that I suddenly knew, though I kept silent about it to absolutely everyone, was that I decided that no matter what happened, I would: 1. Do whatever Bryn wished with his things; 2. Refuse to take any abuse from anyone, nor would I accept the slightest criticism of that decision or course of action; and 3. Do

The Slamming Door

whatever it took to maintain my own sanity, even if it ran counter to her wishes, and not accept her or anyone else's criticism of that choice. That last had some elements of the first two decisions, but that was fine.

Trouble loomed in the future.

Chapter 42

Uncle Damon Dies...on Damon's Birthday

Damon has never liked his birthday.

It's true that there are some serious problems with it.

For one thing, his birthday falls on May 6th, which happens to be Job's birthday, and there was no dearth of bad things that befell him. Job was wealthy, healthy, and had a nice wife and good children. Then he lost his health, his wealth, and his children. Because of that, he cursed the day of his own birth. He did not curse God, even though the story assigns the blame for his troubles to God. Damon has never seen sharing a birthday with Job as a good omen.

For another thing, Damon hates the aging process and aims to defeat it through science.

His birthday is just another yearly reminder of the fact that this may not work.

As if that weren't enough, his father died in a plane crash on his tenth birthday, and Air Force men in uniforms came to inform him and his mother and sisters of the fact. So did his Uncle Rex, his father's younger brother, though I can never remember who got there first.

Damon's father was a famous Harvard-educated psychologist with a Ph.D. from the University of Michigan. He had brought his wife and kids to Turkey for a few years so that he could teach at an American university in Ankara, then they all went back to the States. It was shortly after that that Damon's father came to the infuriating realization that he didn't want children – too much noise. He asked for a divorce.

Unhappily but to satisfy him, Damon's mother granted this request, and thus Henrietta was stuck all on her own with the child care and costs. Unforgiveable, that's what that was. Henrietta went on to study for her Ph.D. in education, and coped admirably, but she shouldn't have had to.

For that, I despise Damon's father. I don't care that the guy continued to write letters to Damon from Ethiopia, where he worked (and died) as some sort of secret psychological profiler for the U.S. military, or so the story goes. I just don't care.

It seems pretty obvious to me, now that I understand how Asperger's works, and that it is hereditary, that Damon got his Asperger's from his father. But that is just no excuse for getting married to a woman who wanted kids, reproducing with her three times, and then suddenly having an epiphany that one didn't like children, noise, and family life. Too damned bad! You have to think all that through and realize it before the fact, before it affects other people.

Damon's father didn't bother to do that.

The Slamming Door

There are some sorts of selfishness I just don't approve of.

Not liking babies is one thing, but not liking them after you've had them is quite another.

Damon's uncle on his mother's side of the family, who shared his first name, was a retired professor who lived in Michigan with his second wife, a nurse whom I had met at our wedding. Aunt Sherry was very nice, and she had made a beautiful chuppah for us when we got married. It had white lace and a pink ribbon through it. I really appreciated it; I'm not Jewish, but some of Damon's relatives were, and we wanted a wedding that incorporated Wiccan, Episcopalian, Catholic, Jewish and Islamic traditions. We managed it nicely, too.

Uncle Damon was sick with brain cancer, and had been for quite some time. He had three children by his first wife, who was living in California. One son lived out there, another somewhere near him, and Nicola, his daughter in the Boston area. It was Nicola's husband Aaron whom I had worked for on the computer via the Internet. Nicola had hosted Thanksgiving in her home the previous fall, and been lucky enough to have her father there.

But now he was getting sicker and sicker.

Damon had wondered about his uncle's opinion of him, because he had disappeared from all contact with his family for a period of twelve years, ending just before he went off to the war in Kuwait in 1990. To see if I could ease his mind, I wrote to Nicola to ask her about it.

She wrote back to say that Damon should call his uncle and talk, but that she really doubted that her father bore him any ill will at all. That wasn't all that she wrote; she added that when Damon had reappeared, the entire family had been very pleased.

Damon had worried over how his uncle viewed him because of his odd and wild behavior as a teenager and even earlier, which was really just a consequence of being an Aspie. But Nicola assured me that the entire generation of kids, with the exceptions of Vianne and her brother Howie, were awful kids, so Damon had company. That was interesting and reassuring.

Nicola concluded by saying that she considered Damon to be an inspiration, and that she often held him up as an example to her kids. So she was telling her two little girls all about Damon, his troubles with college, his eventual successful completion of a double science major with honors, his time as a U.S. Army chemical weapons officer in the war, and then his Ph.D. in immunology. That was pleasing, and yes, he was definitely an inspirational example to tout.

Damon didn't call his uncle, even though I passed this on. He didn't feel the need; he had spoken pleasantly with him earlier in the year by phone. With this missive to share and thus shared, he felt fine...

Uncle Damon Dies...on Damon's Birthday

...which is why I decided not to tell him that his uncle had proceeded to die on May 6th.

Seriously...if I were Damon, with first one then another family member managing to accidentally die on my accursed birthday, I would be taking it rather personally. As it was, I found myself doing that on his behalf, although I shared this thought with no one at the time.

I did tell Damon that his uncle had died that week, but I lied about the date. I think I said it was the next day, or the day before. I knew that he would eventually find out the real date, but why rush into it? Meanwhile, I sent pretty sympathy cards to Aunt Sherry and Nicola, and prepared a list of addresses for Bryn to use on a sheet of paper. He had cards of his own to write.

Soon I was able to think of plenty of other stories to distract Damon with.

Taking care of Bryn's needs, which for now were all about ensuring that his social life and professional activities went as smoothly as possible, was entertaining. Damon liked hearing about what a good time I was having with his cousin.

Bryn was like another dad to me, which was why I wanted to be his care-giver. He was fun, easy-going, and in many ways just the opposite of my father. My father often got enraged over nothing; not Bryn. Of course, my father, because he was another Aspie, did not innately understand how to keep calm. But Bryn did; calmness and a constant willingness to slow down and listen and understand the other person in any situation was Bryn's way of relating to people.

It was at this point that the alumni book from Harvard arrived, a huge, heavy, hard-bound maroon thing with Harvard's crest on the cover, and Radcliffe's too. His Class of 1959 predated the merger of those universities, so the women's section with its alumnae followed the men's.

We looked at the glossy, black-and-white pages and found Bryn's entry. There it was, with the photograph I had shot last fall and the blurb he had written, perfectly typed and reproduced, just as I had sent it into cyberspace for him.

He kept it on the floor next to his chair after perusing the entire volume assiduously.

Before we knew it, he was showing me someone in it, someone from whom he had just received a social invitation. The man was now a wealthy, retired Wall Street stockbroker with a huge apartment on the

The Slamming Door

Upper East Side. He was throwing a party, and Bryn and any other classmate he could find were invited.

He must have been interested in music and opera, because Bryn got the idea of giving him a tie as a gift, one with a musical theme to it. Bryn also wanted another tie, a slightly different one, for someone else who would be there – a mutual friend who knew music. Perhaps it was someone associated with the Mendelssohn Glee Club, but I forget now.

I knew just the tie, I told Bryn. The only problem was locating a source to buy it from.

The tie was one that had been sold for years at Tanglewood, where the Boston Symphony Orchestra spent its summers. We had gotten one there for my father right a few years earlier, right after showing him the scarf version that I had bought for myself. When he saw the scarf, he was impressed; it came in men's ties also, so he wanted it. It was a brilliant sapphire blue with music written all over it, staffs, G-clefs, notes, plus brass, wind and string musical instruments.

I had even seen them for sale in the J.P. Morgan Museum shop recently.

That sounded perfect to Bryn; he wanted one. But he didn't want me to rush all the way back there, so I got on the Internet yet again. In no time at all, I had come across a company in southern Connecticut, called Alynn, Inc., that offered that same tie, plus some other choices.

Bryn came right out to the computer to look at the options.

The tie came in red also, but without the musical instruments; not so exciting.

There was also a dark blue one that depicted people in opera boxes enjoying a performance; definitely of interest, as this other acquaintance conducted music, or some such thing. Bryn had made up his mind, and produced his own credit card for the order.

He left me to it; one blue music tie, one opera tie, plus I already possessed some wrapping paper with a brass, wind, strings and percussion musical instruments pattern. I showed it to him, and he was very pleased indeed.

The order was placed, the merchandise arrived very soon thereafter, I wrapped it, and the Oatman boys went to the party together, both dressed in beige pants and dark blue jackets with ties on. Bryn's tie was his Harvard one.

They had a lovely time, and saw the magnificent library that this classmate had, complete with a balcony overlooking the room, met his beautiful Hungarian wife, ate hors d'oeuvres, mingled and chatted and schmoozed, and finally came home and told me all about it.

Damon heard about it all later and congratulated me on another Bryn-pleasing job. I was satisfied that I could easily forget about that lie

Uncle Damon Dies...on Damon's Birthday

I had told about the date of his uncle's death. He was focused on other things as usual, like work. He was happy to hear the story, and then it was back to article-writing, laboratory experiments, and e-mails.

Good; nothing to worry about, then.

There was already plenty of trouble looming in my future as it was.

Bryn was dying and I wouldn't have him to talk to anymore after that.

In addition, Damon seemed to be trapped in a financial and professional limbo with an unknown duration. When he would become successful was anyone's guess. I wanted him to make it while Bryn was still alive, but doubted that it would work out that way.

Chapter 43

Craigslist and Calligraphy

Back in the winter, I had set up a free account on Craigslist to advertise my services both as an editor/tutor and as a calligrapher. It was free unless you were advertising "erotic services," so I thought I might as well try it. I was proud of the results, and all set with calligraphy supplies.

That wasn't all; another task had been to prepare brochures about both calligraphy and editing. Neither one mentioned the other service. However, both detailed my education and professional background, and both listed rates for my services. The ads I posted on Craigslist mirrored these details. The only drawback surfaced when I attempted to load the images of my scanned calligraphy samples onto the page; the site didn't allow for that.

The whole process had reminded me of all that calligraphy entailed: my hand had gotten tired, and I remembered all of the old frustrations that cropped up as one did this art: a cramped, sweaty right hand, a feeling of being overheated, ink flow problems and pen angle difficulties that must constantly be corrected, worries that someone would speak to me and cause me to write what I heard them say and thus ruin a whole page of art, and nervousness that someone might bump me or the table.

Bryn knew about all this, though, so he wouldn't do that. He was always interested in what I was working on, curious to hear the logistics involved and understand the concentration and pitfalls inherent in any craft that was unfamiliar to him.

I showed Elah the results when she walked into the living room a couple of days later to visit Bryn. She took a good look, and then said, "I'm proud of you." With that, she smiled and went in to see Bryn. That was gratifying.

With my account set up, I began to get some hits after a couple of months. I suspected that the fact that wedding season didn't heat up until the weather did also had something to do with the delay in getting any bites at all, and those were mostly for calligraphy. The editing bites seemed to come mostly in the winter, when school applications were being prepared.

I got rather stressed out over all this in the spring, frantic to earn money. Between pleas from Damon for attention and edits and my own worries about my continuing inability to bring in a regular income, that wasn't exactly surprising.

Craigslist and Calligraphy

Bryn suddenly appeared next to me at the computer, emerging from his room. He was still wearing his jacket, having just returned from another visit with a friend...Claus, I think.

"You have a job," he said, hoping to soothe me.

I looked up at him, startled but appreciative. But I wasn't calm yet. "That's comforting for now, but it'll just end, which means that I'll never be able to talk to you again, and then I'll be fucking miserable!" I replied, actually swearing because I was so upset. I didn't feel calm.

He didn't know what to say to that. What can you say to such a thing? Bryn was a stress reliever, and I was going to lose him. There could be no soothing remark to fix that, and no emotionally intelligent answer. The man who had taught me emotional intelligence was dying, and he knew that there were limits to what emotional intelligence can offer.

He made no reply, and went to sit in front of his TV.

After I felt calmer, I went in to hug and kiss him, and we watched TV and drank tea and relaxed. There was nothing else we could do except enjoy hanging out together.

I had only two calligraphy jobs while I was with Bryn, despite several inquiries.

One was in the spring...in April...and the other over the 4th of July weekend.

Fortunately, for the first calligraphy job, in late April, things went quite smoothly.

Actually, I had a lot of fun. Bryn was away for the weekend, so I could take my time.

It was springtime in Manhattan, the trees had leaves on them and the birds and flowers were out, the sun was shining, and I got a job from a bride who lived in the Carnegie Hill area. It was close to where Damon had lived on West 94th Street as a kid, so I planned to walk down his old street on the way back.

To get there, I took the subway. I found the bride's apartment, chatted with her, complimented her wedding plans, collected the envelopes, promised to check each address thoroughly through the United States Postal Service website and contact her about any uncertain ones before putting pen to paper, and then walked out with the materials in my tote bag.

I had my digital camera with me, and planned to conduct a little low-cost tourism.

The Slamming Door

I headed east, saw Damon's old building, a tall, red-brick structure, and found his across-the-street neighbor's place, a brownstone where we had eaten dinner nearly four years ago. That was where his childhood friend had lived. He was a lawyer now; he and Damon had played in the basement, and we had seen their old Glo-Glue artwork on the walls, untouched after forty years.

From there, I continued on to Central Park, staying on the sidewalk outside as I went south. People were out and about in the park, and I took a photograph of the bridge that was featured in *Enchanted* (Amy Adams movie) and *Wolf* (Jack Nicholson movie), and of the famous Dakota building where John Lennon had lived, and where Yoko Ono still lived.

As I walked, I wasn't entirely decided about walking all of the way home. It was an idea I kept considering as I went along. When I got to Columbus Circle, I was hungry; it was only mid-afternoon, and breakfast had been a long time ago. I went upstairs to the Dean and Deluca café in Borders Books & Music and got a salad and a bottle of water. It was delicious: spinach, goat cheese, apricots, cranberries, and balsamic dressing.

After I ate, I walked around the mall a bit, saw the elaborate Williams-Sonoma again with its framed displays of Chuck Williams' old cook's tools and baker's gadgets, and then headed out again. Yes, I would definitely walk all the way back.

The Slamming Door

    The exercise was good for me, and I had always been a bit lazy about exercise. I just didn't see the point of making all that laundry. Keeping my appetite under control and eating healthy foods seemed easier than gaining weight through sheer carelessness. But a good, long, brisk walk that showed me a beautiful, safe and constantly changing scene was fun.
    When I finally got home, I checked on the naughty cat and put the calligraphy supplies on the table. I sat there for a couple of hours, setting up the Word file of addresses, checking them all. With that finished, I got myself something for dinner, from a take-out place.

Craigslist and Calligraphy

There were plenty of great places to choose from, and this was part of the fun of being home alone. Indian food, British food from Tea & Sympathy (I tried it only once – it was so heavy that that was enough), Cajun food from someplace nearby, and so on. I don't remember which place I chose from that night, just that I enjoyed it.

Damon visited in mid-May so that he and Frank could have an ImmuneACCORD meeting at the NYEEI, leaving me to frantically assemble a catered lunch plus plastic-ware and plates. Bryn helped with choosing a caterer: Mangia To Go. What a lot of stress...

Damon had sent me some stress-inducing e-mails which revealed that, as usual, he wanted me to arrange everything dirt cheap but really had no concept of what was involved. He expected me to borrow cutlery from Dionne, which was ridiculous. She lived all the way in Brooklyn, and I would not go all the way out there and back again. Plus, I hardly knew her. I ended up buying what I needed at a party shop – paper plates, napkins, cups, and plastic cutlery.

The catering reduced me to tears; it was just such short notice, and expensive. We couldn't serve unhealthy, salty, beef and pork-riddled, cheap Chinese food, which was what Damon proposed. ImmuneACCORD was all about healthy food choices and using spices to negate the need for salt. Bryn solved that problem when I told him I was having trouble; he told me that he and Peter liked a place called Mangia To Go, which was on 23rd Street; I could go see what they had and ask questions. In the end, Frank paid for the food. It was delicious, healthy, and included nothing that our Hindu business associate would have trouble eating. We had fruit, little vegetable sandwiches, smoked salmon, and some dessert bars.

But Damon wasn't through driving me crazy. He wanted some super-hot Indian food from East 10th Street, where there were many Indian restaurants, for the general manager of the spice company. Annoyed, I found it online, looked up some stuff called phaal, and ordered some. Berta and Matt surprised me the night before the big meeting by driving me to and from the place to get it. It was something very specific that Damon had read about.

When all was said and done, the meeting went well enough, and the phaal was duly tasted by the Indian visitor, who told Damon that it wasn't authentic; it was a New York trick to impress non-Indian tourists. I was a exhausted and exasperated by the whole fiasco.

Frank was leaving almost immediately by train for Maryland; his elderly mother, who had Alzheimer's, was home alone and he had to get back to her. Damon stayed for another day, and then took a bus back to the university, where he resumed his experiments. What a relief.

Next, there was June's birthday party, on May 15th, which we all celebrated at the Café Loup, an old favorite of hers and Albert's. The place had a lot of wolf (that's *loup* en Français) decorations in the windows on either side of the entrance. A jazz band played in the back, but our table, fortunately, was in the front and to the right, up against the window. We had one long table that extended all the way to the glass, and another short one up against a half-wall.

Albert and June sat there, across from me, facing Albert's former boss and his wife. They had worked at some scholastic publications company, preparing school texts. The wife, who was in her sixties, was dividing her time between enjoying her grandchildren and doing her bachelor's degree in history. They lived near Boston and had come all the way to Manhattan just for this party. I liked her; the husband seemed nice, but he stayed in his seat, and conversation just didn't happen between us, as is often the case at social gatherings.

Bryn enjoyed the party, but the Ground Zero of his bone cancer – the pelvic bone near his right hip joint – was bothering him a lot. It was ominously like he was back to where his illness had left off before the chemotherapy had started, back in the fall when I arrived. He spent a lot of the party standing up, so that his time was spent almost evenly divided between sitting and standing. He also moved around as he did this, using the problem to his advantage so that he could talk to several people. His hair was growing back in at last, now that it wasn't being undermined by chemicals any more.

That was the party when Berta informed me that my penchant for sitting with my back to a wall if at all possible in restaurants, and to otherwise find a spot that felt safe in social situations, was another indicator of Asperger's. I was getting a bit sick of her knowing so much about the condition. When I had time to focus on it, I promised myself that I would find a good book on the topic and read it from cover to cover. Meanwhile, I tried to focus on enjoying the party, which I did by getting a blackberry champagne. Berta had one as well, and it helped.

Late in May, Bryn went to Cassie's place for the weekend, so I had 4 days to myself.

The day before he left, the fridge died. With the fridge broken and a new one not coming until the next week, I had written Elah a pleading e-mail explaining the problem, and she had readily agreed to take in our

Craigslist and Calligraphy

food. Some of it was tacitly understood to be a gift; I never took back every last item.

The dead fridge sat unplugged in the kitchen after Matt looked at it and pulled it out to inspect it. No more hacking ice out of the freezer to speed along defrosting ever again. A refurbished, used one would be arriving the next week. Matt unplugged the old one, saying that it was dangerous, and I ended up throwing out some canned cat food; Nikita sniffed it once and walked off, revolted. I just opened a new one for her each time I fed her; she ate what she could.

Bryn told me to go out to some restaurants and enjoy myself that weekend, so I did.

The beauty of it was that I had to eat dinner out or order in – no cooking. This really felt like a vacation. I found myself eating out even for breakfast. I ate at the French place, Le Grainne Café, and enjoyed a chocolate croissant and a bowl of cut strawberries with fresh-squeezed orange juice and café au lait. The cost was just $12, which was terrific, even with the tip factored in. Another day I got a roll, juice and tea in Amy's Bread at Chelsea Market.

I found an amazing place that looked like the area of France that it was named for – Gascogne – on 8th Avenue. Damon would have loved it. But it wasn't as much fun as I had hoped. I was all alone, watching a couple at the next table eat together as I admired the back terrace, where I was sitting. The ivy, the chairs, tables, candles, window-shutters, everything looking like a piece of France had been transplanted here.

It turned out that everything wasn't roses for that couple; she was a lawyer based in Bermuda and he was a banker based in New York. They were commuter daters. But they were having a good time.

The food was amazing, though, and the wait staff very nice. I didn't have enough cash on me, however, and was determined to pay that way. So I paid the bill, left a meager tip of $2, and dashed home to get more money, which I had hidden in a drawer. Then I went all the way back there and found the waiters. They were delighted to see me, and a bit surprised, but laughed happily when I explained that I had rushed back and forth to get them a larger tip. That was fun.

Bryn insisted upon reimbursing me for it all, too. I hadn't asked him to; he just insisted.

A few days after he got back, the new fridge was delivered. Albert was over, and he and Bryn were almost on their way out somewhere when it arrived. The unfortunate men who brought it had been denied access to our street by the crossing guard lady, and had been forced to

The Slamming Door

park their truck and roll the fridge along most of the block. Bryn gave them each a generous tip - $20, I think – and we sympathized.

Then one of them asked if he might heat up his bagged lunch in our microwave.

With that, we all laughed and ruefully said that we didn't have one.

The men were amazed. But they glanced around and saw that it was true.

Welcome to the bachelor pad of a guy who always ate out.

I got the food back from Elah later and moved in, delighted with the egg and butter compartments, and with a freezer that wouldn't have to be de-iced. Soon our array of ice cream and sorbet was back in place. Bryn's magnets were almost all in place, too – except for the ones that had been permanently glued onto the door of the old one. He had just sighed and said it didn't matter, that they really were stuck forever. I put the others on the front of the new fridge and he was happy.

At one point during the late spring, I forget precisely when, I went across the hall to visit Elah. That was when she told me something about her past that I had not heard before: her mother had died of ovarian cancer rather suddenly when she was fourteen years old.

Elah had grown up in Ohio, and some her relatives still lived there. I had seen photos of her as a child with them, and more on an online webpage that she had recently begun posting family photos to. Her mother had been quiet, and had found out what was wrong shortly before she died, but had not told Elah. I imagined her in her house there, not realizing that everything was about to change, only that her mother suddenly wasn't acting right.

Ovarian cancer is tough to detect; often it isn't even noticed until Stage 4, at which point it is too late to do more than watch the woman die miserably. Elah's mother died back in the 1960s, when medical technology was less advanced, so this wasn't a surprising story…just another very upsetting one.

Elah's mother died 2 weeks after she found out what was wrong with her.

Elah was in her mid-fifties; she smoked a lot, was depressed, and rather quiet. She didn't seem to expect much from life anymore. I hoped she wouldn't die suddenly and without warning. She seemed okay, at least as much as one can be in her situation, but what would happen to Hilda if she were left alone with Rudy?

He acted like his daughter was a pet that he had grown tired of. Would he expect her to move out at age 18? He hadn't gone to college, even though he would have liked very much to study and learn things, it

Craigslist and Calligraphy

seemed to me. Unless Hilda had some help, such as a free place to live, I just didn't how it was going to happen for her. Did Rudy understand that? Did he care?

There was nothing I could do about it.

I had given Bryn the legal advice he had wanted, and he had acted on it when he made up his will; of that I felt certain. Hilda would have that much for cultural events, at least. Berta would have to make sure that she didn't blow it all on crowded rock concerts. Popular culture was not what Bryn had in mind when he set that money aside for his goddaughter.

Sometime during that month, Bryn fell. It might have been a Thursday, but I'm not sure.

It was the middle of the night, at 2 a.m., and I had just sat down on the toilet when I heard him fall. Why he had decided that he needed to go in the dark front hallway to the kitchen just then escaped both of us, but when I heard the thud, I called out to just stay put, that I was coming. I rushed to flush and wash my hands, and found him sitting in his pajamas on the floor.

Did he feel like he had broken anything (like a bone)? Was he in any [new] pain?

No, came the rueful reply. He looked a bit annoyed at himself.

I helped him up carefully, which wasn't difficult because he was able to stand by leaning on the hall table, got him whatever he had wanted from the fridge, and he went back to his chair.

Then I said that I wanted Maggie's boxes of stuff out of that hallway as soon as possible; he had tripped over one of them in the dark. They had been there for months, packed and addressed but ignored while we went through chemotherapy and other distractions. I also said I was going out to buy night-lights the next day for both the front hall and the spot between my room and the back hall.

Bryn said okay, and that he would ask Hilda to get Riley to help me with the boxes.

Soon everything was in order; I got the night-lights at Home Depot the next day, and on Saturday, Riley came over to help carry it all into a cab and out to the UPS store; that was that.

But Bryn never walked about late at night when I was in the bathroom again.

Bryn went away to visit Cassie again for a week in June. That left me home alone, and glad for the break from everything and everyone.

The Slamming Door

Berta didn't come over, and I was left to my own devices. It was nice; I could relax, read and have some time to myself.

Or so I thought...

Berta called to inform me that Alena was visiting, and that the family was going to have a dinner party at East of Eighth on Tuesday evening. Alena had come with her husband and little girls, and the aunts would be there, as would Albert, June, and Alissa.

Suddenly I was angry. Alena was coming because she could afford to do whatever she wanted, and I was apparently expected to just drop everything and show up. Well, I wasn't going to do it. I was anxious, stressed, broke, and didn't want an evening of peace taken away from me.

I told Berta how I felt.

She surprised me by being quite amiable about it all; she said that she would make some sort of pleasant excuse for me, say that I was tired or some such thing. I was relieved. I needed a whole week to myself, especially since I had been led to believe that I could have it. To have any part of it rescinded, especially for a night of shrieking, wild behavior and fawning adoration over it, was infuriating. It would most likely have come with Alena asking me how I was doing in pitying tones, which I didn't want to hear. Better not to go out with them.

If they resented me for this snub, I resented that. I felt snubbed. I was worried that Alena and the aunts thought of me as some sort of interloper or just not all that important...the old thought that I was nothing more than some damned in-law to them all came back.

Add to that the fact that Alena had a penchant for asking, always in the same piteously condescending tone, "And how are YOU?" to either me or Damon. Damon hated it. The tone suggested that she expected an answer that would reveal that things were not well with us. It was insulting, as if she had no expectation of things ever going well for us. I wanted to skip that.

On the evening that this gathering was to take place, I realized that it was time to buy canned cat food. It was raining, and the pet store was in plain sight of the huge upstairs window at East of Eighth. I was sure that they would all be seated at the long rectangular table right in front of it. Perfect; I covered myself with the hood of my rain jacket and took a roundabout route.

At least it was fun once I was inside the shop. The staff was nice, and there was a huge black-and-white, shorthaired, male cat who lived in the store. His name was Bleecker, just like the street, and he was friendly. He allowed customers to pick him up and cuddle him, and he slept on all of the cat condos in the shop. They were probably unsaleable thanks to Bleecker, but the men who ran the place didn't seem to care. I

Craigslist and Calligraphy

loved going there for cat supplies and seeing him lounging in the window without a care in the world.

I went in, bought the cat food, petted Bleecker for a while, and then out again into the pouring rain with my bags. Soon I was home again in the lovely silence, reading and watching whatever I liked as I ate.

It was so much better than seeing rich, comfortable, conformist Alena, the darling of the family, able to afford to live in this country with her husband and enjoy it too while I couldn't do that, and being asked about Damon. I would take any circuitous route to skip that.

The Slamming Door

Berta later confirmed my assessment of this gathering: it had been very noisy the entire time, and all about watching the kids' antics. Too stressful and exhausting; I was glad to have missed out on that and Alena's demeanor, complete with its pitying, quizzing inquiries.

It wasn't until much later in the spring that I was officially hired as a tutor by a student from Empire State College, an actor who had sold me cards and magnets several times over the past few years at the House of Cards on Hudson Street. He needed a tutor to help him prepare his English papers, and was willing and able to pay my rate of $25 per hour.

I enjoyed working with him over the next couple of months, and he taught me some interesting things that I had not known before, such as the fact that the actor Lee Strasberg had started a famous acting school. My new editing client/student had studied with him.

This was so intriguing that I did what I always do when I hear about an actor or actress or director: I looked Strasberg up on the Internet Movie Data Base – www.imdb.com – and found out that he had played Hyman Roth in *The Godfather: Part II* and Roth was shot to death at an airport near the end. That etched him and his school into my memory.

My student was a bit self-conscious. After a couple of lessons, he told me what was bothering him in a phone call: his professors all had academic backgrounds, he didn't, and he was embarrassed to turn his papers in to them.

With that, I proceeded to give him a very frank, reassuring lecture about the fact that they didn't expect him to have what he was going to them to acquire. I added that everyone knows something that other people don't know, and that I was enjoying listening to him inform me about the acting world. It worked; he felt much calmer about his work.

Thus relaxed, he proceeded to get on with writing his papers, and the work started to move along much more efficiently.

One afternoon, Albert was visiting. We found ourselves discussing first names, specifically mine, Berta's, and Alissa's. It turned out that our fathers had each chosen them.

Albert had thought that he was giving his daughter a name that was easy to spell.

As for my father, he just liked the French name that he gave me. So did I.

At some point previously, I had asked Bryn something.

Craigslist and Calligraphy

"Were you trying to please Albert when you chose Berta's name?"
He had said yes.
Interesting; privately, I thought Albert was an attractive name, but that the latter was not.

At some point in early June, on a hot Saturday, Berta and Matt arrived at the apartment after walking around in Greenwich Village for a while in the sunshine. There was some sort of street fair going on, and they had been all over the area, looking around.

Berta was hot, sweaty, and irritable. She began to cool off and settle down as she sat in front of the air conditioner in my room with some ice water. Matt had made her walk briskly all over that street fair, and she didn't like it. She didn't want to exercise. She was wearing long jeans and her favorite, pretty, with three-quarter-length sleeves, sea-green shirt. Matt was in shorts and a tee shirt. Clearly, reaching a healthy weight was low on her list of priorities.

I didn't say anything. What was the point?

At least she now owned some very comfortable Teva sandals, despite the fact that she had teased me about mine. She had gotten hers in Union Square one evening just before we browsed the soon-to-close Virgin megastore of CDs and DVDs.

She drove me crazy before she got them, worrying that they didn't look nice or feel right, checking them out in several stores until she found a great price upstairs in a discount outlet that overlooked the square. They had a pale green pattern, which was one of her favorite colors. Mine were a lovely black pair with dark and light purple tulips for a decorative pattern. I had gotten them on sale during the winter in Greenwich Village. She put them on right after away.

Silly me...I thought that once she was wearing the comfortable sandals, she would be happy and the subject would no longer be of much interest beyond that. But no; I wandered off as we perused the basement wares, then came back and found her chatting with a couple of tall black men who suddenly looked me up and down. Obviously, I was shopping with her.

I didn't see anything particularly odd about the encounter, but when it was over and we were walking around the store again, she insisted that they had thought we were a pair of lesbians because of our Teva sandals!

Whatever...I couldn't tell one way or the other, and we would never see them again. That was what my great-aunt Susan used to say to me when she took me traveling: that we would never see the people that we were with on some tour again, so why worry about what they thought?

The Slamming Door

It wasn't like we had done anything bad, so who cared? It was a bit annoying, though.

Berta cared, though, and carried on and on and on about it, ad nauseum, ad infinitum. She finally dropped the subject when it was time to go home, but when we got there, I was even more annoyed when she recounted the tale to Bryn. I am straight, and I should be able to wear comfortable sandals without any nonsense.

When it was just me and Bryn, I told him how I really felt. He nodded.

Then, a week or so later, Berta showed up hot and sweaty and in long jeans again, and I noticed that she was wearing white sneakers, not the sandals. Where were they? In Long Island at Matt's place, she told me. By then it was mid-June.

Just like her copy of the *Twilight: New Moon* book, I thought – unavailable.

What a nuisance, having one's stuff strewn all over the place, in multiple homes. I could relate: storage unit, parents' place, Bryn's place...I wanted it all consolidated.

Berta was starting to stress me out. She could drop by at any time, and when I had some calligraphy due, it was a problem. The desk could suddenly be usurped, and that was the only surface on which I could do the fussy artwork. Also, the noise would threaten the work; I might write what I heard rather than the addresses on the list.

If the job was editing something on the word processor, none of this mattered. With editing and writing, if I messed it up, I could just redo it with no damage to the end result. Not so with calligraphy; one false pen-stroke and it would be ruined.

I had no place that was truly my own in which to work; that fact was impressed on me often as I tried to make money.

As long as I was there, the only work that I could really focus on was being Bryn's care-giver. Realistically, that was the truth. But people expected me to make money. I needed to make money. I had gone to all of the trouble of setting this up, and now I doubted that the final, crucial ingredient to the successful completion of any assignment, quiet time, would not be available.

I was right; Bryn stopped traveling and stayed home after June. Cassie began to visit him every Thursday instead. The calligraphy clients weren't materializing anyway; the potentials I communicated with wanted obscure alphabets, and each one took time to learn. I needed to get back to writing in order to do any serious work, it seemed. But not yet; it would have to wait.

Chapter 44

Vianne Visits

In the spring, Vianne flew out from Arizona to stay at Aunt Summer's place and visit Bryn one last time before it was too late. She stayed for just over a week, arriving on Monday, June 1st, and leaving on Tuesday, June 9th.

Bryn was getting a lot of visits like that.

At this point, Bryn was starting to make comments like that, too. I responded each time by saying that the party wasn't over for him yet, which would usually improve his mood. I believed, it, too; he was still able to go out and have some fun.

Ominous though that was, the visit was enjoyable and appreciated by all.

Vianne was the sister who resembled her older brother, my husband. She was easily as intelligent as he was, and almost as independent. She had studied at McGill University in Montréal, Canada, where she had majored in linguistics and anthropology, graduated with honors, and later gone on to the University of Arizona for her master's of arts in English.

She had also lived in Shanghai, China and Rome, Italy as she pursued a career teaching English. She was fluent in English, French, Spanish, Hebrew, and Mohawk, and had settled in Arizona to teach English as a second language.

Vianne had once told me that she moved to Arizona to get away from her family and be on her own, but that they – her mother and sister – had followed her there. Interesting; Henrietta had lived near Vianne for a long time. I don't know where Alena lived at first, but she ended up in New Mexico, which was an hour's plane ride away. When Henrietta got sick, she went to a nursing home near Alena.

Sometime after Vianne got settled with a job in Arizona, she met her future husband. But the job was not good, and her mother warned her against staying with it for too long. She didn't listen, much to her own detriment. Henrietta had warned her that it was an abusive work environment that would wear her down terribly. Vianne also got migraine headaches.

But Ron was a plus. He was a postal worker, handsome and friendly, in a rock band, and he shared her love of Golden Retriever dogs. They got married in Arizona, and the wedding was lovely. I had seen the video of it on a previous visit that Vianne made to New York City, on a machine in Hilda's corner of the Ranger-Stone apartment. I really liked Vianne's gown.

The Slamming Door

Ron spoke in it, with a close-up appearance before the ceremony, saying many complimentary things about Vianne and how he was looking forward to being her husband. He was fourteen or fifteen years older than she was, and in his late thirties when they got married.

I had spoken on the phone with Ron a few times, but never met him. His work kept him from traveling much because it had such a tight schedule. He was no longer a postal worker, having quit due to stress, determined to get out before he "went postal," as he had phrased it.

So he had left in the late 1990s, and he took a course in refurbishing corporate jets. He and his classmates had all been guaranteed jobs in that field upon graduation. But come graduation, 9/11 happened, wiping out that possibility. Ron ended up selling used cars for a while, and then getting a horrible job driving a Tucson city bus. It sucked; he had no lunch breaks, not even a rest room break, and the shifts lasted well over eight hours. There was either no union, or it had no clout; he had explained it to me once.

Ron's mother, who was an excellent cook, lived nearby, and Vianne liked her a lot. She and Ron ate at her place often, which was also nice because Vianne said that she herself wasn't a great cook. I guess it ran in the family; Damon said that his mother hadn't been very good at it either, but that he had never blamed her for it.

Poor Ron. His health wasn't great, and the doctors consistently failed to diagnose the cause of his chronic internal bleeding. Vianne was constantly worrying about him, and Damon had tried to help by suggesting that Ron's doctors investigate various rare possibilities.

Ron deserved a better work environment, and he was very nice to Vianne.

They had a house together that Damon and I had yet to visit together. It had an underwater fish scene painted onto the guest room walls. Vianne could take her Golden Retriever and her rescue dog, a black one with floppy ears, to a nearby dog park in their neighborhood.

For a long time, Ron had kept a hilarious message on their answering machine. I was sorry when it was replaced with something more mundane. The fun message had said: "Hello. You've reached our answering machine. Unfortunately, we're not within reach at the moment. Please leave a message and hopefully we'll reach you when we try to."

Vianne had left him home with the dogs and flown to New York City.

She had learned – perhaps at my urging on a previous visit – to insist that Aunt Summer refrain from scheduling her time from the moment of her arrival to the moment of her departure. With all of the migraines that Vianne suffered from, she needed to recover from her flight for a day or

Vianne Visits

so. She was also a bit afraid of flying. At last Aunt Summer understood that, which was good. Yet when Vianne first came over to see Bryn, a day after arriving, she had a headache.

She sat on one of the chairs in Bryn's room to chat for a while, before I went in to join them. Bryn had said that he wanted to talk to her on his own for a while. That was one of the drawbacks to having a caregiver – I was just constantly around. I didn't mind; the only solution to too much togetherness was to speak up when necessary.

I had errands to do, and I timed them to take the pressure off; with me gone they wouldn't imagine that I felt banished, which I didn't. After a little while, I came home and they invited me in.

For some reason – probably because it would be more fun to give her the birthday gift I had gotten for her in person and see her open it than to wait and mail it to her in late June – I went ahead and gave it to her. Vianne's birthday fell the day after my wedding anniversary; I would mail her a card later.

The gift was a Vera Bradley handbag, a white one with a brightly colored floral pattern. Vianne was very pleased, and immediately moved her stuff into it; it was just what she needed. That was nice.

She came back the next day, and I tried to take her photograph as a souvenir, but her head still ached and Bryn said to stop. I had gotten off one or two shots before that. I wondered how I was going to remember this visit, but gave up. Still, she intended to go forward with our plans.

We went out to eat lunch together at The Green Table in Chelsea Market. We had planned to do something nice together, and this was it. Vianne couldn't deal with too much light, noise, or activity. She didn't like museums much, which surprised and disappointed me.

Even Chelsea Market was too loud for her, but she was comfortable and happy enough inside the restaurant, which was quiet. She really liked the food, too. But she insisted upon sticking to fairly cheerful topics of conversation, something that she had shown a penchant for on previous visits.

That was both difficult and disappointing; difficult because most of the news of both my life and Damon's was glum and full of frustration, and disappointing because it felt as though we could never reach any sense of closeness with those restrictions.

I wanted a close friendship out my relationship with this sister-in-law, and distance and other factors seemed to persistently impede that. Vianne ended up sighing that it was too bad that we couldn't spend more time together, and that this visit was too short.

It didn't make much sense to me.

What did she really want? Wasn't she willing to push for whatever it was?

The Slamming Door

Or did she not really want much of anything to do with me at all beyond a brief check-in from time to time? Was she just after a cursory interaction, and then satisfied?

We went back to Bryn's place when lunch was over, with me still feeling bewildered.

He showed her what he had been saving for her, a book that he had at least two copies of. It was about the Otterman family in the nineteenth century, and it focused on a distant branch of relatives. Bryn didn't know exactly how he was related to them, only that he was related to them somehow. These Ottermans had traveled in a covered wagon to the far reaches of Arizona, where some angry Native American warriors had murdered all of them except for Opal and her younger sister.

The two were taken captive, given tattoos on their chins that marked them as prisoners, and set to a brutal schedule of menial labor. Opal survived, but not her sister. Later on, the Mohave tribe took her in a trade, and she had a better time of it with them. After all that, she was finally brought back to her own civilization, to a fort in the Arizona desert. She ended up living as a happily married woman in Ohio, where she hid her face and covered the tattoos with cosmetics as best she could. It was a fascinating story.

There was even a town named for the family in some remote area of Arizona.

The journalist who had written about Opal during her lifetime had deliberately left something out: the possibility that she might have been married to a Mohave man. It was the right thing to do, because raising that issue would have made life among white people unbearable for Opal. Sometimes responsible journalism means not reporting a particular fact.

Bryn had no clear idea as to precisely how he and Opal were related, but the surname was so rare as to leave him with no doubt about it. There was a branch of his family, very distantly related, that had lived in Missouri in the nineteenth century, and that was where Opal's parents had started out.

Bryn particularly wanted Vianne to have a copy of this story because she lived in Arizona, so she happily took the book away with her. I found it all fascinating and read the story on my own as soon as Bryn was finished with his copy, though I forget whether it was before or after Vianne's visit.

Another event on the agenda for the week of Vianne's stay in Manhattan was a party that Aunt Summer threw for the family in her apartment. There was no Jewish Chinese food this time; Albert had

Vianne Visits

called her and faced up to the awkwardness of our family mutiny against it. We couldn't eat that stuff again – only the aunts liked it. Neither of them seemed to be mad at us, though; Aunt Summer served a rotisserie chicken, strawberries, grapes, cheeses, nuts, and cole slaw.

When the visit was over, I had yet another set of photographs from it, and I found an e-mail from my mother asking how Bryn was. We were communicating a bit more now since her visit in April, mostly by e-mail. I had sent her a beautiful card for Mother's Day, too, acquired at the House of Cards. It showed a copy of a nineteenth-century painting of roses; I found similar cards with other flowers – pansies and an iris – for my Aunt Joan and grandmother.

So I wrote back, telling her all about the visit, and sent several of the new photos.

Aunt Summer had asked me (in advance) to work on her computer during this party, so I had brought over some canned air to blow out the dust. She led me into her kitchen, which was a fully equipped, late twentieth-century one. The front of her refrigerator was completely covered with her magnet collection, one from each trip. A lot of them were from the southwest, as were the knick-knacks over her desk, which was just inside on the right.

She needed me to set up her new printer. I sat down on the office chair, which had wheels, and leaned in to concentrate on the task. Suddenly Aunt Summer was shouting in horror; I had bumped into the magnets with the chair. I looked back at the collection, startled, and apologized, but it quickly became obvious that I needed to move around a lot without worrying about this, so she took most of them off the fridge and stashed them in a drawer. The magnets hadn't suffered any damage, at least.

That was a relief; she went back into the living room to enjoy the party, and really did enjoy it now that she wasn't worried about her souvenirs. I couldn't blame her for protecting them, but removing them was the best solution.

It took me about an hour, but I set up the new printer-scanner-copier-fax contraption, inserted its ink cartridges, connected everything properly, and loaded the software to Aunt Summer's hard drive. When it was done, I did the required tests and pronounced it ready. She was very grateful and paid me forty dollars.

On a future trip over there for another quick adjustment, I said that family members shouldn't have to pay for quick little jobs like this. It wasn't like working for Adam, which I did with a prior agreement on a regular basis. Adam's office system was now well-organized and much more efficient thanks to my efforts, and I was out of a job there, but I had accepted payment for that. Meanwhile, Aunt Summer was jubilant over

The Slamming Door

having had my help; a professional computer geek would have cost her $150.

The party was fun. Berta was in a loud, happy mood, and she had a pretty new cellular phone, a dark purple one with an etched floral-and-vine pattern on it. We all passed it around and admired it. Vianne was on the sofa chatting with Bryn, and there was another guest whom we had never met before and would probably not meet again. She was an older English lady, an artist whom Berta and Mike had just met; she was temporarily locked out of her apartment.

It was summertime, the sun was shining, and it was nice and warm, so Aunt Summer had opened her screen door to let the breeze in. She had a small deck that faced east. We each went out there to admire the view, which showed the Fashion Institute of Technology across the street, and the Empire State Building in the distance.

Despite the fact that Bryn was now sleeping upright in his chair all night with his light on the whole time, he had enough energy to enjoy himself. He had sleeping pills, but was afraid to take them. I was appalled; to me, there was nothing as wonderful and relaxing as sleep, and he was missing that feeling out of fear. He even kept his television on low as he slept, waking up from time to time to read and check the news. I had changed his lamp's light bulb to a kind that could be switched between three levels of brightness, and we had night-lights on in his room, the living room, and the front hallway.

At least he was still eating decently, if only in small amounts. He ate some of everything, careful to have a balanced diet with fruits, vegetables, yoghurt and Ensure drinks, and lots of water. That was helping him to continue teaching a class every few weeks, and to enjoy parties.

He was going to have another party that very evening, with Teckla, Karen Krams, Albert and Hilda. It was a Henry George School party, and he was going to hold it in his room so they could all watch a documentary called *The End of Poverty*. It was for the class that he and Teckla were teaching. I had gone out to the Madeleine Patisserie shop to get some financiers, little round chocolate chip cakes. The name had attracted him because his party was related to finances.

We ended up at a big Unitarian church on East 35th Street a couple of weeks later to watch it again. For me, it was the first time; I had worked on an edit for Bryn's friend Peter, the eccentric sociology professor during his party. His room was packed, so after I had served the coffee and cakes and set up the DVD machine, I left them all to it.

Vianne Visits

Vianne got home okay, but was delayed at first from Newark Airport due to thunderstorms. They were probably the next phase of the terrible storm that destroyed that Air France plane that was going from Brazil to France through 50,000-foot high thunderclouds. Nothing that terrible would happen over a continent on a cooler latitude (ours), but at least the airline that Vianne used had chosen to careful.

Now that she was gone, I wondered when I would see her again, but that was typical.

By the time I was writing to my mother, Vianne had gone back to Arizona.

I asked my mother for news about our black-and-white cat, Cookie, and that was it.

Nikita was a cat and she was with me, but she wasn't as nice to me as Cookie was.

Shortly after Vianne's visit, Bryn made a mistake with his pain medication. It wasn't a disaster, but it could have been.

Bryn was now on morphine, a low dose, but it was more powerful than methadone.

That meant that he needed stronger pain medication, and that the tumors were feasting on him. To complicate matters, he had to take the pills at three different times each day. As if that wasn't difficult enough, one dose was 100mg and the other two were 60mg.

When I realized that, I had wanted to make separate entries for it on his pill sheet.

But he didn't want me to devote separate rows to that on the chart; he thought he could just keep track of the times by checking it off, one, two, three, and noting the times when he took them. So I backed off, letting him take charge of the system. It was his illness, I told myself.

Still, I paid attention to what was happening, trying to sound overly inquisitive or nosy.

Bryn didn't seem to mind it.

But one night, that changed.

It had started out pleasantly enough. I had served our raspberry-strawberry milkshakes, and Bryn had taken his shower while I monitored him while passing on the late-night comics' jokes. Letterman's show ended, and Bryn came out of the bathroom with his cane to change.

He had gotten into his polo shirt and lounge pants, all ready for bed, and sat in his chair with his box of medications pulled up close as he worked over the pill sheet with a pen. He didn't like pill boxes with days of the week on them; the one that I had bought months ago sat unused in a bag, rejected.

The Slamming Door

I was in my summer nightgown, getting ready to go into the bathroom at 1 a.m. and take a shower when Bryn called out to me: he had just made a mistake and swallowed not one but two morphine pills.

Wonderful...I threw my street clothes onto the bed to change into and went into his room. He was sitting there looking absolutely disgusted with himself. Well, the deed was done.

"I'm going to check the Internet to see what can happen to you from doing this," I said, and went to the computer." Meanwhile, Bryn announced that he was going to find the Poison Control Center phone number that came with his pills. "Great," I said, "let's do both."

Predictably, both sources revealed the same information: if nothing was done, the person who overdosed on morphine could go to sleep and not wake up. Neither of us was ready for that! Bryn was still enjoying life enough not to want it to end just yet. He was very curious to see how the ruined economy recovered...but back to the overdose.

One suggestion was for Bryn to make himself puke, but he couldn't. He could only do it when he felt nauseated. We each came back with that annoying idea, but Bryn wasn't happy about losing his milkshake and said so. Whenever his appetite was fine and he could take in calories, he wanted to keep them in.

The woman from the Poison Control Center who spoke to him on the phone said that if he went to a hospital, they would have a drug he could take that would counteract the effect of too much morphine. The catch was that he might not need it at all, or he might suddenly need it after a few hours. Was there someone who could stay up all night and watch him?

He thanked her very much and hung up. Then he reported all that to me.

I just looked at him, flabbergasted at the hole in the logic of this plan.

Stay up all night and watch him at home? Sure, I was available, but if he turned out to suddenly and abruptly need the antidote, our information indicated that in order for it not to be too late, he would have to already be at the hospital at that moment, where the antidote was.

That was just plain idiotic. What was I supposed to do, I inquired, stay up and see if you start to expire because you aren't respiring fast enough, panic, call 911, have the EMTs arrive just as you die, and then cry?

He looked at me for a moment, deadpan, clearly seeing the idiocy of that idea.

Without waiting for another hypothetical argument, I said, "All right Bryn, which hospital will it be? When you said you took too much morphine, I immediately threw my street clothes onto my bed to change into."

He looked at me for an instant and then said we could go to St. Vincent's in Greenwich Village. It was a crappy and poorly-equipped place that was going to be closed in the next few months, but it was the closest to us and still in operation.

I got dressed, he got dressed, and we packed his black book-bag. It was after 2 a.m.

I found us a cab and we rode over there, approached the admitting window, and told them what was wrong. The nurses let us right into their office, sat us down, and listened to the whole story. They didn't panic; they just signed Bryn in with his insurance information.

From the odd glances that they gave him at first, it occurred to me that they might be thinking he could have done this deliberately, so I said that he hadn't, and that he loved being alive. He didn't want me to do most of the talking, but he was glad I said that. The nurses looked like they bought it, and stopped with the suspicious glances.

Next, they brought us into the emergency room and sat Bryn on a black rolling bed with his head up. It was very, very crowded. Most of the patients were Hispanic, and some of them looked like they had been injured, but not fatally.

I expected to sit there with him for hours, and had brought a magazine and a book.

The nurse came back and said that it was too late to puke up the pill, and probably had been too late after just a few minutes, which was how long it had taken us to look up all of the information on this problem. Well, good!

There was nothing for it now but to stay awake all night and see what happened.

After a certain number of hours, if nothing happened, then nothing would, and Bryn could just go home again and continue with his routine like he had never screwed up the dosage of any of his pills.

Okay, that sounded reassuring. I had ceased to fear immediate death once we were inside the hospital anyway. Bryn was a reasonable person, and I knew that I would be allowed by him to take whatever precautionary measures I saw fit to ensure that the first time he did this would be the last time. Meanwhile, I said nothing about my plans for doing that.

I settled in, expecting to keep him company all night on the edge of his black, plastic-rubber-coated cushion, and took out the magazine.

But he surprised me by telling me that since he was in a hospital with nurses to watch him, he wanted me to go home, have my shower, and wait there. He wouldn't hear of any protest on my part, so I packed up my stuff, arranged his things within his reach, and said that I would go home, but I that I would not go to sleep.

I planned to stay awake reading, and to keep my cell phone on, and I wanted him to call me and tell me the outcome. Would he promise to tell me whether or not he ended up needing that antidote?

Yes.

Okay. Off I went, finding a cab across the street, and was home again in minutes.

Back upstairs, into the apartment, and over to the computer I went.

I wasted no time in editing that pill sheet.

Whereas before, the morphine had been in black characters just like all the other pills, I changed that row on the chart to three rows, one blue, one purple, and one red in that order. That looked good. The highest dosage was in red. There was no chance he would mess it up with the pill sheet looking like this.

Pleased with myself, I printed up several copies, e-mailed Damon about the night's events, and went to take my shower. I called no one; this was the point of having me, a night owl, staying here. Some weird things would inevitably happen when the rest of the family was asleep.

When I was all cleaned up for the night, I laid down on top of my bed, on the quilt, with a magazine about the *Twilight* cast members and the television on and tuned in to the movie channel. Berta and I had been passing these silly celebrity rags back and forth. I had moved on to reading other books by now, women's history books. One was called *The Commoner*, about the empress of Japan; Damon had read it too. The other was by Iris Chang, about the attack on the women of Nanking, China during World War II.

But tonight I wasn't sure I could concentrate on anything new, so I read junk.

After a little while, I called Bryn on his cell phone to see what was going on.

He was glad to hear from me, but there was nothing new. It was almost 4 a.m.

As the night wore on, I had trouble staying awake, but fought and managed it.

No coffee; I wasn't about to deliberately spin my sleeping schedule around. Once I did that, I would have great difficulty spinning it back. I stubbornly read the stories about Robert Pattinson and Kristen Stewart and Ashley Greene, amused at my ability to remember this nonsense later and discuss it with Berta. At least it would hold her interest.

Lately, she had been sending me some funny messages urging me to go hang out at some spot where Pattinson had been seen frequently, just to catch a glimpse of him. He was filming a movie that included the

Vianne Visits

events of 9/11, *Remember Me*, and had almost been hit by a passing taxicab as he fled some hysterical idiots – also known as fans. No, no way was I going to participate in that.

At 7 a.m., my cell phone rang again. Bryn had been released without needing that antidote and was coming back now in a cab. No, he did not want me to get dressed, get a cab, and rush over to get him. He could handle returning home on his own, and insisted upon it.

Okay, but I pulled on shorts and a tee shirt, put my keys in my pocket and my feet into my sandals and went downstairs. He arrived as the birds were chirping and the sun was rising, and I went out to hug him and grab his bag. He looked okay, which meant about the same as usual despite being too thin, with stubble for hair, and needing a cane.

On the way inside, I picked up his copy of *The New York Times*, and we went up.

I didn't know how he felt, but I was dizzy from staying up all night. I wondered for perhaps the hundredth time in my life how people who liked to stay out all night partying and then had to go to school or work the next day could do it. They couldn't, I realized; they flunked out of college or got into trouble at work.

Upstairs, Bryn sat down in his Lazy Boy chair looking relieved that this night was over.

I showed him what I had done to his pill sheet right away; it didn't matter that sleep was the next item on both of our agendas. He had to see it because his pill-taking schedule would march on relentlessly, regardless of what he did next. We could rest when he had seen the edits.

At first glance, he was confused, but then he caught on to the purpose of listing the morphine by dose rather than by what drug it was. He approved, and said he now rued having objected to the idea of listing it that way in the first place.

I said I had no fear that this would happen again, and I meant it.

Bryn was smart: he only needed to learn important lessons once.

Chapter 45

Hospice, and His Papers Again

Bryn had gotten his final will in order. He and Albert went to the law office of their childhood friend, who had been the boy next door in Yonkers, and took care of it – writing, witnessing, everything. They said that the other elderly law partners came in to witness it.

I don't know where the original was put, but I had a clue: Bryn suddenly became very protective of his top bureau drawer. I really didn't care. Bryn was going to leave whatever money he had to his daughters, minus that sum of $25,000 for Hilda to attend cultural events until she was 21 years old. He had told me so. My reward for being with him was simply that – to spend time with him before the time was all gone – and that was all that I had ever expected.

But the fact that Bryn had made his last will and testament – really his last one – meant that soon I would have to do more than just organize his papers at home. Previously, I had avoided scrutinizing them, deeming it none of my business to know specifically what information about him they contained. There were bills, bank statements, and so on that I hadn't read; I had only filed them as fast as I could – identify, file, put away, and recycle the ad inserts.

Now I would have to be a bit more inquisitive in order to put them in order.

This was because everyone – Bryn, Cassie, Albert, and even Berta – realized that in order for Albert, who had been designated executor of Bryn's estate, to actually do that job, the papers would have to be put in perfect order. The job that I had begun the previous fall would now have to be completed.

The project was nicely set up, but that was all.

Now I put it in order completely.

It was both Cassie's and Berta's idea, oddly enough.

Both of them, on separate visits, told me that I ought to proceed with it.

Bryn was no longer able to move about comfortably.

He was still able to go on visits, and had ridden with Cassie for some more overnight visits, but he was paying less and less attention to his bills, which were piling up in the morass of paper on his old ottoman stool, and also on his white plastic table that he had asked for.

Berta quietly told me that I ought to just move the plastic thing on wheels with 6 drawers into my room, open and organize any and all bills that came in, note the due dates, and present them to Bryn before the

Hospice, and His Papers Again

payments could be late. In short, I was to help him keep the household functioning in ways that I had left up to him until now.

I did it.

That meant organizing things a bit more, but still, I only set up the top drawer. That was the one about household bills.

It was later in the summer, after Bryn truly became chair-ridden, that I finished the job.

Meanwhile, I bided my time with those papers, determined not to be viewed as some meddlesome sort who snooped through the papers. I would only touch them if asked, but halfway through the summer, I was finally asked to finish the job. I did it.

They – Albert, Berta, Cassie, and Bryn – pointed out that I was a lawyer, and said that they trusted me to know how to organize everything. Of course I could do that – the skill came naturally to me anyway.

So one day, I tackled the job with the huge, clear recycling bags next to me, the stapler, a pen, a letter opener, and the 6-drawer-thing-on-wheels pulled up by my bed. I worked all afternoon until I felt dizzy, removing all the irrelevant inserts that come with bills (ads, outer envelopes, return envelopes, etc.) and throwing them into the recycling bags. I laid each item flat, put all of the items in the proper folders, in order by date, and it fit neatly into each drawer.

At dinner-time, I had to stop and eat. I was getting hungry, and I was very dizzy.

I went into Bryn's room and told him I only had one more drawer to do, but I needed a break. Berta was in there with him, sitting by the TV. She was wearing her square glasses, looking right at me, and she didn't smile. I didn't get it; I was just doing what I had been asked to do. I didn't look directly at her; she looked jealous, but there was nothing I could do for her. She would have to sort that out for herself.

But Bryn smiled; next, he was hugging me, kissing me, and giving me the thumbs up.

And he told me to order myself a really nice Indian dinner, dessert and all.

I did; I got coconut shrimp with rice and dahl, mango lassi, and rice pudding.

After all that, I finished the entire job. Now keeping track of bills was absurdly easy.

Bryn called hospice in early June.

He sensed that he was starting to decline faster and faster, and wanted to be more prepared. He added that he could die either in a couple of weeks or a few months, and that he had just found that out. Either way, he wanted to be ready.

Perhaps he would go to a facility in the Bronx. He wanted me to stay on in the apartment, so I started plotting how I would get back and forth on the trains, buying a map of all 5 boroughs of New York City. I showed it to him, and promised to bring him whatever reading material he wanted, and whatever else occurred to him.

He suggested that I could go see the Bronx Botanical Garden. Okay, I said, wondering how I would work that in while getting upset in an unfamiliar area that might not be all that safe.

The most significant things about this call, however, were the facts that a new visiting nurse named Ellen Rosenberg, R.N., and a social worker named Lorie Adagio, M.S.W., came out to meet us. The nurse would be back often. She was very nice, a small, petite woman who wore skirts and dresses with her light brown, straight hair pinned up at the back of her head, bangs hanging almost in her eyes over her glasses. She had been an artist, but switched careers, probably to pay the bills.

The social worker was just vaguely plump, with a pretty face and honey-brown hair. She tended to wear her hair down in waves around her face, with a little makeup, and pants, cotton blouses and sandals. It was Lorie who sat down on the sofa to talk to me as I sat at the computer, where I felt calm. That was probably because I could distract myself from what was happening by reading the news online, or by playing Word Whomp and Poppit, and because it felt familiar.

Lorie had a huge binder that she opened, and she told me that it was her job to describe to me the signs that indicated a person was about to die. First, Bryn would likely fall into a deep sleep from which no one would be able to rouse him. Next, he would make a raspy sound as he breathed, which is called a death rattle. Finally, he would just stop breathing as he slept.

I listened carefully, memorizing it all, trying not to be afraid of it. My expression did not change; I just sat there, intently focused on what I was hearing, trying to imagine what all that would look and sound like. I felt calm mostly because none of this was happening right then, and because I tend to plan ahead as much as possible, including by trying to know what to expect.

What did I make of this information?

I tried to imagine experiencing those symptoms myself, and hoped that it really was the way it sounded: like falling asleep. That didn't sound so bad.

Would Bryn just calmly go to sleep? Or would he feel pain, or sense that he was dying and feel fear? My guess was that he would just calmly go to sleep, and that if he sensed what was happening to himself, he would welcome it. His problems would be over.

He had also set up a do-not-resuscitate order, which I had scanned and saved.

I began to be less afraid, at least for him.

The fear that the social worker was trying to prepare me for, and whomever else she read that description to, seemed to be more likely to be on our end. The fear and anxiety would be from separation and loss – from never again being able to talk to Bryn.

Somehow, I only appreciated all that on an intellectual level just then, as I analyzed it.

Later, when I was on my own to think at night, I felt depressed over it and cried. I think I got most of my crying over Bryn done before the fact than after. I know I did a lot of that alone late at night, silently so that he wouldn't be upset by it, as I sat at that computer.

Staying up late was easy for me; I am a night owl. Add to that the fact that Damon would be available to talk to via Skype late at night, usually during the late-night talk shows that I liked to watch. I began to stay up later and later, watching Bryn from the computer. I couldn't sleep.

Books and movies were a way of escaping from such depressing thoughts, and I clung to David Letterman's and Craig Ferguson's shows as a way of not being alone to think too much about Bryn's impending departure from my life late at night. Of course, after *The Late Late Show*, I had to rely on movies or computer games, and as the summer wore on, it was just games because I was watching Bryn surreptitiously.

I would stay like that until 4 a.m., forgetting how late it was getting, afraid to stop keeping watch on Bryn, until I realized that if I didn't go to bed, I wouldn't be able to function the next day. After talking to Damon, watching the late shows, taking a shower, and making sure that Bryn had taken all of his medicine, I would just sit there and forget how long I was sitting.

But that was how the summer played out. It wasn't like that right away.

It gradually became that way, little by little, as time wore on.

For now, we wondered, Berta and I, how it would go. I repeated everything that the social worker had described to me when she returned from work, and for once she seemed not to have attention deficit disorder. She memorized it all, too.

Then she said, "If you check on him and he has...passed," and here she paused, revealing herself to be one of those people who preferred such irritating euphemisms to directness, "call Albert first, then me.

The Slamming Door

Though I would like to be there at the exact moment that it happens, with him," she added.

I guess she hoped to arrive in time for that somehow.

Odd…something occurred to me, though I kept it myself, sensing that its iteration would be unwelcome: didn't people try to die when they thought that no one was looking? What did I know about that, I thought next…my only direct knowledge of this was with my lovely Charcoal Cat, who had died while I was occupied with signing on the euthanasia line at the vet's office.

Maybe it was just a matter of luck…unless someone was fatally injured, it was logistically difficult to know when to hang around and wait for that moment. Dying of a disease was different; one could wonder for months on end how long it would take someone to die.

And Bryn clearly had more time. He was planning ahead, trying to be as little trouble to others as possible.

True to type, Bryn came out of his room then, stumping along with his cane, and informed us that he wanted his memorial service (he didn't want a funeral) to take place a couple of months after his death. We just listened. He went on to add that his reasoning was that if people had plenty of advance notice about the date, they would be able to plan for it. Plane tickets wouldn't cost them so much because they wouldn't be bought at the last minute.

That was vintage Bryn, really, being so thoughtful of other people even in death.

He really was the saint and the glue of the family. I was certain that we would feel less connected and less likely to get together without him in the picture.

There was another thing that I found myself wondering about at this time: suicide. Had Bryn considered it? He had rejected marijuana from the get-go; what about suicide? Or had he decided against it for similar reasons?

I didn't have to wonder for long; he suddenly talked about that the next day.

Albert was there.

Bryn told us that he had thought about killing himself and decided against it for several reasons, and he was the one who brought it up.

He told us a story he had heard about someone he knew a few years earlier, someone who died of cancer – some other kind but a painful one. Aren't they all painful, I thought? They all have inflammation, caused by tissue swelling around tumors that the body has no room for.

Well…anyway…his friend had saved up his pills, stockpiling them for a suicide attempt. He had read about a reliable method of doing this on the Internet first. He would need a couple of plastic bags and a lot of

Hospice, and His Papers Again

pills. But he had no Dr. Kevorkian to help him, so he just saved the drugs up for the final exit.

He took all of the pills, put the bags over his head, and tried to go to sleep.

He must not have planned this carefully enough, though, because the cops broke into his house, pulled off the bags, revived him, and then he didn't have enough to try again. Bryn said he was furious when he came to. I can't say that I blame him, whoever he was.

"So," I asked Bryn, "you aren't planning to do that?"

"No. I don't want to get anyone else into trouble."

"You mean, you don't want them [the authorities] to say that I killed you."

"Exactly."

So, based on that conversation, he was planning to keep me with him until he died.

We never discussed the idea of his suicide again, and barely referred to his impending death either. It was such a given at that point that it seemed pointlessly depressing, and we were already quite depressed as it was.

Since it was summer, there was nothing on television that compelled my attention, so I just watched a few reruns and a lot of movies. Once, Bryn and I got distracted by *The Nanny Diaries*, a movie about an anthropology graduate from Columbia University who worked as a nanny for an oblivious, clueless, and over-privileged Upper East Side woman.

We were intrigued by the whole thing, disgusted at the woman and wondering when things would improve, which of course they ultimately did. Even if I don't like or want kids, I don't like to think of idiots raising them and making them miserable. We spent a leisurely afternoon watching together in his room, he in the Lazy Boy chair and I flopped on his bed, which he had pretty much abandoned.

It was a lovely afternoon, and for some reason or other, no one came over. There were no errands to do, and I had recently cleaned the entire apartment. So, we enjoyed the movie and the quiet, with no pressure to do anything much.

That happened sometimes; despite the anxiety and unhappiness associated with death and dying, it would punctuated by pleasant and peaceful interludes. We had the good sense to just sit back and enjoy them, but they still felt a bit odd and surreal; how could we be feeling peaceful, calm and happy during this time?

The Slamming Door

Easy: life marches on, regardless of how we feel about our situations.

Albert did something really neat one afternoon: he arrived by cab, alone, carrying in two large, framed political cartoons – Georgist cartoons! – that he had ordered online, moving very carefully. They were from *Puck* magazine, which ran from 1879 to 1918. It was America's first successful humor magazine, and it had been known for caricatures and political cartoons.

The prints were beautiful, in color on an aged paper background, with the captions in German, and Bryn was absolutely delighted with them.

One of them showed two men in a desert leading a donkey to drink out of a trough of papers. The word "LABOR" was written on the donkey's flank, and it was wearing enormous green spectacles, just like Dorothy and her friends did when they got to the Emerald City. The other showed two men on a city rooftop at night, with one peering through a telescope labeled "Henry George Theories" – and the other dripping candle wax onto his own bald head.

I promptly got out the hammer and picture-hanging hooks from under the kitchen sink. There was no time to lose in putting them up to be enjoyed. Bryn stumped around, being careful as usual not to pound his cane too loudly on the floor, directing me as to where to situate each one. When I was finished hanging them – one in the hallway and the other above the little table between Bryn's bed and hat-rack – I got out the digital camera to record the images.

We all stood back and admired the effect, and then I carried out Bryn's next wish: I went online and e-mailed his girlfriend and Henry George colleagues, sending the digital images and inviting them all to come over and see them.

Bryn announced that he would leave the framed cartoons to the Henry George School.

Of course – where else would they belong but there?

Soon we had a couple of afternoons during which Henry George people paraded through the apartment to view the artwork, drink McNulty's coffee, and chat. Claus dropped by, then Desta and her mother, and finally Alfred Mazerati, who brought his wife.

These were all separate visits.

Desta was funny; on prior visits, she hadn't realized that each cup of coffee had to be individually made, and she tried to be polite by saying that she would have whatever everyone else was having. I was standing there with the bags of labeled coffee. Now she understood, and smiled

Hospice, and His Papers Again

and pointed to the toasted praline bag. It was a nice surprise to see her venerable mother along with her, and also an ominous one. It meant that if this great lady was making the effort to trudge on over to Bryn's place, she understood that he wasn't doing very well himself.

Alfred and his wife arrived on a lovely, warm, sunny afternoon, and we all enjoyed the news that the bit of cancer on his lung had been removed during surgery. He would likely live for at least a few more years. We had all been shocked and horrified to find out that he was sick earlier in the year, so this was nice, though not a real thrill. He was still on borrowed time.

I couldn't remember hearing of Alfred smoking, so the mere idea of lung cancer in him infuriated me. Granted, I realize that not smoking is no guarantee that one won't get that particular kind of cancer. However, I always feel as though a person is somehow entitled not to get lung cancer if they never smoke...not that life cares or works out that way.

Alfred's wife was a thin, pretty, and intelligent woman who had, like me, kept her own last name when they got married. Logical though that choice is, it's not what the majority of women do in our culture, so whenever I encounter another woman who has kept her own name – her own identity – I notice and feel a thrill.

She had a red Vera Bradley handbag, and we laughed over our similarities. She also had a graduate degree of some sort, though I forget now what it was. She had dark brown hair that curled and waved and that she had pinned up, and wore no makeup. She even dressed like me – shorts with good pockets, a comfortable, colorful summer shirt, and flat, rubber-soled sandals.

If we had had more time to get to know each other, we might have found more in common, but we just didn't. She told me that she and Alfred had been married for about 5 years, and I vaguely remembered having seen her during a noisy dinner gathering at the 30 at 30 restaurant; she remembered me just as vaguely.

When the excitement over the *Puck* cartoons had blown over, Albert and June's visits resumed with marked regularity. It was as though he wanted to spend all of the time that he possibly could with his brother. Now that Alissa had moved back in with her parents, he found that it was very easy to arrive with June, wait for Alissa to meet us at Bryn's place for a visit, and then let her take her mother home while he stayed on into the evening.

Albert began to be concerned about his daughter, and asked me and Berta to shop for some pretty shirts for her. I knew what he meant; he was sick, her mother had lost a lot of her memory, and Alissa had no

The Slamming Door

boyfriend. Albert was afraid of leaving her all alone. I got around to it promptly, happy for the distraction. Berta was too busy and disinterested, so I did it myself. It was fun.

Both Berta and I were present when her uncle made this request, and Berta always seemed very concerned about her cousin, but I sensed that there would be no action from her end on this count. That was fine with me; I work best alone on such projects. As it was, looking for pretty clothes for someone else was fussy enough; better to tackle the problem independently.

By independently, I meant one-on-one with Alissa, first suggesting that we both shop together, and finding out where she thought she might find pretty tops and other items.

But that wasn't going to work out: she had to work, watch her mother, cook for her parents, attend a writers' group called *paragraph* (the first letter was not capitalized), participate in her French and English literature book clubs – which meant reading the books as well attending their gatherings – and somehow work in her own writing, which was what she wanted to do most. We wouldn't be going out shopping together at all, I quickly realized.

Alissa's time was almost completely spoken for, and very little of it was now her own.

No wonder her father was concerned that he and June would die and leave her utterly alone, with no husband to keep her company. He certainly wasn't counting on her cousins to pick up the slack; they had men to be with already. Albert said that he would pay me back promptly for things, and so would Alissa.

I felt badly for her, even though my own husband couldn't as yet be with me either.

Accordingly, I studied the situation.

Alissa thought she might find pretty shirts and blouses in the Burlington Coat Factory store and in another equally improbable store on 6th Avenue, the name of which I have since forgotten. I walked through them both and came away unimpressed; the merchandise was loud, gaudy, uncomfortable, and labor-intensive to care for. I told Alissa so the next time I saw her.

She seemed nonplussed, but nodded in a way that suggested she was glad to have had someone else investigate the facts on her behalf.

With that, I turned back to my own favorite haunts.

Every afternoon, Bryn was now encouraging me to go out walking in the city and enjoy myself. I think he wanted to be home alone for a while, and we were still comfortable with that idea at that point. As long as I kept my cell phone on, it worked.

Hospice, and His Papers Again

Sometimes he would call me just to see what I was up to, but that was all.

I keep up with his errands for prescriptions so well that he hardly possessed a new one before it was filled, typically the same day or the next afternoon, depending upon how quickly the pharmacy could meet the demand. Bryn stopped looking surprised when I wanted to do that immediately; he was used to my obsession with efficiency by then.

So I now found myself visiting the cats – London and Paris – while I waited for bottles of pills, or traipsing across town to the other place, where the people would ask how Bryn was. The reports weren't too sad as yet, but later in the summer my voice shook a little when I replied.

But not yet; I had plenty of time to boost both my own and Alissa's wardrobe as I wandered about, following an abortive attempt to get her a dress online from Anthropologie's sale items. She tried it on at home, it didn't look good, and I never tried to get her another dress.

But the blue pullover blouse – exactly like my own – was a success.

I found myself copying her father's method of shopping for Alissa, which meant getting clothes for her that resembled my own rather closely. The upside to this was that with me as the model, Alissa was getting some different clothes – feminine ones that were from places other than L.L. Bean. Albert and June looked like twins in polo shirts and beige pants, and their daughter was dressed like a copy of June. Sometimes it was cute – they had matching shoes on once. But it just looked dowdy on their daughter.

The sale racks of Banana Republic, Anthropologie, and a few other places became great sources of pretty blouses, and soon Alissa had several additions to her wardrobe. I found one more – a black pullover with a waved scoop neckline at Banana Republic – and saved it for Bryn to give her for her birthday. He was pleased; I had a black one and a fuchsia one, so he knew how it looked.

With the blouses bought, Alissa looked really happy in them, and wore them often.

It was time to deal with one last detail: her bag.

Her bag was a beige teardrop-shaped thing with a large, bright-green chewing gum stain on the side. It weighed a ton because she carried everything but the kitchen sink in it – including her laptop computer.

It seemed to me that Vera Bradley must have something else, something pretty but utilitarian, and something that was on sale. I went online and found that there was such a thing.

Alissa was visiting when I got the image on the screen: a backpack in some discontinued patterns. Alissa looked with me, and told me which one she liked best. She chose a pale blue-and-green flower pattern. It looked pretty, and her mother approved, of course. June was still obsessed with Vera Bradley, which was cute.

Then Alissa said that she wanted the large backpack, not the regular one. She intended to keep on lugging that laptop around the city. Okay. That meant calling Vera Bradley and cancelling an earlier order, but the company did it. And this was pay dirt, as far as I could see: the large backpack was half off, even cheaper than the discontinued regular one.

When the item arrived, we wasted no time in unpacking it and urging Alissa to move into it, which she did. She was wearing a bright green blouse that I had bought, and she stood in the living room with the monster flowered backpack over her shoulders, looking pretty and happy.

A fait accompli – we were all quite delighted.

There was just one other detail to take care of, this time for June: Albert had replaced her ratty old red Vera Bradley backpack – a regular-sized one – with a new red one. It was another discontinued pattern, marked down, but it was the same size and red, which was what mattered.

He moved her things into it, put the plastic I.D. tag from the old one on it with her name, address, and his phone number on the plastic card, and she seemed to be all set…until she noticed that the invisible magnetic snap on the outer flap was too weak to be of use.

She tucked it into the compartment, tsk-tsking that it was annoying not to be able to use that part of the bag. And it was…

…and I could fix that.

I mentioned it to Bryn that night, and he said, in mock-urgent tones, "Something has got to be done!" He was moving some papers around, just about to sit in his chair, and he gave a big, mischievous grin as he said.

Berta heard about it and wondered what was funny; I replied that it wasn't all that earth-shattering of a problem. I could easily fit the solution into my schedule.

Accordingly, the next afternoon, I walked up 8th Avenue to the Fashion Institute of Technology. Across the street from the school was a sewing supply shop with everything I needed: black remnant rags, a magnetic snap, and thread. I bought the stuff and went home. All together, it was under five bucks.

When June and Alissa arrived, I asked for the bag, and explained why.

June looked delighted and handed it right over.

Hospice, and His Papers Again

I shut myself in my room to do the deed, telling the others that I needed to concentrate on it and not to look for me for a little while, and that it wouldn't take too long. They nodded and left me to it.

When I was finished, the snap was visible, but only when the flap was opened – fixed.

Bryn later remarked, "It's a lot better than hearing June bitch about it Albert for the next several months."

June was happy; she moved on to other things.

Of course, those weren't the only issues that we dealt with in June.

Bryn's osteo-oncologist had pretty much given up on being able to save him at this point and we all knew it, but she seemed to be determined to try to make him comfortable, or to at least seem to be doing something, anything, about him.

Accordingly, she prescribed something awful called Sirolimus (generic name) or Rapamune (the brand name). The cost of a bottle of the pills even in generic form was as horrendous as its effects: $900. I had had to tell Albert and Bryn that if they chose to go ahead with this, I would not be able to charge that up on my credit card and bring it back due to the cost alone. They already knew that I disapproved of it thanks to having heard about its side effects from Damon. Damon is like my human science encyclopedia, and I love that about him.

Albert and Bryn couldn't blame me for any of that; my credit card had a $4,000 limit, and I was only used to charging amounts of perhaps a hundred dollars, maybe a bit more, at a time. They knew that $900 felt like too big a bite to wait for the reimbursement, so Albert had gotten the drug. It wasn't a big deal to them, this reticence of mine to charge that amount up on my card.

Damon was more of a nutraceutical fan than a pharmaceutical one; he never failed to mention the fact that nutraceuticals don't come with side effects, and won't give a patient a slew of other health problems or cost much.

But the side effects of Sirolimus were disturbing. Bryn promptly developed them: whitish sores in his mouth and on his tongue. Damon had made every reasonable effort to dissuade him and Albert from trying this crap, but to no avail. A whole slew of nasty side effects could be seen on the Internet including, but of course not limited to, rapid heartbeat and swollen limbs. Amazing…Bryn already had tachycardia, and but he took a drug that could bring it on.

I don't know what the Otterman brothers' thinking was on this one. Albert researched every cancer treatment that came along extensively on the Internet and printed up reams of paper for others to read, but he still

The Slamming Door

wanted to try this. He respected Damon's knowledge and interpretation of the science, but he wanted to try anything that came along at that point.

I guess the Otterman boys wanted the big guns treatment, which was why they accepted chemotherapy, radiation, and radioactive seeds. As when it had started with Bryn, the image of Dr. Callahan spraying a massive jet stream of poisonous chemicals all over him out of a huge fire hose came back to mind. Now she was using horse pills (Sirolimus pills were a bit oversized).

Well, Bryn took them for a week or so, and they did him absolutely no good; they just inflicted more misery on him. Back to the doctor, who took him right off of it.

When he came home and told me so, I couldn't resist the urge to say, "I am absolutely disgusted. You have been swindled out of 900 bucks and a comfortable mouth."

He nodded soberly and agreed; eating any fruits or vegetables was a stinging, painful experience. Fortunately, his mouth began to improve within a few days of quitting it.

All of the tortures and indignities that I was observing during my time with Bryn was making me terrified of ever getting cancer and absolutely determined to stick with eating habits that would prevent it.

Whatever my ultimate cause of death – excepting suicide, of course – I was most upset by the possibility of it being cancer. It was gross, disfiguring, had smelled sickly sweet when my grandmother had been sick with lung cancer (fortunately, Bryn never developed that symptom), and unless the damned disease was encrypted in one's DNA, quite possibly avoidable.

I certainly hoped so; my DNA, judging from my family history, suggested that if I ate a healthful diet and didn't smoke, I ought to be able to avoid this.

But I was so horrified by all that I was learning about it, and all that I had already known about it after watching my grandmother die of it and my mother work with prostate cancer patients, that food remained an obsession with me for more than just reasons of finickiness.

No fast food, not too much greasy food, no beef, which Damon tells me is carcinogenic (so glad I hate the stuff!), not too much alcohol – especially beer – but some red wine, lots of fresh fruits, vegetables, cinnamon, other spices, fish and plenty of extra-virgin olive oil plus some good vinegars…and a little chocolate, and some desserts. That ought to protect me.

A heart attack didn't seem like such a bad death, or just falling asleep and never waking up. But we don't know how we will die, or when, and there is only so much control we have in the manner of our deaths.

As this tense period stretched on, I took to imagining a new cartoon character tormenting Bryn: the cancer itself, personified as a small, piss-yellow creature with a belly, arms and legs, and a head that had no brain in it, no eyes, ears, or nose, only a large mouth with teeth that chomped and gobbled, and was one entity as well as many identical ones, somewhat like the Marvel Comics character that went by the name of Multiple Man.

Multiple Man is one guy who can replicate himself while staying aware of the actions and thoughts of all copies, then combine all copies into one original individual, with full memories of what all the copies just did. The difference was is that this piss-yellow monster had no sentience whatsoever. It merely existed to feed itself, as it was the ultimate parasite. This was the monster that was now gobbling Bryn up from the inside…out. Cancer was a monster that was feasting on my friend.

Bryn was not going out as much, but his hair had grown back, and his sense of taste and smell appeared to have reverted to normal. So what; he did go out on visits – short ones – and then would come home exhausted and eat very little. It was unsatisfying to watch him pay for fun times with a day or two of utter exhaustion. That just looked like a punishment being meted out for enjoying life.

We had Berta's cat Nikita to keep us company for as long as he enjoyed her.

Bryn told me I was indispensable to him, and that I was doing a wonderful, great job.

Terrific.

I had nowhere to go after this, except to what felt like a tomb: home to Bloomfield, Connecticut, with my stress-inducing 66-year-old parents, away from any public transportation or way to make any money. I wanted to die too.

Bryn loved life and I hated it.

Something was backwards.

Berta was coping strangely, too. She was eating more and was less interested in dieting.

One evening, after we had all eaten dinner, she and Bryn and I had dishes of Hagen Daas ice cream. I went into the kitchen and scooped it out, some strawberry for Bryn, and Swiss chocolate almond for us girls.

The Slamming Door

I just put 3 small scoops into each bowl, enough for a gastronomic thrill and chill in the warm weather without heaping on too many calories.

I threw the empty container in the rubbish bin; there was another pint in the freezer.

When I brought out the bowls, Berta looked in hers and said, "Why so little?!"

I replied, "I want to be thin."

"I don't!" she said.

I was a bit surprised by this; previously she had cried over her weight and dieted.

But I wasn't about to say anything more.

I ate mine, and then got Bryn's dish a few minutes later and washed them both.

Berta seemed to take a bit longer, which was odd, but I went back into my room to read and watch television. She was at the computer, looking at her Facebook account. I read for a while, forgetting what was happening around me.

As I read, I heard some sounds in the kitchen and realized that Berta was in there. The sounds were of water running and a scrub brush being used; she had cleaned up her bowl and spoon. Then silence for a while, during which I read some more. She didn't come out of the kitchen for a while longer.

Hours later, when she had gone home, I went to get some ice out of the freezer, and realized that the extra pint of Swiss chocolate almond ice cream – the unopened one – was gone. Nonplussed, I looked down at the rubbish bin. There it was, emptied. So that was what Berta had been doing in here.

Bryn was disgusted and annoyed.

I just said I would get more tomorrow.

After that, on another evening, Berta commented that she didn't want anyone offering her advice any more about portion sizes and healthy food choices or dieting any more.

Okay, fine. It was her problem.

Piper and Melissa continued to visit until the summer, at which time they prepared to do their usual thing: take off for distant lands and travel as lightly as possible.

In the past, whenever they went away, which was every winter and summer break, Bryn would look after their mail and apartment, collecting everything and leaving it in a box and then watering every plant in their front rooms.

Hospice, and His Papers Again

But that was in the past. I had done it over the winter break, so Melissa asked me to do it again, and gave me a couple hundred dollars in advance. I went upstairs with her and saw the box for the mail, and practiced with her keys again. It was the same routine that I had done in the winter, although this time I decided to keep all of the mail in a huge orange bag with cloth handles (from the Time-Warner cable company), and haul the lot upstairs at the end.

Piper, for his part, had a last-minute (what other kind of work did he ever do?!) typing job for me. He left it for me when I was out, with a hundred dollars in the pages of the journal, his notes, and detailed instructions. Melissa spoke to Bryn about it, exasperated with her husband for being disorganized and hurried, convinced that the only reason the journal in question would publish it was that Piper was one of its founders.

Whatever; it was just a straightforward typing and editing job, and I made short work of it, e-mailed it to Piper after I was finished, and pocketed the cash as agreed.

They were going to England and France for the summer, Piper first, to be followed by Melissa. Montclair College got out first, then the New York City public school that she taught at. She would have to come home ahead of him, too. He always stayed away longer, enjoying his vacation a bit longer than his wife's shorter one.

What with the footnotes, text and cite-checking via Google's search engine, Piper was soon confident that he could enjoy his travels without another thought about the article.

That suited me fine, of course. I had my new student from Empire State College.

Another thing that happened when summer got underway was that we found out what Berta's favorite television shows were at last.

Previously, she had followed along, no doubt observing me and gathering data on me, as I watched the *CSI* forensics dramas, plus the *NCIS* one, and my favorite Aspie one, *Bones*. I had wondered what she liked, but left it at that. She claimed to like what I liked, and although we had both liked *Wonder Woman* as children, I was a bit suspicious of that.

Seriously: she couldn't just like all of the same things that I liked and nothing else.

The first thing that we found out was that she liked AMC's *Mad Men*, something that I had watched a little bit of with my mother back in Connecticut, admiring the artwork during the credits as the advertising executive takes a suicidal dive out the skyscraper and falls to his death

The Slamming Door

in slow motion against a backdrop of other skyscrapers, all of which have ads on them.

We found it out in the most interesting way, because it brought out some information about Bryn's father. Berta had brought over a DVD set of its entire first season for us to watch, and we finally got around to doing so.

Bryn said he just wanted to see the first episode, so we settled for that, though I suspect that both Berta and I would have gladly played a few more if he had been willing to see them.

We let it run, and then Bryn shared some family history with us. They were well worth listening to, and about his father. Franklin Otterman had worked for an advertising agency in Manhattan, just like the Mad Men, but his career had spanned the two and a half decades that had preceded the TV series. It was a smaller firm than Don Draper's, and it had an Irish name.

The really fun part was hearing that Bryn's father had coined the phrase that the Cunard Cruise line had gone with for a long time: "Getting there is half the fun." So…he had been the creative mind behind a famous line; cool.

After that, Bryn went back to watching *The L Word* on Showtime and *The No. 1 Ladies' Detective Agency* on HBO. He was really into those shows, and sorry when *The L Word* ended. I got a kick out of seeing him be so into a television show.

Berta, however, suddenly showed us what she liked best: reality shows and talent shows.

Her favorite reality show was one that I had never noticed before: *Real Housewives of New Jersey*. It was intriguing at first, because it showed NT women with boob jobs – or scheduling them at the plastic surgeon's office with a drooling husband in tow – plus heavy makeup, glued-on lacquered talons for fingernails, and the latest and wildest dresses and skirt suits. All dressed up to…go to each other's houses and chat. Sometimes they went out to eat, but I was intrigued to see just how dressed up and made up they were at all times.

Berta loved it. She would see the previews for each episode and eagerly anticipate it, talking about the upcoming scenes with great enthusiasm. Of course Bryn would let her watch the show on his television; he was the sort of dad who would indulge his daughter in whatever gave her a thrill, which was nice.

The show was anything but nice, however. One of the housewives had been a porn star before marrying a guy from the Jersey Shore. When that fact came up, it wasn't particularly shocking or appalling. In fact, I thought it was nice that a porn star could move on and have a decent life

Hospice, and His Papers Again

after being a sex worker, rather than slink off to loneliness, misery, disgrace and ridicule as "fallen" women did in decades past.

That was so early 20th century, wasn't it?

Sadly, no; the Jersey housewives found out and gave her grief for being around them and their daughters, and Berta just couldn't wait to see the episode in which one of them flipped a table over in a restaurant right in front of her own 12-year-old daughter.

She rushed home that evening, wildly excited to see that, saying, "Dad! Dad! Quick – turn on *Real Housewives*!" which he did right away, of course. It wouldn't have been right not to let her see the show after hearing her talk about it for the past few days...

I had lost interest in it by then. I just couldn't sit through an entire episode of...stupid.

Keeping my expressions neutral and my mouth shut as to my true opinions, I had wandered in and out of Bryn's room on other evenings when it was on, glancing at the screen when I was there, presenting dinner and whatever else but otherwise not settling in to watch.

No one had insisted that I stay and watch it.

I kept going back to the computer, not feeling much urgency about watching anything on the other television. It was just so pleasant in the apartment in the summertime, with the air so warm and plenty of breezes wafting through the screened windows. I have always loved summer weather with no air conditioning on unless it feels truly stifling.

So while they watched, books, the Internet, and movies kept me occupied.

Shrieks of delight emanated from Bryn's room as the table got flipped over, which I missed. I was right outside, but not motivated to go in and see. I suppose it would have been an interesting sight, but it had been on several times in the previews.

Was this how people felt when I got excited about *Star Trek*? Probably. When I wanted to see a movie about some historical figure? Quite likely. Oh well...I was used to it.

If someone wanted to talk to me like I was in the throes of childlike delight when such a thing got me into a happy mood of anticipation, I never let it bother me. Women who are NTs often take a motherly attitude with Aspie women, perhaps feeling unsettled by our interests in intellectual entertainments. Berta had, my own mother had (though it didn't seem condescending when my own mother did it), my college R.A. had, and so on and on.

Berta's choices were so utterly at the opposite end of the mental spectrum that I didn't know what to say, so I chose to say nothing. If you can't think of anything complimentary to say about such things, it's better to just keep your mouth shut, so I did that.

The Slamming Door

Or to paraphrase Mark Twain said, "It is better to keep your mouth shut and appear intellectually snobbish than to open it and remove all doubt."

I was going with tacit appearances.

It was obvious that Berta envied the Jersey housewives on many levels: they didn't have to ride a crowded subway train during rush hour, jammed in like a sardine, to work in an office waiting on wealthy bosses. (Berta had to do that every weekday; she had told me so and that she hated it. She probably resented the fact that I didn't have to do that.) Instead, they were married to wealthy men, they had bodies that Berta wanted and no amount of plastic surgery could give her, and endless leisure time to socialize in ways that Berta understood and enjoyed.

It was all Etruscan to me. (I won't say ancient Greek about Italian people; the pre-Romans, however, spoke Etruscan.) Aspies don't understand nonverbal cues, don't enjoy verbal sparring or have a clue as to how to engage in it, and could care less about anything that those women cared about – fashion, trends, fads, and plastics.

I just couldn't relate.

Her other favorite show was *America's Got Talent*.

It was those teenagers in Kuwait all over again, the wealthy ones who had absorbed the worst aspects of American culture and actually thought that the cheating that went on during *American Idol* contents was of any importance. (But this was summer, so that show wasn't on.)

Somehow, I wound up in Bryn's room when *America's Got Talent* was on, as did Albert.

It came down to a choice between two groups of contestants, which meant that one group won and the other lost. Berta took an unseemly delight in observing the facial expressions of the members of the losing team, which were naturally ones of visible disappointment.

She grinned, cackled, rocked back and forth in her seat, and commented, "Look at the looks on the faces of the losers!" and laughed some more.

That was too much for Albert; he told her that her behavior was appalling.

I kept my mouth shut and left the room sooner than I could invent a reason to.

Give me Bones solving a heinous murder and asking Booth to explain subtle innuendos any day. It taught me new things every time I watched, both facts and social interactions, and no one was a bully to anyone else. If she offended someone, the others all knew that she didn't meant to, and talked her through understanding it.

Hospice, and His Papers Again

Berta's favorite shows were loaded with instances of deliberate nastiness. People who bullied others knew exactly what they were doing, and went ahead with it every time, with malicious enthusiasm.

At least I was observing Berta now rather than merely being observed.

It was as though we were finally starting to show each other our honest selves.

The disturbing part of this was that I had been showing her my true self all along while waiting for her to reciprocate.

What had induced her to reciprocate now?

Perhaps it was a gradual build-up to the truth that was corresponding to her father's decline; as he worsened, she dropped a few more shields.

Chapter 46

20th Precinct Business Cards

In mid-June, Berta invited me out again with her and Leila. We had had a lot of fun the first time, and an interesting evening the second time. Each time, I met them at the appointed places after they got off work.

It was great fun getting to know Leila better.

Some of that came directly from chatting with Leila, and some from Berta. Apparently, Leila was having trouble being single after dumping her two-timing boyfriend, and was not doing a very good job of fending off lusty men.

The plan was to meet at a nearby furniture store, a Danish outlet called Bo Concept that offered cold, modern-looking items with metal frames, leather sofas, and faux fur throws. I didn't like its décor, and had seen it before in Kuwait, of all places. But the focus of the event this time was on the framed artwork that would be hung all over the store.

The place was east of Bryn's place, in Chelsea, and he pushed me to leave on time. I managed it with no problem, but arrived feeling a bit overheated despite my best efforts not to hurry too much. I went right inside to cool off. Soon I was comfortable.

I had dressed nicely, not knowing exactly what to expect, and was relieved when I saw the other partygoers; some were in gorgeous dresses and uncomfortable shoes, but others wore pants. I was in black linen pants with pockets, and a beautiful cobalt blue peasant blouse with floral embroidery around the square-cut neckline. I looked good, and my hair was down long, out of its usual, utilitarian gold matte clip (even the clip was chic; I liked to be presentable at all times). To finish it all off I wore, as a mischievous jab, my Teva sandals.

Leila appeared and did not fail to disappoint me; she immediately commented about my footwear. "I wore them just for you," I said. She laughed and let it drop.

Berta appeared soon after, and we began to enjoy the gourmet goodies and free alcohol.

Berta had amazed me during the winter at first one and then another Mexican restaurant by downing a couple of Margaritas without missing a beat; I could get through one without feeling ill, but only if I ate a full meal. I had to remind myself that my in-laws drank more than I was used to, and could still function efficiently, but it was always a surprise to see it done.

I wandered around the store, which took up two large rooms, looking at the artwork. In the first room, back to the right, was a large black-and-white photograph of Billy Idol at a party in the 1980s. He

20th Precinct Business Cards

looked terrific, thin, young and at the pinnacle of his music career, and was shown enjoying the night life in New York City. I loved several of his songs still, including the one that came to mind on this particular evening: "Hot in the City." It was a hot night.

After a while, I went into the next room to see what else there was to look at and found a row of photos – a set – of outdoor stone artwork, wall carvings, in Venice, Italy. Having just read *City of Falling Angels* the previous fall, about the destruction and reconstruction of the opera house, La Fenice, I was intrigued. A lot of that artwork was literally crumbling off of the walls of Venetian buildings due to acid rain.

I glanced to one side and noticed a tall, thin woman with long blond hair looking at the same set of framed photos and spoke to her about them. Soon we were chatting away about them and about Venice. We had both been to that city at some point, and from there the conversation moved on to other things. We exchanged business cards when I mentioned my editing service. As I was handing mine over, Berta beckoned to me from across the room.

When I saw that, I excused myself and went over to her, wondering what she wanted.

"That woman isn't interested in whatever you are holding her up with," she told me.

Really…I made no reply. This was a bit much. Berta was clearly well out of earshot and couldn't have heard what we were saying to one another. She had some nerve. I just moved on to looking at other art on my own.

But I was annoyed. Berta was lately getting more and more obnoxious over Asperger's, pointing out to me at times this and that little sign of the condition in whatever habit I exhibited or quirk that cropped up.

What had possessed her to interfere in a conversation that I was having with a total stranger?! It was none of her business if I couldn't carry a social interaction off perfectly. That is the risk of living life with Asperger's. Granted, the condition leads me to a more isolated and introverted range of career choices, but I am not a child; I have a right to be left to my own devices and either hit it off with people or not.

Later on, still at that event, I found myself sitting with first Leila and then Berta too at a table with a computer as they chatted with an artists' agent; I was trying out the company's furniture software just out of curiosity. It let the user decorate a virtual living room or bedroom with the wares for sale by Bo Concept. It was a fun thing to do for the odd woman odd; they weren't including me in the conversation much. Sometimes body language helps to exclude an extra person, and sometimes just being at the most distant spot at the table achieves that.

The Slamming Door

When we went outside, we met a handsome young man who was out on the town for the evening with two young women – they were probably all in their late twenties. He was wearing all black and was tanned with dark hair that was slicked straight back; the women wore high-heeled, ankle-breaker shoes. Berta started chatting with him, and he told us that he had attended the La Guardia High School, and that he was both an actor and a mixologist.

We all stared at him, confused. "What's a mixologist?" Berta and Leila asked.

It turned out to be someone who mixed drinks at a bar...a bartender. Apparently, he just liked this glorified name for the profession. He wasn't succeeding as an actor.

He asked me why I was so quiet at one point; I told him I was just listening and observing. It was another Aspie moment that freaked out an NT, one that gave me something constructive to do rather than stumble through an awkward attempt at conversation. There wasn't much that I could have added to this chat, so listening was the best option. The NTs with me had pretty much covered all of the important points. That happened to me a lot, and I didn't mind.

Berta later told us that this was because his face wasn't perfectly symmetrical and therefore wouldn't look good on camera. She had gone just far enough with her curriculum in television production before partying had caused her to flunk out; after that she had changed schools and switched to general studies.

The more time I spent with Berta, the more I understood how she had become the way that she was. She was so undisciplined – physically, mentally, emotionally and otherwise – that she had sealed herself off from a wide range of attractive options in life. She had had all of the opportunities that I had, and wasted them. No wonder she was treating me this way.

I was upset constantly, and expected to feel that way. What I hadn't expected was to feel that it was taboo to talk about it. I felt like another daughter to Bryn at this point, and was certainly doing the work of a daughter as his caregiver. But Berta didn't want to hear about anything remotely upsetting.

She seemed utterly and stubbornly determined to feel nothing but a sense of fun and enjoyment at all times lately, enjoying party after social event after restaurant gathering. I found these to be lovely distractions, but they were only that; when each one was over, the quiet was a relief and I sought it out in order to keep calm.

20ᵗʰ Precinct Business Cards

Not Berta; she thrived on constant activity and social noise; she even demanded it every time she came over. "Turn on your TV, Clarisse!" she said one evening. I had been reading all afternoon in the quiet, and hadn't bothered to switch it on. I don't like daytime programming much anyway, and it was a weekday. "I need constant stimulation," she said with a grin.

Incredible; no wonder she couldn't pay attention to any story that I tried to tell. Lately, she refused to try, saying "I can't pay attention, I have ADD!" It seemed like she was holding that up to compare with Asperger's at every opportunity.

Honestly, I found that to be a bit pathetic; Asperger's focuses one's mind intently on an area of interest and comes with a high I.Q. What it lacks in social savvy it more than compensates for in other ways. Not so with ADD; Attention Deficit Disorder has no redeeming features. It must be fought. What bothered me about this was the fact that Berta never showed any interest in fighting it.

Not so with her uncle; Albert had the same condition and had wrestled into enough submission to study at Hamilton College for a bachelor's degree in French and then later go on to earn a master's degree in creative writing in Iowa. ADD had been a nuisance to him, but it had not defined him. He had gone on to pursue an interesting editing career.

My sympathy for Berta was slipping. I tried to ignore it, but it was getting harder.

Fortunately, Leila provided enough of a distraction from everything that evening.

We all came away from Bo Concept, headed up 8ᵗʰ Avenue, and learned that Leila didn't like dogs. She wasn't particularly drawn to any animals, but she froze in the middle of the sidewalk when a man with two small and benign-looking dogs on long leashes tried to pass us. "I don't like dogs," she said, and didn't seem able to move.

The man's leashes got tangled around us as the dogs unhelpfully walked on either side of us, and he tried to assure us that his pets were harmless. Leila still didn't move.

I found this a bit surprising, but considered my emotional assessment to be irrelevant; we were causing a pileup of foot traffic. So I gripped Leila by the shoulders and tugged, saying "Come here, Leila!" I dragged her over to the wall of the building we were next to. She let me pull her over there, but didn't look at the man as he continued to talk about his dogs.

"I'm sure they are very nice animals, and I like them, but you aren't going to change her mind; she's scared of animals. Just walk on," I replied. He did.

The Slamming Door

Other than that, we had a good time with her that evening, with no problems.

Leila was secure with herself, she had her own apartment, she had a master's degree, she spoke three languages, and she didn't point out social ineptitudes in me. She knew I had Asperger's, and didn't harp on it.

She wasn't perfect, but no one is. Her only significant problem was romantic.

We discussed that some more after yet another visit the following week.

As we walked home together through Greenwich Village, Leila told us that some guy she had just met a few nights earlier had gotten into an elevator with her at the end of a party, and promptly stuck his tongue down her throat.

Lovely.

I never had such problems; it must be an NT thing, related to making eye contact a lot.

I don't do much of that, and have a knack for looking away before men can get the wrong idea. The only time it's the right idea is when Damon is around, and my mind is just closed to the idea of getting into trouble…that would be too much bother and inconvenience.

But getting back to Leila's latest romantic difficulty…

Berta was appalled, and scolded Leila for letting that guy put his mouth all over hers.

But what was she supposed to do when these guys asked for her phone number? Leila asked, sincerely wondering how to deal with that.

Suddenly, I had a bright idea. It was inspired by a joke of my father's from years ago.

I explained it now. Before the advent of the wonderful National Do Not Call List, telemarketers used to call homes during dinner, during favorite television shows, during any time that we would rather not be called.

My father had had the perfect response: "Hello – 46th Precinct."

The caller would hang up abruptly, and it worked every time.

It was great fun.

Berta just looked at me, confused, until I went on to say that I would apply this to Leila's problem, and make for her, free of charge, a set of business cards with a fake phone number on them. The last name would be a variation on her own, so that lying would be easy enough.

"That's brilliant!" they both said.

This was going to be fun. I would change her last name from Haeri, lengthening it.

The next day, I did it. The cards were plain and to the point.

20ᵗʰ Precinct Business Cards

They looked like this:

Leila Haeriani, M.A.

Phone: (212) 580-6411

E-Mail: lalehhaeriani@gmail.com

The phone number was for the 20ᵗʰ precinct of the New York City police department. I had looked the precinct numbers up online, and a list came up obligingly. Then I tested the one nearest to her apartment from Bryn's land line phone. It just rang and rang; no one ever picked up. Perfect; if a horrible guy ever did call it, he would just get a cop and hang up in horror.

I printed up 2 reams of them on business card paper, and tore along the perforated lines.

I felt wicked.

Then I told Bryn all about it, and he laughed appreciatively.

On the weekend of my wedding anniversary, for some insane reason, I decided to clean the two bookcases in the kitchen, white ones that contained a large collection of mugs, plates, cutlery, plastic containers, glasses, spices, teas, and coffees. They really showed the dirt. The insane part of this was the fact that I foolishly stayed up all night on Thursday, the first night that Bryn was gone. He had left for the entire weekend. Berta was going to meet him at Cassie's with Matt in tow, just to spend more time with him. Damon would be arriving to be with me on Friday.

When the job was all done, it looked neater, the contents of the shelves had been checked over carefully, and a colony of yellowed larval eggs were wiped away from under the mugs on the extreme right. Surely, no one had cleaned this area for at least a decade, if not longer.

It was amusing the next Monday evening when Bryn and Albert were back in his room and I told them about the cleaning job. Damon had told me what those eggs were, and I mentioned finding and removing them. Albert had one comment, which he uttered at least twice: "Eww…"

But all that cleaning left me tired the next day.

Before I went to sleep, I thought of all the trash that Hilda was supposed to take out. Bryn had been annoyed at her lately for not being diligent about trash removal; he paid her a weekly allowance plus some extra gift money to take away his garbage and recycling, and she wasn't keeping up with the job to his satisfaction. Now there was a lot to remove, and I hoped to get it out before he came back.

Not entirely convinced that e-mailing Hilda alone would produce any response at all, I wrote to her and her parents, using all three e-mail addresses. If that annoyed the kid, I really didn't care. She clearly had no interest in friendship with me; she hardly spoke to me, and when she saw me, she didn't smile.

I supposed it had something to do with not letting her take over my room while she had to be a teenager in a living room in a one-bedroom apartment, but that wasn't my fault.

The e-mail's subject line read: S.O.S.: 3 Giant Bags of Garbage and 1 Dead Television - MUST GO. In it, I explained that I had stayed up all night cleaning, but that it all had to go and could she please take care of it later in the day. I seriously doubted that she would have wanted to rush in and get it early in the morning anyway.

In any case, she took it the trash away later on in the day.

She left the old TV, though; I had to lug it out to the street myself, but I said nothing.

That was the same day that Leila wrote to me with a surprise: the day before my anniversary, something else had come up: Massoumeh Parsi, my friend, memoir topic and editing client, was in town, and Leila invited me to go with her to Columbia University and attend the talk that she was participating in. It was about the fraud that had just taken place in Iran over the 2009 presidential election, and so the event was also a protest by Iranians and Iranian-Americans.

I was definitely interested, and wrote back that I would be there...with the business cards.

Saturday afternoon, I put on a nice blouse and went to meet Leila.

When I had looked at my blouses, I suddenly paused; all of them were in shades of pink, blue, or white. No green, which was the political color of choice. Muslims like green, so they had chosen a hunter hue for the protest. In the coming days as I mentioned this, I found myself explaining this fact to people in my own country who pointed out that it made them think of environmentalism. Well, no movement could claim a monopoly on a color.

I put on a bright pink blouse with my black pants and took off; I would just have to wear what I had and stand out, which I did: everyone else wore either all black, or some green with it. Massoumeh herself had a pastel green scarf that her sister had sent to her just for the protest.

Leila met me at the appointed subway stop and we walked onto Columbia's beautiful campus. We hugged, and I triumphantly handed her the envelope of phony business cards. She looked at one and started

20th Precinct Business Cards

laughing in delight. Then she thanked me with enthusiasm, saying that she was looking forward to trying them out.

But it was getting close to the time that the event was to start, so we started walking and looking around us. The campus was green with lawns and leaves on the trees, the air smelled cleaner in the enclosed space, surrounded by walls and greenery and leafy trees, and I shot some photographs of it as we hurried along. We didn't know exactly where to go…

It was a lovely evening, and we admired the academic buildings and the library. People were everywhere, but all walking purposefully in different directions. How would we find the place? I spotted a woman wearing a hejab – head scarf – and approached her. As negative as stereotyping is, we were in a hurry, and this seemed like a good bet.

It was; she was headed to the same event. Our destination was across the street in an auditorium, and we found it quickly. Posters with bloodied hands making the victory sign led the way. On the way out afterward, Leila and I took a few with us as souvenirs.

Massoumeh was in there, down at the front, and I walked up to her and said with a grin, "Surprise!" She was definitely surprised. We hugged, and I introduced Leila, explaining that she had told me about this event and invited me to come with her.

The two women gave each other the visual once-over, and I was amused; Leila wore black clothes and her hair showed. She practically had the words "secular" and Pahlavi-era" stamped on her. Massoumeh was covered in cloth as usual, with only her hands and face visible. The Islamic Revolution in Iran had not made Massoumeh feel attacked or limited like it had with Leila. I understood this in an instant but made no comment; Massoumeh knew that not all Iranian woman wanted to veil, and Leila knew who Massoumeh was. They had both chosen to be at this event.

Leila and I sat down, and the panel discussion commenced…in Persian only. "I am *so* sorry!" Leila wrote to me on the letter-sized papers I had brought along (each one had event data and directions on the other side). "I had no idea it would all be in Farsi!"

"Don't be sorry – I'm not!" I wrote back, smiling. "I'm thrilled to be here, and the language is no problem with you writing translations at top speed." Leila was writing as fast as she could, and she graciously kept it up the whole time.

The panel consisted of Massoumeh Parsi, Ph.D., outspoken Reformist and former member of Iran's 6th Islamic *Majlis* (Parliament), a Columbia University professor named Hamid Dabashi, Ph.D., whose book, *Iran: A People Interrupted*, I had read, and an imam, Ayatollah Mohsen Kadivar. Each one of them spoke in turn. Massoumeh had a soft voice, but not when she spoke publicly; she knew she had to speak up. I shot a few photographs to commemorate the event and share with her.

When it was over, a Q-and-A session ensued, during which time people could write in a book at the back of the auditorium. Its title was the same as the panel event: *Where Are Our Votes?* I went up there to see it, and asked the Iranian people who were standing around it whether or not it was okay for any non-Iranian people to write in it. They enthusiastically encouraged me to do so.

I think I was the only non-Iranian person, American or foreign, present. I wrote:

> *I wish the people of Iran luck.*
> *Those in power are cheating and lying while claiming that they would not do so.*
> *Iran will need a new Constitution, one modeled after Cyrus the Great plus modern democratic [principles,] if human rights are to be enjoyed there.*
> *Iran needs a separation of mosque and state.*
> *When law is the top priority, religion and human rights are safe... otherwise they aren't.*
>   - *An American Lawyer*

Some of them smiled at me as I moved away from the table.

Now I understood why Massoumeh hadn't told me about this event; it was in Persian.

It seemed funny after the fact, but Massoumeh said that she was glad to have seen me.

Chapter 47

Wedding Anniversary...and Bryn's Leg Swells

That same evening, Damon came back for our 7th wedding anniversary. I had gone to a grocery store with Suzan right after the event at Columbia University, one in the Upper West Side called Fairway. It was a concrete-floored, utilitarian space, famous in the city for the quality of its wares. Floor-to-ceiling, every which way we looked, we found the best of everything. I came back with fresh raspberries, strawberries, cheeses, green vegetables, garlic, and I forget what else – things that I could cook for Damon that night, all foods that he would enjoy.

Our anniversary falls on the 21st of June, the Summer Solstice.

The morning before our anniversary, Berta came in, left a card with $200 in cash inside on the hall table for us, and disappeared before we got up. She was going to Cassie's place to stay with her father for the weekend. We were all alone together for the anniversary.

There was no question but that Damon and I would accept the money and use it for our anniversary dinner. If she hadn't given it to us, we would have just paid for it ourselves, and still gone to the same place that I had selected. We never asked for it. But it was given, and as a surprise...no advance warning. So we said thank you the first chance we got (over the phone) and that was that.

I wondered whether Berta thought that she might be purchasing my undying loyalty to her by giving it me, or just paying me for taking care of her father when she could not; she had to work and leave it to me or else quit and do it herself. One couldn't quit a job in this economy, and even Bryn had wanted her as his caregiver, he wouldn't have condoned that. Nothing that would injure someone else would have been acceptable to him. He was just a good person and a good parent, but ultimately it also came down to what he did and did not want for himself.

Whatever her thinking was, we made up our minds to be alone and have a good time.

Was it fortuitous or deliberate on Bryn's part that his visit to Cassie was on the weekend of my anniversary? I felt uncomfortable about asking him or anyone else that question, so I never did. I chose to think that it was more fortuitous than anything else, and that it had nothing to do with me and anything that might please me. Part of me felt that I just didn't matter; no doubt it was a consequence of not having a place with Damon and a continuous income.

The Slamming Door

I was constantly depressed and hated life. This anniversary was going to be a bright spot in it all, a break from miserable reality for at least an evening and maybe a weekend.

Before we could go out, Damon needed a shower, and he took a cold one because something was wrong with the hot water – it was spurting all over the place. Fortunately, Damon likes cold showers, and it was summer. But we did call Bryn to tell him about it. And we found out that his right leg had swollen up. He was cranky about the water. What had we done to it?

Done to it?! Nothing! We didn't know why it had suddenly chosen this weekend of all times to start doing that.

Well, we would have to call the superintendent the next day, and early, and that just sucked. Damon promised to take care of it, and I was all too happy to let him. I hardly ever had my husband around to take care of things, and I wanted to enjoy it for once. At one point, I had cried when Bryn sounded annoyed with me. I had said, "It's my anniversary!" feeling dismayed that this was happening, as if timed to ruin it. "I don't care!" he had said, whereupon I cried and Damon talked to him, working out all of the tedious details of meeting with the superintendent.

Bryn was worried that every use of hot water would cause a flood inside the walls. It was summer though, and Damon routinely took cold showers. "I don't believe he's taking a cold shower," Bryn had said, which amazed me. I was absolutely sure that Damon was doing just that, and sure enough, there was no steam in the bathroom when he came out. Sigh…

It ultimately turned out that no water had gotten into the walls, and the plumbers just needed to tighten something on Tuesday afternoon. All was well. Meanwhile, we each took showers upstairs in Piper and Melissa's apartment; suddenly plant-watering duties yielded a convenient benefit. I brought a scratchy sponge and Soft Scrub with me, towels…the works.

Looking through my *Michelin Guide to New York Restaurants 2009*, I had found a wonderful French place called L'Absinthe. Damon had been talking about trying absinthe for years, and it had only just been made legal in the United States. (It turned out that the stuff was not really a hallucinogen, so that was why.) I made a reservation for that evening. The restaurant was owned and operated by a master chef who had trained in France, so it didn't need any further recommendation. There tend to be only fifty master chefs on the planet at any one time.

If Damon and I could be together and live near the food and entertainment – i.e., museums, shows, movies, historic sites – which were what thrilled us, we would eat at a place like that a few times a year and at somewhat less expensive ones every week. I would also cook and bake at home, using my gourmet skills and enjoying doing so. To me, life isn't being lived to its fullest or even worth the bother and upset involved without experiences like gourmet restaurants in it.

I wore a new dress from the Anthropologie store, complete with the pockets I had gotten installed in it. The dress was a gorgeous ivory silk one with huge, butterfly-like sleeves and a garden of pink iris blossoms and butterflies on the skirt and bodice. Damon was impressed with it. He wore a nice shirt with buttons and a collar, and we photographed each other before departing.

I brought the camera along to document the evening; the website for the restaurant had promised a lovely atmosphere, and we weren't disappointed. We arrived by cab for our 7:30 p.m. reservation, leaving enough daylight to take more photos of the outside of the place, and of Damon out there too. The doors were wide open, letting warm breezes inside.

The décor of L'Absinthe was beautiful. It included mirrors on the walls, tiled floors, wood paneling, graceful hanging lamps with early 20th century-style glass shades and similar sconces on the walls, a hanging clock off to one side, hand-painted script en Français on some of the wood panels outside listing the offerings, and some old French advertisements for absinthe, complete with pictures, in frames on the walls.

Naturally, the first order of business was for Damon to try some absinthe. If he didn't do that here, it would have been silly to eat in the place. A menu was brought, one that was devoted to the beverage, and it covered both sides of the spread. Prices averaged to $14 for each serving. Damon chose one called La Fee Absinthe Parisienne; the most memorable thing about it was its green hue. The menu itself bore the heading *L'Heure Vert*.

The waitress then proceeded to set up a tall and ornate contraption on our table and explain it to us: the thing had 4 spigots, only one of which was used. The liquid inside the huge, lamp-like glass compartment above them appeared to be a bit cloudy, but it was colorless. The device looked like it had been crafted in the late 19th century.

She placed a glass below one of the spigots, laid a beautiful piece of silverware over it that resembled a leaf with some openings in it on a long stem, placed a cube of sugar over that, and turned on the spigot. She then instructed us to wait and watch until the glass was reasonably full of absinthe.

We did, and were intrigued to see it turn green as the liquid passed through the cube of sugar. No doubt a chemist could have given us a detailed explanation of what was happening. In any case, she came back and turned it off when the glass was almost full and took the silverware leaf with its sugar and the contraption away.

Damon offered me some of the absinthe, but I didn't want any. He was hoping to get some sort of hallucinogenic buzz off of it, but he just didn't. Perhaps the real deal was only in Paris. At least he got a taste of the essence of wormwood.

From there, we moved on to less bizarre foods.

First up: a couple of on-the-house cheese pastries. They were delicious.

Wedding Anniversary...and Bryn's Leg Swells

Hors d'Oeuvres: vegetarian pea soup with fresh snipped chives for me, and escargots in herbs for Damon. We shared a taste of our choices with each other.

Dinner Entrées: steak tartare with watercress and frites crisps for Damon (none of that raw meat for me!), and salmon with asparagus and fleur de sel for me (I shared a taste with him – we both liked that). We shared orders of frites, sautéed spinach, and haricots verts with sliced almonds. French bread was complimentary. We also shared a glass of Merlot wine.

Desserts: there was a cart full of choices, and we had chocolate mousse. I had more of it than Damon did; he didn't want much dessert, so we took that home with us.

Next, we took a long walk through Lenox Hill, walking straight over to 5th Avenue and on south into Midtown. We walked on the side of the street with the buildings, even though Central Park was right across from us, because it was after dark.

We crossed at the Park Plaza Hotel, and saw the horse-drawn carriages out front, and then went in to see the painting of *Eloise* by Hillary Knight. The Kay Thompson recording of the character was gone, however; a casualty of the hotel's purchase by a foreign Muslim. The sound of a woman's voice is taboo to devout Muslim men unless the woman is a relative. This imposition of Islam on a piece of American culture infuriated us, me in particular. The hotel is a National Historic Landmark, and Eloise is a part of American culture that had been bought out and suppressed by a disapproving foreigner.

We continued on past the window displays of the Bergdorf-Goodman store, where I entertained Damon by making fun of the outrageous outfits behind the glass. They were the sorts of things that only models in magazines would wear for a photo-shoot; once the artistry had been recorded, there would be no reason to wear the outfits except perhaps a costume party.

Eventually, we got home and I had to face the task of making passport photos for Damon.

He had lost his U.S. passport sometime the year before, possibly at a dentist's office in Maryland while under the influence of heavy anesthesia. Roots canals can disorient a person, but I was really annoyed; he would have to pay over a hundred dollars for a new passport so that he could leave for Hungary on time. He was due as visiting faculty at the University of Debrecen in the northeast, near the border of Romania.

It wasn't for lack of trying that he had no acceptable photos ready for the new passport; he had gone to the post office near the University of Connecticut a couple of days earlier and had a set taken. But they were awful; he was wearing a ratty black tee shirt and his face was all swollen

The Slamming Door

up from doing an experiment in the lab. He had opened a package of nettle venom powder and slipped, unleashing a cloud of the stuff in front of him. He was fine by the time he got to Manhattan, but the photos were no good.

Still, I insisted upon seeing them because I needed to see how to frame mine, and how small I would have to cut them. With great reluctance, Damon handed the package with the little squares inside over to me.

Wedding Anniversary...and Bryn's Leg Swells

Now I was sure what to do. I got a light blue sheet and hung it up on the tall bookcases, pinning it down with the statues that were up there. That would be the backdrop. Next, I got Bryn's old footstool, the black leather one from the predecessor to the Lazy Boy chair. The photo would meet the requirements of the passport regulations with no back on the seat.

I called Damon and told him to sit down and try to look pleasant. He didn't want to smile; he was sure he would look silly. But a menacing stare wouldn't work either. That sort of photo would probably just get him inspected at every airport security stop he passed through.

After a few shots, I checked the camera and decided to see how the results looked on the computer, warning Damon to keep that nice shirt on just in case I wasn't satisfied. Fortunately, I was satisfied, and printed the best one up twice, trimmed the prints down to size, and put them in the little cardboard photo holder. There; the passport people would be none the wiser, and Damon was satisfied with the results.

What a hassle. It seemed a lot easier to just not lose one's passport. Mine was safe in Connecticut, and I knew precisely which drawer it was in next to my desk. My mother wouldn't touch a thing; whenever I went back there, my work and things would still be in place.

The day after our anniversary was a hectic one for Damon, and Bryn didn't come home until that night. Albert brought him back. Damon spent the entire morning at the passport office on Hudson Street paying top dollar to replace his lost passport, using the photos I had prepared. Then he met with the ophthalmologists at the New York Eye & Ear Infirmary in the afternoon.

Bryn came home with his right leg swollen up, having been told that the doctors near Cassie couldn't help, and that the ones at Sloan-Kettering couldn't do much of anything about it either. The problem was that the bone cancer had grown a spur that was pressing on a vein or artery, and as if that wasn't enough, the cancer had fractured his pelvis in that spot, or eaten through it. Either way, it was split in that spot, which was the ground zero of his bone cancer.

I asked about surgery; couldn't they file the offending bit down, remove it so that he could be more comfortable? "They don't do that," Bryn said.

I had no further comment after that. At that point, I was infuriated all over again with the current medical technology. It seemed utterly lame and useless. It couldn't make a person comfortable, protect their dignity, refrain from destroying the patient's appearance, or enable a person to move about independently. Little by little, it would make life so completely not worth living that the person – in this case the saint and glue of our family – would hate to be alive.

The Slamming Door

So that was it; I could see that Bryn would be immobilized in a couple more weeks.

He had also been given an appointment for a physical therapy session – in August.

What was he supposed to do in the meantime?!

I looked at his feet. One foot was ballooning a bit; the other was the same size as ever. He was wearing his usual white socks and the dark blue Lands End slippers with the brown nubuck leather sides and soles that I had found for him online. He had asked Albert to get the scissors and cut a slit in the one for his right foot, so he had a 2-inch long v-shape there.

That week, he asked me to get him another pair of those. He intended to give up wearing shoes and just wear the slippers, even when he went out. The soles were a bit tougher than the rest; unless it rained, this seemed like a clever plan. I found the slippers online again, but in dark green only. Bryn said okay and I ordered them. A couple of days later, he had me cut the right one for him.

I didn't put away his shoes though; I just didn't want to think about or face that.

Meanwhile, Damon was due to depart for Hungary the next day, and Bryn was bound and determined to attend a Board of Trustees meeting that afternoon at the Henry George School. It was arranged that Damon would get a cab and drop Bryn off at the school, then continue on to JKF Airport. As before, I was not supposed to be at that school until the secret meeting was over.

Damon called me to say good-bye from the airport – I always like that sort of attention if I can get it – and I kept my cell phone so that Bryn could tell me when to come and get him.

It was actually fun to pick him up, despite that fact that I was feeling so glum about his swollen leg. He came out of there in a triumphant mood, delighted with how it had gone, smiling happily. He had gotten up to speak, and gone on at length about his issues without interruption.

Bryn had gotten up to talk about something that had bothered him: a lack of transparency on the board, combined with an abuse of power. There was an education committee – a separate group – that was in charge of deciding who would teach what and how they would be allowed to do it. The head of the board of trustees had attempted to control such things on his own, using his authority as justification for this. Bryn had vehemently and politely criticized this abuse of power without naming names, and then sat down.

The problem with his victory, though we had shaken each other's hands and grinned from ear to ear over it in the cab as he told me about this, was that it wouldn't last beyond his death, which we expected

Wedding Anniversary...and Bryn's Leg Swells

sometime within the next couple of months. Then all hell would likely break loose. But at least Bryn had lived and fought well while he had the chance.

Just a few days after Damon left, I received my forwarded mail from Connecticut, sent on by my father. In it was a most unwelcome summons for jury duty. To get there, I would have needed a ride from someone else, a thing that I would not want to accept. Either I get somewhere on my own, or I don't go.

Add to that the fact that I was currently out of state and could not return just for that and I had a problem. Bryn came first; I had promised to stick around until he didn't want me to stay any more. He had not changed his mind as yet, had not given the slightest indication that he wished me to depart, and so I intended to remain for the foreseeable future.

Dionne had gone off on a trip to Europe with The Hornsby for weeks on end; she thought I would be taking care of her father all this time. Berta couldn't do it and he didn't want her to. In fact, he really didn't want to leave his apartment. I had to stay, and I wanted to.

I looked at the summons carefully; according to its terms, they could call me at any time until October of 2009. Whether or not they would actually want someone with a law degree once they met me during voir dire was a completely separate consideration, and one that I intended to preempt if at all possible.

It wasn't that I aimed to interfere with the judicial process; it was that I had no idea when Bryn would cease to need me around. I had no crystal ball, my psychic powers were negligible, and I wasn't willing to hazard a guess as to how long he would live.

With that, I went onto the Internet and hunted until I found a name and phone number of the court clerk in Hartford. They don't put that information where anyone can easily find it. You have to be persistent. But I was and I found it, and set up a letter to her, complete with her name, the court's address, and her work phone number. Then I called her and explained the problem. I added that I could provide contact information for Bryn and his osteo-oncologist if she needed my story corroborated.

She was actually very nice and helpful. She did ask how long I thought I would be where I was, how long Bryn might need me, and I said that I couldn't possibly guess how long he would live, and that I didn't want to jinx him by trying. That did it; she stopped asking and gave up on the whole idea. She told me to write her a letter and send it by e-mail explaining the whole thing all over again, and that I would

The Slamming Door

automatically qualify for something called an extreme hardship. She would send a letter back excusing me from jury duty through October, thus cancelling out any chance that I would be called at all.

I sent it off right away, and sure enough, soon got a reply formally excusing me from appearing; problem solved. I had told Bryn what I was doing, and he had agreed to, if necessary, let the court clerk know his name and his doctor's name and whatever else she wanted, but it didn't come to that. I was off the hook. When the reply came, I told Berta, and she just nodded and looked pleased about it. I filed copies of that correspondence away for safekeeping.

Meanwhile, I found a book for Bryn at The Biography Bookshop in Greenwich Village. It was a new one of John Updike poems, and it was an unplanned purchase, but when I showed it to Bryn, he was thrilled. He had wanted that one and had known that it was coming out. That was gratifying.

At least he had something he looked forward to reading now that he was unable to move about easily. With his leg all swollen, and a huge blister forming on the sole of his foot, which was also swollen on the instep and the sole and the top, he was now chair-ridden. Sleeping in his bed wasn't comfortable anymore, so I never thought of him as bed-ridden.

I had gotten him some special socks at the pharmacy, black ones, but they didn't help.

Now he surprised me with another request: he needed me to rub his legs with a special lotion, the brand of which he told me, and then to wrap his leg in paper towels and then with an ace bandage. When the bandage got dirty, I had to wash it out. I went out to the New London Pharmacy, bought all the supplies, and did the deed.

The visiting nurse, Ellen, had specified all of this. She was the only visiting nurse after the spring, assigned to take care of Bryn and several other patients in the area. We had her cell phone number, but I was only to call her in a dire emergency, which didn't come up.

Sitting bent over for several minutes to massage his swollen leg in what seemed like a futile attempt to coax the fluids where they belonged and thus relieve the ever-increasing edema was tiring. I didn't tell him so; I just kept it up until he was satisfied.

Working on Bryn's feet was part of this task, so the first thing I did was commandeer his blue bucket for the task. He wasn't up to going to the tub just for this, although he had started using the bench that we had gotten the previous fall whenever he took a bath. That was another issue; soon he would need someone to help him in the bathtub, and I was worried. I couldn't handle that. It would be embarrassing for us both – plus, I doubted I was strong enough.

Wedding Anniversary...and Bryn's Leg Swells

I didn't know it yet, but he had requested a male home health aide for that.

But for now, it was time to work on Bryn's feet. I washed them off, and found that they were all crusty, with a layer of gritty, dead skin. Damn cancer, I thought to myself. This had to be one of its effects. Cassie had told him a week or so ago to scrub at his feet with the washcloth when he was in the tub, and he said he had done so, but clearly it wasn't doing the trick.

I was revolted by this, but said nothing again. There was nothing to say; Bryn had apologized for the state of his feet, and told me what he had tried. Now he couldn't even reach them. I was plotting a solution though; something along the lines of a home spa treatment.

The next afternoon that I could go out, I went down 8th Avenue, almost to Hudson Street, and into a fancy shop called Soapology that I had browsed in before without buying anything more exciting than an interesting bar of soap. The rest of the wares just seemed overpriced.

Now I meant to spend serious money on a luxury item for Bryn's benefit.

Soapology offered five different scents of lovely oiled bath salts, sold in round jars.

I had tried several of them out before, just for fun.

Fun time was over; I was going to clean up Bryn's feet with this stuff.

I bought, for the sum of thirty-five dollars plus tax, a jar of lavender-vanilla bath salts, turning down the sales woman's attempt to sell me a fancy teaspoon along with it. This was going on Bryn's tab, and he had plenty of teaspoons at home. I was polite to the girl; I didn't laugh. But the idea of buying an extra spoon for this almost made me laugh.

It was probably the glum reason behind the purchase that prevented that laugh. The women tried again to sell me more luxury items, thinking that this stuff was for me, until I told them why I was buying it. Suddenly they sobered up; most of their customers were just playing.

When I got home with it, I explained what I was up to, showing Bryn the salts.

Okay, he would go along with that, he said. He even enjoyed it.

I dunked his feet in the bucket, spooned out some salts with a spoon from the kitchen – he laughed when I mentioned the attempt to sell me another one – and scrubbed both of his feet thoroughly. It worked! His feet were as smooth as could be. Feeling quite pleased with myself, I washed my nail-grooming implements and trimmed his toenails; perfect.

The rest was the usual grind of massaging, then paper towels, then the ace bandage.

I told Bryn that I hoped that this wouldn't bother Cassie.

He said that she wasn't jealous.

"That's not what I meant; I meant that I wondered what she thinks of this idea."

"Don't worry; she's not a girlie girl; she'll just be pleased that you fixed this."

Okay – cool.

Next, I told him I was a bit worried about what his daughters might say about the lovely bath salts, because Bryn wanted me to enjoy them too; my feet were still constantly covered with city dirt, and now that it was warmer, it was worse because I wore sandals when I was out.

"You're contributing to my care with this," he said, "so don't worry about it."

After that, I did my own pedicure; Bryn always found the process amusing for some reason, and admired the results. Berta arrived that evening in sandals, a bit later than usual, and without explaining it. I didn't ask; the answer was on her toenails. She couldn't bend over to work on them, and had therefore gotten a beautiful French-style pedicure. I could think of better uses for money, mostly because I could touch my own toes. But the three of us had neat feet.

I didn't know it, but this would only last a couple of weeks before Nurse Ellen would fire me from this duty for my own good. It wasn't that I had done anything incorrectly; the problem was that Bryn had started to have weeping spots on his swollen leg that she said were infectious.

She and the home health aide took over, wearing gloves.

But before I walked away from this particular duty, I insisted upon showing Ellen the bath salts treatment. Bryn patiently let me go through the whole process.

When I stood up and backed away, Ellen said that it was more like a pedicure than what she had in mind, but that it was great – she knew about the dead skin that it was targeting – and that she would remember it for her other patients. Not bad for a caregiver's initiative.

Still, I didn't want to make a career of this. This was a special gift to Bryn, one that I reserved for family members. I would take care of Bryn, my grandmothers, and whoever else needed me in the future, but no strangers. Ellen understood that.

Chapter 48

Moonwalking with a Cane

Michael Jackson's death on June 25th, 2009 was such ubiquitous news that it made the front page of *The New York Times*.

The death of a pop star was not the sort of news item that Bryn or Albert would normally pay much attention to other than passing notice and comment, but it was written up in each of the periodicals that they read together every afternoon.

Albert had gotten into the habit of coming over with *The New York Post*, which he and Bryn derisively labeled yellow journalism but then proceeded to read for entertainment. They each read *The New York Times*, often together in Bryn's room, while I read the same publication online out in the living room. It was our afternoon routine, complete with milkshakes, tea, and whatever else. We passed many fun afternoons this way, successfully ignoring the stress of impending death. Bryn usually kept the news channels on in the afternoons as well.

That afternoon, all was calm and quiet until I heard Albert say, "They're doing the Moonwalk in Paris," as he sat in Bryn's room holding the paper out in front of him. I thought nothing of it and kept doing whatever I was doing on the computer.

A moment later, Bryn called out to me, "Clarisse – what's the Moonwalk?"

I looked up from the computer, staring at nothing in particular, and suddenly feeling a peculiar sense of elation. It was the sort of elation that one gets when asked to explain a part of one's own repertoire of fun experiences from long ago.

I got up and went into Bryn's room, where I found both Otterman boys staring up at me expectantly. So they did really want to know. I chose a spot in front of Bryn's chair and turned sideways so that they could each see this properly.

"Okay, watch my feet," I told them, and glided backwards across the floor, Moonwalking. Pushing each foot backwards one at a time and lifting the heel upwards as the next foot slid past it, I moved far enough to give them the general idea.

They leaned over and watched intently. When I was done, I said, "If you were an 80s teenager, you learned this."

They loved it. To my surprise and delight, they both got up and started doing the Moonwalk, Albert in his heavy white sneakers and Bryn in his slippers with his cane. They got it right, too.

A couple of minutes later, the phone rang; it was Alissa, and I said, "Your father and uncle are doing the Moonwalk!" Laughter on the other

The Slamming Door

end of the line; the same call and the same line was repeated moments later when Berta called, eliciting the same response. Cool.

Chapter 49

July Birthdays...But the Party's Over

Both Otterman girls had birthdays in July.

Berta said that she had always enjoyed the fact that for one week in July each year, she and Alissa were the same age. As for me, I looked forward to some fun for each of them.

Alissa's birthday was on Friday, July 3rd; Berta's was on Saturday, the 11th. For a week, they were both 39 years old, until Berta turned 40. We had a lovely party for each of them, and each one suited the party girl's personality to a tee.

Berta arranged her own party, announcing via e-mail that it would be in the West Village at a place called Cowgirls USA, and requesting that I prepare calligraphy place cards for the people on the attached list all in one note.

Wow. And whoa; her father was dying and she was planning her own party.

Of course I would make the place cards; it was easy and would provide a nice distraction. I wasn't about to comment about the fact that she was celebrating herself with great enthusiasm or that it looked a bit...unseemly. Included in her summary request was the desire that I find and acquire some *Wonder Woman* stickers for the cards. Where was I going to get those?!

When she came over later, I asked her about cards for Alissa.

She was sitting at the computer, checking her Facebook profile at the time. Without turning around from the screen, she simply said, "No, it's just the family."

That didn't sit right with me at all, but I said nothing. I simply made up my mind that Alissa was getting place cards from me also. That was when I began to feel disgusted by Berta; Berta would take care of Berta, but quiet, retiring Alissa would need some outside help.

I went out that weekend – still with over a week to go before Alissa's party – to get the cards and stickers. No *Wonder Woman* stickers were available. After a couple of false starts, I suddenly thought of going into a comic book store to ask. Manhattan had lots of comic book stores where fans can find anything and everything. I had spent many a fun hour at a time looking for *X-Men* comics in one on 23rd Street, so I tried that place.

The owner was very helpful; he told me that he was the owner, that he did the ordering for the store, and that he had not seen any of those for several years. This gray-haired man certainly looked like he had many hours logged and lots of knowledge in this business. I thanked him

The Slamming Door

and decided that Berta would have to make do with some other decorative effect on her place cards. Her father was dying, and this wasn't crucial – just fun.

A few streets south of there, I found a stationary and craft store, complete with felt-tip art pens, origami supplies, and a whole section of stickers. I found a 24-pack of ivory place cards, some red-and-blue sparkly star stickers, and some pansy stickers. I bought them and went home.

When I got back, both Berta and Alissa were on the sofa in the living room. Right away, I proudly showed off my finds to them. Berta seemed satisfied with what I had found, and kept her mouth shut when I said I was going to make a set of place cards for Alissa's party.

Alissa showed a rare impish streak, asking me, "Are you saying that I am a pansy?"

At first I was horrified; I had only meant to make the cards pretty, and equal to Berta's. But then Alissa laughed and said that she liked and appreciated what I was planning, and that was that. I was the one who engineered her party, and she knew it.

It had become clear to me that Alissa was much too shy, quiet, and self-effacing to speak up for anything that she might want, so I had decided to make it happen for her.

She loved raw foods and was a vegan, so I looked for a restaurant that met both conditions. I found one via the Internet, not far from Union Square, called Pure Food and Wine. It had a full-course menu online, complete with photos of the inside and outside of the place, plus the owner, a stick-thin blond woman with small tattoos of ducks on her biceps, and of food.

This was about 2 weeks ahead of time, so I was planning ahead as usual. As I perused the menu, it occurred to me that this was food porn in its most mesmerizing form. Soon I was mentally drooling over the images on the screen.

After a couple of minutes, I was convinced that this was the right place. Berta thought that it had closed, but I took a chance and called the place. Someone answered, and assured me that they were still very much in business. He made a reservation for me, taking down Albert's name and number. I explained what I was up to; that I would call Albert next and check to make sure that it was all okay.

Sure enough, when I got a hold of Albert, he wanted to throw the party for Alissa. In fact, he told me, she had been trying to get the family to go to that particular restaurant with her for a long time. This was the perfect opportunity to do it.

I think that Albert was particularly keen to do this because the previous year, when he had taken June on that last hurrah of a trip to

July Birthdays...But the Party's Over

France (before she lost too much more of her memory), they had left Alissa at home alone for her birthday.

But Alissa had had to cope with a medical emergency for Pearlie the Sheltie dog, who developed an infection at the base of her tail. The poor animal nearly gnawed the appendage off in dire distress, but Alissa noticed in time and ended up awake all night at the emergency veterinary clinic nearby. Happy Birthday, to the tune of a thousand dollars, no sleep, and a lampshade around the dog's neck.

This year was going to be much better.

Actually, it was a great success.

With the arrangements made and approved (Albert did call the restaurant right away to approve and confirm the reservation), I printed the menu for Bryn. I made sure to include lots of color photos, so that he would see as much of the fabulous presentation as I had just seen.

He sat in his chair looking it all over carefully, trying to decide what he might order. It was fun to think about it with him.

Then he looked up with a grin. "So we're all going to have to eat raw foods?" he said.

I just laughed. "You're not looking at it as any great hardship, eating delectable works of art made of healthy ingredients!"

He threw back his head and gave his signature uproarious but low-volume laugh.

At first, it was to be Alissa, Albert, June, me, Bryn, Berta, and Matt.

Then the aunts got wind of the plans and wanted in on the fun.

I called Albert and told him. He groaned, worried about the cost, but then decided that cost be damned, the only right course of action was to tell them to come. They would be paying for their own food anyway. In the end, he paid for me, for his daughter, his wife, and himself, plus the aunts' drinks because he felt bad when he saw their faces as the bill arrived.

The place was expensive, but Alissa deserved it. It was worth the money. She was just so perfectly behaved at all times that I wondered how she would ever get what she wanted in life, or truly enjoy herself.

But Bryn didn't attend.

His swollen leg had made walking a painful production, and getting in and out of cabs even more of a hassle, that he gave up on the idea two evenings before the fact.

When he announced that he wasn't going, I said quietly, "Oh shit, I can't go."

"Oh yes you can!" he responded without missing a beat, sounding determined.

I thought about that for a moment. "Maybe we could ask Elah to sit with you for the evening," I said. "If you can't go out for fun, none of us

The Slamming Door

feels good about you staying home alone." I kept my expression neutral; the party was now over for him, but I wouldn't say it.

Bryn looked at me for an instant, but then agreed to the idea.

I e-mailed Elah and explained the problem, realizing that part of the reason why Bryn was making sure I went to this party was that I had engineered it. Despite the fact that I have called him this before, it doesn't seem like overkill to saw that he was the family saint yet again.

It was about this time that he called the hospice people and started making arrangements to go away to a facility in the Bronx, and for a home health care aide come over to help him in the afternoons. But he didn't tell us about it until after he had arranged it.

That same evening, Berta said to him, "You're off the hook for my birthday, Dad." By that, she meant that she didn't expect him to attend the party. It sounded so odd and nonchalant, like she was doing him a great favor, but we all knew he hated missing the fun. It seemed a bit odd that she was going ahead with the celebration without him, but the plans marched on.

When Damon looked at the photos of me at Alissa's party afterward, he commented about the one of me sitting next to her, smiling for the camera. "You look like you were under stress in that one," he commented. My eyes were a bit wider than normal; they weren't part of the smile.

Well, I *was* under stress; Bryn was getting worse to the point that the party was over for him. He couldn't go to any more of them. He could only leave the house to go to the doctor, and I had to go down the street to hail a cab for him every time. I would go to 8th Avenue and get one, then ride it up to the front door. Albert would then get in with him and they would ride off together. Bryn was now going to just about all doctors' appointments with his brother.

Once, I forget exactly when, I had a particularly difficult time hailing a cab for Bryn. His had gotten to the point where he could no longer get into one of the high-riding cabs that resembled jeeps, and needed a car-cab. It was a gray afternoon, and a lightning storm was starting. I saw several strikes that looked close by as I stood on 8th Avenue, looking for one.

Like some travesty of authoritarian obedience to Murphy's Law, each and every cab that came by was a jeep-cab. Not one car appeared, yet all these jeeps were available. I had to wave them away, and the drivers looked miffed and confused. I began to get very upset, and sharply gestured at them to just move on. Where were the damned car-cabs?! Full, whenever I saw one. Meanwhile, the lightning kept striking in the near distance.

July Birthdays...But the Party's Over

Hit me, I began to think. By the time I succeeded in getting a car-cab, I was in tears. I was sure that Bryn would be mad at me, wondering where the hell I was with his car-cab, why it was taking so long, and I envied him his impending exit. I was going to hate not having him around to talk to. I felt that going back to Connecticut, to my parents, where Damon was unwelcome, would be unbearable, and I convinced myself that I had nowhere to go after this.

If I couldn't stay with Bryn, I was in trouble, I believed. I got out of the cab and presented it to Bryn and Albert, crying, and said that it had been hard to get a car-cab and that I wished the lightning had gotten me. Then I went inside and upstairs to clean my face and try to calm down. They didn't scold me or criticize me for it. Bryn just couldn't get into the other kind of cab anymore, and I couldn't magically conjure one on cue.

Add to all of this the fact that during Alissa's birthday party Damon was in a hospital in Hungary with an infection in his foot, and I had plenty of reasons to be stressed out. I couldn't even talk to him on Skype for a week. He was just suddenly not there, and then I received an e-mail message from Janos, the Hungarian graduate student whom I had settled into a year-long internship at the UConn Health Center five years earlier. He had his Ph.D. now, and was home.

A week or so then passed in which I fell into a habit of staying home until Albert or someone else came over to sit with Bryn. I just didn't feel that it was safe for Bryn to stay home alone anymore. This meant that I was constantly watching for a chance when someone else was going to stay for a while before I would go out to get basic supplies. When it came, I would gather my list and shopping bags and go. There were no more wanderings around the neighborhood unless someone had convinced me that they would stay for a few hours.

When I wasn't out, I was almost constantly at the computer. I noticed that this meant that whenever Hilda or someone else wanted to talk to Bryn in secret, his door would be shut. I hadn't noticed that before, but it came as no surprise. I was there, so I would hear everything if they didn't shut the door. I might walk in and check Bryn's drinks and see what he needed if the door were open. But I had to stay home at that point.

Hilda didn't understand this. I didn't think about it at the time; I was just doing my duty and upset, unaware of much else. She would give me cold looks and never smile at me, but I just didn't get it. I may have wondered about it, but I was just too preoccupied with Bryn's declining condition to give her much thought.

I couldn't go out if someone dropped by just to chat for a few minutes and then leave. If people couldn't understand that, that was just tough. I wasn't going out every time someone came in, just to preclude

The Slamming Door

any possibility of hearing whatever was said, nor was I going to drop whatever I was doing on the computer or at that desk and then wait for people to leave and come back. Constant interruptions like that would keep me from getting anything finished.

Add to that the fact that I liked to work steadily and not go out much unless I have something specific to do and that meant that I was just constantly there. Eventually, when it was all over, I found out that this was greatly resented by her. Interesting, but I just don't care.

I can't be responsible for everyone's satisfaction; no caregiver can. I wasn't a hired servant; I was a relative. If they wanted it done differently, they could have paid someone and thus further depleted Bryn's or their own bank accounts to pay for it. But they chose not to do so, and that's that.

No doubt, my Asperger's Syndrome played a role in my inability to notice or even understand how other people perceived my constant presence in the apartment. All I can say is that is as good as it would get with me, and that for my efforts, I make no apologies. I did the best I could with a stressful and upsetting set circumstances, so anyone with complaints has a hell of nerve to make them.

Amid all this, the party plans continued.

I really should describe the food at Pure Food and Wine, and how chic the place was. This story doesn't have to be all grimness and misery.

July Birthdays...But the Party's Over

Pure Food and Wine was on Irving Place, just south of Gramercy Park. Its sign on the wall outside was all in lowercase, gold metal letters, with ivy cascading over it. The décor was modern, with straight lines everywhere. The entrance from the street dipped down a few steps, with the door on the left, to a dark interior with a fabulous bouquet just inside. I took a photograph of Alissa by it as she arrived with her parents, which was a few minutes after I met Berta and Matt. We were promptly led past the indoor dining room and out back, to the patio.

The patio seating was up a few steps, which were on the right, with the dining area stretching to the left. A bar with black umbrellas over it was straight ahead of the steps, but we didn't go over there. Our table was against the raised garden along the back of the building, with a long bench built in against that and chairs along the other side. The bench cushion was purple, and the chairs were black metal frames with cherry-red cushions.

Our table at Pure Food and Wine.

Alissa was given the seat of honor in the center of that bench, and I slid in on her left. There were soon 10 of us; the aunts showed up just after Matt's niece and her boyfriend Randall, a Jamaican scientist with long dreadlocks whom she had met at the Rockefeller Institute. Sorcha was wearing a rather shockingly low-cut dress that none of us commented upon at the time, but we all noticed and remarked about it after the fact. She sat directly across from me, with Matt and her boyfriend on the end. The aunts were next to Sorcha, with Berta on their

The Slamming Door

other side across from Albert, and June was next to Alissa. I took out the pretty place cards I had made and passed them out, and everyone admired theirs. The gifts sat by Albert in a pretty stack, wrapped in floral paper.

The table was set for 10 people with a large square, dark napkin in the center of each place and the flatware around it. Menus were brought, and I noticed a little duck shape flanking the design at the bottom center. When we met the restaurant's owner, I realized that it was the same shape that was tattooed onto her biceps. Her name was Jarma, and she was a thin, beautiful blond woman who signed a copy of her recipe book for Alissa, a last-minute gift from Berta.

Rather than go through all of the wonderful things listed in the menu, I will just describe some of what we had. That alone will be detailed enough as it is. Each dish was made of raw food that had been cut into shapes that either aimed at making it taste more delicious or fitting into the overall shape of the concoction or, if at all possible, both. Every plate was full of vibrant, vitamin-rich color, and the profusion of it was tempting and enticing…and delectable.

Each of us ordered a drink, a first course, a second course, and a dessert, and some of us had tea with dessert. The dishes were all huge white ones, either round, square or rectangular, with the items small focal points in the centers.

First courses: fettuccine of zucchini and chopped tomatoes (me); Caesar salad with avocado (Matt); salad with raspberries, strawberries, and herbed cheese (Aunt Johanna Orlov); a salad made up of a rainbow of all colors in the spectrum (Alissa).

July Birthdays...But the Party's Over

Second courses: coconut Thai sauce over curried vegetables (Alissa); hempseed burger with cauliflower purée (Matt and Albert); vegetables and basil cream pesto (Aunt Summer); zucchini and Roma tomato lasagna (June); zucchini blossoms with garlic chive cheese over thick red and orange slices of heirloom tomatoes and strawberries in balsamic sauce with watercress (me).

The Slamming Door

July Birthdays...But the Party's Over

Drinks: coconut water (Alissa); hard apple cider (me and Matt – he ordered seconds and tried to get me to keep drinking – no thanks!); white wine Sangria (Sorcha); mint Mojita (Berta).

Dessert and tea: passion fruit chocolate tart with açai berries, raspberries, and chocolate sorbet (me); almond milk with orange jasmine tea (me); peach cobbler with a small scoop of ice cream over it and rings of hardened nut-sugar like a halo over that (Aunt Summer and Matt); a long rectangular plate of 3 chocolate-covered ice creams: chocolate, cardamom, and coconut (Sorcha); a tray of raspberry, mango and lime fruit sorbets (June). Each dessert, with the exception of the last two, was served in a huge round plate with a small round well in the center.

Each plate was a work of art; for those prices, it ought to have been. Presentation was a big part of the business.

We gave Alissa her presents during dessert. I had given her a Vera Bradley bag just like mine, a mini-hipster in a pretty botanical pattern. Berta immediately chimed in that it was for parties, and that she should leave her huge back-pack at home for those. From Bryn, she got the black cotton blouse with a pretty round shape and slightly loose collar, something I had found on sale at a Banana Republic store. There were more gifts, but I don't remember them all.

At one point during the unwrappings, June asked Alissa what was happening, and she just smiled and said, "I'm having a birthday Momma." We tried not to get depressed, following Alissa's lead and keeping it all cheerful and upbeat. With sad stuff like that going on, it

The Slamming Door

just seemed all the more important to give her a great party and have a fun time.

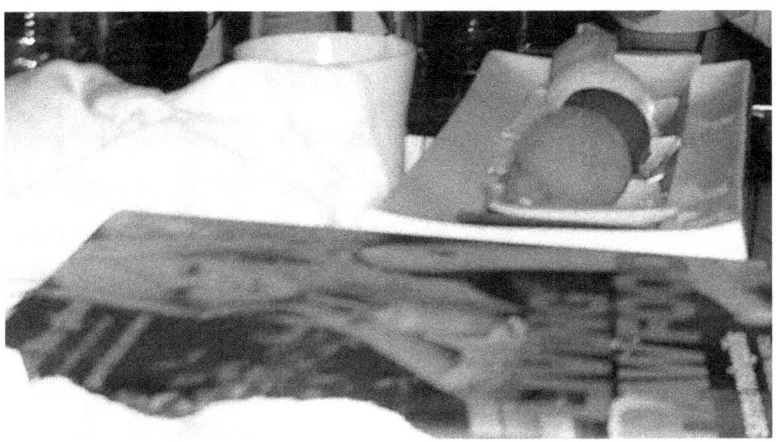

July Birthdays...But the Party's Over

When the party was over, we all dispersed, with Alissa and her parents heading back to TriBeCa and the aunts heading off in a cab to their apartment complex. I wandered out with Berta, Matt, Sorcha and her boyfriend, north to the next block, where they proceeded, despite all of the alcohol just consumed in the restaurant, to sit down in a beautiful bar with wood paneling, stools, and old-style painted offerings on the mirrors.

They attempted to persuade me to join them, and memories of college situations in which I found myself observing groups of people having a wonderful time while feeling utterly puzzled by the excitement immediately resurfaced. I was having a thoroughly Asperger's experience. I didn't stay, of course, and after saying good-bye heading outside and west, towards home.

The phone rang in my pocket as I walked, and I answered it; it was Bryn saying that he hoped I was coming home soon because Elah needed to leave. I knew she had to get back for the next online postings. I told him I was hailing a cab now, and that I had left the others in a bar and was glad to get away and come back to him. I rang off, amazed at Bryn's flawless sense of timing. He seemed to have an almost psychic ability to know when everything that mattered in a birthday celebration had been done, but of course that was just experience with such things.

The next day was July 4th, and he went out with Albert to have another blood transfusion. I was surprised that Albert chose to go with him for that one, but glad because I had over 100 envelopes to address for a bride. They were all on a strange texture of paper by Kate Spade; the nib of my pen kept digging into it rather than moving smoothing across it, slowing me down.

I found myself home alone suddenly with the addresses all checked and spaced on a Word file in front of me, my pen and ink and the

The Slamming Door

envelopes laid out, and the possibility that someone might show up abruptly and make it impossible to work. Would I have to do it all night instead? Would I finish by Monday, as the client wanted?

Perfect; a nasty panic attack was settling in. This sucked. It seized hold of me after I had done only a few envelopes. It was such slow going that I was sure that with all of the visitors coming in and out, I would write whatever I heard them saying in lovely script all over the green envelopes, wasting them. How would I finish on time without infuriating the client?!

When I work on something, I usually go straight out for hours, without much pausing other than to use the bathroom. Writing is different; I can have a drink nearby, but calligraphy is unforgiving that way, and I wouldn't risk the art materials.

I had an idea: call Berta and tell her what I was doing, say that her father wasn't home and would be out for hours, and ask her to please let me alone to work. No answer. I began to cry, convinced that she would appear at any moment and turn on every electronic device in earshot. No wonder I didn't do much creative work that year. I wasn't in control of my own space, and I need that in order to get anything done.

I tried calling Matt to see if he was out walking with her, but he wasn't; he was working and told me that it was not reasonable of me to not want anyone to come over. Thanks so much; I replied that I simply did care whether I was being reasonable or not as long as I got the work done. Then we rang off; there was no point in debating the matter further. I had explained that I was having a nasty panic attack, and knew that he wouldn't harangue me about it later. He was a nice guy and we all liked him.

Sure enough, Berta arrived a bit later and laid herself out on the sofa. It was hot and humid out and she had been walking around in Greenwich Village. She was wearing long jeans and a pale green tee shirt despite the heat. She looked like a beached, green-and-blue whale, and she said, "It's my apartment; I'll come over any time I want," not looking at me but staring up at the ceiling. I felt hopelessly trapped. People thought that I ought to be able to make money while I was in Manhattan, but I just couldn't function under certain circumstances.

She then accused me of never trying to control my Asperger's, but I didn't bother saying that she made no effort to control her attention deficit disorder even though it was true. Control Asperger's....how? Take pills for anxiety and depression again? Get fat like her? No way. I would just make do with whatever Bryn had taught me about emotional intelligence, such as I could with that. I knew I wouldn't always be able to win over the anxiety. We moved on.

July Birthdays...But the Party's Over

Berta got curious about the calligraphy, wondering why it was making me so nervous, so I showed her the texture of the paper and explained what was happening with the nib of the pen. Then she got it. She loved their shade of light green, so the envelopes looked pretty to her, and she admired my work. "That's beautiful," she said.

Eventually, Bryn came home and I helped him settle into his Lazy Boy chair, and told him, still a bit anxious and teary, that I was having trouble with my calligraphy job, and doubted I could go fast enough to finish on time.

"It's the 4th of July," he said. "I don't see why you shouldn't enjoy it just like everyone else," he added. He wanted me to relax and do something else, something fun. He doubted that the job was as urgent as I imagined, too.

Berta wanted to go out to see a movie with me because of the holiday, and we settled on seeing *The Proposal*. Albert was going to stay with Bryn while we did that, so there was no reason not to go. The Otterman brothers insisted, in fact, and said that we could all get take-out together first. It turned into a fun evening, which I hadn't expected. I just gave up on work that afternoon and evening; I wasn't going to finish that night. But when everyone was gone, I went back at it.

While we ate, Berta told us that the restaurant where she was to have her birthday party had called her during the day to confirm some details about it, and that they had baked all of the cupcakes, thinking that the party was that night. It wasn't. "I hope they enjoy eating those red velvet cupcakes," she said. That was an inconvenient mistake; oh well...

The next day, the bride e-mailed that something had come up and could I have the envelopes for Tuesday. Insert image of head smacking desk in exasperation here. Once I knew that I had more time, I remembered that I still had to mail my grandmother's gifts for her 95th birthday...no rest for the birthday preparer that week; but she liked her chocolates and card.

I worked on the job with a sense of urgency on Sunday regardless of the extension, pausing once to get a great photo of Nikita doing something hilarious. I had been stalking that photo for a couple of weeks, and suddenly I was able to tiptoe over the camera, take it out of its case, turn it on, and shoot the photo. Triumphantly, I saved it and e-mailed to everyone I could think of with the subject line: "Caught in the act!" I received several amused replies.

That cat was still providing great amusement and entertainment.

She had set herself up to her satisfaction, complete with a steady routine of sleeping on Bryn's bed, the footrest of his Lazy Boy chair, and the floor, plus sauntering into the kitchen twice a day to be fed canned food by me.

Bryn had won a beer mug at a raffle a few years earlier. It was made of glass, a huge, clear version of a German or Bavarian stein mug. I had long since adopted it as my water glass.

Nikita Cat would sneak into my room every afternoon, put her little white paws up on the small table by the bed where I kept the glass filled with ice water, and like the stealthy cat burglar that she was, take a nice, long drink of it. I suppose it was the lure of the forbidden, and of a successful theft. Cats are great food and drink thieves, and they act like they are entitled to whatever they steal, which is part of what makes them so much fun.

Late in May, on a very quiet, calm, sunny afternoon, I got the photograph that I was after.

Bryn walked by as I did so, stopped, and stood in the doorway, resting on his cane, watching her drink. "Let her do it," he said, with a sober expression on his face.

This calm acceptance of her antics completed the scene.

The next day, I completed the calligraphy job that had stressed me out so much over the weekend. I e-mailed the bride and she arranged for her mother to pick up the envelopes; we would meet on 8th Avenue at Starbucks.

The deed was done quickly the next afternoon, and the mother of the bride even paid me extra. I thanked her, pocketed the cash, and left, somehow knowing that I wouldn't get another contract while I was in New York. They were just so random and hard to get, and my time there seemed to be drawing to an end.

My attention returned to the remaining birthday preparations. We might as well enjoy them; they were going to happen no matter how glum life was.

What gift did I have for her, Bryn asked me? Clearly, he intended to just shop without any further input from his daughter if he could come up with a likely idea. He had forgotten what I told him I had for her, and it wouldn't have helped him brainstorm anyway.

I showed it to him again – it was that *Wonder Woman* doll from Mattel that I had ordered online. The reason I had gotten it for her was that one night as we were hanging out and watching crime shows, she had pried open the lower drawer on the antique bureau that I never touched. I don't know how she got it open; I never could, and it wasn't worth the effort.

Inside were all sorts of relics of her childhood, saved. The drawer was packed tightly with them. Among them were several *Wonder Woman* dolls, all of which had been thoroughly played with. Berta had loved *Wonder Woman* as a kid, and so had I. I told her that I too had had a *Wonder Woman* doll, but just one.

She told me that she wished that she had taken better care her *Wonder Woman* dolls, so that she would have at least one that was in great condition now. With that, I had my gift idea, but of course I kept quiet about it. Berta had then packed the dolls back into the drawer and pushed it shut, not to be seen open again. That had been a few months earlier, but I have a great memory, and so I had my idea.

The Slamming Door

When Bryn saw it in the box (not yet wrapped), he said, "I hate stuff like that."

Oh well. I liked to collect dolls, but not too often. I had saved on shipping costs by getting myself a Wicked Witch of the West doll that looked just like Margaret Hamilton, the actress who had played the character, at the same time that I got the *Wonder Woman* doll. When I went to Kuwait, I had bought a Mattel doll called Fulla; she was dressed like a Kuwaiti woman, complete with black hair and Arab skin tones. She made a great exhibit to show whenever I talk about my experience there; nothing works so well as a prop. Bryn could appreciate that, but he still needed an idea.

I thought about it.

Berta had been surfing the Internet looking at Ficcare hair clips a week or so earlier, so I mentioned that. Bryn looked interested. Could I find that and show him? Sure...but I was already wearing one of those, so I took off the plain matte gold clip that I always wore and showed it to him, tilting it to the side to explain how it gripped the hair. I added that Berta's long hair was so fabulously thick that she would need the largest size clip, and that it would likely cost around $50. He said that was fine; with that, he had made up his mind.

Accordingly, I went out to the computer and brought up an image of a red clip with a design etched into its glaze to print for him. It was the one that Berta had admired most. He approved it, so I ordered it. It arrived in time for her birthday, and I wrapped it up nicely, got him a card to write to her, and he was satisfied; done.

Come to think of it, Berta had wanted to have something with his writing on it to save and look at forever ever; it occurred to me months later that all she needed to do was keep all of the birthday cards that he ever gave her. Bryn was the sort of dad who would never fail to remember her birthday with a personal message and a card, so she had a ready supply of mementos. If she hadn't saved them all, that was her fault. If she wanted to read his other writings, those not meant for her eyes, she was out of luck.

The red hair clip arrived, nearly coinciding with Berta expressed a particular wish to me about a gift from her father. She had a rather specific desire for a last gift with both sentimental and ornamental value. She hoped for a ring like the one that he had given her mother, a ruby with white diamonds on either side, but when I passed this on to Bryn, he said he didn't give people jewelry. I found it all rather odd and disturbing...creepy, even. He was dying and she wanted stuff from him. I kept my opinions to myself and just mediated the situation as best I could.

July Birthdays...But the Party's Over

When she told me, I was a bit deflated by the news; I had thought that we were all set, but now I wondered. Not only that, I felt strange about it all. Bryn was dying and she wanted him to make a shopping effort. He just couldn't do it. Add to that the fact that she was turning 40 and it seemed that she ought to be past wanting such expensive things from a parent, and certainly past requesting them.

At that point, I didn't want to be involved in any further message-passing or hint-dropping; I told Bryn that I felt uncomfortable with the idea. When I told him that I was worried about mediating this gift-hunting business, he told me that I ought to tell her that she should just speak directly to him about it. He said he would deal with Berta, and that I didn't have to worry about that anymore.

That was a relief.

At one point, I had gotten so upset that I had confided in Leila about it, frustrated that Berta might be unhappy with her gift, which I would obviously be involved in acquiring and preparing for her. Leila just agreed with me; it's the thought that counts more than anything else. I decided to just go ahead with the clip and the doll and quit worrying about it.

With that, I relaxed and went back to enjoying this. The place cards were ready, the arrangements were made, and it was going to fun, damnit! And then I was going to come home and relax – no trips out to a stupid bar. It should be easy to avoid that, I thought to myself. They all knew I wasn't interested in getting drunk, and that I had to go home to be with Bryn anyway.

It was also in between the two birthday parties that I wrote a note to Bryn's son-in-law The Hornsby, who would be returning home from Europe a few days ahead of Dionne. I told him how things were, that I hoped he could remove Dionne's paintings and easel that I had found behind the futon frame while cleaning, and that I was getting anxious and depressed thinking of all the packing and organizing that I supposed I would be expected to do. Worries that I would be the target of someone else's fury over the logistics of all were constantly on my mind. I mentioned Asperger's in the letter, too. He didn't write back, which really didn't surprise me. As long as he helped with the stuff, I didn't care.

Berta's party was to be at a place called Cowgirl N.Y.C., which suggested a different theme from that of superheroines. I didn't know anything about it, but had dutifully made all of the place cards that she wanted, complete with the red and blue star stickers, and put them by her gift in a zip-lock bag. I had never been to a birthday party that was planned by the celebrant before, but people do plan their own parties.

The Slamming Door

Elah agreed to come over and sit with Bryn again. I felt bad that he was missing out on the fun, and made sure that he had whatever he wanted to eat that night. He had written his card to Berta, and seen his gift both before and after I had wrapped it up for her. I put both of our gifts in a small Whole Foods bag that Berta had admired, the one with the Sheryl Crow tree design, and had decided that I would let her just keep it.

Just before it was time to go, Rudy came over to talk to Bryn and they shut the door. I thought nothing of it, but Berta noticed that they were talking in there before she arrived. She was wearing jeans a cowgirl hat. Rudy came out and left, Elah came in and turned on my TV, and off we all went, me and Berta riding with Matt in his jeep SUV.

As we drove through Greenwich Village, Berta talked about the legal advice that I had given Bryn months earlier, about that trust fund for Hilda to attend cultural events. She was absolutely convinced that her father had been informing Rudy of the bequest that evening. She went on for a couple of minutes about how that must bother him, and I wondered why it would. She replied that it meant that he wasn't enough of a man to afford that for his daughter himself.

What?! Rudy worked hard to earn a living and took every job, cooking at diners, taking odd gigs with his bass violin or guitar, teaching lessons, and catering events. I had a hard time buying the idea that poverty could be his fault or that poverty and manhood might be connected. Was she implying that poor people were emasculated by their economic status, I wondered? I made no reply to her analysis, deciding that it was pointless to pursue the subject further. Rudy might not be friendly, approachable, or much of a people person, but this was a bit much.

A minute or so later, Matt pulled the vehicle within sight of the restaurant.

It was on the corner of 10th Street and Hudson Avenue, in an old building with huge windows. It could have been rented out to a clothing store just as easily as to a restaurant, I thought, as I looked at the mannequins lined up inside, set up on a long, low shelf. They were all dressed in wild, rainbow-colored dresses, leftover relics from Gay Pride Day.

I hung back to shoot some photos of the place, and got a couple of Berta and Matt entering, then followed. Crossing the street to the place, I noticed more details such as a fake cactus just outside the front door, and a male mannequin in a white suit with a goatee and a white wig. There was some sidewalk seating, but we ignored it.

July Birthdays...But the Party's Over

We went past the bar, which was dim and hung with chandeliers made of antlers. We passed through a couple of back hallways and a little den with low sofas a framed photograph of a slice of an old tree with many rings. Finally, we were led to the left and down a set of perhaps six steps, into a smaller room with a bar and a long table that was a booth on one side and chairs on the other.

The aunts, Albert, June, Alissa, Kandi Kramer, and Sorcha were already there. I took a seat next to Sorcha in a chair. Leila showed up soon after and sat next to me on the end by the stairs. Desta was the last one to arrive, and I called her on my cell phone when the waiter wanted to take our order, reading her the entire list of prix fixe items so that I could place her order with all the others. She arrived soon after that and slid into her seat on the end of the booth next to Matt. Berta was in the center of the booth, presiding happily over her party.

This place and this party were – just as in personality – the exact opposite of her cousin's. It was good, but not as healthful; we had salsa, guacamole, cornmeal-fried and Cajun catfish with corn and peas and rice on the side, a huge salad for Alissa, and red velvet cupcakes with a candle in each one on a 2-tiered tray for Berta to blow out. We sang *Happy Birthday* when it arrived.

She enjoyed opening her gifts, with exaggerated, showy, overblown reactions to each one. Alissa had been comparatively low-key as she had opened her, quietly thanking everyone. Not Berta; she made huge moue faces and posed with things, and got teary for a moment when she opened the *Wonder Woman* doll, mistakenly thinking that it was from her father. I had to jump up slightly and tell her to stop crying, it wasn't what she thought, and then she realized who had given her what. I had added a large bar of French lavender soap to the mix, and Aunt Summer had given her a huge polka-dot mug that said "Goddess," which pleased her.

That was about it.

It was fun but loud, and when all rituals had been completed and we were just sitting there enjoying each other's company, we started to chat, still taking some photos. Sorcha told me that she had a nephew with Asperger's back in Ireland, and that he had just been accepted to a university there. (I had told her that I had it, which was why she mentioned it.) Alissa and I each had our Vera Bradley mini bags with us, so Berta took a silly photo of us with them. Alissa hid behind hers, I noticed later on, when I was labeling the photos. Finally, Albert shot a few of me, saying that I was never in enough of them. Actually, I was in some from each event.

When it was over, we all trouped out, and I headed out, chatting with Leila. We said good-bye to the aunts at one cab and to Albert, June and Alissa at another one, just as we had the week before. With that, the rest of the party headed up the street in the drizzling rain toward a bar, completing the repetition of that pattern of movement.

I hung back, not interested in joining them. Berta was getting rowdy, and I wanted to go home again. No way was I going to follow her into

The Slamming Door

another bar only to have to excuse myself; this time I wanted to just make my escape unnoticed.

As I put my arm up to hail a passing cab, Bryn called me. Perfect timing! I answered and told him I was just stepping into a cab and would be right back. Satisfied, he rang off and I hopped in. Then I called Matt's phone, convinced that Berta was too exuberant to notice the sound of her own cell phone ringing. He answered and said that yes, he had noticed me getting into that cab, and not to worry.

Bryn was fine when I got back, if you could call declining too much to enjoy going to parties anymore fine. I greeted him and told him how it had gone in full detail, trying to remember it all so that he would feel like he hadn't missed anything.

After that, just as the week before, I loaded all of the new photos to the computer, labeled them, and printed up several of them for Bryn to look at. I also found a small, forgotten picture frame and put a photo of Berta at Alissa's party into it for him to have in his room. She had her hair down, cascading prettily over her huge turquoise shirt, and her pose was like a movie star. She was smiling and looked pretty. He liked it.

Next, I burned a CD for Berta of all of the photos I had taken, and sent her an e-mail to tell her about it. I also put a set of copies on Bryn's computer. It seems odd now that I just kept making visual records for him to possess of memories that he wouldn't look at later, but it felt soothing to do it.

The next Monday, while Berta was at work, I received an e-mail from her: she was asking if I could get her some note cards for her to write thank-you notes on, and could I also print out, from my address file, everyone's contact information?

So I was her errand-girl and secretary…fine. I had nothing better to do. When I went out that afternoon, I visited a few stores until I found some fairly inexpensive light green ones at Papyrus. That was her favorite color.

But she complained about the cost that evening when I presented them. Unbelievable…if she didn't like my effort, why not do this herself?! Where would she have shopped for them, I wondered, and what would she have chosen?

Then she saw the ill-used expression on my face and just accepted them, thanked me, and reimbursed me.

I don't know whether or not she actually wrote the notes, but that was her problem.

I went back to thinking about taking care of Bryn.

Berta could and would take care of herself, I was sure.

July Birthdays...But the Party's Over

There was one other thing that happened during this time – something fun.

Bryn told me that he had been one of the people who got to attend the Reverend Doctor Martin Luther King Jr.'s *I Have a Dream* Speech at the Lincoln Memorial in Washington, D.C. on August 28th of 1963.

It took me a lot of searching and fussing, but I finally figured out which one of the spectators was Bryn. But...this is a Roman à Clef novel, so I won't put a circle around his face here. Just look at the men in front of the fence; he's the third above the left guy's hat. ☺

The Slamming Door

Really? That was fascinating. Even more fascinating was the fact that Bryn was in photographs of the audience on that bright, sunny day, smiling and listening. He had gone to work, and he and his social worker colleagues had all been offered a bus ride to hear a speech – a field trip day. So they had accepted the impromptu day off and ridden down there, not knowing what they would find when they got there.

I went onto the Google search engine, doing an image search for his face in that crowd.

It took a lot of scrutiny, but in the portrait-oriented color image, I was able to find him.

He had a crew-cut, his hair was dark brown, his glasses were like magnifying lenses as always, and he was smiling and listening. His face was just above one of two of King's security men in front of the barrier, the one on the left, a few heads above his hat, listening to and watching a piece of history unfolding.

Chapter 50

Alena Visits

Another month passed and Damon's other sister came to visit.

By that time, Bryn's leg had swelled up, Alissa had turned 39 and Berta had turned 40, and Bryn couldn't go out much anymore. I only went out when someone else could stay and sit with him. Bryn-sitting, I called it, because he wasn't a baby but he had to have company just in case of an emergency.

So when she came to see Bryn, things felt a lot different there. Bryn had told me that she was coming to see him, "essentially for the last time." He nodded as he said that to me, and looked deadly serious. Like I hadn't figured out that this was her last visit…

Alena was Damon's youngest sister. She was the corporate executive, the remote one with the smiling façade and the long, straight, dishwater blond hair. She looked like a ringer for their maternal grandmother, Diane Otterman Koren, who was very cold and remote. Damon had never liked either one of them. But it wasn't Alena's fault that she resembled that grandmother.

I wasn't excited to see her, with her disconnected way of relating to others, her corporate demeanor, and knowing that she didn't like me. I didn't particularly like her either. She had everything – money, success, and a home with her husband – and was condescending to me.

Yet I had no wish to emulate a person whose demeanor was so disconnected and callous. Was that why she had those wonderful things, I wondered? Was it because she didn't care about other people's lives? Was it only the coldest people who could afford lovely homes and the material things that made it possible to have a relationship and enjoy togetherness from it too?

I could be as polite and friendly as ever and she would still be cold and distant. I had given up any desire to like her long ago. Being friends with this sister-in-law wasn't possible.

So Alena paid her last-chance-to-see-Bryn visit. She combined it with a business conference that she had to attend in Manhattan, which was at a hotel. Accordingly, for efficiency's sake – quite logical – she stayed at that hotel.

Her visit began the evening after Berta's birthday party. I knew that she was coming, but hadn't thought about entertaining her. I was too distracted and too busy until the day she arrived.

Damon was stuck in the hospital in Hungary with an infected foot, and I still couldn't get him on the Skype phone system. I was a nervous, distracted wreck from checking the computer constantly; I just couldn't

The Slamming Door

go to sleep and see what happened the next day until I had waited as long as I could stand to stay awake. I kept hoping to talk to him on the Skype each night.

The day before Alena arrived I ordered a tee shirt with a cat cartoon for Bryn on Berta's behalf from *The New Yorker.com* store. It was something that she had wanted to give to him; she would reimburse me later. Still busy with so many other, unrelated details for Bryn, I really hadn't given Alena's actual visit much thought.

It was the Monday after Berta's party that Alena was due to arrive, and I had gone out the week before, between Alissa and Berta's birthdays, to get gifts for her daughters from both me and Bryn. Bryn's friend Kandi had sat with him while I went, and suggested the perfect place to shop in, called Lee's Art Shop, on West 57th Street. I even found something for Alena.

Alena arrived on July 12th, in the evening, for a 6 p.m. party. She was coming alone, flying in from Albuquerque, New Mexico, and her first stop was Bryn's place.

She arrived wearing shorts and a tee shirt with her hair tied in 2 unevenly divided braids. I didn't realize that a corporate bigwig could look like a geek, but she managed it. (Damon later said that he had seen that hairstyle on her, and that he thought it looked ridiculous on her too.) She got there after I had come home with the party food and set it up, dumped her bags in the long front hallway and headed in to see Bryn.

After a couple of minutes, she came back out to look through her bags, and I gave her a gift: a Vera Bradley makeup bag. She gave me a cinnamon lotion set. Thank-yous were exchanged. Then I gave her the wrapped boxes from Lee's Art Shop, puzzles and crafts for Roselyn and Lillian. More thanks gushed from Alena, and she stashed them in her suitcase. Good; that was out of the way. Everything was starting to feel like a joyless chore – things that I used to take pleasure from were tasks to be completed and crossed off my list now.

I had gone out and shopped for all of the food that afternoon at Whole Foods and the nearest liquor store. Berta had e-mailed me a list of things to buy for us all to eat at the party, and I had added a few items that I thought ought to be included. Among them was the one thing that I thought her father would eat: chunks of melon. He liked honeydew, cantaloupe, and watermelon, and Whole Foods offered clear containers full of chunks of them. Albert sat with Bryn.

Berta's note was sent just after noon, asking me to shop for all this stuff when I woke up. At that point, I didn't care that it was common knowledge that I didn't wake up until around noon. Between communicating with Damon and watching Bryn, I didn't get to bed until

Alena Visits

4 a.m. any more. If anyone had a problem with that, I just resented their attitude.

Berta mentioned that there were wine glasses above the sink...in that cabinet with the family crystal and china that I couldn't reach. Forget it; she could get those when she arrived. She was tall enough to see inside, and she could be the one to physically handle that fragile stuff. If any of it broke, I wouldn't have anything to do with it.

After heading out early enough to acquire Chardonnay for the aunts plus have enough time to chill it, I went out again to buy the groceries, returning shortly before the event was to start. We already had a lot of beer; between Berta, Albert and me, the place constantly seemed to have a menu of beer options that summer. It was fun. The choices offered me a chance for a mild buzz when I was stressed out, and it only took one bottle to achieve that.

I came back with 2 Whole Foods plastic bags loaded with carrot sticks, conveniently upright in a clear container, roasted red pepper hummus to dip them in, blue corn chips, guacamole, Carr's crackers, Asiago and Brie cheeses, and raspberries as well as the melon chunks. Alissa immediately joined me in the kitchen to help set it all up, which I appreciated.

Quickly, I took out all 4 dinner plates and laid them out on the stove, which was the only place to work. Somehow, we got everything in order and Alissa brought in all into Bryn's room, carefully removing his papers from the ottoman and his white plastic table. The aunts arrived as I set up the food and congregated around Bryn's room, facing him.

Everyone arrived, and soon the party was in full swing.

I positioned the melons in a bowl with a plastic fork that pointed in Bryn's direction, and he did eat a few pieces. Alena and I split one blueberry and one apricot beer so as to taste each flavor. She was surprisingly friendly and congenial toward me, so I later showed her my calligraphy and editing brochures. She made a couple of minor suggestions, so I opened the files and did the edits. Why not? She may not like me, but she wasn't out to get me, either.

Aunt Summer accidentally broke one of Berta's grandmother's etched wine glasses when she forgot it under her chair. Berta was upset, and I felt sorry for her to lose the beautiful piece, so I said so. I was secretly glad to have been nothing more than an observer after the fact, though. Aunt Summer looked a bit mortified, though I was all the way out in the front hall as she sat facing Bryn in his room; poor Aunt Summer.

When at last the party was breaking up and we had all gravitated back into the living room, Berta and Alissa stood by the drop-leaf table with the Tiffany lamp behind them. I sat at the computer. Alena and aunts

The Slamming Door

were still there, chatting, and Bryn stood in the doorway of the back hall, his back to the bathroom. Berta was wearing a red-and-white dress with a floral pattern, which I hadn't seen before. It was different from her usual pale blues and greens.

Somehow, the fact that I was a bit different came up, though I forget how. It might have been about my editing and calligraphy business, my writing, or just my personality. In any case, the point was that my inability to fit into an office environment with its politics and background noise was mentioned. That was brushed aside; I was praised for my accomplishments.

Berta bemoaned the fact that she did not stand out in any particular way, so I said, "Don't worry about it; you're normal."

"I don't want to be normal," she complained. "That sounds like I'm ordinary."

I just looked at her. No one else spoke. The silence stretched on awkwardly.

It was as though we were all tacitly agreeing with her, but unwilling to dig ourselves into any conversational hole. It was already deepening without any of us so much as uttering a word. Finally, someone spoke, though I don't remember who it was or what they said. All that mattered was that the subject was changed, the thread of conversation was picked up, and we moved on.

Chapter 51

Walden

Bryn was declining with obvious speed at this point, and he had decided to get a home health aide to help him with certain things. I couldn't handle all of his physical needs, he found the mere idea of having a female relative doing so awkward, and it turned out that formal training was necessary for this anyway.

It wasn't until Walden started doing this job that I understood that last part, but I hadn't been obsessing over it. When someone is dying, their needs are usually so specific and medically septic that only people with health training and certification would know what to do for them. It doesn't take any great leap of intuition or logic to realize that.

Walden was a black man of medium height and build in his early thirties, very dark, with black stubble for hair, and when he spoke it was apparent that he was from an African nation. He wore jeans, sneakers, a plain tee shirt, a baseball cap and a watch with a huge round face and a leather strap that he put in his pocket when he helped Bryn in the bathroom. He was quiet, and he had large, round eyes with a careful but pleasant expression in them.

I wasted no time in making Walden feel welcome in the apartment. The first thing I did was in response to Bryn's expressed worry that this aide, whoever he was, would spend the afternoon staring at him. No one likes to be stared at, even people who are as secure with themselves as Bryn was.

So I put out books for Walden to look at – picture books, mostly, and not because I labored under any mistaken ideas that he might not be able to read well. The books were about things that he wouldn't have to concentrate on too much, because he was really there to work. There were the Edward Gorey art books, the one from the Morgan Library, and I forget what else, but he seemed to enjoy them, and Bryn and Albert noticed this. It worked out well; he wasn't staring at Bryn, but he was easy to summon if Bryn needed any assistance from him.

The first evening after he left us for the day, Berta came over and asked about the pile of books on the table near the hallway. I told her it was for Walden to look when her father didn't need anything from him. She screwed up her face, making a displeased expression, and said "He's probably just some uneducated…"

I cut in, disgusted and unwilling to let her finish that sentence. "Just because he hasn't had the opportunity to get an education, that doesn't mean that he doesn't have any interest in learning things."

She straightened her face out and dropped the subject.

The Slamming Door

She was sitting in Bryn's room, and he was there. We simply moved on to the next subject. There was no winning way to continue that line of conversation.

As soon as I had the chance to chat with him, I tried to learn a bit about him. Where was he from originally? Liberia. Aha...I had noticed an accent. What languages did he speak? English. Well, I can tell that you speak English, I replied, but you obviously speak an African language, because you have an accent when you speak English, and you are from an African country. What language besides English do you speak? Grebo, he said, sounding surprised and hesitant. Why didn't you say so before? It's not a major, global language; I didn't think it counted. Of course it counts – you can think in more than one language – that's impressive!

Liberia: that was the nation founded by former American slaves after the Civil War, and Walden had grown up there. He said he had attended a high school in which the students sat on the floor, but that the basics seemed to have been covered. He had done his home health care training here.

And so it went. Now he could see that I respected him, and that I didn't see him as just some servant who had come into the family home to do grunt work. He smiled a shy smile.

He usually arrived at 2 p.m., and when he did, I would make him a cup of coffee. I forget precisely how he liked it now – but I do remember that some milk and sugar went into it, and that he liked Bryn's Sumatra blend.

Albert would often give him a few bottles of beer to take home and share with his wife, and they were good brews – Belgian ones, German lagers, and some of the fruit beers that I liked. I would give him cookies and cupcakes from the area bakeries.

At first, I hadn't known that he had an older boy living with him. I had thought that it was just him, his wife, and their baby, so I had been giving him only two sweets at a time, thinking that Walden and his wife were enjoying them. Then he said that his 11-year-old son had just joined them from Liberia, where he had stayed behind with relatives until his parents could afford to send for him.

I scolded Walden, saying that I felt bad about not having sent more cupcakes. He smiled. Then he told us all that the kid was thrilled not only to be here but also not to have to tote a bucket of water two miles each day. He was turning on the bathroom faucets and marveling at the clear water that came out whenever he wanted some. We were happy for the kid, and felt lucky to have always lived with indoor plumbing in our wonderful, developed nation.

Walden

But we kept our mouths shut about that while Walden was visiting. Although we realized that Bryn's health insurance was paying him to be with us, we liked him so much that it really did feel like a visit each day.

It turned out that Walden didn't have any other jobs; usually he would just have one sick man at a time to take care of. I couldn't resist asking him about the other families, if they had been pleasant or friendly to him. "Not like you people," he said, and left it at that. Hmmm...that sucked for him, but it revealed that we were treating him with appreciation. Who cared that he was being paid?! He was helping Bryn to maintain his comfort and dignity.

Another day, I asked him about his family again: did he happen to have any photographs of them? Yes – he had some wallet photos. He took them out and showed me. His wife was a beautiful woman with her hair done in tiny cornrow braids that artfully sloped back from her face. She looked very serious in her photo. The other one was of his older son, who had short hair and looked cheerful. I scanned them both and asked for his e-mail address.

Once I had sent the scans to him, I said, "There – now they are safely in cyberspace, in case anything ever happens to the originals." He looked delighted.

One of the things that he saw me doing was scanning the old family photos that I had found in the drawers of that futon frame, and labeling them carefully on the computer.

The photographs were all framed, and I even took the ones on the wall between the hall closet and my room down and tried to scan them. Some came out okay, others didn't, but I'm glad I tried. That meant that everyone could have a scanned copy: me, Bryn, Albert, Alissa, Dionne, Berta, everyone.

There was a beautiful one of a great-aunt who had lived in Paris in the 1920s, another one of Bryn and Albert's mother as a teenager in the same decade, one of Bryn and Albert as little boys in matching suits of shorts and blazer jackets, various others of the Bryn and Albert in their twenties and thirties surrounded by June, Elvira, and their mother, one portrait of Bryn from when he was thirty years old, and finally, a enormous color photo in a white paper matte frame from the 1990s of Berta. She was twenty-two when that one was taken, thin, beautiful, and smiling. I had to photograph that and then tinker with the framing and cropping of the image rather than scan that one. It was an interesting collection of Otterman family images.

When Berta walked in with Matt later that day, the huge photo of her was laid out on the side table between the stained glass lamp and the Gallic warrior statue. She saw it and said that it was a Glamour Shot, and that she hated it.

The Slamming Door

That surprised me; she was thin and beautiful in it, and even looked a bit glamorous, thus living up to the company's advertising promise. I didn't know how to respond to that, so I just said, "I have a Glamour Shot too from about the same time. I like it though; I'm all in black with a red rose, and Damon and my grandmother kept copies."

She let the matter drop. Her father had enjoyed seeing that photograph.

Meanwhile, Walden and Eve took care of more and more of Bryn's physical needs, and I took care of fewer and fewer of them. The errand-running was still my job, and I timed them for the four hours in which Walden was there.

Bryn was starting to fear being left alone, and he would say, "Don't leave me alone."

When there were no visitors, I didn't.

Chapter 52

Moving Furniture – Berta Freaks Out

Ellen, the visiting nurse, had decided that Bryn should have a hospital bed in his room, but had also announced that she would not place the order unless and until she came over and saw an empty spot where it would go.

That meant a furniture moving day.

It was scheduled for the next Saturday, when Matt, Rudy, and Hilda's boyfriend Riley could come over to do the heavy lifting. It took place on Saturday, July 18th, 2009.

Meanwhile, Walter Cronkite died the day before that, on a Friday, thus clogging the news stations almost as much as Michael Jackson's death had done. At least this wasn't another silly obsession with popular culture. Granted, age 50 was too young to die and Jackson had died from a medical error, but a legendary newscaster with a great sign-off line – "And that's the way it is" – was just much more interesting to me and Bryn and Albert.

Bryn watched the newscasts all day, and I read about it online, saving a copy of the *Associated Press* article for future reference as a matter of routine.

Berta arrived at the end of the day and asked if we had heard about it, to which I replied that it had been on the news all day, and I had read a huge long biographical piece about him online. I must have sounded matter-of-fact and nonchalant, like someone to whom being up on such things is second nature, which must have been irritating, though I only realized that later.

But back to the furniture moving plans.

Berta had been all for simply placing the beautiful new bed that she had bought for her father the previous fall in her storage unit, but Bryn spoke up and said no, he wanted me to have it for the remainder of my stay there. He said that this was the perfect time to throw out the futon.

Okay; Berta just agreed to it without a word. This was all explained to me later, perhaps moments later; I had heard it from the next room as all this came up in the planning. I never asked for things or involved myself in the planning of logistics; it seemed like the best way to avoid conflict. I wouldn't seek conflict out, but neither would I shrink from it if it came at me.

But I just didn't see any trouble coming. What could happen? We were just shifting things around, and on a weekend with no hurry. No boss, no hired delivery people to accommodate, no reason to get anxious. At least, that was what I told myself.

The Slamming Door

I was up and ready to receive people by 10:45 a.m., but no one arrived right away. Well, no problem. I was ready. When they got there, we could start. Somehow though, I didn't get around to eating right away.

Berta and Matt arrived around 11:30 a.m. I still hadn't eaten anything, but she surprised me by wanting to go out for sandwiches with Matt, Rudy, and me. Perfect; I would get something that passed for breakfast food. I always eat breakfast food first no matter when during the day I have my first meal.

Bryn wanted the Rafaella's Moroccan Breakfast – couscous, walnuts, raisins, strawberries, blueberries, and banana. We would get that on the way back, so it would be fresh when he started to eat it.

Sure enough, we all found a nice lunch place, with Berta complaining about the speed at which we walked in the warm, slightly humid sunshine to it. We weren't moving all that fast, but she was uncomfortable. I didn't know what to say, so I just slowed down slightly, but soon we were far behind Rudy and Matt. That was no good; she didn't want to lag behind.

They all got sandwiches and iced tea or juice; I got oatmeal with raisins and orange juice. We ate, with Rudy doing a lot of the talking with Matt. The two men seemed to get along well.

Rudy and Matt went back to Bryn's place ahead of us after we ate while Berta and I went to Rafaella's to get the Moroccan meal. She ordered it, and we sat down to wait for it.

The place was full of people. It was such a lovely, sunny Saturday that couples and friends and families had gathered in there to visit and enjoy the place for a while.

As we sat at one of the small tables off to the side, with Berta's back to the window and me spacing out, waiting with nothing new to talk about, Berta noticed a mother with a little girl who was holding a rag doll. The mother was busy with a stroller. She either had another, smaller girl with her or was pregnant; I don't remember.

She was busy though, paying the bill and getting organized, so they could leave just yet. The little girl stood behind her mother holding the doll, facing out to watch people, and looking a bit bored. She was pretty, with long, brown hair and bangs. She was also very quiet.

Berta suddenly began to talk to her in a high-pitched, silly tone, asking if she could hold her doll. I looked at Berta, nonplussed and disgusted, but without a word, and back at the little girl. Berta was completely oblivious to me, but the girl just clutched her doll and looked at Berta out of the tops of her eyes, saying nothing.

That is exactly how it was with me when I was a little girl. People would make utter fools of themselves talking to me like that, and I would

Moving Furniture – Berta Freaks Out

stare coldly back, saying nothing so as to avoid being scolded for speaking rudely to an adult. I would do nothing to encourage the nonsense, but I was infuriated and insulted at being spoken to as though I were an imbecile simply because I was young. The girl made no reply as Berta continued to insult her intelligence with inanity.

I liked this girl. I couldn't help it; we had something in common – we didn't like stupid adults and stupid behavior from them.

"Berta," I said, trying to help the little girl, "she's not going to let a stranger touch her doll – she doesn't want you to."

"Of course she wants me to," Berta cooed, still oblivious.

She was starting to really irritate me.

I refrained from saying so; we were about to move furniture and I would be stuck with her for the next couple of hours. Hopefully it would all be over soon and everything would be quiet and not stressful.

Well...one could fantasize.

The nonsense continued unabated, however, with the mother also turning to look less than pleased by it but unwilling to say anything and risk offending a stranger. She led her daughter out of the restaurant as soon as she possibly could, and before there could be any more comments exchanged, our package was presented. What a relief – saved by the bill.

Berta paid it and we walked out. The little girl with the doll and her mother were long gone. We went back to the apartment.

I unwrapped the food on the kitchen counter and brought some of it in for Bryn; he was long past wanting to be presented with an entire serving of anything by then, but he looked happy to see the berries and couscous. Then I went in to see what was going on.

First the old futon had to be removed from my room. To prepare, I had pulled out the drawers from the frame the night before and emptied their contents into some boxes that I had found in the closet, being careful to clean and sort it all. Only 2 of the 3 drawers would open, the ones on either side. The middle lacked a handle, and I had given up. The 2 boxes that I had prepared were out in the hallway, full of family photos and all sorts of knick-knacks of Berta's.

I had pointed it out to her, explaining that I had been as careful as I could with it all.

She didn't seem upset, but I didn't see what else I could have done about any of it.

Looking through the holes where the drawers had been, I saw a lot of unreachable filth. That would have to be swept up and the spot mopped before the new bed was put in place, I thought to myself. I brought the broom and stick mop out in anticipation of that.

The Slamming Door

Before the work got started, I tossed my bedding out of the way. The quilt was already folded and out of the way, thanks to the hot summer nights I didn't need it now. Pillows, sheets, and other items were quickly thrown out of the zone of upheaval.

Matt, Rudy and Riley moved in on the futon and hauled away the old avalanche mattress, the disgusting old pillows, and the old quilts that I had used to level it off – all out with the rubbish. Next went the futon pad. Then it was time to get rid of the wooden frame.

I had thought that Berta would have been glad to see it go. She had always hated that thing, and been angry when Bryn and Cassie had gotten it.

Instead, Berta showed no clear emotion one way or the other about its departure. She hung around, not helping with the actual work, bossing Matt around. She limited her remarks to her boyfriend, not daring to push Rudy or Riley. She soon sounded abusive. It was definitely a hot day, and with her girth, she began to sweat…and swear. She used the F-word repeatedly.

Beads of perspiration dripped down her forehead and nose, and she lifted up her tee shirt to fan herself with it, showing her white, lacy bra. I was the only one who saw that; the men and the teenage boy were facing the other way. "Berta, you're flashing us," I said, worried that Rudy or Riley would turn around at the wrong moment and look up.

"Sorry," she said, covering herself. She was wearing jeans and sneakers; no wonder she was overheated. It was over 90 degrees out, she was overweight, and overdressed.

I was in shorts and a sleeveless shirt with my Teva sandals; I had expected to be cleaning and moving about. Bryn sat in his chair, unable to observe what was going on. I wondered what he made of all the sounds he was hearing. It must have sucked to have to stay still while furniture was being shifted around, and not to be up, observing and facing the activities.

Matt turned to the wooden frame. The drawers were taken back out of their slots and carted away, and then the middle one was the only one left. It wouldn't budge, and I explained my efforts of the night before. Matt nodded, then raised his boot and pried at the upper edge, catching it after a moment. He brought his foot down on it hard, trying to dislodge it.

"Kill it, Matt," I said, trying to make light of it.

He did; stomp, stomp, stomp, and the front came off. After that it was easy to pull the drawer out. I got another box and hauled the drawer away to work on the mess later.

Moving Furniture – Berta Freaks Out

Next, I peered under the frame at the filth, and poked the broom under, trying to remove the filth. There was an awful lot of dust, both grit and dust bunnies.

"Clarisse, wait, let us get the frame out of here first," Matt said to me.

I backed off, broom and all, and got out of their way.

Berta was getting more and more irritable now, still ordering Matt about. He was just silently putting up with it, which seemed odd to me, but I wasn't about to say anything. As long as she didn't speak to me like that, I figured it would all be fine and over with soon.

"Hurry the fuck up, Matt," Berta said yet again.

Rudy and Riley were keeping carefully out of it, quietly helping to remove things. I saw Hilda once, but she didn't stick around for long. Elah didn't appear at all; she was probably busy posting stuff on the Internet as usual.

The frame was lifted out of the way, and I managed to get the sweeping done fast.

Next, I came at the mess with the stick mop, hot, wet, and ready to go. The filth was caked onto the blue painted floor, and dated back at least a decade, from what I understood. I had to get rid of it quick before the men were ready to bring the nice new bed.

Berta was making me anxious now, still barking orders at Matt. Now she turned her attention to me. "Hurry up, Clarisse," she said in a rather nasty tone.

That did it. "Don't tell me hurry up," I said, "I'm cleaning as fast as I can."

With that, Berta got obnoxious. "I'll tell you to hurry up if I want to; I'm doin' you a fuckin' favor," she said, still in that nasty tone.

Now I glared at her. I didn't give a damn that she had money from a job to pay for stuff; she seemed to consider me a servant. I wouldn't put up with such insulting treatment. "I am going to clean this spot before the bed is brought. Don't swear at me," I replied in a grating tone.

That did it; she went nuts, screaming and swearing at me, calling me a fucking bitch but still not bothering to completely enunciate the insults, and, yelling her lungs out, dashed into her father's room, where she crashed his door shut.

I was shaking with rage and upset. Damn her.

I started to cry, and sat on one of the wooden chairs in the living room. Rudy and Riley came in and sat down too – Rudy on a chair and Riley on the sofa. I started to talk, still crying. "This is the first death I have dealt with since my grandmother died of lung cancer when I was seventeen," I told them. Matt had slipped into Bryn's room after Berta; he didn't hear this.

The Slamming Door

Rudy and Riley said nothing; they just listened.

"I helped with my grandmother a bit, but nothing like what my mother and the nurses did," I continued. "Teenagers don't see too much or find out much about death and dying. Just because Berta pays for things and has a job is no reason why she should be able to treat me like a damned servant. All along I have wondered whether or not I would be treated as some damned in-law, and I think now it's happening."

Rudy and Riley said nothing. I didn't know what they were thinking. I still don't.

I really don't care now; I have nothing to apologize for. I didn't swear at Berta, I didn't tell her anything terrible, insult her, or otherwise heap misery onto her. I still don't see what more I could have done other than to just stuff it and let her treat me rudely.

That was the one thing that I would never have been able to do for anyone.

Asperger's may very well be the reason for that; I would never take abuse from anyone for any reason in my entire life. I have always, always, refused to accept it from my father, a boss, a bully, or anyone else. If abuse came, I would never feel obligated to accept it, even if the perfect retort eluded me. Often, even after the incident is over, I still can't come up with the perfect retort. I just know that I feel ill-used by the abuse, and would hurt the abuser for what they did to me if I could. Payback is elusive though; the lawyer in me warns me against doing anything that could cause me any further trouble.

My father wished for instant compliance and obedience while I was a child simply because he was the parent and I was the child. He didn't get it if I was in the middle of something, had to go to the bathroom, or was otherwise not instantly ready. When he didn't get it, there would be trouble until my mother intervened. In addition, he was taller and had huge, strong arms. He used them on me when I was a kid, and I never regretted fighting back even when I couldn't adequately get him back for his enraged tirade. That didn't change a thing; I still don't regret any of my responses to any of those incidents. My father knows that.

This still happened occasionally even now, except that after a blow-up, he would realize that he had made a mistake and stop it. We would each move on, get over it, and not the other to accept imperious or nasty behavior. But that was with two Aspies in the equation.

I had explained all of this the previous year to Berta and to Bryn.

Berta knew about the trouble with my father, but when she vented her angst on me – or whatever was driving that outburst – the same response kicked in. It didn't help that she matched up in several ways to my father: taller, huge arms, screaming and nasty and convinced that she

Moving Furniture – Berta Freaks Out

had the right to act that way, paying for things, and dissatisfied with my attitude.

I'm just not subservient, obsequious, silent under a shouted insult, or otherwise tolerant of abusive behavior. When someone who has enough of the cards in a given situation to be able to call the shots, the one thing I insist upon from them is that they not act like they are entitled to behave imperiously towards me. If they can't handle that, all bets are off.

Still, I could not see that I had done anything wrong or bad, and I still don't.

I shut myself in my room, and wouldn't come out until things quieted down.

After screaming and crying in her father's room with him as a captive audience in his Lazy Boy chair, Berta disappeared for over an hour. I didn't know where she had gone.

The men came and finished the moving job; the old crap was gone and the new bed was in my room. I cleaned my face up, finished the mopping, and put back all the bedding. Done.

That one drawer full of filthy junk remained, but I left it for now.

I went in and saw Bryn, who had only eaten part of the Moroccan food. His room looked oddly bare now. A huge empty space filled the corner, and now a row of two chairs faced his like an audience facing a professor, or a pair of kids to be lectured to for naughtiness. I wasn't about to accept it, if that was what was coming.

But of course it wasn't. Bryn saw me still crying and upset, and just soothed me. I wondered what was going to happen next. It wasn't like with my father; my father wasn't sick, wasn't able to handle such situations until they were over, and he wasn't involved. I had no frame of reference for this. I would have to wait and see what happened next.

Albert showed up after a while, and I was glad to see him.

Bryn said to him, "If these girls don't make up, I'm fucked."

So that was it. He wanted us to be friends again because he was stuck with us.

It was even worse for him: he wanted me to be his caregiver, not his daughter. His other daughter hadn't yet returned from Europe, and he didn't want her either anyway. But I was there because Berta had asked me to come and take care of him. If he came out and said what he wanted, another tantrum would ensue, because no daughter would receive the knowledge that her father preferred another girl her age to herself with calmness and acceptance.

That was why he wanted us to make up, so that he could just keep things as they were without any more upsets. That would enable him to

The Slamming Door

continue having me there and not her. It was an unsustainable situation, though. Sooner or later, something was going to change.

I did not break down and call my mother. I was proud of myself for that. But I always kept Damon apprised of my situation. He was in Hungary at this point, and I was worried about him; he had spent the previous week – all of it – in the hospital with a staphylococcus infection in his foot after taking off his shoes at an outdoor faculty picnic. After being hooked up to a continuous drip of IV antibiotics, he was cured.

The university had paid for that; he was visiting faculty, and that had its benefits. The understanding of Hungarians, however, was not one of them. While in the hospital, Damon had had almost no computer access, and so no way to talk to me via Skype. He got depressed and started having nightmares about me, worrying about how I was doing.

Just a day or so before this uproar over moving the furniture, Damon had been released from the hospital and able to resume calling me on Skype. But he had spent a week in a hospital ward comprised of two rows of white metal-framed beds facing each other, limited privacy, and no way to keep working. That was easily a recipe for a massive anxiety attack and depression.

The nurses had let him use their computer a couple of times to write to me, but that had been it. A Hungarian cardiologist had spoken to him once, loudly and blustering, saying that he should just relax, even if he couldn't. Well…he didn't add that last bit. But the problem was that Damon couldn't relax or calm down. He needed to earn money, and he couldn't; he needed to be able to talk to me, and he couldn't.

That's Hungary for you. People there were very nice, but that just didn't help. They only understood their own point of view, and didn't care to see or contemplate another.

I had plenty of my own other problems to think about besides Bryn's impending death, which would severely depress me when it actually happened. The thought of not being able to talk to him any more ever again was terribly upsetting. Who would be so quietly understanding and not criticize me for how I felt about life or dealt with it when he was gone? No one, I thought. Everyone probably thought I would only mourn the lack of a place in Manhattan, which infuriated me. What I wanted was for everyone I enjoyed being with to stay alive.

That's what we all want. But sooner or later, everyone dies and leaves us.

Then what? What are we supposed to do? I didn't want to be the last one alive, with no Bryn, no Damon, no one, and I didn't want kids. I wanted my husband and a cat, and not to be scared about money and stability. None of that was possible. When Bryn died, I felt sure that

Moving Furniture – Berta Freaks Out

going back to my parents would be unbearable and impossible, and Damon had nowhere for us.

I kept thinking, throughout that summer, that when Bryn died, I would have to die too.

Why did I have to be so healthy, with such a long warranty on my DNA?!

This thought went through my mind constantly. I wanted to die too. I was miserable, and it wasn't just because of Bryn. I had no plans to go elsewhere and no clue as to where I ought to go. Home to my parents was an option, but I dreaded it.

I envied Bryn his imminent exit. I didn't envy him the manner of that exit; cancer terrified me. It's disgusting, humiliating, messy, disfiguring, and painful. If I died, my heart murmur was the most likely exit, but even so, my grandmother had just turned 95 and she had had a heart murmur since she was 2 years old.

Perfect; I was probably in for a long, stressful, unhappy life. I spent a lot of time crying and worrying about that, convinced that it would be so, and that old age would be unbearable, either in a state of poverty or, if I actually managed to leap that hurdle, trapped with bullying caregivers who would force me to eat foods that I hated or starve, put me in with a roommate who watched trash TV all day, and early, and with annoying little kids in the room visiting, remarking about me, and staring, and staff making me use the bathroom with the door open.

I do that when I get anxious – project into the future, convinced that life will just be unbearable. Great; life was now promising to be one long series of watching anyone I wanted to be with taken away from me somehow or other, and then being trapped with bullies.

I wanted to die too.

Where the hell had Berta gone anyway?

Matt came back.

I was sitting with Bryn when he appeared, and the moment he walked in, I felt defensive. Even though I didn't know him, I wasn't about to let him think for a moment that he could tell me I had done anything wrong, said anything I shouldn't have, or otherwise scold me.

"If you are here to say that I have done or said anything wrong, you can just forget about that; I won't accept anything like that," I told him, before he could utter a word.

"I'm not going to do that," he said, and actually hugged me.

Fascinating; a guy who didn't want to inflame a conflict, only defuse it. Berta was dating a younger version of her father! Why didn't she appreciate him more?!

Matt told us that Berta was at Hilda's place. Oh.

The Slamming Door

"I did nothing rude, nasty or wrong, I won't take abuse, and if she comes back saying anything other than that she's sorry, I won't be interested," I concluded."

Oddly he had no objection to that, either.

Matt sat down to chat. Something odd was up, but I just waited for it.

I didn't have to wait long. Matt got to it with a slight bit of discomfort, but he went ahead and asked it anyway. "Berta is upset, and sometimes she wonders whether you think that she is a bit stupid."

Really...I stared at him deadpan for a moment, nonplussed. Is that how she took my habitually neutral facial expressions? She who had immediately Blackberried Asperger's Syndrome and then acted like an expert of some sort on the topic? Interesting.

After a moment, I replied, "I think that she is smarter than she thinks she is," and left it at that. No way was I about to incriminate myself over this.

Matt seemed satisfied. He acted like a person who has just been assured that a worry was all in his head or, rather, his girlfriend's head.

We relaxed, greeted Albert, and waited for over an hour. I had plenty of time to clean up Bryn's meal, serve tea, start to calm down for real, and let my mind wander. I cleaned up that last drawer and sorted all of the photos so that I could scan them all later that evening.

Now that I saw all of those things, I was a bit excited to have a chance to study the family history a bit more. I couldn't help it; I'm a historian, and this was my husband's family. The photos were new to me, and I wanted to learn about the family history.

More time went by.

Finally, Berta came back, calm, quiet, and even apologetic. Wow. She came up to me and sobbed, "I love you, Clarisse! I'm sorry!" She hugged me, too. Her breath reeked of booze.

Okay, I would make up with her. I hugged her back, and led her to my room, where we flopped on the nice bed, our heads landing in the corner with all the pillows. I hugged her some more, and suggested that she be nice to Matt, because she was going to have him around for quite a while (at least, that was the hope).

"I don't want Matt, I want my dad!" she wailed.

"But Matt is nice – you need to show him that you appreciate him. What have you been doing all this time? I wondered where you were and what you were doing," I said.

"I had a shot of Jack Daniels and talked with Elah and Hilda," she said.

"Oh."

Moving Furniture – Berta Freaks Out

Well, that about did it for that uproar. We were all thoroughly sick of being upset and wanted to relax. But first, I heard the Skype system beeping at me from the bedroom; with the headphones rigged up, I could hear calls coming in unless I went into the kitchen or bathroom.

I dashed out and answered it, and told Damon to wait, and got Berta to talk to him. Maybe he could joke with her and help her calm down. I had filled him in fast about what was happening, and explained that it was all over. Soon, she was chatting merrily with him, talking about what it was that made life worth living to her: food, drinks, fun, and sex.

I knew that Damon was as close-mouthed about that last topic as I was and that he would just acknowledge what she said and move on. Losing interest in the conversation, I waited my chance to get the headphones back and talk to him.

When I did, he sounded cheerful and okay; we had a nice chat. He had been back at the lab for a few days and was feeling fine again…at least, as fine as he could be with unemployment money and no home.

Take-out was ordered, and we all settled in to relax.

My cell phone rang.

People were everywhere except in the bathroom, so I went in there to take the call.

It was my editing client, the nice actor from the card shop.

He was calling to say that the edits I had done for him and tutoring and consulting for those papers had really helped him a lot, and that the professors at his college were happy with the work. He could continue in the program, all was well, and thank you very much. He also planned to hire me again.

Well – that was terrific! I thanked him for allowing me to work with him, and so on and on. We chatted for a couple of minutes longer before we rang off.

When I came out of the bathroom, putting my phone back in my pocket, the family asked if everything was okay. "Oh yeah, it's great," I said, smiling.

"Really?" Berta said, grinning. "What's going on?"

I started to speak, but she interrupted immediately. "Let me guess; you're pregnant!"

I looked puzzled and outraged. "No! I hate babies – I never want one!"

More interruptions from her; I got annoyed and interrupted with: "Are you going to let me tell what it really is, or not?"

"Oh, all right," she said, laughing. What the hell was the matter with her?!

The Slamming Door

I told them all what it really was, complete with the compliments and thanks from the client, and Bryn and Albert and Berta all congratulated me and said that that was wonderful.

The evening wore on with more chatting about whatever struck our fancy, and at some point, I wandered back into the room after clearing the dishes and detritus of dinner in time to hear Berta fondly remembering life at the Emma Willard School with her high school friends. It was some story of harassing a student who was a loner, after which they all ran off together, laughing uproariously through the stairwell.

I stared at her, appalled. "You were a bully in school; I would have avoided you," I said.

So that was where I recognized her personality type from: the school bully. I had been trying to place it for months, but this simple fact had eluded me. It was a relief to have the question answered, but also alarming; now I would have to be tense around her. There was no doubt in my mind that another assault of some sort was imminent.

All through high school I had wondered about bullies, particularly what their parents were like. Now I had an answer: a monster parent and an easygoing, sweet one who did not enforce any particular demands about good behavior or self-discipline. Of course, there could be other personality types with bullies for children, but I had just learned about one scenario.

After an awkward pause during which I simply went back to my room to organize some now-forgotten detail, the conversation turned to other things, and eventually the evening drew to a close, leaving me home alone with Bryn once more.

He would be sleeping for the next two nights in his Lazy Boy chair with a view of a large empty space, confronted with a row of wooden chairs but no audience in them. It was like one was expected to troop in and sit down expectantly in front of him…creepy.

I moved the chairs back, settling them into less confrontational stances.

The room echoed now with every sound. It felt eerie and ominous.

That stupid hospital bed couldn't arrive soon enough, I thought to myself.

We tuned our televisions in to some soothing and distracting movies.

With Bryn's leg swollen and him unable to go out much, Cassie began to visit regularly. She came every Thursday in the morning, and stayed until about noon. Then she made the long drive, over two hours, north back to Goshen. She had to get back because Chip had vertigo; she didn't know anyone near them who could check on him or sit with him.

I left them to it for as much as they wanted; she had a key and could let herself in. I would greet her when I got up. She was always cheerful and happy to see me. The only bad feature was the smoking; she claimed that she was only having natural tobacco made by Native Americans, but it still made a bad smell. She always dumped her own ashes, and she brought Bryn a fancy cappuccino from Rafaella's on every visit.

On one visit, she borrowed my nail-grooming kit to cut Bryn's toenails for him, washing them carefully before and after the fact. I didn't expect to interact with her in such a short time, but she and Bryn would always call out to me to come in and chat for a little bit at the end.

That week would be a busy one. Hilda's 16th birthday was on Thursday, the 23rd, and I had my gift ready for her, and wrapped. Bryn's was coming soon, and would have to be wrapped as well. The last of his papers were to be dealt with that week. Cassie had encouraged us to go ahead with that and get the place looking as devoid of junk as possible so that Bryn would have no extra decisions sitting around for anyone else to make later on.

So we were at the point of contemplating "later on" now. Terrific.

On another visit, Cassie also tried to clear up some more clutter in Bryn's room, including a pile of winter throw blankets. There was just one problem with that: the little pile served as a cushion for Nikita's ring pillow bed. Cat beds don't have much comfort on the bottoms, and the poor cat suddenly took on an expression that suggested that she felt ill-used and mistreated. She was utterly silent about it, and I sympathized with her.

I pointed this out to Bryn about a half-hour after Cassie had left, and he said to give the cat back her pile of blankets. They were still in the apartment, out in the front hall, waiting to go. I put them back under the cat's bed, and she instantly settled into it, purring. "That wasn't fair," Bryn said. "Don't worry about it; I'll tell Cassie it was too much clearing out."

He was spending a lot of time with that cat now, and the cat seemed to know that he was getting worse and worse; she slept on his footrest with him a lot, and stayed close, deliberately falling asleep in his field of view. That meant on his footrest or on the ring pillow.

The next time Cassie visited, I asked how Louis, her horse was. "Oh, he's fine," she said.

I told her I had a funny horse story for her. She and Bryn perked up and looked at me.

The Slamming Door

A long time ago, when I was a kid, my father had had an assortment of carpentry machines in our basement. They generated a lot of sawdust, which he disposed of periodically by bringing it all in large bags to a horse farm. When he got there, the woman in charge told him to watch out for a particular horse. "He bites," she warned him.

Okay. He started unloading the sawdust, keeping an eye on the wayward animal.

Sure enough, suddenly a menacing equine face invaded his personal space.

Without missing a beat, my father turned around to face the horse, opened his mouth wide to show it his own teeth, and with a giant step toward the animal, chomped his mouth shut.

The horse widened his eyes and backed up fast, hitting the back wall of his stall with a resounding crash. The woman in charge cracked up; she loved it.

So did Bryn and Cassie. "I've never heard of that approach," she said. "That's great."

The next day, it was time to finish up Bryn's papers. That meant getting rid of everything so that it would not be available to read after his death. The Bess Truman anecdote was about to be played out in Bryn's apartment, but with the recycle bin rather than with a fireplace. That was sufficient. I asked him what was to be saved, if anything, and he said anything that Cassie had given him. Okay…ready to proceed.

It had been quite a while, it seemed to me, since I had done the estate papers. Perhaps a few weeks, but I wasn't sure. Now I was just outright disposing of the recreational papers in their entirety. I spent Tuesday afternoon on that, filling 2 huge, clear recycling bags, only to decide that they were too heavy and full to lift, and dividing the contents into yet more bags, for a total of 4. I put them in the hallway by the small round table in front of the boxes of Berta's stuff from the futon and Dionne's easel.

But I had to get them out of here before Berta saw them. She would have a fit if she knew about this. It was Hilda's job to haul stuff away, and Berta's last outburst was only a few days ago. I sent an e-mail to Hilda and her parents asking for help and explaining why it was urgent:

Hi! Got a special request...

Tuesday, July 21, 2009 7:42 PM

Hi Hilda! Hi Elah! Hi Rudy!

Moving Furniture – Berta Freaks Out

I've got a special request: would it be possible to - either this evening or sometime tomorrow before Berta might possibly arrive and see all this - take away 4 bags of paper to be recycled?

I have gone through all of Bryn stuff at his, Albert's, and even Berta's requests.

I did it the way I was requested to.

The reason for this feeling of urgency should be unfortunately and abundantly clear after Berta freaked out on Saturday...she explained it herself: she can't face this.

That's why I did the papers.

One look and I'm afraid she'll make another scene, crying and saying she can't take it.

I hate this too - but it's happening because life doesn't give a shit how we feel.

So...any chance of removal?

Let me know - thanks.

Clarisse.

Sending it to all of them seemed like the best strategy; one of them was bound to get the message in time to get rid of the bags before Berta came back from work.

Meanwhile, Albert arrived, and I told him what I had just done, and why. He approved. Whatever his brother wanted was fine, as was whatever prevented another screaming episode.

Amazingly, Elah and Hilda appeared just minutes later and removed all 4 bags together; apparently they didn't want another episode of Berta sobbing and kicking back shots of hard liquor in their kitchen any time soon either. I thanked them both profusely.

They looked sober and quiet, nodded, and disappeared with the bags.

Just 10 minutes later, Berta came walking in, calmly tossed her keys and purse down onto a wooden chair, and joined us all in the bedroom.

The Slamming Door

The hospital bed was due the next day. Albert turned to me as she ducked into the bathroom and whispered to me, "Just in time."

That was for sure. But Berta wasn't feeling that great, and she didn't even notice that the papers were gone. She had thrown up at work, right into her desk. Was she okay? Yes, nothing contagious, she assured us, she just wasn't very hungry.

That was a new wrinkle, but we didn't worry about it.

Later that evening, a CD got stuck in Bryn's Bose player/radio, one with classical music from the stack he had. Albert had given him that machine. As if it were teasing us, the CD kept coming out only slightly, not far enough to grab. Damnit, I thought, I have to keep all Bryn's entertainment options open to him! Unplugging it, I said I had an idea for fixing it and carried out to my desk in the living room.

I looked it over and realized that I could just unscrew everything, so I got the necessary tool and did so. Then I plugged it in out there, turned it on, and snatched the CD when the machine came to life. I threw it in the recycle bin, hoping that the CD and not the machine was to blame, and then used the screwdriver again. Fixed!

Triumphantly, I brought it back into Bryn's room, put it in its usual spot, and plugged it back in. "Where's the bad CD?" Bryn asked me. "In the recycle bin, so this can't happen to anyone else," I replied. He nodded like I had done exactly what he wanted.

The hospital bed came the next day, and the day after that, the new sheets from Bed, Bath & Beyond. I put them on it. At last everything was organized, but Bryn couldn't stay in it. Albert tried sitting with him a couple of afternoons and timing him for periods of fifteen minutes, but it did no good. Bryn went back to his chair like it was the most inviting spot in the world.

We knew that Nurse Eve had just been doing her job, but what worked for most patients didn't help Bryn. The Ground Zero of his bone cancer made lying down a misery, but sitting was comfortable for him. No one pushed him to use the hospital bed after that, and it just sat there, taking up space in his room.

With the letters and cards gone, I saw that Bryn needed an up-to-date address book.

He showed me what he had: a small, dark-blue, hardcover book full of handwritten entries, many of which were crossed out, plus another book with the same shortcoming, plus a plethora of little bits of paper, mostly the return addresses torn off of envelopes and stuffed into the pages, along with whole envelopes stuffed in as well.

The system was a mess; making sense of any of it promised to be a horrendous, fussy job.

Moving Furniture – Berta Freaks Out

In short, it was just what I was looking for to pass the hours as I watched Bryn get worse and worse, unable to do much for him aside from serve Ensure drinks and mix the vile-tasting, powdery contents of some green-and-white capsules into little dishes of applesauce.

Getting those open had proved to be easy enough; just twist and they opened. But one afternoon Albert and Alissa tried it and got really worked up over the task. The stupid pills just wouldn't open, so they called me in to show them how. So easy it's hard, I said, pouring the stuff into the applesauce and stirring. We all laughed.

Other than that, Bryn was pretty much chair-ridden and I was surreptitiously watching him from the computer table, and I had lost interest in reading and watching movies. I was too distracted, anxious and depressed. No more reading history and literature and art and chatting with him about it, passing the books back and forth.

So I decided to do his address book over as a Word file, which I called Contacts with his name at the start of the title. It was just like my own, but with the data that he needed in it.

It took me a few days, and Walden saw me working on it. "You're always busy," he remarked, one of several times that he did so. It was true; I was determined to be busy rather than spacing out, thinking about the present and future.

I made the new Word file, copy-pasted my own contacts into it for the format, and started cutting my stuff out, leaving only the contacts that we had in common. My own file had a large, graceful letter at the top of each page with a section break between each letter of the alphabet, and I wanted to carry this over to Bryn's contacts without having to recreate that system in this new file. It was more efficient than starting from the very beginning; I may have wanted a project to work on, but I don't believe in deliberately making it take longer than necessary.

After the initial set-up, I started typing it all in: name, address, various phone numbers, and e-mail addresses. Some people had more than one of everything but their names, and for couples with different last names, I listed them twice. One woman was known only by her nickname, and Bryn didn't know any other, so in that went under the nickname.

Finally, after Bryn had checked things over, I made a beautiful cover sheet with that same graceful font, and printed up two copies, one for him and one for Albert. It made sense to give his brother and executor his own copy to take home with him.

Then I went out to the dollar store on 23rd Street to buy clear covers for them. The stacks of paper, printed on both sides, just fit into these, and then the blue gripper part of it slid into place, pinning everything together tightly.

The Slamming Door

Berta checked it over on July 21st and found a couple of errors, which I quickly fixed and printed replacement pages for. There; done. Now I was out of a job again.

I hoped I could find something else to do soon and keep busy.

Meanwhile, I had my four hours each afternoon in which to walk around, and sometimes there were no errands. That left me free to enjoy things like The Chocolate Bar with its spicy hot chocolate drink, or to browse a bookstore, or to see the shops on Broadway. All of these things were good motivators for going for a walk in the sunshine and getting some exercise.

One afternoon, I was walking back down 8th Avenue toward home, which was a change from my usual routine, when I saw Aunt Summer coming in the opposite direction. I had just passed her apartment building.

She saw that I looked depressed and stressed, and asked how things were going, so I told her: Bryn was getting worse. He couldn't go out anymore, he never slept in his bed anymore because it hurt to lie down, and he was eating a bit less. My voice got shaky as I talked, but my facial expression stayed about the same. I have never liked to see or make

Moving Furniture – Berta Freaks Out

contorted facial expressions when I am upset; I always hide my face if I feel the need to really sob.

The Slamming Door

Aunt Summer was sympathetic and pleasant, but I just didn't feel much of a connection with her. She was financially solvent, she had her own apartment, she wasn't an Aspie, she was divorced and I was married, and lived alone. I never wanted to be stuck living alone, but was even less willing to live with another woman. We women like to be the bosses of our homes, so that we each need our own space. Aunt Summer and I were too different from one another, and she was more interested in Vianne and Alena, it seemed to me.

After a couple of minutes, we said our good-byes.

July 21st was a Tuesday, and my own father's birthday.

But I was mad at him; his irascible behavior had led to Damon's clumsy note to my mother, the one that attempted to distract her from the idea of making my father and the cat move out of the house by saying that he had never liked her, and my mother thus banning my husband from the house. To top it all off, my father had made the phone call about that to me.

What a mess; I didn't want to go home after Bryn died. I felt as though I had nowhere to go. I kept muttering to myself like a crazy person: "I want to go home...there isn't one."

There really wasn't – not with Damon, not at my own house (I still thought of my parents' place as my house, having made it what it was along with them for many years, cat, décor and all), not anywhere. I may not literally have been homeless, but I certainly felt that way. If my husband was effectively homeless, then a part of me was as well. Life sucked.

So I had done something for my father that felt like a duty: I had found a book on environmental architecture at a MoMA store in SoHo and mailed it to him with a card. I didn't even write "I love you" on it – just "Happy Birthday."

He left a nice thank-you message on my cell phone just the same.

Chapter 53

Bombshells and Teddy Bears

On the evening of July 23rd, a Thursday, Bryn informed me that Berta and Matt were coming over to tell him something privately, and that they would need his door closed.

I really thought nothing of it at the time. I sat at the computer and clicked away.

I had suddenly had a lot to coordinate that week. It was Hilda's birthday – her 16th – and Bryn wanted to give her a nice present. Berta had guided me to a website called Hot Topic for my gift to her, which was a beautiful, partially lacy, all black mini dress. The business seemed to deal mostly in Goth styles of everything, and Hilda was clearly changing her style in that direction. Bryn had wanted to give her a bag for her computer, but ended up with a scarf set, also from Hot Topic, after having Hilda e-mail us some possibilities. It was more Goth stuff.

The dress had arrived, but the gift from Bryn was a couple of days late. He wasn't concerned. I was; I like to be ready on the day of any event or occasion. Oh well. I decided not to obsess about it, and just bought wrapping paper and cards and explained the delay to Hilda.

Hilda had been acting oddly lately; maybe she was upset that Bryn was dying, maybe it was something else, but I couldn't read the expression on her face whenever she looked at me. Somehow, we had managed to get Hilda in for a quick visit on the afternoon of the 23rd, to give her the dress and explain about what Bryn was getting for her, and that it hadn't yet arrived. She took the dress politely enough. However, she didn't say how she liked it until we asked.

She was taking a geoscience class, and it had been a big deal for just a few high school students to be accepted to this summer academic program…which Bryn had relentlessly urged her to apply for. At the absolute last minute, she had done so. Seeing as I had taken geoscience in college, I had offered to help with the homework. But Hilda never contacted me about it all summer, and except for asking about it once, as Bryn deteriorated, I forgot about it.

Berta and Matt came over, spent a few serious minutes in Bryn's room, and that was it.

But I had enough to worry about. I was the one who was home alone with Bryn all night, and he was dying at his own pace in his Lazy Boy chair. It was scary to observe, but not yet terrifying, because I knew that he would wake up from his naps. He could no longer really sleep.

The next evening, however, I understood the significance of that secret visit with Bryn behind his closed door, when Berta told me that

The Slamming Door

she was pregnant. She told me last of all, and it may have been meant as an insult, but I really didn't care. I don't like babies, and I don't see why everyone on the planet should have to like them.

She told me as I returned from a few errands to shops nearby, including beer for the evening, snacks, and a spare dog dish for Albert and June's Sheltie. It was a hot and humid evening, and I was just unloading the items into the fridge when she informed me of this cursed event. "Guess what?" "What?" "I'm pregnant."

And because she had joked about the idea of me being pregnant the week before, as I had attempted to describe the compliments of my editing client just in over the phone (and annoyed me with inane interruptions about the idea after I thought that our uproar was all over with) I asked her, "Is this a joke?"

I really had thought that it was a distinct possibility.

Alas, it wasn't, and she said so. I took this in for a split second, then said, "That's terrible." And with that I headed into the living room to relax, pausing to enter the data from the receipts and to give Albert the new dog dish.

Unbelievable, I thought; she's not married, so she figures that this will achieve that, and she's probably right. She's using the kid to get herself married, which can't possibly work long-term. After realizing that, I considered it some more: Matt put up with Berta's abusive behavior towards him now, but I couldn't imagine that he would forever, baby or no baby. What a terrible, rotten, selfish thing to do to a child, to use it to get oneself married, I found myself thinking.

As I mulled this revelation over, I was sure that this had been a premeditated pregnancy. Matt had been surprised by the news that he was going to be a father, so he had not known what was in the works until it was a fait accompli.

Berta had told me back in September that she was on birth control pills, so this pregnancy was obviously premeditated, because she would have had to stop taking them in order to get pregnant. Judging from her erratic, volatile behavior of late, she most likely had gone off her anti-depressant and anti-anxiety pills as well. I wondered when she had stopped the other pills; they have half-lives that last months with birth control pills and over two weeks for the others.

Yet she had continued to drink, perhaps because she wasn't yet certain that she was pregnant. She had just found out that very week that she was definitely pregnant, but she had no doubt suspected it when she had had that shot of Jack Daniels over the weekend to calm down.

Would this kid even be healthy? Or would she have multiple health problems? That was why Matt had not wanted to reproduce or get married all along. The kid could have a touch of fetal alcohol syndrome from the booze, Type 1 diabetes due to Berta's obesity, and what about Berta coming down with Type 2 diabetes while pregnant? These seemed like realistic concerns.

And people called me selfish for not liking babies or wanting any! Incredible. I really think that I have the better attitude. My selfishness doesn't hurt anyone else, and leaves me happy with my own choices. I'm not abusive to my husband, and we both love cats as our children. We don't inflict existence on anyone; most people want kids and don't care that earning a living and getting an education will be like climbing Mount Everest. I just don't get it…

It just didn't seem right to risk the kid's health in order to have it, and in order to guarantee getting oneself married. But Berta seemed to have realized that she had no other option if she wanted to get married, and she didn't care who she hurt to accomplish that. How despicable. It was marriage by entrapment.

I had told Albert that I thought that Berta had deliberately gotten pregnant so that Matt would marry her. "Berta wouldn't do that," he said, almost immediately. I disagreed; the kid was a mere pawn to her. But then, Berta had said that her uncle lived in a state of denial.

Soon after that, Dionne had commented about the pregnancy, wondering how the baby could possibly be healthy. "Berta could get Type 2 diabetes from this pregnancy," I told her, "and the baby could be born with Type 1 diabetes, which is childhood diabetes; that's worse."

Dionne was headed down the stairs when I said this; she paused to gawk at me, upset.

And then there was the matter of this news being a cruel tease to Bryn. He loved little girls, and I had the strangest inkling that this baby would turn out female. (Months later, it turned out that I had guessed right.)

But Bryn was obviously dying at what was now a speed that one could gauge. We might not have been able to guess his precise death date, but the essential point was blatantly obvious: he would not live long enough to meet his granddaughter.

What an obnoxious, selfish tease. He would know what he was missing.

Damn Berta.

Any wedding – not that one was being planned, at City Hall or otherwise – would be missed by him, the arrival of his grandchild would be missed, he would not find out her name or birthday, and he would be well aware of all of those facts.

And to think that just the day before I had been sitting at the computer working, with Alissa and Walden and Albert in the room, when I heard a baby yowling annoyingly through the open window! I had said

The Slamming Door

quietly, "Shut up, baby." This elicited sounds of mild outrage from the audience. I told them I didn't care, I hated that sound and so did Damon, so they left me alone.

The relatives were pretty much used to me now.

I just hoped that Alissa wouldn't also decide to reproduce. I wanted some childless female relatives to hang out with. At some point later that week, she actually lamented that she was probably too old to have kids, and that it was too late for her.

With that, I brought up something that I had seen on television lately. It was on several times. It was a biopic tale of the author Sylvia Plath, titled *Sylvia*. I had known that she was an author whose work was on college English course syllabi, and that she had killed herself by sticking her head into a gas oven. Beyond realizing that she had to have been terribly depressed to have done such a thing, I hadn't given it much more thought until this movie came on.

In it, Plath had married another author and had a baby daughter. She continued to write – or try to – but the kid kept interrupting, screaming and crying for attention. She couldn't take it. Her husband didn't understand. So…well, you know the rest.

I told Alissa that she would be utterly miserable, unable to write with a kid.

Alissa listened gravely, nodded, and left it at that.

I doubt that I made much of an impression on her. People just want what they want.

Reproduction is the ultimate selfish act – inflicting life, which is just one big problem, on someone else and expecting and requiring them to be grateful for it – so unreasonable. The planet was overpopulated already, and it wasn't fair to the next generation to just have more kids without a thought for their quality of life just because, damnit, the parents wanted babies.

I did not see what there was to celebrate.

And it was backwards; the parents-to-be weren't married yet, which was a disadvantage for their imminent offspring. I am not some old-fashioned prig who disapproves of premarital sex. What I do disapprove of is a premarital pregnancy or birth. It puts the child, who had no say in the matter, at a distinct legal and social disadvantage, and life is hard enough as it is. Married parents are better for children. But there were many more months in which to rectify that.

If a couple is married at any time before the child is actually born, then that child will be born with full inheritance rights from both the mother and the father, and can claim itself to be "legitimate" – a term which I think needs replacing. It is outdated and libelous. Everyone who exists is legitimate in my view – we all count equally because we all start out the same, having had no say in the fact of our very existence.

I told Matt, as I sat glumly at the computer, that I was not thrilled; it wasn't like this announcement was about a wedding. I loved weddings, I told him, but not babies. It annoyed me that everyone would expect and require that I be delighted over this.

He said that he would expect it and require it anyway, whereupon I said that I wouldn't be cooperating with that. He just sat there, offering no particular response, which came as no great surprise. Undeterred, I went on to add that it was a distinctly unfair situation for the baby, to have unmarried parents, and proceeded to explain that a marriage that took place at any time before her birth would solve that problem. It seemed like the least I could do for the baby, and to help Berta now that the deed was done and there was clearly no going back.

Matt listened to me gravely, and I knew that he was paying attention. (The marriage took place sometime during the next winter, thus solving the baby's potential problem. I guess my anti-social, lawyerly comments weren't a mistake. I'll never regret them.) I never feel any guilt for not responding as social etiquette dictates. What would bother me would be keeping quiet and not voicing my true opinion, especially when an innocent party is part of the equation.

A little while later – maybe it was over the weekend, when Matt wasn't in the apartment – Berta was in my room. I asked her, no doubt sounding incredulous and like I wasn't pleased, "Are you really going to have this baby?"

"Yes. I love Matt, so I will."

Interesting if questionable response; I told her what I had said to Matt about newborns' legal rights depending the marital status of their parents, adding that I had done my best for her to persuade Matt to marry her.

She definitely heard me, but made no particular response.

She knew I didn't like babies. I had said so the week before when she had teased me.

That teasing made diabolical sense now.

Often, when people say something that seems to have nothing to do with the current circumstances, what they are really doing is subtly hinting about their own situation. It was clear that Berta had been doing that the week before. That was another reason why I was so sure that she had been drinking hard liquor while fully cognizant of her own pregnancy.

She stopped once the announcement was made, and I'm sure she didn't drink another drop until Ginger was born, but she had partied on

The Slamming Door

her 40th birthday with beer and who knew what other alcoholic drinks at the bar after the restaurant party.

She had to have suspected that she was pregnant before it was confirmed.

And I wondered, was she expecting, or even just hoping, that I might babysit, and change shitty diapers, and put up with it shrieking? I had just confirmed that I would never do that when I had responded to the news with the words "That's terrible."

Suddenly I found myself remembering that odd, ominous conversation that we had had over dinner the night before Thanksgiving, in which Berta had told me that she was definitely expecting something from me in return when her father's illness was over.

Add to that her offers to have me live in the Long Island house with the cat and her and Matt rather than go back to Connecticut, and it all made a horrific sense to me now.

She had thought she could get me to take care of her baby while she went to work.

Never; I have never changed a diaper in my life, and have always sworn that I never will. Plus I couldn't stand to live in a house with the sound of a baby crying in it. Sleep deprivation, inanity, and stench. If you don't enjoy babies, that's all there is. I was so angry.

Feeling angry whenever I hear of another impending birth has always been the way with me. The planet is grossly overpopulated, there's no justification for adding more, and wanting a child does not constitute a reason to do so. Add to that the fact that I have never liked babies, and I can't feel any other way. I like a romantic life of a married couple with no baby to scream and break the mood. That, and I can't stand the way that people act around babies and little kids: stupid. As if the child is stupid, even though we all know it's not…I used to glare at adults who spoke to me in such insipid tones. This is a rant, but I don't care. It's how I really feel.

I was so glad I had married a man who agreed with me on each and every one of those points. No way would I react the way that society wanted me to react to this news. Not only did I flatly refuse to do so, I just couldn't bring myself to do it.

Bryn heard me crying quietly the next afternoon, and called me into his room. "What's the matter?" he asked me, as I came in flopped onto his unwanted hospital bed.

I told him that it was Berta's pregnancy, and that I felt that our friendship was over because of it. My feelings intrigued me, because my best friend from college, Brandie, had been pregnant once, and then adopted a baby girl from Guatemala, yet we were still best friends. But

Bombshells and Teddy Bears

Brandie had gotten married first, and she knew how I felt about babies, but accepted me as I am.

The problem was rooted in the means to the end, I realized; I had lost all respect for Berta, and was too disgusted. I didn't believe that I could keep up any pretenses with her about this pregnancy. I disapproved, I hated babies, and I didn't like this.

Bryn looked sadly at me and asked, "Are you sure about that?"

I nodded sadly back and said yes. He didn't push me to change my attitude. No wonder I loved and admired him so much. He just accepted me as I was. He even liked me.

When I calmed down, which didn't take too much effort as I wasn't wildly worked up, I made up my mind about something: I would get Berta a Teddy bear at the F.A.O. Schwarz store in the next few days. It was the only socially acceptable response to all of this that I felt capable of, and it was really a gift for the baby anyway.

I told no one of my intention; I simply waited for an opportunity to go there and shop.

The chance to do so came on Tuesday, when Bryn's friend Kandi Kramer, an art teacher at a Manhattan middle school, came over to sit with him for the afternoon. I got their consent to go out for hours on end and get a lot of errands done. (Wilson was there, but he left at 6 o'clock, and I wanted to make sure that I wouldn't need to rush back.)

So I left Bryn and Kandi that afternoon, seeing them settled with whatever drinks they wanted and Bryn in his chair, and headed uptown. It was an awkward situation for Bryn. He was an intelligent adult who couldn't be left home alone for a moment any more. I persisted in calling it Bryn-sitting whenever it had to be labeled, and avoided the necessity as much as possible. Aging and dying can be seriously and decidedly undignified.

It was going to be nice to wander around F.A.O. Schwarz for a while and forget my problems. The store still had the giant piano keys on the upper floor from the movie *Big*, and it was next to several shelves of Teddy bears. There were more stuffed animals on the ground floor, but those were a jungle – literally. Animals from all over the world were represented downstairs, plus a few dragons. Beautiful life-size ones guarded the escalator. Up I went, staring.

I took a while mulling over my options, picking up Teddy bear after Teddy bear, first thinking that one and then another was the right one, and comparing softness and cuteness, but finally I chose one that was a light honey color with a little bow tie and a music box in its butt. I picked that one because I had had a blue Teddy bear with a music box in his butt when I was little, and he had been my favorite. I still have him somewhere, saved carefully.

The Slamming Door

The store didn't offer gift-wrap, which seemed odd for such a famous place, but they did give me a little bit of red tissue paper, so I decided to just go with that. As I got onto the escalator to go back down, Bryn called me on his cell phone. Kandi wanted to go home.

I told him I was just about to leave, and would come right home, which I did by cab. When I arrived, Kandi was satisfied, and I thanked her for staying. Kandi left after admiring the Teddy bear, which I then rushed to set up nicely. I just wanted to settle it into the bag with the red tissue paper pouffed nicely over it so that it would look like a casually wrapped gift. It looked good; the F.A.O. Schwarz bag was red and glossy.

Berta arrived a short while later, with her hair tied up in a bun due to the hot, humid weather. It was a sunny evening, and she was in a good mood – probably due to the success of her pregnancy coup with Matt. She kept going on and on about how he had called her at work several times, asking if she was sitting down. "It's so cool that he's into this," she said happily. And why not? She had tricked him and gotten what she wanted. No doubt the next phase of her plan was to quit the job that hated so much and be a housewife.

I made no reply to that comment. I had done my bit, attempting to induce him to marry her before the unfortunate child was born. More negative thoughts about this situation had since occurred to me: the baby would not be given a college education, which would be nothing less than a regression in circumstances for a member of her family.

Bryn and Albert had been given college educations and come out without loans. Berta, Dionne and Alissa had been given the same. All that any of them had had to do to hold up their end of the bargain was study and graduate on time. Having no loans from one's college education is the most wonderful advantage a family can offer its children, especially when one follows the news of soaring tuition and other costs associated with a bachelor's degree, followed by loans that can easily reach at least one hundred thousand dollars…or more.

I'm not making this up. *The New York Times* and *U.S. News & World Report* have thoroughly documented this trend, which is fueled in significant part by sports. Colleges – including my alma mater, I'm sorry to say – pour tons of money into sports facilities in order to have a distraction for their students. I hate team sports, crowds, and noise, yet if I were in college today my tuition costs would be inflated to support them. It just makes an education at a private (or even a public) institution unaffordable now.

Rich donors don't help with this either. They want to immortalize themselves with a football field, so they just donate them, get their pictures in the alumni publications, grinning from ear to ear, and then the college is stuck with the maintenance costs, absorbed by the students in higher tuition payments whether they like sports or not.

Add to that the problem presented by inflation in general, and you have a recipe for a large percentage of the next generation to miss out on college altogether. As it was, we all wondered how Hilda was going to get a bachelor's degree. Her wealthy boyfriend was looking at private colleges for a nursing degree, and she wanted to go with him, but the costs were like a pie in the sky to her family, who couldn't possibly help her.

Berta's unfortunate kid was going to have to borrow money, and no student could borrow the entire cost. It wasn't not permitted anymore because the bills were just too high for any guarantor to realistically expect one person to ever pay off all of the loans on their own, at least when they result from a mere bachelor's degree program.

So I didn't see how Berta's baby was going to get a college education either, which would be an unacceptable step down for a member of her family. I held out a vague hope that her baby would be more serious than her mother and thus study her way through in precisely four years, and that Matt would somehow be able to help her through, but that was just a big unknown right now…and community college is more like high school than college.

Berta sat down heavily on the hospital bed and started chatting with us.

I have no recollection of what she was saying. That happens a lot when I am about to bring out a gift for someone. The anticipation keeps me focused on the fun of presenting something nice to the person. I enjoy giving people things now more than getting them, so I guess that even Aspies can grow up, despite all the disparaging remarks to the contrary.

Not able to stand the suspense, I got the bag and brought it into Bryn's room. Berta noticed it at once, of course. I carried it right over to her and she took it with her customary glee, pulling out the Teddy bear and exclaiming how cute it was, and posing for a photo with it.

"It's so cute I might not give it to the baby!" she squealed.

I stared at her, astonished but keeping my facial expression as neutral as possible. Only my eyes widened perceptibly. This person was going to be a parent? It was then that I took back what I had thought the week before, when Matt had asked me – on her behalf – if I thought she was stupid. After all that I had discovered this week about her, her decisions, choices and actions, it added up to the realization that she was an idiot and that I had been…polite that day.

Chapter 54

That Son-in-Law

I had never liked The Hornsby. I just thought that he seemed entirely too selfish to be married. He also had an air of entitlement about him that grated on me.

The Hornsby owned the brownstone house in Brooklyn with no mortgage, it had cost something like $10 million, and he treated his wife like a guest in it. Well – that was close enough. The computer was his, the ranch house in Wyoming was his, and he wouldn't get a credit card for Dionne.

Albert had told me about overhearing a conversation between them. Dionne had found out that I had a credit card, not that it was a state secret. So she asked her husband, "When can I get a credit card?" to which he had replied, "When you get a job."

The Hornsby was independently wealthy and had never held a job himself, yet he had the nerve to tell his wife – as if she were a mere guest rather than his wife – to get one in order to have any extra money. How odd; didn't married people share their finances?

Apparently this married person didn't do that. When I had organized the estate papers, I had come across a document that intrigued me: it was a pre-nuptial contract between Dionne and The Hornsby, paid for by Bryn. Without reading it through – not my business to know what was in it! – I had saved it with the legal papers in its drawer.

But its mere existence had gotten me thinking; if they had one, and we all knew that she had no money to speak of while he had inherited lots and never held a job in his life, then its purpose was no doubt to wall off most of his money against any claim she might make in the event of a divorce. That is always the point of a pre-nuptial agreement.

How depressing; Damon and I had never gotten one. We considered a pre-nup to be a no-confidence vote in the future of the marriage by its participants. Never mind that we had no money when we got married, and still had none; we could get some, and when we did, we would share it and stay together. We didn't need or want a pre-nup. And Damon often encouraged me to enjoy small amounts of our shared money – regardless of who had earned it – for my own fun.

Even though we couldn't afford to live in our own home together, he treated me like a wife. I really felt married, and to my best friend. I still felt emotionally safe with him. He was all mine and loyal to me.

The day after the furniture was moved, The Hornsby called. He wanted to come over and visit Bryn. "Of course!" I heard Bryn say into his cell phone. The Hornsby had just returned from the trip to Europe, a couple of days ahead of Dionne. But he was going right on to Colorado or Wyoming before Dionne got back, so he wouldn't see her, and if he was going to see Bryn, he would have to work it in now.

I had e-mailed him about some paintings and an easel of Dionne's that I had found when cleaning, and one painting was a massive black-and-white roll of a nuclear blast that had been down behind the futon bed. Hoping that he would help get it out of the apartment, I had written to explain that, saying that I was getting the impression that I would be expected to figure out the logistics of packing the whole place up at some point, and was getting anxious about it.

When he arrived, he was dressed like someone you would expect to see hanging out at a beach country club, in white shorts, a white oxford shirt, a straw hat with a dark band on it, saddle shoes and dark socks, and his horrid wrist watch. He walked quietly and even a bit primly, and despite the fact that I knew he was an artist, seeing a man who had chosen his wardrobe with such care – a straight man – creeped me out a bit. It wasn't natural.

I let him in, asked about his trip, and he followed me to the living room. He spoke in his usual low tones, tones that showed no apparent emotion yet grated on me. It was the clueless questions that he asked that made me want to smack him.

"Where's Damon now?"

"In Hungary; he is visiting faculty at Debrecen University."

"Oh. Perhaps you will go and visit him."

"No, I doubt it," I said. "Unlike you, I don't have the money to just go wherever I want whenever I want." His assumption that I might have the ability to just up and visit anyone in a foreign country was extremely irritating.

Utterly oblivious to how he came across – or perhaps just starting to comprehend it – he replied, without looking up from something in the living room, "That's unfortunate."

Elah was there for a moment to check on something with Bryn; perhaps that was why he didn't just go in right away, and hung about over my desk, looking at the old notice from his buffalo-skin art exhibit he had put on in Chelsea. That was where I had met him.

I suggested that he go in and see Bryn. Would he like a drink?

He had the gall to ask for iced tea rather than to ask what the choices were.

I stalked off to the kitchen, livid. I boiled some water, laid out a mug and a raspberry-peach tea bag since I had over 40 of them in a jar, and waited. I was glad it would take a while; that meant that I wouldn't have to go back in there and see him for a few more minutes.

The water boiled and I brewed the tea.

The Slamming Door

I got a glass and filled it with ice, then poured the tea in started stirring vigorously.

Elah came in. She saw what I was doing and I griped about the request, saying that he should have asked what was available.

"Well, you offered," she said.

True; I should have immediately followed the offer with a list of specific options.

She left, and I decided that the tea was presentable after a lot of stirring and adding a bit more ice. I went in with it, and brought up the matter of Dionne's stuff again as he took it.

"I was hoping that you would be able to take it, so that she wouldn't be upset at having to move stuff again," I explained. I was determined to preempt more upsets if I possibly could.

He told me he couldn't take any of today after all, despite what he had written back a few days earlier or said over the phone or whatever or however we had planned it, because he was going somewhere else next to see some friends.

What about the next couple of days, before he left and Dionne got back?

"I don't want to discuss it anymore," he said quietly, sounding a bit dismissive.

Fine. I suddenly couldn't stand to be around him for another second.

Without saying anything, I went into my room, changed into my sandals, grabbed my cell phone and handbag, and quietly left the apartment. I slipped out of the building without meeting anyone I knew. It was a Sunday, another gorgeous sunny afternoon, and the people on the street looked like they were enjoying themselves thoroughly, and their dogs were too.

I sat down on the wooden bench outside Rafaella's and felt awful.

My cell phone rang.

I took it out of my pocket and looked at the screen to see who it was. "Unknown" was the only data that came through, but I answered it out of curiosity.

It was Damon, calling me from Hungary on Skype.

I was so upset that I told him everything that was going on, added a bit more detail from the night before about Berta, and how I had fled from The Hornsby. Then he said, "Clarisse, I know that this is the last thing you need to hear right now, but I'm going back to Kuwait."

I just sat there for a moment.

"Why?" I finally asked.

He wasn't making enough money in Hungary; it was summer and there was no teaching for him to do; Saad was setting up a spa clinic in

Kuwait and would do his immunotherapy treatments on the side there, and share the profits for each one with Damon.

Oh. Saad had sent a plane ticket already; he would leave tomorrow.

Oh. Well, Damon wasn't around anyway. What difference did it make whether he was in Hungary or Kuwait? As long as it wasn't Iraq…

He didn't intend to go there, he assured me, so don't worry.

Would he come back in time for Christmas?

He thought so. We would try to have a nice Christmas together, he said to me.

We talked a bit more, then rang off. Later, when I got the bill, I realized that we had just spent $36 on one call. Not free on my end, which was really our end, with our money; Damon swore never to call my cell phone on Skype from a foreign country again.

More depressed than ever, I wandered off and found myself on 10th Avenue at the 192 Books shop, where I bought a small paperback of essays by American and British expatriates who had lived in Paris.

Determined not to return until the damned Hornsby was gone, I drifted off to Chelsea Pier. I didn't go near the Frying Pan, an outdoor restaurant and rusted out little ship that was permanently docked on the northernmost pier. Bryn had brought me and Damon and Toby there with him on July 4th just four years earlier. Hilda and her mother had walked ahead of us all, and we had hung out with Toby and Hilda while Elah flopped on a sofa that was concealed on the stage where Rudy played the electric guitar in a band and sang old sailor songs.

I went the other way, looked listlessly at the history display of huge photos that covered the wall inside the overhang, and then found a vacant bench.

Bryn called to ask where I was. I told him that I had fled the house, and couldn't stand to be in The Hornsby's presence for another moment. That was okay, he said. I told him I would come right back when I knew that he was gone. That was okay too. Where was I, he asked? I told him, and added that I had just gotten a book of Paris essays.

I told him about the call from Damon, too.

We rang off and I tried to read. It was a good book, but I only read part of the first essay.

After another half hour had passed, I went back and put my stuff away.

Fortunately, I had something much more fun to focus on for the next day, the 27th: my Aunt Johanna Rénard was coming to Manhattan for a couple of days to stay with Auburn and visit with me. I would see them for the whole afternoon and evening, and then Aunt Johanna would

The Slamming Door

spend the rest of the visit with Auburn before going back to Rhode Island.

I was really annoyed and confused by Auburn's behavior that summer. She had one more year of college and had chosen to spend her summer living in Washington Heights with a roommate while working at the Discovery Museum in Times Square. That was all well and good, but why hadn't she been willing to say where she was and let me have her address? I could have sent her birthday gift directly to her, a small Vera Bradley bag with a dark blue owl pattern.

Bryn had told me that she clearly was worried that I would try to visit and disrupt her schedule and plans to be on her own, and said that I shouldn't say a word to her about it. I agreed not to, but it was weird. I had ended up sending Aunt Johanna the Vera Bradley handbag in its box, which she then sent on to Auburn's undisclosed location. It was like the Vice President in hiding after 9/11 all over again, except that it was my twenty-one-year-old cousin.

The next day, I served Bryn his breakfast, ate mine, let Walden in, and took off secure in the knowledge that Albert would arrive by 6 o'clock to sit with Bryn so that I wouldn't need to rush back. He knew about this visit, and we had planned for it. I put the tiny green spoonula that I had gotten at Williams-Sonoma for Aunt Johanna in the back pocket of my own Vera Bradley bag and decided to hail a cab; I didn't want to arrive drenched with sweat.

We were going to see the *Lucy* exhibit where Auburn worked, and then spend some more time together. Aunt Johanna had ridden in on the train. At last I knew what had happened: Auburn had found a place to sublet with a classmate for the summer while the owner traveled, and the two of them took care of her cat for her. Aunt Johanna had driven to Manhattan with what Auburn needed for the summer, then dutifully not told me or my parents where she was.

I arrived and found that Auburn was working in a building that formerly housed the printing operation of *The New York Times*, long since removed to the outskirts of the city when the sheer volume of it all just got too huge for one small (!) building. Historic photos with captions explained this in the hallway by the rest rooms. The place was on West 44th Street, just a block away from 1 Times Square, where the reporters once typed up their stories, now also elsewhere – on 8th Avenue.

I rushed in, confused, looking around for my aunt and cousin, glad to be meeting relatives who were not in-laws and who still liked my husband. They were up on the balcony looking down over the escalator, calling to me and waving. I puffed over to the moving stairs and hopped on, in a rush until I could hop off and greet them.

That Son-in-Law

They hugged me, I hugged them, and I noticed that Auburn was using the new Vera Bradley bag that I had given her. We looked like twins, me with my pink-on-black floral one and her with her night-owls-on-blue. I took out the little green spoonula and handed it to, and just as fast, she passed me a large plastic bag with handles that smelled really good; it had a loaf of her homemade cinnamon raisin bread in it.

I was raised on that bread. My grandmother had made that and white bread from scratch every week, and we ate it every time I was at my grandparents' place. Shoving my face into the bag, I took a long, appreciative whiff.

Aunt Johanna took our picture with each of our cameras by an old printing press photo.

Then it was off to the exhibit. Auburn ushered us in past her friends, exchanging greetings as we went. It was her day off and she had come back to work. Well, I had been there and done the exact same thing. When Auburn was 5 years old, I had taken her and Aunt Johanna on a tour of the Mark Twain House.

We saw the *Lucy* exhibit and the Ethiopian history and culture exhibit, which was sandwiched into the *Lucy* exhibit. Aunt Johanna and I read everything in sight, and the Beatles' song *Lucy in the Sky with Diamonds* played in the last section of it. That had nothing to do with the subject matter, but it was a fun detail.

From there, we walked over to 8th Avenue to eat friend oysters and sushi, and I told them what had been going on, and about how Bryn was doing at that point, which was not so good. They listened while I poured out the whole story of Berta's screaming, and her bombshell of a pregnancy. They didn't tell me that I shouldn't say it when I said that I hated life, that it was just one big problem, and that the planet was overpopulated and reproduction was the ultimate selfish act, meant to satisfy the parent while dumping an often impossible problem on the child just because the parent wanted a child.

I was pretty upset at that point, and it was all hanging out. It felt good to be able to talk.

When I said everything that was on my mind to people I trusted not to judge me, I felt a lot better. I calmed down, and we chatted about other things. Auburn showed me a photograph on her cell phone of the silver-gray tuxedo cat that she and her roommate were taking care of. She said it was friendly, and it looked like a nice pet. Its fur was short, and Auburn said that it felt like suede when they petted it. I thought of Mischa, the cat I had met at Thanksgiving.

We went walking back over to Broadway next, and I led them up past the Ed Sullivan Theater where David Letterman's show was recorded. From there, we continued on up to Columbus Circle and wandered around the Time-Warner mall, pausing to use the rest rooms upstairs, and finally sitting in the Circle itself after dark, talking and watching the fountains spraying the statue. The place was full of people out enjoying the night, just sitting there.

We talked until it was time for me to leave and for Aunt Johanna and Auburn to take the subway to Washington Heights. I walked home;

That Son-in-Law

it was a lovely, warm evening, not too hot or humid, and I wanted the time to myself. Walking felt like a constructive use of energy.

Bryn and Albert greeted me cheerfully when I got back, asked how the visit had gone, and I told them all about it. I also assured Bryn that I hadn't bugged Auburn about her secrecy over the summer, and he was glad to hear it.

Dionne came over the next day, back from her trip, exuberant from her time in Europe with her artist friends. She came into my room after a while and suddenly noticed some purple bruises on my forearms; I had gotten them a couple of days after the bed was brought in, when I noticed that the metal frame under the mattresses wasn't properly connected.

I had lifted everything up, fixed it, and put the mattresses back down without feeling the pressure on my arms. Like my maternal grandmother, I was strong despite minimal exercise. Dionne stared with an odd expression on her face, an appalled mixture of disbelief and confusion. I assured her that it didn't hurt and hadn't noticed the bruise until she pointed it out.

She was wearing a beautiful blouse with blue jeans. She was tall and thin and long-waisted, and the filmy white blouse looked incredible on her. It was part lace and part linen, criss-crossing with ribbons and lace here and there. When I asked her where she had gotten it, she said, playing with the accent as usual, "Zara!" She was referring to a store with multiple locations on 5th Avenue. I took a startling photograph of her with Bryn. They both grinned like they were happy, with Dionne as tall and thin as he was, but Bryn looked shocking next to her – skin and bones with a big smile and glasses.

The next afternoon, I went out and found it on the sale rack, but I am short-waisted, so I found a slightly different style of white linen blouse for $19.99 and ended up wearing it often. Berta saw it, found out where I got it and for how much, and said, "That's gorgeous."

Sometime after all that trouble with the furniture and moving things had blown over, I was about to go out on yet another shopping errand when I paused with my list to read it to Bryn and make sure that we had both thought of everything that might possibly belong on it.

"Is there anything else that I should buy while I'm out?" I asked, when the litany had been read in its entirety.

"Yes, a new body," he said from his chair in the corner.

The Slamming Door

For once, his attempt to teach me how to tease and joke paid off. "Okay, I'll get you one of those at T.J. Maxx. They've got a bin of them for $4.95 each," I said, without missing a beat.

Bryn immediately burst out in his silent laugh, shaking a bit with mirth. It was his signature laugh, in which he looked up at the ceiling dramatically with his mouth wide open.

I couldn't believe it; I had amused him. That was exactly the kind of joke that I was usually afraid to make, convinced that it would offend someone in his situation. Instead, he had enjoyed making light of his situation.

Pleased that he was laughing, I said I'd see him later with the stuff on the list and left.

Chapter 55

Anxiety and Cleaning

There was almost no escape or respite from the anxiety that I now felt almost all of the time. Lately, the only way I could take my mind off of it when I was at home was through cleaning, but I was running out of things to clean, organize, sort or otherwise improve.

The legal and estate papers were in perfect order. The recreational papers were gone; Bryn didn't need to worry about anyone reading his deepest, innermost thoughts or other private business after he was dead and gone.

That left the closets, which included the filthy, disorganized upper shelves in my room, and the front hall closet, which looked like an avalanche of boxes and phone books if the door were opened. Fortunately, none of it ever moved at all when that was done.

My closet like a good project, and I had always been annoyed by the falling dust and plaster landing on my clean clothes, and I wanted to be able to use the upper shelves. I lived in that room, and my boxes were stacked in corners. I decided to start with those upper shelves. It was only part of the closet, so it looked like a small job. Better to do the smaller tasks first, get them out of the way, and then tackle the larger ones. It was something to do rather than just watch Bryn expire in his chair.

Albert had criticized the clutter that was taking up space outside of the closet. This, from a man whose office room at home was an utter and complete disaster, but I had agreed; some of the boxes blocked the fire escape, and shifting them around hadn't helped much. With the closet cleaned and emptied of the old junk on those shelves, I could solve both problems.

Lately, Bryn wasn't interested in his coffee or tea, or his pipe. That was an ominous though not at all surprising omen of things to come. "I've lost my taste for it," Bryn told me when I asked about that.

When I kept busy, I forgot my problems. If I could have done some writing, I would have. But I couldn't focus. My options were stupid computer games, movies, or cleaning. Berta had watched me one evening playing Poppit, and asked me to let her play. But that would put tokens on my account, so I had offered to set a new one up just for her. It was free, so she agreed. When it was done, she wanted to create her cartoon avatar, but I told her she had to play and rack up tokens in order to qualify for that. Of course, if you pay, you don't have to wait, but that would be a waste of money, and it wasn't a necessity, so I had waited.

It took me a while to decide to clean the closet.

The Slamming Door

There were more important things do, such as the routine, dreary business of emptying the bitter-tasting contents of those large capsules, too big for Bryn to swallow, into a dish of applesauce for him each night. I felt angry on his behalf that he had to endure that sensation over and over again but die anyway. Such things kept me from focusing on ordinary tasks like cleaning the closet because they upset me, hence the delay. I wasn't thinking too clearly lately.

I tried to make it more interesting for Bryn by buying different flavors of organic applesauce at Whole Foods. They had apricot, blackberry, cherry and plain applesauce. He gave me the thumbs up for it all when I brought the jars home and showed him. Dionne would approve, I thought: she liked food to be organic. Bryn nodded, and gave me the thumbs up sign.

At one point, Bryn found that he really liked something that I did to potatoes, so I kept making them, usually with salmon, cod or chicken, plus green beans or red and yellow bell peppers. The potatoes were just peeled and sliced, then sautéed in extra-virgin olive oil with salt and pepper. Bryn surprised me by wanting some of everything, and I was quite pleased.

The one mistake I tended to make was to pour the cooking oil over the potatoes, sharing it on each plate. The food was drowning in olive oil, but I felt guilty about just throwing it out. I suppose that was silly, but I was anxious and preoccupied. Berta came back into the kitchen after I served dinner this way, got a spoonula, and carefully poured off the excess. Obviously, her father had asked her to do this. She was polite, though; she didn't say a word about it.

Other nights – at least twice a week that summer as Bryn was chair-ridden – I found myself ordering his favorite meal from Rafaella's for him. It was the vegetarian couscous, and it came with a warm, smooth, strained, tomato-based sauce. It didn't look appetizing to me because of all the green peppers on it – I don't like those. If Albert was hanging out with us for the evening, and he often was, we would insist that he eat some of it.

Albert was on that horrid chemotherapy that Cornell was giving him once a month, so he had lost about half of his hair but evenly all over his head. It was just much thinner, and his face had that awful puffed look that cancer patients get. He was nauseated, but not as badly as Bryn had been, and could keep food down if he took an anti-nausea pill. If he protested about eating dinner, we would say "Oh, take an anti-nausea pill and suck it up!" He would laugh and do it.

We spent a lot of evenings together, just the three of us. Alissa would call to check on us. She was watching her mother, getting their dinner, feeding and walking the dog with June in tow, and wondering when she

Anxiety and Cleaning

might get to do some writing and whether or not her sick father had eaten. Each time she called, I would say hi to her and then tell her, unbidden, what we had given Albert to eat. Then I would hand the phone off to Albert. I was trying to ease her mind about him.

The process of slowly dying of an illness compared with a sudden heart attack or just being shot and bleeding out preoccupied me again. Which was easier? The first way was so slow and agonizing, humiliating, unpleasant, and debilitating. The second way gave one no time to mentally or otherwise prepare. Each way was its own kind of terrifying. Neither offered much control. Why couldn't we all just die of extreme age in our sleep?!

Albert, meanwhile, sat down and talked with me in detail one day about Bryn's plans to go stay in the Bronx at a hospice care facility. It had room service, round-the-clock nursing care, social events for the patients, and a pretty website that we all looked at.

Bryn discussed this with me before, and had said that he wanted me to stay in his apartment while he was at that place, visit him, and maybe also visit the Bronx Zoo and Botanical Gardens on my own. I had bought a spiral-bound map of the 5 boroughs of New York City, got familiar with the area, and promised to bring him whatever reading material struck his fancy each day. That suited him just fine. After that discussion, a couple of months had passed.

But the whole idea seemed scarier the more that I thought about it.

When was he going there? He didn't seem able to go anywhere now. He didn't seem to want to go anywhere, either. He was content in his familiar environment, and I couldn't imagine him ever leaving it. His friends could visit him here, and they kept coming in – from the Henry George School, the Mendelssohn Glee Club, his social work job, and wherever else.

But Albert was talking about keeping me here for another 6 months beyond his brother's death. That was very nice of him, telling me that he could "keep things going for me here" for that amount of time, but I had trouble believing that it would actually work. I guessed, silently, that he was hoping to enable me to stay away from Connecticut, where my parents had banned my husband from the house and where I had no car and no way to go out.

Yes, that was very, very nice of him. But it just didn't seem feasible. Aside from that, the thought of living alone here suddenly seemed ominous. Alone, with too much time on my hands, thinking and being scared. How soon before I would have to pack everything up? I was sure that the family was expecting me to do the work of packing up the entire apartment, and that my reward for doing so would be recriminations for not doing it right. Add to that the facts that I couldn't possibly know how

The Slamming Door

to box up what without asking a million questions and that I feel calm working independently and alone and it seemed like a looming recipe for conflict.

Well…at least I might clean up that filthy closet in my room, the one that rained plaster dust on my stuff whenever the building shook in the lightest of breezes. This was my room while I was there, and all year I had lived in bits and pieces of it, avoiding certain areas only to be told – gradually – to take over this area, that area, and another area. It felt like my space now.

The days began to blur as I did this each night, letting Walden in each afternoon and making the coffee, sitting at the computer, going out in the afternoons when Walden and Albert were over for hours, and finally, late at night, crying silently in front of the computer as I played Word Whomp, Mah Jong Safari and Poppit! on www.pogo.com.

From time to time, I would watch Bryn by getting up to check on him, peering in unobtrusively only to see him either dozing in front of Charlie Rose's talk show or watching *The L Word* or *The No. 1 Ladies' Detective Agency*. After that, he would doze off, and of course there was no more tucking him into bed.

Instead, I was setting him up carefully with his chair in the reclining position and the cat stretched out on it between his legs. Once I had taken my shower, we would get everything neatly into place knowing that a little while after I fell asleep, Bryn would probably get up and go to the bathroom and have to fumble it all back into place on his own. The thought of it was maddening, and no doubt to him as well as to me.

It drove me crazy to think about the fact that I didn't have the energy to wake up over and over again on cue, like a psychic who knew exactly when he needed more help, so that I could put him back into that comfortable position again. Bryn needed more and more from me and I couldn't provide all of it on my own.

One morning, he broke a glass and sat with the pieces nearby, unable to get up for a while. I was asleep, having watched him carefully for most of the night, scared and upset, and finally managed to relax and drift off to sleep. I had no idea about that glass.

When I woke up and checked on him, he told me that Leah had come over to check on him in mid-morning, found him trapped with the broken glass, and cleaned it up. So there it was; I wasn't the perfect caregiver. I had to do it all round the clock, waiting my chance to go out in the afternoons and get whatever we needed, perhaps stroll around the block and chat with a few shop-keepers, and then get back, all in the space of 4 hours. I had trouble falling asleep, and I stayed awake and watched Bryn while the rest of the world slept.

Anxiety and Cleaning

I was scared, tense, thinking about the looming stress and upheaval in the near but inexact future, and unable to calm down and sleep. Drugging myself to manipulate my sleeping times was out of the question; that could make me unresponsive if Bryn were ever in dire distress and needed me to wake up quickly. But I couldn't function without sleep, and I needed more than 6 hours of it each night.

That left the mornings. I told myself that it wouldn't hurt Leah to check on Bryn at those times, and willed myself not to obsess about it or ever apologize for getting my sleep then.

The silence, quiet and routine of decline pressed on and on, and it was scary. This did not surprise me in the least; it was exactly what I had expected. But what was I supposed to do to keep calm? The cleaning project looked more and more appealing. At least it would give me some busy work for a little while, and keep my mind off of my life and the end of Bryn's.

So on a hot Thursday afternoon, July 30th, I cleaned that closet.

Walden was over as usual, and Bryn didn't need much. He had his bath early, shortly after Walden arrived, using the bars on the wall by the tub and his white bench. Walden was now into the groove of washing the tub with Soft Scrub before and after each bath, so I stayed out of it altogether, only checking to lay out clean towels and a washcloth and a fresh set of clothing.

Once Bryn was settled into his chair again, I sat at the computer, spacing out for a few minutes. I hadn't really thought consciously about cleaning the closet on this particular day of all days; it just suddenly came to me as I sat there that I had to get moving and busy.

I was dressed in my old black linen shorts and my new white linen blouse from the sale rack at the Zara store. It was quite comfortable in the mild breeze on this hot day, but as I worked, removing things from the closet, I got a bit hotter. At least my hair was up in its clip. Soon I needed the ladder/step-stool and had it pushed up close to the closet shelves.

Walden watched me at it and commented, "Every time I see you, you are always busy." Huh...I guessed that typing at the computer counted too, but he had seen me doing errands and a little cleaning every day as well.

There was a brief interruption when a delivery of bottled water arrived – Berta had ordered it. I had cleared a spot for it earlier, and the delivery man put it all there, on the floor to the left of the food shelves, next to the garbage and recycling and extra bottles of Ensure.

Walden needed some polite attention that afternoon as usual; he helped Bryn with his bath, and helped him get dressed, but there was still the laying out of clothing and towels and making of coffee to do for him.

The Slamming Door

When someone is in a family's home, doing health care work, it is only polite to pay attention and listen carefully when they have the inevitable questions aimed at the sick person's comfort. Everything has to be done just so.

Earlier that day, Berta had sent me an e-mail with an odd, defensive tone. The purpose of it was to inform me that she had bought a large number of Poland springs individual-sized bottles of water and that they would soon be delivered to Bryn's apartment. She wanted him to drink bottled water only from now on, nothing from the tap.

> *Tomorrow, Friday between 2 and 4 pm, Fresh Direct will be coming by to deliver the following water order. I want my father to drink fresh clean, filtered water and I want a few bottles in the fridge at all times for him so they are ice cold the way he likes it and so we can offer to any guests that come in. I do not want to hear any shit from anyone about these taking up space in the apartment. They can be stored in the hallway if necessary, or on the floor in the living room.*
>
> *When the guy comes to deliver, you do not have to tip him.*
>
> *8 Poland Spring Natural Spring Water (8oz bottles 12pk)*
> *2 Poland Spring Natural Spring Water, Half-Liter Case (0.5 liter bottles, case of 24)*

I had looked at the note, puzzled as to why anyone would give her any "shit" about over this, especially since it was meant as a nice thing for her father and a done deed. When the man with the water had come, I had immediately chilled several bottles and served one to Bryn.

Odd though its tone was, I dismissed it. I was busy, and not just with the closet.

When the delivery guy left, I went back to work on the closet. I got everything out and laid it out neatly at the far end of the living room, under the window, around the rocking chair and painted guitar, and on the right half of the sofa, cleaning each dusty thing as I did so.

Finally, I had empty shelves. They were utterly filthy, not having seen a rag or sponge for a couple of decades at best. No wonder plaster shook down onto my stuff every time a big truck rolled by on the street. It was so dirty in there that I could always hear the fragments falling.

It took several back-and-forth trips to the kitchen with the wet floor sponge, but I cleaned every last bit of filth out. Then it was time to put the boxes of my stuff up there. At last, the closet would have all of my stuff in it, and my stuff would be away from the windows.

Anxiety and Cleaning

The boxes with my things inside looked neat and orderly up on those newly cleaned shelves, and not like clutter, once the deed was done. The task had also helped me to forget my problems and anxieties for a couple of hours.

The stuff that I had removed was clearly not all Berta's, I now realized as I looked it over. It was about evenly divided between her, Maggie and Hilda, with a little bit belonging to Maggie's daughter, I was later told. Not bad for an afternoon's work.

The stuff looked like worthless rubbish, I suddenly realized, but it was someone else's rubbish, so I wasn't about to do anything with it other than clean it and lay it out. There was one framed collection of photographs that was falling apart and missing one or two photos; perhaps Berta would tell me more about it. They were family photos, probably from the 1980s, and I was curious. Right along, I had hoped to hear about the events when family photos had been taken.

I got myself an apricot beer, wanting to chill out and get loopy. I felt oddly stressed out, though I wasn't entirely sure why. I should be feeling relaxed now, but I didn't. I put it down to the disappointment at the job being over with and not knowing what else I could clean next.

The front hall closet maybe? It would be fun to go over the 19th-century family photographs with Bryn and Albert and be able to tell my husband what I had seen and learned of his family history. Perhaps I could even scan them for everyone.

Meanwhile, I started playing Poppit and sipping the apricot beer.

Chapter 56

Berta's Meltdown

It was the evening of July 30th, 2009, a Thursday, when Berta came back to Bryn's place after having coffee with the social worker at a nearby Starbucks. It was shortly after 7:30 p.m.

I was sure that I had just done a very nice favor for Berta. Packing was in the near future, and now she would have the luxury of simply collecting it all with no dust, dirt or plaster and putting it into boxes.

My things now occupied the upper part of the closet: boxes, full of things such as a porcelain Alice in Wonderland sugar bowl and creamer, my black winter hat, and other assorted items. At last none of those things crowded the marble-topped bureau by the window with the fire escape. And I had more room to walk around in. Satisfaction to all, I imagined.

Perhaps now I could settle down and let my thoughts turn to pleasant things that did not induce stress. Another cleaning job was done, a burst of activity over with, and that always felt good. Calmness was what I wanted now, and I wondered why that felt elusive.

Bryn came out as I sat at the computer with my apricot beer, trying to relax. He looked at all of that stuff and seemed a bit worried. I couldn't understand it; it was clean and organized. All memory of any possible objection had gone from my mind as I had cleaned, so desperate was I to escape from the anxiety of his worsening condition. Yet next to me sat the two cardboard boxes that Cassie had packed at his request years earlier, full of Berta's things; they served as a shelf for Bryn's stationery and some books.

All of the items that I had removed from the upper reaches of the closet were neatly laid out to my right on the sofa and in front of it. It was easy to see each thing, too. Easy to sort through, easy to identify what was what and therefore what belonged to whom. What could possibly be objectionable about that?

Berta would be pleased, I thought. When I cleaned the hall closet, we could see the old family photographs, some of which Bryn said dated back to the 19th century. That would be fun.

I thought wrong.

Silly, Aspie me; I don't recognize storms of negative human interaction coming.

Albert had his own key, and he arrived in time to say good-bye to Walden, or maybe even a bit earlier. Considering what came next, it is not surprising that I can't remember that detail. In any case, he was in Bryn's room when the trouble started.

Berta's Meltdown

Berta suddenly arrived, came into the living room, and walked right up to the desk. She didn't look at the sofa and window area right away; Bryn appeared, and we started to ask her how the visit with the social worker had gone. That visit had been postponed for a full week due to some extra work that Berta had had to do at the office the previous Thursday.

She started to reply, and then saw the sofa.

An outraged expression spread across her face, and an imperious tone crept into her voice. "What is this?!" she said rather than asked. "What the *hell* is this?!"

Now I was annoyed. I had worked hard on the cleaning effort and on calming myself all afternoon, and then some more with the apricot beer buzz. She was ruining that effect! I looked at her; she had some nerve reacting this way. In a flat and uncompromising tone, I said, "Don't yell at me, even if you want to."

I had been deadly serious from Day One about not accepting this sort of thing, and it suddenly occurred to me that if she got loud and upsetting, she could set off a fatal heart attack in her father, whom she claimed to be so upset about.

Apparently, she wasn't as upset about his condition as she had claimed, or she wouldn't have started in on this. Completely ignoring what I said, or perhaps in response, she immediately escalated her behavior, yelling about how I should not have touched any of her stuff, and that this apartment was hers, the stuff in it was hers, and no one was to touch any of it.

Never mind that only a quarter of the stuff laid out here seemed to be hers, and that her father, the true and current owner of the rest of the stuff in this apartment was still alive and standing right next to us...and I supposed that I wouldn't be learning about the photographs now.

Bryn had his cane, of course. (He had acquired a walker a long time ago, and we had recently set it up next to his chair, but he persisted in using the cane.) Using the cane and quiet, soothing tones, he edged his outsized daughter toward the front hall, trying to get her to leave.

I followed, not saying anything else. Berta was still screaming like a banshee, and I was trying to avoid heaping any more fuel onto her tirade for now. It was a losing battle. I was shaking internally, which was a rare sensation. It was vaguely familiar, and I tried to recall when I had felt this way in the past. That was difficult; the reason for the sensation continued unabated.

"You fuckin' bitch! Fuck you and your Asperger's! Go back to Connecticut – I hope you and Damon kill yourselves!" Berta shrieked at me from just inside the front door. Wow...in all of the times that I had ever gotten mad at my parents, and they had been quite awful from time

The Slamming Door

to time, I had never, ever, wished them dead. I would never say that to anyone. She was a monster.

Her father was standing close to her, quietly, obviously hoping to get her out quickly. His hopes were not to be answered. He looked really frail, standing there with his hair grown back in as a crew cut, not as long as he had always chosen to keep it, with his dark green flannel shirt on over his tee shirt and shorts, his ace bandage tight around his swollen leg, and his socks and slippers, leaning on his cane. Damn her for getting irate over a cleaning job!

I just looked at her expressionlessly and replied, "I hate you."

Then I turned on my heel and went into my room.

I didn't see Albert; I knew he was in the apartment, but I did not notice him as I went.

I moved quickly because I realized that she was coming back in now, and I hoped that she had been careful as she passed her father not to knock him off balance. What the hell was wrong with this monster, this blob of selfishness, that she would go crazy like this when her supposedly beloved father was near death?!

The screaming continued, but I didn't look back. I went into my room with Albert suddenly hot on my heels, dashing in as I turned to hook the pathetic-looking lock. Would it keep Berta out of here, or would she crash her way in? Fortunately, she stayed out.

This was ridiculous. My stuff had barely spent an hour and three-quarters in its newly cleared space, and I couldn't enjoy it. Apparently, I didn't matter; I was nothing but a damned servant to her, and expected to occupy just a small, cramped portion of what felt like my room but perhaps wasn't. I heard a few more epithets of "fuckin' bitch" uttered at the top of her lungs.

Damn her – she claimed possession and control of so much: her mother's apartment, for which she paid half the rent (perfectly understandable); a storage unit (quite reasonable); a house in Oneonta that her mother owned; Matt's house in Hicksville; and her father's apartment, even though she didn't live in it anymore and he never wanted her to again.

I kept it clean and quiet, was an intellectual companion to him, prepared food and created recipes that he liked, and waited on him very carefully. What a nightmare I must have been to her; she could never hope to do all that or as well as I did. She must have hated my guts for it.

This was the first time that I understood that.

Whatever it was that she was shrieking at me, I just took it as so much noise that merely constituted abuse. The bully in her was all that I heard, and I didn't give a damn why she was yelling, or that she imagined

Berta's Meltdown

that she was in any way justified. The moment she got abusive, I just didn't care how she felt or what her position was. I was done with her – permanently.

However, the fact that I was done with her did not mean that I was ready with an exit.

That was why I felt the way that I felt and cried a bit while barricading myself in my room, and why I began tossing whatever I could into my biggest suitcase. People do things when they get upset. Some people injure others in retaliation, but I'm not stupid. Some people pack and try to flee. I was doing that, which was not my usual M.O. Usually, I turned and figuratively bared my teeth like a cornered but enraged and not surrendering cat, my image animal.

But I was so used to battling difficult males that it was only males who failed to inspire fear and panic in me. Not so with a female bully my own age. This was the bane of my Aspie existence: cluelessness and a lack of a suitable rejoinder in the face of an ordinary, no-talent, angry, jealous, hideous female my age.

I should have recognized this pattern repeating.

But I didn't; I had been away from this scenario for so long that it was almost forgotten.

And why not? Who would knowingly expose themselves to this?

Despite keeping quietly to myself in school until college, where I had found that differences were embraced and respected, I did have some memories of being bullied by girls in my classes. There was a bully in 6th grade, another in 7th grade – both at different schools – and in neither case had I known what to say or do. Older people had helped me in both instances. At one camp, the kids put oil in my hair, and at the other they put popcorn in my bed.

So I had no idea what to do with this next screaming and barely coherent bully…yet I suspected that if a calm, sane advisor had been able to speak to me about this, she or he would have recommended doing what I did: I ran into my room and locked the door.

After Albert had dashed in after me, he sat down on the little blue-and-white floral rocking chair, watching me empty the contents of the lower drawer of my bureau into the big blue suitcase. It all just barely fit. Clearly, packing and fleeing wasn't an option. I would need help, something I had dreaded asking for the entire time I had been here. I was still angry with my parents for their utter unwillingness to make up with my husband. But I had to get out of here.

Albert sat there and pleaded with me not to go as I filled that suitcase while the screaming continued. At some point, it receded into Bryn's room, where it was abruptly muffled as Berta rather loudly shut the door and locked it. They were in there, and he was stuck with her.

The Slamming Door

Was she totally heedless of her father's tachycardia? Why wouldn't she just shut up?!

I pulled out my cell phone and called my mother.

It wasn't what I wanted to do, but I saw no other option.

The simple, logistical fact of the matter was that my parents had a car – two, actually – and could drive down here, collect everything I owned, and take it away. No way was I going to leave it lying around for Berta to lay her sticky fingers on. If she was going to spiral out of control over the cleaning and sorting and minor relocation of her possessions, I would be an idiot to trust her around mine.

I had all of it neatly organized and clean at all times; it just needed to be packed.

My mother answered, fortunately. It was a Thursday evening, but at least she wasn't out at a prostate cancer support group. Come to think of it, this was the last Thursday evening of July; why wasn't she out doing that? Well, I was too freaked out to ask and just glad to be able to get her on the phone so fast while the tantrum raged on.

"Mommy, Berta is screaming her head off," I said breathlessly into the phone. "Can I come back and stay with you? I cleaned a closet in my room and she went nuts!"

"Of course you can come back," my mother replied in soothing tones.

Well, that was a relief. I had actually had doubts, though I now realized that I might have created them in my own mind. What I really wanted was to become financially solvent rather than just live with my parents until they aged and couldn't keep me with them anymore. But now was not the time to put off facing the fact that I had to go back there and depend on them.

It made no difference that I didn't want to go back; I had to get out of here.

Albert asked to talk to mother after a moment or two, by which time she understood what was going on, and that it wasn't over yet. "Please don't take Clarisse away," he wailed to her.

I stared at him, a bit shocked. I knew that I had made myself very, very useful to him, but to be appreciated was another thing entirely. Albert was actually feeling a sense of panic about how he was going to manage his brother's care without me around. Clearly, he was laboring under no delusions about either of his nieces being sufficiently available or able to handle the task.

I don't know whether or not he knew that his brother didn't want either of them.

My mother talked with him for a few minutes, and at last we heard Berta depart.

Berta's Meltdown

When the coast was clear, I opened my door slightly and peered out. Yep, she was really gone. I had the phone back now, and was talking to my mother, giving her a blow-by-blow account of what was happening. She was very interested to know when the uproar was over; I had to continue this call to tell her that.

The freeze in my chest was thawing now, yet I did not remember my own heart murmur. I was too focused on what had just happened, and on Bryn's heart trouble. It all seemed surreal; Berta was too old for this sort of horrendous behavior, wasn't she? And we weren't supposed to have screaming fits around a dying guy, were we? Well, I hadn't screamed.

My mother asked to talk to Bryn, so I went in and found him sitting quietly in his chair and told him that she wanted to talk to him. He took the phone, and I went back to Albert.

The open suitcase was still sitting there.

Somehow, I vaguely recalled my mother having said that if I needed help getting my stuff out of here, she and my father would help me with that. She had added that I could always count on them to help me.

I sat on the edge of my bed for a moment as this important information came back to mind, staring at the open suitcase. Then I put everything back in the drawer, closed the big blue suitcase, and returned it to the closet.

As calm returned, minus, alas, the beer buzz, I remembered having worried to my mother that getting out with all of my things by bus was an impossible task; I had acquired more clothes, more books, more other things, and had my winter things sent here. There was no way was I going to be able to get it all out of here by myself, as much as I hated to admit needing help. Plus, there were those two big cardboard boxes of Grandpa Koren's books that my father should never have shipped here to begin with. He had done in 2005. Everything must now go – back.

Albert watched me put the stuff back – it was a drawer full of socks and underwear. What had I been thinking I would do, leave behind my outer clothing and go home with this suitcase, abandoning my books?! It looked like a moot point now.

Albert talked on and on about how indispensable I was, and that we couldn't have a pregnant woman in here. I looked up at him; he was still on the little rocking chair, the only chair in my room. Then I realized why he was talking about the idea of a pregnant woman in here; some of Berta's rantings had been about taking over, but mostly about wanting me out.

The more either of us contemplated the whole thing, the more ludicrous it seemed. How could a morbidly obese woman who was pregnant and subject to wild mood swings even when not in that

The Slamming Door

condition replace me? My job was complex, required a lot of physical labor – fetching and carrying things around the neighborhood, cleaning, cooking (Berta couldn't cook much), watching Bryn, and making sure that his pill sheet was current.

Albert also commented about how insane her reaction had been; he thought that all of that stuff laid out in the living was nothing but junk. It was, I replied, but it wasn't my junk, so I had left it to be picked through by the owner. That should have been okay, we both thought.

Berta needed enough sleep to keep functioning, which she couldn't possibly have as a caregiver and go to work too. That was another thing; her father couldn't be home alone, and she had to work. No, it would never work; I relaxed. It seemed that I would continue at my post.

A little while later, Bryn called out and I took the phone back. After saying good-bye to my mother, who said nothing remotely chastising or upsetting to me, I rang off.

"You knew that it would upset her," Bryn said later on, meaning Berta.

I swore I hadn't thought of that; I told him was upset and anxious, and had thought that I was doing her a great favor, because all of that stuff was so filthy. "I wanted to use the closet," I added, protesting the unreasonableness of the whole thing.

Bryn wasn't one to pursue a conflict, though. He never was, and now he that was very sick, he needed me as his caregiver. He was even getting dependent on me. I was his staunchest ally in his efforts at keeping comfortable and hiding the outward signs of just how debilitating his illness was. He wanted it hidden from his daughters and almost everyone else, and I was still hard at work enabling that. His clothes looked like they always had, except that he had recently begun to wear shorts, something that he hadn't done since childhood.

He wanted me around still, and I hadn't yelled; I had simply refused to take any abuse.

A few days after the first of Berta's meltdowns, after the bed had been moved, he had been in the kitchen drinking a cup of water and Miralax when he brought the incident up. "You could have held your tongue," he said to me.

"I don't do that for people," I had replied.

He had just looked at me and let it go.

I mean it even now: I will not take or accept abuse.

That doesn't mean that I will shriek and yell in front of a dying person and make something worse, but if someone is abusive to me, I will speak up and defend myself, and tell the unpleasant individual to back off. I may not be all that adept at producing the perfect phrase, but I do know enough not to swear and not to yell.

Berta's Meltdown

Unfortunately, that isn't always enough in life. It should be, but it isn't.

What I still find incomprehensible is indirect behavior and avoiding conflict, or fleeing from it rather than meeting and facing it. Why flee? It will just follow you around. Better to face it and deal with it one way or another, so that it will be resolved. Of course, this is the lawyer in me talking. But Bryn and Albert were different; they were old and sick now, but also with different personalities than mine. Of course they found it far easier to avoid conflict, but I sensed that this was a general character component for them, not merely a part of being old and sick.

I couldn't be like them in this way; it went against my nature.

No wonder I stood apart from my in-laws, as did my husband.

After midnight, when I was quietly alone at the computer again, I e-mailed Damon.

He was in Kuwait, and six hours ahead of us, but I didn't care. I wanted to talk to him NOW and to try to feel better. I wrote a detailed account of everything that had happened. Its subject heading read: "Berta was rotten to me again! CALL ME UP!"

Damon called me.

I forget how long I had to wait, but I took my shower and twisted apart the capsule full of vile-tasting medicine that Bryn had to take and mixed it into his applesauce for him before the call came. Bryn and Nikita Cat were in front of the television, and Bryn also knew that I would need a nice, soothing phone call with my husband after such a rotten evening. So I was very glad when Damon's Skype cloud turned green that night.

Our chat wasn't particularly soothing, but it helped and made me feel loved and wanted.

I told him everything that had happened, and he said he never wanted anything to do with Berta again, and that he had been a bit worried when I first went down to New York to take care of Bryn, because he knew Berta. But he also knew that it would mostly be good for me to get out of my house, out of Connecticut where I hardly went out, and to be with Bryn again.

Damon had been happy to think of me in Manhattan, enjoying walks around historic areas, enjoying cafés and patisseries, and sitting with Bryn late at night to chat about books, politics, city life, and life in general.

Now, however, he was worried that I might have to go back to Connecticut, and he was frantic. He thought that that would be awful for me, like death. He didn't want me to have to do that. Damon had hoped all along to achieve a financial success that would make that unnecessary, and before Bryn died so that I could just go straight from being with Bryn to being with him.

That seemed a bit unrealistic to me; it takes a long, long time to do that.

Now Damon described some things to me that he had been keeping back: 2 nightmares.

In one of them, I had killed myself, so he had come back to Manhattan, had me cremated, and was walking around Greenwich Village to whatever favorite places of mine that he knew about, scattering my ashes and crying.

In the other, I was also dead, though it was unclear how that had happened – it was unspecified in this nightmare – and he was sitting in Washington Park on a bench when he felt a warm touch on his arm. It was my ghost. Then he started crying again.

He was sure that we would both have PTSD – Post Traumatic Stress Disorder – soon.

We talked for a while longer and I assured him that I was healthy and well, and that now that Berta had expressed a hope that we kill ourselves, I was cured of that urge. I would stay alive and live well. That is, as Damon and I often said, the best revenge.

I told him how I felt now and he agreed to live and live well; with that, I felt much better.

The next afternoon, my mother sent me a nice note:

From: Nicole B. C. Rénard
Subject: Mom Loves You
To: Clarisse N. Rénard
Date: Friday, July 31, 2009, 3:24 PM

Dear Clarisse;

I just want you to know how much I love you and what a good person I know you are and how much love and effort you have put into helping Bryn all these months.

Mom

At least I felt safe. Having a supportive mother has always induced that. So I wrote back to my mother in great detail, telling her every last

Berta's Meltdown

thought that was on my mind, every move I had made both before and after calling her the night before, and included Damon's nightmares.

My favorite lines from that letter were: "The entire family here finds Berta piggish and unreasonable, just so you know." And "She wants to keep a foothold in her father's place, her mother's place, and her boyfriend's place – by keeping some of her property in each place."

That pretty much summed up the situation.

But I write a lot when I am upset, and I went on to add more of my thoughts:

Finally I have figured out some of what's wrong with her: she can't stand to move ANY of her stuff AT ALL even though it's necessary.

So I'm screwed.

And I need to keep busy and do things in advance of a death. After all, if I am still going to be here during the period after this is over, it will be more hellish if nothing has been done yet.

And the problem area is in the room where I am staying, which scares me. I need to feel a safe territory to retreat to, and I don't have one with this monster and her stuff in there, with an uproar threatening every time anything needs to be done.

The rest of them call me indispensable, invaluable, and many other complimentary things.

I wish you would write to say one thing in particular, because it would be a huge relief: that you and Daddy would, if I really need the help, drive here with the station wagon to help me remove ALL of my stuff and take it back to Bloomfield, if I feel cornered by this problem at some point. Could you possibly help me with that?

Please let me know.

I still love you, even if I really would rather just stay here, and even though I feel deathly depressed about living with you, and want desperately to just live with Damon in Manhattan with no more terror about the future.

The Slamming Door

He is doing okay, and 3 products are moving along very nicely, but these things have long periods of nothing happening with a few promising meetings here and there...normal, because you do work in between the meetings, and then you have the meetings and they go well, and then the executives/investors/whomever need time to go back and do whatever is next.

My mother did it; she told me all that I asked, including that she would help get my stuff out soon, but I had to wait until she saw her e-mail again. She was busy working with patients on the phone at the office, and couldn't keep checking her e-mail.

But I felt better about her.

At some point between watching Berta make a fool of herself to that little girl in the café and her meltdown – her insane, out-of-control shrieking fit – I ceased to care that my attitude about kids, reproduction and what makes life enjoyable differed from hers.

As it was, I had never cared that my point of view differs from that of most people.

I no longer gave a damn that most people would find what mattered to her relevant let alone normal and in the majority and therefore socially acceptable. Berta wanted a baby, I hated babies; Berta liked to talk to little kids as though they were imbeciles, I found that insulting and kept remembering how much I had hated being spoken to that way when I was little myself...and so on. I simply ceased to find her worth catering to.

Berta had made herself utterly irrelevant.

When I was back at home with my mother, she told me that as far as she could see, our personalities just wouldn't work together and that was all there was to it. She was absolutely right. I had sensed this from the get-go and done my best to ignore it and therefore postpone the inevitable. But the inevitable always arrives eventually. Now we hated each other's guts.

I had utterly lost all sympathy for Berta about anything now.

I was done with her, but I didn't consciously realize that yet.

Now I remembered the trouble that my cousin Kumiko had had when she was caregiver to my great-uncle Ron, the retired three-star general in the U.S. Air Force who had lived to be ninety-eight years old.

Berta's Meltdown

Kumiko lived nearest to him, so she was his caregiver – while her own husband was dying. His other ones, Gwenn and Julie, lived elsewhere.

I saw lots of parallels between our situations. Berta was more like Julie than her sister was. The women matched very precisely: Dionne/Gwenn (calmer older sisters); Berta/Julie (irate, off-the-wall younger sisters); Clarisse/Kumiko (adopted daughter figures).

The difference was between the men. Bryn didn't blow up at his off-the-wall daughter and tell her to shut up and stuff it, like my great-uncle the general had. Bryn was a conflict-averse social worker who would always choose to smooth things over. Being in the military isn't what this difference was about; the rest of my relatives, civilians, had no-nonsense personalities.

The point is that tolerating Berta's behavior sent the wrong message to her..

Chapter 57

Being Sent Home...and Seeing the Movie *Adam*

Over the next few days, I stayed quiet and kept taking care of Bryn, and Berta did not come over. Naturally, I was very glad not to see her. It was just me and Bryn, with Albert there in the evening on Friday and Saturday.

Bryn and I had fun making sure that he ate something on Friday evening. As had happened at least three times each week for the past few weeks, that meant insisting that Albert eat half of Bryn's order of vegetarian couscous with tomato dressing from Rafaella's. Bryn had become addicted to that meal, so when I wasn't cooking potatoes and fish, we all ordered our dinners from there. The place even offered delivery services, which we had only just discovered.

On Saturday, June and Alissa came over, but left before dinnertime. Now it was August.

That was really nice, because the two of them decided that we should all go out together to see the new *Julie & Julia* movie, about the blogger who had prepared every recipe in Julia Child's first cookbook over the course of a year.

As we sat there, I noticed that both mother and daughter were wearing identical flip-flops from L.L.Bean, bought online by Albert, of course. He told me that he had bought June's pair first, and then saw them on sale and bought the other pair. He was so funny, shopping for them both.

Then I glanced down and noticed June's toenails. They were all different lengths and jagged. Poor June; she was an attractive woman who had dressed herself to perfection before her memory was attacked. She still worked out at a gym whenever her daughter could take her there, just as she always had. Albert was doing his damnedest to maintain her at the same excellent standard that she had kept up, with expensive hair salon visits.

But a man can only keep track of so much, and he could only know so much about what needed to be done in order to maintain that standard. It wasn't his fault. So I quietly went in my room, got my nail-grooming kit, and came back into Bryn's room where we were all sitting.

"June – how about a quickie pedicure?" I asked her. "I've my tools right here."

She smiled sweetly at me, giggled, and said, "Oh, okay."

So I did it, first one foot on my knees and then the other. Soon her toenails were all evenly and neatly cut and shaped. But there was a problem; one big toenail had a fungal infection. It wasn't very bad, but I

Being Sent Home...and Seeing the Movie Adam

could see the faint yellow tinge. I cleaned up my tools with hot water and soap and put them away.

Later that night, when they had all gone home, I remembered this and e-mailed Albert, telling him that June needed to see a podiatrist and get some medicine for this. I added that her big toe probably felt funny at the very least, but that she was likely forgetting about this when everyone was busy, and that it wasn't surprising that he hadn't noticed this. There; that was probably the most that I could do for her right now. I would tell him face-to-face when I got the chance, probably the next day.

But the next day went differently.

Bryn had been spending a lot of time on the phone over the past couple of days, and I had sensed that it was Berta, so I had avoided the entire scene, not going into his room until each call ended. I didn't want to hear even half of those conversations, not even by accident.

I got up, made my bed with one or two quick moves (a sixty-second job), checked on Bryn, went in the bathroom to brush my teeth and wash my face, and got food for him, the cat, and myself. Elah and Rudy had been leaving *The New York Times* at our door for months if they happened to intercept it before it either got stolen or lost, and I took that in and gave it to Bryn.

When there was nothing else to do, I sat down at the computer to check my e-mail.

For months, Berta and I had communicated daily both by phone and by e-mail.

That had ground to a screeching halt over the weekend, until now.

A long message from her awaited me. Expecting more unpleasantness, I read through it.

The first thing that I noticed was that Berta had used her personal e-mail account, not the one from work. She had written to me directly from work many times in the interest of efficiency, but with her Deutsche Bank e-mail account. She wasn't allowed to access her personal account while at work. I don't know how they blocked her access to it, but they did.

I also noticed that she had written to me in the morning, which meant that she had not been sleeping late. She had told me that she typically spent the entire mornings and longer – often past one o'clock in the afternoon – of her days off asleep. She said she did it because she was depressed. I could relate. Besides, she had to get up early on weekdays and ride the subways like a sardine in rush hour. Of course she was tired. The message was full of typos, too.

From: Berta

The Slamming Door

Subject: Hi
To: Clarisse
Date: Sunday, August 2, 2009, 11:05 AM
Hi Clarisse:

I thought I better write an email as I don't think I would be able to get out everything without crying. I'm really sorry I got so angry at you and yelled and made you feel bad. I said a lot of bad things that I didn't mean, but that's what yelling is. In my heart, I know you were just trying to be helpful, but my brain didn't interpret it that way. To you, I know you were thinking that you were being helpful, as you have been in so many ways. For me, that apartment still represents to me my life living there with my father and I am not ready to let that go yet. That's why I purposely have left things there. This might not make sense to you, but by leaving things there, it makes me feel as if I still belong there, that I still have a presence with my "Daddy". I don't want to remove any of my stuff as it also brings me closer to realizing that he is going to die soon and I will have to move. I feel like there will be time enough to go through things when he's gone. I also felt as if I was being pushed out, which really made me angry. I know that was not your intention at all, but that's how my brain interpreted it. I am not handleing the fact that he is going to die in a matter of weeks, and I am very upset in general every day, on the verge of an emotional breakdown, waiting for the news that he's dead. I'm freaking out that the only person in the world who loves me unconditionally in that way only a father can is going to leave me. I don't want to leave him, and I don't want him to leave me. So as I walk around as an emotional basket case, the slightest thing sets me off, which is the case the other night.

On top of feeling emotional over my father, I am no longer taking the psycho drugs that I usually take to calm my crazy brain because I am pregnant. That in itself is dangerous territory for me, as without them, I do not handle day to day stresses of any kind. On top of not having my meds, being pregnant has given me an influx of hormones pumping through my body and making me feel a bit crazy in itself. The two make a volitile combination and I find myself flying off the handle at the smallest stressor.

Being Sent Home...and Seeing the Movie Adam

I know this all seems so stupid all because you were trying to clean, and be nice, but I have a set of issues that stem deeper than that which you didn't realize. Please do not worry about us, and our friendship. I love having you as not only my cousin, but as my friend, and you have been a great friend to me. Nothing has changed, or will change between us, I just need you to be understanding and forgiving in my current state. I will be there for you when you go through tough times too. Just be patient with me and make me laugh and not cry, as crying is all I feel like doing these days.

I love you!
Berta

After I had read it all, I wrote back, thinking that explaining what I had been thinking might help the situation, and perhaps soothe her and smooth it over a bit. Addressing each of her concerns and ending on what seemed like a pleasant, sociable note, I sent it off, foolishly imagining that it would reassure her and make her feel better.

From: Clarisse N. Rénard
Subject: Re: Hi - Hi.
To: Berta
Date: Sunday, August 2, 2009, 1:34 PM
Hi Berta.

Well...I figured out the part about you not wanting to move ANY of your stuff and why hours later.

It takes a while to figure people out.

I just wanted to use the upper part of the closet, and stop having filth and plaster fall all over my clothes every time a large vehicle passes by - that shakes the building slightly and stuff would fall.

People have commented about how my stuff was close to the window and maybe a fire hazard, so I thought having it hidden up there would be a better way to keep it.

The Slamming Door

And...last winter, on some random night when we were watching Bones, you said (obviously you forgot, because it is much more pleasant to just leave the stuff in place - I get that) that you wanted to go over all that stuff with me carefully at some point and sort out whose is whose.

I found stuff that belongs to you, Maggie, Dionne, Hilda, and Elah. I will have to ask her about that...it's a heavy thing in a box with her name and address.

I thought that other people would want their things back, and be wondering and worrying about whether or not any of us would get around to it.

There is another reason why I cleaned: I am terrified of having all of this sort of work left to do LATER when your father isn't here - be that because of death or going to hospice. I am convinced that it will be much more upsetting to all involved to have to do this then.

That's why I pushed myself through all the papers - aside from the fact that being able to ask him a few questions as I went made it easier to be sure that I wasn't making any mistakes. Albert will need that stuff just ready to work with, because he and June are sick.

As for the other closets, your father wants to go through those while he is here too. He has some old family photos in there, and he said he wants to get them out and identify the people in them. As a historian, I am looking forward to it. As someone who wants to learn all about in-laws that she really likes, I am looking forward to it.

Obviously, we have to do this soon.

When I was 11 years old, my sweet and quiet grandfather (mother's father) was dying of prostate cancer and diabetes. While he was still sleeping upstairs in his same bed - not the hospital bed in the family room downstairs - I asked if he could teach me whatever family history he knew with whatever family photographs he had. It wasn't cheerful to have to ask a dying guy to do this knowing that he would realize that he could not possibly procrastinate,

Being Sent Home...and Seeing the Movie Adam

but he just did it. Of course it was fascinating. He had been in the Marines in the 1930s and gone to Manchuria, China. He had some cool and shocking photos of decapitated Manchu guys with long queue braids. Someday I will figure out, through reading history, what that was about. The family history stuff was interesting too, but no need to list what I saw, photo by photo.

So...having trouble controlling yourself with no medication. I am off medication too. I've had years of practice. When I was on it, I was overweight - felt a water pressure in my face, wheezed going up a mere set of 6 steps indoors, figured I might get diabetes, etc. - and I was mentally so damned calm that I couldn't write or edit and Damon was wondering who I was and what I had done with the person he knew.

You have got to control yourself, even if you don't want to. Your father doesn't need the screaming, and I am not out to get you. And don't worry about the stuff in the left bureau in your room. The drawers are so damned tightly shut that they just won't budge. If you ever want to get whatever is in there out you will need Matt, and he won't be able to just destroy that piece of furniture because it's a nice one that is to be preserved. Good luck...

Whatever we think is yours in now grouped in the corner of the front hall. Hilda very nicely identified her property last night, but she was going out, so it's still in the corner of the living room. Including that rock water fountain thing, which I spent a long time cleaning.

Your cat is fine, doing a great job as therapy pet. I keep finding her purring in your father's lap.

Are we still going out with Alissa to see Julie & Julia next week? I want to. And could we invite my 21-year-old cousin Amber?

Love,
Clarisse.

The Slamming Door

Instead of helping, it only fanned the flames that had been sparked inside both of us.

But I wouldn't know that for certain until she had time to read my reply and respond.

Meanwhile, still feeling suspicious about the ultimate outcome of all this, I wrote to my mother, forwarding both of our letters to her. I suddenly felt the need to put her fully into the loop about what was going on. I had to be realistic; once she was aware that there was trouble, it would be foolish not follow up with whatever information came next.

Fw: Re: Hi – Hi.
Sunday, August 2, 2009 1:54 PM
From: Clarisse N. Rénard
To: Nicole B.C. Rénard

Hi Mommy!

Berta finally got over it and wrote to me, and it's better now.

But I still don't trust her AT ALL - she WILL do another rotten thing like this to me again.

And I still want you to answer my questions from the other long letter I sent to you, for just this reason.

Love,
Clarisse.

Confirmation of my suspicions came a couple of hours after that. Her response was riddled with typos, spacing errors, and block capitals. Those come across like a shout in e-mail. I read through it carefully, and that pounding chill in my chest from the other night returned. This letter wasn't even signed; it had no formal ending whatsoever, not that I doubted that it was over.

From: Berta
Subject: Re: Hi - Hi.
To: Clarisse
Date: Sunday, August 2, 2009, 3:39 PM
Clarisse:

Being Sent Home...and Seeing the Movie Adam

Right off the bat---regardless of the fact that you are a historian and looking foward to it, you are NOT to touch anything in that hall closet. This is MY father, and I WANT TO BE THE ONE TO GO OVER PHOTOS WITH HIM! Save me from freaking out, but this is MY FAMILY history, and these are the moments that I WANT WITH MY DYING FATHER!!! I am sorry if you can't understand that. I will show you everything, all photos, etc., but ALONG WITH MY SISTER, WE ARE THE ONES TO HANDLE THAT. Regardless of what he might have said to you, I will talk to him. I'm sorry, but it is MY father, not yours. I am extremely possivie, and you certainly would not like it if I touched any of your stuff, so try to imagine how I feel.

Also, I am sorry, but you will NOT be doing any packing up of that apartment after he is gone. My sister and I will handle that. I am and have not been comfortable with you even handling his papers at this point, regarldess that he has instructed you to do so. That should be a job for my uncle, for me or my sister. How would you feel if I went to your parents house and did that? You certainly wouldn't like that either.

I know you are not out to "get me" but if you do not follow my wishes, we are going to have serious conflicts which I hope to avoid. Please back off immediately with the idea of getting everyone's stuff out. I will handle all of that after he is gone. Of course he doesn't want to hear the screaming, but you are making it very hard for me. I do not like ANYONE touching my things, am EXTREMELY possessive, and things are to be done on MY TERMS as he is MY FATHER!!!! I hope I have made myself very clear here.

    The first couple of e-mails that Berta and I exchanged that Sunday had lulled me into thinking that things were going to be okay. Then I realized that they were not going to be. It turned out that she wanted me gone, and to take over my job, pregnant or not, capable or not. I suppose that it was just as well, but I felt attacked, cornered, and ill-used.
    So...everything was HERS, ALL HERS.

The Slamming Door

Like it or not, I found myself thinking to her, I have a piece of Bryn too.

And my piece was a positive one; he liked me and wanted me as his caregiver.

I had told him that he was my best friend and that I loved him many times.

I had also told him that he was like another father to me.

Bryn had also told me that I was his best friend now, too.

I really didn't give a damn if that made Berta feel threatened or jealous.

Added to all that baggage was the now glaringly obvious fact that she had no intention of controlling herself when she got upset, which was going to happen more often now that Bryn was getting worse. Instead, she actually expected me to cater to her losses of self-control, all so that she could be off her medications and have a baby, regardless of the fact that her father was near death and couldn't take the upsets. She had no self-discipline whatsoever, and I was utterly sick of her. No wonder her own father didn't like her.

Now I decided to write back one more time, and one more time only.

From: Clarisse N. Rénard
Subject: Re: Hi - Hi.
To: Berta Otterman
Date: Sunday, August 2, 2009, 5:25 PM
Hi Berta.

Stop getting upset and writing like that. I'm not going to work on it without you.

You can drag it all out of wherever it is and get him to tell the stories YOURSELF.

I am just interested and want to learn the family history.

And if you want the stuff scanned – best way to preserve it – I am available for that, too.

Don't forget – YOU asked me to come here and take care of your father. This leaves me here with his death process for most of the time – so I get upset too. And don't forget – YOU are not conflicted about your father. Mine is crazy. He can be very funny and witty and interesting, but most of

Being Sent Home...and Seeing the Movie Adam

the time I just don't care. So this is weird for me, seeing a nice father.

Just promise me that you won't involve me in any fights over who gets what and how it gets packed after he leaves this apartment. That worries me a lot. I don't want to be involved or expected to do the actual packing, because of this. You have said you want everything in the apartment, and I wonder what fights might happen between you and Dionne or whomever else later on. I don't want to be involved. Maybe it will all be fine – but just say you will not involve me. It's time I mentioned this: I am worried that someone might try to involve me even slightly. Tell me you won't. It will be a great relief.

If you want help preserving photos on the computer, I'll be available.

Now relax and don't send any more upset notes. I just want to be calm.

I am the one who is always in here, needing to stay relaxed.

I just looked at your father a little while ago. He was sleeping comfortably, with the footrest part of his blue chair up – I had cranked it up. I wondered if he needed anything, but decided that I couldn't improve his situation. That position was working for him, and he was asleep. He just got up and went into the bathroom. We're expecting Albert soon, so I guess he decided to get up and wait.

Nothing much else is happening right now.

Love,
Clarisse.

After I hit "Send" I suddenly realized something: I never wanted to interact with Berta again. I didn't want to see her, hear from her, cater to a single whim of hers, or have anything to do with her. She hadn't signed her last letter, she hadn't even said "Hi" at its beginning, and she had been completely unyielding, demanding that I cater to her out-of-control

The Slamming Door

mood swings because she was pregnant and therefore could not be expected to control herself.

Well...I expected her to control herself anyway, and had made that clear.

And I didn't give a damn that she wanted to have a baby. If doing so meant that she expected me to put up with abuse, count me out. Being done with her was now in my conscious thought processes.

If I were to invite any further letter-writing, this would just go on and on and on...

...so forget that. I was cutting her off.

The hell with people who thought that they could just scream their lungs out heaping abuse on me and then expect me to forget it. I was no saint and didn't want to apply for the title. Bryn could have that honor. Apparently, being a saint meant taking abuse, never slapping down anyone who needed it, and allowing such people to turn out...awful.

All this time, I had wondered how Berta could have turned out the way that she had: morbidly obese and utterly ordinary, without the necessary skills and education to enjoy a career in the field of her choice.

She had been handed all of the tools necessary to study and train for that.

So had I, but I was thin and well-educated, and working in the field of my choice, writing and editing. It would eventually earn me a living, and meanwhile I was doing what I loved to do.

Both of us had had fathers who knew exactly what we needed to succeed, and they had supplied us with it: private girls' schools, private colleges, and lots of advice and encouragement.

But there was something missing in her equation: an attitude that she had a duty to fulfill her end of the bargain by studying diligently and doing her best.

My father may have had a short fuse and a lack of impulse control, but aside from the confrontations with him over that – in which my character trait of refusing to accept abuse and fighting back was cemented – I thought that I had turned out rather well.

Sometimes the anxiety that came with Asperger's had slowed me down, but I had always fought it, determined to complete any task that I started, including but not limited to my education, and exactly on time. No Berta; she had let ADD slow her down by eight years.

So I didn't care about any of the excuses she had offered up for her behavior, nor did I accept them. And why was that? Because she had demanded that I accept and excuse her tantrums and let her keep it up. She expected me to just take some more abuse, and soon.

No way.

Being Sent Home...and Seeing the Movie Adam

Accessing my e-mail account again, I did something that I had only done once before, when I had a stalker: I blocked both her e-mail addresses. No more of her letters would be getting through to me.

It seemed like the best move; now she wouldn't be able to upset me anymore.

Next, I printed off the whole ream of crap that had gone back and forth through cyberspace to show Albert, whom I knew would arrive soon. Then I e-mailed Damon and my mother each to tell them what was going on. I also told Damon that I wanted him on the phone right away, regardless of the time zone difference, knowing that the only benefit of doing so would be to make myself feel better for a fraction of a second.

Albert arrived soon after that, and sat down on the sofa to chat for a couple of minutes. He had arrived ahead of Alissa and June, whom Bryn had told me were also coming over. I handed Albert the papers with the terrible e-mails when he sat down on the sofa.

He read through them. "It reads like a descent into hell," he commented.

That about summed it up; I told him that I had just blocked Berta's e-mails so that this would stop. He had no argument with that. How could he? He had been with us during her insane, abusive tirade.

Alissa and June walked in a little bit later, and Bryn asked me to come in and sit down with them all in his room. He was in his Lazy Boy chair, of course, and Albert, June and Alissa were arrayed in the wooden chairs around him. I took the remaining one, feeling a sense of dread. What was this about? It couldn't be anything good.

Bryn didn't keep me waiting. "Berta and Dionne would like to move in here at the end of August," he told me. The others were staring at me, gauging my response, and I saw that they were there for moral support. Was Bryn expecting me to dissolve into an insane, shrieking idiot just like his idiot daughter had? They did seem like buffers against another upset.

I began to hyperventilate then and there. "I have to get out of here," I said, and jumped up and dashed into my room, grabbing for the cell phone. There was no reason to sit around in Bryn's room discussing this further; the only thing that was going to calm me down was confirmation that getting out with all of my stuff would not be a problem.

But it was a Sunday, and that meant that my parents were out in the car, driving for hours with my mother's cell phone in her handbag and turned off. She had a maddening habit of keeping it with her but only

The Slamming Door

turning it on to make a call, leave a message, and then shut it off if the person didn't answer. This drove me crazy because she wasn't the one driving; she could have kept it on without risking a traffic accident. My parents loved to go on long country drives.

I left a frantic-sounding message on the home answering machine explaining what the problem was, what kind of help I needed, and insisting that they call me back as soon as they found this message. Then I left a similar message on my mother's cell phone voice mail, even though I was sure she wouldn't notice it for days.

Shutting my cell phone, I sat on my bed with no idea as to what to do next.

I wanted something to do, but there wasn't anything now that the hall closet wasn't an option. Damn Berta and her possessiveness. No wonder this had happened.

Bryn didn't seem like he would last much longer. He was weaker and weaker now, eating less, looking like a living skeleton with skin and hair and clothes on, and I secretly doubted that he would be going to hospice at all. His lovely tenor voice was fading.

By now, I had stopped hyperventilating; the phone calls had made me feel a bit better, because they were an immediate, constructive response to the latest problem. I hadn't yelled or scared anyone, it seemed to me. My response hadn't been particularly loud. Once again, my facial expressions had barely changed, except for a pronounced widening of my eyes as I felt fear about the impending change of environment and concern over transitioning through it as smoothly as possible.

I hate change, and it seemed that a disruption to my environment could still freak me out.

Even though I had done what I could for now, I knew that I would not be happy unless and until I both heard from my parents and heard that they would help me to remove everything I owned – everything.

Until then, my cousins came looking for me. They had seen me make those calls and then sit down, clueless as to my next move. Alissa and June decided that the three of us should go out together later that week and see *Julie & Julia* – and not with Berta. We would eat dinner, too.

It sounded good and comforting, and I went back into Bryn's room. He and Albert would hang out together in his room and watch a DVD on his machine that night, they told me. Perfect; we anticipated satisfaction to all, at least for an evening.

A little while later, my cell phone rang. My parents were back from their marathon of driving on every back road in southern New England – I swear, my father had a street atlas stored in his brain, as clear as files

Being Sent Home...and Seeing the Movie Adam

on a hard drive or a DVD. Aspies tend to have photographic memories, and he and I are no exceptions.

My mother said that I hadn't needed to sound so desperate (Really? She should try functioning calmly while feeling under siege!), that of course they would come with the car on a Wednesday to take away as much of it as they could fit into her station wagon. "Your parents will always come through for you," she added.

That was all that I needed to hear. I relayed this vital information to the others.

My mother wasn't sure yet how soon they would come here; she had to check her schedule to make sure that there were no appointments, and my father would need to take that day off. He still had his job as the planner in a well-known engineering and surveying firm in Connecticut. He worked all week, while my mother had Wednesdays free.

Bryn and Albert talked to her, and Albert seemed resigned to the inevitable.

He didn't plead with my mother not to take me away this time.

But he wasn't happy; he dreaded the thought of having someone else as caregiver.

After they all left, I e-mailed Damon again, telling him of my imminent departure.

I was dreading his response to this most of all.

Just as I predicted, when he had read it, he called me on Skype and sounded really bad, and a bit unhinged. Damon was the one of us with no support system and no place to go, and he was out in the world trying to live on nothing.

He had been calm as long as he thought that I was someplace quiet and comfortable and safe, but now he thought that I was going back to what seemed like prison to him. He thought that it was going to be absolutely unbearable for me back at my house.

Because of that, Damon said that I should never have married him, that he was no good for me, and that he was cutting off communication with me for my own good. I could keep everything we owned in our storage unit, he told me; he would give me a divorce.

I didn't want a divorce! And I told him so; but he hung up on me.

Well, I couldn't deal with that. Having my husband as my best friend and ally was what kept me calm and made me feel as though I had a future. Sure, I could have a professional future someday as a published author, but who would I share my life with? I wanted my husband, and no quitting and starting over with someone else! I wanted Damon.

But I couldn't think, I was so upset.

The Slamming Door

I took off the earphones, stunned and speechless, and got up, unable to think.

Then I ran as fast as I could into the wall between my room and the back hallway, crashing my head into it so hard that I was too dizzy to see or stand. I had forgotten about the old-fashioned molding in that part of the wall, the one that made the three Otterman family photographs stand out against the plaster. It was a long, thin strip of a decorative ridge.

I rushed over to my bed and flopped on it, face down, and stayed like that for several minutes. As I lay there, my head started to hurt, and I could hear Bryn calling me, sounding scared. He had heard half of that conversation, and he had heard my getting up and then hurting myself. I was too upset and dazed to move or to respond to him for a few more minutes.

I really didn't want to live without Damon in my life. He had always been around as my best friend, the person whom I could tell about any and all upsets or happy events, the one who understood and empathized with me no matter what life threw at me, for nearly a decade and a half. Even Bryn couldn't claim that; Damon and I were soul mates, different from most people but alike in our view of the world around us.

I really wasn't interested in life without Damon in it.

Bryn was still calling me.

After I was sure that I could get up and walk steadily, I went in and told him the full story, and that I had been dreading Damon's reaction to my imminent departure most of all. He looked alarmed, but said he doubted that Damon would just cut me off; he was sure that Damon would call back soon. It was so nice to have Bryn's sane point of view assessing this just then.

Why had I hit my head so hard? Bryn wanted to know, not understanding that part.

I told him that I didn't even realize what I was doing until after I had done it.

Suddenly I heard the Skype phone ringing, and dashed out to answer it, telling Bryn what I heard as I did so. It was Damon.

"I love you, Clarisse. I can't leave you," Damon sobbed.

Bryn was right!

Damon and I talked for a while, and he swore never to abandon me, but that he wasn't making any promises about anyone else. He would be loyal to me forever, though, both because of what I had done for Bryn and because he loved me.

Even before I had stayed with Bryn, he would have felt that way, but now even more so.

We talked until we both felt better, and he listened to me when I told him that every last bit of our stuff would be carefully removed and driven back to Connecticut, and that the transition would be fine. He listened when I told him that my parents had said that the house in Connecticut was my house too, the cat was my cat too, and that they had promised to treat me nicely and let me alone to be in my room quietly. They would make noise in the morning, but they wouldn't knock on my door constantly and bother me.

Damon began to understand that it might just be okay for me there.

The next day, my mother and I exchanged a couple more letters.

I told her that I was thinking of what I could do to prepare Bryn and the rest of the family to do what I had been doing. There was the pill sheet, which I called a medication chart when I wrote to her, and a long list of habits and routines to go over. I would have to write it all down for Bryn's daughters, not to make their lives easier, but so that he would have an easier time of it after I left. I was expecting it to be a difficult transition for him.

Frankly, I hoped that they would soon realize just how complex a caregiver's job was, preferably as they struggled to do what I had done. I doubted that they would do it as well as I had, and I was angry with Berta for kicking up this fuss and getting her father to send me away. He had acquiesced to her demands even though it wasn't what he wanted.

My mother had told me that Bryn said to her, on the phone, "I have to let her take care of me. She's my daughter, so I have to let her do it." Always the self-sacrificing parent…

My mother also commented on the letters that Berta and I had exchanged. She remembered her own father's death, which had come when she was thirty-eight years old, so she had talked about showing Berta some sensitivity. That was a nice thought, but I had been doing that for the past ten and a half months, and no longer felt obligated to do so.

I told her I had blocked Berta's e-mails, and explained that Berta hadn't cared about how I felt while I watched Bryn dying. Berta only cared about how she felt, I told my mother, and she expected and required people to cater to that, and to excuse her abusive behavior.

I just couldn't do it anymore.

The next note from my mother told me I ought to make sure that I told Bryn I loved him, to which I replied that I had done so often during my entire stay with him. Did she think that I was foolish enough to miss that opportunity?! I had rushed down here to be his caregiver precisely because I knew that time was precious, and then I had made the most of it.

My mother had said that she and my father would drive down in the station wagon the very next Wednesday, August 5th, to take away the

The Slamming Door

majority of my things. She had checked her schedule, and my father had gotten that day off, and I could always count on them to help me.

I didn't know it then, but she told Dr. Leonardi about Berta's tantrum.

He had said that it was time for me to come home.

I guess I had a place that was mine, then. How odd; I had spent the past eleven months convinced that I had no place that I could think of that way. At least I was getting something that I wanted very much after all this upset: a sense that I could feel proprietary over a living space, and have possession of and control over it. That was crucial to feeling better.

If only my husband had sensed this aspect of the situation.

After that, I wrote more notes for *The Slamming Door*, and the irony of the title I had chosen so many months ago now seemed like the choice of a psychic. Here is what I wrote:

> Bryn's hair has all grown back. He looks good again, with nice thick hair – no bald spots. There's just one cute thing different, that he says he's never had before: a tuft of hair that sticks up at the top back. It sticks straight up, and makes him look sort of like Calvin from the comic strip Calvin and Hobbes...or some European little boy comic book character. It's just cute.

> I'm leaving on Wednesday, August 12th, 2009. His daughters want to take over this job. I wrote them an 8-page letter, a how-to guide. Good luck to them – it's logistically complex to properly take care of a sick person, and it's constant work. But he's always taken care of them, so now they want to take care of him – last chance to do so!

It seems bizarre now that I wrote that he looked good; to me, a man who looks good is simply one who is not bald. But if that man is a skeleton dying of cancer, he doesn't look good. The way that Bryn looked was better, but not good.

At some point the next day, I saw Rudy, and told him that I was "done with her" after the way that Berta had treated me. He knew what had gone on; no doubt through Berta and Hilda. He wasn't the sort who

Being Sent Home...and Seeing the Movie Adam

cared to really listen to people, so I didn't care to enlighten him further. Of course, he just looked at me with no particular expression, and that was that.

The next evening, Berta was coming back to the apartment.

There was absolutely no way that I would see her, I told Bryn. I was going out, so I would like to time things with Albert in such a way as to be able to be gone from not only the building but also this city block before Berta approached. I was that upset at the mere thought of interacting with her, and I did not want to run into her on the street.

The Otterman brothers acquiesced.

How could they not? They had been there for Berta's meltdown, and I had taken great care of Bryn exactly the way he wanted me to for months. Albert promised to arrive before Wilson had to go home.

By the way, I added once that was arranged, I planned to go out to see a movie that I had been planning to see that night. It was called *Adam*, starring Hugh Dancy, and it was about a man in his twenties who had Asperger's.

A few months earlier, Berta and I had seen a preview for it at a movie theater. When the character informed his future girlfriend that he had Asperger's, we both turned to gape at each other. This sort of movie was a new thing, something that no one had been used to even hearing about until recently. It was playing at the Angelika Theater, which meant that it was an Indie film, that I would have trouble finding in Connecticut.

Bryn was intrigued, and asked me to tell him all about it later.

Asperger's was still a new subject to the public; no wonder this movie stood out.

I took off early and found dinner somewhere, though I forget where. I also called Kasey and told her what was going on, and that I was determined not to interact with Berta again. She was a bit concerned when I said that if I had to stay out walking until midnight, I would do it.

"I don't like to think of you wandering the streets of New York City in the dark."

That was nice of her, but I said that I would just find a late-night diner and bring a book each night...whatever it took not to be upset again. She conceded that point.

Adam was a great movie. It was not an in-depth presentation of the character; there wasn't time for that. Instead, it showcased all of the major markers and indicators of Asperger's. Hugh Dancy did a very good job with the role, only slipping up when he up-talked as he told Rose Byrne that he had Asperger's. A true Aspie would have maintained

The Slamming Door

a flat, matter-of-fact tone even as he used what he knew would be an unfamiliar term to his listener, and then just defined it for her.

Adam was fascinated by astronomy and owned a real space suit; he ate the same foods each day and night no matter what; he had gone to an engineering school in Manhattan and so had never been off the island in his life; he did not understand how he seemed to other people when he talked; he had limited social skills, a problem exacerbated by the fact that his mother had died when he was eight years old, thus taking away the time she would have needed to train him; and he hit his head against walls (or mirrors, in this movie) when he was under intense emotional stress.

The movie opened with his father's funeral. So that left him on his own, in the house that he had lived in for his entire life. His father had found him a job making robotic toys, and his work area was in the back of the office, away from the background noise of most of the staff. But he got fired because he would not make low-quality toys; Adam just couldn't understand why sub-standard products could be of any value, even though his toys would cost $5,000 – out of reach for most customers.

I came out of the theater feeling a bit stunned. That was me. I was like Adam.

At this point, I didn't know that Bones was another character with Asperger's; that understanding came later, after I learned about the condition in detail. But *Adam* wasn't subtle, and that was what I needed. The movie directly informed the viewer that he had Asperger's, whereas one is left to figure that out with *Bones*.

Subtlety was not what I needed. I needed to start learning about this intriguing condition that I had, and *Adam* was the perfect way to start because it was a visual experience that gave Asperger's a face. So that was what an Aspie was like, I thought.

I definitely had Asperger's. If hitting my head so damned hard that I was nearly senseless after a major upset hadn't convinced me, this movie had. There was that, and the fact that I had been formally diagnosed by that psychiatrist a decade ago. Why had she been so dismissive of it?! Oh yeah: because she couldn't do anything about it, and psychiatrists are all about using pharmaceuticals to help a patient cope with life.

I headed home – whether Berta liked it or not, Bryn's apartment was home to me – and sat on the steps of P.S. 11, surrounded by the colorful hand-painted murals that the kids had created years earlier. That school had been covered with scaffolding for a year as a new roof was put onto it, and the job had just ended the week before. At last, just as I was leaving the area for good, the pretty colors were fully visible.

Being Sent Home...and Seeing the Movie Adam

Before going any farther, I had to make sure that the coast was clear. I called Bryn and told him that I was about to come back, but I wanted to make sure that Berta wasn't in the building first.

She was gone, he told me. She had left a while ago. So I went home.

Bryn greeted me, curious to hear about the movie I had just seen.

I had wanted to go alone, and so even though Alissa had offered to accompany me, I had turned her down. "Too close to home?" she had asked, trying to make sense of that. I said it might be, and that I wanted to be sure of that by going by myself.

"Are you sure you have Asperger's?" Bryn asked me, after I had given him a detailed account of the highlights of the movie.

"Yes, very sure; Damon too," I added. "We both have it, though I am the only one with a formal diagnosis."

Bryn nodded soberly, absorbing this.

After a few moments, he was done considering the data, and said he agreed.

It was a significant night for me.

The next call with Damon was a lot better. I told him all about the movie *Adam*, and he had the same epiphany. It was too bad he hadn't been there to go and see it with me, but he was all the way in Kuwait, and the current batch of American movies wouldn't get there for quite a while. When they did, the sexy parts would be chopped out, which would kill at least one significant scene with Rose Byrne. Better to wait until we were together again, however long that would take.

Chapter 58

Packing, Shopping, and More Packing

Most of the packing was done in the few days before my parents' first visit with the car, but it wasn't finished yet; I found every last thing the night before I left, and packed that also. There was also some shopping that I did in those few days before my parents took the bulk of my things away. I figured it was my last chance to do certain things for quite a while.

Once I had calmed down enough to pack, having realized that vacating the premises with all of my stuff would in fact be possible, and that my parents were even looking forward to my presence at our place (it still felt like my home, even if I couldn't have my husband in it), I began to think in detail about the logistics of withdrawing as Bryn's caregiver.

By that, I mean that I analyzed the actual process of taking care of him and wrote it all down in a 10-section-long letter addressed to Berta and Dionne. I prefaced it with the demand that they not take offense, and the threat that if they did, I would.

I wasn't writing that letter to make them feel good, though I phrased it in neutral tones thereafter. I was writing it so that they would be able to know exactly what their father needed and wanted on a day-to-day basis, so that when I left, he could have the same level of comfort that he had enjoyed under my care. I put that in the letter, too.

Bryn looked it all over and approved every bit of it.

As an afterthought, also reviewed and approved by Bryn, I attached a blank pill sheet.

But when I tried to show Dionne how to update it whenever a doctor changed a medication, she didn't feel like paying attention. She was on the sofa on a hot summer afternoon. At that point, I figured, "on her own head be it" rather than seeing any point in pushing.

I did say, "I just don't think that you realize how available you have to be," when she wondered why I was bothering with the details, but then I moved on. The look of combined dismay, disbelief and confusion was enough for me. What did it mean, anyway? That she did understand in theory, and was wondering why I pointed the issue out? Who knew?

That was also when I gave her a gift, unwilling to fool around with any more nonsense about anything. A gift would force pleasant behavior out of her. That, and I had hardly interacted with her all year thanks to her constant absences. The only other thing I had given her was a porcelain reproduction of a standard diner cup at Christmas. This was a yellow, Provence-pattern, Williams-Sonoma apron that I had found in a

Packing, Shopping, and More Packing

basket on sale at the 7th Avenue location. (I had kept the blue one for myself, and was looking forward to using it in Connecticut. Funny how stuff like that helped with the upcoming change, but it did.)

Dionne opened the box up and gushed her thanks with enthusiasm. She said that an apron was the one thing that she hadn't gotten either on her own or as a gift when she got married, and that she really liked this one.

Well – that was gratifying. The last time we had talked about anything, she had said that I shouldn't have cleaned the damned closet. Like I cared; her sister was an inexcusable brat, a bully and a monstrosity.

And when I have decided to clean up a mess left by someone like that, someone who repeatedly emphasizes that everything around me is hers and not mine, I cease to care about social norms, niceties, or NT points of view. The hell with Berta and anyone who agreed with any part of her behavior or point of view.

With that taken care of, I didn't see Dionne again. She just wasn't around.

Nurse Ellen came over again, so I took her in my room to explain what had happened and that I was leaving. "You're well out of it," she said.

Hilda was being quiet but pleasant. She told me, when I asked her how she liked her birthday gift, that black mini-dress of black cloth and lace from Hot Topic.com, that she liked it so much that she had been finding excuses to wear it – high praise indeed.

Elah came through the living room the day before my parents came to get most of my stuff, and I told her, steeling myself against a distant or indifferent response, "I'm leaving, Elah. Will you miss me?" She actually said yes, and came over to hug me. That was a relief.

I had packed everything up in boxes – books, stainless steel flatware from Fishs Eddy on Broadway, Alice in Wonderland tea set items from Christmas, winter clothing, beautiful black velvet hat, CDs, DVDs, kitchenware, and so on – and my parents took it all away in the VW station wagon on Wednesday.

Even the 2 boxes of books that my father had sent via UPS, inherited by Damon from his grandfather the New School founder, fit. They had sat in the same spot for exactly four years. My father hadn't asked; he had just sent them on at his own expense, and now he was driving them back to Connecticut. Good riddance; we had never wanted them at Bryn's place.

My mother promised to empty the big blue suitcase in Connecticut and bring it back the next week. There were a very few more things to

The Slamming Door

go, but they would easily fit in the back of the car when I left with my parents a week from that day.

Bryn had asked Hilda for Nikolai's phone number and called him up; he was hiring him to help my father load the car with all of my stuff. Bryn liked that kid, so he wanted to give him the job. I liked that kid, too. He was nice, quiet, and seemed nonjudgmental.

I e-mailed my mother the afternoon before Wednesday and told her about that.

I told her about Nikolai and why Bryn had hired him, worrying that my father would be cranky and difficult about it. None of Hilda's friends had been able to get jobs over the summer; all of their birthdays were right in the middle of it, so when they were legally able to work, the jobs were all gone.

I answered her question about eating lunch at one of the nearby cafés; I hoped to eat at the French one, but Bryn would want take-out brought from the other. My father just wanted to eat first and pack later. Fine; whatever everyone else wanted about timing…why argue?

The only other thing to mention was the cat; I told her that they could meet Nikita Cat, but to watch out, that she was a little bitch who would seem to accept petting and then suddenly hit someone hard with her paw. She liked men, though, so I anticipated that my father would be treated pleasantly by her.

And that was that.

The next day, my parents appeared, and soon Nikolai did as well. We loaded the car first, and my father didn't say a word to Nikolai; I checked with him, still worried. My father was absolutely silent, in fact, just working with Nikolai efficiently. I had warned Nikolai that he would be very particular about loading the car, so Nikolai was just placing the items as close as possible and walking away to get more.

My father plan to first hadn't worked out. Nikolai had appeared right on time, so they had loaded the car first, Bryn paid Nikolai, and then Albert rode with my father to a garage and walked back in the horrid heat, sweating. June and my mother and I waited for him.

It was nice that I was leaving in the summertime, when the street allowed cars on weekdays, I thought to myself. My father had had no trouble parking the car right in front of the building. Any later in the year, and moving out would have become a complicated hassle.

My mother went right into Bryn's room and sat up close to him, talking quietly to him.

Later, back in Connecticut, she told me what he said. He said that he preferred having me there to take care of him, but damnit, Berta was his daughter and he had to let her do it before it was too late. As I said before, Bryn was always the self-sacrificing parent.

Packing, Shopping, and More Packing

I made a mental note to myself to ask my own father how Berta could have turned out the way that she did, which was unacceptable in just about every way. That would be later, when I was out of there. But I was really wondering about it, and even though my father had no patience and a bad temper, and didn't relate well to little kids or noise (he's an Aspie!), I was sure that he would have some insight to offer. He was an Aspie who had wanted a daughter and then had no patience if I got loud or exuberant, which had happened occasionally.

Raising a daughter is partly about what a parent has to work with – what that daughter is like as a person – plus the effort and discipline and personality exerted by her parents. Both of mine were definitely very involved in raising me, and I turned out well. I'm educated, self-disciplined when I eat, skilled at cooking, baking, certain types of artistry, and articulate. I have decent table manners and I don't swear much. When it really matters, I just don't swear.

Berta and I had both had every advantage in terms of access to education and opportunities to learn skills and good manners, plus appreciation of art and music and culture. Yet the result had differed drastically with each of us. What the hell happened?! I needed to ask my own dad about that, because I was still reeling from the shock of data collection. Processing it was going to take me a while.

Being on the autism spectrum, I collect data first and figure out what it means later.

But not this week; it wasn't over yet.

Wilson showed up at noon, just after my father and Albert got back from the garage, which was a couple of blocks away. Albert was sweating buckets, which was a bit upsetting. Here he was puffed up with cancer treatments and losing his hair, but still smiling and friendly, and overheated.

I introduced Wilson to my mother, who immediately smiled and shook his hand.

Then we all headed out to Le Grainne Café, with Bryn's order for yet another round of vegetarian couscous from Rafaella's on 9th written down...we would get it on the way back.

Lunch in there was lovely as usual. The breeze wafted in to the back table that we were seated at, and I had a nice view of the whole room, complete with the gorgeous floral arrangement on the counter. I sat in between my parents, facing June and Albert.

Because I was feeling a bit antsy about the change, I ordered breakfast food, including a dish of cut strawberries. The place was great

The Slamming Door

about letting a customer have that instead of a bowl of mixed fruit, which was what was on the menu.

The others got lunch foods, crêpes and salads, and June just picked at hers as usual, pushing it around on the plate. At one point, June held up her red Vera Bradley backpack with the little front flap open, looking at my mother like she wanted to say something but couldn't remember what; she seemed to be thrusting the snap that I had sewn into it forward.

"Mommy, look – June is trying to show you the snap that I sewed into her handbag," I said. "Albert bought it for her, and the invisible magnetic snap didn't work, so she couldn't use that part of the bag, and it was really annoying her until I fixed it."

June looked relieved. I had guessed correctly. I was going to miss her; odd though it was to realize it, I had actually grown fond of helping her deal with her memory problems.

My mother looked impressed and commented nicely, and the conversation resumed.

Albert spent most of the meal gushing about how helpful I had been, how efficiently I had kept things running, and how sorry he was that I was leaving. That felt good.

When the meal was cleared away, my father said he wanted to try a dessert, and that he wanted a recommendation from me.

"You want a food adventure?" I asked him.

He nodded, silent and serious as usual.

I recommended the chestnut purée crêpe, and he ordered it.

He liked it.

That was the same one that Damon I liked to share at Le Grainne Café.

When at last it was time for my parents to drive off, my father went back alone to get the car and then sat in it, silent, staring straight ahead. I hadn't seen him in nearly 11 months, and now there he was.

I had spoken to him on the phone, having him set up my L'Occitane gifts for my aunt and mother at Christmas. I had shipped his gift with the others for the holidays. I had mailed him a father's day card with pretty calligraphy. I had mailed him a birthday gift of some architecture books from the MoMA store with a card.

And I told him, a few months earlier, in the spring, I hated him for his role in Damon's banishment from our house. He hadn't exactly apologized in the springtime phone conversation, but I definitely heard something in his tone that suggested that he felt a twinge of discomfort about that.

All the while that I had been in Manhattan taking care of Bryn, whenever I mentioned my own father, Berta would say that she didn't

Packing, Shopping, and More Packing

want to hear anything about him because of the times that he had hit me or almost done so.

That annoyed me. I insist on talking about whatever I want to talk about, especially if it's my own baggage. Censorship by other people infuriates me. Even though my parents had banned Damon, I told them that I refused to be told not to talk about my own husband, and they had given up on that idea.

The same goes for my father; there were lots of positive things about him, such as his insistence that I take my education seriously, study hard, and finish it on time, and his diabolical sense of humor. I really enjoy that last trait about him. One example of this is "Jabba the Slutt." But that was after I got home and told him everything that had happened. Thus far, he just knew the basics, and was on my side.

Now he sat in the car, waiting for my mother to come out.

She was upstairs, talking to Bryn again. Bryn hadn't wanted to eat his couscous immediately, so I had come down here to see if there was anything else that I ought to remember to do before my parents drove off.

There really wasn't. I had another week to tie up every last loose end.

But I suddenly commented to my father, "They certainly seem to think that I have done a stellar job of it here."

He glanced up at me, then stared straight ahead while nodding deeply and sincerely.

He tended to do that when he agreed about anything of significance.

At least my parents were proud of me.

The next day, my mother e-mailed me again. She was pleased with the visit, wanted Albert's e-mail address so that they could stay in touch (she liked him, of course – what wasn't to like?!), and added that my Cookie Cat would be waiting for me, and that Nana was looking forward to having me back at home.

That wasn't all; at some point during the time between being told that Berta and Dionne wanted to move in and me actually going home, my mother mentioned that Nana had insisted that I ought to have a car. She didn't think it was good for me to be cooped up at home all the time, unable to go out at all. She knew what she was asking for; it meant that my parents would be buying me a used car.

Wow. Damon and I would have to get the money to pay my mother back.

That would be a huge problem, although Damon was certain that he would soon have a couple of payments from Saad, his co-inventor, for

The Slamming Door

some immunotherapy treatments. That would bring in $2,000 each time, so after paying some bills, I hoped to present my mother with a couple of checks for half that amount. That would at least earn Damon some respect.

But I would be able to go out driving alone in a car again, enjoying the countryside, doing errands on my own, and visiting bookstores and cafés. I loved to do that.

Chapter 59

A Foley Catheter

Bryn woke me up the morning after my parents took away most of my things, unable to pee. He called out to me, and I got up and flopped on his hospital bed, groggy and out of it, but ready to get washed and dressed if he wanted to go out and get help right away.

He surprised me by not wanting to do that; if he did so, he would miss his visit with Cassie, an unacceptable outcome. She was probably en route anyway.

Could we go to the hospital once she arrived?

No. He wanted his visit like usual at home.

Okay…I got dressed and washed anyway, teeth brushed, makeup on, etc.

Did he want anything?

No; just his visit with Cassie. We could go after that.

Cassie typically stayed until noon. We waited for her to arrive.

Walden was called; he arrived early, a bit before noon. He would be going with us.

Albert came over. He sat with us, worried but unable to do anything to help.

Cassie soon arrived, and was told about this latest unpleasant problem.

Some visit; we all sat around, worrying and wondering what more we could do, even though we realized that there was nothing impressive or particularly useful to do until we went to the hospital.

It didn't take a medical degree to figure out how this had happened to Bryn. Obviously, the evil parasite that was growing in his hip had spread into his…well, you know what…and bent it. Damnit – there was no end to the humiliations that this disease managed to inflict.

Granted, I realized that cancer did not have a higher reasoning function, but it was inevitable that I would react with an illogical, emotional assignment of malice to it for what it was doing to Bryn now. The cancer was enjoying the torment it was inflicting!

No, it wasn't. I was just thinking this because I wanted an enemy to torment back. There wasn't one, at least not the kind that I could get revenge upon. But doctors and lawyers spend a huge chunk of their careers fighting monsters that they can't get that satisfaction from.

I got my breakfast and ate and drank it, feeling lucky to be able to pee it out over the course of the morning, and angry that Bryn couldn't do that. He didn't want his food, or to drink much water, which was no surprise. Why take in more if you can't get rid of it?

The Slamming Door

Cassie talked about what they would ultimately do for Bryn at the hospital; she was sure that it would involve drilling a hole through his pelvis and inserting a tube through that.

It sounded awfully dire and drastic; why did she think that would be the solution?

I didn't say anything, but with a mother working as a urology nurse, I knew about a thing called a Foley catheter – no doubt named for the inventor. No drilling was necessary with one of those; the rubber tube could just be inserted up the urethra and left in place.

Either way, I wondered how Bryn could endure the pain and discomfort of a full bladder for hours on end until we not only went to the hospital but also waited and waited until a doctor actually arrived and inserted the device.

But I wasn't in charge of this schedule; Bryn was. It was his illness, so if he wanted to proceed this way, and enjoy something like a normal visit with his sweetheart, and wait for most of the day for relief, then that was his choice and there was nothing we could do about it.

There was, however, something that I could do once we got to the waiting area, and I watched for the appropriate and opportune moment to do it.

It is one of the moments as his caregiver that I look back upon with pride.

I did well for him, if I do say so myself.

Insert smug grin here.

By the time we left for the hospital, it was after two o'clock. Albert didn't come with us.

By the time we were actually there…

…well, a cab had to be hailed, and it had to be a low-to-the-ground car cab, not one of those new-fangled mini SUVs that the city had recently acquired so many of that hailing a cab that Bryn could ease himself into took twice the usual amount of time.

By the time we were there, it was nearing two o'clock. I had to get the cab, get into it and guide the driver to Bryn's door, wait while he and Walden got him settled, then drive diagonally across town. Then we had to get out, grab a wheelchair, settle Bryn into it, and roll him into an elevator, ride up one level, and roll through the maze of hallways to the center of the building on York Avenue. We went to the small waiting area just inside on the right.

Next, Bryn had to announce himself. We sat down to wait.

I had to wait for about an hour before the right moment came up, but I stalked it.

A Foley Catheter

Meanwhile, I sensed that if I didn't wait at all, Bryn would have been embarrassed, so I procrastinated by keeping busy with inane tasks like getting coffee for me and Walden at the gift shop and then accidentally drinking a sip out of his because I was so distracted about Bryn.

Apologizing after tasting the sugar in it, I took the lid off and gave it to him. He hadn't sipped mine yet. We sat there with Bryn, drinking the coffee and watching the goings on in the waiting area. This was a spot that we hadn't sat in yet on previous visits with Bryn.

Previously, Bryn had sat in a bed wearing a hospital Johnny for hours on end. Not now; he was fully dressed and sitting in a chair in the first part of Sloan-Kettering's Urgent Care Center on York Avenue. It was a little area to the right just inside the double doors.

I asked what the agenda was, and Bryn told me that the urology resident on call had to be phoned and told about his problem. Then this doctor would come over here, take Bryn in the back, and probably insert a catheter in him so that he could pee.

Oh. That sounded logical; it was more or less what I expected to hear.

I sat and watched some more; there were several other patients with caregivers sitting in the room with us, and at the desk was one man in his forties, all dressed in brown street clothes, working the phones. He was chatting with a hospital security guard who had come in to get a cup of the awful but free coffee in the back nook to the right of the desk, next to the rest rooms.

They were just socializing.

That was all the excuse I needed to approach them and speak up. There was no reason for the man at the desk to chat but not get on with the call. It was time to check to see whether not that call had been made yet and, if not, induce that man to make it.

But I decided to be just a little bit indirect. Accusing the guy of not caring and delaying for no valid reason would likely slow things down. I would have to be sneaky, and appeal to his sympathies.

I got up without telling either Bryn or Walden what I was up to and approached the desk.

The man looked up at me, and the guard stopped distracting him. They were obviously used to dying people who felt uncomfortable or worse and their worried and upset relatives.

"Hello," I said. They greeted me pleasantly but with expectant tones; I promptly went on and explained that I was there with my cousin, Bryn Otterman, who couldn't pee, and I added that I didn't know for sure, but it seemed likely that a Foley catheter was in his near future.

The man agreed; it was.

The Slamming Door

I nodded; this was going well so far. "So what happens next?"

"I have to call the urology resident; I just haven't had a chance yet."

Aha…just as I had suspected. The guy could pee comfortably, so he was taking his damned sweet time. Well, enough of that already. I looked as unhappy as I could, breathed a sigh, and said that I had been sitting with Bryn, knowing that he couldn't pee, and remembering all of the times that I had ever had to go to the bathroom but had to wait until one was free. I was remembering how much it hurt to have a full bladder and to just have to stay like that for who knew how long.

The response was as if I had waved a magic wand; the man at the desk picked up his phone and called the urologist immediately. I thanked him very nicely and went back to my seat.

Bryn probably heard it all; he didn't scold me for hurrying things along.

He must have really felt uncomfortable to forgo doing that. It was either that, or he thought that I had been so diplomatic that he could see nothing to criticize.

Walden grinned ever so slightly; he approved.

It wasn't long after that the Bryn was called to a back room with a bed and prepped for the doctor's arrival. Walden got him comfortable, Bryn took out money and told us to go get dinner at the hospital cafeteria, and we left him there. We shouldn't be there while the doctor unstopped his drainage system, I thought to myself; just get over here already and do it.

Walden and I left and found spicy catfish, corn, and whatever else in the cafeteria, I paid for it, and we sat down at one of the long, rectangular tables to eat. There were doctors at some tables, nurses at others, and relatives of patients at still others. I don't remember what we talked about, but Walden thought that my departure was a negative thing.

I still had mixed feelings about it, but was resigned to going.

The doubts I had stemmed from the fact that Bryn was going to be stuck with other caregivers for who knew how long; no one likes changes in their environment when they are that far gone with a terminal illness.

Well, he was sending me away. Time to get him organized so as to make it as easy as possible (could I make it easy?) and time to make sure that he could pull away from me emotionally (thought not until we knew that he could pee).

Walden and I went back to see what was going on.

Great news; the deed had been done, it was a Foley catheter, not a drilled-through-the-pelvis catheter (I don't know what those are called, and have no particular desire to learn that gruesome and miserable data), and Bryn was feeling much better. Obviously, his bladder had emptied

A Foley Catheter

into the attached bag like a drain being unclogged with the most effective chemical.

I obligingly turned away while he showed it to Walden; Walden knew how to empty it.

But it didn't need that right now. We were free to go. Walden helped him get dressed, and we were off, making much faster progress with Bryn now that he was more comfortable.

That wasn't saying much. Bryn was moving pretty slowly at this point.

We rolled him out to a cab; he didn't walk.

He could walk with his cane around the apartment still, but long distances were no longer possible. What was really impressive about the way that Bryn now moved was the fact that he was so careful with his cane at home. He took great pains to set it down lightly as he walked from his chair to the bathroom and back again.

Bryn was determined not to thump the cane loudly, oblivious to the quiet enjoyment of the people who had just moved in below us. "It's just not fair," he had said. The renovation of that apartment had been completed a couple of weeks earlier, and a young married couple had moved in. They seemed delighted with the place, and were friendly enough.

We got home not long after Walden was scheduled to leave, but Walden was in no hurry; this was a special day, one with the kind of problems that can't be planned for and scheduled. He stuck around to settle Bryn into his chair again, complete with draping the horrid pee bag over a rung of the walker, which was strategically parked next to the Lazy Boy chair.

Bryn got his shorts back on instead of the pants, and that made his movements easier.

Then he showed me where the bag was, and how he had concealed it with a section of *The New York Times*. Excellent use of a non-sustainable news-gleaning method; right along, I had been in favor of expending trees on Bryn's comfort. Now they were preserving his dignity, too. I know I'm supposed to be environmentally responsible, but I have no qualms about having put Bryn first for the time I was with him.

Weeks ago, Nurse Ellen had left us a Foley catheter apparatus in a cardboard box, warning us not to try to use it ourselves. When the time came to actually have one, she wasn't in the area for the whole day. I suppose the purpose of leaving it was for a weekend, or for a day when she could install it. I now vaguely recalled that I had jammed the box into the darkest and most unnoticed spot in the closet under Bryn's coats and formal clothes that I could find, all so that Berta wouldn't see it. Neither of us had wanted her to see it; she would have flipped out.

The Slamming Door

Well, we didn't need it now, and Walden couldn't have installed it anyway.

I promptly forgot all about it again.

But what else happened that evening? Lorie Adagio, the social worker, dropped by, and I told her everything that had happened with Berta, and she just looked amazed and appalled.

There were plenty of other loose ends to tie up over the next few days.

In addition to all of this reorganizing and packing, I had the welcome lack of pressure in the form of Berta's absence for the entire weekend before I actually left for Connecticut. She, Matt and Dionne all drove up to Oneonta together for the weekend, thus removing any possibility that any of them might show up at Bryn's apartment.

I didn't give a damn about how she felt about the rubbish that she had left rotting in that closet for years, or about how she felt about having it moved, cleaned, touched, whatever. It's a simple fact of life: you leave detritus in an area that you lack full control over, you take your chances with it.

Out of sight, out of mind was how I thought of them.

Albert came over and commented about the weekend excursion to Oneonta, which was to be their last before the Otterman girls officially had to take over my duties and be available 24/7. "To whom do you owe the freedom to go up there?" he had asked them. Of course, he had no reply to report to me.

That wasn't the point; the point was that he had made a minor effort to rub my care-giving services in their noses. I may not have delivered them flawlessly, but they were delivered willingly and with great attention to detail, with each bit as Bryn requested. My services were invaluable; they freed the others up to do as they chose so that they could think about their upcoming misery with the loss of Bryn.

Albert had given me a gift for my computer and all of the data that I saved: an external hard drive, extra storage space, independent of the main computer tower. It works beautifully still, and I have backed up everything I have on it.

That was one of Albert's motives. The other was about record-keeping. He was nervous about his upcoming responsibility as executor of his brother's estate, and he was also nervous about caring for Bryn after I left, and didn't intend to just rely on his nieces for that. He knew that the computer was full of data that helped with that: the pill sheet, the

A Foley Catheter

address book, and who knew what Henry George materials, plus the scans of those *Puck* magazine prints.

Would I please copy everything on Bryn's hard drive to this little machine, this MyBook thing, so that if he had trouble locating something after I was gone, he could just call me up and have me guide him to it over the phone as he clicked around on Bryn's computer?

Of course, I said, and did so. It was nice not to rely on just those memory sticks, too.

Matt had come around once the previous week, alone, to talk to Bryn. I was sitting at the computer at the time. I looked up at him unapologetically, half daring him to engage me in some sort of exchange, but not particularly concerned that he actually would. I still liked him; he was a nice guy who, like Bryn, would not make any trouble. No wonder Berta had hooked him.

I doubted that even with a baby she would be able to keep him forever, unless he turned out to be a self-sacrificing Catholic. But I really had no idea how much religious tenets informed his life choices – clearly not enough to preclude pre-marital sex. The question was, would he stay with Berta forever, no matter how disgustingly, morbidly obese she was now and later became, and no matter how abusive she was toward him? No...I still doubted it.

Matt had gone in, visited with Bryn, and gone out. That was it, and I was glad. I had had enough of Berta, and Matt was tied to her now by that pregnancy. He had no choice but to take her side and live with it. He was being quite reasonable, considering his predicament, which was very much his own stupid fault. He just stayed out of the conflict, doing nothing to escalate it.

When I checked my e-mail on Saturday, I found a very unpleasant message: the father of my best friend from college was in a coma. Beth had sent out a group message to tell us all what had happened. I was upset when I read about it; I really liked Mr. Coe, and had since I had met him nineteen years earlier.

Brandie's father was a mechanical engineer who had studied at MIT and then started his own company, which made tiny metal pellets that were used to test computer boards. The point was to make sure that each computer chip – there were many embedded into each board – functioned properly. It was cheaper to just make the boards, test them, and then either use them or throw them out if a defective chip was found. Mr.

The Slamming Door

Chandler had given me a tour and explained it one summer afternoon when Beth and I were still in college and I went to visit.

He had collapsed in front of his favorite machine – one that he had invented – and an employee who was an EMT had tried CPR on him to no avail. Brandie said that he was on life support in a hospital nearby, just north of Massachusetts, in New Hampshire, near his company.

I think he was in his late seventies, but no one ever seems to live long enough, especially if we like them a lot. Mr. Chandler had given me one of the best compliments I ever got during the visit: "I like you because you're blunt," he had told me as we sat on the den sofa. "Most women beat around the bush, but you just say what you think without worrying about how to say it."

Leave it to an engineer to say that. I loved it. I still love it. I'll always love it.

He gave me lots of honey from his own apiary and homemade seedless raspberry jam. That went on for years, even long after I wasn't making regular visits; he just kept sending more of his wonderful stuff to me through Brandie, and I would send his jars back later.

Saturday evening, I went out with Alissa and June to see *Julie & Julia*, and to eat Japanese food after that. We did both things on West 23rd Street, on either side of 8th Avenue; it was just convenient that way. But with Albert spending the evening with Bryn, we relaxed and took our time. We had cucumber and peanut sushi, salmon and crab sushi, and green tea ice cream with green tea.

Silly us, happily enjoying ourselves with the assumption that the guys were watching a movie in Bryn's room; they couldn't figure out how to work the DVD set-up, and so had watched Charlie Rose talk about the economy all evening!

Sigh. When we came back, I was not pleased to hear about it; wasn't Albert the technically inclined one of the Otterman brothers?! Oh well; I set up a movie for them, and they watched it for a while. Alissa and June went home.

The next day, Albert was back to keep us company.

He had come over to get Bryn's 2008 tax filing in order, which would be late.

And he had what felt like an insurmountable problem that was pressing on him.

A Foley Catheter

Albert had loaned Bryn something like $12,000 for living expenses when it became clear that his brother was declining faster and would not be able to visit his stockbroker or do whatever he needed to do to access his own funds. Albert would have to get that money back later, after Bryn died, as he settled the estate.

At first, I was just listening. Then I was doing more than listening when he added that "those girls wouldn't understand and would get very upset and I would have a lot of trouble over it, but what can I do," he concluded, looking like it he viewed it as a lost cause. He had convinced himself that he would never get his money back, and he needed it back.

It was an awkward situation, because Albert couldn't just give that money away. But this detail wasn't in Bryn's will. There was nothing in writing to account for it, and Albert worried that after Bryn died, his daughters wouldn't care, wouldn't listen, and wouldn't just quietly let him subtract that amount from the inheritance that he would be responsible for disbursing to them. The attorney would not be doing this job; Albert would. I guess that would cost less.

What to do? Albert sat on the sofa, thinking about it, worried.

Okay, time to be a shark again. I might not be able to fight a nasty case in court, but this didn't sound too difficult. We just had to get Bryn to leave a clear paper trail for Albert to hold up as evidence later.

What could he do, indeed?

I knew what he could do. I got a blank folder and a black Sharpie pen and made yet another important folder: "$ owed by Bryn to Albert" and explained that all paper evidence of these transactions must go into it starting now. This would circumvent such unnecessary uproars.

"Oh no, don't show that to my brother – it will upset him!"

No it won't, I thought, and went right in to show it to Bryn.

Surprise, surprise: it didn't upset Bryn AT ALL.

I explained the point of it as I handed it to him. He said he had lots of paper evidence and would put it in there…today. I told him that his brother would suffer later if he didn't, and when I returned from another errand in the neighborhood, Bryn had done it. End of problem.

I had gone out to buy a lot of toilet paper, soap, cleaning supplies for the bathroom, and whatever food items Bryn was still eating a lot of. All this so that he wouldn't need any errands done right away. That would be convenient for Berta, but sometimes helping out nasty people is just a side effect of helping the person you care about. I didn't waste any emotion on that.

Then, later in the evening with Albert still here, I had to say No to Bryn about something.

What fun.

The Slamming Door

Bryn had a chair sore on his butt – because he was chair-ridden. (It is not accurate to say bed-ridden, because he got this sore by being in a chair.) He lied to me and said it was on his back and he didn't want to bandage it now – he wanted to do it in 2 hours. The translation was "later on, when no one else was with us." Albert had just helped him with a sponge bath.

Well, it sounded suspiciously like a 'likely story' to me. I insisted upon seeing the alleged back sore then and there so that I would understand what was going on. If it was someplace where his underwear went, I wanted Albert here to handle this, because he was another guy.

So, Bryn stood up and turned around, and instead of pulling his shirt up he began to pull his pants down. Definitely time for me to leave – both the room and this duty – so I spun around and said: "That's it - I'm out of here! This is something you need another guy to do! You need your brother – and Walden. That's what he comes here for."

Albert had no objection; he agreed with me. I prepared a gauze bandage, and Albert found the spot...with significant difficulty. Bryn had no butt left, just hanging flesh. Poor Bryn; no wonder he had the equivalent of a bed sore. My mother and grandmother may have been used to this, but I wasn't, and I certainly couldn't make a career of it. If that makes me a terrible or spoiled person, so be it. We're not all nurses.

But I was a bit freaked by this experience, and asked Albert what had gotten into Bryn. I just couldn't calmly figure it out all by myself because I felt awkward and upset.

Albert said that Bryn was getting scared and had grown so dependent on me that he was somewhat taking me for granted. Oh. That explained it. But I wasn't mad at him at all. Bryn was really nearing the end, and although actually being dead wasn't inducing panic; it was the unpleasant and unknown details of his final days that were scaring him. How would it go, and how would he get through it all with his dignity intact? He didn't know, so he was being clingy.

Leaving was going to be awful for both of us, and the process of leaving was starting before I actually walked out the door. It was time to pull away a bit. I said what I was thinking.

Albert and I were standing right outside Bryn's door, and he heard everything we said.

We weren't trying to hide it; we were just sharing our thoughts and analyzing what was making both me and Bryn act the way that we were acting now: our fears, our uneasiness...and this was necessary.

If I was leaving, I shouldn't be doing all of these intimate things for him...he had to get used to having other people take care of him. Just as Bryn needed more and more help, and more intimate things done, I was

A Foley Catheter

leaving. If I went ahead and did those things for him, it would just make my departure even more difficult for him.

Better to insist that he rely on people who weren't leaving; it would be easier for us both.

I suspected that Dionne and Berta wouldn't last long doing this job, and that Bryn would have to go to the Bronx Cavalry Hospital soon. I made him promise to go there if things got too bad with them in charge.

He said, "I know," and promised that he would go.

This sucked; he knew he was in for an unpleasant time of it, and unpleasant in a different way than either of us had been used to. Invasive questions and louder and somewhat babying tones were in his near future. I hated it; it was just another layer of dignity being stripped away.

As I had bought those household supplies and whatever else Bryn needed to get ready for my absence, I had wondered how his daughters would pick up when things ran out; Dionne had no credit card to be reimbursed with, but they would just have to figure it out.

I wasn't going to be around to worry about that anymore, and I had to put it out of my mind. Bryn had already reimbursed me for the last of my errands, and Berta still had to pay me back for a few stacks of canned cat food. Bryn promised to take care of that, telling me to just leave a tally sheet for her the next evening.

So I did; it was just one sheet of paper, very simple, and I drew a line across it two-thirds of the way down. I wrote "PAID" above it and "Not yet paid" below it, and tallied up that part.

When I came home, Berta had left me a check with the word "Thanks" and a smiley face written on the sheet. I went to the bank with that the next afternoon. Check that off the list...

But back to the weekend; Alissa was having problems of her own. With her uncle nearer to death, her father was leaving more and more of the work of watching her mother to her. She should have been dating and getting married, but she was in a trap. It was something that she had agreed to accept, but that didn't make it any easier. I didn't envy her; writing preserved her sanity, and she couldn't do enough of it. Albert kept saying that he and June were ruining her life.

That night, she had brought June home, and her mother had announced that she wanted to take a shower. That meant that Alissa wouldn't be able to do any writing, so she protested that showers were part of the morning routine, which they were. June threw a huge fit and cried, so Alissa ended up forced into spending a long time that evening supervising a shower. June always forgot the procedure in there – shampoo, conditioner, once each. At last June fell asleep on the sofa and

The Slamming Door

Alissa called to inform her father of both that fact and that she felt trapped.

I was very glad that I had gotten those pretty blouses for her and then helped her to find that Vera Bradley backpack. On Monday, I bought her a present. Alissa wanted to get her eyebrows shaped, so I made her promise to get it done first at a day spa and then maintain it with a mirror and tweezers – not to just pluck it herself. I looked up a day spa nearby, and she was clearly excited over that. Then I went to a Sephora shop on 5th Avenue and bought her the supplies (tweezers and a magnifying mirror), which the sales lady packed into a pretty bag with bright pink tissue paper. Alissa was thrilled, and thanked me with a hug.

Also, I had written to my mother over the weekend to go over some logistical details about my departure. She wrote back shortly; yes, she really was going to bring my big blue suitcase back empty, and yes, my boxes of books were in my room, so that I could have them, not down in the basement. There was also a surprise that I would like, whatever that might be.

I wrote something to her about a fun thing for us to do together:

We should go out and see Julie & Julia - *I saw it tonight with Alissa and June, and it was wonderful. I'm reading Julia Child and Alex Prud'homme's book about her called* My Life in France *right now - and it has photos. Alex is her husband's twin brother's grandson.*

My mother was very sorry about Mr. Chandler; there wasn't much else to say about that.

She asked me several questions about how Bryn would fare when I left – who would stay with him at night? I wrote back: Berta. Only Berta was moving in; Dionne would come in the mornings when it was time for Berta to leave for work.

Albert certainly wasn't optimistic; he told me, before I took off that evening to eat and see the movie and not be near Berta, that he was worried. "I can see how it will go now; Dionne won't show up on time, and Berta will have to go to work; it's going to be a mess."

Terrific…but I had to leave.

I put post-it notes on Bryn's TV: how to run the DVD player, and how to switch back to be able to watch TV. There wasn't much else I could do, but I kept finding a few more things here and there, and fitting them in.

A Foley Catheter

On the Monday before it was time to go home to Connecticut, I went out to see the 6th *Harry Potter* movie for the second time. Part of my reason for doing so was to make damned sure – for yet another evening – that I would not see Berta. That meant getting out before dinner time and having to find a meal out.

For a moment, when Bryn seemed to be trying to keep me around a bit longer, I got worried and asked him, "You're not trying to force a meeting between me and Berta, are you?"

His brother had already arrived, so I was a bit suspicious, but he just said, "No."

So I went out before anyone else could arrive.

This time I found it was easier to eat at East of Eighth, of all places. I had shellfish paella and gazpacho with sangria followed by flan, a full Spanish/Mexican gourmet meal. It was an early bird special, prix fixe. Why not? I was about to be out of this city, unable to do such things again for a long time.

That was one reason for eating there. The other was that East of Eighth was right next door to the movie theater, thus ensuring that I could get back in there exactly on time. I did, too. I had been thoroughly excited to see this movie the first time, as was usual whenever a new movie in a series of magic, comic book super heroes, or other interest of mine came out.

Now I was getting ready to go home to my mother again. I found my thoughts turning to her, and to things that she had observed to me in the past. She had once commented that I had the ability to wonder at and enjoy things immensely, something that she lacked. She also talked about her own maturity whenever such things came up in conversation.

To me, maturity is grossly overrated, especially when it becomes linked, as it typically does in her estimation, to the loss of one's ability to wonder. I refuse to lose that ability.

Come to think of it, as an Aspie, I am probably stuck with the ability to wonder.

It's not going to go away, and I'm glad.

I still get very, very excited with rapt and happy anticipation whenever a new movie is advertised if it seems well put together and acted. Once I am in the theater, I almost always love the music, the special effects, the story line, the care in following the original story line developed by the book's author, and the cleverness of the entire combination.

If maturity means losing that ability to be so happily thrilled, I don't want it.

Chapter 60

A Good-Bye Party

Bryn, Albert, Alissa and June threw me a lovely good-bye party the night before I left.

But there was something else that I wanted to do with the last bit of time leading up to my final departure from Bryn's apartment that I remember. I wanted to go outside and visit various spots in the neighborhood, enjoy a few places that I really liked, and accumulate a few more significant memories before leaving for good.

I headed down 9th Avenue, went into The Three Tarts, and chatted with the nice gay sales clerk that I had taken a liking to. He had told me all about the Easter brunch that he was going to prepare for a large group of guests, and we had henceforth talked about gourmet cooking and baking every time I went in there. The place sold flavored hot chocolates for a week that spring – a different flavor each day – and little dark chocolate cookies and cardamom-apricot ones cut into flawless shapes depending upon the season. Thanks to having been in the area for nearly a year, I had bought bats at Halloween, hearts for Valentine's Day, rabbits at Easter, and so on.

A Good-Bye Party

From there, I wandered down the street to Chelsea Market for a last tour of the shops.

On the way out, I ran into Hilda and her boyfriend Riley. I told her that I was leaving tomorrow, and my voice shook when I said I doubted I would ever see Bryn again. She didn't smile or say anything much. At the time, I didn't think much about that because I don't read facial expressions well, but later I wished I hadn't chatted with her at all.

I took off in another direction after that, across to 8th Avenue and down to Hudson Street, where I stopped for a last spicy hot chocolate at The Chocolate Bar. It was just a few steps away from House of Cards, but my writing student, the actor, wasn't there. I had already called him to explain that I was leaving the city and why. He was sorry to hear that, and wanted to keep working with me. That was nice, I had thought to myself, but it sounded unrealistic.

As I sat in the chocolate place enjoying my drink, a black couple in their forties (a man and a woman; this was close to Chelsea, so specifying this seems like a reasonable idea), both with long dreadlocks, sat down at the next table. With my usual penchant for chatting with strangers, I struck up a conversation with them. They were tourists.

I was upset about leaving and about the way that I had been treated, so I told them all about it. They thought it was all quite awful of course, and they were also sorry to hear about how Damon had to be away all of the time. That led to showing each other our wallet wedding photos, which was fun. The husband had a photo of them both in his own wallet, but the wife didn't like it because she had smiled with her eyes closed. Oh well...

They wanted to find something in Greenwich Village, and I was going that way to buy some more coffee to take home with me at McNulty's, so I showed them how to get there, referring to my *Manhattan: Block by Block* map for perhaps the thousandth time.

It was a pleasant walk, the sun was shining, and I suppose that it was perfect for a last day in Manhattan while Bryn was still there to come back to. When I had seen and wandered enough, I went home for the last time.

The plan was to be back by dinnertime, because Albert, June and Alissa were coming over to throw me a good-bye party. They had asked me what kind of food I would most like to have, and I had said Indian, thinking of the inexpensive take-out menus I had ordered off of so often.

In Connecticut, there were hardly any Indian restaurants; I usually cooked my own Indian food. That meant no naan bread, no mango lassi, and always chicken curry, not shrimp curry and not bindhi masala. My

The Slamming Door

parents loved my recipe of chicken legs and basmati rice, but it wasn't as much fun that way, never eating Indian food out.

But Albert and June would have none of that cheap menu when I mentioned it.

This was a special occasion, and thank-you party as well as a good-bye party.

They insisted upon getting our dinners from the fancy place around the corner on 9th Avenue, called Bombay Talkie. That was the fabulous place with the large-as-life, museum-quality oil paintings of Bollywood movie scenes. Damon and I had been there once, and its food was delectable.

Like many other restaurants in Manhattan, this one had its menu online, which made it easy for all five of us to just decide what we wanted, write up a list, and give it to Alissa. A phone call was made, and after waiting a reasonable amount of time, she and June went out to get the food. They were only gone for twenty minutes.

The meal was delicious, of course, and we all took our time over it. Another lovely, companionable evening with take-out food and all of us sitting together in Bryn's room...but Bryn was looking pretty frail.

Over the past day or so, his voice had started to get quieter. The change felt abrupt and startling to us all. He still had a voice left, but I had to be in his room now to hear what he said. The previous night, packing the very last few items to go, I had not heard him calling me over the sounds of the television, which I never ran particularly loudly, and the crackling of newspaper as I used it for padding.

I found out that he had been calling to me to put his medicine in the apple sauce when I went in to check on him. Damnit, I thought. I'm never going to be the perfect, flawless caregiver. Maybe that was silly; maybe no one can be perfect, but I wanted a record that reflected all of the attention to detail that I had invested in his care.

Aloud, I just said, "Cancer has stolen your lovely tenor voice," looking furious about life in general. "I'll get the applesauce and come right back." Bryn just nodded. This cancer-driven laryngitis had crept up on him gradually, so that he didn't realize how bad it was either.

It was easy to see how he hadn't noticed, because right along – for years, I was told by both of the Otterman brothers – Albert had been telling Bryn that he couldn't hear him when the two of them were in the same room together. "You're deaf as a post!" Bryn would say to him in frustration. Albert would never forget that.

There was one other lovely surprise that evening from Albert, June and Alissa: a cake.

It wasn't just any cake, either. It was a chocoholic torte, one layer of thick, rich delectability with edible gold icing for garnish, which read

A Good-Bye Party

"Thank you Clarisse" on it, plus an extra dusting of edible gold over the whole top of the cake. It was beautiful, and Albert and I took a few photographs, with that cake. We had a close-up of it, plus one of Bryn holding it up, and a couple of me and Bryn together as he sat in his comfortable blue chair.

It was a pleasant evening, and it kept me from thinking too much about the next day.

That evening, I took my shower, e-mailed Damon, looked around the whole apartment carefully, and packed whatever I wouldn't need during breakfast the next morning. I would be getting up a bit earlier, so that my parents could take me away shortly after they arrived. It was a 3-hour drive each way, so we intended to be gone by eleven o'clock.

That was one part of the agenda, but the other one was that Bryn was going out just before eleven to have a physical therapy session. He had been given this hard-to-get appointment when his leg had first swelled up, and been waiting all summer for it. It was at noon, and there had been no way to change it. The whole idea seemed like an exercise in futility now. His voice was failing, and Albert had told me that their mother's voice went just before she died of bladder cancer at the age of seventy-one.

Bryn was seventy-one.

My grandmother, the one who had died of lung cancer, lost her voice at the end, too.

So the day that I was leaving, he was going to be half-dragged out of there for some exercises that would probably not do him the slightest bit of good, and would likely hurt. Wonderful; the ideas that the medical profession had to offer Bryn just got more ludicrous as this illness at away at him.

There was just one other item of interest that night: a special gift from Bryn.

He gave me one of his high school CDs, so that I could hear him singing with his lovely tenor voice any time I wanted to, and he wrote to me on the insert, the thing that I had made for the jewel cases.

He wrote me a personal note on one side, and he addressed the other side of the fold-out sheet to me, just about the lists of songs. His name was next to the ones that he had had solos for:

To Clarisse,

The Slamming Door

The Hackley Octet and The Hackley Glee Club
"Bidin' My Time" by Gershwin
"Steal Away"

And the note:

August 2009

Dear Clarisse,

It's been quite a year, hasn't it? Under your wonderful care, I have not just survived, but have thrived! Words cannot convey what your being here has meant to me. Much love forever to a great cousin whose presence has brought new spice to an already interesting family.

Love Bryn.

This was the best gift he could have given me in terms of a physical object; the other one was the eleven months as his caregiver. It was the best compliment, being the person that he preferred to have with him when life was awful.

Chapter 61

Home Again

When I woke up on the morning of August 12th, I was anxious, which was typical for a day with an impending change of environment and transition time (the drive). I couldn't face anything that would intensify that feeling, so I kept to myself, getting ready quickly, and avoiding everyone.

Albert had come over early.

As quickly as I could, to get it over with, I rushed into the bathroom, cleaned myself up, and then went back into my room to put on my face cream and makeup so I could pack that stuff. Then I got my breakfast and coffee and sat at the computer, eating and drinking it. I had already signed out of my e-mail, out of the pogo.com game site, and taken away my memory sticks and the new MyBook machine.

There was nothing to do but eat.

Bryn called out to me to come in and sit, but I said I was too anxious, and needed to eat as quickly and calmly as I could. They were all in there; Albert had let Walden in. I didn't get anyone else anything to eat or drink that morning. I just let the others take over those duties; it was time to do that.

As I cleaned up my dishes and put them away, Albert came into the kitchen to chat with me. He watched as I straightened every last item in the kitchen, the garbage, the recycling, the dishes and cutlery, the kitchen scrub brush...everything.

"Your job has been a very detailed one, and you have done it so efficiently that we never saw anything out of place for more than an instant. Things are going to fall apart when you're gone," he said unhappily.

I just nodded and agreed with him, and went to sit at the computer and stare into space.

It was weird; just last week I had been so angry with Berta about this that I had said that I hoped they would have trouble doing this job properly, get stressed out over the details, and start to understand what was involved. I had said it with a demonic tone, and Albert had chided me.

But now he was echoing all that with a rueful, anxious tone (except that he was sure of it rather than hopeful about it), while I was focused on the transition that I was facing today. It was true; he went on about it for a few more minutes, saying that those same things were probably going to happen soon with the daughters in charge, until he had to go into Bryn's room.

The Slamming Door

Suddenly Bryn came out of his room, slowly and with difficulty, supported on both sides by Walden and Albert. I looked up at him, wide-eyed and lost, but didn't make eye contact. I was freaking out. I often look at but don't see people clearly when I am about to go somewhere.

Bryn put his arms out toward me as he ambled forward, and I got up and hugged him. When we let go, the procession toward the front door resumed. That was less than a minute later so that he wouldn't collapse from too much standing.

Such a short, last hug, and he was gone.

I sat back down at the computer and fidgeted in my seat, wondering how soon my parents would appear. I don't remember what I did while I sat there. Perhaps I surfed the Internet…or maybe I just stared at my cell phone.

It wasn't long before Albert came back upstairs with my mother. She had the big empty blue suitcase; I quickly loaded it and we moved things down to the car. When all that was done, my father came up to use the bathroom. It was still summertime, so he could leave the car there for a few minutes. I went again, too.

I looked around once more, to make sure that I was forgetting nothing, but I wasn't. The last thing I did was to go into Bryn's room to say good-bye to the naughty cat. Nikita was curled up in her little green ring pillow bed under the air conditioner. She looked at me sleepily, and didn't get hissy or snippy with me; she knew I was leaving for good. She had seen all of the packing, and cats understand what that means.

"Good-bye Nikita; you have to take care of Bryn now," I told her, petting her.

She looked sideways up at me, and said nothing, but she understood. My mother stood watching me with the cat; of course she thought I should say good-bye to her before taking off.

Albert came out with us to say good-bye, and I took the little ring of keys to Bryn's apartment off of my keychain; it had spent at least four years there. He took it, and it felt final: I was never going inside that apartment again.

His cell phone rang, and it was Alissa, calling to say good-bye. "Cousins forever," she said to me. That was nice. I gave the phone back to Albert and hugged him, then got into the car.

That was it; we took off.

Off in the car, west on 21st Street to 10th Avenue, past the 192 Books shop, which I pointed out to my parents as we went. We were in my mother's silver Volkswagen Jetta station wagon again. I tended to turn into a tour guide whenever there was something to show them.

Home Again

They seemed interested, so I kept it up for a while as we moved north, until my father turned northwest to get onto the Henry Hudson Parkway. It was a gray, overcast, drizzly day, perfect for leave-taking.

We went over a bridge and onto the New York State side of the river, and continued on north until we were on the country roads that led to Sleepy Hollow. I asked if we were going to pass through there, and my father thought we might. I thought of the photograph of Bryn and his friends in that town with the metal statue of Rip Van Winkle, one of Washington Irving's characters.

A couple of times, I had to ask my parents to speak up. They tended to mumble in the front seats, and I was a bit deaf. There's nothing like talking quietly in some other direction when they want me to respond; of course I can't until they repeat it more loudly.

It was a nice drive, but my father couldn't find the statue, and we didn't really care. Maybe we would plan a drive to see it another time, my mother said. We found a place in a hilly town, an Irish pub, and ate lunch. I had sweet potato fries and a crab cake, and they had heavy, multi-layered sandwiches.

My mother admired my smaller lunch as she got half of hers to go; she was tall and thin and didn't need to eat much. But my father ate all of his as usual; he was a big guy, with the same shape as me. We were both short-waisted, with big calves, the same shape to our hands and noses, and the same gait. But both of my parents were taller than me; it made me feel like a little kid next to them.

At one point on the way home, I found my father alone; my mother had wandered off somewhere. It was then that I asked him, bewildered, how Berta could have turned out so awful after having the same advantages in life as me: an ivy-league-educated father, private school, college, and emphasis on all that.

He said that Bryn was a laissez-faire dad. That made sense; being such a sweet guy who wouldn't insist on things and get enraged at a failure to make an effort in school had contributed to the outcome. But I suspected that the basic raw material – Berta herself – was even more to blame for the outcome. She was too old now to just say it was someone else's fault.

When we went back to the car, my phone rang. It was Bryn!

I was thrilled that he had called me.

He was back from the physical therapy appointment, which had gone okay. No one expected him to go back, but he had been determined to go there after waiting all summer. What he wanted to know was, how was I doing, and where were we at this point?

The Slamming Door

I told him I was okay, and that we had just eaten lunch in some hilly town, and paused to ask my father which one it was, relaying it to Bryn. But I don't remember the name now.

That was about it.

Bryn was just checking in with me.

We had discussed phone calls a week and a half earlier, on that Sunday when he had essentially told me that he was sending me away, after my parents had called back to say that I could go home to them.

"You don't like to talk on the phone much," I had said. "Usually you seem to be in a big hurry with everyone, saying that you've got to go after just a minute or two."

"For you, I'll break my rule and talk longer," he had promised me.

He had said that I was his best friend now; I guess this was the proof of that.

We made a plan to talk at roughly three or half-past three o'clock each afternoon, depending upon when we could get on the phone. We chose that time because Berta would be out at work during our calls.

My father drove north until my mother and I insisted that we couldn't wait much longer for a bathroom, certainly not while we drove all the way home.

He used to be impossible about that, refusing to stop until it suited his schedule, following an itinerary that he had worked out in his mind without telling us until we were on route, and with rigid disregard for variables like bathroom use.

No more; my mother wouldn't put up with it, and had read him a riot act the last time he tried it. He found us a place, a really nice place in, of all towns, Katonah, the one that his mother had grown up in.

We dashed into the restaurant he pulled up to and went, and when we came out, the rain had stopped. It was a nice town, with pretty boutique shops and a nice pharmacy that doubled as a little gift shop. My father agreed to stay for a little while.

Off we went, poking around and exploring just across the street and no farther.

We were a bit curious about Grandma Barnes Rénard's childhood stomping grounds, even though we realized that eighty years had passed since she had lived here. The people in the restaurant had looked intrigued when we mentioned that we were using their place as a rest stop so that we could pass through her old hometown.

After about forty minutes, we got back into the car and drove around the town, trying to recognize the house that Grandma had grown up in, but it was no use. Maybe it was completely renovated, or maybe it was gone. There was no way to know without searching land records, and they had rented the place anyway.

Home Again

We continued on home, and arrived in the evening.

The moment I walked into the kitchen, my Cookie Cat heard me talking and walked in to look for me. He was happy to see me again, and let me pick him up and kiss him and cuddle him.

His fur was perfect; the red lesions that he had had the previous fall were all healed. My father showed me how to feed him; the pet allergist had prescribed a specific diet of duck and green pea cat food, both canned and dry, measured and mixed, and it had cured our cat.

My boxes of books were up in my room, and my mother rushed up there with me to show me my surprise: it was a 26-inch flat-screen TV, mounted on the wall just above my computer monitor, and hooked up to the cable system!

That was terrific; when I had left, the entire state was about to switch over to digital cable. Anyone with an antiquated antennae TV would either have to pay for a special box or be out of luck. I had only had an old black antennae TV in there, which was now gone. Granted, this helped with the value of the property, but we weren't moving anytime soon.

In fact, there were no such plans in the works. This was for me to enjoy.

I thanked them both happily; they wanted me there, they said, and were looking forward to enjoying my cooking and baking again. My father had stayed home from work one day to meet the cable guy and get this set up properly.

This was going to be okay. I unpacked a few things, including a little Virginia Woolf finger puppet from House of Cards on Hudson Street, which I put on the top of a wooden ruler from same shop. It was a ruler on one side and a list of Hollywood screen stars on the other.

Now I felt set up to write. I powered up my desktop to computer to check it; it ran beautifully. I settled all of the things I had collected over the past year – the MyBook machine and the memory sticks, and new books – around the desk, connecting and arranging it all.

Later that night, I called Damon and described it to him. He felt much better, too.

So when it was over, I found myself in my old room, with my old cat, my old but still very new computer, my books, my things stacked around me waiting to be put away, the familiar kitchen downstairs with its beautiful décor that I had helped choose and oversee the installation of, complete with its state-of-the-art equipment, and the small garden outside that faced north.

I had planted many pink and blue flowering bulbs and bushes there over the years: iris bulbs were my favorite, a pastel pink rose bush, dark

The Slamming Door

and light pink and blue hyacinths, a bleeding heart shrub, blue delphiniums, and a beautiful pale pink peony bush.
   But the shade would not allow my favorites to grow and thrive.
   I was back in the dark and quiet, alone again.
   It felt like a metaphor for my life.

Chapter 62

Bryn Died

Bryn died at St. Vincent's Hospital at 8:17 a.m., on Monday, August 17th, 2009.

That was when it was declared official, for record-keeping purposes.

Bryn's voice had been fading a bit while I was still taking care of him.

After I had come home to Connecticut, Bryn was true to his word about making an exception for me and being available for a real phone call – not a hurried, how-fast-can-we-end-this-conversation-and-ring-off call – at 3 p.m. each day.

We had three of those.

When I think about it now, it was actually two phone calls that we had, and the third was by proxy. The first two were on Thursday and Friday. When I had called, he had sounded hoarse, as though speech were difficult for him.

I had asked Bryn a couple of questions aimed at understanding what was going on with him just then. Was Walden hanging out with him? Yes. It was hard for him to say much, I could hear, so I had asked easy yes-no questions. I don't remember what else I asked him, but despite the unhurried feel to the calls, I didn't want to strain him by prolonging the conversation.

For some reason, I forget exactly why, we didn't have a call on Saturday. Perhaps Berta was with him all day and I missed my chance, but in any event, there was no call that day. I was thinking about the call, but neither Bryn nor I had attempted a phone call on Saturday.

On Sunday, I was out on a beautiful day in Avon at the brick strip mall on Route 44 with my mother and aunt, who had driven from Rhode Island for the day to visit us. I had my cell phone on and in my pocket, and we were walking around outside, between stores, when it rang.

It said "Bryn W. Otterman" on the notice, but when I answered, it was Albert. He was calling on his brother's behalf, at his request, and he told me so. He also told me that Bryn had completely lost his voice and was speaking in a whisper now. Albert relayed what Bryn and I wanted to say to each other. We kept it short; it's hard to enjoy a conversation by proxy.

So those were our phone calls, aside from the one that Bryn had happily surprised me with as I rode home through downstate New York with my parents. He was sorry to see me go and have a change of caregiver; I couldn't imagine any other reaction to his situation.

The Slamming Door

I was sorry to go, even though it was time to get out of what had become a hideous and unmanageable situation. But I still had wanted to know how his appointment had gone, and how he was doing, so I was glad to have a chance to find out so soon after it. I was also very glad that Bryn had called me while I was on the road because once I was underway, in transition, the panic attack over the change of environment was starting to fade. I could enjoy talking with him, be calm, and really understand what was happening in the call.

When we had last seen each other, I had been too anxious, and I had not wanted to be particularly conscious of the experience of our separation. Not in the morning, not while I was eating, not just then. That hug he had given me as they helped him shuffle out of the apartment – a team effort by then – was what I had really wanted. It was just enough just then.

On Monday, I called again, at 3 or 3:30 p.m. – I didn't note the exact time – and Dionne had answered. She was in the apartment alone, answering the endless stream of calls from his friends, telling them the news as they attempted to say hello to her father. What a miserable task she had, telling them all that they couldn't, and why not.

I told her why I was calling, about our phone call arrangement, and she said that Bryn had "passed away" that morning. She added that she was in shock, because it felt so sudden.

After a stunned pause, I replied, "Okay, I'm in shock too."

For a moment, I wasn't sure what to say next, but then I realized that I needed to ask questions, so I did. I found out that he had died at St. Vincent's Hospital, at what time, and so on. That he had fallen into that coma that the social worker had described to me a couple of months earlier, and wouldn't wake up, at around 4 a.m.

I thanked her for the information and said good-bye. One thing that I simply refused to do, and have no regrets about, was to talk or act like some outsider who owed sympathy remarks, letters, e-mails, or cards to either of his daughters.

As far as I was concerned, I was one of them – not a daughter, but a close relative of Bryn's. There was that, and the fact that I owed no duty to them after doing what they were so utterly unqualified and unwanted for, and after Berta had been so abusive and Dionne had pretty much ignored me. Bryn had had his illness on his own terms, and they had their inheritance coming. It would have been eaten up without me, in hospice costs.

I never told them that he didn't want them to be his caregivers. I guess I'm just not that mean, and that that is probably one of the reasons why I did not end up practicing law.

Bryn Died

But I am mean enough to have been accepted to a top-tier law school, and I wasn't about to give them anything that they didn't deserve...plus it didn't occur to me to even think in such terms until much later. I never think of such details when something shocking happens; at first, I freeze up as I absorb the shock of change and how new it feels.

I was so upset that I turned quiet and had few words to say. I don't talk out loud much when I've had a shock. E-mailing friends to say that Bryn had died was another matter, and I did that right away, with the subject heading "Bryn died" on the message.

If there's one thing about the language of death that I can't stand, it's the words "passed away." I just don't approve of using them, and I won't. I hate euphemisms. I won't mask the facts in soft terms. Bryn died. Whenever someone dies, that's what I say to convey the fact.

So I sent that e-mail out and of course got lots of nice, sympathetic replies from all of my friends. Later that evening, I got a somewhat different reply: Brandie's father had died at 8:30 p.m. – roughly 12 hours apart from Bryn on the same day. My alternate father-figure and her father, both gone on the same day; off went another e-mail, with sympathy for her.

Later that week – perhaps the next day – I wrote sympathy cards, one for her and one for her mother. I used the calligraphy pen, naturally.

But back to Bryn's death...I wanted to know more about it. That was easier said than done. I called Albert's phone and got nowhere. He had probably turned the damned thing off; it must have rung too much for him.

When that didn't work, I called Alissa's cell phone. She answered. She said, "It's still pretty raw," and told me that they were eating in a restaurant. Maybe the next day I would be able to get him to talk to me.

Great. Who else? Cassie – would she talk to me? She was impossibly tricky to actually get on the phone with. All she had was a land line phone out on her porch with an answering machine. Chip either remembered to give her its messages or he didn't, and he was in charge of that thing. Cassie really couldn't hear it in the kitchen. Eventually, I discovered that the best hit-or-miss time to try her was in the evenings between 7 and 8 p.m. Sure enough, by the next day, I was able to get people on the phone. I talked to Albert and Cassie, and between them, pieced together what had happened:

Berta had set her alarm clock and made a practice of waking up every hour on the hour to check her father. Rather than do all of her sleeping at once, she had attempted this insane schedule while pregnant. I don't think professional nurses do that. But Berta wanted to do this.

The Slamming Door

She had checked and gone back to bed when Nikita woke her up, pounding her door and meowing incessantly. The cat had stayed in Bryn's room as usual, watching him or sleeping near him, and his breathing must have sounded ominously different to her, no doubt with that death rattle that the social worker had described to me.

Of course Berta woke up and went to see what was happening. She found Bryn deeply asleep in his chair, and he absolutely would not wake up. She called Albert, who got dressed and came over. That took him a while; he must have arrived about an hour later.

Some time passed, perhaps an hour as they considered what to do and summoned an ambulance. Cassie was called; she got into her car and started driving to Manhattan.

Bryn had set up that do-not-resuscitate order, so I could understand the dilemma and the delay. What to do? You can't just do nothing, and watch someone die. There could be legal consequences for just pacing around wringing your hands, and the inaction itself is far more upsetting than doing something like departing for a hospital.

They arrived with Bryn at the hospital at 8:02 a.m.

Cassie arrived too late to see him, but it didn't make much difference to her…he wouldn't have talked to her anyway. He couldn't have talked to her. She told me that they had talked – sort of – the night before, on the phone. She had called him and Albert had held the phone up to his ear. Cassie had said, "I love you," and Bryn had huffed back twice into the phone. That was all he could do; his voice was completely gone.

I was worried about something; had they bothered Bryn at that emergency room, pushing on his chest trying to do CPR to cover their own legal behinds, or what? I hoped not, but I was worried that they had, despite his wishes that they just let him be.

No, they hadn't, she assured me. They just officially declared his death. It was okay.

That was a relief. I had been sure that Berta would put up a futile resistance, not wanting to let her father escape from his illness if it meant dying and leaving her. I wouldn't have been able to stop her if I had been there; I would have had to just watch, but I wanted to know what had happened. It was better that I had missed her recriminations; what if I had been there when he fell asleep for the last time? Berta would have second-guessed me and heaped abuse on me.

Cassie added that she had found a place to park a couple of blocks away and rushed over to the hospital to find everyone, so Albert had insisted upon walking her back to her car. She had tried to talk him out of it, but he had insisted, exhausting himself somewhat in the humid heat.

Cassie hailed Albert a cab when they got to her car, and stowed her car someplace else for the day. She had to get back to Goshen by the end

Bryn Died

of the day, however, and make sure that Chip was okay; he couldn't be unattended for long. Now she just had one guy to take care of, but she would have given anything to have had both of them still. Bryn was over a decade younger than Chip, but he had died first. Life never makes any sense – it just is.

Albert went back to the hospital and from there, from what I understand, met up with Cassie, Matt, and Berta. Matt couldn't have worked that day with all of this to deal with; he brought his jeep-SUV and they all rode around in it together dealing with the immediate consequences of Bryn's death.

The immediate consequences were, gruesome as this is, dealing with the disposal of his body. The hospital required that it be claimed and removed, and promptly. New York City is full of people getting sick or injured daily, and dying. Its hospitals – especially one that was failing like St. Vincent's – can't afford to keep any space unnecessarily occupied for long.

Accordingly, Albert had to see that his brother's body was sent on to its next stop right away, with no time to sit and cry. Some funeral home in Yonkers, where they had lived as children, was chosen, and it did the cremation. The ashes were divided into three urns, one for Cassie, one for Berta, and one for Dionne. I don't know whether anyone planned to scatter or bury the ashes or not, but cremation and three shares of the ashes was what Bryn had ordered.

Next, the family rode around Yonkers, drove past the childhood home, which Albert said looked a lot like it had when he and Bryn had lived in it, and saw a few other memorable sights. Then Cassie had to get ready to go home; I hope she got out of the city before rush hour.

Albert told me that Alissa had used his bound paper copy that I had made of Bryn's contacts to inform everyone listed in it of his death, via her cell phone. That took care of most of it; perhaps Dionne had fielded a lot of condolence calls as well as attempts to talk with Bryn.

And that was it.

The memorial service would be in a couple of months – nearly two full months later.

All was expected to proceed as Bryn had wished.

I intended to go back to Manhattan and attend, and see all of the in-laws again, including many whom I had never met, because they had been unable to come to my wedding. (That was the last time that I had been at any large gathering that might have made such meetings likely.)

Meanwhile, I had some adjusting and planning to do.

For over a year after Bryn's death, I had constant dreams that I was back there taking care of him again. The dreams always included Bryn, usually with brief appearances by him, and then just me wandering

The Slamming Door

silently around the premises. Those premises were typically in a state of flux. They felt familiar but looked unrecognizable. Always, I had been asked specifically by Bryn to come back and take care of him.

I guess I felt as though I hadn't stayed with him long enough, even though I had stayed as long as he asked me to. The problem was that I had not stayed as long as he wished me to. He did not get to do what he wished.

He did not get to keep me as his caregiver until the end, and he did not get a long enough life. Seventy-one and a half years is not long enough. Bryn wanted eighty years, and had planned on a ten-year retirement in which to teach, write, and watch the economy.

He missed all that.

Perhaps I am comparing his life – the quantity of it – with the amount that many of my own blood relatives have gotten. They have lived into their nineties, some almost to a hundred years old, so when I think of how much time Bryn got, it seems like a rip-off. Also, I often find out about people via the news who lived longer than Bryn, or who are still alive and a lot older.

It always seems like a rip-off when a nice person doesn't get more time.

Chapter 63

Aspie and Proud of It

One of the first things I did after that was fulfill that promise to myself to acquire and read a book about Asperger Syndrome. When I found one written by a person who had the condition, I wanted that one.

It was called *Asperger's from the Inside Out*, and it was published in 2008, and written by Michael John Carley. Carley directs G.R.A.S.P., the Global and Regional Asperger Syndrome Partnership. I spent the remainder of the month of August reading that book very carefully, then searched online for more data.

That book was extremely helpful, and it validated my life's experiences, but there was just one thing missing from it: more about female Aspies.

It wasn't the author's fault; he was a busy person who did very well to provide as much information as he did, but most of it was what it had to be: tales from his own life. One term I took away from all this analysis is Aspie; some people with Asperger's like the term, and others don't. I like it. The other term I learned is NT, which stands for neurotypical, or normal type. Both terms refer to human brain patterns.

Being an Aspie seems like the coolest thing, no matter how hard that makes my life.

Combined with what I discovered from my online research, I learned that women with Asperger's are outnumbered by males 4 to 1. Some famous women with Asperger's include: Marie Curie, who won the Nobel Prize for discovering the element radium; Jane Austen, who wrote what is still considered to be the best novel ever written, *Pride & Prejudice*; and Virginia Woolf, whose thesis *A Room of One's Own*, which stated that women must have money and a room of their own if they are to write fiction, pointed out the value of a woman having her own space and the respect for her work and creativity that that demonstrates.

Male Aspies include: Wolfgang Amadeus Mozart, one of my favorite classical composers; Thomas Jefferson, the author of our Declaration of Independence, an inventor, lawyer, free-thinking theist, politician, ambassador, and botanist; Albert Einstein; Isaac Newton; Hans Christian Anderson; and Nikola Tesla.

I found it really cool and inspiring to be able to say that my brain patterns functioned as theirs did. It gave me reason to hope that what I planned to accomplish – becoming a published author whose books make points that not only I but also the rest of the world deem worthy of consideration – is indeed possible and likely.

The Slamming Door

For years, not knowing what Asperger's is or being aware that we had it, Damon and I had joked with each other that he stopped maturing emotionally at age 9 and I stopped at perhaps age 15. Now that we knew about Asperger's, we looked at those statements much more soberly, and felt a certain sense of seriousness about the idea.

Despite that, we both realized that even if we would never become "mature," as most of the population did, we would gather experience and knowledge as time passed, and our natural, human desire to do the best that we could would enable us to respond to situations better and better as time went on. As we were so fond of saying, maturity is grossly overrated.

Fitting in has never been something that I aspired to; getting by on my own terms as a functioning, unique individual has always been my intention.

Learning what Asperger's is and how it works made me feel freer than ever.

I realized that life in a cubicle was more than not for me; since I couldn't make a success of a job in one that meant that I wouldn't have to go to one. I would hate to report to one of those things. My mother did it, and she was good at what she did, and that was impressive, but I saw no alternative but to do something else.

Knowing that a thing that I hated so much was closed off to me was liberating.

I'm glad that my mother has always been the sort of NT who could spot deficits in my abilities and respond by coaching me to compensate for them as best as we could together, and that she had always viewed me as valuable and not broken or defective. She was satisfied with the daughter that DNA gave her. She told me that she knew I was different, but still wanted me.

Maybe that's why I had managed so well thus far.

Aside from the research that I did, I began to look at my life – habits, likes, dislikes, hobbies – differently. Thus informed about Asperger's, I realized why I was so particular about food, about arranging the mugs in the kitchen cabinet so neatly, the dinner plates in the dish rack according to a precise pattern, and my obsession with routines.

The most common difficulty that cropped up in my life involved communication.

Most of the world is made up of NTs, not Aspies.

As an Aspie, I strive to be comprehensible, sincere, and polite.

But I noticed that many NTs (I won't accuse all of them of this character flaw) were disingenuous, and dissembled when they talk. By that, I mean that they lied a lot. They used false inflections in their tones, they blinked excessively when listening while not really paying attention to others, they expected NT behavior from everyone even though that was not logical or reasonable or realistic, and they used formulaic phrases that sounded like a foreign language and also smacked of insincerity.

Navigating through that is confusing at best and alarming at worst.

There isn't much that Aspies can do about this, but betraying ourselves by adopting such phrases is a big mistake. It makes me uncomfortable, and to do so would feel like a lie. It is a language that I cannot adopt, most particularly when I am able to make sense of it, because it is not honest and is often aimed at putting another person at a disadvantage. I don't like it.

It seems much wiser, and better, if I never try to make another person feel weaker, less important, or otherwise at a disadvantage. If someone asks me about something that they do not know, I just tell them what they want to know in flat tones, hoping that those tones don't suggest that they should have known the thing. Why should they? There is so much to know in life.

Now that I understood what was going on with me, I decided to enjoy it. I had never wished to blend in, fit in, and conform, so learning about Asperger's had not upset me. I had always rejoiced at not being ordinary, at standing out from the crowd, at being unique. I started looking at the pastimes that I enjoyed in a new light, such as television shows like *Bones*.

Most fun was my newfound ability to see that Bones, a.k.a. Dr. Temperance Brennan, was an Aspie female. The show never came out and said that she had Asperger's, but it was so obvious. And yet it was so cool! She is based on someone real, she can take care of herself, she has unique skills and great talents plus an appreciation for life and culture, and she has friends who understand and accept her. She is an Aspie female who gets respect…cool.

Add to that another show that I had not noticed before but now wished I had: *The Big Bang Theory*. It was a sitcom that showcased Asperger's, mostly in males, contrasting it with an NT female, Penny. It was great fun to watch – hilarious, even, considering that I had the benefit of all of my mother's coaching in social skills, plus I read so much that I could see when differing perceptions of reality conflicted and caused difficulties. I loved comic book heroes and heroines, so I had that in common with the characters.

The show parodied Asperger's a bit, but also did a lot to point it out and make it understandable to the viewing public, and less odd. It was made almost normal by making it familiar, which can only make life easier for people with Asperger's. Understanding us makes it easier to feel at ease with us and even respect us.

The Slamming Door

My mother ordered a basic Netflix service for me, something that Albert had repeatedly told me I would like while I was in New York. He and June had it. So I caught up on back episodes of *The Big Bang Theory* via Netflix.

I also loved to watch *Bones* episodes over and over again on TNT. My research on Asperger's, brief though it was, had mentioned that Aspies find such activities comforting. We watch movies over and over again, enjoying the familiar dialogue, action, events, and scenes. That was certainly true of me.

So...I had Asperger's. But was I spoiled? All my life, whenever my obsession with routines and control over food has surfaced, I had been told that I was spoiled, and it infuriated me. It made me determined to hide these quirks as much as I possibly could. Learning gourmet cooking and baking helped a lot. Cleaning helped, too. When it wasn't enough and I heard that accusation again, I would always get very upset. All that work to circumvent such criticism hadn't been enough.

Then I would just get annoyed.

The only way it will ever cease is if I eat what others eat – beef, cabbage, pork, etc. – and endure noise and disruption. In other words, the only way to avoid this is the feign being an NT and eat an unhealthy diet. No thanks.

But I'm unique, erudite, talented, and odd.

And I don't want to be an NT.

I can't lie.

I can't feign being an NT.

Forget it; I'm an Aspie and proud of it.

Once I understood all this about Asperger's, there was something else: an understanding that I because I don't like what most people like, I could not have much human companionship or friendship. Loneliness was part of this equation.

The few friends I had all lived far away.

I couldn't get to them because even though my parents had surprised me by getting me a car – which Damon and I had to pay them back for and which we were able to pay my mother 2 installments of $1,000 each after Damon's immunotherapy treatment was administered twice in Kuwait – I couldn't drive out of state. That was my mother's condition. And I had to pay for insurance on it. I was stuck in Connecticut.

It made me angry. Paying her back was going to take years, it seemed.

Applying for jobs produced no offers in this ruined economy. I wasn't going anywhere, and my mother kept expecting me to do something to produce the costs of living. My husband wasn't succeeding at it, and I couldn't just live like this forever. Parents – even ones who are willing to keep their daughters forever – don't live forever.

It made me angry not to be able to afford to exist.

I loved cable television, shopping for groceries, cooking from scratch with fresh ingredients, eating out, sharing my efforts at the table with my family and finding that they loved everything I made and never found anything wrong with it or extravagant about it…and I couldn't pay for it myself.

If my husband could have paid for it, I would have felt a lot better.

If I could have paid for it after publishing my own work, that would have felt a lot better.

But neither of those things showed any sign of happening any time soon.

We were well-educated and capable of just about anything but earning a living.

It was especially upsetting when I realized that this was a typical problem for Aspies.

I didn't know what to do.

All this time later, and I didn't know what to do.

Once again, I was very glad to have no maternal instinct whatsoever – except for a pet cat. That way, I would not long for a child, because even if I did I would deny myself any such thing rather than raise one with any less material advantages in life than I had enjoyed: skating lessons, music lessons, private school, tutors, private college, and so on and on. It would have been even worse if I had actually had a child, with no income. Forget the whole damned thing.

I began organizing my notes so that I could begin writing books, but those efforts would not pay off for a long time. Writing, re-writing, finding an agent, waiting for a publisher, and then going through the process of preparing a book for to go to press would take a couple of years. There would be no money from my efforts unless and until all that happened.

The feeling that my blood relatives and my in-laws were staring at me with disgust and disapproval never went away. They somehow blamed me and Damon for not earning money no matter what we tried to do about it.

Albert had said many times, "I know how to get money: get a job," referring to Damon.

I was certain that my mother expected me to just report to a cubicle.

It took a while longer to realize that no cubicle wanted me out of the few that remained. The economy had shrunk. There was no way that I would move away from home and live alone, without my husband or parents, to get a job. If I did, I would have to pay to exist there, and that would just eat up all of my money in return for even more unhappiness.

I remembered Brandie crying on the phone with me years ago when she lived alone in graduate school, and how I had sworn never to do that. Law school had been 12 minutes away from home, and then I had gotten married. So had Brandie; but she was all set with an NT husband.

Long after all of this, I met a social worker and began to visit him in his office – just to chat – every couple of weeks. Oddly, my mother had set it up. He was married to an American woman, a Cockney British guy who had decided to stay in the United States permanently 20 years earlier. He wasn't quite like Bryn, but he dressed sort of like him and astonished me by being completely accepting of me as I am.

He even seemed to admire me. He told me that he looked forward to talking with me, thought I was rich in many ways – such as intellectually and with my outlook on life – and said that I was exceptionally bright.

Most amazingly, he said that I already had a career: as an author.

He said that writing was my career, not a job with a boss in a cubicle, and to forget about that. This was coming from a guy who understood that Damon and I needed a permanent, continuous source of income and didn't have one yet.

By this time, I had completed the manuscripts for 2 books and was hard at work on 2 more, including this one. It was his idea to go ahead and complete *The Slamming Door*.

Frankly, I was bewildered by all this. How could any mental health care professional be validating me? Without an income, how could anyone be giving me that?

Was this really happening?

I wasn't used to good things happening any more.

Bryn has been gone for quite a while now, and I'm still angry, and not just about that.

Chapter 64

Memorial Service Plans

Even though Bryn had directed that his memorial service be held a couple of months after his death, the planning for it got underway immediately. Albert was in charge of the details, and he told me that he had contacted the same Unitarian church that we had gone to view *The End of Poverty* at in the spring. It was on East 35th Street, and called the Community Church of New York. I intended to speak at the service.

I saw no reason why I shouldn't; I had been his caregiver.

Accordingly, on September 6th, I wrote something to read at the event, and e-mailed it to Albert, telling him that my mother had rented us a hotel room so that we could attend the service. My mother was determined that I should be there, and wanted to help me.

I followed the same format I had used when my nice great-uncle died in 2001.

Here is what I prepared:

10 Great Things About Bryn

1. There is nothing negative to say about Bryn. This is a really unique thing to be able to say about anyone, but for him it is objectively true.

2. He was a great listener. No wonder he had so many friends.

3. He loved life.

4. He hated to be the reason why others might be either inconvenienced or missing out on having a good time.

5. He was interested in many things, and as a result, he was very interesting. He was intellectually curious…fascinated by national and international news, and enjoyed discussing a variety of academic fields – in addition to his own.

6. He loved people, and welcomed any and every opportunity to visit with his friends and family.

7. He had a lovely tenor singing voice, and enjoyed using it with or without a specific reason for doing so.

The Slamming Door

8. He was, as his daughter Berta said, a rock star of a professor at The Henry George School of Social Science. This meant that he made sure that the students got what they wanted and therefore wanted to be there, learning Henry George's message. The best teachers make learning fun, and Bryn was one of them, using documentaries as well as purely entertaining movies to achieve this. He also did everything he could to make sure that people got along there and remembered to put education before politics and personal differences.

9. He was what I like to call a secular saint – a social worker. He was someone who spent his career helping people who needed him, and he enjoyed it.

10. He was a man who loved cats, and cats are the sort of creatures who only decide that they love a person after considering the matter carefully. And cats loved Bryn.

    What would I do about Berta at that event? I supposed that I would have to see her; it was unavoidable. I could do that once, to properly honor Bryn with my list, and by reading it for everyone present. This happened all the time, didn't it? People had trouble with each other, but behaved okay for the sake of a funeral or memorial service. I had to plan on attending and speaking, it seemed. That would be normal and right.

    Accordingly, I e-mailed Albert to tell him that I had something special that I written about his brother, and shared it with him on the condition that he show to NO ONE until the event, because I was to be the one to do so.

    He was utterly trustworthy with someone else's writing. This was the man who would not even look at his daughter's writing unless and until she was ready to present it herself, because he did not want to risk upsetting her and thus ruining her creativity as applied to any particular piece or work...or worse, all of it. Albert was a writer and editor himself, too.

    He would understand this restriction.
    I was right; he never leaked it to anyone.

Chapter 65

Blocked

Albert read it, and wrote back that it was just right because it wouldn't take too much time, perhaps just three or four minutes, and that it described and honored his brother perfectly. When he saw it, he wrote back that it would fit into the program perfectly, and promised not to show it to anyone without my express consent.

Good.

Not good.

The note went on at length about the issue of me actually speaking at the event:

Clarisse,

I love this list---esp. the kicker about cats. This would read under four minutes, I'd think. Perfect length.

However.... you know the however.... You're just not going to be able to read it at the service. You said you might email it around after the service, which I think a fine backup idea. People should see this list and learn how highly you regarded him and, by reading how he loved people, reminding us all of how much he loved you, too. There's no doubt his life would have been shorter and more painful if you hadn't been around. That's a truism I'll be talking about until I croak. But Berta (and Dionne, in her way) just won't permit you to get in stage. They're his daughters, and there's no way I, as the brother, can prevent them from saying who they want to read and in fact who they want at the service. Berta suggests an alternative (or at least suggested---don't know where she stands on this now): your write up the list, maybe calligraphically, and print up about 100 copies for congregants to pick up and take home.

This is a great list. But I'm truly sorry---it's not going to make the stage. We've got to remember this is Bryn's moment, not ours; all the attention needs to be on him, not on a diversion no matter how petty. I know you can see that and, for the sake of Bryn's memory, I hope you can try to live with it for a while.

The Slamming Door

Love,
Albert

A printed copy?!

Absolutely not, and especially not anything that Berta thought of.

That ran the risk that someone who was allowed to speak would steal an idea of off it.

No way...and I was just livid. This monstrous brat was using her position as Bryn's daughter to prevent me from speaking, because she was angry and couldn't speak eloquently.

I called my friends and told them what was going on. They all liked the list, and one of them, a nice lady who was my mother's age that I had worked with at Williams-Sonoma, said that Berta was jealous because she hadn't thought of this herself, and couldn't write her own beautiful remembrance of her father.

Berta obviously hated my guts, and the feeling was cemented in my psyche right back.

A frenzied slew of e-mails promptly ensued that made it all more upsetting.

As if that weren't complex enough, the date of the memorial service got postponed by a week, and my mother had to cancel the hotel plans. Dr. Leonardi offered to let us stay for free in his apartment; he always returned to Connecticut on weekends and wouldn't need the place.

At first, my mother accepted, but as the spate of e-mail continued, she changed her mind.

She didn't think that I ought to be there and subject myself to any further abuse.

She wasn't the only one who imagined that Berta might scream and yell and make a scene at the event, and she kept saying that she should have brought me home sooner, and that I should never have been subjected to any of the abuse that Berta had heaped upon me.

How nice, but avoiding that abuse would have required a crystal ball; when someone is dying, often there is no way to know how badly the interpersonal relations will go or when that will happen until one has the annoying luxury of hindsight.

Aaron, Damon's cousin-in-law in Roslindale, Massachusetts, decided to try to help me.

He was the only one of Damon's relatives who actively made any effort to see that I attended the service, which was very nice of him, but ultimately futile. His wife, Nicola, refused to get in the middle of anything, and kept out of it.

When I realized that I was being shunted to the side and that none of my New York in-laws had any intention of objecting, I wrote a letter

Blocked

to the family – not just to the New Yorkers – because I didn't want them discussing the situation in my absence, leaving me no way to make my own case. That would be like losing a case by default for not showing up, and for sending no attorney or proxy. My letter was all I could send for a proxy.

In it, I explained what had happened with the closet-cleaning, and how I really felt about everything, telling them that I wouldn't be attending the memorial service, and why. When I say that I wrote to tell them why, I mean that I shared the whole awful story in an e-mail letter. And I told them that I was disappointed, because I had only met some of them once, at my wedding, and had expected to meet a few others for the first time at the memorial service. They all lived quite far away.

Berta had been so awful – and offal – to me that she had completely sacrificed any right to consideration of her wishes or feelings, so I made my mind up. She had made herself irrelevant to me, and to my decision-making process.

I was rather annoyed at Nicola when she responded by writing that she didn't understand why I was telling her all this. Incredible; it had seemed perfectly obvious. I wrote back and told her why: so that when she attended the service and inevitably talked with the others, she would know something of my side of the whole mess, not only whatever they told her. The idea of having them all unaware of that, and thinking only of whatever Berta and Dionne chose to say to them, galled me, and I intended to circumvent that possibility.

Now she understood; she wrote to me again, still saying that she wanted to stay out of it.

Thanks so much for your lack of support, I thought.

That made it all the more interesting that her husband chose to get involved.

He tried to help me find a place to stay. Bryn's place was out, of course, and Alena and her family would stay at Aunt Summer's place. Aunt Summer would go with Aunt Johanna, and neither of them would help me. It was infuriating to think that they would give wealthy, successful Alena a free place to stay while I would have to pay for a hotel room if I had no offers. This, after I had been the caregiver, and this, while Alena was on the list of speakers at the service. It wasn't that I wanted to stay with either of the aunts; it was just galling that they were accommodating Alena and backing her up in every way while I was left out in the cold.

Desta had people staying in her place, or at least claimed to. There was no way to confirm or deny this; she may have been staying out this mess with a carefully crafted excuse. She did write to me that after Bryn had died, Claus had been nasty to her and so she would not be teaching

The Slamming Door

at the Henry George School again. It wouldn't be any fun without her friend.

Aaron was appalled by all this, and wrote to Albert, demanding that he tell Berta that I had to be there, that Bryn would be apoplectic if he knew that I wasn't going to attend, and that it was wrong to spoil her this way by acquiescing to her wishes. By that time, Berta had decided that she didn't want me at the event at all. But Albert wouldn't do it.

The upshot of it all was that she was using her grief, her pregnancy, and her mood problems as a convenient excuse to behave just as badly as she wanted, and that she was just a rotten, nasty, selfish individual.

At that point, going to the service seemed to be more trouble than it was worth, even to Bryn and his memory. But Aaron wasn't done yet; he even added something about Bryn being aware of all this, watching, but that was a bit over the top to me.

I told him that Bryn was an atheist, he was blissfully unaware of all this, and that his problems were now over. Aaron didn't bring that up again. Bryn was going to get his Unitarian, non-theistic memorial service without an afterlife being dragged into the discussion.

I was close to being an atheist also.

I told Aaron that I just wanted to share my list on my own terms, and thus honor his memory properly. "When I figure out how to accomplish that, I will do it," I promised him. I thanked Aaron for trying to help me but said that it was time to stop. He wasn't even going to attend himself; he had to stay home and work.

All the while, Damon was stuck working in Kuwait, unable to help. I called him up on Skype, crying, begging him to come home even though I knew that he couldn't do that. What would he do at home? He had no place to stay now. Bryn had died and that was the end of a place for Damon; my mother wouldn't let him in the house.

"I can't come home," he said, sounding miserable.

He did make me feel better though, just by being on my side about every bit of this mess.

If the aunts couldn't – or wouldn't – make room for me, I was just too upset and feeling too isolated to go. My mother almost went with me, and we would have stayed in Dr. Leonardi's apartment, but then we changed our minds. Interesting turn of events; Berta unhappy with her mother and wishing she would die, me unhappy with mine for repudiating my husband, and now we were aligning ourselves with our mothers.

Something about mothers…unless they have tried to murder their children, they usually are the ones that the children want when things don't go well. That seems to be keeping the bar a bit low, but it's still true. Berta's mother may have been abusive, but she wouldn't kill her.

Blocked

We didn't go to the memorial service. Sitting silently and feeling like I was under siege by a non-supportive group of in-laws held no lure for me. I probably would have glared at the aunts and Alena. I thought back to August, after Berta's meltdown, when I had been utterly unwilling to re-enter the building unless and until I was sure that she had left the premises.

No – this was all on her. She was the one who was blocking me from attending the memorial service. She would have everything as she liked it, with both me and Cassie absent, me because I was blocked and Cassie had to take care of Chip. Berta could simulate the family structure that she wished for, one with her mother but no girlfriend of her father, and no surrogate daughter figure. She could pretend that her mother had been the only woman in her father's life, and that none of the annoying, Aspie women he had preferred had ever existed.

Vianne spoke to me on the phone shortly after reading that long letter from me. "You are so articulate!" she gushed. Interesting response; at least she took in my entire letter and got my point. She didn't like what Berta had said about Asperger's and killing myself one bit, she made sure to mention.

Vianne wasn't coming either; she couldn't afford to fly out from Arizona again so soon. It was more important that she had had a last visit with Bryn while he was alive, and I agreed with her. She put in a good word for me about attending, and that was about it. I didn't blame her; what could she do from that distance?

Albert was sick and not feeling well as usual, plus he had a lifetime of avoiding conflict rather than meeting it. His standard way of dealing with the women in his life, he had often told me, was to keep them happy. So that was the problem, I realized: now that I was back in Connecticut, I was out of sight, and out of his life. He had to deal with them, not me, so he was taking the easy way out and acquiescing to his nieces.

Wimp. I can't help it even now – I meet fights rather than fleeing from them, so I expected him to do so as well. Even as Berta had screamed at me, I had told her not to and then, when she wouldn't shut up, said one, final thing to her: "I hate you." Such an Aspie response, but so well-deserved in this case: tell me you hope I will kill myself, and I will say that.

So I expected Albert to just tell her I would be there, speaking, and to shut up already.

All of the elders that I had been raised with would have done that.

That was why I found his concessions to her so traitorous and pathetic.

Later, he asked me, "What was I supposed to do, risk her making a scene?"

The Slamming Door

To which I had replied, "Yes, and then to have told her to just stuff it."

I didn't have a chance to communicate with Cassie much, but I managed to get her on the phone a couple of times and tell her what was going on. It was tricky, because there wasn't much of a cell phone signal at the condominium where I lived. I drove to the Whole Foods in West Hartford Center and sat in my car to talk to her just as the sun went down.

Cassie was only within earshot of her phone at that hour, making dinner. The phone and its answering machine were out on the porch, near where Chip slept, and he checked the messages…sometimes. Cassie was out most of the day, and elsewhere in the house at other times. When someone is that difficult to reach, I tend to give up on the relationship; they just don't have any time or inclination to deviate from their rigid routines, I assume.

She didn't think much of the way that my in-laws were treating me, and listened and talked to me. That was all that I wanted from her. She was the one who told me that Bryn's ashes had been divided into three urns; one for each of his daughters, and one for her. Hers was on the mantelpiece in her house.

I had a passing thought about Leila; she worked with Berta, so I would probably never interact with her again. Oh well…if that meant no Berta either, the friendship with Leila had been nice while it had lasted. We would just have to leave it at that and be satisfied.

Damon was the most upset of all, aside from me.

He hated Berta more than ever now, if that was possible, and had followed the developments via Skype and e-mail as they occurred. He was very upset, and he reminded me of the fact that he had cut himself off from his entire family for twelve years. Now I understood why, and now he was going to do it again.

"I should never have listened to Jane Setlow and contacted them again," he complained.

"Yes, should have, and I'm glad you did," I contradicted him. "Because of that, I got to know Bryn, and to learn in detail about your family. I learned much more than I would have from just hearing about them. Besides, meeting your uncle Bob was fun, and he was an in-law to all of these people." Uncle Rex, Damon's father's younger brother, and he had died four years before Bryn, in Florida.

Damon conceded all of my points, especially the part about knowing Bryn; it was worth getting back in touch with them so that I could be friends with Bryn and his caregiver.

During all this, Damon had asked Alena to cede the floor to me at the memorial service, and give me some of the time allotted to her for

Blocked

speaking. She had refused, and written to my mother that perhaps I needed medication if I was having trouble dealing with all of this.

That's right, Alena, just drug anyone who shows any sign of discontent with life into silent submission, I thought. She had already done so with her own daughter, and I hoped that the kid wouldn't develop an eating disorder or a weight problem as a result. Asking her to do anything to help me had seemed ridiculous, but Damon had insisted upon trying it.

For his part, Damon had some choice parting words for Alena, forwarded to me:

Under the subject line "Congratulations Alena" Damon sent this to her on the 20th:

Alena:

Everything else aside in this sad and ugly chapter in our family's history, your assertion that Clarisse should be drugged and "counseled" for not accepting the condescending attitude being directed at her was a critical event.

Congratulations. You have driven my wife from the memorial service of a person she loved and cared for deeply and selflessly. How very Soviet of you. Your philosophical brethren in the medical establishment of the Third Reich would also have been pleased with your therapeutic approach.

I will not contact you again. Please do not contact me.

Good Bye.

When it was all over, he had some helpful, comforting words for me:

"You made Bryn's final days much better than they would have otherwise been," Damon told me for the hundredth time. He also thought that if I had not been there, Bryn would have had to leave his home, go to hospice, and spend lots of money on that. So I had saved him a lot of money, money that his daughters could thank me for being able to inherit. I hadn't thought of that until he mentioned it. Oh well…everything has side effects.

The Slamming Door

But before it became clear that I couldn't attend the memorial service, when that idiotic idea was suggested by Albert: that I just attend, and have copies of my eulogy list passed out for people to look at during the memorial service, he had added that Alena would "speak for the family," in what was an obvious attempt to be dismissive and therefore avoid conflict.

Apparently, he figured that if he just wrote that, I would accept that and drop the matter of speaking and reading what I had prepared.

He thought wrong. Dismissiveness never works on me.

I was insulted, infuriated, and not about to just roll over and die.

It never occurred to me to just shut up and go along; that is not in my nature. In fact, to respond that way has always seemed like a dishonorable cop-out, a disgrace, and a reason to lose all self-respect. That was just not going to happen.

I called Albert and asked him a few direct questions, trying to find out what was going on, what he was thinking, and so on. So what if he was afraid that if I attended and participated in the service, Berta would make a scene as I read my list, and then it would be all about a cat-fight and not about his brother. That didn't make it okay. I still expected him to tell Berta to stuff it.

Albert was sick, his wife was sick, his brother was dead, his nieces were being awful, and he didn't want to deal with any more uproars. Damon wouldn't forgive or accept that. As for me, I would forgive it eventually, but I certainly wouldn't accept that or acquiesce to it.

I began to plot my next move, silently, and without telling anyone. If you share your plans with anyone – *anyone* – you vastly increase the odds of failure. That was not an option with me. I was too upset and too determined. It was only much later that I would understand enough about Aspies to realize that this stealth was part of our general modus operandi.

So what was I going to do about sharing my list for Bryn's memorial service?

Allowing anyone to see it – especially Alena – before the fact and perhaps read from it was an utterly unacceptable outcome. "Speaking for the family" would have included me, from what Albert's note had suggested. Not surprisingly, that was unpalatable to me.

It was such a galling idea from Albert, to have Alena read my list when she spoke. I wrote back, irate but polite: absolutely not, no way, Alena would emote the tones all wrong and ruin it. By now I understood that she was an NT and I an Aspie, and I realized why her phony tones grated on me so much. No; if the list couldn't be read with flat, level tones, it would go out another way...certainly not as a stolen part of Alena's speech.

I would have none of that.

I had to simulate being there and reading that list myself.

And I had the tools with which to do it.

That address book that I had made for Bryn was the most important tool, as was the fact that he had been willing to share his contacts with me. He had even had me e-mailing people on his behalf from my own account while he was alive, and had said that he wanted to put me in touch with some of them for my writing career.

Well, too late for that, and I had never really counted upon it. He was too sick to bother, and I wasn't taking care of him for a bunch of professional connections. I was doing it to spend time with him.

I decided to e-mail the eulogy list that I had written to everyone I could get an e-mail address for – his and my contacts. If that bothered Berta, so much the better; the big moment of Bryn's memorial service, the spotlight, would have just ended when the list went out.

If only I had known about a convenient function of e-mail systems known as "Bcc" – it doesn't let groups of addressees see each other's names and e-mail addresses. But I didn't. I just put the list of names into the "To" line and hit "Send" – in three batches. It wouldn't go in one big batch – the system thought it was a spamming attempt that way. But sending it in three batches was fine; it did the job nicely.

The best part was that no one knew that I intended to send it out to everyone I could get an e-mail address for – absolutely everyone. That was precisely the point of this: to simulate attendance at the memorial service. Simply sending it to the relatives would be like acquiescing to the evisceration that Berta had sought. She had sought to expunge my presence in her father's life from the record and from the knowledge of most of those present at that service.

There was no way that I would cooperate with that.

And I gave no warning. Warnings just make it possible to be stopped before the deed is done. That was not an option, and I would not allow it to be.

Off it went, and I felt a sense of satisfaction. It was like Uncle Mort's memorial service all over again. Everyone had been allowed to get up and speak about him, and the stories had been wonderfully interesting and colorful. I had read a list of 10 great things about Uncle Mort, and now I had shared another one about Bryn.

I prefaced the list with an explanation of who I was, just to give context to Bryn's friends and professional colleagues when they received the e-mail, refraining from explaining what was going on behind the scenes among the relatives. It was none of their business anyway; the point was to get the list out to them.

Sending it out just felt so damned…good. I had thwarted all efforts to stop me from sharing it on my own terms. It was a flattering list, and no one had been able to edit a word of it, to read it in my stead, to emote a single tone in any way differently from its author's intent, and it had properly honored this saint of a father figure.

To top it all off, I had done an end-run around conflict, thus letting the memorial service proceed as Albert wished, without the "cat-fight" that he feared. It had been – however it had gone – all about Bryn. This eulogy list went out later, but only moments later. The vicious shunting away that I had felt had been shoved back just as hard. It felt strange to simultaneously honor Bryn while also tossing a grenade into the mix, but so be it.

Eulogy List for Bryn W. Otterman by his cousin and caregiver.

Tuesday, October 20, 2009 12:37 AM
From: Clarisse N. Rénard
To: Everyone on my own and Bryn's contacts list that I wanted to share this with.

Hello Everyone.

For those of you who don't know me, I am Clarisse N. Rénard, J.D., Bryn's cousin and caregiver. I lived with him for the last 11 months of his life, took care of him, got his medicines, went to doctors and chemotherapy with him, sat with him while he puked and got him whatever food he could deal with when everything tasted like poison, and had a good time with him when he felt okay. He was my best friend aside from my husband, Damon Hardy, whom Bryn babysat when he was a kid.

Bryn was the family saint - the glue of our family plus all of his friends.

I wanted to go to his memorial service today, but was prevented from doing so.

Below is what I would have read had I not been prevented from attending.

Blocked

10 Great Things About Bryn

1. There is nothing negative to say about Bryn. This is a really unique thing to be able to say about anyone, but for him it is objectively true.

2. He was a great listener. No wonder he had so many friends.

3. He loved life.

4. He hated to be the reason why others might be either inconvenienced or missing out on having a good time.

5. He was interested in many things, and as a result, he was very interesting. He was intellectually curious...fascinated by national and international news, and enjoyed discussing a variety of academic fields – in addition to his own.

6. He loved people, and welcomed any and every opportunity to visit with his friends and family.

7. He had a lovely tenor singing voice, and enjoyed using it with or without a specific reason for doing so.

8. He was, as his daughter Berta said, a rock star of a professor at The Henry George School of Social Science. This meant that he made sure that the students got what they wanted and therefore wanted to be there, learning Henry George's message. The best teachers make learning fun, and Bryn was one of them, using documentaries as well as purely entertaining movies to achieve this. He also did everything he could to make sure that people got along there and remembered to put education before politics and personal differences.

9. He was what I like to call a secular saint – a social worker. He was someone who spent his career helping people who needed him, and he enjoyed it.

10. He was a man who loved cats, and cats are the sort of creatures who only decide that they love a person after considering the matter carefully. And cats loved Bryn.

The Slamming Door

Sincerely,
Clarisse.

Now all that I wanted was a full and detailed accounting – immediately! – of the memorial service. Alissa and Albert had been there; that was the least that they could do for me after not bothering to stand up for me. I had taken care of Bryn, thus easing their minds for months on end. Now I wanted to know what had happened at the service, and not days later: NOW. I wondered how difficult it would be to get that.

It did in fact take me several more days to get what I wanted out of Albert and Alissa, a precise account of what had happened at the memorial service by phone. A few quick e-mail lines was not acceptable; I wanted details, and I wanted them spoken in a conversation.

What I was looking for was not, as one might wonder, dirt or gossip about nasty behavior by Berta. I didn't want to hear a word about that.

What I wanted was a blow-by-blow description of the event as it unfolded: who attended, what was done in what order, what food-and-drink arrangements were part of it all, how long it took, how many people there were altogether, and what people did as they dispersed…just the usual sorts of things that happen at death rituals.

I called that evening, and Alissa told me they were too tired to talk and tell me about it.

So I let that go, but I was angry with them.

I didn't care that they were tired; they got to attend, and they had done nothing to see that I attended and was treated with respect. It was as though I didn't matter at all to them.

Upset over the death or not, I still view them as appallingly selfish for that.

I was upset about Bryn's death too, and they knew it. It was my loss, too, not just theirs.

Albert kept talking about some sort of thank-you visit and party for me for months afterward, but that seemed absurd to me. They had already fêted me the night before I left, and going back to Manhattan now seemed too difficult to pull off.

The next night was no better; Alissa still wouldn't tell me much.

I was losing patience with them at this point.

At some point, perhaps then or perhaps later, I blew up at her over phone, saying that I wanted Berta to be completely and utterly miserable and right now. This was all her fault, after all. That merely elicited a shriek of horror from Alissa, and I decided that talking with her would never make me feel good – ever.

Blocked

She was just too fragile a personality to hold up the other end of an emotional connection, and it snapped at this point. It's too bad, because I liked her and enjoyed her talents and ambition, and encouraging her with them. We have since talked nicely again, but it was a long time later, and I didn't trust her anymore.

Finally, days later, Albert told me what had happened: Rudy had catered the event, 200 people showed up, Alena did indeed speak though he didn't detail the contents of her talk (and I found that I didn't care), and he and Alissa had both spoken. It lasted a couple of hours, and he was tired from having to stay and speak to every last person as they left. Cassie had been unable to attend because Chip had vertigo and couldn't be left alone, though I had known that.

Alissa got to speak?! That had never been mentioned to me before the fact. Yet I had been blocked from the event entirely. Well, that was just perfect. I had no problem with the fact that Alissa got to speak. The problem was that I had been blocked.

Some family.

I had always wondered why Damon had felt so alienated by his relatives as to have cut them all out of his life, to have cut off all contact for 12 years.

Not anymore.

I was glad to know. I am a curious person, and always want to find out all about whatever intrigues me. I wanted to understand my in-laws, and now I had gotten somewhere with that. Nothing like an emotionally jarring experience to help with that, I realized now.

Curiosity can kill a cat, or give it a nasty shock.

I am like the cat who had had her curiosity satisfied in exchange for a bolt of electricity.

That's fine with me. If knowing Bryn and helping him with his terminal illness must be paid for with a shock, he was worth it – every bit.

Chapter 66

Glowing Letters

On Monday, the responses to the eulogy list began to roll in. Most of the letters were responses to the eulogy list that I had sent out about Bryn; a couple of them were in response to another one sent out by Damon, with the subject line "A Soldier's Tribute."

Some letters glowed with praise, understanding, and friendship; others glowed with what can only be characterized as virtual radioactivity. I sat back and watched the "fun."

Bryn's Henry George colleague, the one who had gotten lung cancer earlier in the year, called me a saint. Someone who knew how it felt to be scared with cancer appreciated me!

Another Henry George colleague wrote to me from Australia, because he had been there when the memorial service took place, and so couldn't attend it either. Bryn had asked me to send him articles and other information via e-mail several times. He sent a nice note telling me how they had become friends.

But when I saw the one that Hilda wrote, it certainly glowed with something vile – vitriol seems like a good word for it. Wow, that just validates my dislike of children, I thought when I saw what it said. It arrived on October 20th, after the eulogy list had had a week to circulate.

Leading off with the line, "first off, ANYTHING DAMON AND/OR CLARISSE SAYS MUST BE COMLPETELY DISMISSED." The block capitals were just as they appear here, and the whole thing was barely articulate. If I were reading that letter and thus finding out about the upset surrounding this event, I would be all the more interested in what Clarisse and Damon had said or might later say. Thanks for the extra hype and publicity, I thought.

Hilda spewed recrimination at me, criticized the food that she found when Albert had her clean out the refrigerator of Bryn's apartment after he died (and he wasn't satisfied with her efforts, he told me), condemned me for sleeping in the mornings, accused of having microwaved a kitten, and accused me of not keeping in touch with my husband. To top it all off, her note made it clear that she and Berta had gone through the "Expenses for Taking Care of Bryn" file and scrutinized the grocery shopping, substituting their judgment for mine about it all.

Damn kid.

Brandie, my best friend from college and who had been the matron of honor at my wedding, whose father had died at 8:30 p.m. on August 12th, just twelve hours after Bryn died, wrote back to her: "My dad died on the same day as Bryn. One thing I learned is that anger is not something you should carry around with you all your life. Please, just live your life in peace, and don't include all these people in abusive e-mails."

Then she called me up to tell me that she had sent that, and added, "I don't care *what* you did; that not was just completely out of line. She had no right to send that note."

But of course I thought about the details. I always think about the details.

Damon and I called each other every day. Sometimes we talked more than once, depending on our whims or whatever we had to do. And he loved cats – no way would he hurt one! What the hell was the matter with this kid?!

Sleeping in the morning and leaving Bryn alone while other people with keys were awake to check on him was perfectly reasonable after staying up and watching him, worrying that he might suddenly die in his chair. I had to sleep sometime. If the time that I was able to do that didn't meet with a teenager's approval, I just didn't give a damn.

And then there was the food issue. Gourmet food?! If she meant the contents of the freezer, its contents certainly represented the greatest, most obviously gourmet of choices. Bryn had wanted Hagen Daas. The green tea ice cream was for June, and it just so happened that Hagen Daas was the only company that made that flavor, and I had searched the area grocery stores for it. As for the sorbets, Alissa could eat those without compromising her vegan diet. And I would happily eat any of those frozen treats.

The refrigerator was another story, but her nasty remarks just confused me. Was she suggesting that I should have eaten and liked beef, beets, cabbage, tomato sauce with meat in it, and whatever else her father kept making that Bryn would try to eat but was unable to finish before it rotted? If so, too bad – I would never eat any of those things. I hate cabbage; it stinks.

Everyone has their opinions about food.

Mine was that when Hilda's dad treated her like a pet that he had grown tired of. He had said that he was making dinner for him and her mother but not her, and she had come across the hall hungry, so she had no right to get nasty about what I had served. I thought I was very nice, feeding a kid whose father had cruelly told her to leave the apartment for the evening. Having a daughter but not feeding her just does not compute with me.

My own parents, difficult though they had been to me, not liking my husband, not wanting him around, and before that getting nasty and combative over random things, had never told me that they wouldn't feed me or that I must eat something that bothered me.

The Slamming Door

My mother had been quite reasonable about food. As long as I tried everything when I was a kid, and sincerely found out how each thing tasted, I was never expected to either eat it or go without. They also taught me not to tell other people that their food choices reflected badly upon their characters. What the hell was this letter about?!

Anger? Definitely.
Resentment? Quite possibly.
Jealously? Without a doubt.

Hilda knew that I had been raised with my own room, private school, private college of the quality that she wished to attend but couldn't afford and perhaps wouldn't be admitted to in this competitive day and age thanks to human overpopulation, having attended public school and not studying enough...and as if that weren't infuriating enough, I hadn't wasted my opportunities.

Berta had had all that and partied. She had squandered her chances, much as Hilda was now doing before the fact. No wonder she was such good friends with Berta, and it was no wonder that her father, who worked so hard as a chef and loved to study and write and teach music, was disappointed in her.

So here I was after this upbringing, fussy about food, determined not to judge others, and with plenty of my own food issues. Learning to be a gourmet-level, at home cook and baker was partly an exercise in concealment; if I did the work, my fussiness would be less noticeable, or so I had always thought. One thing that I had never counted upon was that someone would inventory a refrigerator that I had used after my departure and pillory me for its contents. I felt no guilt over that, only rage. I was absolutely incensed over it.

Bryn wanted what he wanted, so had I acquired it and served it to him. That included Rudy's contributions, ordering in, and whatever I cooked that Bryn said he wanted to have again. He liked my potatoes, and when the chemicals had gotten out of his system, he wanted my fish, asparagus, red-and-yellow bell peppers, and the sliced potatoes with salt and pepper in olive oil.

I thought that my efforts to feed Bryn delicious food had gone rather well; he had reviewed each item that I bought and approved the expense, too. Nothing was sneaked into the budget. I had shown the purchases to him every time, boring though it may have seemed to trot it all before him. The nerve of someone else to second-guess my efforts after the fact!

Vianne saw Hilda's nasty letter and called to say that she thought that it was extremely insulting to me to have looked through the expenses file and critiqued where I shopped for the food and what I had bought. Who was this kid to have anything to say about that? I was trying to tempt a dying guy with nutritious foods, and even he knew it. If a

Glowing Letters

particular food failed to entice him, he didn't blame me for that; he blamed his illness and the treatments for it. Instead, he appreciated my attempt to get more good food into him.

Death can bring out the worst in people (Hilda and Berta), not just the good (Bryn).

When I think of food and death simultaneously, I become even more determined not to bend my attitudes about food. What if the last thing you have to eat before death is awful? I don't want a life of regret, and food is a big deal to me, because it is one of the chief pleasures of life.

And after having listened to my Depression-raised grandmother talk, I fear awful food. It suggests poverty and misery. Even worse, it suggests a loss of control over one's environment and living situation. Poverty wasn't the only factor that could inspire such anxieties.

Reports about the environment with biodiversity loss and rising sea levels terrify me into thinking that fresh fruits and vegetables might not be readily available in my lifetime, and I tended to project into the future and panic. My nice Aunt Johanna Rénard said that I shouldn't do that; that it wasn't good for me, but sometimes my thoughts ran away with me and I would freak out.

Damn that stupid, obnoxious kid; the hell with Hilda. My aunt called her a brat and said to forget about her. But first, I needed to understand why she would write such a rotten letter. Was she angry and afraid about her own future, and her own present? Without Bryn, her quality of life was about to take a sharp dive. It was just an objective fact.

Bryn was a great listener. He also gave generously from the wad of cash he habitually kept in his pocket so that Hilda could see the latest movies with a friend, or visit a museum, or eat out. He invited her to many restaurants, and took her to Broadway shows. Before he got sick, he let her entertain her girlfriends in his guest room; it was like having her own room. That was all over now. Her parents couldn't afford that for her. And Berta wouldn't be as attentive about giving her the money from that cultural events fund that Bryn had left for her.

She had lost all access to that when I moved in to be Bryn's caregiver.

Naturally, she hated and resented me for that.

Add to that the fact that I had been educated at a private high school, a private college, and a top-tier law school, traveled in Europe and one Middle Eastern country, had a fairy tale of a wedding to a stubbornly unique and equally well-educated guy who was my best friend, and there seemed to be plenty of reasons for that kid to wish me ill.

She had cast her lot in with Berta, and shared in her hatred and jealousy of me.

The Slamming Door

Damon told me, over the phone as he tried to make me see that I had nothing to feel bad about aside from the fact that Bryn was dead and gone, that all of the reasons why they hated me were complimentary to me. Many were just objective realities of life, realities of differences in opportunity and access to its benefits, especially where Hilda's feelings were concerned.

Not so with Berta; her hatred and jealousy of me were entirely her fault. The nastiness from her seemed to validate a truth that I had been taught long ago: it was all really about her own insecurities and inadequacies, and her every remark revealed the details of those deficits.

Berta had been given every advantage by her father that my parents had given me, yet she had squandered her opportunities for an education, and grown morbidly obese. I only disparage obesity in nasty people, and she had earned it. She had turned out ordinary to the point of common, ignorant to the point of disinterest, and willfully uncouth and stupid.

Yes – willfully stupid. She had the requisite DNA to be as intelligent as I was, but she had not bothered to develop it. Partying had been preferable to study; she had flunked out of college, failed to acquire the credentials necessary to work in television production, and refused to wrestle her Attention Deficit Disorder into submission, allowing it to rule her mind instead. She made no effort to pay attention to anything that did not hold her interest; only gossip about celebrities, reality TV stars, and data on people she knew personally held her attention.

For months on end, I had made a determined policy of not thinking of her as stupid, basing that judgment solely on her DNA and innate abilities. No more. Now, I thought of her as an adult who was the sum of her decisions…and a bully. We are what we decide to do with what we have been given after a certain point.

Hopefully, Hilda would develop her lovely soprano singing voice, and hopefully, her father wouldn't insist that she move out upon reaching the ripe young age of eighteen, which was less than 2 years away. If she could manage to get an education at Hunter College, which offered a free or at least low-cost bachelor's degree to New Yorkers, she might be okay.

But I had a grim sense that Rudy would not enable that to happen.

I doubted that he would shelter her enough to get that crucial credential under her belt. That kid would not be able to afford a private college, and perhaps not even a state one. Rudy and Elah would not be able to help; they just barely managed to eke out a living in their rent-controlled apartment as it was. Rudy's hours at the place where he cooked had been cut, thanks to the terrible economy.

He hadn't gone to college – for whatever reason, be it economic or his own choice or both – so why would he enable his daughter to go? He was too cranky, quiet, and unfriendly to decipher on these points, and I couldn't expend any further effort on it anyway.

He had replied to my eulogy list for Bryn with a terse, "Not interested. Deleted."

Damon had wished him ill for that, literally…and in writing. I had to block Rudy's account from Damon's to put a stop to that nonsense. It wasn't pleasant, but it didn't the trick.

As for Berta, I had blocked her e-mail accounts back on August 2nd when her letters had degenerated into block capitals, which translate as shouts in cyberspace. The only way I could find out what rottenness she was transmitting over the Internet was through others who passed it on to me, and they were passing it on, just for my information.

She and Hilda had that list of the first batch of e-mail addresses that I sent that *List of 10 Great Things About Bryn* to. It was only when Elah told me about the Bcc function and said in an e-mail of her own not to hit "Reply All" that I realized how I could have kept it from them. But I didn't care that they had those e-mail addresses; they were just making fools of themselves.

Albert disapproved of using the Bcc function for e-mails, he told me; he thought it was wrong to conceal the fact that one was sharing anything with others. Damon and I disagreed; interestingly, so did quite a few other people: my mother, several friends, etc.

My father surprised me by dreaming of sending her all sorts of outrageous and disturbing things, none of which he actually intended to go ahead with. He was just expressing his support for me. He asked to see a photograph of her, looked, and said he had just lost his appetite.

The Hornsby surprised me by writing to say that he understood that I was feeling underappreciated, but that Bryn had told him that he appreciated me very much.

Berta had certainly made good on her promise to have a complete breakdown once her father actually died. I just wasn't willing to be the target of its effects, and never had been. If that was what was to happen when she got upset, I just didn't care how she felt. Not if I had to be an object of condemnation and persecution. By all means, be upset about your father dying, I had thought, but don't ever think of me as a target on which to take out your misery. Do that, and I will wish your misery to intensify.

Apparently, I had gotten to her but good without even planning to do it.

When I sent that e-mail out, intensifying her misery had not been on my mind. What had been on my mind was not allowing anyone to silence me or control my behavior while properly honoring Bryn in the process.

The Slamming Door

If that bothered her, all I could think when this fact was later brought to my attention was: good. I felt no guilt. She had earned that. Silencing me by blocking me was her intent, and her reasons for it were that she was jealous, and that the knowledge that speaking at Bryn's memorial service had been important to me. Because it was important to me, she felt a sense of satisfaction at blocking it.

My mother spelled that out to me later. There's nothing like an observer who does not hate you to help you understand something faster than you would ever have done so on your own. I didn't want to wait to figure that out, and my neurotypical mother enabled me to reach that point with the desired speed and efficiency.

NTs can be lovely people for Aspies to be with as long as they don't hate or resent them.

Actually, when Berta's hate mail got to me – through Damon's e-mail and from my confused and surprised friends – it seemed funny. That's not to say that I wasn't also stressed and angry, but a conscious part of me saw something profoundly satisfying in her reaction, as well as amusing. That she would even imagine that I might find her wishes relevant after the way she had treat me in August was the epitome of absurdity.

She was outraged that I had done what I wanted, ignored her wishes, and satisfied my own desire for a forum with which to share that eulogy list on my own terms: the Internet.

When you put something out into the Internet, it is forever.

Didn't she know that?

Perhaps she forgot.

Her nasty letters went out through, of all systems, her Deutsche Bank e-mail account.

Why not use her private, non-work-related one? Oh yeah: she wasn't allowed to access it while at work. She had no other option, and she just couldn't control herself and wait until later in the day, when she was at home with her own computer and her personal e-mail account.

Well…yes, she could have waited – she just chose not to. She chose the instant gratification of sending terrible notes out to Damon, who gleefully wrote stuff back that further inflamed her.

I didn't want him to do it.

He didn't care; she had given him a golden opportunity to bait her after she had been venomously rotten to his wife, who had taken care of her father, and at her request.

I had the password for his e-mail account. And I knew how to block e-mails. I went in and did so. He didn't know how to do that. I told him what I did and why, and that as his lawyer I thought it advisable to put a stop to further temptation. He had reluctantly desisted…

Glowing Letters

...but not before various examples of nastiness had been traded back and forth.

So the nonsense between Berta and Damon went a bit farther, producing some really silly exchanges, and revealing yet more samples that beautifully illustrated Berta's inarticulateness, written or otherwise. At least it provided more entertainment during the time before I realized I could just block the messages.

Among the samples was the statement that Damon was an "udder liar" – he wrote back that it was "an interesting choice of language, considering the source" and left it at that.

She didn't want me to have that address book, and was carrying on and on about it.

She didn't want me to share anything about Bryn's death and last days, as if the knowledge of it were her personal property. Never mind that I had spent that time with him and had my own memories to relate, which had thus become my own intellectual property.

To paraphrase Craig Ferguson: Take that, you vengeful, insane venom-spewer!

When it started, the first thing I had checked was the e-mail address: YES! It was her work e-mail, complete with letterhead all over it. What was she doing, I had thought, handing us material for a lawsuit on a silver platter? Maybe, but she didn't get fired; I suspect that that was because she was pregnant. Either that, or she was quietly downsized later on and given some unrelated reason as the excuse, such as the economy.

She left me a lovely collection that demonstrated her inarticulateness and impotent rage. Much of it was addressed directly to Damon with the assumption (correct) that he would pass it all on to me for my information and, she vainly hoped, obedience.

The way that she phrased some of her attacks were hilarious: "Neither you nor Clarisse will..." and so on. She was particularly worked up over her father's address book, specifically my (assumed) use of it to extract e-mail addresses for sending out that list. Perhaps she thought that I would use it over and over again, contacting people whom I did not know in the future.

Why would I do that? I had simulated attending the memorial service with it, and now I was done. As for possessing a copy of it, Bryn knew I had it, Albert had asked me to take it, and she had ceded all realistic expectation that I consider what she wanted or didn't want by being abusive to me. I should never have been sorry to be blocked from the event. What a gift she had given me – this tale to tell! A tale of intolerance, jealousy, and mentally unfocused venom.

The Slamming Door

Even funnier was her rant that I hadn't sent her a sympathy card. Why would I do that? The loss of Bryn was mine too, and she had been monstrous. No one who acts like that will ever get a sympathy card out of me.

She really had nothing to recommend her side of this rift, but continued petulantly to rave on and on, becoming more and more incoherent, inane and unbalanced with each succeeding e-mail, all on Deutsche Bank letterhead.

The first communication that Damon got from Berta was quite obnoxious.

She presumed to edit me in two ways: one for using the word puking, which I had not meant as any assault on Bryn's dignity...I simply don't approve of euphemisms, and the other for saying that it was not my "place" to send anything out. When I had sent that out, it had been the lines about having been prevented from attending that seemed more significant.

The moment that anyone starts talking about what is "appropriate" for me or their view of my "place" – or otherwise using the formulaic tone and wording of corporate and traditional-minded attitudes – is the moment that I want to hurt them.

The funny thing was, I didn't have to make any further effort to hurt Berta. She had invited it all along, just by being a jealous, nasty, undisciplined, obese failure. What came at me now were the effects of her own self-loathing.

She had done this to herself.

She told Damon that we were not her family, so he wrote that he guessed he had better check his own DNA for authenticity. Then she went right back to using lots of block capitals to scream at us about that address book. Since Damon wouldn't give her an inch, she then proceeded to do her worst, such as it was, but still on Deutsche Bank letterhead. When I saw that letter, this was the first detail that I checked. Despite what followed, I felt only glee when I got this letter.

It was addressed to everyone I knew, using the list of the people whose e-mail addresses had been in the first batch of the eulogy list mailings – the one that Hilda had shared with Berta.

From: Berta Otterman [mailto:berta.otterman@db.com]
Sent: Monday, October 26, 2009 4:48 PM
To: undisclosed-recipients
Subject: Please Block from your email from following two emails: Clarisse Rénard: cnrjdqueenbee@xxxx.com and Damon Haines: ddhardy@xxxx.com
Importance: High

Glowing Letters

The email was sent by Berta Otterman
berta.otterman@db.com

Dear Everyone:

I am truly sorry for the incontinence, but my mentally ill cousin and his also mentally ill wife have stolen my father's (Bryn Otterman) address book and they are saying some horrible things about me and my sister and I am afraid that they will approach all of you for money, or email you something untrue and horrible. Please block the following two email addresses or delete them if they come through but please do not correspond with them on any level as they are acting inappropriately and are not respecting neither my nor my sister's wishes for them to cease usage of my father's private information.

Apologies for the inconvenience.

Please block: Clarisse Rénard: cnrjdqueenbee@xxxx.com
and Damon Hardy: ddhardy@xxxx.com

Sincerely,

Berta Otterman

```
This communication may contain confidential and/or
privileged information.
If you are not the intended recipient (or have received
this communication
in error) please notify the sender immediately and
destroy this
communication. Any unauthorized copying, disclosure or
distribution of the
material in this communication is strictly forbidden.

Deutsche Bank does not render legal or tax advice, and
the information
contained in this communication should not be regarded
as such.
```

    Well...that was when I decided that I had to stop Damon from writing to her.
    The only way to pull that off – the only tool at my disposal – was to go into his e-mail account and block Berta's e-mail addresses, both her

The Slamming Door

AOL and Deutsche Bank ones. I blocked e-mails from Dionne, The Hornsby, Matt, Hilda, Elah and Rudy. After that, no more inflammatory crap could come from anyone. That would mean that Damon could no longer receive anything by or about Berta. Without having anything to respond to, I figured that he would stop writing.

That note was full of typos, incorrect grammar, and lies. The first rule of libel is that it be published; otherwise it's just slander, which is merely spoken. The second part of libel is that it's not libel if it's true, and it is libel if it's not true. It's also useful to couch a lie in correct grammar, but she didn't even bother to dress her libel properly.

People with autism spectrum conditions are not mentally ill; we are different.

Damon and I never asked our friends for money; we just toughed it out with almost nothing as usual. We would not break down and beg for money. We would just be careful and resourceful, and go without certain things in order to get by without asking for that.

As for horrible things to say about Berta, try this: the truth. One of the things that she wrote to Damon was that she hoped we would both kill ourselves, the sooner the better. Apparently, saying it out loud to me wasn't enough for her. We had not said anything that was untrue, nor had we done so in an uncouth manner – no swearing, no embellishment.

We didn't need to do that. She did it all for us.

Albert called to say that we were still family. He told me that Berta kept calling him up and carrying on about how my e-mails were going all over the world, including to Australia. He said that she would just have to go "apeshit" for a while.

The part about not respecting her or her sister's wishes made me roar with inward laughter. Of course I was not respecting their wishes! They did not deserve it. In signature Asperger fashion (which I now understood to a function of that brain pattern), I had deemed them not worthy of respect and therefore ignored their wishes. Another point about respect: why would I give it when there was nothing to respect?

I was done with them. They were irrelevant, so I been stealthy and given no warning.

That was precisely what she hated about me: Asperger's. She hated my outlook on life, my honest responses to things, and my refusal to feign respect when I saw merit for it. I have never in my life granted respect to anyone in any position of authority who clearly showed that they did not deserve to have it. I was not about to start, most particularly not now.

If in my refusal to cooperate with her effort to crush me like a bug, I instead seemed to rear up and sting her leaving venom that itched and

Glowing Letters

irritated or even burned, then that was just completely her problem. That she would rail against my show of self-respect was laughable.

And that was another crucial thing that the eulogy list had meant to me.

She was just too stupid and unwilling to accept that. The best she had been able to do for a rejoinder was to accuse me of "talking shit" about her after ignoring her. Well, she deserved to be ignored. Her feelings and actions were just completely her fault.

Naturally, my friends starting contacting me after receiving this demand that they not do so, and they all thought that Berta sounded mentally unstable. It was very satisfying after all the abuse that had been coming my way.

Dr. Leonardi said that he briefly considered contacting Deutsche Bank to report her, then said to himself, "No, her father just died and she's upset," and hit the Delete button.

Mack wrote back to Berta to say that anyone who would take care of a dying person out of the goodness of their heart must be a horrible person, signing it "demonically yours" with a laugh. Then he wrote to Deutsche Bank to complain, as a shareholder of its stock, about having received that note, and asking whether it was company policy to send out such things.

Artemis wrote to Deutsche Bank to complain also. She had forwarded the note from Berta to me, saying that she sounded like a "psycho bitch" and added that she now had her e-mail address, and wasn't that an interesting thought.

Brandie was disgusted, too. This note had come so soon after Hilda's that she just told me what she had written, and that she meant it for both of them.

I lost no friends over that note from Berta. Not one. They were particularly disgusted by Berta's venom for Asperger's; it was just plain nasty to attack someone for that, they said.

I looked at that ridiculous note again. One thing it would not achieve was its purpose.

I had been satisfied with just sending out the eulogy list. That was enough; it did its job, and once I had blocked those e-mail accounts from both my own and my husband's addresses, I had thought that that would be it…until Berta started leaving me terrible messages on my cell phone and sending nasty notes to my friends, plus trading more with Damon.

My parents seemed amazed and disgusted by all this; they were proud of me for having taken care of Bryn. They had spoken to him directly a week before they took me home, and he had told them that he was happy with what I had done for him – no complaints. With a mother who was a professional nurse hearing this, I had thought that all was well on that count.

Then this nonsense began.

Berta even left me a voice mail saying that I was the most selfish person in the world.

Funny – that's what I had thought about her for months.

My mother insisted that I write one more note to all of the relatives plus that same group of people who had been the first to receive the eulogy. I was surprised; I thought I was done with communicating with them. But I did it.

What she wanted me to do was to share a couple of notes sent between herself and Albert. I was skeptical, but I was home with her and wanted to be comfortable with her. There was that, the fact that there was nothing awful about any of it – these notes were all quite nice.

Like a classic Aspie, I prefaced it with this:

Hello Everyone.

My mother has insisted that I share this set of notes with you, so here it is below.

Sincerely,
Clarisse.

My mother's message was a bit old by then – two months old:

From: Nicole B.C. Rénard
To: Albert Otterman
Sent: 8/24/2009 7:20:45 AM
Subject: How Are You?

Dear Albert;

Just a note to ask how you are doing. Your care of Bryn was nothing short of phenomenal - the love, caring, support of everyone in the family was without comparison. I know how much he relied on you for everything - a great burden. There certainly is no greater gift someone could give to a loved one than that. Thank you for everything you did for Clarisse, especially. She loves you dearly. I hope now you will focus, at least a little bit, on taking care of yourself. Please e-mail me or call work (# provided), *home* (# provided), *cell* (# provided) *for*

Glowing Letters

anything. I want you to know I am here for you and your family any time for anything.

With love always,
Nicole

That wasn't all that she wanted sent – this was Albert's response, prefaced by my mother:

Clarisse - This says it all from Albert, I think.
Love, Mom

From: **Albert Otterman**
Subject: RE: How Are You?
To: Nicole B. C. Rénard
Date: Thursday, August 27, 2009, 5:45 AM

Nicole,

Thanks so much for the warm and caring note. You can see I'm not getting to my emails too quickly these days. This procrastination (Bryn and I both sinners here) will I hope pass.... Yes, Bryn and I were best friends. Would be much easier if we were Cain and Abel. Clarisse returned everything we did for her . . . and more. It was a valuable exchange on both sides, and Bryn (me too) loved her for all she did and told her so. I hope she realizes how much she contributed to the family. And I hope yours is steaming along nicely with a third voice in the house. I miss hearing Clarisse's cranky orders to stay away from her computer. Again, thanks so much for your advice and offer of help. Just what I need....

Fondly,
Albert

I was really done sending stuff out to large groups at that point, but now Dionne put her two cents in, and her letter came across as ridiculous. Its tone was what did it. She too assumed that I had been maligning her. I hadn't bothered to say much of anything about her. My attention really wasn't occupied by her at all, until she wrote to me.

She too complained that I hadn't had the courtesy to call either of them after their father had died, or send them cards. That was absurd considering the way that Berta had treated me, and that Dionne herself

The Slamming Door

had not bothered with me much for the whole year, yelled at me once over the phone without cause, and then had said that I shouldn't have cleaned out that closet after her sister had been so viciously abusive and voiced the hope that I would kill myself.

I had spoken to her on the phone when Bryn died – she had answered it when I called to speak to him and stunned me with the news that he was dead. I had said that I was in shock too, and that was that. It was my loss too, and I still have no interest in the idea that their loss might possibly have felt worse than my share of it after the way that they had [mis]behaved.

Dionne now stressed some other points that were on her mind: her uncle was sick and not in charge – they the daughters were. Odd; she was not the executor. She used that odious word repeatedly: "inappropriate" and complained about me keeping a copy of the address book. The Hornsby wrote me separately: "Stop contacting me immediately!"

I didn't care, I didn't respond, and I blocked her e-mail address from my account. I was done with them all – Berta, Matt, Dionne, The Hornsby, and Hilda's family. All blocked...no more glowing letters would be exchanged. The only reason why I didn't write again was because I was done, not because they wished it to be so.

What a relief to just be done with it all. I would stay in touch with Albert and Vianne, Aaron and Nicola, and perhaps Alissa. But not with the others; they weren't worth it.

Albert was ready to talk again a few days into this mess. I told him that Berta was an utterly useless, worthless girl. I just couldn't help it; she was still leaving horrid voice mails. He replied, "I can't argue with you."

It was at this point that my mother told me that Bryn had said that he didn't like Berta.

"Her own father didn't like her?"

That was what he had told her when we had all gone out to lunch together in April. My mother went on to add that on the night of Berta's meltdown, Bryn had told her over the phone that he felt that he had to let her try to take care of him because she wanted to do it. So he had, she said, and then just arranged to die as soon as possible after I left.

Chapter 67

Not My Family – The Door Has Been Slammed

What a rotten week that was. The door had now been literally and figuratively slammed.

Berta declared that I was not family in a message left on my voice mail. Fine; I didn't want her for family. And now that Bryn was gone, I didn't feel a burning desire to keep most of the others as family, either. Family is not always about blood or marriage. It is about loyalty and understanding and acceptance. Without that, you don't have any ties. No wonder Damon had left for twelve years. Still, I was glad to have known Bryn. He would always be family to me.

When all was said and done, I thought about Berta's appellation of me: "a creepy, psycho bitch." Keeping in mind that negativity from a hostile source constitutes a compliment, I considered what that translated to.

The use of the adjective "creepy" as applied to me suggested various things.

My facial expressions stay neutral most of the time, with only my eyes widening when I feel stress, amazement, or some other strong emotion. That's hardly a bad thing. In fact, it gives me a tactical advantage, because other people can't be entirely sure what I am thinking unless I choose to enlighten them. I can see how that might be perceived as creepy, but when I consider it from that angle, I have no inclination to change. It's who I am.

My point of view about life and what I find enjoyable differs from that of most people. I don't like what most people like, I don't find acceptable what most people find acceptable, and I can't live my life the way that most people do. I don't fawn over celebrities; I see them as people who happen to be very lucky in that they have fun and lucrative careers. I would rather read, write, and walk around historic sites and museums that go anywhere near a loud ball game. And I cannot function socially in an office or retail environment without strain or for very long.

All of that could be taken as both "creepy" and "psycho" – and that's just fine.

I guess I am a normal-looking version of a member of the Addams family, that macabre group created by the American cartoonist Charles Addams, who drew for *The New Yorker*. I've always admired them for their attitude about life, summed up nicely by Morticia in the 1991 movie when she said: "We would gladly feast on those who would subdue us."

If witches were still being persecuted, I would certainly be a target. Those hunts were never entirely about earlier versions of Wicca; they

The Slamming Door

were about destroying any person whom the majority perceived as different. Those who are different are often feared and loathed by those who are most ordinary. Yesterday's witches are today's Aspies.

So that leaves the word "bitch" to consider. It was another compliment; end of story.

Asperger's rules and bullies drool! I felt better just by writing that.

Chapter 68

My Home Feels Like Home Now

After more than a year went by, I decided to go ahead and write this story.

My mother had an observation that made the trouble with Berta seem like just a normal part of life and nothing to feel bad about: she said that Berta's and my personalities were so different and opposite that they just don't work together.

It's no one's fault; it's just the way it is.

Another thing that my mother kept saying was that she should have taken me home the first time that she and my father drove down to get my stuff. She has since gone even farther than that, and suggested that she should have done it a whole month earlier. I disagree; if I had left sooner, Bryn would have been stuck with Berta and Dionne for a whole month. He would have hated that. It was far better to have stayed so that he only had four days like that.

So what if I had to experience a bit of abuse? At least Bryn had only four days of a caregiver that he didn't want. It was worth sticking around. It was also worth being able to tie up every last loose end for him before departing, leaving a detailed account of how he liked and needed things, how to edit his pill sheet, and to leave ample supplies of whatever he needed.

Before all this happened, my mother used to say that when she got old and unable to take care of herself, she wouldn't want me to take care of her because she thought I would be too bossy. That had bothered me; not the bossy part – the not wanting me to take care of her part.

Not anymore; since I took care of Bryn and Albert spoke so well of me and begged and pleaded with her not to take me away, she had done a complete about-face. Now she said that she would want me to take care of her, because I would be a great advocate for her quality of care, and I wouldn't let the hospital staff do anything wrong.

That's certainly gratifying.

I'll probably still be bossy, but I won't let anything bad happen to her, other than the horrible process of aging, and that's because I have no real weapons against that. Can't fight nature...but I still think of cancer as something unnatural, a despicable, disgusting, abomination.

At some point, science will figure out a way to defeat it.

I sure hope so. No one should have to rot while they are still alive like that.

No one should have to lose body parts to a parasite, or look strange.

Dr. Leonardi wrote to me about it recently:

The Slamming Door

Your experience with Bryn has given you a starkly realistic picture of the end of life for most of these cancer patients who do not benefit from treatment and revealed the impotence of the medical system (more than the patient) in this situation. The importance of a nurturing caretaker in this circumstance cannot be overstated. You filled that role when it was clear others could not for a variety of reasons. That was a very good thing, perhaps the most important of things, for Bryn.

I had written to him that I was angry at the medical profession for not having something better to offer patients, something that would prevent indignity, humiliation, mutilation, and discomfort. There is no excuse for the way that things are now.

I don't care that doctors and scientists haven't figured out better ways to take care of patients yet. It is their fault that they haven't done so.

As the wife of someone who works in the life sciences researching such problems, I have another inside view of this situation. Grants must be laboriously written and filed, and not all of them get funded. Many of the ones that do get funded are given money for political reasons rather than scientific merit, and many others are funded to do more of the same projects rather than any adventurous, out-of-the-box, risky ventures.

It is the risky ones – the ones that take rule-breaking leaps – that have historically proven to be the most beneficial. I want more of those, and I want them now and continuously.

What are all these cancer research charities doing with the money that they take in?

I don't want a tote bag, or a mug, or any souvenir that even mentions cancer. I won't wear a tee shirt that reminds me of this hideous parasite. I want solutions. Save the money for that. Don't waste a cent on useless junk. I don't want to wear anything that says "cancer."

What's wrong with people, buying and buying into this nonsense?

Consumers, politicians, funding agencies…it's like they are all in cahoots to misdirect money, resources, and time to put the race for the cure into stasis. Why would they do this?

To keep those who currently benefit financially and politically swimming in money and influence in perpetuity. What an indictment of the current system.

No wonder a secular saint like Bryn is dead. His good deeds for homeless people and AIDS patients in New York City seem to have gone punished rather than unpunished. A great intellectual and listener is gone. Whenever I do a crossword puzzle – a hobby enjoyed by both of us – and the answer is the name of a person who is still alive but was born before Bryn, I find myself wondering why Bryn isn't still alive. How could he not have been as healthy with the same high quality of medical technology available to him?! DNA, environment, diet, all useless…the medical technology applied to him was wrong.

Committing waste is a crime, and that's what the current medical system did.

I still have lots of dreams about Bryn, usually set in his apartment in Chelsea, but sometimes in some other building that I nonetheless sense are in that neighborhood. Usually I am almost awake when the dreams come, and I try to just watch and see where the subconscious plot will take me. It helps me to remember it all later.

In many of these dreams, I am walking silently around, keeping track of Bryn and going to great lengths to bring in more supplies to keep him comfortable. Sometimes these lengths seem absurd when I wake up and contemplate what was in the dream: a decaying building, painted white, with a tall, balconied courtyard and lots of staircases plus a small cliff in back that I slowly and carefully lowered myself down to get to street level, or an old industrial building full of shops with his apartment somewhere inside, or 9th Avenue closed off and completely taken up with high-end shops, such as Chanel and other trendy, over-the-top boutiques.

My wanderings go on for seemingly long times, and I have ample opportunity to study my surroundings, wondering how things could have changed so much in the short time that I have been away from Bryn's neighborhood.

When I wake up and think about the dreams, I realize that they mean that if I were to go back there to look around, I would most likely see many changes and consciously understand that things there can never be the same again.

The most interesting dream I had was the most recent: I was in Bryn's apartment, but it looked different. Different in layout, décor, furnishings, and with pale blue walls…but Bryn was there and the place felt like his. It was still sparsely but adequately furnished with what seemed to be old family possessions, just as before – except that I didn't recognize them.

In the dream, Bryn gave me a small stack of photographs of the place to keep.

They were his only copies, and there were no negatives.

When I woke up, I could think of only one interpretation: when he was alive, Bryn had talked about somehow taking care of me, and not just for the time that I was taking care of him. Was the fact that I have

The Slamming Door

all these memories of him, many of which are mine alone, his way of taking care of me?

He knew I intended to write books and that his story was to be one of them.

I can think of no other explanation.

As I wrote this book, I thought of the fact that Mark Twain said that when he wrote his autobiography, it was as if he were writing from the grave. This story is very grave indeed, and because of its events, I found myself cut off from most of my in-laws, not just Bryn.

That took away any concern about the reactions of people whom I would not see again.

This book is by, for and of another kind of grave: the loss of Bryn and what he knew.

Epilogue

No Regrets

To tolerate someone who is different is to insult them. The only tolerable way of relating to a different person – especially from that person's point of view – is to accept them.

I speak from experience.

Bryn was an expert at doing this. I don't recall him tolerating anyone.

He didn't need to because he was so accepting and accommodating towards everyone.

He was also very good at holding back when something displeased him, though a large part of that ability was rooted in his extreme distaste for conflict of any kind.

I don't shrink from conflict. I hate discord and upsets, but I won't just take abuse.

Taking care of him meant taking care of my best friend.

I have no regrets about that, or about how I handled any of it.

Taking care of someone who is dying is a huge commitment.

When the inevitable criticisms start rolling in, they have no value.

Which brings me to my next thought: I left just in time.

Just in time for Bryn's daughter to be the one who was there when he fell asleep, never to wake up again. It was what she wanted, and it protected me legally and emotionally, though I only realized this a year later. If I hadn't been so upset by the whole death process and aftermath, I might have come to that realization sooner, but it came much later. I guess it had to be that way. That's okay.

With her there instead of me, I didn't have to be accused of mishandling the death, or worse. It was all up to her to handle it as she chose. Plus, if I had been there, she would have melted down then and there and treated me horribly, finding some excuse to do so even if she had to make one up. I would not have accepted that any more than I would ever accept the meltdown that she actually had.

One of the best thoughts that I can take away from this experience is that Bryn got to die on his own terms, at home, with food that he chose, and people he loved. I'm very glad that he never got around to moving into a hospice facility. The best possible way to die is at home, in familiar territory, without being surrounded by lots of strangers and other terminally ill people.

Bryn never had to leave the home that he loved, and I know I enabled that.

About the Author

Clarisse N. Rénard is a pseudonym. She is an author, holds a law degree, and has written many other books.

www.ingramcontent.com/pod-product-compliance
Lightning Source LLC
Chambersburg PA
CBHW052005070526
44584CB00016B/1621